Whitaker's Scottish Almanack
2001

LONDON
THE STATIONERY OFFICE

©The Stationery Office Ltd
51 Nine Elms Lane, London SW8 5DR

ISBN 011 702258 6

A CIP catalogue record for this book is available
in the British Library

Editorial Staff
Publisher: Tim Probart
Consulting Editor: Magnus Linklater
Editor: Lauren Hill
Deputy Editor: Vanessa Taylor
Contributing Editor: Mandy Macdonald
Editorial Staff: Neil Mackay, Tara West
Database Co-ordinator: Arlene Zuccolo

Contributors
Prof. Peter McGregor, Department of
Economics, University of Strathclyde
(Economy); Alan Boyd, McGrigor Donald
(Government in Scotland); Diana Clayton
(Education); Robson McLean, WS (Legal
Notes); Gordon Taylor (Astronomical Data)

Text and Jacket designed by Compendium
Jacket Photographs © PA Photos, Superstock
    Ltd, Telegraph Colour Library
Maps by Oxford Cartographers
Typeset by Eclipse Design, Norwich, Great
    Britain
Printed and Bound in Great Britain by Bell and
    Bain Ltd, Glasgow

Published by the Stationery Office and available
from:

The Publications Centre
(mail telephone and fax orders only)
PO Box 276, London SW8 5DT
General enquiries 0870-600 5522
Telephone orders 0870-600 5522
Fax orders 0870-600 5533

The Stationery Office Bookshops
123 Kingsway, London WC2B 6PQ
020-7242 6393; Fax 020-7242 6394
68–69 Bull Street, Birmingham B4 6AD
0121 236 9696; Fax 0121 236 9699
33 Wine Street, Bristol BS1 2BQ
0117 926 4306; Fax 0117 929 4515
9–21 Princess Street, Manchester M60 8AS
0161 834 7201; Fax 0161 833 0634
16 Arthur Street, Belfast BT1 4GD
028-9023 8451; Fax 028-9023 5401
The Stationery Office Oriel Office
18–19 High Street, Cardiff CF1 2BZ
029-2039 5548; Fax 029-2038 4347
71 Lothian Road, Edinburgh EH3 9AZ
0870 606 5566; Fax 0870 606 5588

WHITAKER'S SCOTTISH ALMANACK 2001

FOREWORD

Scotland celebrated the first year of its new parliament on 1 July 2000, in low-key style. A birthday cake was cut, there was a rash of newspaper post-mortems, and the Presiding Officer, Sir David Steel, pronounced cautiously that it had been "a learning experience". There was a marked absence of ceremony to hail the early achievements of Scottish devolution – in contrast to the crowds, processions, and stirring speeches which had greeted the state opening by the Queen just one year earlier.

The reasons were not hard to find: it had been, by general consent, a testing period for this new exercise in democracy. The 129 members of the Scottish parliament – most of them new to national politics – had been subjected to hostile comment almost from week one, when they met in their temporary quarters in the Church of Scotland's Assembly Hall in Edinburgh to discuss such matters as their own holidays, salaries, expenses and work practices. The criticism was unfair, since at this early stage there was no real political agenda in place. But the discussions gave the unfortunate impression that the people's representatives were more intent on looking after their own interests than that of the nation.

Perhaps not surprisingly, the early proceedings gave an impression of amateurism, with ministers reading out written answers to a string of parochial questions. The staged debates were often stilted affairs, and the set-piece question-time seemed a pale imitation of its House of Commons equivalent. But from the beginning, it was clear that the Scottish Parliament was a more open, approachable, and informal affair than its counterpart at Westminster. The public gallery was regularly full, the exchanges between Members were relaxed, and gradually some speakers of real distinction began to emerge. The weekly jousting between the First Minister, Donald Dewar, and his Scottish Nationalist opponent, Alex Salmond, became a regular attraction. The committee system, which allows discussion of pre-legislative matters, as well as acting as Scotland's equivalent of a revising chamber, demonstrated a robust independence on the part of MSPs, and was counted a success. Above all, a range of subjects, which had rarely been aired at Westminster, were argued out in a Scottish forum, by elected Scottish members, and reported at length in the Scottish press.

Not all of this, however, appeared to be of immediate benefit to the Scottish Executive, a governing coalition between Labour and the Liberal Democrats resulting from the system of proportional representation that had been used for the first time in Britain. As with most coalitions, a certain amount of horse-trading on policies had been done, and this presented the Executive with its first serious crisis — over student tuition fees. The leader of the Liberal Democrats, Jim Wallace, had committed his party to outright abolition of the fees. Labour ministers were reluctant to agree a reform so early on in the life of the parliament, which would put Scotland on a different footing from England and Wales. A detailed report was commissioned on various options for university funding, and after much debate a compromise was adopted, whereby fees would be scrapped for Scottish and European (but not English) students, and replaced with a graduate tax. In the end, the changes went through with surprisingly little opposition, and the coalition had passed its first test.

The leadership of Donald Dewar, First Minister in the Executive, came under scrutiny when he lost two senior advisers in controversial circumstances, and he was subjected to personal criticism when it emerged that the cost of the new parliament building at Holyrood, designed by the Barcelona architect Enric Miralles, had been grossly underestimated. The initial £40 million estimate which Mr Dewar had approved was revised upwards to £195 million, and when Miralles himself tragically died of a brain tumour, there was widespread uncertainty about the whole future of the project. Earlier, Mr Dewar himself was taken into hospital for major heart surgery, though he was expected to resume office later in the year, after making a satisfactory recovery. His place was filled temporarily by his deputy, the Liberal Democrat Jim Wallace.

It was, however, a decision by one of Mr Dewar's cabinet colleagues, Wendy Alexander, to scrap the contentious Section 28 — legislation barring the promotion of homosexuality in schools, originally introduced under the government of Margaret Thatcher — that sparked the most divisive row the parliament had seen. Ms Alexander had seen the Section as an act of blatant discrimination against homosexuals, and she assumed that its abolition would be welcomed as a symbol of tolerance in the new Scotland. What she had not anticipated was the hostility her proposal would engender amongst parents and the Roman Catholic Church, whose leader in Scotland, Cardinal Thomas Winning, attacked it as an attempt to subvert traditional values. A rich entrepreneur, Brian Souter, founder of the Stagecoach bus company, professed outrage at the notion that homosexual relations would be given the same status as marriage and a stable family life, and committed part of his considerable fortune to mounting a very public campaign to retain the Section, culminating in a privately financed referendum to test public opinion.

From the outset, the Executive found itself on the defensive, assailed by a high-powered PR machine, which characterised Ministers as indifferent and even hostile to majority opinion. The referendum, though boycotted by many, resulted in a substantial majority in favour of retaining rather than scrapping the Section, and the pressure on the Executive to back down was intense. Throughout the controversy, however, the parliament itself, with the exception of its Tory members, remained convinced that the Section should go. It had, however, been a salutary lesson for a new and inexperienced government in the importance of listening to the people rather than simply taking them for granted. It also demonstrated that the principal opposition party, the Scottish Nationalists, were able to stick to a principled line — namely supporting abolition of Section 28 — despite the fact that Mr Souter was one of their main funders. When, in the summer of 2000, the SNP leader, Alex Salmond, announced that he would be standing down after ten years as the head of the party, he was able to claim that it was in better shape to challenge Labour and advance the cause of independence than ever before.

It is probably too early to reach any long-term view about the impact of Scotland's new parliament on the life of the nation. Some relatively minor legislation has come before it — the abolition of the ancient feudal system of land tenure, the end of warrant sales whereby household goods are forcibly sold to pay debts, an act to prevent the release of potentially violent mental patients, and so on — but there has yet to be any substantial reform in the key areas of health or education. Critics still argue that so long as the block grant to Scotland is controlled at Westminster, the parliament itself will be unable to effect major change; an opinion poll, taken at the end of its first year, suggested that some 80 per cent of Scots thought that it had made no difference to their lives; and many of those polled appeared to make little distinction between the performance of the Executive and the parliament itself.

But there is no doubt that, at the end of an eventful year, there has been a sea change in the political climate north of the border, with Scottish issues dominating the agenda to an extent that few had predicted. The focus of national attention has shifted palpably from Westminster to Edinburgh, and even some of the more hostile commentators have conceded that, despite the rows, the Scottish Parliament has bedded in remarkably smoothly. Once again, the much-criticised British constitution has demonstrated that it can adapt to change, even of a fundamental kind, with its traditional qualities of flexibility and resilience.

Magnus Linklater

——— PREFACE ———

Welcome to the second edition of *Whitaker's Scottish Almanack*, the reference book for Scotland. One year on from devolution, this new edition looks at the political and governmental changes of the last 12 months and the changes that the devolution process has had on the running of Scotland.

In addition, the editorial team have revised and updated *Whitaker's Scottish Almanack* to keep you fully abreast of the many contact and personnel changes that have occurred in the last year to the many organisations and public bodies, companies, charities and businesses that are integral to Scottish life.

New information for this edition includes school term dates, more in depth coverage of the arts, listings of parks, gardens and archaeological sites; a fully comprehensive section on sport, details of each local authority's councillors and their political affiliations and coverage of the voluntary sector.

Readers familiar with the first edition will notice that *Whitaker's Scottish Almanack* has undergone a change of structure and format. Sections have been placed within "umbrella" chapters such as Governed Scotland, Legal Scotland, Business Scotland and so on, and it is hoped that this will make the publication more user-friendly and ensure that data flows in the most logical order. Each chapter has its own title page so you can see at a glance what it contains. The editorial team have made every effort to ensure the accuracy and completeness of content and we thank all those who supplied data on time and responded to our editorial enquiries.

Whitaker's Scottish Almanack and The Stationery Office Ltd are also pleased to welcome Magnus Linklater, newspaper columnist and Chairman of the Scottish Arts Council, as Consulting Editor to this edition.

I hope that *Whitaker's Scottish Almanack* provides all you need to know about the government, politics, business, environment and heritage of Scotland, plus a lot more besides. As ever, the editorial team welcomes any comments or suggestions you may have.

Lauren Hill
Editor
The Stationery Office Ltd
51 Nine Elms Lane
London
SW8 5DR
Tel: 020-7873 8442
Fax: 020-7873 8723
Email: whitakers.almanack@theso.co.uk
Web: http://www.the-stationery-office.co.uk
  and http://whitakers-almanack.co.uk

—— KEY DATES IN 2001 ——

PUBLIC HOLIDAYS

STATUTORY PUBLIC HOLIDAYS

New Year	1, 2 January
Good Friday	13 April
May Day	7 May
Spring	28 May
Summer	6 August
Christmas	25, *26 December

*Subject to proclamation

LOCAL AND FAIR HOLIDAYS

In most parts of Scotland there are local and fair holidays; dates vary according to the locality. Dates can usually be obtained from the local authority; the only central source is Glasgow Chamber of Commerce (tel: 0141-204 2121) which publishes each January a diary of holiday dates for the year.

LEGAL CALENDAR

LAW TERMS

The terms of the Court of Session for the legal year 2000–1 are:

Winter	26 September to 22 December 2000
Spring	4 January to 23 March 2001
Summer	24 April to 13 July 2001

TERM DAYS

Candlemas	28 February
Whitsunday	28 May
Lammas	28 August
Martinmas	28 November
Removal Terms	28 May, 28 November

RELIGIOUS CALENDARS

CHRISTIAN

Epiphany	6 January
Ash Wednesday	28 February
Maundy Thursday	12 April
Good Friday	13 April
Easter Day (western churches)	15 April
Easter Day (Eastern Orthodox)	15 April
Ascension Day	24 May
Pentecost (Whit Sunday)	3 June
Trinity Sunday	10 June
Corpus Christi	14 June
All Saints' Day	1 November
Advent Sunday	2 December
Christmas Day	25 December

HINDU

Makara Sankranti	14 January
Vasant Panchami (Sarasvati-puja)	29 February
Mahashivaratri	21 February
Holi	9 March
Chaitra (Hindu new year)	26 March
Ramanavami	2 April
Raksha-bandhan	4 August
Janmashtami	12 August
Ganesh Chaturthi, first day	22 August
Ganesh festival, last day	1 September
Durga-puja	17 October
Navaratri festival, first day	17 October
Sarasvati-puja	22 October
Dasara	26 October
Diwali, first day	12 November
Diwali, last day	16 November

JEWISH

Purim	9 March
Passover, first day	8 April
Feast of Weeks, first day	28 May
Jewish new year (AM 5762)	18 September
Yom Kippur (Day of Atonement)	27 September
Feast of Tabernacles, first day	2 October
Chanucah, first day	10 December

MUSLIM

Muslim new year (AH 1422)	26 March
Ramadan, first day	17 November

SIKH

Birthday of Guru Gobind Singh Ji	5 January
Baisakhi Mela (Sikh new year)	13 April
Martyrdom of Guru Arjan Dev Ji	16 June
Birthday of Guru Nanak Dev Ji	11 November
Martyrdom of Guru Tegh Bahadur Ji	24 November

OTHER SIGNIFICANT DATES

Burns Night	25 January
Chinese Year of the Snake	24 January
Commonwealth Day	12 March
Europe Day	9 May
Remembrance Sunday	11 November
St Andrew's Day	30 November
Hogmanay	31 December

CONTENTS

GOVERNED

SCOTLAND

THE GOVERNMENT OF SCOTLAND

In May 1999 the people of Scotland elected the first Parliament to sit in Scotland since the Act of Union 1707 and the newly elected Members of the Scottish Parliament (MSPs) met for the first time shortly thereafter. The Scottish Parliament was officially opened by the Queen on 1 July 1999, from which date devolution became effective, the Scottish Parliament and Scottish Administration assuming their full powers under the Scotland Act 1998.

PRE-DEVOLUTION GOVERNMENT

Scotland's parliament and administration developed in medieval times and were firmly established by 1603, when James VI of Scotland acceded to the English throne following the death of Elizabeth I of England. Despite the union of the crowns, the independence of the two countries' parliamentary systems was unaffected until 1707, when the Act of Union unified the two parliaments and transferred the government of Scotland to Westminster.

From the late 19th century the office of Secretary of State for Scotland (formerly the Secretary for Scotland) increased in importance, and became a Cabinet post in 1926. Over that period the Scottish Office also grew in size and importance. It provided the government departments in Scotland for education, health, local government, housing, economic development, agriculture and fisheries, home affairs, and law and order. Although required to operate within overall levels of funding set down by Westminster, the Scottish Office under the Secretary of State for Scotland and the Scottish Office ministers enjoyed a freedom of operation and flexibility of budget far greater than the departments of state in Whitehall. The 'Scottish Block' comprised a total allocation of money to Scotland with the Secretary of State being able to set his own spending priorities within the overall budget.

Movement Towards Devolution

However, the concept of Scottish home rule did not die with the Union. Following the general election in October 1974 which saw the Scottish National Party return 11 MPs to Westminster, the Scottish home rule movement gained fresh momentum. Legislation was put in place to establish a Scottish assembly (the Scotland Act 1978) but the required qualified majority did not materialise at the referendum held in March 1979. During the 1980s, support for a measure of home rule continued and a Scottish Constitutional Convention was established in 1989. The Convention, which included representatives from many political parties and other bodies representative of Scottish public life, produced a blueprint for a Scottish Parliament. The Labour government returned at the general election in May 1997 promised constitutional reform as one of its legislative priorities and an early referendum on the establishment of a Scottish Parliament.

The new Labour government published a White Paper, *Scotland's Parliament*, in July 1997. This document set out in detail the Government's proposals to devolve to a Scottish Parliament the power to legislate in respect of all matters not specifically reserved to Westminster. It further proposed limited tax-raising powers, a single-chamber Parliament with powerful committees, and also considered the Scottish Parliament's relationship with Westminster and the European Union. It proposed a measure of proportional representation for the first time in a British parliamentary election.

In a referendum on 11 September 1997, almost 75 per cent of those voting agreed 'that there should be a Scottish Parliament'. On the question that 'the Scottish Parliament should have tax-varying powers', almost two-thirds voted for the proposition. The Scotland Bill was introduced to the House of Commons on 17 December 1997. The Bill completed its Commons stages on 20 May 1998 after 32 days of debate and was subjected to 17 days of line-by-line scrutiny in the House of Lords before receiving royal assent on 19 November 1998. The Government itself tabled 670 amendments to the Bill.

In November 1997 the Government announced the establishment of an all-party Consultative Steering Group to take forward consideration of how the Scottish Parliament might operate in practice and to develop proposals for rules of procedure and standing orders; the Group reported to the Secretary of State in January 1999. The report enshrined four main principles: sharing the power; accountability; accessibility and participation; and equal opportunities. It proposed a modern, accessible and participative Parliament which would operate in a different manner from Westminster.

4   Governed Scotland

POST-DEVOLUTION GOVERNMENT
The Scottish Parliament is a subordinate legislature and can only legislate in respect of matters devolved to it. Westminster is sovereign and could, in theory, repeal the Scotland Act and do away with the Scottish Parliament, although all political parties have stated their commitment to ensure that the new Parliament works effectively. The role of the monarch is unchanged and Acts of the Scottish Parliament require royal assent before becoming law.

Devolved powers
The Scottish Parliament is empowered to pass primary legislation (known as Acts of the Scottish Parliament) and Scottish Ministers can also make secondary legislation in respect of devolved matters. The principal devolved matters are: health, education, local government, social work and housing, planning, economic development, tourism, some aspects of transport, most aspects of criminal and civil law, the criminal justice and prosecution system, police and fire services, environment, natural and built heritage, agriculture and fisheries, food standards, forestry, sport, and the arts. The Scottish Parliament is also responsible for implementing European Community legislation in respect of matters devolved to it. It is an absolute requirement that all laws of the Scottish Parliament, whether in the form of primary or secondary legislation, and all actions of the Scottish Executive must comply with the European Convention on Human Rights, which has been given effect by the Human Rights Act, as well as being consistent with EU law.

Reserved powers
Despite the extent of devolved powers, a substantial range of matters are reserved to Westminster, including the constitution, foreign affairs, defence, the civil service, financial and economic matters, transport regulation, social security, employment and equal opportunities. If the Scottish Parliament attempts to legislate in respect of these reserved areas, the Secretary of State and the law officers may challenge in the courts the right of the Parliament to make a law. Such challenges will ultimately be dealt with by the Judicial Committee of the Privy Council, which has assumed a new role as Scotland's principal constitutional court and will be the final arbiter in disputes between Westminster and Edinburgh regarding legislative competence.

THE SCOTTISH EXECUTIVE
The Scottish Executive is the government in Scotland in respect of all devolved matters. The Scottish Executive comprises the First Minister, the law officers (the Lord Advocate and the Solicitor-General for Scotland) and other ministers appointed by the First Minister. The members of the Scottish Executive are referred to collectively as the Scottish Ministers. The Scottish Ministers assumed their full powers on 1 July 1999, the day on which were transferred to them powers and duties and other functions relating to devolved matters which were previously exercised by the then UK Ministers in Scotland. The transfer of powers was achieved by a series of Statutory Instruments.

The Lord Advocate and Solicitor-General for Scotland are entitled to participate, but not vote, in the proceedings of the Parliament even if they are not MSPs. In addition to being the senior law officer in Scotland, the Lord Advocate continues to be the independent head of the systems of criminal prosecution and investigation of deaths in Scotland and this independence is entrenched in the Scotland Act 1998.

The Secretary of State for Scotland continues to be appointed as a member of the UK Government and is not a member of the Scottish Executive. The Scotland Act recognises that the UK Government will continue to need advice on Scots law, whether relating to reserved or devolved matters. To that end, a new law officer post in the UK Government, the Advocate-General for Scotland, is created; the first holder of this post is Lynda Clark, QC the first ever female law officer.

The Scottish Ministers are supported by staff largely drawn from the staff of the Scottish Office and its agencies. On 1 July 1999 the departments of the Scottish Office transferred to the Scottish Executive. This name reflects the fact that the departments of the Scottish Office now work to the First Minister and his ministerial team. The structure of the Scottish Executive now reflects Scottish ministerial portfolios.

All officials of the Executive hold office under the Crown on terms and conditions of service determined in accordance with the provisions of the Civil Service Management Code and remain members of the Home Civil Service. Established arrangements for interchange with other government departments also remain in place.

THE LEGISLATURE

The Scottish Parliament is a single-chamber legislature with 129 members. Of these, 73 represent constituencies and are elected on a first-past-the-post system. These constituencies are the same as for elections to Westminster with the exception of Orkney and Shetland, which comprise separate constituencies in the Scottish Parliament. In addition, 56 regional members (seven members for each of the eight former Scottish constituencies in the European Parliament) are elected on a proportional basis; this is intended to ensure that the overall composition of the Scottish Parliament reflects closely the total number of votes cast for each of the political parties. Each elector casts two votes, one for a constituency member and one for the party of their choice.

The Scottish Parliament has a fixed term of four years; governments will not be able to hold snap general elections. Elections will normally be held on the first Thursday in May, although there is a limited measure of flexibility should this date prove unsuitable. Extraordinary general elections can be held in exceptional circumstances, such as failure of the Parliament to nominate a First Minister within 28 days or if the Parliament itself resolves that it should be dissolved with the support of at least two-thirds of the members.

The Parliament is responsible for agreeing its own methods of operation and has adopted its own standing orders in place of the transitional standing orders made by Westminster before the transfer of devolved functions.

The Legislative Process

There are three stages to the legislative process: pre-parliamentary procedure, parliamentary procedure, and procedure leading up to royal assent.

Under the pre-parliamentary procedure, before a Bill may be introduced to the Parliament, a member of the Scottish Executive must make a written statement to the effect that the Bill is within the legislative competence of the Scottish Parliament. Furthermore, the Presiding Officer must also certify that the provisions of the Bill would be within the legislative competence of the Parliament.

All Bills on introduction must be accompanied by a Financial Memorandum setting out the best estimates of the administrative, compliance and other costs to which the provisions of the Bill give rise, best estimates of time-scales over which such costs are expected to arise, and an indication of the margins of uncertainty in such estimates.

Furthermore, government Bills must be accompanied by explanatory notes summarising the provisions of the Bill, and a Policy Memorandum which sets out the policy objectives of the Bill, what alternative ways of meeting these objectives were considered, a summary of any consultation undertaken on the objectives of the Bill, and an assessment of the effects of the Bill on equal opportunities, human rights, island communities, local government, sustainable development and any other matter which the Scottish Ministers consider relevant.

The parliamentary procedure has three stages: a general debate on the principle of the Bill with an opportunity to vote (analogous to the second reading debate in the House of Commons); detailed consideration of the Bill with the opportunity to move amendments (analogous to the Committee stage); and a final stage at which the Bill can be passed or rejected (analogous to the third reading).

After a Bill completes its parliamentary procedure, the Presiding Officer submits it for royal assent. There is an in-built delay of four weeks before royal assent is granted to allow one of the law officers or the Secretary of State to challenge the competency of the Parliament to pass the Act.

Committees

As the Scottish Parliament is a single chamber, there is no body such as the House of Lords to undertake detailed scrutiny of legislation. Instead, the Scottish Parliament has powerful all-purpose committees to undertake substantial pre-legislative scrutiny. These committees combine the role of Westminster standing and select committees and:
— consider and report on policy and administration of the Scottish Administration
— have the power to conduct enquiries
— scrutinise primary, secondary and proposed EU legislation
— initiate legislation
— scrutinise financial proposals of the Scottish Executive (including taxation, estimates, appropriation and audit)
— scrutinise procedures relating to the Parliament and its members

Ministers are required to inform committees of the Government's legislative intentions in its area, including discussions about which relevant bodies should be involved in the pre-legislative consultation process. During the first year of the Parliament's operation the Committees have operated with considerable success and have taken evidence from interested bodies and individuals on a wide range of matters. Scottish Ministers have also been required to account to the Committees for matters within their portfolios. Most Committee business is taken in public.

Management of Parliament

The management of the business of the Parliament is undertaken by the Parliamentary Bureau. This meets in private and its main functions are:
— to prepare the programme of business of the Parliament
— to timetable the daily order of business for the plenary session
— to timetable the progress of legislation in committees
— to propose the remit, membership, duration and budget of parliamentary committees

The Parliamentary Bureau gives priority on certain days to business of the committees, to business chosen by political parties which are not represented in the Scottish Executive, and to private members' business.

The management of the business of Parliament as a corporate entity is the responsibility of the Scottish Parliamentary Corporate Body. This has legal powers to hold property, make contracts and handle money and also to bring or defend legal proceedings by or against the Scottish Parliament. It also employs staff engaged in the running of the Parliament who are not civil servants.

BUDGET AND RUNNING COSTS

The budget of the Parliament for 2000–1 is £16.7 billion and the UK Government has agreed to the continuing application of the Barnett Formula to allow for uprating of the Parliament's budget in line with increases for corresponding matters for the rest of the UK. In addition, the Parliament has limited powers to vary the basic rate of income tax by a maximum of 3 pence. The only other financial powers held by the Scottish Parliament relate to the manner in which local authorities raise revenue, presently by way of council tax and business rates.

The Scottish Parliament will be permanently housed in a custom-built building under construction at Holyrood, Edinburgh. The project has been beset by problems and completion is not now expected until late 2002. The cost has risen from £40 million to around £230 million although in April 2002 the Scottish Parliament agreed that the cost should be capped at £195 million. Until the new Parliament building is completed, the Scottish Parliament is occupying the Church of Scotland General Assembly buildings at The Mound, Edinburgh.

The total running costs of the Parliament for 2000–1 as set out in the Budget (Scotland) Act including salaries and allowances for MSPs, staff costs, accommodation costs and payments in respect of the Scottish Parliamentary Commissioner for Administration, are estimated at around £90 million.

Salaries and allowances

The initial salaries of MSPs were set at Westminster, but in future the setting of salaries will be a matter for the Scottish Parliament. Enhanced salaries are payable to the Scottish Ministers and there is a system of allowances to cover MSPs' expenses in carrying out constituency and parliamentary work.

THE JUDICIARY

The role of the judiciary is specifically acknowledged in the Scotland Act and there are detailed proposals for the appointment and removal of judges. Judges are likely to be increasingly involved in matters of political significance, including legal challenges to legislation made by the Scottish Parliament and issues arising out of the European Convention on Human Rights.

Because of their increasing involvement in matters of political sensitivity, the procedures for removing judges have been made more rigorous. Judges can only be removed from office by the Queen on the recommendation of the First Minister following a resolution of the Parliament. Parliament may only pass such a motion following a written report by an independent tribunal concluding that the person in question is unfit for office by reason of inability, neglect of duty or misbehaviour.

RELATIONSHIP WITH THE UK GOVERNMENT

The devolution settlement has resulted in changes to the UK constitutional framework. The role of the Secretary of State for Scotland is diminished to the extent that he or she will only represent Scotland's interests with regard to reserved matters; there is no guarantee that the Secretary of State will continue to have a place in the Cabinet.

A system of concordats has been put in place to ensure that the business of government in Scotland and at the UK level is conducted smoothly. The concordats are non-statutory bilateral agreements between the Scottish Executive and the UK Government which cover a range of administrative procedures relating to devolution. They are intended to ensure that good working relationships and communications continue between the Scottish administration and UK government departments.. They set out the principles on which working relationships will be based rather than prescribe the details of what those relationships should be. Concordats are intended to ensure that consultation takes place in relation to proposals for legislative and executive action, including advance notification.

There are likely to be further changes in future, for example, the number of Scottish MPs at Westminster is expected to be reduced following the next review of electoral areas carried out by the Boundary Commission for Scotland. As the legislation stands, this would also have the consequence of reducing the number of MSPs. Exact numbers will only be known after the Boundary Commission completes its work, but estimates suggest that the number of MSPs could drop from 129 to around 110. This possible reduction in numbers is already causing concern in view of the extent of the workload of Committees of the Scottish Parliament in particular. The UK Government has appointed Dr John Reid, The Secretary of State for Scotland to review this matter.

RELATIONSHIP WITH THE EUROPEAN UNION

Relations with the EU remain a reserved matter. While the Scottish Parliament has the responsibility of scrutinising European legislation affecting Scotland, and the Scottish Executive has the responsibility for applying that legislation in Scotland, it is the UK Government that represents Scottish interests in the Council of Ministers; this includes areas such as farming and fishing, where Scottish Office ministers may previously have led UK delegations. The Government has indicated that Scottish Ministers might be able to participate, on behalf of the UK, in EU meetings. It has indicated that it sees UK and Scottish Ministers agreeing a common line prior to negotiating with other EU member states.

One of the concerns expressed about the proposed relationship between the Scottish Executive and the EU institutions is accountability. Scottish Ministers are not members of the UK Parliament and are therefore not accountable to Westminster. As Scotland is not a member state of the EU, the responsibility for ensuring compliance with EU legislation rests with the UK Government. There is potential for conflict between the Scottish Parliament and Westminster with regard to the implementation of European legislation. In that event the proposed concordats between the Scottish Parliament and Westminster will be tested.

Any financial penalties imposed by the EU for non-observance of an EU measure, even in respect of devolved matters, will be met by the UK. Where the fault is due to the failure of the Scottish Executive to implement EU legislation in respect of devolved matters, the financial consequences will be met out of the Scottish Block.

LEGISLATIVE PROGRAMME FOR THE FIRST YEAR

In June 1999 the First Minister, Donald Dewar identified a number of priorities for the Scottish Parliament and announced its first legislative programme comprising eight Bills to tackle these priorities.

These were:

Land Reform Bill
Feudal Reform Bill
National Parks Bill
Local Government (Ethical Standards) Bill
Incapable Adults (Scotland) Bill
Transport Bill
Financial Procedures and Auditing Bill
Education Bill

As at June 2000 the Parliament had passed the following legislation:-

Mental Health (Public Safety and Appeals) (Scotland) Act 1999
Public Finance and Accountability (Scotland) Act 2000
Abolition of Feudal Tenure etc. (Scotland) Act 2000
Adults with Incapacity (Scotland) Act 2000
Census (Amendment) (Scotland) Act 2000
Budget (Scotland) Act 2000

At that date the Parliament also had a total of 12 Bills in Progress. These comprised a combination of Executive and Members Bills (the Scottish equivalent of a private members bill) as follows:-

Abolition of Poindings and Warrant Sales Bill (Members Bill)
Bail, Judicial Appointments etc (Scotland) Bill (Executive Bill)

Education and Training (Scotland) Bill
    (Executive Bill)
Ethical Standards in Public Life etc. (Scotland)
    Bill (Executive Bill)
Family Homes and Homelessness (Scotland) Bill
    (Members Bill)
Leasehold Casualties (Scotland) Bill (Members
    Bill)
National Parks (Scotland) Bill (Executive Bill)
Protection of Wild Mammals (Scotland) Bill
    (Members Bill)
Regulation of Investigatory Powers (Scotland)
    Bill (Members Bill)
Sea Fisheries (Shellfish) Amendment (Scotland)
    Bill (Members Bill)
Standards in Scotland's Schools etc. Bill
    (Executive Bill)
Transport (Scotland) Bill (Executive Bill)

Up to date information on the progress of all Bills
can be found on the Scottish Parliament website
at http://www.scottish.parliament.uk

THE SCOTTISH EXECUTIVE

The Scottish Executive is the government of Scotland in respect of all devolved matters. The Scottish Executive consists of the First Minister, the law officers (the Lord Advocate and the Solicitor-General for Scotland), and the other Scottish Ministers appointed by the First Minister. The First Minister is also able to appoint junior ministers to assist the Scottish Ministers.

The Secretary of State for Scotland continues to be appointed as a member of the UK Government and is not a member of the Scottish Executive.

Certain UK Ministers continue to have a degree of responsibility for reserved matters.

THE SCOTTISH MINISTERS

First Minister: The Rt. Hon. Donald Dewar, MP, MSP (Lab.)
Deputy First Minister and Minister for Justice: Jim Wallace, QC, MP, MSP (LD)
Minister for Finance: Jack McConnell, MSP (Lab.)
Minister for Health and Community Care: Susan Deacon, MSP (Lab.)
Minister for Communities: Wendy Alexander, MSP (Lab.)
Minister for Transport and the Environment: Sarah Boyack, MSP (Lab.)
Minister for Enterprise and Lifelong Learning: Henry McLeish, MP, MSP (Lab.)
Minister for Rural Affairs: Ross Finnie, MSP (LD)
Minister for Children and Education: Sam Galbraith, MP, MSP (Lab.)
Minister for Parliament: Tom McCabe, MSP (Lab.)
Lord Advocate: Colin Boyd, QC (Lab.)

JUNIOR MINISTERS

COMMUNITIES
Deputy Minister for Local Government: Frank McAveety, MSP (Lab.)
Deputy Minister for Communities: Jackie Baillie, MSP (Lab.)

EDUCATION AND CHILDREN
Deputy Minister for Culture and Sport: Rhona Brankin, MSP (Lab Co-op.)
Deputy Minister for Children and Education: Peter Peacock, MSP (Lab.)

ENTERPRISE AND LIFELONG LEARNING
Deputy Minister for Enterprise and Lifelong Learning: Nicol Stephen, MSP(LD)
Deputy Minister for Highlands and Islands and Gaelic: Alasdair Morrison, MSP (Lab.)

HEALTH AND COMMUNITY CARE
Deputy Minister for Community Care: Iain Gray, MSP (Lab.)

JUSTICE
Deputy Minister for Justice: Angus Mackay, MSP (Lab.)

PARLIAMENT
Deputy Minister for Parliament and Whip: Iain Smith, MSP (LD.)

RURAL AFFAIRS
Deputy Minister for Rural Affairs: John Home Robertson, MSP (Lab.)

LORD ADVOCATE
Solicitor-General for Scotland: Neil Davidson, QC

DEPARTMENTS OF THE SCOTTISH EXECUTIVE

St Andrew's House, Regent Road, Edinburgh
EH1 3DG
Tel: 0131-556 8400; enquiry line: 0345-741741
Fax: 0131-244 8240
E-mail: ceu@scotland.gov.uk;
scottish.ministers@scotland.gov.uk
Web: http://www.scotland.gov.uk

The Scottish Executive Ministers are supported by staff largely drawn from the staff of the Scottish Office, as constituted before devolution, and its agencies. On 1 July 1999 the departments of the Scottish Office transferred to the Scottish Executive and now work to the First Minister and his Ministerial team. All officials of the Executive hold office under the Crown on terms and conditions of service determined in accordance with the provisions of the Civil Service Management Code and remain members of the Home Civil Service.

On 1 July 1999 the Scottish Office changed its name to the Scottish Executive and its departments were renamed; some reassignment of responsibilities also took place.

Scottish Executive Development Department — social inclusion, housing, local government, transport, planning and building control, European structural funds

Scottish Executive Education Department – pre-school, primary and secondary education, childcare, social work and legal provisions for young people (including justice), development of the arts, cultural and built heritage, sports and recreation, Gaelic, broadcasting and architectural policy

Scottish Executive Enterprise and Lifelong Learning Department — further and higher education, lifelong learning, and business and industry functions of Education and Industry Department, the New Deal

Scottish Executive Health Department — Health Department, community care functions of the Social Work Services Group

Scottish Executive Justice Department - police, fire, emergency planning, courts group, civil law, criminal justice, parole and legal aid, criminal justice social work

Scottish Executive Rural Affairs Department — Agriculture; Environment and Fisheries Department

Scottish Executive Finance — replaces Finance Division

Scottish Executive Corporate Services — central support functions, including human resources, equal opportunities, the Modernising Government agenda

Scottish Executive Secretariat — parliamentary liaison, co-ordination of relations with UK Government, support to Scottish Ministers

The information given below reflects the situation at the time of going to press a few weeks after the Scottish Parliament and Scottish Executive had assumed their responsibilities. It is possible that some further reorganisation of the Scottish Executive departments may take place. The most recent information can be obtained from the contact points at the main Scottish Executive offices at St Andrew's House.

The following includes details of the departments of the Scottish Executive; details of the executive agencies of the Scottish Executive departments can be found in the Other Government Departments and Public Bodies section.

SCOTTISH EXECUTIVE CORPORATE SERVICES

16 Waterloo Place, Edinburgh EH1 3DN
Tel: 0131-556 8400

Principal Establishment Officer: C. C. MacDonald, CB
Head of Personnel: D. F. Middleton

DIRECTORATE OF ADMINISTRATIVE SERVICES

Saughton House, Broomhouse Drive, Edinburgh EH11 3XD
Tel: 0131-556 8400

Director of Administrative Services: Jim Meldrum
Chief Estates Officer: J. A. Andrew
Head of Information Technology: Ms M. McGinn
Director of Telecommunications: K. Henderson, OBE
Chief Quantity Surveyor: A. J. Wyllie

Director of Procurement and Commercial Services: N. Bowd

DIRECTORATE OF CORPORATE DEVELOPMENT
Director: Ken Thompson

SCOTTISH EXECUTIVE FINANCE

Victoria Quay, Edinburgh EH6 6QQ
Tel: 0131-556 8400

Principal Finance Officer: Dr P. S. Collings
Assistant Secretaries: M. T. S. Batho; J. G. Henderson; D. G. N. Reid; W. T. Tait
Head of Accountancy Services Unit: I. M. Smith
Assistant Director of Finance Strategy: I. A. McLeod

SCOTTISH EXECUTIVE SECRETARIAT

St Andrew's House, Regent Road, Edinburgh EH1 3DG
Tel: 0131-556 8400

Chief Executive: Robert Gordon
Constitutional Policy and Parliamentary Liaison Division : Michael Lugton
Head of Cabinet Secretariat Division: I. N. Walford
Legal Adviser: J. L. Jamieson, CBE
Chief Economic Adviser: Dr A. W. Goudie
Legal Secretary to the Lord Advocate: P. J. Layden

EXTERNAL RELATIONS DIVISION
Head of Division: Mrs B. Doig

BRUSSELS OFFICE
Head of Office: G. Calder

INFORMATION DIRECTORATE
For the Scottish Executive and certain UK services in Scotland

Head of Information Directorate: Roger Williams
Head of News: O. D. Kelly
Chief Publicity Officer: S. Sutherland

SOLICITOR'S OFFICE
Solicitor: R. M. Henderson
Deputy Solicitor: J. S. G. Maclean

EQUALITY AND VOLUNTARY ISSUES
Head of Group: Mrs V. M. Macniven
Head of Equality Unit: Y. Strachan
Head of Voluntary Issues: S. Adams

SCOTTISH EXECUTIVE DEVELOPMENT DEPARTMENT

Victoria Quay, Edinburgh EH6 6QQ
Tel: 0131-556 8400

Secretary: K. Mackenzie, CB

Under-Secretaries: D. J. Belfall; J. Breslin; C. Imrie; N. Jackson; J. Mackinnon; J. S. B. Martin; A. Rennie; Ms L. Rosborough
Assistant Secretaries: E. C. Davidson; R. A. Grant; Mrs D. Mellon; W. J. R. McQueen; C. Smith; R. Tait
Senior Economic Adviser: C. L. Wood

Professional Staff
Chief Planner: A. Mackenzie, CBE
Deputy Chief Architect: Dr J. P. Cornish
Chief Statistician: C. R. Maclean

Inquiry Reporters
2 Greenside Lane, Edinburgh EH1 3AG
Tel: 0131-244 5649

Chief Reporter: R. M. Hickman
Deputy Chief Reporter: J. M. McCulloch

SCOTTISH EXECUTIVE EDUCATION DEPARTMENT

Victoria Quay, Edinburgh EH6 6QQ
Tel: 0131-556 8400

Secretary: J. Elvidge
Under-Secretaries: Dr M. Ewart; Ms I. Low; Mrs G. Stewart
Assistant Secretaries: A. Brown; Mrs E. Emberson; Mrs J. Fraser; J. Gilmour; R. N. Irvine; G. McHugh; Mrs R. Menlowe; Ms J. Morgan
Chief Statistician: R. C. Wishart
Chief Architect: J. E. Gibbons, Ph.D. FSA Scot.
Chief Inspector of Social Work Services: A. Skinner
Assistant Chief Inspectors: Mrs G. Ottley; D. Pia; I. Robertson

HM Inspectors of Schools
Senior Chief Inspector: D. A. Osler
Depute Senior Chief Inspectors: G. H. C. Donaldson; C. R. Maclean
Chief Inspectors: P. Banks; J. Boyes; W. C. Calder; F. Crawford; Miss K. M. Fairweather; A. S. McGlynn; H. M. Stalker
There are 86 Grade 6 Inspectors

SCOTTISH EXECUTIVE ENTERPRISE AND LIFELONG LEARNING DEPARTMENT

Meridian Court, 5 Cadogan Street, Glasgow G2 6AT
Tel: 0141-248 2855

Secretary: E. W. Frizzell

ECONOMIC DEVELOPMENT, ADVICE
AND EMPLOYMENT ISSUES
Meridian Court, 5 Cadogan Street, Glasgow
G2 6AT
Tel: 0141-248 2855
Under-Secretary: M. B. Foulis
Assistant Secretaries: A. Aitken, OBE; A. K.
Macleod; Dr J. Rigg; D. Wilson

LIFELONG LEARNING GROUP
Europa Building, 450 Argyle Street, Glasgow
G2 8LG
Tel: 0141-248 2855
Under-Secretary: E. J. Weeple
Assistant Secretaries: G. F. Dickson; K. Doran;
C. M. Reeves; D. A. Stewart; D. Stephen

ENTERPRISE AND INDUSTRIAL
AFFAIRS
Meridian Court, 5 Cadogan Street, Glasgow
G2 6AT
Tel: 0141-248 2855
Under-Secretary: G. Robson
Industrial Adviser: D. Blair
Assistant Secretaries: J. A. Brown; I. J. C.
Howie, W. Malone; J. K. Mason; C. L. Wood

LOCATE IN SCOTLAND
120 Bothwell Street, Glasgow G2 7JP
Tel: 0141-248 2700
Director: D. Macdonald

SCOTTISH TRADE INTERNATIONAL
120 Bothwell Street, Glasgow G2 7JP
Tel: 0141-248 2700
Director: L. Brown

EXECUTIVE AGENCY

Student Awards Agency for Scotland

SCOTTISH EXECUTIVE HEALTH
DEPARTMENT
St Andrew's House, Regent Road, Edinburgh
EH1 3DG
Tel: 0131-556 8400

NATIONAL HEALTH SERVICE IN
SCOTLAND MANAGEMENT
EXECUTIVE
Chief Executive: G. R. Scaife, CB
**Director of Strategy and Performance
Management:** Dr K. J. Woods
Director of Primary Care: Mrs A. Robson
Director of Finance: J. Aldridge
Director of Human Resources: G. Marr
Director of Nursing: Miss A. Jarvie

Head of Community Care: Ms E. Lewis
Medical Director: Dr A. Fraser
Director of Trusts: P. Wilson
Head of Information Services, NHS: C. B.
Knox
Head of Estates: H. R. McCallum
Chief Pharmacist: W. Scott
Chief Scientist: Prof. G. R. D. Catto
Chief Dental Officer: T. R. Watkins

PUBLIC HEALTH POLICY UNIT
Head of Unit and Chief Medical Officer: Prof.
Sir David Carter, FRCSE, FRCSGlas.,
FRCPE
Deputy Chief Medical Officer: Dr A. Fraser
Head of Group: Mrs N. Munro
Assistant Secretary: J. T. Brown
Principal Medical Officers: Dr J. B. Louden
(part-time); Dr A. Macdonald (part-time); Dr
R. Skinner; Dr E. Sowler
Senior Medical Officers: Dr A. Anderson; Dr
E. Bashford; Dr K. G. Brotherston; Dr D.
Campbell; Dr J. Cumming; Dr B. Davis; Dr
D. J. Ewing; Dr D. Findlay; Dr G. R. Foster;
Dr A. Keel; Dr P. Madden; Dr H. Whyte; Dr
D. Will

STATE HOSPITAL
Carstairs Junction, Lanark ML11 8RP
Tel: 01555-840293; Fax: 01555-840024
E-mail: info@tsh.org.uk

The State Hospital provides high security mental
health services to patients from Scotland and
Northern Ireland.
Chairman: D. N. James
General Manager: R. Manson

COMMON SERVICES AGENCY
Trinity Park House, South Trinity Road,
Edinburgh EH5 3SE
Tel: 0131-552 6255
Chairman: G. R. Scaife, CB
General Manager: Dr F. Gibb

SCOTTISH EXECUTIVE JUSTICE
DEPARTMENT
Saughton House, Broomhouse Drive, Edinburgh
EH11 3XD
Tel: 0131-556 8400

Secretary: J. Hamill, CB
Under-Secretaries: C. Baxter; N. G. Campbell
Assistant Secretaries: Mrs M. H. Brannan; D.
Carmichael; Mrs E. Carmichael; Mrs M. B.
Gunn; I. Snedden; R. S. T. MacEwen; J.
Rowell

Chief Research Officer: Dr C. P. A. Levein
Senior Principal Research Officer: Mrs A. Millar

COURTS GROUP
Hayweight House, 23 Lauriston Street, Edinburgh EH3 9DQ
Tel: 0131-229 9200
Head of Civil Law and International Division: P. M. Beaton
Judicial Appointments and Finance: D. Stewart

HM INSPECTORATE OF CONSTABULARY
2 Greenside Lane, Edinburgh EH1 3AH
Tel: 0131-244 5614
HM Chief Inspector of Constabulary: W. Taylor, QPM

SCOTTISH POLICE COLLEGE
Tulliallan Castle, Kincardine, Alloa FK10 4BE
Tel: 01259-732000
Commandant: D. Garbutt

HM INSPECTORATE OF FIRE SERVICES
Saughton House, Broomhouse Drive, Edinburgh EH11 3XD
Tel: 0131-244 2342
HM Chief Inspector of Fire Services: D. Davis, QFSM

SCOTTISH FIRE SERVICE TRAINING SCHOOL
Main Street, Gullane, East Lothian EH31 2HG
Tel: 01620-842236
Commandant: D. Grant, QFSM

HM CHIEF INSPECTOR OF PRISONS FOR SCOTLAND
Saughton House, Broomhouse Drive, Edinburgh EH11 3XD
Tel: 0131-244 8481; Fax: 0131-244 8446
HM Chief Inspector of Prisons: C. Fairweather, OBE

OFFICE OF THE SCOTTISH PARLIAMENTARY COUNSEL
Victoria Quay, Edinburgh EH6 6QQ
Tel: 0131-556 8400
First Scottish Parliamentary Counsel: J. C. McCluskie, CB, QC
Scottish Parliamentary Counsel: G. M. Clark; C. A. M. Wilson
Depute Scottish Parliamentary Counsel: J. D. Harkness; Miss M. Mackenzie
Assistant Scottish Parliamentary Counsel: A. C. Gordon

PRIVATE LEGISLATION OFFICE
under the Private Legislation Procedure (Scotland) Act 1936
50 Frederick Street, Edinburgh EH2 1EN
Tel: 0131-226 6499
Senior Counsel: G. S. Douglas, QC
Junior Counsel: N. M. P. Morrison

EXECUTIVE AGENCIES

NATIONAL ARCHIVES OF SCOTLAND

REGISTERS OF SCOTLAND

SCOTTISH COURT SERVICE

SCOTTISH PRISON SERVICE

SCOTTISH EXECUTIVE RURAL AFFAIRS DEPARTMENT

Pentland House, 47 Robb's Loan, Edinburgh EH14 1TY
Tel: 0131-556 8400
Head of Department: J. S. Graham
Group heads: D. J. Crawley (Food and Agriculture); Dr P. Brady (Fisheries); S. F. Hampson (Environment); A. J. Rushworth (Agricultural and Biological Research); A. J. Robertson (Chief Agricultural Officer)
Division/unit heads: Dr J. R. Wildgoose; I. R. Anderson; D. R. Dickson; Ms J. Polley; D. J. Greig; W. M. Ferguson (Food and Agriculture Group); A. G. Dickson; Ms J. Dalgleish; Ms B. Campbell; P. Wright; M. Neilson; A. J. Cameron; Dr J. Miles (Environment Group)
Division heads: D. Feeley; G. M. D. Thomson (Fisheries Group)
Assistant Chief Agricultural Officers: W. A. Aitken; J. Henderson; A. Robb
Chief Agricultural Economist: vacant

EXECUTIVE AGENCIES

FISHERIES RESEARCH SERVICES

SCOTTISH AGRICULTURAL SCIENCE AGENCY

SCOTTISH FISHERIES PROTECTION AGENCY

GENERAL REGISTER OFFICE FOR SCOTLAND

New Register House, Edinburgh EH1 3YT
Tel: 0131-334 0380; Fax: 0131-314 4400
E-mail: records@gro-scotland.gov.uk
Web: http://www.gro-scotland.gov.uk

The General Register Office for Scotland is a department forming part of the Scottish Executive. It is the office of the Registrar-General for Scotland, who has responsibility for civil registration and the taking of censuses in Scotland and has in his custody the following records: the statutory registers of births, deaths, still births, adoptions, marriages and divorces; the old parish registers (recording births, deaths and marriages, etc., before civil registration began in 1855); and records of censuses of the population in Scotland.

Hours of public access: Monday—Friday 9—4.30. Web: http://www.origins.net

Registrar-General: J. N. Randall
Deputy Registrar-General: B. V. Philp
Census Manager: D. A. Orr
Heads of Branch: D. B. L. Brownlee; R. C. Lawson; F. D. Garvie; G. Compton; G. W. L. Jackson; F. G. Thomas

THE SCOTTISH PARLIAMENT

Edinburgh Assembly Hall, Edinburgh EH99 1SP
Tel: 0131-348 5000 (switchboard);
0845-278 1999 (general enquiries)
E-mail:
sp.info@scottish.parliament.uk (public information)
sp.media@scottish.parliament.uk (media enquiries)
education.service@scottish.parliament.uk (schools and colleges)
chamber.office@scottish.parliament.uk (business in the debating chamber)
committee.office@scottish.parliament.uk (business in committees)
petitions@scottish.parliament.uk (petitions)
presiding.officer@scottish.parliament.uk (office of the Presiding Officer)
webmaster@scottish.parliament.uk
Web: http://www.scottish.parliament.uk

Elected: 6 May 1999; turnout was 59 per cent of the electorate
First session: 12 May 1999
Official opening: 1 July 1999 at Edinburgh Assembly Hall
Budget: £16 billion
Devolved responsibilities: education, health, law, environment, economic development, local government, housing, police, fire services, planning, financial assistance to industry, tourism, some transport, heritage and the arts, sport, agriculture, forestry, fisheries, food standards
Powers: can introduce primary legislation; can raise or lower income tax by up to three pence in the pound
Number of members: 129

STATE OF THE PARTIES
as at end May 2000

	Constituency MSPs	Regional MSPs	Total
Labour	52	3	55
SNP	7	28	35
Conservative	1	18	19
Liberal Democrats	12	4*	16*
Green	0	1	1
Socialist	0	1	1
Independent	1	0	1
Presiding Officer	0	1	1
Total	73	56	129

* Excludes the Presiding Officer, who has no party allegiance while in post

SALARIES
from 1 April 2000

MSPs and officers are paid by the Scottish Parliamentary Corporate Body; ministers are paid out of the Scottish Consolidated Fund.

First Minister	£66,173*
Ministers	£34,327*
Lord Advocate	£44,849
Solicitor-General for Scotland	£32,429
Junior Ministers	£17,807*
MSPs	£41,255†
Presiding Officer	£34,327*
Deputy Presiding Officers	£17,807*

* In addition to salary as an MSP
† Reduced by two-thirds (to £13,364) if the member is already an MP or an MEP

OFFICERS
The Presiding Officer, The Rt. Hon. Sir David Steel, KBE, MSP, QC
Deputy Presiding Officers, George Reid, MSP (SNP); Patricia Ferguson, MSP (Lab.)

THE PARLIAMENTARY BUREAU
The Presiding Officer
Tom McCabe, MSP (Lab.)
Mike Russell, MSP (SNP)
The Rt. Hon. Lord James Douglas Hamilton, MSP, QC (C.)
Iain Smith, MSP (LD)

SCOTTISH PARLIAMENTARY CORPORATE BODY
The Presiding Officer
Robert Brown, MSP (LD)
Des McNulty, MSP (Lab.)
Andrew Welsh, MSP (SNP)
John Young, MSP (C.)

THE COMMITTEES
The committees of the Scottish Parliament are:

MANDATORY COMMITTEES

PROCEDURES
Convenor, Murray Tosh, MSP
Committee Clerk: John Patterson

STANDARDS
Convenor: Mike Rumbles, MSP
Committee Clerk: Vanessa Glynn

FINANCE
Convenor: Mike Watson, MSP
Committee Clerk: Sarah Davidson

AUDIT
Convenor: Andrew Welsh, MP, MSP (SNP)
Committee Clerk: Gillian Baxendine

EUROPEAN
Convenor: Hugh Henry, MSP (Lab.)
Committee Clerk: Stephen Imrie

EQUAL OPPORTUNITIES
Convenor: Kate MacLean, MSP
Committee Clerk: Martin Verity

PUBLIC PETITIONS
Convenor: John McAllion, MP, MSP (Lab.)
Committee Clerk: Steve Farrell

SUBORDINATE LEGISLATION
Convenor: Kenny MacAskill, MSP (SNP)
Committee Clerk: Alasdair Rankin

SUBJECT COMMITTEES

JUSTICE AND HOME AFFAIRS
Convenor: Roseanna Cunningham, MP, MSP (SNP)
Committee Clerk: Andrew Mylne

EDUCATION, CULTURE AND SPORT
Convenor: Mary Mulligan, MSP (Lab.)
Committee Clerk: Gillian Baxendine

SOCIAL INCLUSION, HOUSING AND VOLUNTARY SECTOR
Convenor: Margaret Curran, MSP (Lab.)
Committee Clerk: Martin Verity

ENTERPRISE AND LIFELONG LEARNING
Convenor: John Swinney, MP, MSP (SNP)
Committee Clerk: Simon Watkins

HEALTH AND COMMUNITY CARE
Convenor: Margaret Smith, MSP (LD)
Committee Clerk: Jennifer Stuart

TRANSPORT AND THE ENVIRONMENT
Convenor: Andy Kerr, MSP (Lab.)
Committee Clerk: Lynn Tullis

RURAL AFFAIRS
Convenor: Alex Johnstone, MSP (C.)
Committee Clerk: Richard Davies

LOCAL GOVERNMENT
Convenor: Patricia Godman, MSP (Lab.)
Committee Clerks: Craig Harper; Lynn Tullis

SCOTTISH PARLIAMENT CONSTITUENCIES AND REGIONS

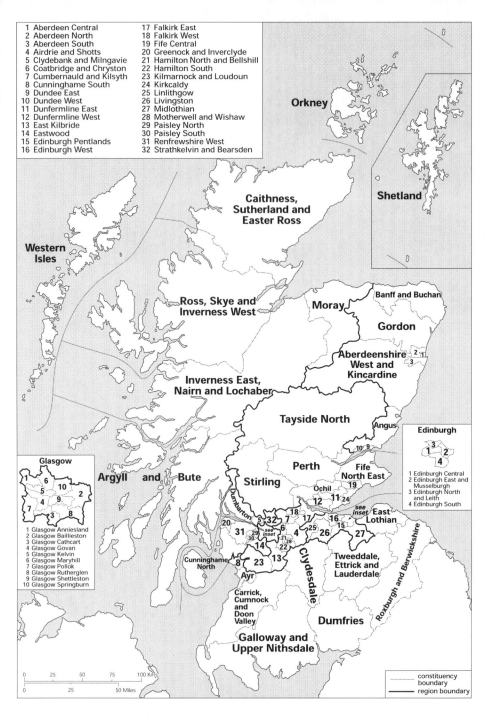

1 Aberdeen Central
2 Aberdeen North
3 Aberdeen South
4 Airdrie and Shotts
5 Clydebank and Milngavie
6 Coatbridge and Chryston
7 Cumbernauld and Kilsyth
8 Cunninghame South
9 Dundee East
10 Dundee West
11 Dunfermline East
12 Dunfermline West
13 East Kilbride
14 Eastwood
15 Edinburgh Pentlands
16 Edinburgh West

17 Falkirk East
18 Falkirk West
19 Fife Central
20 Greenock and Inverclyde
21 Hamilton North and Bellshill
22 Hamilton South
23 Kilmarnock and Loudoun
24 Kirkcaldy
25 Linlithgow
26 Livingston
27 Midlothian
28 Motherwell and Wishaw
29 Paisley North
30 Paisley South
31 Renfrewshire West
32 Strathkelvin and Bearsden

Orkney

Shetland

Western
Isles

Caithness,
Sutherland and
Easter Ross

Ross, Skye and
Inverness West

Moray

Banff and Buchan

Gordon

Aberdeenshire
West and
Kincardine

Inverness East,
Nairn and Lochaber

Tayside North

Angus

Edinburgh

1 Edinburgh Central
2 Edinburgh East and
  Musselburgh
3 Edinburgh North
  and Leith
4 Edinburgh South

Glasgow

Argyll   and   Bute

Perth

Stirling

Fife
North East

Ochil

East
Lothian

1 Glasgow Anniesland
2 Glasgow Baillieston
3 Glasgow Cathcart
4 Glasgow Govan
5 Glasgow Kelvin
6 Glasgow Maryhill
7 Glasgow Pollok
8 Glasgow Rutherglen
9 Glasgow Shettleston
10 Glasgow Springburn

Cunninghame
North

Clydesdale

Tweeddale,
Ettrick and
Lauderdale

Carrick,
Cumnock
and
Doon
Valley

Dumfries

Galloway and
Upper Nithsdale

Roxburgh and Berwickshire

0   25   50   75   100 Kms
0   25   50 Miles

constituency
boundary
region boundary

SCOTTISH PARLIAMENT ELECTIONS

on 6 May 1999

CONSTITUENCIES

ABERDEEN CENTRAL
(Scotland North East region)
E. 52,715 T. 50.26%

L. Macdonald, Lab.	10,305
R. Lochhead, SNP	7,609
Ms E. Anderson, LD	4,403
T. Mason, C.	3,655
A. Cumbers, SSP	523

Lab. majority 2,696

ABERDEEN NORTH
(Scotland North East region)
E. 54,553 T. 51.00%

Ms E. Thomson, Lab.	10,340
B. Adam, SNP	9,942
J. Donaldson, LD	4,767
I. Haughie, C.	2,772

Lab. majority 398

ABERDEEN SOUTH
(Scotland North East region)
E. 60,579 T. 57.26%

N. Stephen, LD	11,300
M. Elrick, Lab.	9,540
Ms N. Milne, C.	6,993
Ms I. McGugan, SNP	6,651
S. Sutherland, SWP	206

LD majority 1,760

ABERDEENSHIRE WEST AND
KINCARDINE
(Scotland North East region)
E. 60,702 T. 58.87%

M. Rumbles, LD	12,838
B. Wallace, C.	10,549
Ms M. Watt, SNP	7,699
G. Guthrie, Lab.	4,650

LD majority 2,289

AIRDRIE AND SHOTTS
(Scotland Central region)
E. 58,481 T. 56.79%

Ms K. Whitefield, Lab.	18,338
G. Paterson, SNP	9,353
P. Ross-Taylor, C.	3,177
D. Miller, LD	2,345

Lab. majority 8,985

ANGUS
(Scotland North East region)
E. 59,891 T. 57.66%

A. Welsh, SNP	16,055
R. Harris, C.	7,154
I. McFatridge, Lab.	6,914
R. Speirs, LD	4,413

SNP majority 8,901

ARGYLL AND BUTE
(Highlands and Islands region)
E. 49,609 T. 64.86%

G. Lyon, LD	11,226
D. Hamilton, SNP	9,169
H. Raven, Lab.	6,470
D. Petrie, C.	5,312

LD majority 2,057

AYR
(Scotland South region)
E. 56,338 T. 66.48%

I. Welsh, Lab.	14,263
P. Gallie, C.	14,238
R. Mullin, SNP	7,291
Ms E. Morris, LD	1,662

Lab. majority 25

BANFF AND BUCHAN
(Scotland North East region)
E. 57,639 T. 55.06%

A. Salmond, SNP	16,695
D. Davidson, C.	5,403
M. Mackie, LD	5,315
Ms M. Harris, Lab.	4,321

SNP majority 11,292

CAITHNESS, SUTHERLAND AND
EASTER ROSS
(Highlands and Islands region)
E. 41,581 T. 62.60%

J. Stone, LD	10,691
J. Hendry, Lab.	6,300
Ms J. Urquhart, SNP	6,035
R. Jenkins, C.	2,167
J. Campbell, Ind.	554
E. Stewart, Ind.	282

LD majority 4,391

CARRICK, CUMNOCK AND DOON
VALLEY
(Scotland South region)
E. 65,580 T. 62.66%

Ms C. Jamieson, Lab. Co-op.	19,667
A. Ingram, SNP	10,864
J. Scott, C.	8,123
D, Hannay, LD	2,441

Lab. Co-op. majority 8,803

CLYDEBANK AND MILNGAVIE
(Scotland West region)
E. 52,461 T. 63.55%

D. McNulty, Lab.	15,105
J. Yuill, SNP	10,395
R. Ackland, LD	4,149
Ms D. Luckhurst, C.	3,688

Lab. majority 4,710

CLYDESDALE
(Scotland South region)
E. 64,262 T. 60.61%

Ms K. Turnbull, Lab.	16,755
Ms A. Winning, SNP	12,875
C. Cormack, C.	5,814
Ms S. Grieve, LD	3,503

Lab. majority 3,880

COATBRIDGE AND CHRYSTON
(Scotland Central region)
E. 52,178 T. 57.87%

Ms E. Smith, Lab.	17,923
P. Kearney, SNP	7,519
G. Lind, C.	2,867
Ms J. Hook, LD	1,889

Lab. majority 10,404

CUMBERNAULD AND KILSYTH
(Scotland Central region)
E. 49,395 T. 61.97%

Ms C. Craigie, Lab.	15,182
A. Wilson, SNP	10,923
H. O'Donnell, LD	2,029
R. Slack, C.	1,362
K. McEwan, SSP	1,116

Lab. majority 4,259

CUNNINGHAME NORTH
(Scotland West region)
E. 55,867 T. 59.95%

A. Wilson, Lab.	14,369
Ms K. Ullrich, SNP	9,573
M. Johnston, C.	6,649
C. Irving, LD	2,900

Lab. majority 4,796

CUNNINGHAME SOUTH
(Scotland South region)
E. 50,443 T. 56.06%

Ms I. Oldfather, Lab.	14,936
M. Russell, SNP	8,395
M. Tosh, C.	3,229
S. Ritchie, LD	1,717

Lab. majority 6,541

DUMBARTON
(Scotland West region)
E. 56,090 T. 61.86%

Ms J. Baillie, Lab.	15,181
L. Quinan, SNP	10,423
D. Reece, C.	5,060
P. Coleshill, LD	4,035

Lab. majority 4,758

DUMFRIES
(Scotland South region)
E. 63,162 T. 60.93%

Ms E. Murray, Lab.	14,101
D. Mundell, C.	10,447
S.Norris, SNP	7,625
N. Wallace, LD	6,309

Lab. majority 3,654

DUNDEE EAST
(Scotland North East region)
E. 57,222 T. 55.33%

J. McAllion, Lab.	13,703
Ms S. Robison, SNP	10,849
I. Mitchell, C.	4,428
R. Lawrie, LD	2,153
H. Duke, SSP	530

Lab. majority 2,854

DUNDEE WEST
(Scotland North East region)
E. 55,725 T. 52.19%

Ms K. MacLean, Lab.	10,925
C. Cashley, SNP	10,804
G. Buchan, C.	3,345
Ms E. Dick, LD	2,998
J. McFarlane, SSP	1,010

Lab. majority 121

DUNFERMLINE EAST
(Scotland Mid and Fife region)
E. 52,087 T. 56.94%

Ms H. Eadie, Lab. Co-op.	16,576
D. McCarthy, SNP	7,877
Ms C. Ruxton, C.	2,931
F. Lawson, LD	2,275

Lab. Co-op. majority 8,699

DUNFERMLINE WEST
(Scotland Mid and Fife region)
E. 53,112 T. 57.75%

S. Barrie, Lab.	13,560
D. Chapman, SNP	8,539
Ms E. Harris, LD	5,591
J. Mackie, C.	2,981

Lab. majority 5,021

EAST KILBRIDE
(Scotland Central region)
E. 66,111 T. 62.49%

A. Kerr, Lab.	19,987
Ms L. Fabiani, SNP	13,488
C. Stevenson, C.	4,465
E. Hawthorn, LD	3,373

Lab. majority 6,499

EAST LOTHIAN
(Scotland South region)
E. 58,579 T. 64.16%

J. Home Robertson, Lab.	19,220
C. Miller, SNP	8,274
Ms C. Richard, C.	5,941
Ms J. Hayman, LD	4,147

Lab. majority 10,946

EASTWOOD
(Scotland West region)
E. 67,248 T. 67.51%

K. Macintosh, Lab.	16,970
J. Young, C.	14,845
Ms R. Findlay, SNP	8,760
Ms A. McCurley, LD	4,472
M. Tayan, Ind.	349

Lab. majority 2,125

EDINBURGH CENTRAL
(Lothians region)
E. 65,945 T. 56.73%

Ms S. Boyack, Lab.	14,224
I. McKee, SNP	9,598
A. Myles, LD	6,187
Ms J. Low, C.	6,018
K. Williamson, SSP	830
B. Allingham, Ind. Dem.	364
W. Wallace, Braveheart	191

Lab. majority 4,626

EDINBURGH EAST AND
MUSSELBURGH
(Lothians region)
E. 60,167 T. 61.48%

Ms S. Deacon, Lab.	17,086
K. MacAskill, SNP	10,372
J. Balfour, C.	4,600
Ms M. Thomas, LD	4,100
D. White, SSP	697
M. Heavey, Ind. You	134

Lab. majority 6,714

EDINBURGH NORTH AND LEITH
(Lothians region)
E. 62,976 T. 58.19%

M. Chisholm, Lab.	17,203
Ms A. Dana, SNP	9,467
J. Sempill, C.	5,030
S. Tombs, LD	4,039
R. Brown, SSP	907

Lab. majority 7,736

EDINBURGH PENTLANDS
(Lothians region)
E. 60,029 T. 65.97%

I. Gray, Lab.	14,343
D. McLetchie, C.	11,458
S. Gibb, SNP	8,770
I. Gibson, LD	5,029

Lab. majority 2,885

EDINBURGH SOUTH
(Lothians region)
E. 64,100 T. 62.61%

A. MacKay, Lab.	14,869
Ms M. MacDonald, SNP	9,445
M. Pringle, LD	8,961
I. Whyte, C.	6,378
W. Black, SWP	482

Lab. majority 5,424

EDINBURGH WEST
(Lothians region)
E. 61,747 T. 67.34%

Ms M. Smith, LD	15,161
Lord J. Douglas-Hamilton, C.	10,578
Ms C. Fox, Lab.	8,860
G. Sutherland, SNP	6,984

LD majority 4,583

FALKIRK EAST
(Scotland Central region)
E. 57,345 T. 61.40%

Ms C. Peattie, Lab.	15,721
K. Brown, SNP	11,582
A. Orr, C.	3,399
G. McDonald, LD	2,509
R. Stead, Soc. Lab.	1,643
V. MacGrain, SFPP	358

Lab. majority 4,139

FALKIRK WEST
(Scotland Central region)
E. 53,404 T. 63.04%

D. Canavan, Falkirk W.	18,511
R. Martin, Lab.	6,319
M. Matheson, SNP	5,986
G. Miller, C.	1,897
A. Smith, LD	954

Falkirk W. majority 12,192

FIFE CENTRAL
(Scotland Mid and Fife region)
E. 58,850 T. 55.82%

H. McLeish, Lab.	18,828
Ms P. Marwick, SNP	10,153
Ms J. A. Liston, LD	1,953
K. Harding, C.	1,918

Lab. majority 8,675

FIFE NORTH EAST
(Scotland Mid and Fife region)
E. 60,886 T. 59.03%

I. Smith, LD	13,590
E. Brocklebank, C.	8,526
C. Welsh, SNP	6,373
C. Milne, Lab.	5,175
D. Macgregor, Ind.	1,540
R. Beveridge, Ind.	737

LD majority 5,064

GALLOWAY AND UPPER NITHSDALE
(Scotland South region)
E. 53,057 T. 66.56%

A. Morgan, SNP	13,873
A. Fergusson, C.	10,672
J. Stevens, Lab.	7,209
Ms J. Mitchell, LD	3,562

SNP majority 3,201

GLASGOW ANNIESLAND
(Glasgow region)
E. 54,378 T. 52.37%

D. Dewar, Lab.	16,749
K. Stewart, SNP	5,756
W. Aitken, C.	3,032
I. Brown, LD	1,804
Ms A. Lynch, SSP	1,000
E. Boyd, Soc. Lab.	139

Lab. majority 10,993

GLASGOW BAILLIESTON
(Glasgow region)
E. 49,068 T. 48.32%

Ms M. Curran, Lab.	11,289
Ms D. Elder, SNP	8,217
J. McVicar, SSP	1,864
Ms K. Pickering, C.	1,526
Ms J. Fryer, LD	813

Lab. majority 3,072

GLASGOW CATHCART
(Glasgow region)
E. 51,338 T. 52.55%

M. Watson, Lab.	12,966
Ms M. Whitehead, SNP	7,592
Ms M. Leishman, C.	3,311
C. Dick, LD	2,187
R. Slorach, SWP	920

Lab. majority 5,374

GLASGOW GOVAN
(Glasgow region)
E. 53,257 T. 49.52%

G. Jackson, Lab.	11,421
Ms N. Sturgeon, SNP	9,665
Ms T. Ahmed-Sheikh, C.	2,343
M. Aslam Khan, LD	1,479
C. McCarthy, SSP	1,275
J. Foster, Comm. Brit.	190

Lab. majority 1,756

GLASGOW KELVIN
(Glasgow region)
E. 61,207 T. 46.34%

Ms P. McNeill, Lab.	12,711
Ms S. White, SNP	8,303
Ms M. Craig, LD	3,720
A. Rasul, C.	2,253
Ms H. Ritchie, SSP	1,375

Lab. majority 4,408

GLASGOW MARYHILL
(Glasgow region)
E. 56,469 T. 40.75%

Ms P. Ferguson, Lab.	11,455
W. Wilson, SNP	7,129
Ms C. Hamblen, LD	1,793
G. Scott, SSP	1,439
M. Fry, C.	1,194

Lab. majority 4,326

GLASGOW POLLOCK
(Glasgow region)
E. 47,970 T. 54.37%

J. Lamont, Lab. Co-op.	11,405
K. Gibson, SNP	6,763
T. Sheridan, SSP	5,611
R. O'Brien, C.	1,370
J. King, LD	931

Lab. Co-op. majority 4,642

GLASGOW RUTHERGLEN
(Glasgow region)
E. 51,012 T. 56.89%

Ms J. Hughes, Lab.	13,442
T. Chalmers, SNP	6,155
R. Brown, LD	5,798
I. Stewart, C.	2,315
W. Bonnar, SSP	832
J. Nisbet, Soc. Lab.	481

Lab. majority 7,287

GLASGOW SHETTLESTON
(Glasgow region)
E. 50,592 T. 40.58%

F. McAveety, Lab. Co-op.	11,078
J. Byrne, SNP	5,611
Ms R. Kane, SSP	1,640
C. Bain, C.	1,260
L. Clarke, LD	943

Lab. Co-op. majority 5,467

GLASGOW SPRINGBURN
(Glasgow region)
E. 55,670 T. 43.77%

P. Martin, Lab.	14,268
J. Brady, SNP	6,375
M. Roxburgh, C.	1,293
M. Dunnigan, LD	1,288
J. Friel, SSP	1,141

Lab. majority 7,893

GORDON
(Scotland North East region)
E. 59,497 T. 56.51%

Ms N. Radcliffe, LD	12,353
A. Stronach, SNP	8,158
A. Johnstone, C.	6,602
Ms G. Carlin-Kulwicki, Lab.	3,950
H. Watt, Ind.	2,559

LD majority 4,195

GREENOCK AND INVERCLYDE
(Scotland West region)
E. 48,584 T. 58.95%

D. McNeil, Lab.	11,817
R. Finnie, LD	7,504
I. Hamilton, SNP	6,762
R. Wilkinson, C.	1,699
D. Landels, SSP	857

Lab. majority 4,313

HAMILTON NORTH AND BELLSHILL
(Scotland Central region)
E. 53,992 T. 57.82%

M. McMahon, Lab.	15,227
Ms K. McAlorum, SNP	9,621
S. Thomson, C.	3,199
Ms J. Struthers, LD	2,105
Ms K. McGavigan, Soc. Lab.	1,064

Lab. majority 5,606

HAMILTON SOUTH
(Scotland Central region)
E. 46,765 T. 55.43%

T. McCabe, Lab.	14,098
A. Ardrey, SNP	6,922
Ms M. Mitchell, C.	2,918

J. Oswald, LD	1,982

Lab. majority 7,176

INVERNESS EAST, NAIRN AND LOCHABER
(Highlands and Islands region)
E. 66,285 T. 63.10%

F. Ewing, SNP	13,825
Ms J. Aitken, Lab.	13,384
D. Fraser, LD	8,508
Ms M. Scanlon, C.	6,107

SNP majority 441

KILMARNOCK AND LOUDOUN
(Scotland Central region)
E. 61,454 T. 64.03%

Ms M. Jamieson, Lab.	17,345
A. Neil, SNP	14,585
L. McIntosh, C.	4,589
J. Stewart, LD	2,830

Lab. majority 2,760

KIRKCALDY
(Scotland Mid and Fife region)
E. 51,640 T. 54.88%

Ms M. Livingstone, Lab. Co-op.	13,645
S. Hosie, SNP	9,170
M. Scott-Hayward, C.	2,907
J. Mainland, LD	2,620

Lab. Co-op. majority 4,475

LINLITHGOW
(Lothians region)
E. 54,262 T. 62.26%

Ms M. Mulligan, Lab.	15,247
S. Stevenson, SNP	12,319
G. Lindhurst, C.	3,158
J. Barrett, LD	2,643
Ms I. Ovenstone, Ind.	415

Lab. majority 2,928

LIVINGSTON
(Lothians region)
E. 62,060 T. 58.93%

B. Muldoon, Lab.	17,313
G. McCarra, SNP	13,409
D. Younger, C.	3,014
M. Oliver, LD	2,834

Lab. majority 3,904

MIDLOTHIAN
(Lothians region)
E. 48,374 T. 61.51%

Ms R. Brankin, Lab. Co-op.	14,467
A. Robertson, SNP	8,942
J. Elder, LD	3,184

G. Turnbull, C.	2,544
D. Pryde, Ind.	618
Lab. Co-op. majority 5,525	

MORAY
(Highlands and Islands region)
E. 58,388 T. 57.50%

Mrs M. Ewing, SNP	13,027
A. Farquharson, Lab.	8,898
A. Findlay, C.	8,595
Ms P. Kenton, LD	3,056
SNP majority 4,129	

MOTHERWELL AND WISHAW
(Scotland Central region)
E. 52,613 T. 57.71%

J. McConnell, Lab.	13,955
J. McGuigan, SNP	8,879
W. Gibson, C.	3,694
J. Milligan, Soc. Lab.	1,941
R. Spillane, LD	1,895
Lab. majority 5,076	

OCHIL
(Scotland Mid and Fife region)
E. 57,083 T. 64.58%

R. Simpson, Lab.	15,385
G. Reid, SNP	14,082
N. Johnston, C.	4,151
Earl of Mar and Kellie, LD	3,249
Lab. majority 1,303	

ORKNEY
(Highlands and Islands region)
E. 15,658 T. 56.95%

J. Wallace, LD	6,010
C. Zawadzki, C.	1,391
J. Mowat, SNP	917
A. Macleod, Lab.	600
LD majority 4,619	

PAISLEY NORTH
(Scotland West region)
E. 49,020 T. 56.61%

Ms W. Alexander, Lab.	13,492
I. Mackay, SNP	8,876
P. Ramsay, C.	2,242
Ms T. Mayberry, LD	2,133
Ms F. Macdonald, SSP	1,007
Lab. majority 4,616	

PAISLEY SOUTH
(Scotland West region)
E. 53,637 T. 57.15%

H. Henry, Lab.	13,899
W. Martin, SNP	9,404

S. Callison, LD	2,974
Ms S. Laidlaw, C.	2,433
P. Mack, Ind.	1,273
Ms J. Forrest, SWP	673
Lab. majority 4,495	

PERTH
(Scotland Mid and Fife region)
E. 61,034 T. 61.27%

Ms R. Cunningham, SNP	13,570
I. Stevenson, C.	11,543
Ms J. Richards, Lab.	8,725
C. Brodie, LD	3,558
SNP majority 2,027	

RENFREWSHIRE WEST
(Scotland West region)
E. 52,452 T. 64.89%

Ms P. Godman, Lab.	12,708
C. Campbell, SNP	9,815
Ms A. Goldie, C.	7,243
N. Ascherson, LD	2,659
A. McGraw, Ind.	1,136
P. Clark, SWP	476
Lab. majority 2,893	

ROSS, SKYE AND INVERNESS WEST
(Highlands and Islands region)
E. 55,845 T. 63.42%

J. Farquhar-Munro, LD	11,652
D. Munro, Lab.	10,113
J. Mather, SNP	7,997
J. Scott, C.	3,351
D. Briggs, Ind.	2,302
LD majority 1,539	

ROXBURGH AND BERWICKSHIRE
(Scotland South region)
E. 47,639 T. 58.52%

E. Robson, LD	11,320
A. Hutton, C.	7,735
S. Crawford, SNP	4,719
Ms S. McLeod, Lab.	4,102
LD majority 3,585	

SHETLAND
(Highlands and Islands region)
E. 16,978 T. 58.77%

T. Scott, LD	5,435
J. Wills, Lab.	2,241
W. Ross, SNP	1,430
G. Robinson, C.	872
LD majority 3,194	

STIRLING
(Scotland Mid and Fife region)
E. 52,904 T. 67.68%

Ms S. Jackson, Lab.	13,533
Ms A. Ewing, SNP	9,552
B. Monteith, C.	9,158
I. Macfarlane, LD	3,407
S. Kilgour, Ind.	155

Lab. majority 3,981

STRATHKELVIN AND BEARSDEN
(Scotland West region)
E. 63,111 T. 67.17%

S. Galbraith, Lab.	21,505
Ms F. McLeod, SNP	9,384
C. Ferguson, C.	6,934
Ms A. Howarth, LD	4,144
Ms M. Richards, Anti-Drug	423

Lab. majority 12,121

TAYSIDE NORTH
(Scotland Mid and Fife region)
E. 61,795 T. 61.58%

J. Swinney, SNP	16,786
M. Fraser, C.	12,594
Ms M. Dingwall, Lab.	5,727
P. Regent, LD	2,948

SNP majority 4,192

TWEEDDALE, ETTRICK AND
LAUDERDALE
(Scotland South region)
E. 51,577 T. 65.37%

I. Jenkins, LD	12,078
Ms C. Creech, SNP	7,600
G. McGregor, Lab.	7,546
J. Campbell, C.	6,491

LD majority 4,478

WESTERN ISLES
(Highlands and Islands region)
E. 22,412 T. 62.26%

A. Morrison, Lab.	7,248
A. Nicholson, SNP	5,155
J. MacGrigor, C.	1,095
J. Horne, LD	456

Lab. majority 2,093

REGIONS

GLASGOW
E. 531,956 T. 48.19%

Lab.	112,588 (43.92%)
SNP	65,360 (25.50%)
C.	20,239 (7.90%)
SSP	18,581 (7.25%)
LD	18,473 (7.21%)
Green	10,159 (3.96%)
Soc. Lab.	4,391 (1.71%)
ProLife	2,357 (0.92%)
SUP	2,283 (0.89%)
Comm. Brit.	521 (0.20%)
Humanist	447 (0.17%)
NLP	419 (0.16%)
SPGB	309 (0.12%)
Choice	221 (0.09%)

Lab. majority 47,228
(May 1997, Lab. maj. 166,061)

Additional members
W. Aitken, C.
R. Brown, LD
Ms D. Elder, SNP
Ms S. White, SNP
Ms N. Sturgeon, SNP
K. Gibson, SNP
T. Sheridan, SSP

HIGHLANDS AND ISLANDS
E. 326,553 T. 61.76%

SNP	55,933 (27.73%)
Lab.	51,371 (25.47%)
LD	43,226 (21.43%)
C.	30,122 (14.94%)
Green	7,560 (3.75%)
Ind. Noble	3,522 (1.75%)
Soc. Lab.	2,808 (1.39%)
Highlands	2,607 (1.29%)
SSP	1,770 (0.88%)
Mission	1,151 (0.57%)
Int. Ind.	712 (0.35%)
NLP	536 (0.27%)
Ind. R.	354 (0.18%)

SNP majority 4,562
(May 1997, LD maj. 1,388)

Additional members
J. MacGrigor, C.
Mrs M. Scanlon, C.
Ms M. MacMillan, Lab.
P. Peacock, Lab.
Ms R. Grant, Lab.
Mrs W. Ewing, SNP
D. Hamilton, SNP

LOTHIANS
E. 539,656 T. 61.25%

Lab.	99,908 (30.23%)
SNP	85,085 (25.74%)
C.	52,067 (15.75%)
LD	47,565 (14.39%)
Green	22,848 (6.91%)
Soc. Lab.	10,895 (3.30%)

SSP	5,237 (1.58%)
Lib.	2,056 (0.62%)
Witchery	1,184 (0.36%)
ProLife	898 (0.27%)
Rights	806 (0.24%)
NLP	564 (0.17%)
Braveheart	557 (0.17%)
SPGB	388 (0.12%)
Ind. Voice	256 (0.08%)
Ind. Ind.	145 (0.04%)
Anti-Corr.	54 (0.02%)

Lab. majority 14,823
(May 1997, Lab. maj. 101,991)

Additional members
Rt. Hon. Lord James Douglas Hamilton, C.
D. McLetchie, C.
Rt. Hon. Sir David Steel, LD
K. MacAskill, SNP
Ms M. MacDonald, SNP
Ms F. Hyslop, SNP
R. Harper, Green

SCOTLAND CENTRAL
E. 551,733 T. 59.90%

Lab.	129,822 (39.28%)
SNP	91,802 (27.78%)
C.	30,243 (9.15%)
Falkirk W.	27,700 (8.38%)
LD	20,505 (6.20%)
Soc. Lab.	10,956 (3.32%)
Green	5,926 (1.79%)
SSP	5,739 (1.74%)
SUP	2,886 (0.87%)
ProLife	2,567 (0.78%)
SFPP	1,373 (0.42%)
NLP	719 (0.22%)
Ind. Prog.	248 (0.08%)

Lab. majority 38,020
(May 1997, Lab. maj. 143,376)

Additional members
Mrs L. McIntosh, C.
D. Gorrie, LD
A. Neil, SNP
M. Matheson, SNP
Ms L. Fabiani, SNP
A. Wilson, SNP
G. Paterson, SNP

SCOTLAND MID AND FIFE
E. 509,387 T. 60.01%

Lab.	101,964 (33.36%)
SNP	87,659 (28.68%)
C.	56,719 (18.56%)
LD	38,896 (12.73%)

Green	11,821 (3.87%)
Soc. Lab.	4,266 (1.40%)
SSP	3,044 (1.00%)
ProLife	735 (0.24%)
NLP	558 (0.18%)

Lab. majority 14,305
(May 1997, Lab. maj. 54,087)

Additional members
N. Johnston, C.
B. Monteith, C.
K. Harding, C.
K. Raffan, LD
B. Crawford, SNP
G. Reid, SNP
Ms P. Marwick, SNP

SCOTLAND NORTH EAST
E. 518,521 T. 55.05%

SNP	92,329 (32.35%)
Lab.	72,666 (25.46%)
C.	52,149 (18.27%)
LD	49,843 (17.46%)
Green	8,067 (2.83%)
Soc. Lab.	3,557 (1.25%)
SSP	3,016 (1.06%)
Ind. Watt.	2,303 (0.81%)
Ind. SB	770 (0.27%)
NLP	746 (0.26%)

SNP majority 19,663
(May 1997, Lab. maj. 17,518)

Additional members
D. Davidson, C.
A. Johnstone, C.
B. Wallace, C.
R. Lochhead, SNP
Ms S. Robison, SNP
B. Adam, SNP
Ms I. McGugan, SNP

SCOTLAND SOUTH
E. 510,634 T. 62.35%

Lab.	98,836 (31.04%)
SNP	80,059 (25.15%)
C.	68,904 (21.64%)
LD	38,157 (11.99%)
Soc. Lab.	13,887 (4.36%)
Green	9,468 (2.97%)
Lib.	3,478 (1.09%)
SSP	3,304 (1.04%)
UK Ind.	1,502 (0.47%)
NLP	775 (0.24%)

Lab. majority 18,777
(May 1997, Lab. maj. 79,585)

Additional members
P. Gallie, C.
D. Mundell, C.
M. Tosh, C.
A. Fergusson, C.
M. Russell, SNP
A. Ingram, SNP
Ms C. Creech, SNP

SCOTLAND WEST
E. 498,466 T. 62.27%

Lab.	119,663 (38.55%)
SNP	80,417 (25.91%)
C.	48,666 (15.68%)
LD	34,095 (10.98%)
Green	8,175 (2.63%)
SSP	5,944 (1.91%)
Soc. Lab.	4,472 (1.44%)
ProLife	3,227 (1.04%)
Individual	2,761 (0.89%)
SUP	1,840 (0.59%)
NLP	589 (0.19%)
Ind. Water	565 (0.18%)

Lab. majority 39,246
(May 1997, Lab. maj. 115,995)

Additional members
Miss A. Goldie, C.
J. Young, C.
R. Finnie, LD
L. Quinan, SNP
Ms F. McLeod, SNP
Ms K. Ullrich, SNP
C. Campbell, SNP

ABBREVIATIONS OF PARTY NAMES

Anti-Corr.	Anti-Corruption, Mobile Home Scandal, Roads
Anti-Drug	Independent Anti-Drug Party
AS	Anti-sleaze
C.	Conservative
Ch. U.	Christian Nationalist
BNP	British National Party
Comm. Brit.	Communist Party of Britain
D. Nat.	Democratic Nationalist
Falkirk W.	MP for Falkirk West
Green	Green Party
Highlands	Highlands and Islands Alliance
Ind.	Independent
Ind. Dem.	Independent Democrat
Ind. Ind.	Independent Independent
Ind. Prog.	Independent Progressive
Ind. R.	Independent Robertson
Ind. SB	Independent Sleaze-Buster
Ind. Voice	Independent Voice for Scottish Parliament
Ind. Water	Independent Labour Keep Scottish Water Public
Ind. Watt.	Independent Watt
Individual	Independent Individual
Ind. You	Independent of London: Independent for You
Lab.	Labour
Lab. Co-op.	Labour Co-operative
LD	Liberal Democrat
Mission	Scottish People's Mission
NLP	Natural Law Party
ProLife	ProLife Alliance
Ref.	Referendum Party
SCU	Scottish Conservative Unofficial
SFPP	Scottish Families and Pensioners Party
SLI	Scottish Labour Independent
SLU	Scottish Labour Unofficial
Soc. Lab.	Socialist Labour Party
SPGB	Socialist Party of Great Britain
SSA	Scottish Socialist Alliance
SNP	Scottish National Party
SSP	Scottish Socialist Party
SUP	Scottish Unionist Party
SWP	Socialist Workers Party
UK Ind.	UK Independence Party
Witchery	Witchery Tour Party
WRP	Workers' Revolutionary Party

MEMBERS OF THE SCOTTISH PARLIAMENT

Adam, Brian, SNP, Scotland North East region
Aitken, William, C., Glasgow region
Alexander, Ms Wendy, Lab., Paisley North, maj. 4,616
Baillie, Ms Jackie, Lab., Dumbarton, maj. 4,758
Barrie, Scott, Lab., Dunfermline West, maj. 5,021
Boyack, Ms Sarah, Lab., Edinburgh Central, maj. 4,626
Brankin, Ms Rhona, Lab. Co-op., Midlothian, maj. 5,525
Brown, Robert, LD, Glasgow region
Campbell, Colin, SNP, Scotland West region
Canavan, Dennis A., MP, Lab., Falkirk West, maj. 12,192
Chisholm, Malcolm G. R., MP, Lab., Edinburgh North and Leith, maj. 7,736
Craigie, Ms Cathy, Lab., Cumbernauld and Kilsyth, maj. 4,259
Crawford, Bruce, SNP, Scotland Mid and Fife region

Cunningham, Ms Roseanna, MP, SNP, Perth, maj. 2,027

Curran, Ms Margaret, Lab., Glasgow Baillieston, maj. 3,072

Davidson, David, C., Scotland North East region

Deacon, Ms Susan, Lab., Edinburgh East and Musselburgh, maj. 6,714

Dewar, Rt. Hon. Donald C., MP, Lab., Glasgow Anniesland, maj. 10,993

Douglas Hamilton, Rt. Hon. Lord James (The Lord Selkirk of Douglas), QC, C., Lothians region

Eadie, Ms Helen, Lab. Co-op., Dunfermline East, maj. 8,699

Elder, Ms Dorothy, SNP, Glasgow region

Ewing, Fergus, SNP, Inverness East, Nairn and Lochaber, maj. 441

Ewing, Mrs Margaret A., MP, SNP, Moray, maj. 4,129

Ewing, Dr Winnifred, SNP, Highlands and Islands region

Fabiani, Ms Linda, SNP, Scotland Central region

Farquhar-Munro, John, LD, Ross, Skye and Inverness West, maj. 1,539

Ferguson, Ms Patricia, Lab., Glasgow Maryhill, maj. 4,326

Fergusson, Alex, C., Scotland South region

Finnie, Ross, LD, Scotland West region

Galbraith, Samuel L., MP, Lab., Strathkelvin and Bearsden, maj. 12,121

Gallie, Phil, C., Scotland South region

Gibson, Kenneth, SNP, Glasgow region

Gillon (elected as Turnbull), Ms Karen, Lab., Clydesdale, maj. 3,880

Godman, Ms Patricia, Lab., Renfrewshire West, maj. 2,893

Goldie, Miss Annabel, C., Scotland West region

Gorrie, Donald C. E., OBE, MP, LD, Scotland Central region

Grahame (elected as Creech), Ms Christine, SNP, Scotland South region

Grant, Ms Rhoda, Lab., Highlands and Islands region

Gray, Iain, Lab., Edinburgh Pentlands, maj. 2,885

Hamilton, Duncan, SNP, Highlands and Islands region

Harding, Keith, C., Scotland Mid and Fife region

Harper, Robin, Green, Lothians region

Henry, Hugh, Lab., Paisley South, maj. 4,495

Home Robertson, John D., MP, Lab., East Lothian, maj. 10,946

Hughes, Ms Janice, Lab., Glasgow Rutherglen, maj. 7,287

Hyslop, Ms Fiona, SNP, Lothians region

Ingram, Adam, SNP, Scotland South region

Jackson, Gordon, Lab., Glasgow Govan, maj. 1,756

Jackson, Dr Sylvia, Lab., Stirling, maj. 3,981

Jamieson, Ms Cathy, Lab. Co-op., Carrick, Cumnock and Doon Valley, maj. 8,803

Jamieson, Ms Margaret, Lab., Kilmarnock and Loudoun, maj. 2,760

Jenkins, Ian, LD, Tweeddale, Ettrick and Lauderdale, maj. 4,478

Johnston, Nicholas, C., Scotland Mid and Fife region

Johnstone, Alex, C., Scotland North East region

Kerr, Andy, Lab., East Kilbride, maj. 6,499

Lamont, Johann, Lab. Co-op., Glasgow Pollock, maj. 4,642

Livingstone, Ms Marilyn, Lab. Co-op., Kirkcaldy, maj. 4,475

Lochhead, Richard, SNP, Scotland North East region

Lyon, George, LD, Argyll and Bute, maj. 2,057

McAllion, John, MP, Lab., Dundee East, maj. 2,854

MacAskill, Kenny, SNP, Lothians region

McAveety, Frank, Lab. Co-op., Glasgow Shettleston, maj. 5,467

McCabe, Tom, Lab., Hamilton South, maj. 7,176

McConnell, Jack, Lab., Motherwell and Wishaw, maj. 5,076

Macdonald, Lewis, Lab., Aberdeen Central, maj. 2,696

MacDonald, Ms Margo, SNP, Lothians region

MacGrigor, Jamie, C., Highlands and Islands region

McGugan, Ms Irene, SNP, Scotland North East region

Macintosh, Ken, Lab., Eastwood, maj. 2,125

McIntosh, Mrs Lindsay, C., Scotland Central region

Mackay, Angus, Lab., Edinburgh South, maj. 5,424

Maclean, Ms Kate, Lab., Dundee West, maj. 121

Mcleish, Henry B., MP, Lab., Fife Central, maj. 8,675

McLeod, Ms Fiona, SNP, Scotland West region

McLetchie, David, C., Lothians region

McMahon, Michael, Lab., Hamilton North and Bellshill, maj. 5,606

MacMillan, Ms Maureen, Lab., Highlands and Islands region

McNeil, Duncan, Lab., Greenock and Inverclyde, maj. 4,313

McNeill, Ms Pauline, Lab., Glasgow Kelvin, maj. 4,408

McNulty, Des, Lab., Clydebank and Milngavie, maj. 4,710

Martin, Paul, Lab., Glasgow Springburn, maj. 7,893

Marwick, Ms Tricia, SNP, Scotland Mid and Fife region

Matheson, Michael, SNP, Scotland Central region

Monteith, Brian, C., Scotland Mid and Fife region

Morgan, Alasdair N., MP, SNP, Galloway and Upper Nithsdale, maj. 3,201

Morrison, Alasdair, Lab., Western Isles, maj. 2,093

Muldoon, Bristow, Lab., Livingston, maj. 3,904

Mulligan, Ms Mary, Lab., Linlithgow, maj. 2,928

Mundell, David, C., Scotland South region

Murray, Ms Elaine, Lab., Dumfries, maj. 3,654

Neil, Alex, SNP, Scotland Central region

Oldfather, Ms Irene, Lab., Cunninghame South, maj. 6,541

Paterson, Gil, SNP, Scotland Central region

Peacock, Peter, Lab., Highlands and Islands region

Peattie, Ms Cathy, Lab., Falkirk East, maj. 4,139

Quinan, Lloyd, SNP, Scotland West region

Radcliffe, Ms Nora, LD, Gordon, maj. 4,195

Raffan, Keith, LD, Scotland Mid and Fife region

Reid, George, SNP, Scotland Mid and Fife region

Robison, Ms Shona, SNP, Scotland North East region

Robson, Euan, LD, Roxburgh and Berwickshire, maj. 3,585

Rumbles, Mike, LD, Aberdeenshire West and Kincardine, maj. 2,289

Russell, Michael, SNP, Scotland South region

Salmond, Alex E. A., MP, SNP, Banff and Buchan, maj. 11,292

Scanlon, Mrs Mary, C., Highlands and Islands region

Scott, John, C., Ayr, maj. 3,344

Scott, Tavish, LD, Shetland, maj. 3,194

Sheridan, Tommy, SSP, Glasgow region

Simpson, Richard, Lab., Ochil, maj. 1,303

Smith, Ms Elaine, Lab., Coatbridge and Chryston, maj. 10,404

Smith, Iain, LD, Fife North East, maj. 5,064

Smith, Ms Margaret, LD, Edinburgh West, maj. 4,583

Steel, Rt. Hon. Sir David (The Lord Steel of Aikwood), KBE, QC, LD, Lothians region

Stephen, Nicol, LD, Aberdeen South, maj. 1,760

Stone, Jamie, LD, Caithness, Sutherland and Easter Ross, maj. 4,391

Sturgeon, Ms Nicola, SNP, Glasgow region

Swinney, John R., MP, SNP, Tayside North, maj. 4,192

Thomson, Ms Elaine, Lab., Aberdeen North, maj. 398

Tosh, Murray, C., Scotland South region

Ullrich, Ms Kay, SNP, Scotland West region

Wallace, Ben, C., Scotland North East region

Wallace, James R., MP, LD, Orkney, maj. 4,619

Watson, Mike (The Lord Watson of Invergowrie), Lab., Glasgow Cathcart, maj. 5,374

Welsh, Andrew P., MP, SNP, Angus, maj. 8,901

White, Ms Sandra, SNP, Glasgow region

Whitefield, Ms Karen, Lab., Airdrie and Shotts, maj. 8,985

Wilson, Allan, Lab., Cunninghame North, maj. 4,796

Wilson, Andrew, SNP, Scotland Central region

Young, John, OBE, C., Scotland West region

BY-ELECTION (16 March 2000)

AYR
T. 57.0%
J. Scott, C. 12,580
SNP, 9,236
Lab., 7,054
Scottish Socialist Party, 1,345
LD, 800
Green, 460
Independent, 186
UK Independence Party, 113
Pro-Life Alliance, 111
Independent, 15
Majority, 3,344
(Conservative gain from labour)

SCOTTISH CONSTITUENCIES IN UK PARLIAMENT

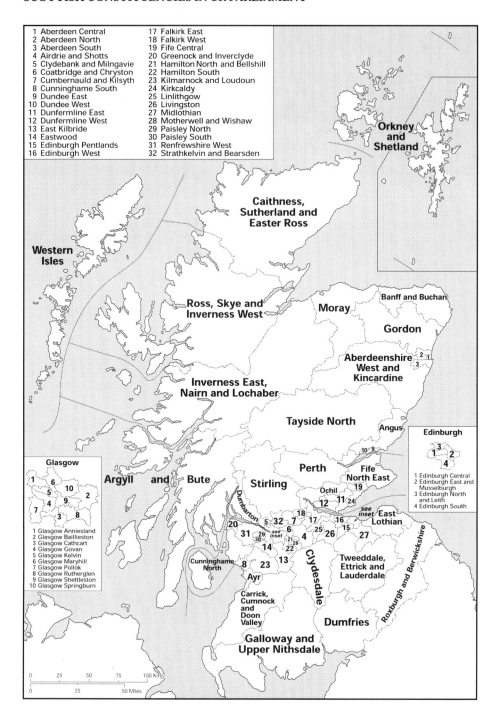

1 Aberdeen Central	17 Falkirk East	
2 Aberdeen North	18 Falkirk West	
3 Aberdeen South	19 Fife Central	
4 Airdrie and Shotts	20 Greenock and Inverclyde	
5 Clydebank and Milngavie	21 Hamilton North and Bellshill	
6 Coatbridge and Chryston	22 Hamilton South	
7 Cumbernauld and Kilsyth	23 Kilmarnock and Loudoun	
8 Cunninghame South	24 Kirkcaldy	
9 Dundee East	25 Linlithgow	
10 Dundee West	26 Livingston	
11 Dunfermline East	27 Midlothian	
12 Dunfermline West	28 Motherwell and Wishaw	
13 East Kilbride	29 Paisley North	
14 Eastwood	30 Paisley South	
15 Edinburgh Pentlands	31 Renfrewshire West	
16 Edinburgh West	32 Strathkelvin and Bearsden	

Orkney and Shetland

Caithness, Sutherland and Easter Ross

Western Isles

Ross, Skye and Inverness West

Moray

Banff and Buchan

Gordon

Aberdeenshire West and Kincardine

2 1
3

Inverness East, Nairn and Lochaber

Tayside North

Angus

Edinburgh

3
1 2
4

1 Edinburgh Central
2 Edinburgh East and Musselburgh
3 Edinburgh North and Leith
4 Edinburgh South

Glasgow

1 6 10
5 2
4 9
7 3 8

1 Glasgow Anniesland
2 Glasgow Baillieston
3 Glasgow Cathcart
4 Glasgow Govan
5 Glasgow Kelvin
6 Glasgow Maryhill
7 Glasgow Pollok
8 Glasgow Rutherglen
9 Glasgow Shettleston
10 Glasgow Springburn

Argyll and Bute

Dumbarton

Stirling

Perth

Fife North East

Ochil

19

12 11 24

18 17 16 15
20
5 32 7
31 29 see 6 25 26 27
30 inset
14 28
22
13

see inset East Lothian

Cunninghame North

8 23

Ayr

Clydesdale

Tweeddale, Ettrick and Lauderdale

Roxburgh and Berwickshire

Carrick, Cumnock and Doon Valley

Dumfries

Galloway and Upper Nithsdale

0   25   50   75   100 Kms
0   25   50 Miles

UK PARLIAMENT ELECTIONS

as at 1 May 1997

SCOTTISH CONSTITUENCIES

* Member of the last Parliament in unchanged constituency
† Member of the last Parliament in different constituency or
one affected by boundary changes
For abbreviations, see pages 40

ABERDEEN CENTRAL
E.54,257 T.65.64%
F. Doran, Lab.	17,745
Mrs J. Wisely, C.	6,944
B. Topping, SNP	5,767
J. Brown, LD	4,714
J. Farquharson, Ref.	446
Lab. majority 10,801
(Boundary change: notional Lab.)

ABERDEEN NORTH
E.54,302 T.70.74%
M. Savidge, Lab.	18,389
B. Adam, SNP	8,379
J. Gifford, C.	5,763
M. Rumbles, LD	5,421
A. Mackenzie, Ref.	463
Lab. majority 10,010
(Boundary change: notional Lab.)

ABERDEEN SOUTH
E.60,490 T.72.84%
Ms A. Begg, Lab.	15,541
N. Stephen, LD	12,176
† R. Robertson, C.	11,621
J. Towers, SNP	4,299
R. Wharton, Ref.	425
Lab. majority 3,365
(Boundary change: notional C.)

ABERDEENSHIRE WEST AND
KINCARDINE
E.59,123 T.73.05%
Sir Robert Smith, LD	17,742
† G. Kynoch, C.	15,080
Ms J. Mowatt, SNP	5,639
Ms Q. Khan, Lab.	3,923
S. Ball, Ref.	805
LD majority 2,662
(Boundary change: notional C.)

AIRDRIE AND SHOTTS
E.57,673 T.71.40%
† Mrs H. Liddell, Lab.	25,460
K. Robertson, SNP	10,048
Dr N. Brook, C.	3,660

R. Wolseley, LD	1,719
C. Semple, Ref.	294
Lab. majority 15,412
(Boundary change: notional Lab.)

ANGUS
E.59,708 T.72.14%
† A. Welsh, SNP	20,792
S. Leslie, C.	10,603
Ms C. Taylor, Lab.	6,733
Dr R. Speirs, LD	4,065
B. Taylor, Ref.	883
SNP majority 10,189
(Boundary change: notional SNP)

ARGYLL AND BUTE
E.49,451 T.72.23%
* Mrs R. Michie, LD	14,359
Prof. N. MacCormick, SNP	8,278
R. Leishman, C.	6,774
A. Syed, Lab.	5,596
M. Stewart, Ref.	713
LD majority 6,081
(April 1992, LD maj. 2,622)

AYR
E.55,829 T.80.17%
Mrs S. Osborne, Lab.	21,679
† P. Gallie, C.	15,136
I. Blackford, SNP	5,625
Miss C. Hamblen, LD	2,116
J. Enos, Ref.	200
Lab. majority 6,543
(Boundary change: notional Lab.)

BANFF AND BUCHAN
E.58,493 T.68.69%
† A. Salmond, SNP	22,409
W. Frain-Bell, C.	9,564
Ms M. Harris, Lab.	4,747
N. Fletcher, LD	2,398
A. Buchan, Ref.	1,060
SNP majority 12,845
(Boundary change: notional SNP)

CAITHNESS, SUTHERLAND AND
EASTER ROSS
E.41,566 T.70.18%
† R. Maclennan, LD	10,381
J. Hendry, Lab.	8,122
E. Harper, SNP	6,710
T. Miers, C.	3,148
Ms C. Ryder, Ref.	369
J. Martin, Green	230
M. Carr, UK Ind.	212
LD majority 2,259
(Boundary change: notional LD)

CARRICK, CUMNOCK AND DOON VALLEY
E.65,593 T.74.96%
† G. Foulkes, Lab. Co-op.	29,398
A. Marshall, C.	8,336
Mrs C. Hutchison, SNP	8,190
D. Young, LD	2,613
J. Higgins, Ref.	634

Lab. Co-op. majority 21,062
(Boundary change: notional Lab. Co-op.)

CLYDEBANK AND MILNGAVIE
E.52,092 T.75.03%
† A. Worthington, Lab.	21,583
J. Yuill, SNP	8,263
Ms N. Morgan, C.	4,885
K. Moody, LD	4,086
I. Sanderson, Ref.	269

Lab. majority 13,320
(Boundary change: notional Lab.)

CLYDESDALE
E.63,428 T.71.60%
* J. Hood, Lab.	23,859
A. Doig, SNP	10,050
M. Izatt, C.	7,396
Mrs S. Grieve, LD	3,796
K. Smith, BNP	311

Lab. majority 13,809
(April 1992, Lab. maj. 10,187)

COATBRIDGE AND CHRYSTON
E.52,024 T.72.30%
† T. Clarke, Lab.	25,697
B. Nugent, SNP	6,402
A. Wauchope, C.	3,216
Mrs M. Daly, LD	2,048
B. Bowsley, Ref.	249

Lab. majority 19,295
(Boundary change: notional Lab.)

CUMBERNAULD AND KILSYTH
E.48,032 T.75.00%
Ms R. McKenna, Lab.	21,141
C. Barrie, SNP	10,013
I. Sewell, C.	2,441
J. Biggam, LD	1,368
Ms J Kara, ProLife	609
K. McEwan, SSA	345
Ms P. Cook, Ref.	107

Lab. majority 11,128
(April 1992, Lab. maj. 9,215)

CUNNINGHAME NORTH
E.55,526 T.74.07%
* B. Wilson, Lab.	20,686
Mrs M. Mitchell, C.	9,647
Ms K. Nicoll, SNP	7,584
Ms K. Freel, LD	2,271
Ms L. McDaid, Soc. Lab.	501
I. Winton, Ref.	440

Lab. majority 11,039
(April 1992, Lab. maj. 2,939)

CUNNINGHAME SOUTH
E.49,543 T.71.54%
* B. Donohoe, Lab.	22,233
Mrs M. Burgess, SNP	7,364
Mrs P. Paterson, C.	3,571
E. Watson, LD	1,604
K. Edwin, Soc. Lab.	494
A. Martlew, Ref.	178

Lab. majority 14,869
(April 1992, Lab. maj. 10,680)

DUMBARTON
E.56,229 T.73.39%
* J. McFall, Lab. Co-op.	20,470
W. Mackechnie, SNP	9,587
P. Ramsay, C.	7,283
A. Reid, LD	3,144
L. Robertson, SSA	283
G. Dempster, Ref.	255
D. Lancaster, UK Ind.	242

Lab. Co-op. majority 10,883
(April 1992, Lab. maj. 6,129)

DUMFRIES
E.62,759 T.78.92%
R. Brown, Lab.	23,528
S. Stevenson, C.	13,885
R. Higgins, SNP	5,977
N. Wallace, LD	5,487
D. Parker, Ref.	533
Ms E. Hunter, NLP	117

Lab. majority 9,643
(Boundary change: notional C.)

DUNDEE EAST
E.58,388 T.69.41%
† J. McAllion, Lab.	20,718
Ms S. Robison, SNP	10,757
B. Mackie, C.	6,397
Dr G. Saluja, LD	1,677
E. Galloway, Ref.	601
H. Duke, SSA	232
Ms E. MacKenzie, NLP	146

Lab. majority 9,961
(Boundary change: notional Lab.)

DUNDEE WEST
E.57,346 T.67.67%

† E. Ross, Lab.	20,875
J. Dorward, SNP	9,016
N. Powrie, C.	5,105
Dr E. Dick, LD	2,972
Ms M. Ward, SSA	428
J. MacMillan, Ref.	411

Lab. majority 11,859
(Boundary change: notional Lab.)

DUNFERMLINE EAST
E.52,072 T.70.25%

† Rt. Hon. G. Brown, Lab.	24,441
J. Ramage, SNP	5,690
I. Mitchell, C.	3,656
J. Tolson, LD	2,164
T. Dunsmore, Ref.	632

Lab. majority 18,751
(Boundary change: notional Lab.)

DUNFERMLINE WEST
E.52,467 T.69.44%

† Ms R. Squire, Lab.	19,338
J. Lloyd, SNP	6,984
Mrs E. Harris, LD	4,963
K. Newton, C.	4,606
J. Bain, Ref.	543

Lab. majority 12,354
(Boundary change: notional Lab.)

EAST KILBRIDE
E.65,229 T.74.81%

† A. Ingram, Lab.	27,584
G. Gebbie, SNP	10,200
C. Herbertson, C.	5,863
Mrs K. Philbrick, LD	3,527
J. Deighan, ProLife	1,170
Ms J. Gray, Ref.	306
E. Gilmour, NLP	146

Lab. majority 17,384
(Boundary change: notional Lab.)

EAST LOTHIAN
E.57,441 T.75.61%

† J. Home Robertson, Lab.	22,881
M. Fraser, C.	8,660
D. McCarthy, SNP	6,825
Ms A. MacAskill, LD	4,575
N. Nash, Ref.	491

Lab. majority 14,221
(Boundary change: notional Lab.)

EASTWOOD
E.66,697 T.78.32%

J. Murphy, Lab.	20,766
P. Cullen, C.	17,530
D. Yates, SNP	6,826
Dr C. Mason, LD	6,110
D. Miller, Ref.	497
Dr M. Tayan, ProLife	393
D. McPherson, UK Ind.	113

Lab. majority 3,236
(Boundary change: notional C.)

EDINBURGH CENTRAL
E.63,695 T.67.09%

† A. Darling, Lab.	20,125
M. Scott-Hayward, C.	9,055
Ms F. Hyslop, SNP	6,750
Ms K. Utting, LD	5,605
Ms L. Hendry, Green	607
A. Skinner, Ref.	495
M. Benson, Ind. Dem.	98

Lab. majority 11,070
(Boundary change: notional Lab.)

EDINBURGH EAST AND MUSSELBURGH
E.59,648 T.70.61%

† Dr G. Strang, Lab.	22,564
D. White, SNP	8,034
K. Ward, C.	6,483
Dr C. MacKellar, LD	4,511
J. Sibbet, Ref.	526

Lab. majority 14,530
(Boundary change: notional Lab.)

EDINBURGH NORTH AND LEITH
E.61,617 T.66.45%

† M. Chisholm, Lab.	19,209
Ms A. Dana, SNP	8,231
E. Stewart, C.	7,312
Ms H. Campbell, LD	5,335
A. Graham, Ref.	441
G. Brown, SSA	320
P. Douglas-Reid, NLP	97

Lab. majority 10,978
(Boundary change: notional Lab.)

EDINBURGH PENTLANDS
E.59,635 T.76.70%

Ms L. Clark, Lab.	19,675
† Rt. Hon. M. Rifkind, C.	14,813
S. Gibb, SNP	5,952
Dr J. Dawe, LD	4,575
M. McDonald, Ref.	422
R. Harper, Green	224
A. McConnachie, UK Ind.	81

Lab. majority 4,862
(Boundary change: notional C.)

EDINBURGH SOUTH
E.62,467 T.71.78%

† N. Griffiths, Lab.	20,993
Miss E. Smith, C.	9,541
M. Pringle, LD	7,911
Dr J. Hargreaves, SNP	5,791
I. McLean, Ref.	504
B. Dunn, NLP	98

Lab. majority 11,452
(Boundary change: notional Lab.)

EDINBURGH WEST
E.61,133 T.77.91%

D. Gorrie, LD	20,578
† Rt. Hon. Lord J. Douglas-Hamilton, C.	13,325
Ms L. Hinds, Lab.	8,948
G. Sutherland, SNP	4,210
Dr S. Elphick, Ref.	277
P. Coombes, Lib.	263
A. Jack, AS	30

LD majority 7,253
(Boundary change: notional C.)

FALKIRK EAST
E.56,792 T.73.24%

† M. Connarty, Lab.	23,344
K. Brown, SNP	9,959
M. Nicol, C.	5,813
R. Spillane, LD	2,153
S. Mowbray, Ref.	326

Lab. majority 13,385
(Boundary change: notional Lab.)

FALKIRK WEST
E.52,850 T.72.60%

† D. Canavan, Lab.	22,772
D. Alexander, SNP	8,989
Mrs C. Buchanan, C.	4,639
D. Houston, LD	1,970

Lab. majority 13,783
(Boundary change: notional Lab.)

FIFE CENTRAL
E.58,315 T.69.90%

† H. McLeish, Lab.	23,912
Mrs P. Marwick, SNP	10,199
J. Rees-Mogg, C.	3,669
R. Laird, LD	2,610
J. Scrymgeour-Wedderburn, Ref.	375

Lab. majority 13,713
(Boundary change: notional Lab.)

FIFE NORTH EAST
E.58,794 T.71.16%

* M. Campbell, LD	21,432
A. Bruce, C.	11,076
C. Welsh, SNP	4,545
C. Milne, Lab.	4,301
W. Stewart, Ref.	485

LD majority 10,356
(Boundary change: notional LD)

GALLOWAY AND UPPER NITHSDALE
E.52,751 T.79.65%

A. Morgan, SNP	18,449
† Rt. Hon. I. Lang, C.	12,825
Ms K. Clark, Lab.	6,861
J. McKerchar, LD	2,700
R. Wood, Ind.	566
A. Kennedy, Ref.	428
J. Smith, UK Ind.	189

SNP majority 5,624
(Boundary change: notional C.)

GLASGOW ANNIESLAND
E.52,955 T.63.98%

† Rt. Hon. D. Dewar, Lab.	20,951
Dr W. Wilson, SNP	5,797
A. Brocklehurst, C.	3,881
C. McGinty, LD	2,453
A. Majid, ProLife	374
W. Bonnar, SSA	229
A. Milligan, UK Ind.	86
Ms G. McKay, Ref.	84
T. Pringle, NLP	24

Lab. majority 15,154
(Boundary change: notional Lab.)

GLASGOW BAILLIESTON
E.51,152 T.62.27%

† J. Wray, Lab.	20,925
Mrs P. Thomson, SNP	6,085
M. Kelly, C.	2,468
Ms S. Rainger, LD	1,217
J. McVicar, SSA	970
J. McClafferty, Ref.	188

Lab. majority 14,840
(Boundary change: notional Lab.)

GLASGOW CATHCART
E.49,312 T.69.17%

† J. Maxton, Lab.	19,158
Ms M. Whitehead, SNP	6,913
A. Muir, C.	4,248
C. Dick, LD	2,302
Ms Z. Indyk, ProLife	687
R. Stevenson, SSA	458
S. Haldane, Ref.	344

Lab. majority 12,245
(Boundary change: notional Lab.)

GLASGOW GOVAN
E.49,836 T.64.70%

M. Sarwar, Lab.	14,216
Ms N. Sturgeon, SNP	11,302
W. Thomas, C.	2,839
R. Stewart, LD	1,915
A. McCombes, SSA	755
P. Paton, SLU	325
I. Badar, SLI	319
Z. J. Abbasi, SCU	221
K. MacDonald, Ref.	201
J. White, BNP	149

Lab. majority 2,914
(Boundary change: notional Lab.)

GLASGOW KELVIN
E.57,438 T.56.85%

† G. Galloway, Lab.	16,643
Ms S. White, SNP	6,978
Ms E. Buchanan, LD	4,629
D. McPhie, C.	3,539
A. Green, SSA	386
R. Grigor, Ref.	282
V. Vanni, SPGB	102
G. Stidolph, NLP	95

Lab. majority 9,665
(Boundary change: notional Lab.)

GLASGOW MARYHILL
E.52,523 T.56.59%

† Ms M. Fyfe, Lab.	19,301
J. Wailes, SNP	5,037
Ms E. Attwooll, LD	2,119
S. Baldwin, C.	1,747
Ms L. Blair, NLP	651
Ms A. Baker, SSA	409
J. Hanif, ProLife	344
R. Paterson, Ref.	77
S. Johnstone, SEP	36

Lab. majority 14,264
(Boundary change: notional Lab.)

GLASGOW POLLOK
E.49,284 T.66.56%

† I. Davidson, Lab. Co-op.	19,653
D. Logan, SNP	5,862
T. Sheridan, SSA	3,639
E. Hamilton, C.	1,979
D. Jago, LD	1,137
Ms M. Gott, ProLife	380
D. Haldane, Ref.	152

Lab. Co-op. majority 13,791
(Boundary change: notional Lab. Co-op.)

GLASGOW RUTHERGLEN
E.50,646 T.70.14%

† T. McAvoy, Lab. Co-op.	20,430
I. Gray, SNP	5,423
R. Brown, LD	5,167
D. Campbell Bannerman, C.	3,288
G. Easton, Ind. Lab.	812
Ms R. Kane, SSA	251
Ms J. Kerr, Ref.	150

Lab. Co-op. majority 15,007
(Boundary change: notional Lab. Co-op.)

GLASGOW SHETTLESTON
E.47,990 T.55.87%

† D. Marshall, Lab.	19,616
H. Hanif, SNP	3,748
C. Simpson, C.	1,484
Ms K. Hiles, LD	1,061
Ms C. McVicar, SSA	482
R. Currie, BNP	191
T. Montguire, Ref.	151
J. Graham, WRP	80

Lab. majority 15,868
(Boundary change: notional Lab.)

GLASGOW SPRINGBURN
E.53,473 T.59.05%

† M. Martin, Lab.	22,534
J. Brady, SNP	5,208
M.Holdsworth, C.	1,893
J. Alexander, LD	1,349
J. Lawson, SSA	407
A. Keating, Ref.	186

Lab. majority 17,326
(Boundary change: notional Lab.)

GORDON
E.58,767 T.71.89%

† M. Bruce, LD	17,999
J. Porter, C.	11,002
R. Lochhead, SNP	8,435
Ms L. Kirkhill, Lab.	4,350
F. Pidcock, Ref.	459

LD majority 6,997
(Boundary change: notional C.)

GREENOCK AND INVERCLYDE
E.48,818 T.71.05%

† Dr N. Godman, Lab.	19,480
B. Goodall, SNP	6,440
R. Ackland, LD	4,791
H. Swire, C.	3,976

Lab. majority 13,040
(Boundary change: notional Lab.)

HAMILTON NORTH AND BELLSHILL
E.53,607 T.70.88%
† Dr J. Reid, Lab.   24,322
  M. Matheson, SNP   7,255
  G. McIntosh, C.   3,944
  K. Legg, LD   1,924
  R. Conn, Ref.   554
Lab. majority 17,067
(Boundary change: notional Lab.)

HAMILTON SOUTH
E.46,562 T.71.07%
† G. Robertson, Lab.   21,709
  I. Black, SNP   5,831
  R. Kilgour, C.   2,858
  R. Pitts, LD   1,693
  C. Gunn, ProLife   684
  S. Brown, Ref.   316
Lab. majority 15,878
(Boundary change: notional Lab.)
* See also page 38

INVERNESS EAST, NAIRN AND
LOCHABER
E.65,701 T.72.71%
  D. Stewart, Lab.   16,187
  F. Ewing, SNP   13,848
  S. Gallagher, LD   8,364
  Mrs M. Scanlon, C.   8,355
  Ms W. Wall, Ref.   436
  M. Falconer, Green   354
  D. Hart, Ch. U.   224
Lab. majority 2,339
(Boundary change: notional LD)

KILMARNOCK AND LOUDOUN
E.61,376 T.77.24%
  D. Browne, Lab.   23,621
  A. Neil, SNP   16,365
  D. Taylor, C.   5,125
  J. Stewart, LD   1,891
  W. Sneddon, Ref.   284
  W. Gilmour, NLP   123
Lab. majority 7,256
(April 1992, Lab. maj. 6,979)

KIRKCALDY
E.52,186 T.67.02%
† L. Moonie, Lab. Co-op.   18,730
  S. Hosie, SNP   8,020
  Miss C. Black, C.   4,779
  J. Mainland, LD   3,031
  V. Baxter, Ref.   413
Lab. Co-op. majority 10,710
(Boundary change: notional Lab. Co-op.)

LINLITHGOW
E.53,706 T.73.84%
† T. Dalyell, Lab.   21,469
  K. MacAskill, SNP   10,631
  T. Kerr, C.   4,964
  A. Duncan, LD   2,331
  K. Plomer, Ref.   259
Lab. majority 10,838
(Boundary change: notional Lab.)

LIVINGSTON
E.60,296 T.71.04%
† Rt. Hon. R. Cook, Lab.   23,510
  P. Johnston, SNP   11,763
  H. Craigie Halkett, C.   4,028
  E. Hawthorn, LD   2,876
  Ms H. Campbell, Ref.   444
  M. Culbert, SPGB   213
Lab. majority 11,747
(Boundary change: notional Lab.)

MIDLOTHIAN
E.47,552 T.74.13%
† E. Clarke, Lab.   18,861
  L. Millar, SNP   8,991
  Miss A. Harper, C.   3,842
  R. Pinnock, LD   3,235
  K. Docking, Ref.   320
Lab. majority 9,870
(Boundary change: notional Lab.)

MORAY
E.58,302 T.68.21%
† Mrs M. Ewing, SNP   16,529
  A. Findlay, C.   10,963
  L. Macdonald, Lab.   7,886
  Ms D. Storr, LD   3,548
  P. Mieklejohn, Ref.   840
SNP majority 5,566
(Boundary change: notional SNP)

MOTHERWELL AND WISHAW
E.52,252 T.70.08%
  F. Roy, Lab.   21,020
  J. McGuigan, SNP   8,229
  S. Dickson, C.   4,024
  A. Mackie, LD   2,331
  C. Herriot, Soc. Lab.   797
  T. Russell, Ref.   218
Lab. majority 12,791
(Boundary change: notional Lab.)

OCHIL
E.56,572 T.77.40%
† M. O'Neill, Lab.   19,707
  G. Reid, SNP   15,055

A. Hogarth, C. — 6,383
Mrs A. Watters, LD — 2,262
D. White, Ref. — 210
I. McDonald, D. Nat. — 104
M. Sullivan, NLP — 65
Lab. majority 4,652
(Boundary change: notional Lab.)

ORKNEY AND SHETLAND
E.32,291 T.64.00%
* J. Wallace, LD — 10,743
J. Paton, Lab. — 3,775
W. Ross, SNP — 2,624
H. Vere Anderson, C. — 2,527
F. Adamson, Ref. — 820
Ms C. Wharton, NLP — 116
A. Robertson, Ind. — 60
LD majority 6,968
(April 1992, LD maj. 5,033)

PAISLEY NORTH
E.49,725 T.68.65%
† Mrs I. Adams, Lab. — 20,295
I. Mackay, SNP — 7,481
K. Brookes, C. — 3,267
A. Jelfs, LD — 2,365
R. Graham, ProLife — 531
E. Mathew, Ref. — 196
Lab. majority 12,814
(Boundary change: notional Lab.)

PAISLEY SOUTH
E.54,040 T.69.12%
† G. McMaster, Lab. Co-op. — 21,482
W. Martin, SNP — 8,732
Ms E. McCartin, LD — 3,500
R. Reid, C. — 3,237
J. Lardner, Ref. — 254
S. Clerkin, SSA — 146
Lab. Co-op. majority 12,750
(Boundary change: notional Lab. Co-op.)
See also page 38

PERTH
E.60,313 T.73.87%
† Ms R. Cunningham, SNP — 16,209
J. Godfrey, C. — 13,068
D. Alexander, Lab. — 11,036
C. Brodie, LD — 3,583
R. MacAuley, Ref. — 366
M. Henderson, UK Ind. — 289
SNP majority 3,141
(Boundary change: notional C.)

RENFREWSHIRE WEST
E.52,348 T.76.00%
† T. Graham, Lab. — 18,525
C. Campbell, SNP — 10,546
C. Cormack, C. — 7,387
B. MacPherson, LD — 3,045
S. Lindsay, Ref. — 283
Lab. majority 7,979
(Boundary change: notional Lab.)

ROSS, SKYE AND INVERNESS WEST
E.55,639 T.71.81%
† C. Kennedy, LD — 15,472
D. Munro, Lab. — 11,453
Mrs M. Paterson, SNP — 7,821
Miss M. Macleod, C. — 4,368
L. Durance, Ref. — 535
A. Hopkins, Green — 306
LD majority 4,019
(Boundary change: notional LD)

ROXBURGH AND BERWICKSHIRE
E.47,259 T.73.91%
† A. Kirkwood, LD — 16,243
D. Younger, C. — 8,337
Ms H. Eadie, Lab. — 5,226
M. Balfour, SNP — 3,959
J. Curtis, Ref. — 922
P. Neilson, UK Ind. — 202
D. Lucas, NLP — 42
LD majority 7,906
(Boundary change: notional LD)

STIRLING
E.52,491 T.81.84%
Mrs A. McGuire, Lab. — 20,382
† Rt. Hon. M. Forsyth, C. — 13,971
E. Dow, SNP — 5,752
A. Tough, LD — 2,675
W. McMurdo, UK Ind. — 154
Ms E. Olsen, Value Party — 24
Lab. majority 6,411
(Boundary change: notional C.)

STRATHKELVIN AND BEARSDEN
E.62,974 T.78.94%
† S. Galbraith, Lab. — 26,278
D. Sharpe, C. — 9,986
G. McCormick, SNP — 8,111
J. Morrison, LD — 4,843
D. Wilson, Ref. — 339
Ms J. Fisher, NLP — 155
Lab. majority 16,292
(Boundary change: notional Lab.)

TAYSIDE NORTH
E.61,398 T.74.25%
J. Swinney, SNP — 20,447
† W. Walker, C. — 16,287
I. McFatridge, Lab. — 5,141
P. Regent, LD — 3,716
SNP majority 4,160
(Boundary change: notional C.)

TWEEDDALE, ETTRICK AND
LAUDERDALE
E.50,891 T.76.64%
M. Moore, LD — 12,178
K. Geddes, Lab. — 10,689
A. Jack, C. — 8,623
I. Goldie, SNP — 6,671
C. Mowbray, Ref. — 406
J. Hein, Lib. — 387
D. Paterson, NLP — 47
LD majority 1,489
(Boundary change: notional LD)

WESTERN ISLES
E.22,983 T.70.08%
* C. Macdonald, Lab. — 8,955
Dr A. Lorne Gillies, SNP — 5,379
J. McGrigor, C. — 1,071
N. Mitchison, LD — 495
R. Lionel, Ref. — 206
Lab. majority 3,576
(April 1992, Lab. maj. 1,703)

BY-ELECTIONS

since the last general election

PAISLEY SOUTH
(6 November 1997)
E.54,040 T.42%
D. Alexander, Lab. — 10,346
I. Blackford, SNP — 7,615
Ms E. McCartin, LD — 2,582
Ms S. Laidlaw, C. — 1,643
J. Deighan, ProLife — 578
F. Curran, Soc. All.
   Fighting Corruption — 306
C. McLauchlan, Scottish Ind. Lab. — 155
C. Herriot, Soc. Lab. — 153
K. Blair, NLP — 57
Lab. majority 2,731

HAMILTON SOUTH
(24 August 1999)
E. 47,081 T. 41.3%
B. Tynan, Lab. — 7,172
A. Ewing, SNP — 6,616
S. Blackall, SSP — 1,847

C. Ferguson, C. — 1,406
S. Mungall, HAHWA — 1,075
M. MacLaren, LD — 634
M. Burns, ProLife — 257
T. Dewar, Soc. Lab. — 238
J. Reid, Scot. Union. — 113
A. McConnachie, UK Ind. — 61
G. Stidolph, Nat. Law — 18
J. Moray, Stat. Quo — 17
Lab. majority 556

THE UK PARLIAMENT

MEMBERS FOR SCOTTISH SEATS

*Member of last Parliament
†Former Member of Parliament

*Adams, Mrs K. Irene (b. 1948), Lab., Paisley North, majority 12,814

†Alexander, Douglas G. (b. 1967), Lab., Paisley South, majority 2,731

Begg, Ms Anne (b. 1955), Lab., Aberdeen South, majority 3,365

*Brown, Rt. Hon. J. Gordon, Ph.D. (b. 1951), Lab., Dunfermline East, majority 18,751

Brown, Russell L. (b. 1951), Lab., Dumfries, majority 9,643

Browne, Desmond (b. 1952), Lab., Kilmarnock and Loudoun, majority 7,256

*Bruce, Malcolm G. (b. 1944), LD, Gordon, majority 6,997

*Campbell, Rt. Hon. W. Menzies, CBE, QC (b. 1941), LD, Fife North East, majority 10,356

*Canavan, Dennis A. (b. 1942), Lab., Falkirk West, majority 13,783

*Chisholm, Malcolm G. R. (b. 1949), Lab., Edinburgh North and Leith, majority 10,978

Clark, Ms Lynda M. (b. 1949), Lab., Edinburgh Pentlands, majority 4,862

*Clarke, Eric L. (b. 1933), Lab., Midlothian, majority 9,870

*Clarke, Rt. Hon. Thomas, CBE (b. 1941), Lab., Coatbridge and Chryston, majority 19,295

*Connarty, Michael (b. 1947), Lab., Falkirk East, majority 13,385

*Cook, Rt. Hon. R. F. (Robin) (b. 1946), Lab., Livingston, majority 11,747

*Cunningham, Ms Roseanna (b. 1951), SNP, Perth, majority 3,141

*Dalyell, Tam (b. 1932), Lab., Linlithgow, majority 10,838

*Darling, Rt. Hon. Alistair M. (b. 1953), Lab., Edinburgh Central, majority 11,070

*Davidson, Ian G. (b. 1950), Lab. Co-op., Glasgow Pollok, majority 13,791

*Dewar, Rt. Hon. Donald C. (b. 1937), Lab., Glasgow Anniesland, majority 15,154

*Donohoe, Brian H. (b. 1948), Lab., Cunninghame South, majority 14,869

Doran, Frank (b. 1949), Lab., Aberdeen Central, majority 10,801

*Ewing, Mrs Margaret A. (b. 1945), SNP, Moray, majority 5,566

*Foulkes, George (b. 1942), Lab. Co-op., Carrick, Cumnock and Doon Valley, majority 21,062

*Fyfe, Ms Maria (b. 1938), Lab., Glasgow Maryhill, majority 14,264

*Galbraith, Samuel L. (b. 1945), Lab., Strathkelvin and Bearsden, majority 16,292

*Galloway, George (b. 1954), Lab., Glasgow Kelvin, majority 9,665

*Godman, Norman A., Ph.D. (b. 1938), Lab., Greenock and Inverclyde, majority 13,040

Gorrie, Donald C. E. (b. 1933), LD, Edinburgh West, majority 7,253

*Graham, Thomas (b. 1944), SLI, Renfrewshire West, majority 7,979

*Griffiths, Nigel (b. 1955), Lab., Edinburgh South, majority 11,452

*Home Robertson, John D. (b. 1948), Lab., East Lothian, majority 14,221

*Hood, James (b. 1948), Lab., Clydesdale, majority 13,809

*Ingram, Rt. Hon. Adam P. (b. 1947), Lab., East Kilbride, majority 17,384

*Kennedy, Charles P. (b. 1959), LD, Ross, Skye and Inverness West, majority 4,019

*Kirkwood, Archibald J. (b. 1946), LD, Roxburgh and Berwickshire, majority 7,906

*Liddell, Rt. Hon. Helen (b. 1950), Lab., Airdrie and Shotts, majority 15,412

*McAllion, John (b. 1948), Lab., Dundee East, majority 9,961

*McAvoy, Thomas M. (b. 1943), Lab. Co-op., Glasgow Rutherglen, majority 15,007

*Macdonald, Calum A., Ph.D. (b. 1956), Lab., Western Isles, majority 3,576

*McFall, John (b. 1944), Lab. Co-op., Dumbarton, majority 10,883

McGuire, Mrs Anne (b. 1949), Lab., Stirling, majority 6,411

McKenna, Ms Rosemary (b. 1941), Lab., Cumbernauld and Kilsyth, majority 11,128

*McLeish, Henry B. (b. 1948), Lab., Fife Central, majority 13,713

*Maclennan, Rt. Hon. Robert A. R. (b. 1936), LD, Caithness, Sutherland and Easter Ross, majority 2,259

*Marshall, David, Ph.D. (b. 1941), Lab., Glasgow Shettleston, majority 15,868

*Martin, Michael J. (b. 1945), Lab., Glasgow Springburn, majority 17,326

*Maxton, John A. (b. 1936), Lab., Glasgow Cathcart, majority 12,245

*Michie, Mrs J. Ray (b. 1934), LD, Argyll and Bute, majority 6,081

*Moonie, Dr Lewis G. (b. 1947), Lab. Co-op., Kirkcaldy, majority 10,710

Moore, Michael K. (b. 1965), LD, Tweeddale, Ettrick and Lauderdale, majority 1,489

Morgan, Alastair N. (b. 1945), SNP, Galloway and Upper Nithsdale, majority 5,624

Murphy, James (b. 1967), Lab., Eastwood, majority 3,236

*O'Neill, Martin J. (b. 1945), Lab., Ochil, majority 4,652
Osborne, Mrs Sandra C. (b. 1956), Lab., Ayr, majority 6,543
*Reid, Rt. Hon. John, Ph.D. (b. 1947), Lab., Hamilton North and Bellshill, majority 17,067
*Robertson, Rt. Hon. George I. M. (b. 1946), Lab., Hamilton South, majority 15,878
*Ross, Ernest (b. 1942), Lab., Dundee West, majority 11,859
Roy, Frank (b. 1958), Lab., Motherwell and Wishaw, majority 12,791
*Salmond, Alexander E. A. (b. 1954), SNP, Banff and Buchan, majority 12,845
Sarwar, Mohammad (b. 1952), Lab., Glasgow Govan, majority 2,914
Savidge, Malcolm K. (b. 1946), Lab., Aberdeen North, majority 10,010
Smith, Sir Robert, Bt. (b. 1958), LD, Aberdeenshire West and Kincardine, majority 2,662
*Squire, Ms Rachel A. (b. 1954), Lab., Dunfermline West, majority 12,354
Stewart, David J. (b. 1956), Lab., Inverness East, Nairn and Lochaber, majority 2,339
*Strang, Rt. Hon. Gavin S., Ph.D. (b. 1943), Lab., Edinburgh East and Musselburgh, majority 14,530
Swinney, John R. (b. 1964), SNP, Tayside North, majority 4,160
*Wallace, James R. (b. 1954), LD, Orkney and Shetland, majority 6,968
*Welsh, Andrew P. (b. 1944), SNP, Angus, majority 10,189
*Wilson, Brian D. H. (b. 1948), Lab., Cunninghame North, majority 11,039
*Worthington, Anthony (b. 1941), Lab., Clydebank and Milngavie, majority 13,320
*Wray, James (b. 1938), Lab., Glasgow Baillieston, majority 14,840

ABBREVIATIONS OF PARTY NAMES

Anti-Corr.	Anti-Corruption, Mobile Home Scandal, Roads
Anti-Drug	Independent Anti-Drug Party
AS	Anti-sleaze
C.	Conservative
Ch. U.	Christian Nationalist
BNP	British National Party
Comm. Brit.	Communist Pary of Britain
D. Nat.	Democratic Nationalist
Falkirk W.	MP for Falkirk West
Green	Green Party
Highlands	Highlands and Islands Alliance
Ind.	Independent
Ind. Dem.	Independent Democrat
Ind. Ind.	Independent Independent
Ind. Prog.	Independent Progressive
Ind. R.	Independent Robertson
Ind. SB	Independent Sleaze-Buster
Ind. Voice	Independent Voice for Scottish Parliament
Ind. Water	Independent Labour Keep Scottish Water Public
Ind. Watt.	Independent Watt
Individual	Independent Individual
Ind. You	Independent of London: Independent for You
Lab.	Labour
Lab. Co-op.	Labour Co-operative
LD	Liberal Democrat
Mission	Scottish People's Mission
NLP	Natural Law Party
ProLife	ProLife Alliance
Ref.	Referendum Party
SCU	Scottish Conservative Unofficial
SFPP	Scottish Families and Pensioners Party
SLI	Scottish Labour Independent
SLU	Scottish Labour Unofficial
Soc. Lab.	Socialist Labour Party
SPGB	Socialist Party of Great Britain
SSA	Scottish Socialist Alliance
SNP	Scottish National Party
SSP	Scottish Socialist Party
SUP	Scottish Unionist Party
SWP	Socialist Workers Party
UK Ind.	UK Independence Party
Witchery	Witchery Tour Party
WRP	Workers' Revolutionary Party

OTHER GOVERNMENT DEPARTMENTS AND PUBLIC OFFICES

This section covers executive agencies of the Scottish Executive, regulatory bodies, tribunals and other statutory independent organisations and non-governmental public bodies. UK Civil Service departments and public bodies are included where their remit continues to extend to Scotland.

The information given below reflects the situation at the time of going to press a few weeks after the Scottish Parliament and Scottish Executive had assumed their responsibilities. It is possible that some further reorganisation of the Scottish Executive departments may take place. The most recent information can be obtained from the contact points at the main Scottish Executive offices at St Andrew's House.

ADJUDICATOR'S OFFICE

Haymarket House, 28 Haymarket, London SW1Y 4SP
Tel: 020-7930 2292; Fax: 020-7930 2298
E-mail: adjudicators@gtnet.gov.uk
Web: http://www.open.gov.uk/adjolt/acctemo1.htm

The Adjudicator's Office investigates complaints about the way the Inland Revenue (including the Valuation Office Agency) and Customs and Excise have handled an individual's affairs.

The Adjudicator: Dame Barbara Mills, DBE, QC
Head of Office: C. Gordon

ADVISORY COMMITTEE ON SITES OF SPECIAL SCIENTIFIC INTEREST

c/o Scottish Natural Heritage, 2 Anderson Place, Edinburgh EH6 5NP
Tel: 0131-446 2436; Fax: 0131-446 2405

The Committee advises Scottish Natural Heritage in cases where there are sustained scientific objections to the notification of Sites of Special Scientific Interest.
Chairman: Prof. W. Ritchie
Secretary: D. Howell

ADVISORY, CONCILIATION AND ARBITRATION SERVICE

Regional Office
Franborough House, 123–157 Bothwell Street, Glasgow G2 7JR
Tel: 0141 2042677; Fax: 0141-221 4697
Web: http://www.acas.org.uk

The Advisory, Conciliation and Arbitration Service (ACAS) promotes the improvement of industrial relations in general, provides facilities for conciliation, mediation and arbitration as means of avoiding and resolving industrial disputes, and provides advisory and information services on industrial relations matters to employers, employees and their representatives.
Director, Scotland: F. Blair

ANCIENT MONUMENTS BOARD FOR SCOTLAND

Longmore House, Salisbury Place, Edinburgh EH9 1SH
Tel: 0131-668 8764; Fax: 0131-668 8765

The Ancient Monuments Board for Scotland advises the Scottish Ministers on the exercise of their functions, under the Ancient Monuments and Archaeological Areas Act 1979, of providing protection for monuments of national importance.
Chairman: Prof. Michael Lynch, Ph.D. FRSE, FSA Scot.
Members: M. Baughan; Ms J. Cannizzo, Ph.D.; Ms Jill Harden, FSA Scot.; John C. Higgitt, FSA, FSA Scot.; Jean McFadden, CBE; Roger J. Mercer, FRSE, FSA, FSA Scot.; Prof. Christopher D. Morris, FRSE, FSA, FSA Scot., FRSA; Dr Scott Peake, Ph.D.; Dr Anna Ritchie, OBE, Ph.D., FSA, FSA Scot.; Cllr Eoin F. Scott, FSA Scot.; Dr Carol Swanson, Ph.D., FSA Scot.; Malcolm J. Taylor, TD, FRICS; Miss Lisbeth M. Thoms, FSA Scot.; Andrew Wright, FRSA
Secretary: Ronald A. J. Dalziel
Assessor: Dr David J. Breeze, Ph.D., FRSE, FSA, FSA Scot., FRSA

THE APPEALS SERVICE

Whittington House, 19–30 Alfred Place, London WC1E 7LW
Tel: 020-7712 2600

The Service (formerly the Independent Tribunal Service) is responsible for the functioning of tribunals hearing appeals concerning child support assessments, social security benefits and vaccine damage payments. Judicial authority for the service rests with the President, while administrative responsibility is exercised by the Appeals Service Agency, which is an executive agency of the Department of Social Security.
President: His Hon. Judge Michael Harris
Chief Executive: Appeals Service Agency: N. Ward

AUDIT SCOTLAND

110 George Street, Edinburgh EH2 4LH
Tel: 0131-477 1234Fax: 0131-477 4567

Audit Scotland was set up on 1 April 2000. It audits the accounts of the Scottish Executive and other public sector bodies in Scotland to ensure the proper, efficient and effective use of public funds. Audit Scotland carries out financial and regularity audits to ensure that public sector bodies adhere to the highest standards of financial management and governance and performance audits to ensure that these bodies achieve the best possible value for money. All of Audit Scotland's work concerning the 32 local authorities, fire and police boards is carried out for the Accounts Commission while its other work is undertaken for the Auditor General.
Auditor General: Robert W. Black
Controller of Audit: Ronnie Hinds
Secretary: William F. Magee

THE BANK OF ENGLAND

Threadneedle Street, London EC2R 8AH
Tel: 020-7601 4444; Fax 020-7601 4771
Web: http://www.bankofengland.co.uk

The Bank of England is the banker of the UK Government and manages the note issue. Since 1997 its Monetary Policy Committee has had responsibility for setting short-term interest rates to meet the Government's inflation target. As the central reserve bank of the country, the Bank keeps the accounts of British banks, who maintain with it a proportion of their cash resources, and of most overseas central banks.
Governor: The Rt. Hon. E. A. J. George
Monetary Policy Committee: The Governor; the Deputy Governors; Mr D. Clementi; Prof. C. Goodhart; Dr D. Julius; I. Plenderleith; J. Vickers; Dr S. Wadhwani
Chief Cashier and Deputy Director, Banking and Market Services: Ms M. V. Lowther

SCOTLAND AGENCY

19 St Vincent Place, Glasgow G1 2DT
Tel: 0141-2217972; Fax: 020-7601 4771
Scotland Agent: Ms J. Bulloch
Deputy Agent: Ms C. Brown

BENEFITS AGENCY

Quarry House, Quarry Hill, Leeds LS2 7UA
Tel: 0113-232 4000

The Agency is an executive agency of the Department of Social Security. It administers claims for and payments of social security benefits.
Chief Executive: Ms A. Cleveland
Directors: Charlie Mackinnon (Field Operations, Scotland and North); Tony Edge (Field Operations, South); Peter Ward (Performance Management); Phil Bartlett (Business Management)

MEDICAL POLICY
Principal Medical Officers: Dr M. Aylward; Dr P. Dewis; Dr P. Sawney; Dr A. Braidwood; Dr P. Stidolph; Dr R. Thomas; Dr M. Allerton; Dr S. Reed; Dr P. Wright; Dr M. Henderson

BOUNDARY COMMISSION FOR SCOTLAND

3 Drumsheugh Gardens, Edinburgh EH3 7QJ
Tel: 0131-538 7200; Fax: 0131-538 7240

The Commission is required by law to keep the parliamentary constituencies in Scotland under review. The latest review was completed in 1995 and its proposals took effect at the 1997 general election. The next review is due to be completed between 2002 and 2006.

Chairman (*ex officio*): The Speaker of the House of Commons
Deputy Chairman: The Hon. Lady Cosgrove
Secretary, R. Smith

BRITISH BROADCASTING CORPORATION

Broadcasting House, Portland Place, London W1A 1AA
Tel: 020-7580 4468; Fax: 020-7637 1630

The BBC is the UK's public broadcasting organisation. It is financed by revenue from receiving licences for the home services and by grant-in-aid from Parliament for the World Service (radio). For services, *see* Media section.

BBC SCOTLAND
BBC Broadcasting House, Queen Margaret Drive, Glasgow G12 8DG
Tel: 0141-339 8844

National Governor for Scotland: N. Drummond
Director, National and Regional Broadcasting: M. Thompson
Controller, BBC Scotland: J. McCormick

BRITISH WATERWAYS

Willow Grange, Church Road, Watford, Herts
WD1 3QA
Tel: 01923-226422; Fax: 01923-201400
E-mail: info@canalshq.demon.co.uk
Web: http://www.britishwaterways.co.uk

British Waterways conserves and manages over
2,000 miles/3,250 km of canals and rivers in
Great Britain. Its responsibilities include
maintaining the waterways and structures on and
around them; looking after wildlife and the
waterway environment; and ensuring that canals
and rivers are safe and enjoyable places to visit.
Chairman (part-time): G. Greener
Chief Executive: D. Fletcher

Scottish Office
Canal House, Applecross Street, Glasgow G4
9SP
Tel: 0141-354 7501; Fax: 0141-331 1688

BUILDING STANDARDS ADVISORY
COMMITTEE

Scottish Executive Building Control Division, 2-
H Victoria Quay, Edinburgh EH6 6QQ
Tel: 0131-244 7440; Fax: 0131-244 7454

The Committee advises the Scottish Ministers on
questions relating to their functions under Part II
of the Building (Scotland) Act 1959.
Chairman: Mr S. Thorburn
Secretary: J. Carter

CENTRAL ADVISORY COMMITTEE ON
JUSTICES OF THE PEACE (SCOTLAND)

Spur W1(E), Saughton House, Broomhouse
Drive, Edinburgh EH11 3XD
Tel: 0131-244 2691; Fax: 0131-244 2623

The Committee advises and makes
recommendations as to problems arising in
relation to the appointment and distribution of
justices of the peace and the work of JPs in
general and of the district court in particular.
Chairman: The Rt. Hon. Lord Cullen
Secretary: Mr R. Shiels

CERTIFICATION OFFICE FOR TRADE
UNIONS AND EMPLOYERS'
ASSOCIATIONS

180 Borough High Street, London SE1 1LW
Tel: 020-7210 3734/5; Fax: 020-7210 3612

The Certification Office is an independent
statutory authority responsible for receiving and
scrutinising annual returns from trade unions and
employers' associations; for investigating
allegations of financial irregularities in the affairs
of a trade union or employers' association; for
dealing with complaints concerning trade union
elections; for ensuring observance of statutory
requirements governing political funds and trade
union mergers; and for certifying the
independence of trade unions.
Certification Officer: E. G. Whybrew

Scottish Office
58 Frederick Street, Edinburgh EH2 1LN
Tel: 0131-226 3224; Fax: 0131-200 1300
Assistant Certification Officer for Scotland: J.
L. J. Craig

CHILD SUPPORT AGENCY

DSS Long Benton, Benton Park Road,
Newcastle upon Tyne NE98 1YX
Tel: 0191-213 5000

The Agency is an agency of the Department of
Social Security. It is responsible for implementing
the 1991 and 1995 Child Support Acts and for
the assessment and collection (or arrangement of
direct payment) of child support maintenance.
From June 1999 the Chief Executive took over
the responsibilities of the Chief Child Support
Officer when that office was abolished.
Chief Executive: Ms F. Boardman
Directors: M. Davison; M. Di Ciacca; V.
Gaskell; P. Hedley; M. Isaac; J. Lutton

CIVIL SERVICE COLLEGE

Branch Offices
Suite 19, 1 St Colme Street, Edinburgh EH3
6AA
Tel: 0131-220 8267; Fax: 0131-220 8367
199 Cathedral Street, Glasgow G4 0QU
Tel: 0141-553 6021; Fax: 0141-553 6171

The College provides training in management
and professional skills for the public and private
sectors.

COMMISSION FOR RACIAL EQUALITY

Regional Office
Hanover House, 45–51 Hanover Street,
Edinburgh EH2 2PJ
Tel: 0131-226 5186; Fax: 0131-226 5243

The Commission was established in 1977, under
the Race Relations Act 1976, to work towards the
elimination of discrimination and promote
equality of opportunity and good relations

between different racial groups. It is funded by the Home Office.
Head of CRE, Scotland: Dharmandra Kanani

COMMISSIONER FOR LOCAL ADMINISTRATION IN SCOTLAND

23 Walker Street, Edinburgh EH3 7HX
Tel: 0131-225 5300; Fax: 0131-225 9495

The Local Commissioner for Scotland is the local government ombudsman for Scotland, responsible for investigating complaints from members of the public against local authorities and certain other authorities. The Commissioner is appointed by the Crown on the recommendation of the First Minister.
Local Commissioner: vacant
Deputy Commissioner and Secretary: Ms J. H. Renton

COMPANIES HOUSE (SCOTLAND)

37 Castle Terrace, Edinburgh EH1 2EB
Tel: 0131-535 5800; Fax: 0131-535 5820
Web: http://www.companieshouse.gov.uk

Companies House is an executive agency of the Department of Trade and Industry. It incorporates companies, registers company documents and provides company information.
Registrar for Scotland: J. Henderson

Edinburgh Search Room
Tel: 0131-535 5868; Fax: 0131-535 5820

Glasgow Satellite Office
7 West George Street, Glasgow G2 1BQ
Tel: 0141-221 5513

COPYRIGHT TRIBUNAL

Harmsworth House, 13–15 Bouverie Street, London EC4Y 8DP
Tel: 020-7596 6510; Fax: 020-7596 6526

The Copyright Tribunal resolves disputes over copyright licences, principally where there is collective licensing.
   The chairman and two deputy chairmen are appointed by the Lord Chancellor. Up to eight ordinary members are appointed by the Secretary of State for Trade and Industry.
Chairman: C. P. Tootal
Secretary: Miss J. E. M. Durdin

COURT OF THE LORD LYON

HM New Register House, Edinburgh EH1 3YT
Tel: 0131-556 7255; Fax: 0131-557 2148

The Court of the Lord Lyon is the Scottish Court of Chivalry (including the genealogical jurisdiction of the Ri-Sennachie of Scotland's Celtic Kings). The Lord Lyon King of Arms has jurisdiction, subject to appeal to the Court of Session and the House of Lords, in questions of heraldry and the right to bear arms. The Court also administers the Scottish Public Register of All Arms and Bearings and the Public Register of All Genealogies. Pedigrees are established by decrees of Lyon Court and by letters patent. As Royal Commissioner in Armory, the Lord Lyon grants patents of arms (which constitute the grantee and heirs noble in the Noblesse of Scotland) to 'virtuous and well-deserving' Scots and to petitioners (personal or corporate) in the Queen's overseas realms of Scottish connection, and issues birthbrieves.
Lord Lyon King of Arms: Sir Malcolm Innes of Edingight, KCVO, WS

Heralds
Albany: J. A. Spens, MVO, RD, WS
Rothesay: Sir Crispin Agnew of Lochnaw, Bt., QC
Ross: C. J. Burnett, FSA Scot.

Pursuivants
Kintyre: J. C. G. George
Unicorn: Alastair Campbell of Airds, FSA Scot.
Carrick: Mrs C. G. W. Roads, MVO, FSA Scot.

Lyon Clerk and Keeper of Records: Mrs C. G. W. Roads, MVO, FSA Scot.
Procurator-Fiscal: W. L. K. MacLeod, WS
Herald Painter: Mrs J. Phillips
Macer: A. M. Clark

CRIMINAL INJURIES COMPENSATION AUTHORITY

Tay House, 300 Bath Street, Glasgow G2 4LN
Tel: 0141-331 2726; Fax: 0141-331 2287

All applications for compensation for personal injury arising from crimes of violence in Scotland are dealt with by the Board and are assessed under a tariff-based scheme which took effect on 1 April 1996. Any applications received before 1 April 1996 and still outstanding at 31 March 2000, when the Criminal Injuries Compensation Board (the Authority's predecessor) was formally wound up, have been transferred for resolution by the legally qualified members of the Criminal

Injuries Appeals Panel (CICAP). There is a separate avenue of appeal to the CICAP.
Chief Executive of the Criminal Injuries Compensation Authority: H. Webber
Chairman of the Criminal Injuries Compensation Appeals Panel: M. Lewer, QC
Secretary to the Panel: Miss V. Jenson

CROFTERS COMMISSION

4–6 Castle Wynd, Inverness IV2 3EQ
Tel: 01463-663450; Fax: 01463-711820
E-mail: crofters_commission@cali.co.uk

The Crofters Commission is a non-departmental public body established in 1955. It advises the Scottish Ministers on all matters relating to crofting, and works with other organisations and with communities to develop and promote thriving crofting communities and simplify legislation. It administers the Crofting Counties Agricultural Grants Scheme, Croft Entrant Scheme, and livestock improvement schemes.
Chairman: I. MacAskill
Secretary: M. Grantham

CROWN ESTATE

Scottish Estates
10 Charlotte Square, Edinburgh EH2 4DR
Tel: 0131-226 7241; Fax: 0131-220 1366
Web: http://www.crownestate.co.uk

The land revenues of the Crown in Scotland were transferred to the predecessors of the Crown Estate Commissioners in 1833. The Scottish office manages a variety of agricultural, forest and marine resources and commercial property.
Head of Scottish Estates: M. J. P. Cunliffe

CUSTOMS AND EXCISE

Scottish Collection
44 York Place, Edinburgh EH1 3JW
Tel: 0131-469 2000; Fax: 0131-469 7340
Web: http://www.hmce.gov.uk
and
http://www.open.gov.uk/customs/c&ehome.htm

HM Customs and Excise is responsible for collecting and administering customs and excise duties and VAT, and advises the Chancellor of the Exchequer on any matters connected with them. The Department is also responsible for preventing and detecting the evasion of revenue laws and for enforcing a range of prohibitions and restrictions on the importation of certain classes of goods. In addition, the Department undertakes certain agency work on behalf of other departments, including the compilation of UK overseas trade statistics from customs import and export documents.
Collector of HM Customs and Excise for Scotland: I. Mackay

DATA PROTECTION TRIBUNAL

c/o The Home Office, Queen Anne's Gate, London SW1H 9AT
Tel 020-7273 3755

The Data Protection Tribunal determines appeals against decisions of the Data Protection Commissioner. The chairman and deputy chairman are appointed by the Lord Chancellor and must be legally qualified. Lay members are appointed by the Home Secretary to represent the interests of data users or data subjects.

A tribunal consists of a legally-qualified chairman sitting with equal numbers of the lay members appointed to represent the interests of data users and data subjects.
Chairman: J. A. C. Spokes, QC
Secretary: R. Hartley

DEER COMMISSION FOR SCOTLAND

Knowsley, 82 Fairfield Road, Inverness IV3 5LH
Tel: 01463-231751; Fax: 01463-712931
E-mail: deercom@aol.com
Web: http://www.dcs.gov.uk

The Deer Commission for Scotland has the general functions of furthering the conservation, control and sustainable management of deer in Scotland. It has the statutory duty, with powers, to prevent damage to agriculture, forestry and the habitat by deer. It is funded by the Scottish Executive.
Chairman (part-time): A. Raven
Members: G. Campbell; R. Callander; D. Irwin-Houston, R. Cooke; R. Dennis; J. Duncan-Millar; S. Gibbs; Dr J. Milne; Sir M. Strangstell BT; J. MacKintosh; Dr P. Ratcliffe
Director: N. Reiter
Technical Director: R. W. Youngson

DRIVER AND VEHICLE LICENSING AGENCY

Longview Road, Morriston, Swansea SA6 7JL
Tel: 0870-240 0009 (drivers); 0870-240 0010 (vehicles)

The Agency is an executive agency of the Department of the Environment, Transport and the Regions. It is responsible for the issuing of driving licences, the registration and licensing of

vehicles in Great Britain, and the collection and enforcement of vehicle excise duty in the UK. The Agency also offers for sale attractive registration marks through the sale of Marks scheme.
Chief Executive: Dr S. J. Ford, CBE

Edinburgh Vehicle Registration Office
Saughton House, Broomhouse Drive, Edinburgh EH11 3XE
Tel: 0131-455 7919; Fax: 0131-443 2478
Scottish Area Manager: D. Drury

DRIVING STANDARDS AGENCY

Stanley House, Talbot Street, Nottingham NG1 5GU
Tel: 0115-901 2500; Fax: 0115-955 7334

The Agency is an executive agency of the Department of the Environment, Transport and the Regions. Its role is to carry out driving tests and approve driving instructors.
Chief Executive: Gary Austin

EMPLOYMENT APPEAL TRIBUNAL

Divisional Office
52 Melville Street, Edinburgh EH3 7HF
Tel: 0131-225 3963

The Employment Appeal Tribunal hears appeals on a question of law arising from any decision of an employment tribunal. A tribunal consists of a high court judge and two lay members, one from each side of industry.
Scottish Chairman: The Hon. Lord Johnston
Registrar: Miss V. J. Selio

THE EMPLOYMENT SERVICE

Argyll House, 3 Lady Lawson Street, Edinburgh EH3 9SD
Tel: 0131-221 4000; Fax: 0131-221 4004
Web: http://www.employmentservice.gov.uk

The Employment Service is an executive agency of the Department for Education and Employment. Its aims are to help people without jobs to find work and employers to fill their vacancies.
Director for Scotland: A. R. Brown

EMPLOYMENT TRIBUNALS

Central Office (Scotland)
Eagle Building, 215 Bothwell Street, Glasgow G2 7TS
Tel: 0141-204 0730

Employment tribunals deal with matters of employment law, redundancy, dismissal, contract disputes, sexual, racial and disability discrimination, and related areas of dispute which may arise in the workplace. A central registration unit records all applications and maintains a public register.
Chairmen are appointed by the Lord President of the Court of Session and lay members by the Secretary of State for Trade and Industry.
President: C. Milne

EQUAL OPPORTUNITIES COMMISSION

St Stephens House
279 Bath Street, Glasgow, G2 4JL
Tel: 0141-248 5833; Fax: 0141-248 5834
E-mail: scotland@eoc.org.uk
Web: http://www.eoc.org.uk

The Commission works towards the elimination of discrimination on the grounds of sex or marital status and to promote equality of opportunity between men and women generally. It is responsible to the Department for Education and Employment.
Director, Scotland: Ms M. Alexander

EXTRA PARLIAMENTARY PANEL

The Scotland Office, Dover House, Whitehall, London SW1A 2AU
Tel: 020-7270 6758; Fax: 020-7270 6730

The Panel hears evidence for and against draft provision orders in private legislation procedure at an inquiry, and makes recommendations as to whether an order should proceed, be amended or be refused. This is a reserved function and the secretariat for the panel is based at the Scotland Office.

FISHERIES COMMITTEE (ELECTRICITY)

Pentland House, Robb's Loan, Edinburgh EH14 1TY
Tel: 0131-244 6229

The Committee advises and assists the Scottish Ministers and any person engaging in, or proposing to engage in, the generation of hydro-electric power on any question relating to the effect of hydro-electric works on fisheries or stocks of fish.
Chairman: R. McGillivray
Secretary: Miss J. Dunn

FISHERIES RESEARCH SERVICES

Marine Laboratory, PO Box 101, Victoria Road, Aberdeen AB11 9DB
Tel: 01224-876544; Fax: 01224-295511

The Agency provides scientific information and advice on marine and freshwater fisheries, aquaculture and the protection of the aquatic environment and its wildlife.
Director: Dr A. D. Hawkins, FRSE
Deputy Director: Dr J. M. Davies

Freshwater Fisheries Laboratory
Faskally, Pitlochry, Perthshire PH6 5LB
Tel: 01796-472060

Senior Principal Scientific Officers: Dr R. M. Cook; Dr J. M. Davies; Dr A. E. Ellis; R. G. J. Shelton; Dr R. Stagg; Dr C. Moffat
Inspector of Salmon and Freshwater Fisheries for Scotland: D. A. Dunkley

FORESTRY COMMISSION

231 Corstorphine Road, Edinburgh EH12 7AT
Tel: 0131-334 0303; Fax: 0131-334 3047

The Forestry Commission is the government department responsible for forestry policy in Great Britain. It reports directly to forestry ministers to whom it is responsible for advice on forestry policy and for the implementation of that policy. The Scottish Ministers have responsibility for forestry in Scotland, the Minister of Agriculture, Fisheries and Food for forestry in England, and the National Assembly for Wales for forestry in Wales. For matters affecting forestry in Britain as a whole, all three ministers have equal responsibility but the Minister of Agriculture, Fisheries and Food takes the lead.
      The Commission's principal objectives are to protect Britain's forests and woodlands; expand Britain's forest area; enhance the economic value of the forest resources; conserve and improve the biodiversity, landscape and cultural heritage of forests and woodlands; develop opportunities for woodland recreation; and increase public understanding of and community participation in forestry.
Chairman (part-time): Sir Peter Hutchison, Bt., CBE
Director-General: D. J. Bills
Secretary to the Commissioners: F. Strang

FORESTRY COMMISSION NATIONAL OFFICE FOR SCOTLAND

231 Corstorphine Road, Edinburgh EH12 7AT
Tel: 0131-334 0303; Fax: 0131-314 6152
Chief Conservator: D. Henderson-Howat

FOREST ENTERPRISE

231 Corstorphine Road, Edinburgh EH12 7AT
Tel: 0131-334 0303

Forest Enterprise, a trading body operating as an executive agency of the Commission, manages its forestry estate on a multi-use basis.
Chief Executive: Dr B. McIntosh

FOREST ENTERPRISE SCOTLAND

North — 21 Church Street, Inverness IV1 1EL.
Tel: 01463-232811; Fax: 01463-243846
South — 55–57 Moffat Road, Dumfries DG1 1NP. Tel: 01387-2724400; Fax: 01387-251491

FOREST RESEARCH

Alice Holt Lodge, Wrecclesham, Farnham, Surrey GU10 4LU
Tel: 01420-22255
Forest Research provides research, development and advice to the forestry industry in support of the development and implementation of forestry policy.
Chief Executive: J. Dewar

Northern Research Station
Roslin, Midlothian EH25 9SY
Tel: 0131-445 2176

HEALTH AND SAFETY EXECUTIVE

Scotland Office
Belford House, 59 Belford Road, Edinburgh EH4 3UE
Tel: 0131-247 2000; Fax: 0131-247 2121

The Health and Safety Executive enforces health and safety law in the majority of industrial premises. The Executive advises the Health and Safety Commission in its major task of laying down safety standards through regulations and practical guidance for many industrial processes. The Executive is also the licensing authority for nuclear installations and the reporting officer on the severity of nuclear incidents in Great Britain.

HM Inspectorate of Mines
Daniel House, Trinity Road, Bootle L20 7HE
Tel: 0151-951 4000; Fax: 0151-951 3758
HM Chief Inspector of Mines: D. Mitchell

Nuclear Safety Directorate
Rose Court, 2 Southwark Bridge, London
SE1 9HS
Tel: 020-7717 6000; Fax: 020-7717 6717

HM Chief Inspector of Nuclear Installations:
Dr L. G. Williams

Railway Inspectorate
Rose Court, 2 Southwark Bridge, London SE1
9HS
Tel: 020-7717 6000; Fax: 020-7717 6717
HM Chief Inspecting Officer of Railways: V.
Coleman

HEALTH APPOINTMENTS ADVISORY COMMITTEE

Room 181, St Andrews House, Edinburgh
EH1 3DG
Tel: 0131-244 2579

The Committee advises on non-executive
appointments to health boards, NHS Trusts and
health non-departmental public bodies.
Chairman: vacant
Secretary: Mrs E. Gray

HERITAGE LOTTERY FUND (SCOTLAND)

28 Thistle Street, Edinburgh EH2 1EN
Tel: 0131-225 9450; Fax: 0131-225 9454
Web: http://www.hlf.org.uk

The Heritage Lottery Fund is the designated
distributor of the heritage share of proceeds from
the National Lottery. The Scottish office receives
and assesses all applications for projects based in
Scotland. A Committee for Scotland makes
decisions on grant requests up to £1 million; the
main board of trustees in London is responsible
for decisions on larger applications, with input
from the Committee for Scotland.
Chairman, Committee for Scotland: Sir Angus
Grossart, CBE
Manager, Scotland: C. McLean

HIGHLANDS AND ISLANDS ENTERPRISE

Bridge House, 20 Bridge Street, Inverness IV1
1QR
Tel: 01463-234171; Fax: 01463-244469
E-mail: hie.General@hient.co.uk
Web: http://www.hie.co.uk

Highlands and Islands Enterprise (HIE) was set
up under the Enterprise and New Towns
(Scotland) Act 1991. Its role is to design, direct
and deliver enterprise development, training,
environmental and social projects and services.
HIE is made up of a strategic core body and ten
local enterprise companies to which many of its
individual functions are delegated.
Chairman: Dr J. Hunter
Chief Executive: I. A. Robertson, CBE

HILL FARMING ADVISORY COMMITTEE FOR SCOTLAND

c/o Room 239, Pentland House, Robb's Loan,
Edinburgh EH14 1TW
Tel: 0131-244 6417; Fax: 0131-244 6277

The Committee advises the First Minister on the
exercise of his powers under the Hill Farming
Act.
Chairman: Mr D. Crawley
Secretary: Miss A. Greig

HISTORIC BUILDINGS COUNCIL FOR SCOTLAND

Longmore House, Salisbury Place, Edinburgh
EH9 1SH
Tel: 0131-668 8600; Fax: 0131-668 8788
Web: http://www.historic-scotland.go.uk

The Historic Buildings Council for Scotland is
the advisory body to the Scottish Ministers on
matters related to buildings of special
architectural or historical interest and in
particular to proposals for awards by them of
grants for the repair of buildings of outstanding
architectural or historical interest or lying within
outstanding conservation areas.
Chairman: Sir Raymond Johnstone, CBE
Members: R. Cairns; Mrs P. Chalmers; Bishop
M Conti; Miss L. Davidson; Mrs A. Dundas-
Bekker; Revd. G. Forbes; Dr J. Frew; D. Gauci;
M. Hopton; E. Jamieson; Mrs P. Robertson; Ms
F. Sinclair
Secretary: Mrs S. Williamson

HISTORIC SCOTLAND

Longmore House, Salisbury Place, Edinburgh
EH9 1SH
Tel: 0131-668 8600; Fax: 0131-668 8699
Web: http://www.historic-scotland.gov.uk

Historic Scotland is an executive agency of the
Scottish Executive Education Department. The
agency's role is to protect Scotland's historic
monuments, buildings and lands, and to promote
public understanding and enjoyment of them.
Chief Executive: G. N. Munro
Directors: F. J. Lawrie; I. Maxwell; B. Naylor; B.
O'Neil; L. Wilson

Chief Inspector of Ancient Monuments: Dr D. J. Breeze
Chief Inspector, Historic Buildings: R. Emerson, FSA, FSA Scot.

IMMIGRATION APPELLATE AUTHORITIES

Taylor House, 88 Rosebery Avenue, London EC1R 4QU
Tel: 020-7862 4200

The Immigration Appeal Adjudicators hear appeals from immigration decisions concerning the need for, and refusal of, leave to enter or remain in the UK, refusals to grant asylum, decisions to make deportation orders and directions to remove persons subject to immigration control from the UK. From 2 October 2000 its powers will derive principally from the Immigration and Asylum Act 1999. The Immigration Appeal Tribunal hears some appeals direct. Its principal jurisdiction is, however, the hearing of appeals from adjudicators by the party who is aggrieved by the decision. Appeals are subject to leave being granted by the tribunal.

An adjudicator sits alone. The tribunal sits in divisions of three, normally a legally qualified member and two lay members.

Immigration Appeal Tribunal
President: The Hon. Mr Justice Collins
Deputy President: C. M. G. Ockleton
Chief Adjudicator: His Hon. Judge Dunn, QC
Deputy Chief Adjudicator: J. Latter

INDEPENDENT REVIEW SERVICE FOR THE SOCIAL FUND

4th Floor, Centre City Podium, 5 Hill Street, Birmingham B5 4UB
Tel: 0121-606 2100; Fax: 0121-606 2180

The Social Fund Commissioner is appointed by the Secretary of State for Social Security. The Commissioner appoints Social Fund Inspectors, who provide an independent review of decisions made by Social Fund Officers in the Benefits Agency of the Department of Social Security.
Social Fund Commissioner: J. Scampion

INDEPENDENT TELEVISION COMMISSION (SCOTLAND)

123 Blythswood Street, Glasgow G2 2AN
Tel: 0141-226 4436; Fax: 0141-226 4682
Web: http://www.itc.org.uk

The Independent Television Commission is responsible for licensing and regulating all commercially funded television services broadcast from the UK. Members are appointed by the Secretary of State for Culture, Media and Sport.
Head of ITC (Scotland) and Controller, Regions: B. Marjoribanks

INLAND REVENUE (SCOTLAND)

The Board of Inland Revenue administers and collects direct taxes and advises the Chancellor of the Exchequer on policy questions involving them. The Department's Valuation Office is an executive agency responsible for valuing property for tax purposes.
Regional Executive Office (Income Taxes)
Clarendon House, 114–116 George Street, Edinburgh EH2 4LH
Tel: 0131-473 4000
Director: I. S. Gerrie

Capital Taxes Office (Scotland)
Mulberry House, 16 Picardy Place, Edinburgh EH1 3NF
Tel: 0131-556 8511; Fax: 0131-556 9894
Registrar: Mrs J. Templeton

Edinburgh Stamp Office
16 Picardy Place, Edinburgh EH1 3NF
Tel: 0131-556 8998

Financial Intermediaries and Claims Office (Scotland)
Trinity Park House, South Trinity Road, Edinburgh EH5 3SD
Tel: 0131-551 8127
Assistant Director: Ms L. Clayton

Solicitor's Office (Scotland)
Clarendon House, 114—116 George Street, Edinburgh EH2 4LH
Tel: 0131-473 4053; Fax: 0131-473 4143
Solicitor: I. K. Laing

Valuation Office Agency
50 Frederick Street, Edinburgh EH2 1NG
Tel: 0131-465 0700; Fax: 0131-465 0799
Chief Valuer, Scotland: A. Ainslie

INTERVENTION BOARD

PO Box 69, Reading RG1 3YD
Tel: 0118-958 3626; Fax: 0118-953 1370

The Intervention Board is an executive agency of the four agriculture ministries in the UK; in Scotland it is an agency of the Scottish Executive Rural Affairs Department. It is responsible for the implementation of European Union regulations covering the market support

arrangements of the Common Agricultural Policy. Members are appointed by and are responsible to the four agriculture ministers.
Chairman: I. Kent
Chief Executive: G. Trevelyan

Regional Verification Office
Room E1/5, Saughton House, Broomhouse Drive, Edinburgh EH11 3XA
Tel: 0131-244 8382; Fax: 0131-244 8117
Regional Verification Officer: P. R. Drummond

JUDICIAL COMMITTEE OF THE PRIVY COUNCIL

Downing Street, London SW1A 2AJ
Tel: 020-7270 0483

Following devolution, the Judicial Committee of the Privy Council assumes a new role as Scotland's principal constitutional court and will be the final arbiter in disputes raising issues as to the legal competence of things done or proposed by The Scottish Parliament or Executive.

The members of the Judicial Committee include the Lord Chancellor, the Lords of Appeal in Ordinary, other Privy Counsellors who hold or have held high judicial office and certain judges from the Commonwealth.
Registrar of the Privy Council: J. A. C. Watherston
Chief Clerk: F. G. Hart

JUSTICES OF THE PEACE ADVISORY COMMITTEES

c/o Spur W1(E), Saughton House, Broomhouse Drive, Edinburgh EH11 3XD
Tel: 0131-244 2222; Fax: 0131-244 2623

The committees, of which there are 32, keep under review the strength of the Commissions of the Peace in Scotland and advise on the appointment of new justices of the peace. Each committee has its own chairman and secretary. The Scottish Executive provides central advice to the committees.

LANDS TRIBUNAL FOR SCOTLAND

1 Grosvenor Crescent, Edinburgh EH12 5ER
Tel: 0131-225 7996

The Lands Tribunal for Scotland determines questions relating to the valuation of land, rating appeals from valuation committees, the discharge or variation of land obligations, questions of disputed compensation following compulsory purchase, and questions relating to tenants' rights to buy. The president is appointed by the Lord

President of the Court of Session.
President: The Hon. Lord McGhie, QC
Members: J. Devine, FRICS; A. R. MacLeary, FRICS
Member (part-time): R. A. Edwards, CBE, WS
Clerk: N. M. Tainsh

LOCAL GOVERNMENT BOUNDARY COMMISSION FOR SCOTLAND

3 Drumsheugh Gardens, Edinburgh EH3 7QJ
Tel: 0131-538 7510; Fax: 0131-538 7511

The Commission keeps under review the boundaries of local government administrative and electoral areas.
Chairman: The Hon. Lord Osborne
Secretary: R. Smith

LORD ADVOCATE'S OFFICE

Crown Office, 25 Chambers Street, Edinburgh EH1 1LA
Tel: 0131-226 2626; Fax: 0131-226 6910

Lord Advocate: The Rt. Hon. Colin Boyd, QC
  Private Secretary: J. Gibbons
Solicitor-General for Scotland: Neil F. Davidson, QC
  Private Secretary: J. Gibbons
Legal Secretary to the Law Officers: P. J. Layden, TD

MARITIME AND COASTGUARD AGENCY

Spring Place, 105 Commercial Road, Southampton SO15 1EG
Tel: 023-8032 9100

The Agency is an executive agency of the Department of the Environment, Transport and the Regions, formed in 1998 by the merger of the Coastguard Agency and the Marine Safety Agency. Its role is to develop, promote and enforce high standards of marine safety; to minimise loss of life amongst seafarers and coastal users and to respond to maritime emergencies 24 hours a day.
Chief Executive: M. Storey

HM COASTGUARD
North and East Scotland Search and Rescue District

Aberdeen Maritime Rescue Coordination Centre
HM CoastguardMarine House, Blaikies Quay Aberdeen, AB11 5PB
Tel: 01224 592334; Fax: 01224 575920
HM Regional Inspector: R. Crowther

West of Scotland and Northern Ireland Search and Rescue Region

Clyde Maritime Rescue Coordination Centre
HM Coastguard, Navy Buildings,Greenock PA16
Tel: 01475-784621; Fax: 01475-724006
Regional Inspector: B. Cunningham

MENTAL WELFARE COMMISSION FOR SCOTLAND

K Floor, Argyle House, 3 Lady Lawson Street, Edinburgh EH3 9SH
Tel: 0131-222 6111

The Commission protects the mentally disordered by the investigation of irregularities and by visiting patients in hospitals and in the community, and reports as appropriate to the relevant authorities.
Chairman: I. J. Miller, OBE
Vice-Chairman: Mrs N. Bennie
Commissioners (part-time): C. Campbell, QC; Mrs F. Cotter; W. Gent; Dr P. Jauhar; Dr S. Jiwa; Dr E. McCall-Smith; D. J. Macdonald; Dr J. Morrow; M. D. Murray; Dr L. Pollock; A. Robb; Mrs M. Ross; Dr M. Thomas; Dr M. Whoriskey
Director: Dr J. A. T. Dyer

NATIONAL ARCHIVES OF SCOTLAND

HM General Register House, Edinburgh EH1 3YY
Tel: 0131-535 1314; Fax: 0131-535 1360
E-mail: research@nas.gov.uk

The history of the national archives of Scotland can be traced back to the 13th century. The National Archives of Scotland (formerly the Scottish Record Office) is an executive agency of the Scottish Executive Justice Department. It keeps the administrative records of pre-Union Scotland, the registers of central and local courts of law, the public registers of property rights and legal documents, and many collections of local and church records and private archives. Certain groups of records, mainly the modern records of government departments in Scotland, the Scottish railway records, the plans collection, and private archives of an industrial or commercial nature, are preserved in the branch repository at the West Register House in Charlotte Square. The National Register of Archives (Scotland) is based in the West Register House.

The search rooms in both buildings are open Monday–Friday, 9–4.45. A permanent exhibition at the West Register House and changing exhibitions at the General Register House are open to the public on weekdays, 10–4.
Keeper of the Records of Scotland: P. M. Cadell
Deputy Keeper: Dr P. D. Anderson

NATIONAL AUDIT OFFICE

22 Melville Street, Edinburgh EH3 7NS
Tel: 0131-244 2739; Fax: 0131-244 2721
E-mail: edin.nao@gtnet.gov.uk
Web: http://www.open.gov.uk/nao.home.htm

The National Audit Office provides independent information, advice and assurance to Parliament and the public about all aspects of the financial operations of government departments and many other bodies receiving public funds. It does this by examining and certifying the accounts of these organisations and by regularly publishing reports to Parliament on the results of its value-for-money investigations of the economy, efficiency and effectiveness with which public resources have been used. The National Audit Office is also the auditor by agreement of the accounts of certain international and other organisations. In addition, the Office authorises the issue of public funds to government departments.
Director, Value-for-Money Audit: A. Roberts
Director, Financial Audit: R. Frith

NATIONAL GALLERIES OF SCOTLAND

The Mound, Edinburgh EH2 2EL
Tel: 0131-624 6200; Fax: 0131-343 3250
E-mail: pressinfo@natgalscot.ac.uk
Web: http://www.natgalscot.ac.uk

The National Galleries of Scotland comprise the National Gallery of Scotland, the Scottish National Portrait Gallery, the Scottish National Gallery of Modern Art and the Dean Gallery. There are also outstations at Paxton House, Berwickshire, and Duff House, Banffshire. Total government grant-in-aid for 1999–2000 was £10.197 million.
Chairman: The Countess of Airlie, CVO
Trustees: Ms V. Atkinson; J. H. Blair; G. Gemmell, CBE; Lord Gordon of Strathblane, CBE; A. Leitch; Prof. C. Lodder; Dr I. McKenzie Smith, OBE; Dr M. Shea; G. Weaver; Prof. I. Whyte
Director: T. Clifford
Keeper of Conservation: M. Gallagher
Head of Press and Information: Ms C. Black
Keeper of Education: M. Cassin
Registrar: Miss A. Buddle
Secretary: Ms S. Edwards
Buildings: R. Galbraith
Keeper, National Gallery of Scotland: M. Clarke

Keeper, Scottish National Portrait Gallery: J. Holloway
Curator of Photography: Miss S. F. Stevenson
Keeper, Scottish National Gallery of Modern Art and of Dean Gallery: R. Calvocoressi

NATIONAL HEALTH SERVICE TRIBUNAL (SCOTLAND)

66 Queen Street, Edinburgh EH2 4NE
Tel: 0131-226 4771

The tribunal considers representations that the continued inclusion of a doctor, dentist, optometrist or pharmacist on a health board's list would be prejudicial to the efficiency of the service concerned. The tribunal sits when required and is composed of a chairman, one lay member, and one practitioner member drawn from a representative professional panel. The chairman is appointed by the Lord President of the Court of Session, and the lay member and the members of the professional panel are appointed by the First Minister.
Chairman: M. G. Thomson, QC
Lay member: J. D. M. Robertson
Clerk: D. G. Brash, WS

NATIONAL LIBRARY OF SCOTLAND

George IV Bridge, Edinburgh EH1 1EW
Tel: 0131-226 4531; Fax: 0131-622 4803
E-mail: enquiries@nls.uk
Web: http://www.nls.uk

The Library, which was founded as the Advocates' Library in 1682, became the National Library of Scotland in 1925. It is funded through the Scottish Executive. It contains about seven million printed and new media items, 1.6 million maps, 25,000 periodicals and annual titles and 120,000 volumes of manuscripts. It has an unrivalled Scottish collection.

The Reading Room is for reference and research which cannot conveniently be pursued elsewhere. Admission is by ticket issued to an approved applicant.

Opening hours
Reading Room, weekdays, 9.30–8.30
  (Wednesday, 10–8.30); Saturday 9.30–1
Map Library, weekdays, 9.30–5 (Wednesday,
  10–5); Saturday 9.30–1
Exhibition, Monday-Saturday 10–5; Sunday 2–5
  Scottish Science Library, weekdays, 9.30–5
  (Wednesday, 10–8.30)

Chairman of the Trustees: vacant
Librarian and Secretary to the Trustees: I. D. McGowan

Secretary of the Library: M. C. Graham
Director of General Collections: vacant
Director of Special Collections: M. C. T. Simpson, Ph.D.
Director of Public Services: A. M. Marchbank, Ph.D.
Director, Information and Communications Technology: R. F. Guy

NATIONAL LOTTERY CHARITIES BOARD (SCOTLAND)

Norloch House, 36 King's Stables Road, Edinburgh EH1 2EJ
Tel: 0131-221 7100; Fax: 0131-221 7120
Web: http://www.nlcb.org.uk

The Board is one of six independent bodies set up to distribute funds from the Lottery. It aims to help meet the needs of those at greatest disadvantage in society and to improve the quality of life in the community by supporting projects run by charitable, benevolent and philanthropic organisations. Grants can be for up to three years; the smallest award is £500 and the average award is around £120,000.
Director for Scotland: Adrienne Kelbie

NATIONAL MUSEUMS OF SCOTLAND

Chambers Street, Edinburgh EH1 1JF
Tel: 0131-225 7534; Fax: 0131-220 4819
E-mail: feedback@nms.ac.uk
Web: http://www.nms.ac.uk

The National Museums of Scotland comprise the Royal Museum of Scotland, the National War Museum of Scotland, the Scottish Agricultural Museum, the Museum of Flight, Shambellie House Museum of Costume and the Museum of Scotland. Total funding from the Scottish Executive for 1999–2000 was £19.9 million.
Board of Trustees
Chairman: R. Smith, FSA Scot.
Members: Prof. T. Devine; Dr L. Glasser, MBE, FRSE; S. G. Gordon, CBE; G. Johnston, OBE, TD; Ms C. Macaulay; N. McIntosh, CBE; Prof. A. Manning, OBE; Prof. J. Murray; Sir William Purves, CBE, DSO; Dr A. Ritchie, OBE; The Countess of Rosebery; I. Smith; Lord Wilson of Tillyorn, GCMG

Officers
Director: M. Jones, FSA, FSA Scot., FRSA
Depute Director and Keeper of History and Applied Art: Miss D. Idiens, FRSA, FSA Scot.
Development Director: C. McCallum
Keeper of Archaeology, D. V. Clarke, Ph.D., FSA, FSA Scot.

Keeper of Geology and Zoology: M. Shaw, D. Phil.
Keeper of Social and Technological History: G. Sprott
Head of Public Affairs: Ms M. Bryden
Head of Technical Services: S. R. Elson, FSA Scot.

NORTHERN LIGHTHOUSE BOARD

84 George Street, Edinburgh EH2 3DA
Tel: 0131-473 3100; Fax: 0131-220 2093
E-mail: nlb@dial.pipex.com

The Lighthouse Board is the general lighthouse authority for Scotland and the Isle of Man. The present board owes its origin to an Act of Parliament passed in 1786. At present the Commissioners operate under the Merchant Shipping Act 1894 and are 19 in number.
The Commissioners control 83 major automatic lighthouses, 117 minor lights and many lighted and unlighted buoys. They have a fleet of two motor vessels.

Commissioners
The Lord Advocate
The Solicitor-General for Scotland
The Lord Provosts of Edinburgh, Glasgow and
    Aberdeen
The Provost of Inverness
The Convener of Argyll and Bute Council
The Sheriffs-Principal of North Strathclyde,
    Tayside, Central and Fife, Grampian,
    Highlands and Islands, South Strathclyde,
    Dumfries and Galloway, Lothians and
    Borders, and Glasgow and Strathkelvin
Capt. D. M. Cowell
Adm. Sir Michael Livesay, KCB
The Lord Maclay
P. Mackay, CB
Capt. Kenneth MacLeod
Chief Executive: Capt. J. B. Taylor, RN
Director of Finance: D. Gorman
Director of Engineering: M. Waddell
Director of Operations and Navigational Requirements: P. J. Christmas

OFFICE OF THE ACCOUNTANT IN BANKRUPTCY

George House, 126 George Street, Edinburgh EH2 4HH
Tel: 0131-473 4600; Helpline 0845-7626171;
Fax: 0131-473 4737

The Office is responsible for the administration of personal bankruptcies in Scotland.
Accountant in Bankruptcy: S. Woodhouse

OFFICE OF THE DATA PROTECTION COMMISSIONER

Wycliffe House, Water Lane, Wilmslow, Cheshire SK9 5AF
Tel: 01625-545745; Fax: 01625-524510

The Data Protection Act 1998 came into force in March 2000. It sets rules for processing personal information and applies to some paper records as well as those held on computers. It is the Commissioner's duty to compile and maintain the register of data controllers and provide facilities for members of the public to examine the register; promote observance of the data protection principles; and disseminate information to the public about the Act and her function under the Act. The Commissioner also has the power to produce codes of practice. The Commissioner reports annually to parliament on the performance of her functions under the Act and has obligations to assess the breaches of the Act.
Commissioner: Mrs E. France

OFFICE OF GAS AND ELECTRICITY MARKETS (SCOTLAND)

Regent Court, 70 West Regent Street, Glasgow G2 2QZ
Tel: 0141-331 2678; Fax: 0141-331 2777

The Office of Gas and Electricity Markets (Ofgem) is the independent regulatory body for the gas and electricity supply industries following the merger of the Office of Gas Supply and the Office of Electricity Regulation in 1999. Its functions are to promote competition and to protect customers' interests in relation to prices, security of supply and quality of services.
Director-General for Electricity and Gas Supply: C. McCarthy
Deputy Director-General for Scotland: C. Coulthard

OFFICE OF THE SOCIAL SECURITY AND CHILD SUPPORT COMMISSIONERS

23 Melville Street, Edinburgh EH3 7PW
Tel: 0131-225 2201; Fax: 0131-220 6782

The Social Security Commissioners are the final statutory authority to decide appeals relating to entitlement to social security benefits. The Child Support Commissioners are the final statutory authority to decide appeals relating to child support. Appeals may be made in relation to both matters only on a point of law.

Chief Social Security Commissioner and Chief Child Support Commissioner (London): His Hon. Judge Machin, QC
Commissioners (Edinburgh): W. M. Walker, QC; D. J. May, QC
Legal Officers: C. F. Smith; Miss L. Hansford
Secretary (Edinburgh): Ms S. M. Niven

OFFICE OF TELECOMMUNICATIONS

50 Ludgate Hill, London EC4M 7JJ
Tel: 020-7634 8700; Fax: 020-7634 8943

The Office of Telecommunications (Oftel) is responsible for supervising telecommunications activities and broadcast transmission in the UK. Its principal functions are to ensure that holders of telecommunications licences comply with their licence conditions; to maintain and promote effective competition in telecommunications; and to promote the interests of purchasers and other users of telecommunication services and apparatus in respect of prices, quality and variety.

The Director-General has powers to deal with anti-competitive practices and monopolies. He also has a duty to consider all reasonable complaints and representations about telecommunication apparatus and services.
Director-General: D. Edmonds

PARLIAMENTARY COMMISSIONER FOR ADMINISTRATION AND HEALTH SERVICE COMMISSIONER

The Parliamentary Commissioner for Administration (the Parliamentary Ombudsman) is independent of Government and is an officer of Parliament. He is responsible for investigating complaints referred to him by MPs from members of the public who claim to have sustained injustice in consequence of maladministration by or on behalf of UK government departments and certain non-departmental public bodies. The Parliamentary Commissioner also investigates complaints, referred by MPs, about wrongful refusal of access to official information.

The Health Service Commissioner (the Health Service Ombudsman) for Scotland is responsible for investigating complaints against National Health Service authorities and trusts that are not dealt with by those authorities to the satisfaction of the complainant. The Ombudsman's jurisdiction now covers complaints about family doctors, dentists, pharmacists and opticians, and complaints about actions resulting from clinical judgment. The Health Service Ombudsman is also responsible for investigating

complaints that information has been wrongly refused under the Code of Practice on Openness in the National Health Service 1995. The office is presently held by the Parliamentary Commissioner (*see also* Scottish Parliamentary Commissioner for Administration).

Parliamentary Commissioner's Office
Millbank Tower, Millbank, London SW1P 4QP
Tel: 0845-015 4033; Fax: 020-7217 4000
Web: http://www.ombudsman.org.uk
Parliamentary Commissioner and Health Service Commissioner: M. S. Buckley
Deputy Parliamentary Commissioner: A. Watson
Directors of Investigations: N. Cleary; Mrs S. P. Maunsell; G. Monk; D. Reynold

Health Service Commissioners' Office
Millbank Tower, Millbank, London SW1P 4QP
Tel: 0845-015 4033; Fax: 020-7217 4000
28 Thistle Street, Edinburgh EH2 1EN
Tel: 0845-601 0456; Fax: 0131-226 4447
Web: http://www.ombudsman.org.uk
Health Service Commissioner: M. S. Buckley
Deputy Health Service Commissioner: Ms H. Scott
Director of Investigations for Scotland: N. J. Jordan

PAROLE BOARD FOR SCOTLAND

Saughton House, Broomhouse Drive, Edinburgh EH11 3XD
Tel: 0131-244 8755; Fax: 0131-244 6974

The Board is an independent body which directs and advises Scottish Ministers on the release of prisoners on licence, and related matters.
Chairman: D. J. J. McManus
Vice-Chairmen: H. Hyslop
Secretary: H. P. Boyle

PATENT OFFICE

Cardiff Road, Newport NP10 8QQ
Tel: 08459-500505 (enquiries); 01633-811010 (search and advisory service); Fax: 01633-814444
E-mail: enquiries@patent.gov.uk
Web: http://www.patent.gov.uk

The Patent Office is an executive agency of the Department of Trade and Industry. The duties of the Patent Office are to administer the Patent Acts, the Registered Designs Act and the Trade Marks Act, and to deal with questions relating to the Copyright, Designs and Patents Act 1988. It aims to stimulate the innovation and competitiveness of industry. The Search and Advisory Service carries out commercial searches through patent information.

There are two Patents Information Network (PIN) centres in Scotland (which are not connected to the Patent Office itself) where patent searches can be conducted:

Business and Technical Department
Central Library, Rosemount Viaduct, Aberdeen AB25 1GW
Tel: 01224-652500

Business Users' Service
Mitchell Library, North Street, Glasgow G3 7DN
Tel: 0141-287 2905

PENSIONS APPEAL TRIBUNALS FOR SCOTLAND

20 Walker Street, Edinburgh EH3 7HS
Tel: 0131-220 1404

The Pensions Appeal Tribunals are responsible for hearing appeals from ex-servicemen or women and widows who have had their claims for a war pension rejected by the Secretary of State for Social Security. The Entitlement Appeal Tribunals hear appeals in cases where the Secretary of State has refused to grant a war pension. The Assessment Appeal Tribunals hear appeals against the Secretary of State's assessment of the degree of disablement caused by an accepted condition. The tribunal members are appointed by the President of the Court of Session
President: C. N. McEachran, QC

POST-QUALIFICATION EDUCATION BOARD FOR HEALTH SERVICE PHARMACISTS IN SCOTLAND

c/o Scottish Centre for Post-Qualification Pharmaceutical Education, Room 163, SIBS Todd Wing, 27 Taylor Street, University of Strathclyde, Glasgow G4 0NR
Tel: 0141-548 4273; Fax: 0141-553 4102
E-mail: scppe@strath.ac.uk

The Board advises on the post-qualification educational requirements of all registered pharmacists working in the NHS in Scotland.
Chairman: Dr G. Jefferson
Secretary: Ms R. M. Parr

REGISTERS OF SCOTLAND

Meadowbank House, 153 London Road, Edinburgh EH8 7AU
Tel: 0845 607 0161; Fax: 0131-479 3688
E-mail: keeper@ros.gov.uk
Web: http://www.ros.gov.uk

Registers of Scotland is the executive agency responsible for framing and maintaining records relating to property and further legal documents in Scotland. Information from these public registers can be obtained through personal visits, by post, fax or via e-mail.

The agency holds 15 registers; two property registers (General Register of Sasines and Land Register of Scotland), which form the chief security in Scotland of the rights of land and other heritable (or real) property; and the remaining 13 grouped under the collective name of the Chancery and Judicial Registers (Register of Deeds in the Books of Council and Session; Register of Protests; Register of Judgments; Register of Service of Heirs; Register of the Great Seal; Register of the Quarter Seal; Register of the Prince's Seal; Register of Crown Grants; Register of Sheriffs' Commissions; Register of the Cachet Seal; Register of Inhibitions and Adjudications; Register of Entails; Register of Hornings).
Keeper of the Registers: A. W. Ramage
Deputy Keeper: A. G. Rennie
Managing Director: F. Manson

REGISTRY OF FRIENDLY SOCIETIES (SCOTLAND)

58 Frederick Street, Edinburgh EH2 1NB
Tel: 0131-226 3224

The Registry of Friendly Societies is a non-ministerial government department comprising the Central Office of the Registry of Friendly Societies, together with the Assistant Registrar of Friendly Societies for Scotland. The Central Office of the Registry of Friendly Societies provides a public registry for mutual organisations registered under the Building Societies Act 1986, Friendly Societies Acts 1974 and 1992, and the Industrial and Provident Societies Act 1965.

The Registry will be subsumed into the Financial Services Authority at a date to be fixed following the enactment of the Financial Services and Markets Bill.
Assistant Registrar for Scotland: J. L. J. Craig, WS

ROYAL BOTANIC GARDEN EDINBURGH

20A Inverleith Row, Edinburgh EH3 5LR
Tel: 0131-552 7171; Fax: 0131-248 2901
E-mail: press@rbge.org.uk
Web: http://www.rbge.org.uk

The Royal Botanic Garden Edinburgh (RBGE) originated as the Physic Garden, established in 1670 beside the Palace of Holyroodhouse. The Garden moved to its present 28-hectare site at Inverleith, Edinburgh, in 1821. There are also three specialist gardens: Younger Botanic Garden Benmore, near Dunoon, Argyllshire; Logan Botanic Garden, near Stranraer, Wigtownshire; and Dawyck Botanic Garden, near Stobo, Peeblesshire. Since 1986, RBGE has been administered by a board of trustees established under the National Heritage (Scotland) Act 1985. It receives an annual grant from the Scottish Executive Rural Affairs Department.

RBGE is an international centre for scientific research on plant diversity and for horticulture education and conservation. It has an extensive library and a herbarium with over two million dried plant specimens.

Public opening hours
Edinburgh site – daily (except Christmas Day and New Year's Day) November–January 9.30–4; February and October 9.30–5; March and September 9.30–6; April–August 9.30–7; admission free
Specialist gardens – 1 March–31 October 9.30–6; admission charge

Chairman of the Board of Trustees: Dr P. Nicholson
Regius Keeper: Prof. S. Blackmore

ROYAL COMMISSION ON THE ANCIENT AND HISTORICAL MONUMENTS OF SCOTLAND

John Sinclair House, 16 Bernard Terrace, Edinburgh EH8 9NX
Tel: 0131-662 1456; Fax: 0131-662 1477
E-mail: postmaster@rcahms.gov.uk
Web: http://www.rcahms.gov.uk

The Royal Commission was established in 1908 and is appointed to provide for the survey and recording of ancient and historical monuments connected with the culture, civilisation and conditions of life of people in Scotland from the earliest times. It is funded by the Scottish Executive.

The Commission compiles and maintains the National Monuments Record of Scotland as the national record of the archaeological and historical environment. The National Monuments Record is open for reference Monday–Friday 9.30–4.30.

Chairman: Sir William Fraser, GCB, FRSE
Commissioners: Prof. J. M Coles, Ph.D., FBA; Prof. R. Cramp, CBE, FSA; Dr B. Crawford, FSA, FSA Scot.; Dr D. Howard, FSA; Prof. M. Mackay, Ph.D.; R. A. Paxton, FRSE; Miss A. Riches; J. Simpson, FSA Scot.; Prof. T. C. Smout, CBE, FRESE, FBA
Secretary: R. J. Mercer, FSA, FRSE

ROYAL FINE ART COMMISSION FOR SCOTLAND

Bakehouse Close, 146 Canongate, Edinburgh EH8 8DD
Tel: 0131-556 6699; Fax: 0131-556 6633
E-mail: rfacscot@gtnet.gov.uk

The Commission was established in 1927 and advises ministers and local authorities on the visual impact and quality of design of construction projects. It is an independent body and gives its opinions impartially.
Chairman: The Rt. Hon. the Lord Cameron of Lochbroom, PC, FRSE
Commissioners: Prof. G. Benson; W. A. Cadell; Mrs K. Dalyell; Ms J. Malvenan; R. G. Maund; M. Murray; D. Page; B. Rae; Prof. R. Russell; M. Turnbull; A. Wright
Secretary: C. Prosser

SCOTLAND OFFICE

Dover House, Whitehall, London, SW1A 2AU
Tel: 020-7270 3000; Fax: 020-7270 6730

The Scotland Office is the Office of the Secretary of State for Scotland, who represents Scottish interests in the Cabinet on matters reserved to the UK Parliament, i.e. national financial and economic matters, social security, defence and international relations, and employment.
Secretary of State for Scotland: The Rt. Hon. Dr John Reid, MP
   Private Secretary: Ms J. Coulquhoun
Minister of State: Brian Wilson, MP
   Private Secretary: D. Ferguson
Advocate-General for Scotland: Dr Lynda Clark, QC, MP
Head of Office: I. Gordon

SCOTTISH ADVISORY COMMITTEE ON DRUG MISUSE

Public Health Policy Unit, Department of Health, St Andrews House, Edinburgh EH1 3DG

Tel: 0131-244 2496; Fax: 0131-244 2689

The Committee advises and reports on policy, priorities and strategic planning in relation to drug misuse in Scotland.
Chairman: The Deputy Minister for Justice
Secretary: Mrs M. Robertson

SCOTTISH ADVISORY COMMITTEE ON THE MEDICAL WORKFORCE

Room 140, St Andrews House, Edinburgh EH1 3DG
Tel: 0131-244 2486

The Committee advises on all matters relating to medical workforce planning in Scotland, other than matters concerning terms and conditions of service. (The Committee's status as a non-departmental public body is under review.)
Chairman: Dr D. Ewing
Secretary: Mr S. Miller

SCOTTISH AGRICULTURAL SCIENCE AGENCY

East Craig, Edinburgh EH12 8NJ
Tel: 0131-244 8876; Fax: 0131-244 8988

The Agency is an executive agency of the Scottish Executive Rural Affairs Department. It provides scientific information and advice on agricultural and horticultural crops and the environment, and has various statutory and regulatory functions.
Director: Dr R. K. M. Hay
Deputy Director: S. R. Cooper
Senior Principal Scientific Officer: Dr K. J. O'Donnell

SCOTTISH AGRICULTURAL WAGES BOARD

Pentland House, 47 Robb's Loan, Edinburgh EH14 1TY
Tel: 0131-244 6392

The Board fixes minimum wage rates, holiday entitlements and other conditions for agricultural workers in Scotland.
Chairman: Mrs C. Davis, CBE
Secretary: Miss F. Anderson

SCOTTISH ARTS COUNCIL

12 Manor Place, Edinburgh EH3 7DD
Tel: 0131-226 6051; Fax: 0131-225 9833
E-mail: administrator@scottisharts.org.uk
Web: http://www.sac.org.uk

The Scottish Arts Council (SAC) aims to create a dynamic arts environment which enhances the quality of life for the people of Scotland. It achieves this by providing leadership; developing new ideas and initiatives; working in partnership; promoting the arts and artists; providing information and advice; investing in the arts for the people of Scotland. SAC is one of the main channels of public funding for the arts in Scotland and receives funding from two main sources: revenue funding from the Scottish Executive (£29.7m) and Lottery funding through the Department of Culture, Media and Sport (£19.7m).
Chairman: Magnus Linklater
Members: Sam Ainsley; Elizabeth Cameron; Richard Chester; Jim Faulds; Bill English; Dale Idiens; Maud Marshall; Ann Matheson; Robin Presswood; John Scott Moncrieff; Bill Speirs;
Director: Tessa Jackson

SCOTTISH CHARITIES OFFICE

25 Chambers Street, Edinburgh EH1 1LA
Tel: 0131-226 2626; Fax: 0131-226 6912

The Scottish Charities Office is responsible for the supervision and regulation of charities in Scotland with the aim of enhancing the integrity and effectiveness of charities.
Director: B. M. Logan

SCOTTISH CHILDREN'S REPORTER ADMINISTRATION

Ochil House, Springkerse Business Park, Stirling FK7 7XE
Tel: 01786-459500; Fax: 01786-495933

The Scottish Children's Reporter Administration supports the Principal Reporter in his statutory functions in relation to children who may be in need of care, and provides suitable accommodation and facilities for children's hearings.
Chairman: Ms S. Kuenssberg

SCOTTISH COMMITTEE OF THE COUNCIL ON TRIBUNALS

44 Palmerston Place, Edinburgh EH12 5BJ
Tel: 0131-220 1236; Fax: 0131-225 4271
E-mail: sccot@gtnet.gov.uk

The Council on Tribunals is an independent body that advises on and keeps under review the constitution and working of administrative tribunals, and considers and reports on administrative procedures relating to statutory inquiries. Some 70 tribunals are currently under the Council's supervision. It is consulted by and advises government departments on a wide range

of subjects relating to adjudicative procedures. The Scottish Committee of the Council generally considers Scottish tribunals and matters relating only to Scotland.
Chairman: R. J. Elliot, DKS
Members: The Parliamentary Commissioner for Administration (ex officio); Mrs P. Y. Berry, MBE; Mrs B. Bruce; I. J. Irvine; Mrs A. Middleton; I. D. Penman, CB; D. Graham
Secretary: Mrs E. M. MacRae

SCOTTISH CRIMINAL CASES REVIEW COMMISSION

5th Floor, Portland House, 17 Renfield Street, Glasgow G2 5AH
Tel: 0141-270 7030; Fax: 0141-270 7040
E-mail: info@sccrc.co.uk

The Commission is a non-departmental public body which started operating on 1 April 1999. It took over from the Secretary of State for Scotland powers to consider alleged miscarriages of justice in Scotland and refer cases meeting the relevant criteria to the Appeal Court for review. Members are appointed by Her Majesty The Queen on the recommendation of the First Minister; senior executive staff are appointed by the Commission.
Chairperson: Prof. S. McLean
Members: A. Bonnington; Prof. P. Duff; Very Revd G. Forbes; A. Gallen; Sir G. Gordon, CBE, QC; W. Taylor, QC
Chief Executive: C. A. Kelly

SCOTTISH ENTERPRISE

120 Bothwell Street, Glasgow G2 7JP
Tel 0141-248 2700; Fax 0141-221 3217
E-mail: scotent.co.uk
Web: http://www.scotent.co.uk

Scottish Enterprise was established in 1991 and its purpose is to create jobs and prosperity for the people of Scotland. It is funded largely by the Scottish Executive and is responsible to the Scottish Minister for Enterprise and Lifelong Learning. Working in partnership with the private and public sectors, Scottish Enterprise aims to further the development of Scotland's economy, to enhance the skills of the Scottish workforce and to promote Scotland's international competitiveness. Through Locate in Scotland, Scottish Enterprise is concerned with attracting firms to Scotland, and through Scottish Trade International helps Scottish companies to compete in world export markets. Scottish

Enterprise has a network of 13 local enterprise companies that deliver economic development services at local level.
Chairman: Sir Ian Wood, CBE
Chief Executive: C. Beveridge, CBE

SCOTTISH ENVIRONMENT PROTECTION AGENCY

Erskine Court, The Castle Business Park, Stirling FK9 4TR
Tel: 01786-457700; Fax: 01786-446885
E-mail: publicaffairs@sepa.org.uk
Web: http://www.sepa.org.uk

The Scottish Environment Protection Agency is Scotland's environmental regulator, responsible for preventing and controlling pollution to land, air and water. Its main aim is to provide an efficient and integrated environmental protection system for Scotland which will improve the environment and contribute to the Government's goal of sustainable development. It has regional offices in East Kilbride, Riccarton and Dingwall, and 18 offices throughout Scotland. It receives funding from the Scottish Executive.
The Board
Chairman: K. Collins
Members: Mrs D. Hutton; Prof. B. D. Clark; S. Clark; S. Dagg; F. Edwards; Mr B. Furness; Mr D. Hallett; B. Howatson; Mr N. Kiensberg; C. McChord; A. Paton
The Executive
Chief Executive: A. Paton
Director of Finance: J. Ford
Director of Environmental Strategy: Ms P. Henton
Director, North Region: Prof. D. Mackay
Director, East Region: W. Halcrow
Director, West Region: J. Beveridge

SCOTTISH FISHERIES PROTECTION AGENCY

Pentland House, 47 Robb's Loan, Edinburgh EH14 1TY
Tel: 0131-556 8400; Fax: 0131-244 6086

The Agency is an executive agency of the Scottish Executive Rural Affairs Department. It enforces fisheries law and regulations in Scottish waters and ports.
Chief Executive: Capt. P. Du Vivier, RN
Director of Corporate Strategy and Resources: J. B. Roddin
Director of Operations: R. J. Walker
Marine Superintendent: Capt. W. A. Brown

SCOTTISH HOMES

Thistle House, 91 Haymarket Terrace, Edinburgh EH12 5HE
Tel: 0131-313 0044; Fax: 0131-313 2680

Scottish Homes, the national housing agency for Scotland, aims to improve the quality and variety of housing available in Scotland by working in partnership with the public and private sectors. The agency is a major funder of new and improved housing provided by housing associations and private developers. It is currently transferring its own rented houses to alternative landlords. It is also involved in housing research. Board members are appointed by the First Minister.
Chairman: J. Ward, CBE
Chief Executive: vacant

SCOTTISH HOSPITAL ENDOWMENTS RESEARCH TRUST

Saltire Court, 20 Castle Terrace, Edinburgh EH1 2EF
Tel: 0131-473 7516; Fax: 0131-228 8118
Web: http://www.shert.com/www.shert.org.uk

The Trust holds endowments, donations and bequests and makes grants from these funds to improve health standards by funding research into the cause, diagnosis, treatment and prevention of all forms of illness and genetic disorders and into the advancement of medical technology. It also engages in fundraising activities.
Chairman: The Lord Kilpatrick of Kincraig, CBE
Secretary: T. Connell, WS

SCOTTISH INDUSTRIAL DEVELOPMENT ADVISORY BOARD

Meridian Court, 5 Cadogan Street, Glasgow G2 6AT
Tel: 0141-242 5674

The Board advises the Scottish Ministers on the exercise of their powers under Section 7 of the Industrial Development Act 1982.
Chairman: Ian Good, CBE
Secretary: Peter Ford

SCOTTISH LAW COMMISSION

140 Causewayside, Edinburgh EH9 1PR
Tel: 0131-668 2131; Fax: 0131-662 4900
E-mail: info@scotlawcom.gov.uk

The Commission keeps the law in Scotland under review and makes proposals for its development and reform. It is responsible to the Scottish Ministers through the Scottish Executive Justice Department.
Chairman (part-time): The Hon. Lord Gill
Commissioners (full-time): Prof. G. Maher; Prof. K. G. C. Reid; Prof. J. Thomson; (part-time) P. S. Hodge, QC
Secretary: N. Raven

SCOTTISH LEGAL AID BOARD

44 Drumsheugh Gardens, Edinburgh EH3 7SW
Tel: 0131-226 7061; Fax: 0131-220 4878
E-mail: general@slab.org.uk
Web: http://www.scotlegalaid.gov.uk and http://www.slab.org.uk

The Scottish Legal Aid Board was set up under the Legal Aid (Scotland) Act 1986. It is responsible for ensuring that advice and assistance and representation are available in accordance with the Act. The Board is a non-departmental public body whose members are appointed by the First Minister.
Chairman: Mrs J. Couper
Members: B. C. Adair; Mrs K. Blair; W. Gallagher; Prof. P. H. Grinyer; Sheriff A. Jessop; N. Kuenssberg; D. O'Carroll; Mrs Y. Osman; Prof. J. P. Percy; Ms M. Scanlan; M. C. Thomson, QC; A. F. Wylie, QC
Chief Executive: L. Montgomery

SCOTTISH LEGAL SERVICES OMBUDSMAN

Mulberry House, 16–22 Picardy Place, Edinburgh EH1 3JT
Tel: 0131-556 5574; Fax: 0131-556 1519
E-mail: complaints@scot-legal-ombud.org.uk
Web: http://www.scot-legal-ombud.org.uk

The Legal Services Ombudsman oversees the handling of complaints against solicitors, advocates, licensed conveyancers and legal executives by their professional bodies. A complainant must first complain to the relevant professional body before raising the matter with the Ombudsman. The Ombudsman is independent of the legal profession and his services are free of charge.
Scottish Legal Services Ombudsman: G. S. Watson

SCOTTISH MEDICAL PRACTICES COMMITTEE

Scottish Health Service Centre, Crewe Road South, Edinburgh EH4 2LF
Tel: 0131-623 2532

The Committee ensures that there is an adequate number of GPs providing general medical services in Scotland.
Chairman: Dr G. McIntosh, MBE
Secretary: Mrs K. McGeary

SCOTTISH NATURAL HERITAGE

12 Hope Terrace, Edinburgh EH9 2AS
Tel: 0131-447 4784; Fax: 0131-446 2277
Web: http://www.snh.org.uk

Scottish Natural Heritage was established in 1992 under the Natural Heritage (Scotland) Act 1991. It provides advice on nature conservation to all those whose activities affect wildlife, landforms and features of geological interest in Scotland, and seeks to develop and improve facilities for the enjoyment and understanding of the Scottish countryside. It is funded by the Scottish Executive.
Chairman: Dr J. Markland, CBE
Chief Executive: Prof. R. Crofts, CBE
Chief Scientific Adviser: Prof. M. B. Usher
Directors of Operations: J. Thomson (West); Dr. I. Jardine (East); Dr. J. Watson (North)
Director of Corporate Services: Dr I. Edgeler

SCOTTISH OCEANIC AREA CONTROL CENTRE

Atlantic House, Sherwood Road, Prestwick KA9 2NR
Tel: 01292-479800; Fax: 01292-692733

The Centre is the Scottish division of the Civil Aviation Authority, which is responsible for the economic regulation of UK airlines, for the safety regulation of UK civil aviation, and (through its subsidiary company National Air Traffic Services Ltd) provides air traffic control and telecommunications services.

SCOTTISH PARLIAMENTARY COMMISSIONER FOR ADMINISTRATION

28 Thistle Street, Edinburgh EH2 1EN
Tel: 0845-601 0456; Fax: 0131-226 4447
Web: http://www.ombudsman.org.uk

The Scottish Parliamentary Commissioner for Administration (the Scottish Commissioner) is responsible for investigating complaints referred to him by Members of the Scottish Parliament on behalf of members of the public who have suffered an injustice through maladministration by the Scottish Executive, the Parliamentary Corporation and a wide range of public bodies involved in devolved Scottish affairs. The Scottish Commissioner also investigates complaints, referred by MSPs, about wrongful refusal of access to official information.
Scottish Parliamentary Commissioner: M. S. Buckley
Head of Scottish Office: G. Keil

SCOTTISH POST OFFICE BOARD

102 West Port, Edinburgh EH3 9HS
Tel: 0131-228 7300; Fax: 0131-228 7218
Web: http://www.ukpo.com

The Post Office is a public corporation required by Parliament to provide a network of post offices. Legislation currently proceeding through parliament will make The Post Office a plc with all shares held by Parliament, appoint a regulator, the Commission of Postal Services, and a consumer for Postal Services to look after customer interests.

The Post Office Board represents The Post Office in Scotland especially to the Scottish Parliament and opinion former groups.
Chairman: J. Ward, CBE
Secretary to the Scottish Post Office Board: M. Cummins

SCOTTISH PRISONS COMPLAINTS COMMISSION

Government Buildings, Broomhouse Drive, Edinburgh EH11 3XD
Tel: 0131-244 8423; Fax: 0131-244 8430

The Commission was established in 1994. It is an independent body to which prisoners in Scottish prisons can make application in relation to any matter where they have failed to obtain satisfaction from the Prison Service's internal grievance procedures. Clinical judgments made by medical officers, matters which are the subject of legal proceedings and matters relating to sentence, conviction and parole decision-making are excluded from the Commission's jurisdiction. The Commissioner is appointed by the First Minister.
Commissioner: Joan N. Aitken

SCOTTISH PUBLIC PENSIONS AGENCY

St Margaret's House, 151 London Road, Edinburgh EH8 7TG
Tel: 0131-556 8400; Fax: 0131-244 3334

The Agency is an executive agency of the Scottish Executive Education Department. It is responsible for the pension arrangements of some

300,000 people, mainly NHS and teaching services employees and pensioners.
Chief Executive: R. Garden
Directors: G. Mowat (Policy); J. MacDermott (Resources/Training Scheme Manager); J. Nelson (IT and Finance); G. Taylor (NHS Scheme Manager)

SCOTTISH RECORDS ADVISORY COUNCIL

HM General Register House, Edinburgh EH1 3YY
Tel: 0131-535 1314; Fax: 0131-535 1360
E-mail: alisonrosie@nas.gov.uk

The Council was established under the Public Records (Scotland) Act 1937. Its members are appointed by the First Minister and it may submit proposals or make representations to the First Minister, the Lord Justice-General or the Lord President of the Court of Session on questions relating to the public records of Scotland.
Chairman: Prof. A. Crowther
Secretary: Dr A. Rosie

SCOTTISH SCREEN

249 West George Street, Glasgow G2 4RB
Tel: 0141-302 1700; Fax: 0141-302 1711
E-mail: info@scottishscreen.com
Web: http://www.scottishscreen.com

Scottish Screen is responsible to the Scottish Parliament for developing all aspects of screen industry and culture in Scotland through script and company development, short film production, distribution of Lottery film production finance, training, education, exhibition funding, the film Commission locations support and the Scottish Film and Television Archive.
Chairman: J. Lee
Chief Executive: J. Archer

SCOTTISH SOLICITORS' DISCIPLINE TRIBUNAL

22 Rutland Square, Edinburgh EH1 2BB
Tel: 0131-229 5860

The Scottish Solicitors' Discipline Tribunal is an independent statutory body with a panel of 18 members, ten of whom are solicitors; members are appointed by the Lord President of the Court of Session. Its principal function is to consider complaints of misconduct against solicitors in Scotland.
Chairman: J. W. Laughland
Clerk: J. M. Barton, WS

SCOTTISH TOURIST BOARD

23 Ravelston Terrace, Edinburgh EH4 3EU
Tel: 0131-332 2433; Fax: 0131-343 1513
Thistle House, Beechwood Park North, Inverness IV2 3ED
Tel: 01463-716996; Fax: 01463-717233
Web: http://www.visitscotland.com

The Scottish Tourist Board is responsible for developing and marketing the tourist industry in Scotland. The Board's main objectives are to promote holidays and to encourage the provision and improvement of tourist amenities.
Chief Executive: T. Buncle

SCOTTISH VALUATION AND RATING COUNCIL

c/o LG3A-Area 3-J, Victoria Quay, Edinburgh EH6 6QQ
Tel: 0131-244 7003; Fax: 0131-244 7058

The Council advises on any matter pertaining to valuation and rating, including evaluation of representations and recommendations made to the First Minister, the identification of issues requiring consideration, and advice in the preparation of legislation.
Chairman: Prof. G. Milne
Secretary: P. A. Hancock

SEA FISH INDUSTRY AUTHORITY

18 Logie Mill, Logie Green Road, Edinburgh EH7 4HG
Tel: 0131-558 3331; Fax: 0131-558 1442
E-mail: seafish@seafish.demon.uk

Established under the Fisheries Act 1981, the Authority is required to promote the efficiency of the sea fish industry. It carries out research relating to the industry and gives advice on related matters. It provides training, promotes the marketing, consumption and export of sea fish and sea fish products, and may provide financial assistance for the improvement of fishing vessels in respect of essential safety equipment. It is responsible to the Ministry of Agriculture, Fisheries and Food.
Chairman: E. Davey
Chief Executive: A. C. Fairbairn

SECRETARY OF COMMISSIONS FOR SCOTLAND

Spur W1 (E), Saughton House, Broomhouse Drive, Edinburgh EH11 3XD
Tel: 0131-244 2691; Fax: 0131-244 2623

The Secretary of Commissions deals with the appointment of justices of the peace and of general commissioners of income tax, and with lord lieutenancy business.
Secretary of Commissions for Scotland:
R. Shiels

SPECIAL COMMISSIONERS OF INCOME TAX

15-19 Bedford Avenue, London WC1B 3AS
Tel: 020-7631 4242

The Special Commissioners are an independent body appointed by the Lord Chancellor in conjunction with the Lord Advocate to hear complex appeals against decisions of the Board of Inland Revenue and its officials. In addition to the Presiding Special Commissioner there is one full-time and 11 part-time special commissioners; all are legally qualified.
Presiding Special Commissioner: His Hon. Stephen Oliver, QC
Special Commissioner: T. H. K. Everett
Clerk: R. P. Lester

SPORTSCOTLAND

Caledonia House, South Gyle, Edinburgh EH12 9DQ
Tel: 0131-317 7200; Fax: 0131-317 7202

Sportscotland is responsible for the development of sport and physical recreation in Scotland. It aims to increase participation in sport among young people and to provide the highest level of coaching and support for aspiring top performers. It advises the Scottish Parliament on sports matters, and it administers the Lottery Sports Fund in Scotland.
Chairman: A. Dempster
Chief Executive: F. A. L. Alstead, CBE

STUDENT AWARDS AGENCY FOR SCOTLAND

Gyleview House, 3 Redheughs Rigg, Edinburgh EH12 9HH
Tel: 0131-476 8212; Fax: 0131-244 5887

The Agency is an executive agency of the Scottish Executive Enterprise and Lifelong Learning Department. It awards grants to Scottish students undertaking full-time or sandwich course courses.
Chief Executive: K. MacRae

TRAFFIC COMMISSIONER (SCOTLAND)

Argyle House, J Floor, 3 Lady Lawson Street, Edinburgh EH3 9SE
Tel: 0131-529 8500; Fax: 0131-529 8501

The Traffic Commissioners are responsible for licensing operators of heavy goods and public service vehicles. They also have responsibility for appeals relating to the licensing of operators and for disciplinary cases involving the conduct of drivers of these vehicles. Each Traffic Commissioner constitutes a tribunal for the purposes of the Tribunals and Inquiries Act 1971.
Scottish Traffic Commissioner: M. W. Betts, CBE

TRANSPORT TRIBUNAL

48-49 Chancery Lane, London WC2A 1JR
Tel: 020-7947 7493

The Transport Tribunal hears appeals against decisions of Traffic Commissioners/licensing authorities on passenger or goods vehicle operator licensing applications. The tribunal consists of a legally-qualified president, two legal members who may sit as chairmen, and five lay members. The president and legal members are appointed by the Lord Chancellor and the lay members by the Secretary of State for the Environment, Transport and the Regions.
President (part-time): H. B. H. Carlisle, QC
Legal member (part-time): His Hon. Judge Brodrick
Lay members: L. Milliken; P. Rogers; Ms P. Steel; J. W. Whitworth; D. Yeomans
Secretary: P. J. Fisher

UK PASSPORT AGENCY

Regional Office
3 Northgate, 96 Milton Street, Cowcaddens, Glasgow G4 0BT
Tel: 0990-210410
Central telephone number: 0870-521 0410
Central Fax number: 020-7271 8581
Web site: http://www.ukpa.gov.uk

The UK Passport Agency is an executive agency of the Home Office. It is responsible for the issue of British passports. The passport offices are open Monday-Friday 8.30-6.00, Saturday 9.00-3.00. The majority of telephone calls are now handled by a call centre, but where it is essential that customers speak directly to a particular regional office calls are transferred. The call centreoperates 24 hours a day.
Head of Glasgow Regional Office: R. D. Wilson

VALUATION APPEAL PANELS

c/o Convention of Scottish Local Authorities, Rosebery House, Haymarket Terrace, Edinburgh EH12 5XZ
Tel: 0131-474 9200; Fax: 0131-474 9292

The valuation panels and valuation appeal panels drawn from them hear and determine council tax and non-domestic rating appeals. Members of the local valuation panels are appointed by the Sheriff Principal for the area and are required to live or work in the area covered by the panel. A central secretariat service to the valuation appeal panels is provided by COSLA.

COSLA contact: Mrs B. Campbell

VAT AND DUTIES TRIBUNALS

44 Palmerston Place, Edinburgh EH12 5BJ
Tel: 0131-226 3551

VAT and Duties Tribunals are administered by the First Minister in Scotland. They are independent, and decide disputes between taxpayers and Customs and Excise. Chairmen in Scotland are appointed by the Lord President of the Court of Session.

President: His Hon. Stephen Oliver, QC
Vice-President: Scotland, T. G. Coutts, QC
Registrar: R. P. Lester

WAR PENSIONS AGENCY

Norcross, Blackpool, Lancs FY5 3WP
Tel: 0800-169 2277

The Agency is an executive agency of the Department of Social Security. It administers the payment of war disablement and war widows' pensions and provides welfare services and support to war disablement pensioners, war widows and their dependants and carers.

Chief Executive: G. Hextall

Central Advisory Committee on War
PensionsWar Pensions Agency
Norcross, Blackpool, Lancs FYS 3WP
Tel: 0800-169 2277
Secretary: Mrs V. Clark

THE EUROPEAN PARLIAMENT

European Parliament elections take place at five-yearly intervals; the first direct elections to the Parliament were held in 1979. In mainland Britain MEPs were elected in all constituencies on a first-past-the-post basis until the elections of 10 June 1999, when a 'closed-list' regional system of proportional representation was used for the first time. Scotland constitutes a region.

Parties submitted a list of candidates for each region in their own order of preference. Voters voted for a party or an independent candidate, and the first seat in each region was allocated to the party or candidate with the highest number of votes. The rest of the seats in each region were then allocated broadly in proportion to each party's share of the vote. The Scotland region returned eight members.

British subjects and citizens of the Irish Republic are eligible for election to the European Parliament provided they are 21 or over and not subject to disqualification. Since 1994, nationals of member states of the European Union have had the right to vote in elections to the European Parliament in the UK as long as they are entered on the electoral register.

MEPs currently receive a salary from the parliaments or governments of their respective member states, set at the level of the national parliamentary salary and subject to national taxation rules (the salary of British MEPs is £48,371). A proposal that all MEPs should be paid the same rate of salary out of the EU budget, and subject to the EC tax rate, was under negotiation between the European Parliament and the Council of Ministers at the time of going to press.

SCOTTISH MEMBERS

Attwooll, Ms Elspeth M.-A. (b. 1943), LD, Scotland
* Hudghton, Ian (b. 1951), SNP, Scotland
MacCormick, Prof. D. Neil, FBA (b. 1941), SNP, Scotland
* Martin, David W. (b. 1954), Lab., Scotland
* Miller, William (b. 1954), Lab., Scotland
Purvis, John R., CBE (b. 1938), C., Scotland
Stevenson, Struan (b. 1948), C., Scotland
Stihler, Ms Catherine D. (b. 1973), Lab., Scotland

*Member of the last European Parliament
For party abbreviations, see pages 27

SCOTLAND REGION

at election on 10 June 1999
E. 3,979,845 T. 24.83%

Lab.	283,490 (28.68%)
SNP	268,528 (27.17%)
C.	195,296 (19.76%)
LD	96,971 (9.81%)
Green	57,142 (5.78%)
SSP	39,720 (4.02%)
Pro Euro C.	17,781 (1.80%)
UK Ind.	12,549 (1.27%)
Soc. Lab.	9,385 (0.95%)
BNP	3,729 (0.38%)
NLP	2,087 (0.21%)
Lower Tax	1,632 (0.17%)

Lab. majority 14,962
(June 1994, Lab. maj. 148,718)

EU INFORMATION

Scotland's relations with the European Union (EU) remain a reserved power after devolution. However, since EU policies and legislation affect many of the matters for which the Scottish Parliament and Executive are responsible, the Parliament may choose to scrutinise EU proposals to ensure that Scotland's interests are taken into consideration.

Where national legislation is required to fulfil the UK's obligation to implement EC legislation, the Scottish Parliament and Executive may choose whether to implement EC obligations which cover devolved matters in Scotland, or to agree on compliance with the relevant British or UK legislation. The Scottish Ministers will be actively involved in decision-making on EU matters.

The Scottish Executive has its own office in Brussels to help represent Scotland's interests and complement the work of the UK Permanent Representative to the EU (UKREP). The office may also gather information on behalf of the Scottish Executive and Parliament and act as a base for visits to Brussels by Scottish Ministers and officials of the Scottish Executive.

SCOTTISH EXECUTIVE EU OFFICE

Scotland House, 6 Rond Point Schuman, B-1040 Brussels, Belgium
Tel: 00-322-282 8330; Fax: 00-322-282 8345

INFORMATION SOURCES

Information about the EU is available from a variety of sources at different levels. The European Commission is developing a decentralised information network which aims to meet both general and specialised needs. The following are available in Scotland:

EUROPEAN COMMISSION REPRESENTATION IN SCOTLAND

Alva Street, Edinburgh EH2 4PH
Tel: 0131-225 2058; Fax: 0131-226 4105
Web: http://www.europa.eu.int

EUROPEAN PARLIAMENT INFORMATION OFFICE

see above address
Web: http://www.europarl.org.uk

EURO INFO CENTRES

The centres provide information on Europe relevant to business (particularly small and medium-sized businesses), such as company law, relevant European legislation, taxation, public contracts, opportunities and funding. They can also offer an advisory service, for which a charge may be made.

GLASGOW
Franborough House, 123 Bothwell Street, Glasgow G2 7JP
Tel: 0141-221 0999; Fax 0141-221 6539
E-mail: euroinfocentre@scotent.co.uk
Web: http://www.euro-info.org/centres/glasgow

INVERNESS
20 Bridge Street, Inverness IV1 1QR
Tel: 01463-702560; Fax: 01463-715600
E-mail: eic@sprite.co.uk

EUROPEAN DOCUMENTATION CENTRES

Based in university libraries, the documentation centres hold reference collections of major official documents of the EU institutions, and other publications.

UNIVERSITY OF ABERDEEN

The Taylor Library EDC, Dunbar Street, Aberdeen AB24 3JB
Tel: 01224-273334; Fax: 01224-273819
E-mail: e.a.mackie@abdn.ac.uk
Web:
 http://www.abdn.ac.uk/diss/infoserv/sites/taylor
European and Business Information Officer: Ms L. Mackie

UNIVERSITY OF DUNDEE

The Law Library, Perth Road, Dundee DD1 4HN
Tel: 01382-344102; Fax: 01382-344102
E-mail: a.duncan@dundee.ac.uk
Senior Library Assistant: Ms A. Duncan

UNIVERSITY OF EDINBURGH

Law and Europa Library, Old College, South Bridge, Edinburgh EH8 9YL
Tel: 0131-650 2043; Fax: 0131-650 6343
E-mail: europa.library@ed.ac.uk
Web: http://www.lib.ed.ac.uk/lib/sites/law.shtml
Law and European Documentation Librarian: K. Taylor

UNIVERSITY OF GLASGOW

The Library, Hillhead Street, Glasgow G12 8QE
Tel: 0141-330 6722; Fax: 0141-330 4952
E-mail: gxlr30@gla.ac.uk
Web: http://www.lib.gla.ac.uk/Depts/MOPS/
EU/index.html
Director of Library Services: A. Wale

EUROPEAN REFERENCE CENTRES

The reference centres keep less comprehensive
collections of publications.
The Library, Stirling University, Stirling FK9
4LA
Tel: 01786-467231; Fax: 01786-466866
E-mail: d.j.gardiner@stir.ac.uk
Web: http://www.stir.ac.uk/infoserv
Director of Information Services: Dr P. Kemp

CARREFOUR CENTRES

The Carrefour centres are based in rural areas.
They provide information on EU policy
concerning rural areas and rural issues, and
promote awareness of rural development.

HIGHLANDS AND ISLANDS RURAL CARREFOUR CENTRE

Business Information Source, 20 Bridge Street,
Inverness IV1 1QR
Tel: 01463-715400; Fax: 01463-715600
E-mail: bis.enquiries@bis.uk.com

PUBLIC INFORMATION RELAY

These are information points at a number of
public libraries where general reference
documents about the EU are held and free
information leaflets are available. At present there
are public information relay points at about 34
local public libraries in Scotland, at least one in
each local authority area.

EUROPEAN RESOURCE CENTRES

The resource centres hold printed and electronic
information on Europe for schools, and stocks of
free publications on European affairs, the EU
institutions, and the countries of the EU.

EURODESK SCOTLAND

Community Learning Scotland, Rosebery
House, 9 Haymarket Terrace, Edinburgh EH12
5EZ
Tel: 0131-313 2488; Fax: 0131-313 6800
E-mail: UK001@cls.dircon.co.uk
Web: http://www.ercscotland.eurodesk.org

CITIZENS FIRST

Citizens First is a free telephone service
providing public information on various aspects
of European citizenship. Callers can order free
guides and factsheets on living, working and
travelling in the EU, study and training in
another EU country, equal opportunities, the
single market, and other subjects. The materials
are published in all EU languages, including
Gaelic.
Freephone: 0800-581591
Web: http://europa.eu.int/citizens

POLITICAL PARTIES

Financial support for opposition parties has been set at £5,000 per MSP until 31 March 2000 in a draft SI laid at Westminster. The Scottish Parliament has no statutory power to overturn this level, although some MSPs are pressing for it to be reviewed by the Neill Committee as opposition parties at Westminster get £10,000 per MP. From 1 April 2000, the Scottish Parliament has set the level of financial support.

Although there are Liberal Democrat MSPs in the Executive, the party is deemed an opposition party because its members make up less than 20 per cent of the total number of ministers (four out of 22).

SCOTTISH CONSERVATIVE AND UNIONIST CENTRAL OFFICE

83 Princess Road, Edinburgh EH2 2ER
Tel 0131-247 6890; Fax: 0131-247 6891
E-mail: centraloffice@Scottish.torys.org.uk
Web: http://www.scottish.torys.org.uk

Chairman: Raymond Robertson
Deputy Chairman: W. Walker
Hon. Treasurer: D. Mitchell, CBE
Director: Simon Turner

SCOTTISH GREEN PARTY

14 Albany Street, Edinburgh EH1 3QB
Tel 0131-478 7896; Fax: 0131-478 7890
E-mail: info@scottishgreens.org.uk
Web: http://www.scottishgreens.org.uk

Party Leaders: Ms M. Coyne; Robin Harper, MSP
Convener: C. Hoffmann
Treasurer: I. Baxter

SCOTTISH LABOUR PARTY

Delta House, 50 West Nile Street, Glasgow G1 2NA
Tel 0141-572 6900; Fax: 0141-572 2566
E-mail: general@scottish-labour.org
Web: http://www.scottish.labour.co.uk

Party Leader in Scottish Parliament: Rt. Hon. Donald Dewar, MP, MSP
Chair: John Lambie
Vice-chair: Anne McLean
Treasurer: Susan Morton
General Secretary: Lesley Quinn

SCOTTISH LIBERAL DEMOCRATS

4 Clifton Terrace, Edinburgh EH12 5DR
Tel 0131-337 2314; Fax: 0131-337 3566
E-mail: scotlibdem@cix.co.uk
Web: http://www.scotlibdems.org.uk

Party President: Malcolm Bruce, MP
Party Leader: Jim Wallace, MP, MSP
Convener: I. Yuill
Treasurer: D. R. Sullivan
Chief Executive: Kilvert Croft

SCOTTISH NATIONAL PARTY

6 North Charlotte Street, Edinburgh EH2 4JH
Tel 0131-226 3661; Fax: 0131-225 9597
E-mail: snp.administration@snp.org.uk
Web: http://www.snp.org.uk

Parliamentary Party Leader: Alex Salmond, MP, MSP
Chief Whip: Bruce Crawford, MSP
National Convener: Alex Salmond, MP, MSP
Senior Vice-Convener: John Swinney, MP, MSP
National Treasurer: I. Blackford
National Secretary: Stewart Hosie

SCOTTISH SOCIALIST PARTY

73 Robertson Street, Glasgow G2 8QD
Tel: 0141-221 7714; Fax: 0141-221 7715
Web: http://www.scotsocialistparty.org

Convener: T. Sheridan
Treasurer: K. Baldasara
General Secretary: A. Green

UK INDEPENDENCE PARTY

268 Bath Street, Glasgow G2 4JR
Tel: 0141-332 2214; Fax: 0141-353 6900

Organiser: A. D. McConnachie

LOCAL GOVERNMENT

The Local Government etc. (Scotland) Act 1994 abolished the two-tier structure of nine regional and 53 district councils which had existed since 1975 and replaced it, from 1 April 1996, with a single-tier structure consisting of 29 unitary authorities on the mainland; the three islands councils remain. Each unitary authority has inherited all the functions of the regional and district councils, except water and sewerage (now provided by public bodies whose members are appointed by the Scottish Ministers) and reporters panels (now a national agency).

On taking office, the Scottish Parliament assumed responsibility for legislation on local government.

REVIEW OF LOCAL GOVERNMENT

The Commission on Local Government (the McIntosh Commission), reported to the First Minister in June 1999. Subsequently the Scottish Executive established the Renewing Local Democracy working group to consider how to make council membership more attractive, make councils more representative of their communities and advise on appropriate numbers of members for each council. It will also consider possible alternative electoral systems and remuneration of councillors.

As recommended in the *McIntosh Report*, the Scottish executive has also set up the Leadership Advisory Panel. All Scottish local authorities are conducting reviews of their policy development and decision-making structures, working closely with the Panel. The Panel will assess each council's proposals for openness, transparency and accessibility.

ELECTIONS

The unitary authorities consist of directly elected councillors. Elections take place every three years, normally on the first Thursday in May. The 1999 local government elections were held on 6 May, simultaneously with the elections for the Scottish Parliament.

Generally, all British subjects and citizens of the Republic of Ireland who are 18 years or over and resident on the qualifying date in the area for which the election is being held, are entitled to vote at them. A register of electors is prepared and published annually by local electoral registration officers. Candidates, who are subject to various statutory qualifications and disqualifications designed to ensure that they are suitable persons to hold office, must be nominated by electors for the electoral area concerned. The electoral roll that came into effect in 16 February 2000 showed 4,009,424 people registered to vote.

The Local Government Boundary Commission for Scotland is responsible for carrying out periodic reviews of electoral arrangements and making proposals to the Scottish Ministers for any changes found necessary.

INTERNAL ORGANISATION AND FUNCTIONS

The council as a whole is the final decision-making body within any authority. Councils are free to a great extent to make their own internal organisational arrangements. Normally, questions of policy are settled by the full council, while the administration of the various services is the responsibility of committees of councillors. Day-to-day decisions are delegated to the council's officers, who act within the policies laid down by the councillors.

The functions of the councils and islands councils are: education; social work; strategic planning; the provision of infrastructure such as roads; consumer protection; flood prevention; coast protection; valuation and rating; the police and fire services; emergency planning; electoral registration; public transport; registration of births, deaths and marriages; housing; leisure and recreation; development control and building control; environmental health; licensing; allotments; public conveniences; and the administration of district courts.

The chairman of a local council in Scotland may be known as a convenor; a provost is the equivalent of a mayor. The chairman of the council in the cities of Aberdeen, Dundee, Edinburgh and Glasgow are Lord Provosts.

LORD-LIEUTENANTS

The Lord-Lieutenant of a county is the permanent local representative of the Crown in that county. They are appointed by the Sovereign on the recommendation of the Prime Minister. The retirement age is 75.

The office of Lord-Lieutenant dates from 1557, and its holder was originally responsible for the maintenance of order and for local defence in the county. The duties of the post include attending on royalty during official visits to the county, performing certain duties in connection with armed forces of the Crown (and in particular the reserve forces), and making presentations of honours and awards on behalf of the Crown.

Lord-Lieutenants

Title	Name
Aberdeenshire	A. D. M. Farquharson, OBE
Angus	The Earl of Airlie, KT, GCVO, PC, LLD
Argyll and Bute	The Duke of Argyll
Ayrshire and Arran	Maj. R. Y. Henderson, TD
Banffshire	J. A. S. McPherson, CBE
Berwickshire	vacant
Caithness	Maj. G. T. Dunnett, TD
Clackmannan	Lt.-Col. R. C. Stewart, CBE, TD
Dumfries	Capt. R. C. Cunningham-Jardine
Dunbartonshire	Brig. D. D. G. Hardie, TD
East Lothian	Sir Hew Hamilton-Dalrymple, Bt., KCVO
Eilean Siar/ Western Isles	vacant
Fife	Mrs C. M. Dean
Inverness	The Lord Gray of Contin, PC
Kincardineshire	J. D. B. Smart
Lanarkshire	vacant
Midlothian	Capt. G. W. Burnet, LVO
Moray	Air Vice-Marshal G. A. Chesworth, CB, OBE, DFC
Nairn	Ewen J. Brodie
Orkney	G. R. Marwick
Perth and Kinross	Sir David Montgomery, Bt.
Renfrewshire	C. H. Parker, OBE
Ross and Cromarty	Capt. R. W. K. Stirling of Fairburn, TD
Roxburgh, Ettrick and Lauderdale	Dr June Paterson-Brown, CBE, MBChB
Shetland	J. H. Scott
Stirling and Falkirk	Lt.-Col. J. Stirling of Garden, CBE, TD, FRICS
Sutherland	Maj.-Gen. D. Houston, CBE
The Stewartry of Kirkcudbright	Lt.-Gen. Sir Norman Arthur, KCB
Tweeddale	Capt. David Younger
West Lothian	The Earl of Morton
Wigtown	Maj. E. S. Orr-Ewing

The Lord Provosts of the four city districts of Aberdeen, Dundee, Edinburgh and Glasgow are Lord-Lieutenants for those districts *ex officio.*

COMMUNITY COUNCILS

Unlike the parish councils and community councils in England and Wales, Scottish community councils are not local authorities. Their purpose as defined in statute is to ascertain and express the views of the communities which they represent, and to take in the interests of their communities such action as appears to be expedient or practicable. Over 1,000 community councils have been established under schemes drawn up by district and islands councils in Scotland.

Since 1996 community councils have had an enhanced role, becoming statutory consultees on local planning issues and on the decentralisation schemes which the new councils have to draw up for delivery of services.

FINANCE

Local government is financed from four sources: the council tax, non-domestic rates, government grants, and income from fees and charges for services.

COUNCIL TAX

Under the Local Government Finance Act 1992, from 1 April 1993 the council tax replaced the community charge, which had been introduced in April 1989 in place of domestic rates. The council tax is a local tax levied by each local council. Liability for the council tax bill usually falls on the owner-occupier or tenant of a dwelling which is their sole or main residence.

Each island council and unitary authority sets its own rate of council tax. The tax relates to the value of the dwelling. Each dwelling is placed in one of eight valuation bands, ranging from A to H, based on the property's estimated market value as at 1 April 1991.

The valuation bands and ranges of values in Scotland are:

A	Up to £27,000
B	£27,001–£35,000
C	£35,001–£45,000
D	£45,001–£58,000
E	£58,001–£80,000
F	£80,001–£106,000
G	£106,001–£212,000
H	Over £212,000

The council tax within a local area varies between the different bands according to proportions laid down by law. The charge attributable to each band as a proportion of the Band D charge set by the council is approximately:

A	67%
B	78%
C	89%
D	100%
E	122%
F	144%
G	167%
H	200%

The Band D rate for each council is given in the individual local council entries. There may be variations from the given figure within each district council area because of different community precepts being levied.

NON-DOMESTIC RATES

Non-domestic (business) rates are collected by the billing authorities, which in Scotland are the local authorities. Rates are levied in accordance with the Local Government (Scotland) Act 1975. From 1995–6, the Secretary of State for Scotland prescribed a single non-domestic rates poundage to apply throughout the country at the same level as the uniform business rate (UBR) in England. The UBR for 1998–9 was 48p for property up to a rateable value of £10,000 and 48.9p for property over a rateable value of £10,000. Rate income is pooled and redistributed to local authorities on a per capita basis.

Rateable values for the current rating lists came into force on 1 April 1995. They are derived from the rental value of property as at 1 April 1993 and determined on certain statutory assumptions by Regional Assessors. New property which is added to the list, and significant changes to existing property, necessitate amendments to the rateable value on the same basis. Valuation rolls remain in force until the next general revaluation. Such revaluations take place every five years. New ratings lists came into force on 1 April 2000, based on rental levels as at 1 April 1998.

Certain types of property, such as places of public religious worship and agricultural land and buildings, are exempt from rates. Charities, other non-profit-making organisations, sole village shops and post offices, and certain other businesses may receive full or partial relief. Empty property is liable to pay rates at 50 per cent, except for certain specified classes which are entirely exempt.

In 1998–9, total receipts were £1,441 million (provisional) from non-domestic rates and £1,046 million from the council tax. The amount of council tax budgeted to be collected in 1999–2000 was £1,470.1 million.

GOVERNMENT GRANTS

In addition to specific grants in support of revenue expenditure on particular services, central government pays revenue support grant to local authorities. This grant is paid to each local authority so that if each authority budgeted at the level of its standard spending assessment, all authorities in the same class can set broadly the same council tax.

EXPENDITURE

Local authority current budgeted expenditure, supported by aggregate external finance (AEF), for 2000–1 was:

Service	£000s
Education	2,997,406
Arts and Libraries	121,652
Social Work Services	1,223,442
Law, Order and Protective Services	950,668
Roads and Transport	352,681
Other Environmental Services	720,495
Tourism	8,778
Housing	4,222
Sheltered Employment	9,679
Administration of Housing Benefit	34,988
Consumer Protection	17,006
TOTAL	6,441,017

COMPLAINTS

Commissioners for Local Administration are responsible for investigating complaints from members of the public who claim to have suffered injustice as a consequence of maladministration in local government or in certain local bodies.

Complaints are made to the relevant local authority in the first instance and are referred to the Commissioners if the complainant is not satisfied.

NB: In the entries for Local Councils, (LP)= Lord Provost, (P)= Provost and (C)= Convenor.

LOCAL AUTHORITY AREAS

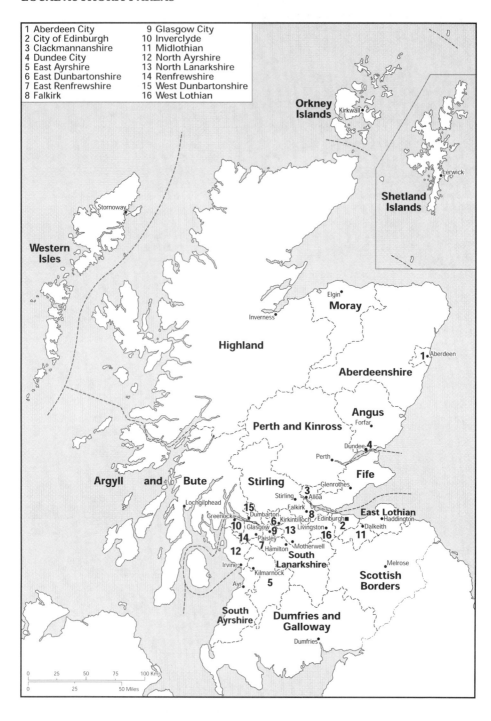

1 Aberdeen City
2 City of Edinburgh
3 Clackmannanshire
4 Dundee City
5 East Ayrshire
6 East Dunbartonshire
7 East Renfrewshire
8 Falkirk

9 Glasgow City
10 Inverclyde
11 Midlothian
12 North Ayrshire
13 North Lanarkshire
14 Renfrewshire
15 West Dunbartonshire
16 West Lothian

Orkney Islands
Kirkwall

Shetland Islands
Lerwick

Western Isles
Stornoway

Moray
Elgin
Inverness

Highland

Aberdeenshire
Aberdeen

Angus
Forfar

Perth and Kinross
Dundee
Perth

Fife
Glenrothes

Argyll and Bute
Lochgilphead

Stirling
Stirling
Alloa

East Lothian
Haddington
Dalkeith

Falkirk
Edinburgh
Livingston

Greenock
Dumbarton
Kirkintilloch
Glasgow
Paisley
Hamilton
Motherwell

South Lanarkshire

Scottish Borders
Melrose

Irvine
Kilmarnock

Ayr

South Ayrshire

Dumfries and Galloway
Dumfries

0   25   50   75   100 Kms
0   25   50 Miles

COUNCIL DIRECTORY

ABERDEEN CITY COUNCIL

Town House, Broad Street, Aberdeen AB10 1FY
Tel: 01224-522000; Fax: 01224-627213
Web: http://www.aberdeencity.gov.uk

Area: 184.47 sq. km
Population (1998 estimate): 213,070
   population density (2000): 1,691 persons per sq. km
   projected population in 2006 (1999-based): 208,714
   number of households (1998): 96,661

Council tax (average Band D per two-person household), as at 1 April 2000: £1,173.08
Non-domestic rateable value (1999–2000): £265,073,312

Education (pupils on register, 1998–9):
   primary: 15,387
   secondary: 10,907
   special: 694
   entitled to free meals: 12.9%

MEMBERS OF THE COUNCIL

Adam, George	(Lab.)
Allan, Yvonne	(Lab.)
Anderson, Janetta	(LD)
Cassie, Scott	(LD)
Clark, Ronald	(LD)
Clyne, David	(Lab.)
Cormack, Irene	(LD)
Dean, Katherine	(LD)
Dempsey, John	(C.)
Falconer, David	(LD)
Gordon, Stewart	(C.)
Graham, Gordon	(Lab.)
Graham, Marjorie	(C.)
Harris, Edward	(Lab.)
Hutcheon, Raymond	(LD)
Irons, Maureen	(Lab.)
Ironside, Leonard	(Lab.)
Jaffrey, Muriel	(SNP)
Lamond, James	(Lab.)
Lamond, June	(Lab.)
Leslie, Gordon	(LD)
MacDonald, Pamela	(LD)
MacLean, Allan	(Lab.)
Maitland, David	(Lab.)
McIntosh, Allan	(Lab.)
Milne, Alan	(C.)
Milne, Ramsay	(Lab.)
Pirie, Charles	(Lab.)
Porter, John	(C.)
Reynolds, John	(LD)
Rutherford, Brian	(Lab.)
Shirron, Karen	(SNP)
Smith, Margaret (LP)	(Lab.)
Stephenson, John	(LD)
Stewart, Kevin	(SNP)
Stewart, Marianne	(Lab.)
Thomaneck, Jurgen	(Lab.)
Traynor, William	(Lab.)
Urquhart, George	(Lab.)
Webster, Ronald	(Lab.)
Wisley, Jillian	(C.)
Wyness, James	(Lab.)
Yuill, Ian	(LD)

Total: 43 (Lab.22; LD.12; C.6; SNP.3)

CHIEF OFFICERS
Chief Executive: D. Paterson
Director of Contracting Services: D. Gordon
Director of Education: J. Stodter
Director of Finance and Information Technology: G. Edwards
Director of Housing: M. Scot
Director of Legal and Corporate Services: C. Langley
Director of Personnel: L. Common
Director of Planning: P. Cockhead
Director of Property and Technical Services/Environmental and Consumer Protection Services: D Murdoch
Director of Social Work and Community Development: J. Tomlinson
Local Agenda 21 contact: G. Robertson

SCOTTISH AND UK PARLIAMENTARY CONSTITUENCIES
Aberdeen Central; Aberdeen North; Aberdeen South

ABERDEENSHIRE COUNCIL

Woodhill House, Westburn Road, Aberdeen AB16 5GB
Tel: 01467-620981; Fax: 01224-665444
Web: http://www.aberdeenshire.gov.uk

Area: 6,318 sq. km
Population (1998 estimate): 226,260
   population density (1998): 36 persons per sq. km
   projected population in 2006 (1998-based): 227,267
   number of households (1998): 89,000

Council tax (average Band D per two-person household), as at 1 April 2000: £777.00
Non-domestic rateable value (2000): £129,631,270

Education (pupils on register, 1999):
  primary: 21,286
  secondary: 15,510
  special: 800
  entitled to free meals: 5.6%

MEMBERS OF THE COUNCIL

Anderson, James	(LD)
Anderson, William	(LD)
Argyle, Peter	(LD)
Barnes, George	(SNP)
Benzie, Kenneth	(SNP)
Bisset, Alan	(C.)
Bisset, Heather	(LD)
Bisset, Raymond (C)	(LD)
Buchan, Alexander	(SNP)
Burnett, Mitchell	(SNP)
Cameron, Alan	(SNP)
Cameron, Douglas	(C.)
Carmichael, Kathryn	(LD)
Cormack, Harald	(Ind.)
Coull, Samuel	(LD)
Cowie, Norman	(Ind.)
Cox, John	(SNP)
Davidson, James	(SNP)
Duguid, Douglas	(SNP)
Ewing, Doreen	(C.)
Findlay, Audrey	(LD)
Findlay, Walter	(LD)
Ford, Martin	(SNP)
Fowler, Helen	(Ind.)
Frain, Ian	(Ind.)
Howatson, William	(LD)
Humphrey, James	(C.)
Johnston, Paul	(LD)
Leitch, Alister	(LD)
Lonchay, Sheena	(LD)
Loveday, John	(LD)
Luffman, Bruce	(C.)
MacLeod, Alice	(SNP)
Mair, Stuart	(Ind.)
Mair, Sydney	(SNP)
Makin, Norma	(Ind.)
McGregor, John	(LD)
McHugh, Denis	(SNP)
McInnes, Alison	(LD)
McKee, Jeanette	(SNP)
McLean, John	(Ind.)
McRae, Margaret	(SNP)
Millar, Colin	(LD)
Morrison, John	(LD)
Nash, Mairi	(LD)
Nelson, Carl	(C.)
Norrie, Alisan	(Ind.)
Pratt, Stuart	(SNP)
Raeburn, Michael	(LD)
Robertson, Elizabeth	(LD)
Saluja, Gurudeo	(LD)
Sheridan, James	(LD)
Smith, David	(LD)
Storr, Debra	(LD)
Strachan, Agnes	(SNP)
Strathdee, Joanna	(SNP)
Stroud, Richard	(LD)
Swapp, George	(Ind.)
Tait, Ian	(SNP)
Taylor, Sandra	(SNP)
Tennant, Stanley	(SNP)
Thomson, Norma	(SNP)
Topping, Brian	(SNP)
Towers, James	(SNP)
Tunstall, Anne	(LD)
Wallace, Alexander	(C.)
Watson, Jenny	(Ind.)

Total: 67 (LD.27; SNP.23; Ind.10; C.7)

CHIEF OFFICERS
Chief Executive: A. G. Campbell
Director of Education and Recreation: H. Vernal
Director of Finance: C. Armstrong
Director of Law and Administration: N. McDowall
Director of Personnel and Information Technology: P. Hay
Director of Planning and Environmental Services: E. Melrose
Director of Social Work and Housing: Mrs M. Wells
Director of Transportation and Infrastructure: I. Gabriel
Local Agenda 21 Officer: Ms D. Burroughs

SCOTTISH AND UK PARLIAMENTARY CONSTITUENCIES
Aberdeenshire West and Kincardine; Banff and Buchan; Gordon

ANGUS COUNCIL

The Cross, Forfar, Angus DD8 1BX
Tel: 01307-461460; Fax: 01307-461874
Web: http://www.angus.gov.uk

Area: 2,181 sq. km
Population (1998 estimate): 110,070
    population density (1998): 50 persons per sq. km
    projected population in 2006 (1996-based): 110,130
    number of households (1996): 46,200

Council tax (average Band D per two-person household), as at 1 April 2000: £734
Non-domestic rateable value (1997–8): £51,395,000

Education (pupils on register, 1997–8):
    primary: 9,373
    secondary: 7,069
    entitled to free meals: 10.4%

MEMBERS OF THE COUNCIL

Angus, Ian	(SNP)
Crowe, Bill	(SNP)
Duncan, Frances (P)	(SNP)
Ellis, Frank	(SNP)
Gibb, Jack	(SNP)
Gray, Alistair	(SNP)
Henderson, John	(SNP)
King, Alex	(SNP)
Leslie, Stephen	(SNP)
Lumgair, David	(C.)
Mackintosh, Ian	(C.)
McGlynn, Stewart	(SNP)
Melville, Ruth	(Ind.)
Middleton, Bill	(SNP)
Middleton, Glennis	(SNP)
Milne, Brian	(SNP)
Mowatt, Joy	(SNP)
Murphy, Peter	(Lab.)
Murray, Rob	(SNP)
Myles, Robert	(Ind.)
Nield, Peter	(LD)
Norrie, George	(Ind.)
Oswald, Helen	(SNP)
Ritchie, Kitty	(SNP)
Robertson, Bill	(SNP)
Selfridge, David	(SNP)
Spiers, Richard	(LD)
Welsh, Sheena	(SNP)
West, Sandy	(SNP)

Total: 29 (SNP.21; Ind.3; C.2; LD.2; Lab.1)

CHIEF OFFICERS
Chief Executive: A. B. Watson

Director of Contract Services: M. Graham
Acting Director of Cultural Services: N. Atkinson
Director of Education: J. Anderson
Director of Environmental and Consumer Protection: S. Heggie
Director of Finance: D. Sawers
Director of Housing: R. Ashton
Director of Information Technology: A. Greenhill
Director of Law and Administration: Ms C. Coull
Director of Personnel: Ms J. Torbet
Director of Planning and Transport: A. Anderson
Director of Property Services: M. Lunny
Director of Recreation Services: J. Zimny
Director of Roads: R. McLellan
Director of Social Work: W. Robertson
Local Agenda 21 Officer: Ms P. Coutts

SCOTTISH AND UK PARLIAMENTARY CONSTITUENCIES
Angus; Tayside North

ARGYLL AND BUTE COUNCIL

Kilmory, Lochgilphead, Argyll PA31 8RT
Tel: 01546-602127; Fax: 01546-604138
Web: http://www.argyll-bute.gov.uk

Area: 6,930 sq. km
Population (1998 estimate): 89,980
    population density (1998): 13 persons per sq. km
    projected population in 2006 (1996-based): 89,461
    number of households (1996): 37,700

Council tax (average Band D per two-person household), as at 1 April 2000: £1,070.10
Non-domestic rateable value (1997–8): £65,985,000

Education (pupils on register, 1997–8):
    primary: 7,747
    secondary: 5,390
    special: 54
    entitled to free meals: 13.4%

MEMBERS OF THE COUNCIL

Banks, Robin	(Ind.)
Blair, Alastair	(Ind.)
Cameron, Campbell	(SNP)
Coleshill, Paul	(LD)
Currie, Douglas, (C)	(Ind.)
Currie, Robin	(LD)

Findlay, John	(Ind.)
Freeman, George	(Ind.)
Gillies, Ian	(Ind.)
Gray, Stephen	(Lab.)
Hay, Alison	(LD)
Kinloch, Ronnie	(Ind.)
MaCallum, Archie	(C.)
Mackaskill, Allan	(Ind.)
MacDougall, Alistair	(Ind.)
Macintyre, Duncan	(Ind.)
Macintyre, Robert	(SNP)
MacKinnon, Dugie	(Ind.)
MacMillan, Donnie	(Ind.)
Marshall, Bruce	(C.)
McIntosh, David	(SNP)
McKinley, Alistair	(Ind.)
McQueen, James	(Ind.)
McTaggart, Elspeth	(SNP)
Petrie, William	(Ind.)
Robertson, Bruce	(Ind.)
Scoullar, Len	(Ind.)
Strong, Isobel	(SNP)
Walsh, Dick	(Ind.)
Webster, David	(Ind.)

Total: 30 (Ind.19; SNP.5; LD.3; C.2; Lab.1)

CHIEF OFFICERS
Chief Executive: J. A. McLellan
Director of Corporate and Legal Services: N. Stewart
Director of Development and Environment Services: G. Harper
Director of Education: A. Morton
Director of Finance: S. MacGregor
Director of Housing and Social Work: D. Hendry
Director of Information Technology: G. Williamson
Local Agenda 21 Officer: vacant

SCOTTISH AND UK PARLIAMENTARY CONSTITUENCIES
Argyll and Bute; Dumbarton

CITY OF EDINBURGH COUNCIL

Wellington Court, 10 Waterloo Place, Edinburgh EH1 3EG
Tel: 0131-200 2000; Fax: 0131-529 7477
Web: http://www.edinburgh.gov.uk

Area: 262 sq. km
Population (1998 estimate): 450,180
   population density (1998): 1,716 persons per sq. km
   projected population in 2006 (1996-based): 455,608
   number of households (1996): 198,200

Council tax (average Band D per two-person household), as at 1 April 2000: £915.00
Non-domestic rateable value (1997–8): £520,273,000

Education (pupils on register, 1999–2000):
   primary: 29,813
   secondary: 19,503
   pecial: 802
   entitled to free meals: 22.8%

MEMBERS OF THE COUNCIL

Aitken, Ewan	(Lab.)
Anderson, Donald	(Lab.)
Attridge, Philip	(Lab.)
Burns, Andrew	(Lab.)
Cairns, Robert	(Lab.)
Cardownie, Stephen	(Lab.)
Child, Maureen	(Lab.)
Cunningham, Bill	(Lab.)
Fallon, Edward	(Lab.)
Fitzpatrick, William	(Lab.)
Forrest, Moyra	(LD)
Gilchrist, James	(C.)
Gilmore, Sheila	(Lab.)
Grubb, George	(LD)
Guest, David	(C.)
Henderson, Ricky	(Lab.)
Hinds, Lesley	(Lab.)
Houston, Brian	(Lab.)
Jackson, Allan	(C.)
Kennedy, Sheila	(Lab.)
Mackintosh, Fred	(LD)
Maclaren, Marilyne	(LD)
Marshall, Lawrence	(Lab.)
Milligan, Eric (LP)	(Lab.)
Munn, Robert	(SNP)
Perry, Ian	(Lab.)
Pringle, Michael	(LD)
Russell, Frank	(Lab.)
Tritton, Susan	(LD)
Wallis, James	(C.)
Wardlaw, Elizabeth	(LD)
Weddell, Brian	(Lab.)

Williamson, Paul   (Lab.)
Wilson, Donald   (Lab.)
Total: 34 (Lab.22; C.4; LD.7; SNP.1)

CHIEF OFFICERS
Chief Executive: T. N. Aitchison
Director of City Development: A. Holmes
Director of Corporate Services: D. Hume
Director of Education: R. Jobson
Director of Environmental and Consumer Services: M. Drewry
Director of Finance and Information Technology: D. McGougan
Director of Housing: M. Turley
Director of Recreation: H. Coutts
Director of Social Work: L. McEwan
Local Agenda 21 Officer: D. Hume

SCOTTISH AND UK PARLIAMENTARY CONSTITUENCIES
Edinburgh Central; Edinburgh East and Musselburgh; Edinburgh North and Leith; Edinburgh Pentlands; Edinburgh South; Edinburgh West

CLACKMANNANSHIRE COUNCIL

Greenfield, Alloa, Clackmannanshire FK10 2AD
Tel: 01259-450000; Fax: 01259-452230

Area: 157 sq. km
Population (1999 estimate): 48,530
    population density (1998): 310 persons per sq. km
    projected population in 2006 (1998-based): 48,183
    number of households (1997): 20,200

Council tax (average Band D per two-person household), as at 1 April 2000: £913.00
Non-domestic rateable value (April 2000): £29,690,025

Education (pupils on register, 1998–9):
    primary: 4,512
    secondary: 2,956
    special: 58
    entitled to free meals: 23.0%

MEMBERS OF THE COUNCIL
Alexander, William   (SNP)
Balsillie, Donald   (SNP)
Brown, Keith   (SNP)
Calder, Billy   (Lab.)
Campbell, Alastair   (C.)
Douglas, William   (SNP)
Elder, Robert   (Lab.)

Forbes, Charles   (SNP)
Holden, Craig   (SNP)
Lindsay, Alison   (SNP)
McAdam, Walter (P)   (SNP)
Murphy, Tina   (SNP)
Paterson, Margaret   (Lab.)
Ross, Joanne   (Lab.)
Scobbie, Alex   (Lab.)
Stewart, Derek   (Lab.)
Wallace, William   (SNP)
Watson, Jim   (Lab.)
Total: 18 (SNP.10; Lab.7; C.1)

CHIEF OFFICERS
Acting Chief Executive: Keir Bloomer
Executive Director of Corporate Services: R. Dunbar
Executive Director of Development Services: G. Dallas
Executive Director of Education and Community Services: K. Bloomer
Executive Director of Environmental and Contract Services: W. Cunningham
Executive Director of Housing and Social Services: Ms B. Dickie
Head of Housing and Advice Services: C. J. Thirkettle
Head of Information Technology: Ms A. Easton
Head of Administration and Legal Services: Mrs J. McGuire
Head of Personnel: B. Hutchison
Local Agenda 21 contact: A. Shaw

SCOTTISH AND UK PARLIAMENTARY CONSTITUENCY
Ochil

DUMFRIES AND GALLOWAY · COUNCIL

Council Offices, English Street, Dumfries DG1 2DD
Tel: 01387-260000; Fax: 01387-260034
Web: http://www.dumgal.gov.uk

Area: 6,439 sq. km
Population (1999 estimate): 146,800
    population density (1998): 23 persons per sq. km
    projected population in 2006 (1998-based): 145,311
    number of households (1998): 63,000

Council tax (average Band D per two-person household), as at 1 April 2000: £817.00
Non-domestic rateable value (1997–8): £82,164,205

Education (pupils on register, 1999–2000):
primary: 12,699
secondary: 9,717
special: 48
entitled to free meals: 12.0%

MEMBERS OF THE COUNCIL

Agnew, John	(Ind.)
Bell, Helen	(Ind.)
Bell-Irving, Andrew	(C.)
Callender, Ian	(Ind.)
Cameron, Ken (P)	(Ind.)
Campbell, Andrew	(Ind.)
Conchie, Brian	(Lab.)
Davidson, Kathleen	(SNP)
Dempster, Jim	(Lab.)
Dinwoodie, John	(LD)
Forster, Grahame	(Lab.)
Forteath, John	(Lab.)
Geddes, Alistair	(SNP)
Gilbey, Anthony	(C.)
Gilroy, Patsy	(C.)
Gordon, Beth	(Ind.)
Higgins, Robert	(SNP)
Holmes, Thomas	(Ind.)
Hyslop, Ivor	(C.)
Little, Billy	(SNP)
Lockhart, William	(Ind.)
Maitland, Jane	(Ind.)
Male, Denis	(LD)
Marshall, Sean	(Lab.)
McAughtrie, Thomas	(Lab.)
McBurnie, George	(Lab.)
McDowall, Sandra	(LD)
McKay, Neil	(C.)
McKie, David	(Lab.)
McQueen, Marjory	(C.)
Mitchell, Joan	(LD)
Murray, Fred	(SNP)
Nimmo, Bill	(Ind.)
Paterson, Wilma	(Lab.)
Pennie, Ian	(Ind.)
Prentice, George	(Ind.)
Purdie, Jock	(Ind.)
Ramage, John	(LD)
Saunders, Bert	(Lab.)
Scobie, Willie	(Lab.)
Sloan, Tommy	(Lab.)
Sword, David	(Lab.)
Thomson, Michael	(Ind.)
Turner, Tony	(LD)
Urquhart, Donald	(Ind.)
Vaughan, Lavinia	(C.)
Wright, Allan	(C.)

Total: 47 (Ind.15; Lab.13; C.8; LD.6; SNP.5)

CHIEF OFFICERS

Chief Executive: P. N. Jones
Director of Community Resources: L. Jardine
Director of Commercial Services: R. Blackburn
Acting Director of Education: F. Sanderson
Director of Environment and Infrastructure: Dr R. Guy
Director of Environmental Health: D. A. Grant
Director of Finance and Corporate Services: J. Cowie
Director of Housing Services: Ms Y. MacQuarrie
Director of Information Services: Dr J. Pearson
Director of Legal Services: B. Kearney
Head of Personnel Services: D. Archibald
Director of Social Services: K. Makin
Local Agenda 21 Officer: Ms J. Muir

SCOTTISH AND UK PARLIAMENT CONSTITUENCIES

Dumfries; Galloway and Upper Nithsdale

DUNDEE CITY COUNCIL

21 City Square, Dundee DD1 3BY
Tel: 01382-434000; Fax: 01382-434666
Web: http://www.dundeecity.gov.uk

Area: 65 sq. km
Population (1998 estimate): 146,690
population density (1998): 2,252 persons per sq. km
projected population in 2006 (1996-based): 141,965
number of households (1996): 67,500

Council tax (average Band D per two-person household), as at 1 April 2000: £1,056
Non-domestic rateable value (1999–2000): £136,097,125

Education (pupils on register, 1998–9):
primary: 11,708
secondary: 8,917
special: 163
entitled to free meals: 27.02%

MEMBERS OF THE COUNCIL

Beattie, David	(SNP)
Beattie, Richard	(SNP)
Borthwick, Ian	(Ind.)
Bowers, David	(SNP)
Corrigan, John	(SNP)
Dawson, Andrew	(SNP)
de Gernie, George	(Lab.)

Farquhar, Charles	(Lab.)
Fitzpatrick, Joe	(SNP)
Fordyce, Elizabeth	(SNP)
Glen, Neil	(Lab.)
Grant, Fiona	(Lab.)
Guild, Ken	(SNP)
Kemp, John	(Lab.)
Letford, John	(Lab.)
Luke, Iain	(Lab.)
Mackie, Bruce	(C.)
Petrie, Allan	(SNP)
Powrie, Neil	(C.)
Presswood, Robin	(Lab.)
Regan, George	(Lab.)
Rolfe, Mervyn	(Lab.)
Sawers, Willie	(SNP)
Scott, Derek	(C.)
Shimi, Jill	(Lab.)
Sturrock, Julie	(Lab.)
Wallace, Rod	(C.)
Ward, Betty	(Lab.)
Wright, Helen (P)	(Lab.)

Total: 29 (Lab.14; SNP.10; C.4; Ind.1)

CHIEF OFFICERS
Chief Executive: A. Stephen
Director of Arts and Heritage: S. Grimmond
Director of Contract Services: R. Jackson
Director of Corporate Planning: C. Ward
Director of Economic Development: D. Grimmond
Director of Education: Ms A. Wilson
Director of Environmental and Consumer Protection: R. Gabriel
Director of Finance: D. Dorward
Director of Housing: Mrs E. Zwirlein
Director of Information Technology: A. Allan
Director of Leisure and Parks: A. Stuart
Director of Neighbourhood Resources: F. Patrick
Director of Personnel and Management Services: J. Petrie
Director of Planning and Transportation: M. Galloway
Director of Public Relations: L. Roy
Director of Social Work: Ms J. Roberts
Director of Support Services: Ms P. McIlquham
Local Agenda 21 Officer: Ms A. Anderson

SCOTTISH AND UK PARLIAMENTARY CONSTITUENCIES
Dundee East; Dundee West

EAST AYRSHIRE COUNCIL

Council Headquarters, London Road, Kilmarnock, Ayrshire KA3 7BU
Tel: 01563-576000; Fax: 01563-576500
Web: http://www.east-ayrshire.gov.uk

Area: 1,252 sq. km
Population (1998 estimate): 121,300
    population density (1998): 97 persons per sq. km
    projected population in 2006 (1996-based): 115,597
    number of households (1996): 50,100

Council tax (average Band D per two-person household), as at 1 April 2000: £1,101.60
Non-domestic rateable value (1997-8): £55,385,000

Education (pupils on register, 1997-8):
    primary: 11,414
    secondary: 7,611
    special: 187
    entitled to free meals: 20.5%

MEMBERS OF THE COUNCIL
Boyd, James (P)	(Lab.)
Carmichael, James	(Lab.)
Campbell, Alan	(SNP)
Coffey, William	(SNP)
Darnborough, Jane	(Lab.)
Dinwoodie, Elaine	(Lab.)
Farrell,Thomas	(Lab.)
Fauld, Julie	(SNP)
Hall, Kathleen	(SNP)
Hay, Ann	(SNP)
Jackson, Eric	(Lab.)
James, Raymond	(Lab.)
Kelly, James	(Lab.)
Knapp, John	(Lab.)
Linton, Iain	(SNP)
Macrae, David	(Lab.)
McDill, Robert	(SNP)
McIntyre, Andrew	(Lab.)
McLean, Finlay	(SNP)
McNeil, Brian	(SNP)
Menzies, William	(Lab.)
Reeves, Brian	(Lab.)
Reid, Douglas	(SNP)
Ross, Eric	(Lab.)
Smith, George	(Lab.)
Taylor, Robert	(Lab.)
Walsh, Alexander	(Lab.)
Weir, John	(SNP)
Wilson, Henry	(SNP)
Young, Stephanie	(C.)

Total: 32 (Lab.17; SNP.12; C.1; V.2)

CHIEF OFFICERS
Chief Executive: D. Montgomery
Director of Community Services: W. Stafford
Director of Education: J. Mulgrew
Director of Finance: A. McPhee
Director of Housing and Technical Services: J. Lavery
Director of Social Work: D. Bulloch
Head of Information Technology: M. Roulston
Head of Legal Services: Ms K. McVey
Head of Personnel: G. Hough
Head of Planning: A. Neish
Head of Protective Services: J. Crawford
Local Agenda 21 Officer: M. Buchanan

SCOTTISH AND UK PARLIAMENTARY CONSTITUENCIES
Carrick, Cumnock and Doon Valley; Kilmarnock and Loudoun

EAST DUNBARTONSHIRE COUNCIL

Tom Johnston House, Civic Way, Kirkintilloch, Glasgow G66 4TJ
Tel: 0141-578 8000; Fax: 0141-777 8576

Area: 172 sq. km
Population (1998 estimate): 109,570
population density (1998): 638 persons per sq. km
projected population in 2006 (1996-based): 109,761
number of households (1996): 40,006

Council tax (average Band D per two-person household), as at 1 April 2000: £830.00
Non-domestic rateable value (1997–8): £41,320,000

Education (pupils on register, 1997–8):
primary: 10,614
secondary: 8,412
special: 143
entitled to free meals: 10.0%

MEMBERS OF THE COUNCIL
Baillie, Stephen	(Lab.)
Brown, Alan	(C.)
Cameron, Anne	(Lab.)
Dempsey, John	(Lab.)
Divers, Barry	(Lab.)
Duncan, Robert	(LD)
Geekie, Rhondda	(Lab.)
Gotts, Eric	(LD)
Hannah, Alex	(Lab.)
Hendry, Billy	(C.)
Jarvis, Anne	(C.)
Kennedy, Charles	(Lab.)
McGaughrin, Edward	(Lab.)
McInnes, Cathy	(LD)
McSkimming, Robert (P)	(LD)
Moody, Keith	(LD)
Moody, Vaughan	(LD)
Morrison, John	(LD)
O'Donnell, Michael	(Lab.)
Risk, Fiona	(LD)
Smith, Tom	(Lab.)
Southcott, Julia	(LD)
Steel, Pat	(LD)
Walker, Una	(Lab.)

Total: 24 (Lab.11; LD.10; C.3)

CHIEF OFFICERS
Chief Executive: Dr V. Nash
Assistant Chief Executive: V. Watts
Head of Environmental Health and Consumer Services: A. McNicol
Head of Finance: K. Mitchell
Head of Human Resources: Ms A. Macpherson
Head of Planning and Building Control: Don Jamie
Strategic Director of Commercial: J. Mundell
Strategic Director of Community: vacant
Strategic Director of Development and Environmental: G. Thom

SCOTTISH AND UK PARLIAMENTARY CONSTITUENCIES
Clydebank and Milngavie; Coatbridge and Chryston; Strathkelvin and Bearsden

EAST LOTHIAN COUNCIL

John Muir House, Court Street, Haddington, East Lothian EH41 3HA
Tel: 01620-827827; Fax: 01620-827888
Web: http://www.eastlothian.gov.uk

Area: 678 sq. km
Population (1998 estimate): 89,570
  population density (1998): 132 persons per sq. km
  projected population in 2006 (1996-based): 91,649
  number of households (1996): 36,300

Council tax (average Band D per two-person household), as at 1 April 2000: £858.00
Non-domestic rateable value (1997–8): £61,920,000

Education (pupils on register, 1997–8):
  primary: 7,961
  secondary: 4,640
  entitled to free meals: 13.3%

MEMBERS OF THE COUNCIL

Berry, David	(SNP)
Broun-Lindsay, Ludovic	(C.)
Costello, David	(Lab.)
Crawford, Frances	(C.)
Ferguson, Tom	(Lab.)
Ford, Peter	(C.)
Grant, Donald	(Lab.)
Hampshire, Norman	(Lab.)
Ingle, Charles	(Lab)
Innes, Willie	(Lab.)
Jarvie, Kevin	(Lab.)
Kennedy, Simon	(Lab.)
Kinnear, Diana	(C.)
Lawrie, Tom	(Lab.)
McCarthy, Ann	(Lab.)
McNeil, John	(Lab.)
Meikle, Gilbert	(C.)
Murray, Norman	(Lab.)
O'Brien, Pat (P)	(Lab.)
O'Donnell, Patrick	(Lab.)
Ross, John	(Lab.)
Shepherd, Bishop	(Lab.)
Talac, Maureen	(Lab.)

Total: 23 (Lab.17; C.5; SNP.1)

CHIEF OFFICERS
Chief Executive: J. Lindsay
Chief Environmental Services Officer: D. Evans
Council Solicitor: K MacConnachie
Director of Education and Community Services: A. Blackie
Director of Environment and Technical Services: R. Hannah
Director of Finance: A. McCrorie
Director of Social Work and Housing: B. Walker
Head of Community Services: T. Shearer
Head of Environment: P. Collins
Head of Information Technology: R. Dowie
Head of Personnel: G. Britain
Local Agenda 21 Officer: Ms L. Wason

SCOTTISH AND UK PARLIAMENTARY CONSTITUENCY
East Lothian

EAST RENFREWSHIRE COUNCIL

Council Offices, Eastwood Park, Rouken Glen Road, Giffnock G46 6UG
Tel: 0141-577 3000; Fax: 0141-620 0884
Web: http://www.eastrenfrewshire.gov.uk

Area: 173 sq. km
Population (1998 estimate): 87,980
  population density (1998): 509 persons per sq. km
  projected population in 2006 (1996-based): 90,854
  number of households (1996): 33,100

Council tax (average Band D per two-person household), as at 1 April 2000: £810.00
Non-domestic rateable value (as at April 2000): £28,805,312

Education (pupils on register, 1999–2000):
  primary: 8,763
  secondary: 7,073
  special: 45
  entitled to free meals: 11%

MEMBERS OF THE COUNCIL

Collins, Daniel	(Lab.)
Cunningham, Elizabeth	(Lab.)
Drysdale, Iain	(C.)
Fletcher, James	(Lab.)
Forbes, Ian	(Lab.)
Garscadden, Roy	(Lab.)
Gilbert, Charlie	(C.)
Grant, Barbara	(C.)
Hutchison, Ian	(C.)
Lafferty, Alan	(Lab.)
MacDonald, Gordon	(C.)
McGee, Frank	(C.)
Montague, Mary	(Lab.)

Napier, George	(LD)
Pearce, Ian	(R)
Phillips, Edward	(Lab.)
Rosin, Leslie	(C.)
Shaw, James	(C.)
Steele, Allan (P)	(LD)
Taylor, Owen	(Lab.)

Total: 20   (Lab.9;   C.8;   LD.2;   R.1)

CHIEF OFFICERS
Chief Executive: P. Daniels
Assistant Chief Executive: Mrs C. Innes
Deputy Chief Executive: C. Dalrymple
Director of Central Services: J. Hawkins
Director of Commercial Operations: R. A. Russell
Director of Community and Leisure: Mrs A. Saunders
Director of Education: Mrs E. Currie
Director of Environment: A. Cahill
Director of Finance: D. Dippie
Director of Social Work: Dr S. Ross
Local Agenda 21 Officer: M. Valenti

SCOTTISH AND UK PARLIAMENTARY CONSTITUENCY
Eastwood

COMHAIRLE EILEAN SIAR/WESTERN ISLES COUNCIL

Council Offices, Sandwick Road, Stornoway, Isle of Lewis HS1 2BW
Tel: 01851-703773; Fax: 01851-705349
Web: http://www.w-isles.gov.uk

Area: 3,134 sq. km
Population (1998 estimate): 27,940
   population density (1998): 9 persons per sq. km
   projected population in 2006 (1996-based): 27,554
   number of households (1996): 11,600

Council tax (average Band D per two-person household), as at 1 April 2000: £1023.00
Non-domestic rateable value (1997-8): £12,563,000

Education (pupils on register, 1997-8):
   primary: 2,535
   secondary: 2,002
   entitled to free meals: 12.5%

MEMBERS OF THE COUNCIL

Blaney, David	(Ind.)
Bremner, Mary	(Ind.)
Campbell, Angus	(Lab.)
Campbell, Archibald	(Ind.)
Graham, Angus	(Ind.)
Graham, Malcolm	(Ind.)
Lonie, George	(Lab.)
Macarthur, James	(Ind.)
Macdonald, Alexander (C)	(Ind.)
Macdonald, Donald	(Ind.)
Macdonald, Norman A.	(Lab.)
Macdonald, Norman L.	(Ind.)
Mackay, Donald	(Ind.)
Mackenzie, Katie	(Ind.)
Mackinnon, Ronald	(Ind.)
Maclean, Donald	(Ind.)
Maclean, Philip	(SNP)
Macleod, Ian	(Ind.)
Macleod, Malcolm	(Lab.)
Macleod, Norman	(Ind.)
Macleod, Murdo	(Ind.)
Macrae, Alasdair	(Ind.)
Macsween, Doanld	(Ind.)
Manford, Donald	(SNP)
Morrison, Finlay	(Ind.)
Morrison, Iain	(Ind.)
Morrison, Roderick	(Ind.)
Munro, Morag	(Ind.)
Murray, Roderick	(Lab.)
Nicholson, Donald	(Ind.)
Nicolson, Angus	(SNP)

Total: 31   (Ind. 23;   Lab. 5;   SNP 3)

CHIEF OFFICERS
Acting Chief Executive: N. Galbraith
Director of Corporate Services: D. O'Loan
Acting Director of Education: M. Macleod
Acting Director of Environmental Health: M. Gold
Director of Finance: R. Bennie
Director of Housing: A. Lamont
Director of Social Services: M. Smith
Director of Technical Services: M. Murray
Local Agenda 21 Officer: D. McKim

SCOTTISH AND UK PARLIAMENTARY CONSTITUENCY
Western Isles

FALKIRK COUNCIL

Municipal Buildings, West Bridge Street, Falkirk
FK1 5RS
Tel: 01324-506070; Fax: 01324-506071

Area: 299 sq. km
Population (1998 estimate): 144,110
　population density (1998): 482 persons per
　sq. km
　projected population in 2006 (1996-based):
　142,109
　number of households (1996): 59,100

**Council tax (average Band D per two-person
household), as at 1 April 2000:** £757.00
Non-domestic rateable value (1997–8):
　£115,964,000

Education (pupils on register, 1997–8):
　primary: 12,316
　secondary: 8,551
　special: 297
　entitled to free meals: 18.1%

MEMBERS OF THE COUNCIL
Alexander, David	(SNP)
Anderson, William	(Lab.)
Bryson, David	(SNP)
Buchanan, William	(Ind.)
Coleman, Thomas	(SNP)
Connolly, John	(Lab.)
Constable, Harry	(SNP)
Constable, John	(SNP)
Eaglesham, Elizabeth	(SNP)
Forsyth, David	(SNP)
Fowler, Alexander	(Lab.)
Goldie, Dennis (P)	(Lab.)
Goldie, Gerald	(Lab.)
Gow, Linda	(Lab.)
Gray, Alan	(Lab.)
Jenkinson, John	(Lab.)
Johnston, James	(Ind.)
Kenna, Lynda	(SNP)
Martin, Craig	(Lab.)
McCafferty, Patrick	(Ind.)
Miller, Ian	(Lab.)
Milne, James	(Lab.)
O'Brien, Lezley Cameron	(Lab.)
O'Dea, Thomas	(Ind.)
Paisley, Alastiar	(C.)
Patrick, John	(C.)
Pollock, Mary	(Lab.)
Short, James	(Lab.)
Spears, Robert	(Ind.)
Spiers, David	(Lab.)
Williamson, Diane	(SNP)
Wilson, James	(Ind.)

Total: 32 (Lab.15; C.3; SNP.9; Ind.5;

CHIEF OFFICERS
Chief Executive: Ms M. Pitcaithly
**Director of Community and Environmental
Services:** S. Dunlop
Director of Contract Services: vacant
Director of Corporate Services: S. Ritchie
Director of Education: Dr G. Young
Director of Finance: A. Jannetta
Director of Housing: I. Walker
Director of Law and Administration: Ms E. S.
Morton
Director of Social Work Services: Ms C.
Wilkinson
Director of Strategic Services: G. Peart
Local Agenda 21 contact: D. Gorman

SCOTTISH AND UK PARLIAMENTARY CONSTITUENCIES
Falkirk East; Falkirk West

FIFE COUNCIL

Fife House, North Street, Glenrothes, Fife KY7
5LT
Tel: 01592-414141; Fax: 01592-414142
Web: http://www.fife.gov.uk

Area: 1,323 sq. km
Population (1998 estimate): 348,900
　population density (1998): 264 persons per
　sq. km
　projected population in 2006 (1996-based):
　349,020
　number of households (1996): 145,600

**Council tax (average Band D per two-person
household), as at 1 April 2000:** £849
Non-domestic rateable value (1997–8):
　£258,076,000

Education (pupils on register):
　primary: 29,935
　secondary: 22,761
　special: 590
　entitled to free meals: 17.5%

MEMBERS OF THE COUNCIL
Aitken, William	(Lab.)
Alexander, David	(SNP)
Allan, George	(Lab.)
Arbuckle, Andrew	(LD)
Arnott, David	(Lab.)

Ballantyne, Fraser	(Lab.)	Sawers, Alexander	(Lab.)
Beveridge, Isabella	(Lab.)	Scott-Hayward, Michael	(C.)
Blyth, Henry	(Lab.)	Simpson, James	(LD)
Bradie, Jack	(LD)	Simpson, John	(Lab.)
Brand, William	(Lab.)	Smith, Agnes	(Lab.)
Brennan, James	(Lab.)	Stocks, Barbara	(Lab.)
Brown, Andrew	(Lab.)	Taylor, Margaret	(LD)
Cameron, John	(Lab.)	Taylor, Robert	(Lab.)
Clark, Susan	(LD)	Thacker, Bryan	(SNP)
Clarke, William	(O)	Thomson, Alexander	(Lab.)
Connelly, Irene	(Lab.)	Tolson, James	(LD)
Cook, James	(SNP)	Torrance, David	(SNP)
Coyne, Michael	(Lab.)	Toye, Anne	(LD)
Dair, Thomas	(Lab.)	Watters, Ann	(LD)
Dodds, May	(Lab.)	Woods, Michael	(SNP)
Doig, Margot	(Lab.)	Young, Robert	(Lab.)

Douglas, Peter (LD)
Dow, Allan (LD)

Total: 77 (Lab.42; LD.21; SNP.9; C.2; O.2; Ind.1)

Duff, Gordon (Lab.)
Eadie, Robert (Lab.)
Edward Drew (Lab.)
Farmer, John (Lab.)
Garrett, Anthony (LD)
Grant, Fiona (SNP)
Grant, Peter (SNP)
Gunn, Theresa (Lab.)
Gunstone, Eleanor (LD)
Harris, Elizabeth (LD)
Hill, Sheila (LD)
Hunter-Blair, Jane (LD)
Kay, William (Lab.)
Keddie, Andrew (Lab.)
Kenney, Alan (Lab.)
Latto, Catherine (Lab.)
Law, Helen (Lab.)
Leslie, George (SNP)
Liston, Jane Ann (LD)
Logan, Margaret (Lab.)
Lothian, David (LD)
McCallum, Angel (Lab.)
MacDougall, John (C) (Lab.)
McFee, Edith (LD)
McGarry, Alice (SNP)
McGovern, Anne (Lab.)
Martin, Anthony (LD)
Maxwell, Alexander (O)
May, Christine (Lab.)
Melville, Frances (LD)
Morrison, Kay (Lab.)
O'Sullivan, Bill (Lab.)
Paterson, Andrew (Lab.)
Randall, Stuart (C.)
Riches, Elizabeth (LD)
Rodger, Andrew (Ind.)
Rougvie, David (Lab.)
Rumney, Robert (Lab.)

CHIEF OFFICERS
Chief Executive: D. Sinclair
Head of Community Services: D. Somerville
Head of Corporate Procurement: J. McHugh
Head of Education: A. McKay
Head of Environmental Health: J. Stark
Head of Finance: P. Ritchie
Head of Housing: A. Davidson
Head of Information Technology: E. Brewster
Head of Law and Administration: S. Allan
Head of Personnel: M. Burnell
Head of Planning: D. Rae
Head of Social Work: M. Sawyer
Local Agenda 21 Co-ordinator: Ms S. Keast

SCOTTISH AND UK PARLIAMENTARY CONSTITUENCIES
Dunfermline East; Dunfermline West; Fife Central; Fife North East; Kirkcaldy

GLASGOW CITY COUNCIL

City Chambers, George Square, Glasgow G2 1DU
Tel: 0141-287 2000; Fax: 0141-287 5666
Web: http://www.glasgow.gov.uk

Area: 175 sq. km
Population (1999 estimate): 611,440
    population density (1999): 3,494 persons per sq. km
    projected population in 2008 (1999-based): 591,911
    number of households (1998): 274,615

Council tax (average Band D per two-person household), as at 1 April 2000: £1,317.20
Non-domestic rateable value (1997–8): £633,729,769

Education (pupils on register, 1997–8):
    primary: 46,105
    secondary: 29,238
    special: 3,100
    entitled to free meals: 43.7%

MEMBERS OF THE COUNCIL

Baird, Susan	(Lab.)
Beckett, Mary	(Lab.)
Burns, Kenneth	(Lab.)
Butler, William	(Lab.)
Butt, Shaukat	(Lab.)
Cameron, Elizabeth	(Lab.)
Chalmers, Patricia	(Lab.)
Coleman, James	(Lab.)
Colleran, Aileen	(Lab.)
Davey, Ronald	(Lab.)
Devine, Christine	(Lab.)
Dingwall, Tommy	(Lab.)
Dodds, Josephine	(Lab.)
Dornan, Stephen	(Lab.)
Fitzgerald, Eamon	(Lab.)
Flanagan, John	(Lab.)
Gaughan, Deirdre	(Lab.)
Gibson, Iris	(SNP)
Glass, Alexander	(Lab.)
Gordon, Charles	(Lab.)
Gould, Robert	(Lab.)
Graham, Archie	(Lab.)
Graham, Irene	(Lab.)
Gray, John	(Lab.)
Gray, Robert	(Lab.)
Green, Malcolm	(Lab.)
Hurcombe, Ellen	(Lab.)
Kelly, Christopher	(Lab.)
Kernaghan, Michael	(Lab.)
Lee, Martin	(Lab.)
Leonard, Gerald	(Lab.)
Lynch, John	(Lab.)
Lyon, Catherine	(C.)
McCafferty, Charles	(Lab.)
McCafferty, Margaret	(Lab.)
McCann, Gaille	(Lab.)
McCarron, James	(Lab.)
McDougall, Elaine	(Lab.)
McFadden, Jean	(Lab.)
McKenzie, John	(Lab.)
McLean, Malcolm	(Lab.)
McMaster, Catherine	(Lab.)
McNally, James	(Lab.)
McNicol, Colin	(Lab.)
MacBean, Robert	(Lab.)
Macdiarmid, Gordon	(Lab.)
Mackechnie, James	(Lab.)
MacLellan, Walter	(Lab.)
Macrae, Hugh	(Lab.)
Maan, Bashir	(Lab.)
Macey, Jean	(Lab.)
Malik, Hanzala	(Lab.)
Marshall, Robert	(Lab.)
Mason, Christopher	(LD)
Mason, John	(SNP)
Matheson, Gordon	(Lab.)
Mosson, Alex (LP)	(Lab.)
Moynes, John	(Lab.)
Mutter, James	(Lab.)
O'Neill, Marjorie	(Lab.)
O' Rourke, William	(Lab.)
Purcell, Stephen	(Lab.)
Quinn, Ronald	(Lab.)
Redmond, George	(Lab.)
Renton, Catriona	(Lab.)
Roberton, Craig	(Lab.)
Ryan, George	(Lab.)
Sheridan, Tommy	(Soc.)
Shoaib, Muhammad	(Lab.)
Simpson, Ruth	(Lab.)
Sinclair, Margaret	(Lab.)
Smith, Elaine	(Lab.)
Stevenson, David	(Lab.)
Stewart, Alan	(Lab.)
Stewart, Allan	(Lab.)
Timoney, Bill	(Lab.)
Watson, Alistair	(Lab.)
Watson, Allan	(Lab.)
Winter, Robert	(Lab.)

Total: 79 (Lab.74; SNP.2; C.1; LD.1; Soc.1)

CHIEF OFFICERS

Chief Executive: J. Andrews
Acting Director of Building Services: S. Fallis
Director of Cultural and Leisure Services: Ms B. McConnell

**Director of Development and Regeneration
Services:** R. McConnell
Director of Direct and Care Services: F.
Chambers
Director of Education Services: K. Corsar
Director of Financial Services: G. Black
Director of Housing Services: D. Comley
Director of Land Services: A. Young
Director of Personnel and Administration: H.
Burke
Director of Protective Services: B. Kelly
Director of Social Work Services: R.
O'Connor
Local Agenda 21 Officer: S. Gillon

SCOTTISH AND UK PARLIAMENTARY CONSTITUENCIES

Glasgow Anniesland; Glasgow Baillieston;
Glasgow Cathcart; Glasgow Govan; Glasgow
Kelvin; Glasgow Maryhill; Glasgow Pollok;
Glasgow Rutherglen; Glasgow Shettleston;
Glasgow Springburn

HIGHLAND COUNCIL

Glenurquhart Road, Inverness IV3 5NX
Tel: 01463-702000; Fax: 01463-702111
Web: http://www.highland.gov.uk

Area: 25,784 sq. km
Population (1998 estimate): 208,300
population density (1998): 8 persons per sq.
km
projected population in 2006 (1996-based):
214,031
number of households (1996): 85,800

**Council tax (average Band D per two-person
household), as at 1 April 2000:** £839.00
Non-domestic rateable value (2000-1):
£161,178,865

Education (pupils on register, 1999-2000):
primary: 18,854
secondary: 14,787
special: 178

MEMBERS OF THE COUNCIL

Alexander, James	(Ind.)
Allan, Duncan	(Ind.)
Alston, David	(Ind.)
Anderson, Andrew	(SNP)
Balfour, Roderick	(Ind.)
Beaton, Allan	(Ind.)
Black, Stuart	(LD)
Briggs, Douglas	(Ind.)
Bruce, George	(Ind.)
Cairns, Peter	(SNP)
Campbell, Isabelle	(LD)
Clark, Neil	(Ind.)
Cole, John	(LD)
Corbett, Peter	(Ind.)
Coutts, Garry	(Ind.)
Cumming, Christina	(Lab.)
Davidson, Margaret	(Ind.)
Deirdrie, Steven	(Lab.)
Dick, Angus	(LD)
Downie, Morris	(Ind.)
Dunlop, Basil	(Ind.)
Durham, Richard	(Ind.)
Finlayson, Michael	(Ind.)
Finlayson, Rita	(Ind.)
Flear, David	(LD)
Foxley, Michael	(LD)
Fraser, David	(Ind.)
Fulton, William	(Ind.)
Goodman, Clive	(Lab.)
Gordon, Angus	(Ind.)
Green, David	(Ind.)
Home, Janet	(Ind.)
Jardine, Barbara	(LD)
Keith, Francis	(Ind.)
King, Charles	(Ind.)
Lyon, Ron	(Ind.)
MacDonald, Alistair	(LD)
MacDonald, Eilidh	(Lab.)
MacDonald, Liz	(SNP)
Macdonald, Olwyn	(Ind.)
Macintyre, Roy	(Ind.)
MacKenzie, Sandy	(Ind.)
Mackinnon, Ewen	(Ind.)
MacLachlan, William	(Ind.)
MacLennan, Margaret	(Ind.)
MacRae, Ella	(Ind.)
Magee, Alison	(Ind.)
Matheson, John	(Ind.)
Matheson, Kathleen	(Ind.)
McCreath, Gillian	(SNP)
McFarlane, Andrew	(Ind.)
Millar, Andrew	(Ind.)
Moncrieff, Gavin	(SNP)
Mowat, William	(Ind.)
Munro, David	(Lab.)
Murphy, Brian	(Lab.)
Norrie, Donald	(Ind.)
Oag, James	(Ind.)
Park, Alexander	(Ind.)
Paterson, Andrew	(Ind.)
Paterson, James	(Ind.)
Paterson, Margaret	(SNP)
Philip, Russell	(Ind.)
Rhind, Alasdair	(Ind.)
Rosie, John	(Lab.)
Ross, William	(Ind.)

Russel, Alexander (LD)
Salmon, Bernard (LD)
Saxon, Roger (Lab.)
Severn, Robert (SNP)
Shiels, Simon (Ind.)
Simpson, Dick (LD)
Smith, Graeme (LD)
Smith, William (P) (Ind.)
Sutherland, Angus (Ind.)
Thomson, James (Lab.)
Waters, Donald (Ind.)
Wilkerson, Lou (Lab.)
Wilson, Carolyn (Ind.)
Wynd, Robert (SNP)
Total: 80 (Ind.50; LD.12; Lab.10; SNP.8)

CHIEF OFFICERS
Chief Executive: A. D. McCourt
Director of Commercial Operations: C. Mackenzie
Director of Corporate Services: A. Dodds
Director of Culture and Leisure: A. Jones
Director of Education: B. Robertson
Director of Finance: A. Geddes
Director of Housing: G. Fisher
Director of Information Systems: R. Metcalfe
Director of Planning and Development: J. Rennilson
Director of Property and Architectural Services: Dr A. Coutts
Director of Protective Services: D. Thompson
Acting Director of Roads and Transport: P. Shimin
Director of Social Services: H. Dempster
Local Agenda 21 contact: A. Dorin

SCOTTISH AND UK PARLIAMENTARY CONSTITUENCIES
Caithness, Sutherland and Easter Ross; Inverness East, Nairn and Lochaber; Ross, Skye and Inverness West

INVERCLYDE COUNCIL
Municipal Buildings, Clyde Square, Greenock, Renfrewshire PA15 1LY
Tel: 01475-717171; Fax: 01475-712010

Area: 162 sq. km
Population (1998 estimate): 85,400
  population density (1998): 528 persons per sq. km
  projected population in 2006 (1996-based): 77,840
  number of households (1996): 38,000

Council tax (average Band D per two-person household), as at 1 April 2000: £933.00
Non-domestic rateable value (1997–8): £47,829,000

Education (pupils on register, 1997–8):
  primary: 7,791
  secondary: 5,583
  special: 145
  entitled to free meals: 23.9%

MEMBERS OF THE COUNCIL
Blair, Alan (LD)
Calvert, Alex (C.)
Campbell, Robert (LD)
Hunter, Jim (LD)
Jackson, Robert (Lab.)
McCabe, Stephen (Lab.)
McCormick, Patrick (Lab.)
McGhee, Alex (Lab.)
Mitchell, Jim (LD)
Moody, John (LD)
Morrison, Daniel (Lab.)
Nimmo, Sandy (LD)
O'Rourke, Jim (Lab.)
Rebecchi, Ciano (LD)
Roach, Robert (P) (Lab.)
Robertson, Allan (Lab)
Robertson, Yvonne (Lab.)
White, George (LD)
Total: 20 (Lab. 9; LD. 8; C. 1; V. 2)

CHIEF OFFICERS
Chief Executive: R. Cleary
Deputy Chief Executive/Director of Economic Development Services: G. Malone
Director of Community and Protective Services: N. Graham
Director of Education Services: B. McLeary
Director of Information Services: M. Russell
Director of Legal and Support Services: E. Paterson
Director of Resource Services: M. McCrossan

Director of Social Work and Housing Services:
T. Keenan
Local Agenda 21 Officer: D. Hall

SCOTTISH AND UK PARLIAMENTARY CONSTITUENCIES
Greenock and Inverclyde; West Renfrewshire

MIDLOTHIAN COUNCIL

Midlothian House, 40–46 Buccleuch Street, Dalkeith, Midlothian EH22 1DJ
Tel: 0131-271 7500; Fax: 0131-271 3050
Web: http://www.midlothian.gov.uk

Area: 355 sq. km
Population (1998 estimate): 80,860
  population density (1998): 228 persons per sq. km
  projected population in 2006 (1998-based): 82,305
  number of households (2000): 31,800

Council tax (average Band D per two-person household), as at 1 April 2000: £963.00
Non-domestic rateable value (1999–2000): £45,657,386

Education (pupils on register, 1999–2000):
  primary: 7,424
  secondary: 5,402
  special: 150
  entitled to free meals: 17.6%

MEMBERS OF THE COUNCIL
Aitchinson, Jackie	(Lab.)
Anderson, Maureen	(Lab.)
Boyes, Peter	(Lab.)
Campbell, Sam (P)	(Lab.)
Dunsmuir, James	(Lab.)
Fletcher, David	(LD)
Hamilton, David	(Lab.)
Harkness, Sandy	(Lab.)
Imrie, Russell	(Lab.)
Marr, Graham	(Lab.)
Martin, Maira	(Lab.)
Milligan, Derek	(Lab.)
Molloy, Danny	(Lab.)
Montgomery, Adam	(Lab.)
Pottinger, Bryan	(Lab.)
Purcell, George	(Lab.)
Russell, Margot	(Lab.)
Small, Richard	(Lab.)

Total: 18 (Lab. 17; LD 1)

CHIEF OFFICERS
Chief Executive: T. Muir
Director of Community Services: G. Marwick
Director of Contract Services: B. Page
Director of Corporate Services: I. Jackson
Director of Education: D. MacKay
Director of Social Services: S. Adams
Director of Strategic Services: J. Allan
Local Agenda 21 Officer: vacant

SCOTTISH AND UK PARLIAMENTARY CONSTITUENCIES
Midlothian; Tweeddale, Ettrick and Lauderdale

MORAY COUNCIL

Council Office, High Street, Elgin, Morayshire IV30 1BX
Tel: 01343-543451; Fax: 01343-540183
Web: http://www.moray.gov.uk

Area: 2,238 sq. km
Population (1999 estimate): 85,870
  population density (1999): 38 persons per sq. km
  projected population in 2006 (1998-based): 85,871
  number of households (1997): 35,300

Council tax (average Band D per two-person household), 1 April 2000: £724.00
Non-domestic rateable value (2000): £55,839,686

Education (pupils on register, 1997–8):
  primary: 8,048
  secondary: 5,542
  special: 22
  entitled to free meals: 9.4%

MEMBERS OF THE COUNCIL
Aldridge, Eddie (C)	(Ind.)
Bisset, Alastair	(Ind.)
Burgess, Alan	(Lab.)
Coutts, Eddie	(Ind.)
Drivers, John	(Lab.)
Ettles, Muriel	(Lab.)
Farquharson, Ali	(Lab.)
Fleming, Alistair	(Ind.)
Flynn, Wilma	(Ind.)
Gorn, Linda	(LD)
Hogg, John	(Ind.)
Howe, Tom	(SNP)
Jappy, Bill	(Lab.)
Keith, Sandy	(Lab.)
Leslie, John	(Lab.)
Longmore, Sinclair	(Ind.)

McIntosh, Rex	(Ind.)	Donn, John	(Lab.)
Paul, Pearl	(SNP)	Gallagher, David	(Lab.)
Shaw, Jennifer	(Ind.)	Gooding, Samuel	(Lab.)
Shepherd, Ronald	(Ind.)	Gorman, Jane	(Lab.)
Towns, George	(LD)	Gray, Elliot	(Lab.)
Urquhart, Alasdair	(Ind.)	Hill, Alan	(SNP)
Watt, Percy	(Ind.)	Jennings, James	(Lab.)
Wilson, Bob	(Ind.)	Marshall, Elisabethe	(C.)
Young, Iain	(C.)	McDougall, Margaret	(Lab.)

Total: 25 (Ind.13; Lab.7; LD.2; SNP.2; C.1)

McKinney, Joseph (Lab.)
McLardy, Elizabeth (Ind.)

CHIEF OFFICERS
Chief Executive: A. Keddie
Deputy Chief Executive: Ms K Williams
Director of Community Services: M. Martin
Director of Education: D. Duncan
Chief Financial Officer: D. Clark
Director of Environmental Services: R. Stewart
Local Agenda 21 Officer: G. Templeton

SCOTTISH AND UK PARLIAMENTARY CONSTITUENCIES
Gordon; Moray

McNamara, Peter	(Lab.)
Moffat, John	(Lab.)
Munn, David	(Lab.)
Munn, Margaret	(Lab.)
Munro, Alan	(Lab.)
O' Neill, David	(Lab.)
Rae, Robert	(SNP)
Reid, John	(Lab.)
Reilly, Robert	(Lab.)
Sillars, John	(Lab.)
Taylor, Samuel (C)	(Lab.)
Wilkinson, Richard	(C.)

Total: 30 (Lab. 25; C. 2; SNP 2; Ind.1)

NORTH AYRSHIRE COUNCIL

Cunninghame House, Irvine, Ayrshire KA12 8EE
Tel: 01294-324100; Fax: 01294-324144

Area: 884 sq. km
Population (1998 estimate): 139,660
  population density (1998): 158 persons per sq. km
  projected population in 2008 (1998-based): 139,621
  number of households (1998): 58,500

Council tax (average Band D per two-person household), as at 1 April 2000: £1,050.20
Non-domestic rateable value (2000): £100,492,807

Education (pupils on register, 1999):
  primary: 12,408
  secondary: 9,063
  special: 192
  entitled to free meals: 26.7%

MEMBERS OF THE COUNCIL

Barr, Tom	(Lab.)
Bell, John	(Lab.)
Browne, Jacqueline	(Lab.)
Carson, Jack	(Lab.)
Clarkson, Gordon	(Lab.)
Clarkson, Ian	(Lab.)
Dewar, Stewart	(Lab.)

CHIEF OFFICERS
Chief Executive: B. Devine
Assistant Chief Executive, Development and Promotion: B. MacDonald
Assistant Chief Executive, Finance: A. Herbert
Assistant Chief Executive, Information Technology: J. Barrett
Assistant Chief Executive, Legal and Regulatory: I. Mackay
Assistant Chief Executive, Personnel: J. M. MacFarlane
Corporate Director, Educational Services: J. Travers
Corporate Director, Property Services: T. Orr
Corporate Director, Social Services: G. Irving
Local Agenda 21 Officer: Ms S. King

SCOTTISH AND UK PARLIAMENTARY CONSTITUENCIES
Cunninghame North; Cunninghame South

NORTH LANARKSHIRE COUNCIL

PO Box 14, Civic Centre, Motherwell, Lanarkshire ML1 1TW
Tel: 01698-302222; Fax: 01698-275125
Web: http://www.northlan.gov.uk

Area: 474 sq. km
Population (1998 estimate): 326,720
  population density (1998): 690 persons per sq. km
  projected population in 2006 (1996-based): 317,922
  number of households (1996): 128,500

Council tax (average Band D per two-person household), as at 1 April 2000: £1099.20
Non-domestic rateable value (1997–8): £181,228,000

Education (pupils on register, 1997–8):
  primary: 29,843
  secondary: 22,383
  special: 692
  entitled to free meals: 24.7%

MEMBERS OF THE COUNCIL

Barrie, Tom	(Lab.)
Brady, Brian	(Lab.)
Brooks, James	(Lab.)
Burns, Andrew	(Lab.)
Cameron, Campbell	(SNP)
Carmichael, William	(SNP)
Cassidy, John	(Lab.)
Cefferty, Charles	(Lab.)
Chadha, Bob	(Lab.)
Clark, Anthony	(Lab.)
Connelly, Patrick	(Lab.)
Cox, Sandra	(SNP)
Coyle, James	(Lab.)
Curley, Thomas	(Lab.)
Curran, Harry	(Lab.)
Devine, George	(Lab.)
Donnelly, Patrick	(Lab.)
Glavin, Faye	(SNP)
Gordon, John	(Lab.)
Gorman, Joe	(Lab.)
Gormill, Frank	(Lab.)
Grant, Stephen	(Lab.)
Gray, Charles	(Lab.)
Griffin, Francis	(Lab.)
Hebenton, Charles	(Lab.)
Hogg, William	(Lab.)
Holloway, Ernest	(Lab.)
Horner, William	(SNP)
Irvine, Elizabeth	(SNP)
Jones, Jean	(Lab.)
Lefferty, John	(Lab.)
Logue, James	(Lab.)
Love, Sam	(Lab.)
Lunny, Thomas	(Lab.)
Lyle, Richard	(SNP)
Maginnis, Thomas	(Lab.)
Martin, James	(Lab.)
Martin, William	(Lab.)
Mathison, Vincent	(Lab.)
McCabe, James	(Lab.)
McCallum, Neil	(SNP)
McCulloch, Barry (P)	(Lab.)
McElroy, Gerald	(Lab.)
McGee, John	(Lab.)
McGuigan, Harry	(Lab.)
McGuigan, James	(Lab.)
McKendrick, David	(Ind.)
McKeown, Kevin	(Lab.)
McKinlay, James	(Lab.)
McLaughlin, Gerard	(Lab.)
Moran, John	(Lab.)
Morgan, Thomas	(Lab.)
Morris, Donna	(Lab.)
Murray, Gordon	(SNP)
Murray, Margaret	(SNP)
Nolan, Thomas	(Lab.)
Pentland, John	(Lab.)
Robertson, James	(Lab.)
Ross, Michael	(Lab.)
Saunders, David	(Lab.)
Scott, Bernard	(Lab.)
Selfridge, Thomas	(Lab.)
Shaw, Joseph	(Lab.)
Shields, Bill	(Lab.)
Smith, James	(Lab.)
Stocks, David	(SNP)
Sullivan, Peter	(Lab.)
Valentine, Alan	(SNP)
Wallace, Brian	(Lab.)
Wilson, William	(Lab.)

Total: 70 (Lab.57; SNP.12; Ind.1)

CHIEF OFFICERS

Chief Executive: A. Cowe
Director of Administration: J. O'Hagan
Director of Community Services: P. Jukes
Director of Education: M. O'Neill
Director of Finance: R. Hinds
Director of Housing and Property Services: G. Whitefield
Director of Planning and Environment: D. Porch
Director of Social Work: J. Dickie
General Manager of Contracting Services: R. Ellerby
Local Agenda 21 Officer: A. Hendry

SCOTTISH AND UK PARLIAMENTARY CONSTITUENCIES

Airdrie and Shotts; Coatbridge and Chryston; Cumbernauld and Kilsyth; Hamilton North and Bellshill; Motherwell and Wishaw

ORKNEY ISLANDS COUNCIL

Council Offices, School Place, Kirkwall, Orkney KW15 1NY
Tel: 01856-873535; Fax: 01856-874615

Area: 992 sq. km
Population (2000 estimate): 19,534
    population density (1998): 20 persons per sq. km
    projected population in 2010 (2000-based): 19,181
    number of households (1998): 8,200

Council tax (average Band D per two-person household), as at 1 April 2000: £690.00
Non-domestic rateable value (2000–1): £15,203,557

Education (pupils on register, 1999–2000):
    primary: 1,757
    secondary: 1,366
    special: 20
    entitled to free meals: 7.5%

MEMBERS OF THE COUNCIL

Annal, C. A.	(Ind.)
Annal, J,	(Ind.)
Brown, J. F.	(Ind.)
Cormack, R.	(Ind.)
Drever, M. J.	(Ind.)
Foubister, J.	(Ind.)
Groundwater, F. J.	(Ind.)
Hagan, T. S.	(Ind.)
Halcro-Johnson, H. (C)	(Ind.)
Hamilton, J. M.	(Ind.)
Johnson, A. K.	(Ind.)
McLeod, R. R.	(Ind.)
Moodie, J.	(Ind.)
Murray, B. M.	(Ind.)
Petrie, M. A.	(Ind.)
Sclater, R. C.	(Ind.)
Scott, E. F.	(Ind.)
Scott, S. T.	(Ind.)
Sinclair, J.	(Ind.)
Sutherland, K. A.	(Ind.)
Taylor, B. A.	(Ind.)

Total: 21 (Ind. 21)

CHIEF OFFICERS

Chief Executive: A. Buchan
Chief Administrative Officer: M. Burr
Chief Environmental Services Officer: D. Tonge
Chief Legal Officer: D. Fairnie
Chief Trading Standards Officer: I. Watt
Director of Community Social Services: H. Garland
Director of Development and Planning: J. Baster
Director of Education and Recreational Services: W. L. Manson
Director of Finance and Housing: D. A. Robertson
Director of Technical Services: J. Panton
Personnel Officer: B. Evans

SCOTTISH PARLIAMENT CONSTITUENCY
Orkney
UK PARLIAMENT CONSTITUENCY
Orkney and Shetland

PERTH AND KINROSS COUNCIL

PO Box 77, 2 High Street, Perth PH1 5PH
Tel: 01738-475000; Fax: 01738-475710
Email: enquiries@pkc.gov.uk
Web: http://www.pkc.gov.uk

Area: 5,311 sq. km
Population (1998 estimate): 134,030
    population density (1999): 25 persons per sq. km
    projected population in 2006 (1996-based): 136,454
    number of households (2000): 61,792

Council tax (average Band D per two-person household), as at 1 April 2000: £795.00
Non-domestic rateable value (1997–8): £107,929,000

Education (pupils on register, 2000):
    primary: 10,852
    secondary: 7,413
    special: 49
    entitled to free meals: 8.0%

MEMBERS OF THE COUNCIL

Anderson, Hugh	(C.)
Baird, Kathleen	(C.)
Barnacle, Michael	(LD)
Barr, Alistair	(SNP)
Bushby, Sandy	(C.)

Caddell, Lorraine	(LD)
Cook, Michael	(SNP)
Crabbie, Colin	(C.)
Crawford, Bruce	(SNP)
Culliven, John	(SNP)
Doig, James	(Ind.)
Dow, David	(C.)
Ellis, Bob	(SNP)
Flynn, John	(Lab.)
Gilles, Callum	(Lab.)
Grant, Alan	(SNP)
Howie, Eleanor	(SNP)
Hulbert, John	(SNP)
Hunter, Gordon	(SNP)
Hunter, Iain	(SNP)
Jack, Alan	(C.)
Kelly, Jack	(Lab.)
Lennie, Margo	(Lab.)
Livingstone, Chris	(LD)
Lloyd, John	(Ind.)
Lumsden, Bob	(SNP)
Lyall, Ken	(SNP)
Mair, John	(C.)
McDonald, Helen	(C.)
McEwen, Joan	(Lab.)
Miller, Ian	(SNP)
Mulheron, Peter	(SNP)
O'Malley, Mike (P)	(Lab.)
Robertson, William	(LD)
Scott, Bob	(LD)
Scott, Dave	(SNP)
Stewart, Alexander	(C.)
Stewart, Heather	(C.)
Telfer, Alan	(SNP)
Wilson, William	(LD)
Young, Colin	(C.)

Total: 41 (SNP.16; C.11; LD.6; Lab.6; Ind.2)

CHIEF OFFICERS

Chief Executive: H. Robertson
Director of Education and Children's Services: B. Frew
Director of Environment: J. Milne
Director of Finance: A. R. McArthur
Director of Housing and Social Work Services: I. Manson
Director of Human Resources: G. Farquhar
Director of Information Systems and Technology: A. J. Nair
Director of Planning and Development Services: D. Munro
Director of Roads, Transport and Architectural Services: J. Irons
Director of Social Work Services: Mrs B. Bridgeford

SCOTTISH AND UK PARLIAMENTARY CONSTITUENCIES

Angus; Ochil; Perth; Tayside North

RENFREWSHIRE COUNCIL

Council Headquarters, North Building, Cotton Street, Paisley PA1 1BU
Tel: 0141-842 5000; Fax: 0141-840 3335
Web: http://www.renfrewshire.gov.uk

Area: 261 sq. km
Population (1999 estimate): 178,340
   population density (1998): 680 persons per sq. km
   projected population in 2006 (1996-based): 175,632
   number of households (1996): 75,100

Council tax (average Band D per two-person household), as at 1 April 2000: £846.00
Non-domestic rateable value (2000): £141,617,861

Education (pupils on register, 1999–2000):
   primary: 15,332
   secondary: 11,859
   special: 318
   entitled to free meals: 23.6%

MEMBERS OF THE COUNCIL

Adams, Barbara	(Lab.)
Anderson, Marion	(SNP)
Burns, Ronnie	(Lab.)
Cameron, Lorraine	(SNP)
Cowan, Michele	(Lab.)
Glen, Roy	(Lab.)
Goldie, Jean	(Lab.)
Green, Jackie	(Lab.)
Hall, Ann	(Lab.)
Harkins, Jim	(Lab.)
Hogg, Iain	(Lab.)
Jackson, Nancy	(C.)
Kelly, Terry	(Lab.)
Kenny, John	(Lab.)
Lawson, Brian	(SNP)
Lawson, Celia	(SNP)
Macgregor, Nan	(LD)
Mackay, Derek	(SNP)
Macmillan, Mark	(Lab.)
Manser, Richard	(Lab.)
Martin, Bill	(SNP)
McCartin Eileen	(LD)
McDowell, John (P)	(Lab.)
McFee, Bruce	(SNP)

McGerty, Bob	(Lab.)
McGuinness, William	(SNP)
McGurk, Marie	(LD)
McMillan, Iain	(Lab.)
McNally, Robert	(Lab.)
Murrin, Alex	(Lab.)
Mylet, David	(SNP)
Nicolson, Iain	(SNP)
Nimmo, Alastair	(SNP)
Noon, Allan	(SNP)
Oldrey, Brian	(Lab.)
Pathucheary, Carol	(SNP)
Sheridan, James	(Lab.)
Vassie, Richard	(SNP)
Williams, Tommy	(Lab.)

Total: 39 (Lab.21; SNP.14; LD.3; C.1)

CHIEF OFFICERS

Chief Executive: T. Scholes
Director of Corporate Services: Ms M. Quinn
Director of Education and Leisure Services: Ms S. Rae
Director of Environmental Services: B. Forteath
Director of Finance and Information Technology: W. Hughes
Director of Housing and Property Services: M. Bailey
Director of Planning and Transport: I. Snodgrass
Director of Social Work: Ms S. Duncan
Head of Legal Services: D. Sillars
Head of Personnel Services: Ms C. Proudfoot
Local Agenda 21 Officer: Ms J. Brooke

SCOTTISH AND UK PARLIAMENTARY CONSTITUENCIES
Paisley North; Paisley South; Renfrewshire West

SCOTTISH BORDERS COUNCIL

Council Headquarters, Newtown St Boswells, Melrose, Roxburghshire TD6 0SA
Tel: 01835-824000; Fax: 01835-825001

Area: 4,734 sq. km
Population (1998 estimate): 106,400
　population density (1999): 22 persons per sq. km
　projected population in 2006 (1998-based): 106,914
　number of households (1998): 45,700

Council tax (average Band D per two-person household), as at 1 April 2000: £725.00
Non-domestic rateable value (1997–8): £50,069,000

Education (pupils on register, 1999–2000):
　primary: 8,877
　secondary: 6,666
　entitled to free meals: 6.6%

MEMBERS OF THE COUNCIL

Angus, Oliver	(LD)
Borthwick, Anne	(LD)
Brockie, Bryan	(Lab.)
Dumble, Thomas	(Ind.)
Elliot, John	(Ind.)
Evans, Geoffrey	(LD)
Forrest, W. Logan	(Ind.)
Hardie, William	(Ind.)
Henderson, Thomas	(Ind.)
Hewat, Alastair	(Ind.)
Home Robertson, Catherine	(O.)
Jack, Robert	(LD)
Jones, David	(LD)
Lamb, William	(LD)
Law, John	(Ind.)
Lindores, David	(LD)
Meikle, John	(Ind.)
Mitchell, John	(SNP)
Nairn, James	(LD)
Nicol, Alexander	(LD)
Parker, David	(SNP)
Paterson, David	(SNP)
Pender, Norman	(LD)
Renton, Christopher	(SNP)
Rutherford, Robert	(LD)
Scott, James	(LD)
Scott, John	(LD)
Smith, Patricia	(LD)
Smith, William	(Ind.)
Suckling, David	(Ind.)
Tulley, Andrew (C)	(Ind.)
Waddell, Ian	(Ind.)

Wight, John   (O.)
Younger, Anne   (Ind.)
Total: 34 (LD.14; Ind.12; SNP.4; Lab.1; O. 2)

CHIEF OFFICERS
Chief Executive: A. M. Croall
Director of Central Services: vacant
Director of Education: J. Christie
Director of Finance: J. Campbell
Director of Housing: H. Blacklaws
Director of Leisure and Recreation: I. Yates
Director of Planning: P. Gregory
Director of Protective Services: W. Lillico
Director of Social Services: C. Johnson
Director of Technical Services: I. Brown
Head of Information Technology: Ms G. Hanham
Head of Personnel: D. Hunter
Local Agenda 21 Officer: vacant

SCOTTISH AND UK PARLIAMENTARY CONSTITUENCIES
Roxburgh and Berwickshire; Tweeddale, Ettrick and Lauderdale

SHETLAND ISLANDS COUNCIL
Town Hall, Hillhead, Lerwick, Shetland ZE1 0HB
Tel: 01595-693535; Fax: 01595-744509
Web: http://www.shetland.gov.uk

Area: 1,438 sq. km
Population (1998 estimate): 22,910
   population density (1998): 16 persons per sq. km
   projected population in 2006 (1996-based): 22,383
   number of households (1996): 8,900

Council tax (average Band D per two-person household), as at 1 April 2000: £621.00
Non-domestic rateable value (1997–8): £37,429,000

Education (pupils on register, 1997–8):
   primary: 2,313
   secondary: 1,596
   entitled to free meals: 7.7%

MEMBERS OF THE COUNCIL
Anderson, Robert   (LD)
Angus, Leslie   (LD)
Begg, Christine   (LD)
Black, Robert   (Ind.)
Cluness, Alexander   (LD)

Colligan, Mary   (Ind.)
Eunson, Cecil   (Ind.)
Goodlad, Charles   (Ind.)
Grains, Florence   (Ind.)
Hawkins, Iris   (Ind.)
Hutchison, Loretta   (Ind.)
Irvine, James   (Ind.)
Malcolmson, Peter   (LD)
Manson, William   (Ind.)
Mitchell, Gordon   (Ind.)
Nicolson, John   (LD)
Ratter, William   (Ind.)
Ritch, James   (LD)
Robertson, Frank   (LD)
Stove, Thomas (C)   (Ind.)
Stove, William   (Ind.)
Tate, William   (Ind.)
Total: 22 (Ind.14; LD.8)

CHIEF OFFICERS
Chief Executive: M. Goodlad
Director of Education and Community Services: J. Halcrow
Director of Environment and Transportation: G. Spall
Director of Finance and Housing: A. Matthews
Director of Social Services: vacant
Local Agenda 21 Officer: A. Hamilton
Manager of Information Technology: J. Smith

SCOTTISH PARLIAMENTARY CONSTITUENCY
Shetland
UK PARLIAMENTARY CONSTITUENCY
Orkney and Shetland

SOUTH AYRSHIRE COUNCIL

County Buildings, Wellington Square, Ayr KA7 1DR
Tel: 01292-612000; Fax: 01292-612143
Web: http://www.south-ayrshire.gov.uk

Area: 1,202 sq. km
Population (1998 estimate): 114,440
  population density (1998): 95 persons per sq. km
  projected population in 2006 (1996-based): 113,577
  number of households (2000): 49,475

Council tax (average Band D per two-person household), as at 1 April 2000: £832.00
Non-domestic rateable value (1997–8): £71,833,000

Education (pupils on register, 1997–8):
  primary: 9,458
  secondary: 7,622
  special: 102
  entitled to free meals: 15.5%

MEMBERS OF THE COUNCIL

Baillie, John	(Lab.)
Bowie, Sadie	(Lab.)
Cairns, Alexander	(Lab.)
Campbell, Brenda	(Lab.)
Campbell, Douglas	(Lab.)
Campbell, Robert	(Lab.)
Convery, Peter	(C.)
Cree, John	(Lab.)
Davies, Agnes	(Lab.)
Duncan, David	(Lab.)
Fitzsimmons, Ian	(C.)
Foulkes, Elizabeth (P)	(Lab.)
Hill, Andrew	(Lab.)
Hunter, Hugh	(C.)
Kerr, Alistair	(C.)
Kilpatrick, Mary	(C.)
Macdonald, Gibson	(C.)
McIntosh, Bill	(C.)
McKenzie, Gordon	(Lab.)
McNally, Bill	(C.)
McNicol, Lorraine	(Lab.)
Miller, Rita	(Lab.)
Murray, Alan	(Lab.)
Paterson, Pam	(C.)
Reid, Robin	(C.)
Sloan, Winifred	(C.)
Stewart, Ian	(Lab.)
Toner, Margaret	(C.)
Torrance, Paul	(Lab.)
Young, Cherry	(C.)

Total: 30 (Lab.17; Con.13)

CHIEF OFFICERS
Chief Executive: G. W. F. Thorley
Director of Community Services: Ms E. Noad
Director of Commercial Operations: R. Sheed
Director of Education: M. McCab
Director of Finance: T. Cairns
Director of Strategic Services: A. Harkness
Director of Support Services: J. G. Peterkin
Head of Housing: P. Whyte
Head of Information Technology: Ms I. Gillespie
Head of Legal Services: D. Russell
Head of Personnel: A. Stewart
Head of Social Services: Ms J. Thompson
Local Agenda 21 Officer: K. Gibb

SCOTTISH AND UK PARLIAMENTARY CONSTITUENCIES
Ayr; Carrick, Cumnock and Doon Valley

SOUTH LANARKSHIRE COUNCIL

Council Offices, Almada Street, Hamilton, Lanarkshire ML3 0AA
Tel: 01698-454904; Fax: 01698-454949
Web: http://www.southlanarkshire.gov.uk

Area: 1,771 sq. km
Population (1998 estimate): 306,860
  population density (1998): 173 persons per sq. km
  projected population in 2006 (1996-based): 303,554
  number of households (1996): 122,300

Council tax (average Band D per two-person household), as at 1 April 2000: £1124.20
Non-domestic rateable value (1997–8): £175,979,000

Education (pupils on register, 1997–8):
  primary: 26,810
  secondary: 19,821
  special: 490
  entitled to free meals: 20.4%

MEMBERS OF THE COUNCIL

Addison, Lindsay	(SNP)
Ahmad, Mushtaq	(Lab.)
Buchanan, Archie	(SNP)
Burns, Jackie	(Lab.)
Caldwell, May	(Lab.)
Carlin, Anthony	(Lab.)
Clearie, Pamela	(Lab.)
Clearie, Russell	(Lab.)
Convery, Gerry	(Lab.)
Craw, Lorraine	(Lab.)

Crawford, Stewart	(Lab.)
Daisley, James	(Lab.)
Dick, Alan (P)	(Lab.)
Docherty, Gerald	(Lab.)
Docherty, James	(Lab.)
Duffy, Margaret	(Lab.)
Dunsmuir, Hugh	(Lab.)
Falconer, Alan	(Lab.)
Ferguson, Robert	(Lab.)
Forrest, Beith	(C.)
Gauls, Bev	(SNP)
Gibb, Richard	(Lab.)
Handibode, Elizabeth	(Lab.)
Handibode, James	(Lab.)
Hughes, Carol	(Lab.)
Keirs, David	(Lab.)
Logan, Eileen	(Lab.)
Lowe, Joseph	(Lab.)
Maggs, Anne	(SNP)
Malloy, James	(Lab.)
McAlpine, T.	(SNP)
McAvoy, Edward	(Lab.)
McCaig, William	(Lab.)
McCann, Michael	(Lab.)
McDonald, Dugald	(Lab.)
McDonald, H.	(C.)
McGlynn, Michael	(Lab.)
McGuinness, John	(Lab.)
McGuire, Alex	(Lab.)
McInnes, Alexander	(Lab.)
McKenna, Brian	(Lab.)
McKenna, Denis	(Lab.)
McKenna, Patrick	(Lab.)
McKeown, Jean	(Lab.)
McLachlan, David	(Lab.)
McNab, William	(Lab.)
McNeil, Mary	(Lab.)
Mitchell, Alice Marie	(Lab.)
Morgan, Patrick	(Lab.)
Murray, Robertson	(SNP)
Ormiston, John	(Lab.)
Roberts, Ian	(Lab.)
Rooney, Robert	(Lab.)
Ross, Gretel	(LD)
Ross, William	(Lab.)
Scott, Graham	(Lab.)
Shearer, D.	(SNP)
Smith, Mary	(Lab.)
Smith, May	(Lab.)
Smith, Rita	(Lab.)
Thompson, Christopher	(Lab.)
Walls, Joseph	(Lab.)
Wardhaugh, James	(SNP)
Watson, D.	(SNP)
Watters, Patrick	(Lab.)
Winning, Ann	(SNP)

Total: 66　(Lab.53; SNP.10; C.2; LD.1)

CHIEF OFFICERS
Chief Executive: vacant
Executive Director of Community Resources: Ms G. Pain
Executive Director of Corporate Resources: A. Cuthbertson
Executive Director of Education Resources: Ms M. Allan
Executive Director of Enterprise Resources: M. Docherty
Executive Director of Finance and Information Technology Resources: W. Kirk
Executive Director of Housing and Technical Resources: S. Gilchrist
Executive Director of Social Work: S. Cameron
Head of Enforcement: R. Howe
Head of Information Technology: Ms K. Brown
Head of Legal Services: Ms S. Dickinson
Local Agenda 21 Officer: K. Boag

SCOTTISH AND UK PARLIAMENTARY CONSTITUENCIES
Clydesdale; East Kilbride; Glasgow Rutherglen; Hamilton North and Bellshill; Hamilton South

STIRLING COUNCIL

Viewforth, Stirling FK8 2ET
Tel: 01786-443322; Fax: 01786-443078
Web: http://www.stirling.gov.uk

Area: 2,196 sq. km
Population (1998 estimate): 83,130
　　population density (1998): 38 persons per sq. km
　　projected population in 2006 (1996-based): 86,120
　　number of households (1996): 33,100

Council tax (average Band D per two-person household), as at 1 April 2000: £992.00
Non-domestic rateable value (1997–8): £66,907,000

Education (pupils on register, 1997–8):
　　primary: 6,817
　　secondary: 5,446
　　special: 58
　　entitled to free meals: 16.0%

MEMBERS OF THE COUNCIL

Beaton, Alastair	(C.)
Brisley, Margaret	(Lab.)
Brookes, Tommy (P)	(Lab.)
Coll, Tom	(Lab.)

Dickson, Ann	(C.)
Finch, Tony	(C.)
Greenhill, Pat	(C.)
Harding, Keith	(C.)
Hazel, Tom	(Lab.)
Hendry, John	(Lab.)
Holliday, John	(C.)
Kelly, Pat	(Lab.)
Love, Susan	(SNP)
McChord, Corrie	(Lab.)
O'Brien, Colin	(Lab.)
Organ, Catherine	(C.)
Paterson, John	(Lab.)
Power, Gerard	(C.)
Reid, Alastair	(C.)
Scott, Helen	(C.)
Strang, Ann	(Lab.)
Thomson, Gillie	(Lab.)

Total: 22 (Lab.11; C.10; SNP; 1)

CHIEF OFFICERS

Chief Executive: K. Yates
Director of Civic Services: R. Jack
Director of Community Services: Ms H. Munro
Director of Education Services: G. Jeyes
Director of Environmental Services: D. Martin
Director of Finance and Information Services:
    W. Dickson
Director of Housing and Social Services: vacant
**Director of Technical and Commercial
    Services:** A. Nicholls
Head of Personnel: Ms J. Jones
Local Agenda 21 Officer: A. Speedie

SCOTTISH AND UK PARLIAMENTARY CONSTITUENCIES
    Ochil; Stirling

WEST DUNBARTONSHIRE COUNCIL

Garshake Road, Dumbarton G82 3PU
Tel: 01389-737000; Fax: 01389-737582/737070
Web: http://www.west-dunbarton.gov.uk

Area: 17,792 hectares
Population: 94,390
    population density: 538 persons per sq. km
    projected population in 2006 (1996-based):
    90,596
    number of households (1999): 42,500

**Council tax (average Band D per two-person
    household), as at 1 April 2000:** £1,222.20
Non-domestic rateable value (1999–2000):
    £52,022,179

Education (pupils on register, 1998–9):
    primary: 8,809
    secondary: 6,417
    special: 180
    entitled to free meals: 22.6%

MEMBERS OF THE COUNCIL

Bollan, James	(Ind.)
Calvert, Geoffrey	(Lab.)
Campbell, Mary	(Lab.)
Collins, Mary	(Lab.)
Devine, Anthony	(Lab.)
Flynn, James	(Lab.)
Macdonald, Alistair (P)	(Lab.)
McCafferty, Daniel	(Lab.)
McCallum, James	(Lab.)
McColl, Linda	(Lab.)
McColl, Ronald	(SNP)
McCutcheon, John	(SNP)
McDonald, Duncan	(Lab.)
McDonald, John	(SNP)
McElhill, James	(SNP)
McGregor, Margaret	(SNP)
McLaughlin, Craig	(SNP)
O'Sullivan, Connie	(Lab.)
Robertson, Iain	(SNP)
Syme, John	(Lab.)
Trainer, John	(Lab.)
White, Andrew	(Lab.)

Total: 22 (Lab.14; SNP.7; Ind. 1)

CHIEF OFFICERS
Chief Executive: T. Huntingford
**Director of Commercial and Technical
    Services:** David McMillan
**Director of Economic, Planning and
    Environmental Services:** Dan Henderson
Director of Education and Cultural Services:
    I. McMurdo
Director of Corporate Services: E. Walker

Director of Social Work and Housing:
Alexis Jay
Head of Corporate Policy and Public Relations:
Ms M. Cullen
Head of Information Services: Ms A. Clements
Manager of Personnel and Training: vacant
Local Agenda 21 Officer: T. Moan

SCOTTISH AND UK PARLIAMENTARY CONSTITUENCIES
Clydebank and Milngavie; Dumbarton

WEST LOTHIAN COUNCIL

West Lothian House, Almondvale Boulevard,
Livingston, West Lothian EH54 6QG
Tel: 01506-777000; Fax: 01506-777102
Web: http://www.westlothian.gov.uk

Area: 425 sq. km
Population (1998 estimate): 153,090
   population density (1998): 360 persons per
   sq. km
   projected population in 2006 (1996-based):
   160,620
   number of households (1996): 60,300

**Council tax (average Band D per two-person
   household), as at 1 April 2000:** £1115.00
Non-domestic rateable value (1997–8):
   £108,235,000

Education (pupils on register, 1997–8):
   primary: 14,987
   secondary: 9,510
   special: 152
   entitled to free meals: 18.5%

MEMBERS OF THE COUNCIL

Anderson, Frank	(SNP)
Bartholomew, Carol	(Lab.)
Constance, Angela	(SNP)
Davidson, Alexander	(Lab.)
Day, Martin	(SNP)
Dickson, Jim	(SNP)
Dunn, Willie	(Lab.)
Ferrie, Bruce	(Lab.)
Fitzpatrick, Lawrence	(Lab.)
Gamble, Bert	(Lab.)
Gordon, Audrey	(SNP)
Johnston, Peter	(SNP)
Kerr, Tom	(C.)
King, Dave	(Lab.)
Lee, Robert	(Lab.)
Logue, Danny	(Lab.)

Mackie, Allister	(Lab.)
Maclean, Duncan	(SNP)
Malcolm, Eddie	(SNP)
McGinty, John	(Lab.)
McGrouther, David	(Lab.)
Miller, Andrew	(SNP)
Graeme, Morrice	(Lab.)
Muldoon, Cathy	(Lab.)
Mutch, Wendy	(Lab.)
Owens, Hugh	(Lab.)
Russell, William	(Lab.)
Sibbald, Jim	(SNP)
Smart, Heather	(Lab.)
Smith, Tam	(SNP)
Swan, Jim	(Lab.)
Thomas, Joe (P)	(Lab.)

Total: 32   (Lab. 20; SNP. 11; C.1)

CHIEF OFFICERS
Chief Executive: A. M. Linkston
Corporate Manager, Community Services:
   D. Kelly
Corporate Manager, Education Services:
   R. Stewart
Corporate Manager, Strategic Services:
   J. Dickson
Corporate Manager, Environmental Services:
   B. Dixon
Head, Housing Services: J. Ritchie
Head, Social Work: G. Blair
Local Agenda 21 Officer: Ms C. Braithwaite
Manager, Administration and Legal: G. Blair
Manager, Development and Building Control:
   R. Hartland
**Manager, Environmental Health and Trading
   Standards:** A. Campbell
Manager, Finance: A. Logan
Manager, Human Resources: J. Nowak
Manager, Information Technology: Ms S. Aird

SCOTTISH AND UK PARLIAMENTARY CONSTITUENCIES
Linlithgow; Livingston

DEFENCE

Defence is one of the powers reserved to Westminster and the Scottish Parliament has no jurisdiction over it. However, there are a number of important armed forces installations in Scotland. In particular, all the UK's nuclear weaponry is held at the Clyde naval base.

The following gives details of the main commands and forces in Scotland.

SCOTTISH COMMANDS

FLAG OFFICER SCOTLAND, NORTHERN ENGLAND AND NORTHERN IRELAND

HM Naval Base Clyde, Helensburgh, Dunbartonshire G84 8HL
Tel: 01436-674321
Flag Officer Scotland, Northern England and Northern Ireland: Rear-Adm. A. M. Gregory, OBE

GENERAL OFFICER COMMANDING 2ND DIVISION
Army HQ Scotland, Annandale Block, Craigiehall, South Queensferry, West Lothian EH30 9TN
Tel: 0131-336 1761
General Officer Commanding 2nd Division: Maj.-Gen. R. D. S. Gordon, CBE
HQ 51 Highland Brigade, Highland House, 7 St Leonard's Bank, Perth PH2 8EB
HQ 52 Lowland Brigade, Edinburgh Castle, Edinburgh EH1 2YT

AIR OFFICER SCOTLAND AND NORTHERN IRELAND

RAF Leuchars, St Andrews, Fife KY16 0JX
Tel: 01334-839471
Air Officer Scotland and Northern Ireland: Air Cdre J. H. Haines, OBE

NAVAL BASE

HM NAVAL BASE CLYDE
Helensburgh, Dunbartonshire G84 8HL
Tel: 01436-674321

THE ARMY

ROYAL ARMOURED CORPS
The Royal Scots Dragoon Guards (Carabiniers and Greys)
Home HQ, The Castle, Edinburgh EH1 2YT
Tel: 0131-310 5100
Colonel-in-Chief: HM The Queen

INFANTRY

SCOTS GUARDS
Regimental HQ, Wellington Barracks, Birdcage Walk, London SW1E 6HQ
Tel: 020-7414 3324
Colonel-in-Chief: HM The Queen

SCOTTISH DIVISION
Divisional Offices, The Castle, Edinburgh EH1 2YT. Tel: 0131-310 5001
HQ Infantry, Imber Road, Warminster, Wilts BA12 0DJ. Tel: 01985-222674
Training Centre, Infantry Training Centre, Vimy Barracks, Catterick, N. Yorks DL9 4HH
Colonel Commandant: Maj.-Gen. Ash Irwin, CBE
Divisional Lieutenant-Colonel: Lt.-Col. R. M. Riddell

THE ROYAL SCOTS (THE ROYAL REGIMENT)
Regimental HQ, The Castle, Edinburgh EH1 2YT
Tel: 0131-310 5014
Colonel-in-Chief: HRH The Princess Royal, KG, GCVO

THE ROYAL HIGHLAND FUSILIERS (PRINCESS MARGARET'S OWN GLASGOW AND AYRSHIRE REGIMENT)
Regimental HQ, 518 Sauchiehall Street, Glasgow G2 3LW
Tel: 0141-332 0961/5639
Colonel-in-Chief: HRH The Princess Margaret, Countess of Snowdon, CI, GCVO

THE KING'S OWN SCOTTISH BORDERERS
Regimental HQ, The Barracks, Berwick-on-Tweed TD15 1DG

Tel: 01289-307426
Colonel-in-Chief: HRH Princess Alice, Duchess of Gloucester, GCB, CI, GCVO, GBE

THE BLACK WATCH (ROYAL HIGHLAND REGIMENT)
Regimental HQ, Balhousie Castle, Perth PH1 5HR
Tel: 01738-621281; 0131-310 8530
Colonel-in-Chief: HM Queen Elizabeth the Queen Mother
THE HIGHLANDERS (SEAFORTH, GORDONS AND CAMERONS)
Regimental HQ, Cameron Barracks, Inverness IV2 3XD. Tel: 01463-224380
Outstation, Viewfield Road, Aberdeen AB15 7XH. Tel: 01224-318174
Colonel-in-Chief: HRH The Prince Philip, Duke of Edinburgh, KG, KT, OM, GBE

THE ARGYLL AND SUTHERLAND HIGHLANDERS (PRINCESS LOUISE'S)
Regimental HQ, The Castle, Stirling FK8 1EH
Tel: 01786-475165
Colonel-in-Chief: HM The Queen

ARMY PERSONNEL CENTRE
Kentigern House, 65 Brown Street, Glasgow G2 8EX
Tel: 0141-248 7890
Chief Executive: Maj.-Gen. Ash Irwin, CBE

MAIN RAF BASES

RAF KINLOSS
Kinloss, Forres, Moray IV36 3UH
Tel: 01309-672161

RAF LEUCHARS
St Andrews, Fife KY16 0JX
Tel: 01334-839471

RAF LOSSIEMOUTH
Lossiemouth, Moray IV31 6SD
Tel: 01343-812121

RESERVE FORCES

ROYAL NAVY RESERVES
There are two Royal Naval Reserve units in Scotland, with a total of 395 members at April 2000.

HMS DALRIADA
Navy Buildings, Eldon Street, Greenock PA16 7SL
Tel: 01475-724481

HMS SCOTIA
c/o HMS Caledonia, Hilton Road, Rosyth, Fife KY11 2XT
Tel: 01383-425794

TERRITORIAL ARMY
The post-Strategic Defence Review establishment of the Territorial Army in Scotland, including the Officers' Training Corps, is 4,794, with effect from 1 July 2000.
  There are TA/reservist centres in Aberdeen, Arbroath, Cumbernauld, Cupar, Dumbarton, Dundee, Dunfermline, Dunoon, Elgin, Forfar, Glenrothes, Grangemouth, Invergowrie, Inverness, Keith, Kirkcaldy, Kirkwall, Lerwick, Leuchars, Perth, Peterhead, St Andrews, Stirling, Stornoway and Wick (Highlands), and Ayr, Bathgate, Dumfries, East Kilbride, Edinburgh, Galashiels, Glasgow, Irvine, Livingston, Hamilton, Motherwell and Paisley (Lowlands).

HIGHLANDS RESERVE FORCES AND CADETS ASSOCIATION
Seathwood, 365 Perth Road, Dundee DD2 1LX
Tel: 01382-668283
Secretary: Col. J. R. Hensman, OBE

LOWLANDS RESERVE FORCES AND CADETS ASSOCIATION
Lowland House, 60 Avenuepark Street, Glasgow G20 8LW
Tel: 0141-945 4951
Secretary: Col. R. S. B. Watson, OBE

ROYAL AUXILIARY AIR FORCE (RAUXAF)
There are three units of the RAuxAF in Scotland, with a total of about 280 members at April 1999.

603 (CITY OF EDINBURGH) MARITIME HQ SQUADRON
25 Learmonth Terrace, Edinburgh EH4 1NZ
Tel: 0131-332 2333

NO. 2622 (HIGHLAND) SQUADRON, RAUXAF REGIMENT
RAF Lossiemouth, Moray IV31 6SD
Tel: 01343-812121

AIR TRANSPORTABLE SURGICAL SQUADRON, RAUXAF
RAF Leuchars, St Andrews, Fife KY16 0JY
Tel: 01334-839471

PUBLIC SERVICE

SCOTLAND

EDUCATION
THE ENERGY INDUSTRIES
THE FIRE SERVICE
HEALTH
AMBULANCE SERVICE
POLICE SERVICE
PRISON SERVICE
SOCIAL SERVICES
TRANSPORT

PUBLIC SERVICE SCOTLAND

EDUCATION

Overall responsibility for all aspects of education in Scotland lies with the Scottish Ministers acting through the Scottish Executive Education Department and the Enterprise and Lifelong Learning Department (formerly the Scottish Office Education and Industry Department (SOEID); references to SOEID occur below where data, e.g. statistics, refer to the period before 1 July 1999).

The main concerns of the Scottish Executive Education Department are the formulation of policy for primary and secondary education, its administration and the maintenance of consistency in educational standards in schools. It is responsible for the broad allocation of resources for school education, the rate and distribution of educational building and the supply, training and superannuation of teachers. The Enterprise and Lifelong Learning Department is concerned with post-16 education, qualifications and student support.

EXPENDITURE

Expenditure on education by central government, in real terms, was £1,860.8 million in 1999–2000, with a planned expenditure of £1,944.6 million for 2000–1.

The major elements of central government expenditure are: support for higher and further education in universities and colleges (through the funding councils), grant-aided special schools, student awards and bursaries (through the Students Awards Agency for Scotland), curriculum development, special educational needs and community education.

Significant expenditure is incurred by local authorities, which make their own expenditure decisions according to their local situations and needs. Local authority net expenditure on education (provisional) for 1999-2000 was £2,637.1 million; planned net expenditure for 2000-1 is £2,717.1 million.

LOCAL EDUCATION ADMINISTRATION

The education service at present is a national service in which the provision of most school education is locally administered.

The duty of providing education locally in Scotland rests with the education authorities. They are responsible for the construction of buildings, the employment of teachers and other staff, and the provision of equipment and materials. Devolved School Management (DSM) is in place for all primary, secondary and special schools.

Education authorities are required to establish school boards consisting of parents and teachers as well as co-opted members. These are responsible, among other things, for the appointment of staff.

THE INSPECTORATE

HM Inspectors of Schools in Scotland inspect schools and publish reports on a wide range of education provision including pre-school, nursery, primary, secondary and special schools, further education institutions, teacher education and community education. HMIs work in teams alongside lay members and associate assessors, who are practising teachers seconded for the inspection. HMIs monitor how well schools, colleges and other providers of education are performing and lead and support the development of educational initiatives designed to improve the standards and quality of education. In 1999–2000 there were 84 HMIs and eight Chief Inspectors in Scotland.

The inspection of higher education is the responsibility of inspectors appointed by the Scottish Higher Education Funding Council.

SCHOOLS AND PUPILS

Schooling is compulsory for all children between five and 16 years of age. Provision is being increased for children under five and many pupils remain at school after the minimum leaving age. No fees are charged in any publicly maintained school in Scotland.

Throughout the UK, parents have a right to express a preference for a particular school and to appeal if dissatisfied. The policy, known as more open enrolment, requires schools to admit children up to the limit of their capacity if there is a demand for places, and to publish their criteria for selection if they are over-subscribed, in which case parents have a right of appeal.

The 'Parents' Charter', available free from education departments, is a booklet which tells parents about the education system. Schools are now required to make available information about themselves through the school handbook, their public examination results, truancy rates, and destination of leavers. Corporal punishment is no longer legal in publicly maintained schools in the UK.

The number of schools by sector in 1998–9 was:

Publicly maintained schools:

Pre-school centres	1,186
Primary	2,291
Secondary	392
Special	185
Independent schools	207
Total	4,261

Education authority schools (known as public schools) are financed by local government, partly through revenue support grants from central government and partly from local taxation. There is a small number of grant-aided schools, mainly in the special sector, which are conducted by boards of managers and receive grants direct from the Scottish Executive Education Department. Under the previous government a category of self-governing schools was created. Such schools opted to be managed entirely by a board of management, but remained in the public sector and were funded by direct government grant set to match the resources the school would have received under education authority management. Two schools were established, one of which has been returned to the education authority framework.

Independent schools charge fees and receive no direct grant, but are subject to inspection and registration.

THE STATE SYSTEM

PRE-SCHOOL EDUCATION

Pre-school education is for children from two to five years and is not compulsory. It takes place in play groups, private nurseries, nursery schools or nursery classes in primary schools.

Local authorities are responsible for the funding and management of services. All providers of pre-school education are subject to inspection.

LOCAL AUTHORITY PRE-SCHOOL CENTRES 1998-9

No. of centres	1,186
No. of pupils	63,072
No. of teachers	1,200
(full-time equivalent)	
Staff to child ratio	8.9

Primary Education

Primary education begins at five years and is almost always co-educational. The primary school course lasts for seven years and pupils transfer to secondary courses at about the age of 12.

Primary schools consist mainly of infants' schools for children aged five to seven, junior schools for those aged seven to 12, and combined junior and infant schools for both age groups. Many primary schools provide nursery classes for children under five.

PRIMARY SCHOOLS 1998-9

No. of schools	2,291
No. of pupils	437,014
No. of teachers	22,508
(full-time equivalent)	
Pupil-teacher ratio	19.4

SECONDARY EDUCATION

Secondary schools are for children aged 11 to 16 and for those who choose to stay on to 18. Most secondary schools in Scotland are co-educational. All pupils in Scottish education authority secondary schools attend schools with a comprehensive intake. Most of these schools provide a full range of courses appropriate to all levels of ability from first to sixth year.

SECONDARY SCHOOLS 1998-9

No. of schools	392
No. of pupils	313,247
No. of teachers	24,085
(full-time equivalent)	
Pupil-teacher ratio	13.0

SPECIAL EDUCATION

Special education is provided for children with special educational needs, usually because they have a disability which either prevents or hinders them from making use of educational facilities of a kind generally provided for children of their age in schools within the area of the local authority concerned.

It is intended that pupils with special education needs should have access to as much of the curriculum as possible, but there is provision for them to be exempt from it or for it to be modified to suit their capabilities. The number of full-time pupils with statements of special needs in January 1997 was:

In publicly funded special schools	8,300
In public sector primary and secondary schools	5,800

The school placing of children with special needs is a matter of agreement between education authorities and parents. Parents have the right to say which school they want their child to attend, and a right of appeal where their wishes are not being met. Whenever possible, children with special needs are integrated into ordinary schools. However, for those who require a different environment or specialised facilities, there are special schools, both grant-aided by central government and independent, and special classes within ordinary schools. Education authorities are required to respond to reasonable requests for independent special schools and to send children with special needs to schools outside Scotland if appropriate provision is not available within the country.

The Scottish Executive funds "Enquire", a national information helpline on special educational needs.

SPECIAL SCHOOLS 1998–9

Maintained schools	
No. of schools	185
No. of pupils	8,264
No. of teachers	1,875
(full-time equivalent)	
Pupil-teacher ratio	4.4
Non-maintained schools	
No. of schools	33
No. of pupils	1,081
No. of teachers	328
(full-time equivalent)	
Pupil-teacher ratio	3.3

ALTERNATIVE PROVISION

There is no legal obligation on parents anywhere in the UK to educate their children at school, provided that the local education authority is satisfied that the child is receiving full-time education suited to its age, abilities and aptitudes. The education authority need not be informed that a child is being educated at home unless the child is already registered at a state school, in which case the parents must arrange for the child's name to be removed from the school's register before education at home can begin. Neither are parents educating their children at home required to be in possession of a teaching qualification.

Information and support on all aspects of home education can be obtained from Education Otherwise.

INDEPENDENT SCHOOLS

Independent schools receive no grants from public funds. They charge fees, and are owned and managed under special trusts, with profits being used for the benefit of the schools concerned. There is a wide variety of provision, from kindergartens to large day and boarding schools, and from experimental schools to traditional institutions. A number of independent schools have been instituted by religious and ethnic minorities.

Most independent schools offer a similar range of courses to state schools and enter pupils for the same public examinations. Those in Scotland tend to follow the English examination system, i.e. GCSE followed by A-levels, although some take the Scottish Education Certificate at Standard Grade followed by Highers or Advanced Highers.

Most Scottish independent schools in membership of the Headmasters' and Headmistresses' Conference, the Governing Bodies Association or the Governing Bodies of Girls' Schools Association are single-sex, but there are some mixed schools, and an increasing number of schools have mixed sixth forms.

INDEPENDENT SCHOOLS 1998–9

No. of schools	134
No. of pupils	29,633
No. of teachers	2,885
(full-time equivalent)	
Pupil-teacher ratio	11.7

ASSISTED PLACES SCHEME

The Assisted Places Scheme began to be phased out after the September 1997 entry. It enabled children to attend independent secondary schools which their parents could not otherwise afford, by providing help with tuition fees and other expenses, except boarding costs, on a sliding scale depending on the family's income. The scheme is administered and funded in Scotland by the Scottish Executive through the Education Department. In the 1999–2000 academic year, about 2,054 pupils participated in the scheme in 49 schools in Scotland.

Pupils in secondary education holding their places at the beginning of the 1997–8 school year will keep them until they have completed their education at their current school. Those at the primary stage will hold them until they have completed that phase of their education, although some may exceptionally be allowed to hold their places until they have completed their secondary education.

Further information can be obtained from the Independent Schools Information Service.

THE CURRICULUM

The content and management of the curriculum in Scotland are not prescribed by statute but are the responsibility of education authorities and individual headteachers. Advice and guidance are provided by the Scottish Executive Education Department and Learning and Teaching Scotland (formerly the Scottish Consultative Council on the Curriculum), which also has a developmental role. The Scottish Executive Education Department has produced guidelines on the structure and balance of the curriculum for the five to 14 age group, as well as for each of the curriculum areas for this age group, although they are currently under review. There are also guidelines on assessment across the whole curriculum, on reporting to parents, and on standardised national tests for English language and mathematics at five levels.

The curriculum for 14- to 16-year-olds includes study within each of eight modes: language and communication; mathematical studies; science; technology; social studies; creative activities; physical education; and religious and moral education. There is a recommended percentage of class time to be devoted to each area over the two years. Provision is made for teaching in Gaelic in Gaelic-speaking areas. Testing is carried out on a voluntary basis when the teacher deems it appropriate; most pupils are expected to move from one level to the next at roughly two-year intervals. National testing is largely in place in most primary schools but secondary school participation rates are lower.

For 16- to 18-year-olds, a new unified framework of courses and awards, known as 'Higher Still', which brings together both academic and vocational courses, was introduced in 1999. The Scottish Qualifications Authority (SQA) awards the new certificates.

THE PUBLIC EXAMINATION SYSTEM

Scotland has its own system of public examinations, separate from that in England, Wales and Northern Ireland. At the end of the fourth year of secondary education, at about the age of 16, pupils take the Standard Grade of the Scottish Certificate of Education. Standard Grade courses and examinations have been designed to suit every level of ability, with assessment against nationally determined standards of performance.

For most courses there are three separate examination papers at the end of the two-year Standard Grade course. They are set at Credit (leading to awards at grade 1 or 2), General (leading to awards at grade 3 or 4) and Foundation (leading to awards at grade 5 or 6) levels. Grade 7 is available to those who, although they have completed the course, have not attained any of these levels. Normally pupils will take examinations covering two pairs of grades, either grades 1–4 or grades 3–6. Most candidates take seven or eight Standard Grade examinations.

Above Standard Grade, Higher Grade will be available after a one-year course in the fifth or sixth year of secondary school until 2000–1. The one-year Certificate of Sixth Year Studies (CSYS) will be available until 2001–2.

A new system of courses and qualifications is being phased in under the 'Higher Still' reforms, bringing together academic and vocational qualifications. By 2004 National Qualifications will replace Highers, CSYS and National Certificate modules, and General Scottish Vocational Qualifications for everyone studying beyond Standard Grade in Scottish schools, and for non-advanced students in further education colleges. Standard Grade and Scottish Vocational Qualifications will remain. National Qualifications will be available at five levels: Access, Intermediate 1, Intermediate 2, Higher and Advanced Higher, the latter from 2000–1. Courses will be made up of internally assessed units, with external assessment of the full course determining the grade (A to C). The core skills of communication, numeracy, problem-solving, information technology and working with others are embedded in the 'Higher Still' qualifications although the skills and levels covered vary between subjects; there are also separate core skill units.

All of these qualifications are awarded by the Scottish Qualifications Authority (SQA).

At the end of the 1997–8 academic year, 62,483 pupils left school, 30 per cent of them at the school leaving age (34 per cent of boys, 26 per cent of girls). Their achievement, by highest Scottish Certificate of Education qualification held, was:

Higher grades A–C	
1 or 2	8,692 (13.2%)
3 or 4	8,064 (12.9%)
5 or over	10,817 (17.3%)
Standard grades 1–3	
1 or 2	8,926 (14.2%)
3 or 4	6,257 (10%)
5 or over	8,189 (13.1%)
Standard grades 4–7	7,422 (11.8%)
None	4,116 (7%)

THE INTERNATIONAL BACCALAUREATE

The International Baccalaureate is an internationally recognised two-year pre-university course and examination designed to facilitate the mobility of students and to promote international understanding. Candidates must offer one subject from each of six subject groups, at least three at higher level and the remainder at subsidiary level. Single subjects can be offered, for which a certificate is received. The International Baccalaureate diploma is offered by 33 schools and colleges in the UK, of which one school, the International School of Aberdeen, is in Scotland.

RECORDS OF ACHIEVEMENT

The Scottish Qualification Certificate replaced the National Record of Achievement (NRA) from the academic year 1999-2000. It is issued by the Scottish Qualifications Authority and records all qualifications achieved at all levels. The school report card gives parents information on their child's progress in school.

TEACHERS

All teachers in publicly maintained schools must be registered with the General Teaching Council for Scotland. They are registered provisionally for a two-year probationary period, which can be extended if necessary. Only graduates are accepted as entrants to the profession; primary school teachers undertake either a four-year vocational degree course or a one-year postgraduate course, while teachers of academic subjects in secondary schools undertake the latter. Most initial teacher training is classroom-based. Colleges of education provide both in-service and pre-service training for teachers which is subject to inspection by HM Inspectors. The colleges are funded by the Scottish Higher Education Funding Council.

The Scottish Qualifications for Headship (SQH) is aimed at aspiring headteachers and is both a development programme and a qualification.

The General Teaching Council advises the Scottish Executive Education Department on the professional suitability of all training courses in colleges of education.

TEACHERS IN PUBLICLY MAINTAINED SCHOOLS 1998—9

(full-time equivalent)

	Total	Male	Female
Primary			
Headteacher	2,261	515	1,746
Deputy headteacher	972	87	885
Assistant headteacher	600	56	544
Senior teacher*	3,175	207	2,968
Unpromoted teacher	15,500	736	14,761
Secondary			
Headteacher	389	351	38
Deputy headteacher	389	306	83
Assistant headteacher	1,044	710	334
Principal teacher	7,044	4,225	2,819
Assistant principal teacher	3,024	1,312	1,713
Senior teacher*	1,721	680	1,041
Unpromoted teacher	10,480	3,679	6,801

Includes other promoted posts

SALARIES

Teachers in Scotland are paid on a ten-point scale. The entry point depends on type of qualification, and additional allowances are payable under certain circumstances.

Salaries
from 1 April 2000

Head	£34,407–£54,774
Deputy head	£33,708–£40,986
Principal teacher	£26,301–£30,681
Teacher	£14,022–£23,313

FURTHER EDUCATION

Further education covers all provision outside schools to people aged over 16. It comprises National Qualifications, SVQ work-based awards and occasionally GCE A-level and its equivalent. Courses are taught mainly at colleges of further education, but may also be provided in schools, in higher education institutions and in the work place.

Responsibility for further education lies with the Scottish Executive under the Minister for Enterprise and Lifelong Learning, through the Scottish Further Education Funding Council.

There are 47 further education colleges, of which 43 are self-governing incorporated colleges run by their own boards of management. The boards include the principal, staff and student representatives among their ten to 16 members; at least half the members must have experience of commerce, industry or the practice of a profession. Two colleges, on Orkney and Shetland, are under Islands Council control, and two others, Sàbhal Mor Ostaig (the Gaelic college on Skye) and Newbattle Abbey College, are managed by trustees.

The Scottish Qualifications Authority (SQA) is the statutory awarding body for qualifications in the national education system in schools and colleges; the national accrediting body for work-based SVQs; and the main awarding body for work-related and work-based qualifications. It awards at non-advanced level the National Certificate, which is available in over 4,000 individual modules embracing a wide range of subjects and covers the whole range of non-advanced further education provision. Students may study for the National Certificate on a full-time, part-time, open learning or work-based learning basis. National Certificate modules can be taken in further education colleges, secondary schools and other centres, normally from the age of 16 onwards. New unified National Qualifications will be available at five levels (Access, Intermediate 1, Intermediate 2, Higher and Advanced Higher), and will replace Higher Grades, CSYS, General Scottish Vocational Qualifications (GSVQ) and National Certificate modules, but not Standard Grade or Scottish Vocational Qualifications (SVQ).

SQA also offers modular advanced-level HNC/HND qualifications, which are available in further education colleges and higher education institutions. SQA accredits and awards Scottish Vocational Qualifications (SVQs), which have mutual recognition with the NVQs available in the rest of the UK. SVQs are work-place assessed in the work-place, but can also be taken in further education colleges and other centres where work-place conditions can be simulated.

In the academic year 1998–9 there were 36,874 full-time and sandwich-course students and 253,411 part-time students on non-advanced vocational courses of further education in further education colleges (excluding Newbattle Abbey College). In the same year at the 43 incorporated colleges there were 5,019 full-time teaching staff and 8,546 part-time. Salaries are determined at individual college level.

COURSE INFORMATION

Applications for further education courses are generally made directly to the colleges concerned. Information on further education courses in the UK and addresses of colleges can be found in the *Directory of Further Education* published annually by the Careers Research and Advisory Centre.

HIGHER EDUCATION

The term 'higher education' is used to describe education above A-level, Higher and Advanced Higher grade and their equivalent, which is provided in universities, colleges of higher education and some further education colleges.

The Further and Higher Education (Scotland) Act 1992 removed the distinction between higher education provided by the universities and that provided by the former central institutions and other institutions, allowing all higher education institutions which satisfy the necessary criteria to award their own taught course and research degrees and to adopt the title of university. All the central institutions, the art colleges and some colleges of higher education have since adopted the title of university. The change of name does not affect the legal constitution of the institutions.

All higher education institutions are funded by the Scottish Higher Education Funding Council. The funding allocated for higher education in 2000–1 was £609.4 million (£601.8 in 1999–2000).

The number of students in higher education in Scotland in 1997–8 was:

Full-time	162,332
Postgraduate	17,847
first degree	104,533
other HE	39,952
Part-time	85,324
postgraduate	25,450
first degree	8,439
other HE	51,435
Undergraduates	144,485
overseas	9,440
Postgraduates	17,847
overseas	5,965

In the 1997–8 academic year, there were 39,139 full-time first degree entrants to higher education institutions; 18,150 were male and 20,989 female. Forty eight per cent of all undergraduates were mature students entering full-time higher education courses in 1997–8 were: engineering and technology (7,724), business administration (6,088), multi-disciplinary studies (5,973), physical sciences (3,393), biological sciences (3,068), architecture and planning (2,794) and social studies (2,775). Among female students entering full-time higher education in 1997–8, the most heavily subscribed first degree subjects were: business administration (8,353), multi-disciplinary studies (7,058), biological sciences

(5,454), subjects allied to medicine (5,223), social studies (4,478), languages (3,427) and education (3,420).

UNIVERSITIES AND COLLEGES

The Scottish Higher Education Funding Council (SHEFC) funds 21 institutions of higher education, including 13 universities. Responsibility for universities in Scotland rests with the Scottish Ministers. Advice to the Government on matters relating to the universities is provided by the SHEFC. The SHEFC receives a block grant from central government which it allocates to the universities and colleges.

The universities each have their own system of internal government, but most are run by two main bodies: the senate, which deals primarily with academic issues and consists of members elected from within the university; and the council, which is the supreme body and is responsible for all appointments and promotions, and bidding for and allocation of financial resources. At least half the members of the council are drawn from outside the university. Joint committees of senate and council are becoming increasingly common.

The institutions of higher education other than universities are managed by independent governing bodies which include representatives of industrial, commercial, professional and educational interests.

Each body appoints its own academic staff on its own conditions. The salary structure in the 'pre-1992' universities is in line with the rest of the UK.

SALARIES FOR NON-CLINICAL ACADEMIC STAFF IN UNIVERSITIES
1999–2000 (1 April 1999)

Professor	from £36,401
Senior lecturer	£31,563–£38,561
Lecturer grade B	£24,479–£30,065
Lecturer grade A	£16,286–£23,521

The salary scales for staff in the 'post-1992' universities and colleges of higher education in Scotland are as follows (1 April 1998):

Head of Department	£34,861–£46,508
Senior lecture	£26,146–£38,037
Lecturer	£15,885–£31,658

Although universities and colleges are expected to look to a wider range of funding sources than before, and to generate additional revenue in collaboration with industry, they are still largely financed, directly or indirectly, from government resources.

COURSES

In the UK all universities, including the Open University, and some colleges award their own degrees and other qualifications and can act as awarding and validating bodies for neighbouring colleges which are not yet accredited.

Higher education courses last full-time for at least four weeks or, if part-time, involve more than 60 hours of instruction. Facilities exist for full-time and part-time study, day release, sandwich or block release. Most of the courses outside the universities have a vocational orientation and a substantial number are sandwich courses.

Higher education courses comprise:
— first degree and postgraduate (including research)
— Diploma in Higher Education (Dip.HE), a two-year diploma usually intended to serve as a stepping-stone to a degree course or other further study
— Higher National Diploma (HND), awarded after two years of full-time or three years of sandwich-course or part-time study
— Higher National Certificate (HNC), awarded after two years part-time study
— preparation for professional examinations
— in-service training of teachers

In some Scottish universities the title of Master is sometimes used for a first degree in arts subjects; otherwise undergraduate courses lead to the title of Bachelor. Most undergraduate courses at universities and colleges of higher education run for four years. Professional courses in subjects such as medicine, dentistry and veterinary science take longer. Post-experience short courses are also forming an increasing part of higher education provision.

Details of courses on offer and of predicted entry requirements for the following year's intake are provided in *University and College Entrance: Official Guide*, published annually by the Universities and Colleges Admissions Service (UCAS) and available from bookshops. It includes degree, Dip.HE and HND courses at all universities (excluding the Open University) and most colleges of higher education.

Postgraduate studies vary in length, with taught courses which lead to certificates, diplomas or masters degrees usually taking less time than research degrees. Details of taught postgraduate courses and research degree opportunities can be found in the *Directory of Graduate Studies,* published annually for the Careers Research and Advisory Centre (CRAC) by Hobsons Publishing PLC.

ADMISSIONS

For admission to a degree, Dip.HE or HND, potential students apply through a central clearing house. All universities and most colleges providing higher education courses in the UK (except the Open University, which conducts its own admissions) are members of the Universities and Colleges Admission Service (UCAS).

Most applications for admission as a postgraduate student are made to individual institutions but there are two clearing houses of relevance. Applications for postgraduate teacher training courses may be made direct to the institution or through the Graduate Teacher Training Registry. For social work the Social Work Admissions System operates.

Details of initial teacher training courses in Scotland can be obtained from colleges of education and those universities offering such courses, and from the Committee of Scottish Higher Education Principals (COSHEP).

FEES

Since September 1998, new entrants to undergraduate courses have been liable for an annual contribution to their fees (up to £1,050 in 2000–1), depending on their own level of income and that of their spouse or parents. From autumn 2000 the student liability for tuition fees has been abolished for all eligible Scottish domiciled and EU students studying on a full-time higher education course at a Scottish institution. Those from the rest of the UK, in the fourth year of a four-year degree course at a Scottish institution may also be exempt from payment.

For postgraduate students on non loan-bearing courses, the maximum tuition fee to be reimbursed through the awards system in 2000–1 is £2,740.

STUDENT SUPPORT

Student Grants

Students who started a full-time or sandwich undergraduate course of higher education from the academic year commencing September 1998 are no longer eligible for a grant. Grants for such students have been replaced entirely by loans which are partly means-tested. Students who started designated courses prior to that date continue to be eligible for means-tested maintenance grants from which a parental contribution is deductible on a sliding scale dependent on income or, for married students, from a spouse's income. However, a parental contribution is not deducted from the grant to students who have reached the age of 25 before the start of the academic year for which the assistance is being assessed or who are over 25 years of age and have been self-supporting for any three years before the start of their course. Some categories of student, including single parents and those with dependants, are entitled to a means-tested non-repayable supplementary grants for help in meeting certain living costs. Disabled students are eligible for non-means tested disabled students allowances.

In Scotland grants are made by the Scottish Executive through the Student Awards Agency. Application forms are normally available around early May for the following academic year. The Student Awards Agency should be consulted for advice about eligibility for a grant and designated courses.

A means-tested maintenance grant, usually paid once a term, covers periods of attendance during term as well as the Christmas and Easter vacations, but not the summer vacation. The basic grant rates for 2000–1 for domiciled students are:

Living in	Existing students
College/lodgings in London area	£2,255
College/lodgings outside London area	£1,825
Parental home	£1,395

Additional allowances are available if, for example, the course requires a period of study abroad. Expenditure on student fees and maintenance in 1998–9 was £283 million; about 107,452 mandatory awards were made.

Access funds are allocated by education departments to the appropriate funding council and administered by further and higher education institutions. They are available to students whose access to education might otherwise be inhibited by financial considerations or where real financial difficulties are faced. For the academic year 1998–9, provision in Scotland was £8.7 million (£4.3 million in 1997–8).

A revised student support package is proposed from 2000-1 including the introduction of non-payable access payments for students from low-income families and from 2001–2 a graduate endowment payable on graduation.

STUDENT LOANS

In the academic year 2000–1, students were eligible to apply for indexed loans of up to £4,590 through the Students Awards Agency. Loans are available to students on designated courses, which are those full-time courses leading to a degree, Dip.HE, HND, initial teacher-training qualification, or other qualification specifically designated as being comparable to a first degree. Certain residency conditions also apply. From autumn 2000 loans of up to £500 were made available to part-time students on low incomes.

POSTGRADUATE AWARDS

Postgraduate students, with the exception of students on loan-bearing diploma courses such as teacher training, are not eligible to apply for student loans, but can apply for grants for postgraduate study. These are of two types, both discretionary: 30-week bursaries, which are means-tested and apply to certain vocational and diploma courses; and studentship awards, which are dependent on the class of first degree, especially for research degrees, are not means-tested, and cover students undertaking research degrees or taught master's degrees.

Postgraduate funding is provided by the Enterprise and Lifelong Learning Department through the Students Awards Agency for Scotland, the Scottish Executive Rural Affairs Department, and government research councils. An increasing number of scholarships are also available from research charities, endowments, and particular industries or companies.

The Scottish rates for 30-week bursaries for professional and vocational training in 2000–1 are:

Living in

College/lodgings in London area	£3,853
College/lodgings outside London area	£3,032
Parental home	£2,291

Studentship awards are payable at between £6,620 and £8,265 a year (2000–1).

ADULT AND CONTINUING EDUCATION

The term 'adult education' covers a broad spectrum of educational activities ranging from non-vocational courses of general interest, through the acquiring of special vocational skills needed in industry or commerce, to degree-level study at the Open University.

The Scottish Executive Enterprise and Lifelong Learning Department funds adult education, including that provided by the universities and the Workers' Educational Association, at vocational further education colleges (47 in 2000) and evening centres. In addition, it provides grants to a number of voluntary organisations.

Courses are provided by the education authorities, further and higher education colleges, universities, residential colleges, the BBC, independent television and local radio stations, and several voluntary bodies.

Although the lengths of courses vary, most courses are part-time. Newbattle Abbey College, the only long-term residential adult education college in Scotland, offers one-year full-time diploma courses in European studies and Scottish studies which normally provide a university entrance qualification. Some colleges and centres offer short-term residential courses, lasting from a few days to a few weeks, in a wide range of subjects. Local education authorities sponsor many of the colleges, while others are sponsored by universities or voluntary organisations.

Adult education bursaries for students at the long-term residential colleges of adult education are the responsibility of the colleges themselves. In Scotland the awards are funded by central government and administered by the education authorities. Information is available from the Scottish Executive Enterprise and Lifelong Learning Department.

The involvement of universities in adult education and continuing education has diversified considerably and is supported by a variety of administrative structures ranging from dedicated departments to a devolved approach. Membership of the Universities Association for Continuing Education is open to any university or university college in the UK. It promotes university continuing education, facilitates the interchange of information, and supports research and development work in continuing education.

Of the voluntary bodies, the biggest is the Workers' Educational Association (WEA), which operates throughout the UK, reaching about 150,000 adult students annually. As well as the Scottish Executive, LEAs make grants towards provision of adult education by WEA Scotland.

Advice on adult and community education, and promotion thereof, is provided by Community Learning Scotland.

LOCAL EDUCATION AUTHORITY TERM DATES

(for session 2000–1)

The table below gives term dates for Local Education Authority schools in Scotland, along with Autumn, Spring and Summer mid-term holiday dates. In addition to the dates shown there may be in-service days or local holidays to be taken at the discretion of the local education authority and/or school. For further information on term dates, please contact your local education authority or visit http://www.scotland.gov.uk

AUTUMN TERM Local Education Authority	From	Mid-term holiday inclusive	To
Aberdeen City	15/08/00	22/09/00 - 25/09/00 09/10/00 - 20/10/00	22/12/00
Aberdeenshire	15/08/00	09/10/00 - 20/10/00	22/12/00
Angus	15/08/00	02/10/00 - 13/10/00 30/11/00 - 04/12/00	22/12/00
Argyll & Bute (except Cowal)	16/08/00	16/10/00 - 24/10/00	22/12/00
Cowal	16/08/00	12/10/00 - 20/10/00	22/12/00
Clackmannanshire	22/08/00	02/10/00 09/10/00 - 13/10/00	20/12/00
Comhairle Nan Eilean Siar (Western Isles)	15/08/00	16/10/00 - 27/10/00	22/12/00
Dumfries and Galloway	22/08/00	16/10/00 - 20/10/00 29/11/00 - 01/12/00	22/12/00
Dundee City	15/08/00	02/10/00 - 13/10/00 09/11/00 - 10/11/00 30/11/00 - 01/12/00	22/12/00
East Ayrshire	21/08/00	15/09/00 - 19/09/00 16/10/00 - 23/10/00	22/12/00
East Dunbartonshire	21/08/00	22/09/00 - 25/09/00 16/10/00 - 20/10/00	22/12/00
East Lothian	17/08/00	18/09/00 - 19/09/00 16/10/00 - 20/10/00	22/12/00
East Renfrewshire	21/08/00	22/09/00 - 25/09/00 16/10/00 - 23/10/00	22/12/00
Edinburgh City	16/08/00	18/09/00 - 19/09/00 16/10/00 - 23/10/00	22/12/00
Falkirk	22/08/00	11/09/00 09/10/00 - 13/10/00 20/11/00 - 21/11/00	22/12/00
Fife	22/08/00	02/10/00 16/10/00 - 20/10/00	22/12/00
Glasgow City	21/08/00	22/09/00 - 25/09/00 16/10/00 - 20/10/00	22/12/00
Highland	15/08/00	16/10/00 - 27/10/00	22/12/00
Inverclyde	16/08/00	16/10/00 - 20/10/00	22/12/00
Midlothian	21/08/00	15/09/00 - 19/09/00 16/10/00 - 23/10/00	22/12/00
Moray	22/08/00	09/10/00 - 20/10/00	21/12/00
North Ayrshire (except Arran)	21/08/00	18/09/00 16/10/00 - 23/10/00 17/11/00 - 20/11/00	21/12/00
Arran	21/08/00	18/09/00 09/10/00 - 24/10/00	21/12/00
North Lanarkshire	21/08/00	16/10/00 - 20/10/00	22/12/00
Orkney Islands	22/08/00	13/10/00 - 24/10/00	21/12/00

Local Education Authority	From	Mid-term holiday inclusive	To
Perth and Kinross	15/08/00	02/10/00 - 13/10/00	22/12/00
Renfrewshire	21/08/00	16/10/00 - 20/10/00	22/12/00
Scottish Borders	22/08/00	09/10/00 - 13/10/00	22/12/00
Shetland Islands	22/08/00	16/10/00 - 23/10/00	20/12/00
South Ayrshire	21/08/00	15/09/00 - 18/09/00	22/12/00
		16/10/00 - 23/10/00	
South Lanarkshire	17/08/00	22/09/00 - 25/09/00	22/12/00
		16/10/00 - 20/10/00	
Stirling	22/08/00	09/10/00 - 13/10/00	22/12/00
West Dunbartonshire	21/08/00	22/09/00 - 25/09/00	22/12/00
		16/10/00 - 20/10/00	
West Lothian	22/08/00	18/09/00 - 19/09/00	22/12/00
		23/10/00 - 30/10/00	

SPRING TERM

Local Education Authority	From	Mid-term holiday inclusive	To
Aberdeen City	08/01/01	19/02/01	30/03/01
Aberdeenshire	08/01/01	19/02/01	30/03/01
Angus	08/01/01	16/02/01 - 19/02/01	30/03/01
Argyll & Bute (except Cowal)	08/01/01	19/02/01	06/04/01
Cowal	08/01/01	19/02/01	06/04/01
Clackmannanshire	04/01/01	12/02/01	30/03/01
Comhairle Nan Eilean Siar (Western Isles)	08/01/01		30/03/01
Dumfries and Galloway	08/01/01	14/02/01 - 19/02/01	30/03/01
Dundee City	08/01/01		30/03/01
East Ayrshire	08/01/01	16/02/01 - 20/02/01	06/04/01
East Dunbartonshire	08/01/01	20/02/01	06/04/01
East Lothian	08/01/01	16/02/01 - 23/02/01	06/04/01
East Renfrewshire	08/01/01	20/02/01	06/04/01
Edinburgh City	08/01/01	16/02/01 - 23/02/01	06/04/01
Falkirk	08/01/01	08/02/01 - 12/02/01	30/03/01
Fife	08/01/01	15/02/01 - 16/02/01	30/03/01
Glasgow City	08/01/01	19/02/01 - 20/02/01	06/04/01
Highland	08/01/01	09/02/01 - 12/02/01	30/03/01
Inverclyde	08/01/01	19/02/01	06/04/01
Midlothian	04/01/01	15/02/01 - 23/02/01	06/04/01
Moray	08/01/01	12/02/01	30/03/01
North Ayrshire (except Arran)	04/01/01	16/02/01 - 20/02/01	05/04/01
Arran	04/01/01	19/02/01 - 20/02/02	05/04/01
North Lanarkshire	08/01/01		06/04/01
Orkney Islands	08/01/01	08/02/01 - 12/02/01	30/03/01
Perth and Kinross	08/01/01		30/03/01
Renfrewshire	08/01/01	19/02/01	06/04/01
Scottish Borders	08/01/01		30/03/01
Shetland Islands	08/01/01		30/03/01
South Ayrshire	08/01/01	16/02/01 - 20/02/01	06/04/01
South Lanarkshire	08/01/01	16/02/01 - 19/02/01	06/04/01
Stirling	08/01/01		30/03/01
West Dunbartonshire	08/01/01	16/02/01 - 19/02/01	10/04/01
West Lothian	08/01/01	16/02/01 - 20/02/01	06/04/01

114 Public Service Scotland

SUMMER TERM Local Education Authority	From	Mid-term holiday inclusive	To
Aberdeen City	18/04/01	07/05/01	29/06/01
Aberdeenshire	17/04/01		29/06/01
Angus	16/04/01	07/05/01 25/05/01	28/06/01
Argyll & Bute (except Cowal)	23/04/01	07/05/01	29/06/01
Cowal	23/04/01	07/05/01	29/06/01
Clackmannanshire	17/04/01	07/05/01 - 08/05/01	29/06/01
Comhairle Nan Eilean Siar (Western Isles)	17/04/01		29/06/01
Dumfries and Galloway	17/04/01	07/05/01	29/06/01
Dundee City	16/04/01	07/05/01 25/05/01 - 28/05/01	27/06/01
East Ayrshire	24/04/01	07/05/01 25/05/01 - 28/05/01	29/06/01
East Dunbartonshire	23/04/01	25/05/01 - 28/05/01	29/06/01
East Lothian	23/04/01	07/05/01 - 08/05/01	29/06/01
East Renfrewshire	23/04/01	07/05/01 25/05/01 - 28/05/01	29/06/01
Edinburgh City	23/04/01	07/05/01 - 08/05/01 21/05/01 - 22/05/01	28/06/01
Falkirk	17/04/01	07/05/01 - 08/05/01	29/06/01
Fife	16/04/01	07/05/01 04/06/01	29/06/01
Glasgow City	23/04/01	07/05/01 25/05/01 - 28/05/01	29/06/01
Highland	17/04/01	07/05/01	28/06/01
Inverclyde	23/04/01	07/05/01	27/06/01
Midlothian	23/04/01	07/05/01 - 08/05/01	29/06/01
Moray	16/04/01	07/05/01	06/07/01
North Ayrshire (except Arran)	23/04/01	07/05/01 25/05/01 - 28/05/01	29/06/01
Arran	23/04/01	07/05/01	29/06/01
North Lanarkshire	23/04/01	07/05/01	29/06/01
Orkney Islands	17/04/01	07/05/01	29/06/01
Perth and Kinross	17/04/01	07/05/01	28/06/01
Renfrewshire	23/04/01	07/05/01	29/06/01
Scottish Borders	16/04/01	07/05/01	28/06/01
Shetland Islands	17/04/01		04/07/01
South Ayrshire	23/04/01	07/05/01 - 08/05/01 25/05/01 - 28/05/01	29/06/01
South Lanarkshire	23/04/01	07/05/01 25/05/01 - 28/05/01	28/06/01
Stirling	17/04/01		29/06/01
West Dunbartonshire	23/04/01	07/05/01 25/05/01 - 28/05/01	28/06/01
West Lothian	23/04/01	07/05/01 - 08/05/01	29/06/01

Source: Scottish Executive Education Department

ADMISSIONS AND COURSE INFORMATION

Careers Research and Advisory Centre
Sheraton House, Castle Park, Cambridge
CB3 0AX
Tel: 01223-460277
Fax: 01223-311708
E-mail: enquiries@crac.org.uk
Web: http://www.crac.org.uk
Chief Executive: D.Thomas

Committee of Scottish Higher Education Principals (COSHEP)
53 Hanover Street, Edinburgh EH2 2PJ
Tel: 0131-226 1111
Fax: 0131-226 1100
E-mail: d.caldwell@coshep.ac.uk
Web: http://www.coshep.gcal.ac.uk/default.html
Director: D. Caldwell

General Teaching Council for Scotland
Clerwood House, 96 Clermiston Road,
Edinburgh EH12 6UT
Tel: 0131-314 6000
Fax: 0131-314 6001
E-mail: gtcs@gtcs.org.uk
Web: http://www.gtcs.org.uk
Registrar: D. I. M. Sutherland

Graduate Teacher Training Registry
Rosehill, New Barn Lane, Cheltenham, Glos.
GL52 3LZ
Tel: 01242-544788
Web: http://www.gttr.ac.uk
Registrar: Mrs J. Pearce

Social Work Admissions System
Rosehill, New Barn Lane, Cheltenham, Glos.
GL52 3LZ
Tel: 01242-544600
Admissions Officer: Mrs J. Pearce

Universities and Colleges Admissions Service
Rosehill, New Barn Lane, Cheltenham, Glos.
GL52 3LZ
Tel: 01242-222444
Fax: 01242-544960
E-mail: info@ucas.ac.uk
Web: http://www.ucas.com
Chief Executive: M. A. Higgins

ADULT AND CONTINUING EDUCATION

Community Learning Scotland
Rosebery House, 9 Haymarket Terrace,
Edinburgh EH12 5EZ
Tel: 0131-313 2488
Fax: 0131-313 6800
E-mail: info@cls.dircon.co.uk
Web: http://www.communitylearning.org
Chief Executive: C. McConnell

The Open University
Walton Hall, Milton Keynes MK7 6AA
Tel: 01908-274066
Fax: 01908-653744
E-mail: ces-gen@open.ac.uk
Web: http://www.open.ac.uk/
Vice-Chancellor: Sir John Daniel

UNIVERSITIES ASSOCIATION FOR CONTINUING EDUCATION

University of Cambridge Board for Continuing Education
Madingley Hall, Madingley, Cambridge
CB3 8AQ
Tel: 01954-280279
Fax: 01954-280200
E-mail: smi20@cam.ac.uk
Web: http://www.vace.org.uk
Chair: Prof. Sir Graeme Davies

University of Cambridge Board for Continuing Education
Madingley Hall, Madingley, Cambridge
CB3 8AQ
Tel: 01954-280279
Administrator: Ms S. Irwin

WEA Scotland (Workers' Educational Assocation)
Riddle's Court, 322 Lawnmarket, Edinburgh
EH1 2PG
Tel: 0131-226 3456
Fax: 0131-220 0306
E-mail: hq@weascotland.org.uk
Scottish Secretary: Ms J. Connon

ADVISORY BODIES

Education Otherwise
PO Box 7420, London N9 9SG
Tel: 0870-730 0074

International Baccalaureate Organisation
Peterson House, Fortran Road, St Mellons,
Cardiff CF3 0LT
Tel: 029-2077 4000
Fax: 029-2077 4001
E-mail: ibca@ibo.org
Web: http://www.ibo.org
Director of Academic Affairs: Dr H. Drennan

Scottish Council for Educational Technology
74 Victoria Crescent Road, Glasgow G12 9JN
Tel: 0141-337 5000
Fax: 0141-337 5050
E-mail: enquiries@scet.com
Web: http://www.scet.com
Chief Executive: R. Pietrasik

Scottish Council of Independent Schools
21 Melville Street, Edinburgh EH3 7PE
Tel: 0131-220 2106
Fax: 0131-225 8594
E-mail: scis@btinternet.com
Web: http://www.scis.org.uk
Director: Mrs J. Sischy

Scottish Studentship Advisory Group
c/o Student Awards Agency for Scotland
Gyleview House, 3 Redheughs Rigg, Edinburgh
EH12 9HH
Tel: 0131-244 5153
Fax: 0131-244 5104
E-mail: SAS-8@scotland.gov.uk
Web: http://www.student-support-saas.gov.uk
Chairman: Prof. D. Harding

CURRICULUM COUNCIL

**Scottish Consultative Council on the
Curriculum**
Gardyne Road, Broughty Ferry, Dundee
DD5 1NY
Tel: 01382-443600
Fax: 01382-443645/6
E-mail: reception@sccc.ac.uk
Web: http://www.sccc.ac.uk
Chief Executive: M. Baughan

EXAMINING BODY

Scottish Qualifications Authority
Hanover House, 24 Douglas Street, Glasgow
G2 7NQ
Tel: 0141-248 7900
Fax: 0141-242 2244
E-mail: mail@sqa.org.uk
Web: http://www.sqa.org.uk
Chief Executive: R. Tuck

FUNDING BODIES

Scottish Further Eduction Funding Council
Donaldson House, 97 Haymarket Terrace,
Edinburgh EH12 5HD
Tel: 0131-313 6500
Fax: 0131-313 6501
E-mail: info@sfc.ac.uk
Web: http://www.sfefc.ac.uk
Chief Executive: Prof. J. Sizer, CBE

Scottish Higher Education Funding Council
Donaldson House, 97 Haymarket Terrace,
Edinburgh EH12 5HD
Tel: 0131-313 6500
Fax: 0131-313 6501
E-mail: info@sfc.ac.uk
Web: http://www.shefc.ac.uk
Chief Executive: Prof. J. Sizer, CBE

Student Awards Agency for Scotland
Gyleview House, 3 Redheughs Rigg, Edinburgh
EH12 9HH
Tel: 0131-244 5868
Fax: 0131-244 5717
E-mail: saas.geu@scotland.gov.uk
Web: http://www.student-support-saas.gov.uk
Chief Executive: D. Stephen

Student Loans Company Ltd
100 Bothwell Street, Glasgow G2 7DJ
Tel: 0141-306 2000
Fax: 0141-306 2006
E-mail: colin_ward@slc.co.uk
Web: http://www.slc.co.uk
Chief Executive: C. Ward

LOCAL EDUCATION AUTHORITIES

Aberdeen
Summerhill Education Centre
Stronsay Drive, Aberdeen AB15 6JA
Tel: 01224-346060
Fax: 01224-346061
Web: http://www.aberdeen-education.org.uk
Director of Education: J. Stodter

Aberdeenshire
Woodhill House Annexe
Westburn Road, Aberdeen AB16 5GN
Tel: 01224-664630
Fax: 01224-664615
Web: http://www.aberdeenshire.gov.uk
Director of Education and Recreation:
   H. Vernal

Angus
County Buildings, Market Street, Forfar
DD8 3WE
Tel: 01307-461460
Fax: 01307-461848
Director of Education: J. Anderson

Argyll and Bute
Argyll House, Alexandra Parade, Dunoon
PA23 8AG
Tel: 01369-704000
Fax: 01639-708584
E-mail: suzanne.kerr@ecsumail1.ecsu.org
Web: http://www.argyll-bute.gov.uk
Director of Education: A. C. Morton

City of Edinburgh
Wellington Court, 10 Waterloo Place,
Edinburgh EH1 3EG
Tel: 0131-469 3000
Fax: 0131-469 3322
Director of Education: R. Jobson

Clackmannanshire
Lime Tree House, Alloa FK10 1EX
Tel: 01259-452435
Fax: 01259-452440
**Executive Director of Education and
   Community Services:** K. Bloomer

Dumfries and Galloway
30 Edinburgh Road, Dumfries DG1 1JG
Tel: 01387-260000
Fax: 01387-260453
Director of Education: F. Sanderson

Dundee
8th Floor, Tayside House, Crichton Street
Dundee DD1 3RJ
Tel: 01382-434000
Fax: 01382-433080
E-mail: education@dundeecity.gov.uk
Web: http://www.dundeecity.gov.uk
Director of Education: Ms A. Wilson

East Ayrshire
Council Headquarters, London Road,
Kilmarnock KA3 7BU
Tel: 01563-576017
Fax: 01563-576210
E-mail: john.mulgrew@east-ayrshire.gov.uk
Web: http://www.east-ayrshire.gov.uk
Director of Education: J. Mulgrew

East Dunbartonshire
Boclair House, 100 Milngavie Road, Bearsden,
Glasgow G61 2TQ
Tel: 0141-578 8000
Fax: 0141-578 8653
Director of Community Services: Ms S. Bruce

East Lothian
John Muir House, Haddington EH41 3HA
Tel: 01620-827562
Fax: 01620-827291
Director of Education A. Blackie

East Renfrewshire
Council Offices, Eastwood Park, Rouken Glen
Road, Giffnock G46 6UG
Tel: 0141-577 3431
Fax: 0141-577 3405
E-mail: curriee@eastrenfrewshire.gov.uk
Web: http://www.eastrenfrewshire.gov.uk
Director of Education Mrs E. J. Currie

Eilean Siar/Western Isles
Council Offices, Sandwick Road, Stornoway,
Isle of Lewis HS1 2BW
Tel: 01851-703773
Acting Director of Education: M. Macleod

Falkirk
McLaren House, Marchmont Avenue, Polmont,
Falkirk FK2 0NZ
Tel: 01324-506600
Fax: 01324-506601
Director of Education Dr G. Young

118   Public Service Scotland

Fife
Fife House, North Street, Glenrothes KY7 5LT
Tel: 01592-413656
Fax: 01592-413696
E-mail: mjohnson@itasdarc.demon.co.uk
Head of Education: A. McKay

Glasgow
Nye Bevan House, 20 India Street, Glasgow
G2 4PF
Tel: 0141-287 6898
Fax: 0141-287 6892
E-mail: education@glasgow.gov.uk
Web: http://www.glasgow.gov.uk
Director of Education Services: K. Corsar

Highland
Council Buildings, Glenurquhart Road,
Inverness IV3 5NX
Tel: 01463-702802
Fax: 01463-702828
Web: http://www.highland.gov.uk/educ/
default.htm
Director of Education: B. Robertson

Inverclyde
105 Dalrymple Street, Greenock PA15 1HT
Tel: 01475-712824
Fax: 01475-712875
E-mail: invereduc@ecsumaill.ecsu.org
Web: http://www.inverdlyde.gov.uk
Director of Education Services B. McLeary

Midlothian
Fairfield House, 8 Lothian Road, Dalkeith
EH22 3ZG
Tel: 0131-270 7500
Fax: 0131-271 3751
E-mail: education-services@midlothian.gov.uk
Director of Education D. MacKay

Moray
Council Offices, High Street, Elgin IV30 1BX
Tel: 01343-563097
Fax: 01343-563478
Director of Educational Services:
D. M. Duncan

North Ayrshire
Cunninghame House, Irvine KA12 8EE
Tel: 01294-324411
Fax: 01294-324444
Corporate Director, Educational Services:
J. Travers

North Lanarkshire
Municipal Buildings, Kildonan Street,
Coatbridge ML5 3BT
Tel: 01236-812222
Fax: 01236-812247
E-mail: education@northlan.gov.uk
Director of Education: M. O'Neill

Orkney Islands
Council Offices, School Place, Kirkwall, Orkney
KW15 1NY
Tel: 01856-873535
Fax: 01856-870302
E-mail: education@orkney.gov.uk
Director of Education L. Manson

Perth and Kinross
Blackfriars, Perth, PH1 5LU
Tel: 01738-476211
Fax: 01738-476210
Director of Education and Children's Services:
B. Frew

Renfrewshire
Council Headquarters, South Building,
Cotton Street, Paisley PA1 1LE
Tel: 0141-842 5663
Fax: 0141-842 5699
E-mail: education.leisure@renfrewshire.gov.uk
Web: http://www.renfrewshire.gov.uk
Director of Education and Leisure Services:
Ms S. Rae

Scottish Borders
Council Headquarters, Newtown St Boswells,
Melrose, Roxburghshire TD6 0SA
Tel: 01835-824000
Fax: 01835-825091
Director of Education: J. Christie

Shetland
Hayfield House, Hayfield Lane, Lerwick,
Shetland ZE1 0QD
Tel: 01595-744000
**Director of Education and Community
Services:** J. Halcrow

South Ayrshire
County Buildings, Wellington Square, Ayr
KA7 1DR
Tel: 01292-612000
Fax: 01292-612258
Director of Education: M. McCabe

South Lanarkshire
Council Headquarters, Almada Street, Hamilton
ML3 0AE
Tel: 01698-454545
Fax: 01698-454465
E-mail: maggi.allan@southlanarkshire.gov.uk
Web: http://www.southlanarkshire.gov.uk
Executive Director of Education Resources:
Ms M. Allan

Stirling
Viewforth, Stirling FK8 2ET
Tel: 01786-442678
Fax: 01786-442782
E-mail: jeyesg@stirling.gov.uk
Director of Children's Services: G. Jeyes

West Dunbartonshire
Garshake Road, Dunbarton, G82 3PU
Tel: 01389-737301
Fax: 01389-737348
Director of Education and Cultural Services:
I. McMurdo

West Lothian
Lindsay House, South Bridge Street, Bathgate
EH48 1TS
Tel: 01506-776000
Fax: 01506-776378
E-mail: education@westlothian.gov.uk
Corporate Manager, Education Services:
R. Stewart

UNIVERSITIES

Glasgow Caledonian University
Cowcaddens Road, Glasgow G4 0BA
Tel: 0141-331 3000
Web: http://www.gcal.ac.uk
Chancellor: The Lord Nickson, KBE
Vice-Chancellor and Principal:
Dr I. A. Johnston
Secretary: B. M. Murphy

Heriot-Watt University
Ricarton Campus, Edinburgh EH14 4AS
Tel: 0131-449 5111
Fax: 0131-451 3744
Web: http://www.hw.ac.uk
Chancellor: The Rt Hon. The Lord Mackay of
Clashfern, PQ, QC, FRSE
Vice-Chancellor and Principal:
Prof. J. S. Archer, FREng.
Secretary: P. L. Wilson
Academic-Registrar: Mrs R. J. Moir

Napier University
219 Colinton Road, Edinburgh EH14 1DJ
Tel: 0131-444 2266;
Student enquiries: 0500-353570
Fax: 0131-455 6333
E-mail: info@napier.ac.uk
Web: http://www.napier.ac.uk
Chancellor: Lord Younger of Leckie, KT,
KCVO, TD, PC, FRSE
Vice-Chancellor and Principal: Prof. J. Mavor
Secretary: Dr G. Webber
Academic Registrar: Ms L. Fraser

Robert Gordon University
Schoolhill, Aberdeen AB10 1FR
Tel: 01224-262000
Web: http://www.rgu.ac.uk
Chancellor: Sir Bob Reid
Vice-Chancellor and Principal: Prof. W. Stevely
Secretary: Dr A. Graves
Academic-Registrar: Mrs H. Douglas

University of Aberdeen
King's College, Aberdeen AB24 3FX
Tel: 01224-272000
Fax: 01224-273664
E-mail: senoff@abdn.ac.uk
Web: http://www.abdn.ac.uk
Chancellor: The Lord Wilson of Tillyorn
GCMG
Vice-Chancellor and Principal: Prof. C. D. Rice
Secretary: S. Cannon
Registrar: Dr T. Webb
Rector: Miss C. Dickson Wright

University of Abertay Dundee
Bell Street, Dundee DD1 1HG
Tel: 01382-308000
Fax: 01382-308118
Web: http://www.abertay-dundee.ac.uk
Chancellor: The Earl of Airlie, KT, GCVO, PC
Vice-Chancellor and Principal: Prof. B. King
Secretary: D. Hogarth
Registrar: Dr D. Button

University of Dundee
Dundee DD1 4HN
Tel: 01382-344000
Fax: 01382-201604
E-mail: secretary@dundee.ac.uk
Web: http://www.dundee.ac.uk
Chancellor: Sir James Black, FRCP, FRS
Vice-Chancellor and Principal:
   Sir Alan Langlands
Secretary: R. Seaton
Rector: T. Slattery

University of Edinburgh
Old College, South Bridge, Edinburgh
EH8 9YL
Tel: 0131-650 1000
Web: http://www.ed.ac.uk
Chancellor: HRH The Prince Philip, Duke of
   Edinburgh, KG, KT, OM, GBE, PC, FRS
Vice-Chancellor and Principal: Prof. Sir
   Stewart Sutherland, FBA, FRSE
Secretary: M. J. B. Lowe, Ph.D.
Director of Registry: Dr V. O'Halloran
Rector: R. Harper

University of Glasgow
University Avenue, Glasgow G12 8QQ
Tel: 0141-339 8855
Fax: 0141-330 4808
E-mail: postmaster@gla.ac.uk
Web: http://www.gla.ac.uk
Chancellor: Sir William Fraser, GCB, FRSE
Vice-Chancellor: Prof. Sir Graeme Davies,
   FREng, FRSE
Academic Secretary: Ms J. Hulme
Secretary of Court: D. Mackie, FRSA
Rector: R. Kemp

University of St Andrews
College Gate, North Street, St Andrews, Fife
KY16 9AJ
Tel: 01334-476161
Web: http://www.st-and.ac.uk
Chancellor: Sir Kenneth Dover, D. Litt, FRSE,
   FBA
Vice-Chancellor: Prof. C. A. Vincent
Secretary and Registrar D. J. Corner
Rector: A. Neil

University of Paisley
Paisley PA1 2BE
Tel: 0141-848 3000
Web: http://www.paisley.ac.uk
Chancellor: Sir Robert Easton, CBE
Vice-Chancellor: Prof. R. W. Shaw, CBE
Secretary: J. Fraser
Registrar: D. Rigg

University of Stirling
Stirling FK9 4LA
Tel: 01786-473171
Fax: 01786-463000
E-mail: pr-office@stir.ac.uk
Web: http://www.stir.ac.uk
Chancellor: Dame Diana Rigg, DBE
Vice-Chancellor: Prof. A. Miller, CBE, FRSE
Secretary: K. J. Clarke
Academic Registrar: D. G. Wood

University of Strathclyde
John Anderson Campus, 16 Richmond Street,
Glasgow, G1 1XQ
Tel: 0141-552 4400
Fax: 0141-552 0775
Web: http://www.strath.ac.uk/campus/info.html
Chancellor: The Rt Hon. Lord Hope of
   Craighead, PC
Vice-Chancellor and Principal: Prof. Sir John
   Arbuthnott, FRSE, FRCPath
Secretary: P. W. A. West
Academic Registrar: Dr S. Mellows

COLLEGES

Bell College of Technology
Crichton University Campus, Dudgeon House,
Bankend Road, Dumfries DG1 4SG
Principal: Dr K. MacCallum

Bell College of Technology
Almada Street, Hamilton, Lanarkshire
ML3 0JB
Tel: 01698-283100
Fax: 01698-282131
Principal: Dr K. MacCallum

Dumfries and Galloway College
Heathhall, Dumfries DG1 3QZ
Tel: 01387-261261
Fax: 01387-250006
E-mail: info@dumgal.ac.uk
Web: http://www.dumgal.ac.uk
Principal: T. Jakimciw

Fife College of Further and Higher Education
St Brycedale Avenue, Kirkcaldy, Fife
KY1 1EX
Tel: 01592-268591
Fax: 01592-640225
E-mail: enquiries@fife.ac.uk
Web: http://www.fife.ac.uk
Principal: Mrs J. S. R. Johnston

Glasgow School of Art
167 Renfrew Street, Glasgow G3 6RQ
Tel: 0141-353 4500
Fax: 0141-353 4528
Web: http://www.gsa.ac.uk
Director: Prof. S. Reid

Inverness College
3 Longman Road, Longman South, Inverness
IV1 1SA
Tel: 01463-237000
Fax: 01463-711977
E-mail: inverness.college@groupwise.uhi.ac.uk
Web: http://www.uhi.ac.uk
Principal: Dr G. Clark

Lews Castle College
Stornoway, Isle of Lewis HS2 0XR
Tel: 01851-770000
Fax: 01851-770001
Web: http://www.lews.uni.ac.uk/
Principal: D. R. Green

Moray College
Moray Street, Elgin, Moray IV30 1JJ
Tel: 01343-576000
Fax: 01343-576001
E-mail: greg.cooper@moray.uni.ac.uk
Web: http://www.moray.ac.uk
Acting Principal: B. G. Cooper

Newbattle Abbey College
Dalkeith, Midlothian EH22 3LL
Tel: 0131-443 1921
Fax: 0131-654 0598
E-mail: office@nac.sol.co.uk
Principal: W. M. Conboy

The North Highland College
Ormlie Road, Thurso, Caithness KW14 7EE
Tel: 01847-896161
Fax: 01847-893872
E-mail: r.masonth@groupwise.uhi.ac.uk
Web: http://www.uhi.ac.uk/thurso/
Principal: H. Logan

Northern College
Dundee Campus, Gardyne Road, Dundee
DD5 1NY
Tel: 01382-464000
Web: http://www.norcol.ac.uk
Principal: D. Adams

Northern College
Hilton Place, Aberdeen AB24 4FA
Tel: 01224-283500
Fax: 01224-283900
Web: http://www.norcol.ac.uk
Principal: D. Adams

Orkney College
Kirkwall, Orkney KW15 1LX
Tel: 01856-872839
Fax: 01856-875323
E-mail: orkney.college@groupwise.uhi.ac.uk
Principal: P. Scott

Queen Margaret University College
Duke Street, Edinburgh EH6 8HF
Tel: 0131-317 3000
Fax: 0131-317 3256
E-mail: admissions@qmuc.ac.uk
Web: http://www.qmuc.ac.uk
Principal: Prof. J. Stringer

Queen Margaret University College
Corstorphine Campus, Clerwood Terrace
Edinburgh EH12 8TS
E-mail: admissions@qmuc.ac.uk
Web: http://www.qmuc.ac.uk
Principal: Prof. J. Stringer

Queen Margaret University College
Scottish International Drama Centre, 41 Elm
Row, Edinburgh EH7 4AH
E-mail: admissions@qmuc.ac.uk
Web: http://www.qmuc.ac.uk
Principal: Prof. J. Stringer

Royal Scottish Academy of Music and Drama
100 Renfrew Street, Glasgow G2 3DB
Tel: 0141-332 4101
Fax: 0141-332 8901
E-mail: registry@rsamd.ac.uk
Web: http://www.rsamd.ac.uk
Principal: Sir Philip Ledger, CBE, FRSE

Sàbhal Mor Ostaig
Sleat, Isle of Skye IV44 8RQ
Tax: 01471-888000
Fax: 01471-888001
E-mail: oifis@smo.nhi.ac.uk
Web: http://www.smo.nhi.ac.uk
Director: N. N. Gillies

SAC (Scottish Agricultural College)
Central Office, Kings Buildings, West Mains
Road, Edinburgh EH9 3JG
Tax: 0131-535 4000
Fax: 0131-667 2601
Web: http://www.sac.ac.uk
Principal and Chief Executive:
   Prof. K. Linklater

THE ENERGY INDUSTRIES

The main primary sources of energy in Britain are oil, natural gas, coal, nuclear power and water power. The main secondary sources (i.e. sources derived from the primary sources) are electricity, coke and smokeless fuels, and petroleum products.

Policy and legislation on the generation and supply of electricity from coal, oil and gas, and nuclear fuels, remains a matter reserved to the UK Government after devolution. The Department of the Environment, Transport and the Regions is responsible for promoting energy efficiency.

INDIGENOUS PRODUCTION OF PRIMARY FUELS (UK)
Million tonnes of oil equivalent

	1997	1998p
Coal	31.5	27.0
Petroleum	140.4	145.2
Natural gas	86.2	90.3
Primary electricity		
Nuclear	22.99	23.28
Natural flow hydro	0.41	0.50
Total	281.9	286.2

p provisional

INLAND ENERGY CONSUMPTION BY PRIMARY FUEL (UK)
Million tonnes of oil equivalent, seasonally adjusted

	1997	1998p
Coal	42.9	43.1
Petroleum	77.0	76.7
Natural gas	88.7	92.2
Primary electricity	24.83	25.19
Nuclear	22.99	23.28
Natural flow hydro	0.42	0.50
Net imports	1.42	1.41
Total	233.5	237.2

p provisional

UK TRADE IN FUELS AND RELATED MATERIALS 1997p

	Quantity*	Value†
Imports		
Coal and other solid fuel	15.1	687
Crude petroleum	40.0	2,170
Petroleum products	17.8	1,414
Natural gas	0.4	43
Electricity	1.1	335
Total	74.5	4,648
Total (fob)‡	—	4,105

Exports		
Coal and other solid fuel	0.9	69
Crude petroleum	79.6	4,441
Petroleum products	37.1	2,886
Natural gas	1.5	76
Electricity	—	3
Total	119.0	7,475
Total (fob)‡	—	7,475

p provisional
* Million tonnes of oil equivalent
† £ million
‡ Adjusted to exclude estimated costs of insurance, freight, etc.
Source: Department of Trade and Industry, Energy Trends, May 1999 (Crown copyright)

OIL AND GAS

The United Kingdom Continental Shelf (UKCS) is treated as a separate region in official economic statistics. Calculation of Scottish oil and gas outputs and revenue deriving from the UKCS is difficult and controversial. Recent research from Aberdeen University suggests that there is considerable variation from year to year in the Scottish proportion of UK tax revenue from oil and gas, depending on a number of factors, including division of the North Sea, relative expense of developing the North Sea fields, and oil price fluctuations. According to this analysis, Scotland's share of UK oil and gas revenue was 80 per cent in 1996–7, but the drop in oil prices over the last two years has reduced this to an estimated 75 per cent for 1997 and 66 per cent for 1998 (calendar years). The following table shows the total value of UKCS oil and gas production and investment in 1997–8.

	1997 £m	1998p £m
Total income	18,955	16,950
Operating costs	4,150	4,190
Exploration expenditure	1,194	762
Gross trading profits*	13,832	11,289
Contribution to GDP	1.9%	1.5%
Capital investment	4,333	5,086
Contribution to industrial investment	18%	18%

* Net of stock appreciation
p provisional

OIL
Until the 1960s Britain imported almost all its oil supplies. In 1969 oil was discovered in the Arbroath field of the UKCS. The first oilfield to be brought into production was the Argyll field in 1975, and since the mid-1970s Britain has been a major producer of crude oil.

There are estimated to be reserves of 2,015 million tonnes of oil in the UKCS. Royalties are payable on fields approved before April 1982 and petroleum revenue tax is levied on fields approved between 1975 and March 1993.

Licences for exploration and production are granted to companies by the Department of Trade and Industry; the leading British oil companies are British Petroleum (BP) and Shell Transport and Trading. At the end of 1998, 1,021 offshore licences and 150 onshore licences had been awarded, and there were 121 offshore oilfields in production in the UK.

There are four oil terminals and two refineries in Scotland.

OIL COMING ASHORE AT SCOTTISH TERMINALS 1997*
Million tonnes

Sullom Voe	31.7
Flotta, Orkney Islands	9.8
Forties Leeward	38.1
Nigg Bay, Cromarty Firth	0.4
Total	80.0

* Figures do not reflect total oil production in Scotland, because some oil produced is exported directly by tanker from offshore fields

CAPACITY OF SCOTTISH REFINERIES 1997
Million tonnes p.a.

Grangemouth	8.9
Dundee	0.7
Total	9.6

GAS
In 1965 gas was discovered in the North Sea off the South Yorkshire coast, in the West Sole field, which became the first gasfield in production in 1967.

By the end of 1998 there were 80 offshore gasfields producing natural gas and associated gases (mainly methane). There are estimated to be 1,795,000 million cubic metres of recoverable gas reserves in existing discoveries. Two new North Sea fields, Elgin-Franklin and Shearwater, are due to come into operation in 2000; their production will be piped to terminals at Bacton, Norfolk.

There are three gas terminals in Scotland, at St Fergus, Aberdeenshire.

GAS BROUGHT ASHORE AT SCOTTISH TERMINALS 1998*
Million cubic m

Far North Liquids and Associated Gas System (FLAGS)	7,400
Frig, Fulmar and Miller Lines	21,300
Scottish Area Gas Evacuation (SAGE)	9,800
Total	38,500

* Figures do not reflect total Scottish gas production, because some gas produced is piped to terminals in England
Source: Department of Trade and Industry

Since 1986 the British gas industry, nationalised in 1949, has been progressively privatised. Competition was introduced into the industrial gas market from 1986, and supply of gas to the domestic market was opened to companies other than British Gas from April 1996 onwards. Gas companies can now also sell electricity to their customers. Similarly, electricity companies can also offer gas.

The Office of Gas and Electricity Markets is the regulatory body for the gas and electricity industries in Britain; for its office in Scotland.

NATURAL GAS PRODUCTION AND SUPPLY (UK)
GWh

	1997	1998p
Gross gas production	998,343	1,048,353
Exports	21,666	31,604
Imports	14,062	10,582
Gas available	927,790	956,076
Gas transmitted‡	911,798	948,401

p provisional
‡ Figures differ from gas available mainly because of stock changes

NATURAL GAS CONSUMPTION
GWh

	1997	1998p
Electricity generators	243,361	253,348
Iron and steel industry	20,725	22,754
Other industries	174,763	175,747
Domestic	341,347	360,266
Public administration, commerce and agriculture[1]	[1]12,347	118,860
Total	892,544	930,975

p provisional
Source: Department of Trade and Industry

ELECTRICITY

ELECTRICITY

There are currently 27 electricity generating companies in Britain. The 12 regional electricity companies (RECs) formed under the Electricity Act 1989 currently have a monopoly on sales of 100 kW or less to consumers in their franchise areas; over this limit competition has been introduced. Competition was introduced into the domestic electricity market in 1998–9. Electricity companies can now also sell gas to their customers. Similarly, gas companies can also offer electricity. Generators sell the electricity they produce into an open commodity market (the Pool) from which buyers purchase.

In Scotland, three new companies were formed under the Electricity Act 1989: ScottishPower PLC and Scottish Hydro-Electric PLC (now Scottish and Southern Energy PLC), which are responsible for generation, transmission, distribution and supply; and Scottish Nuclear Ltd. ScottishPower and Scottish Hydro-Electric were floated on the stock market in 1991 (the latter merged with Southern Electric plc to form Scottish and Southern Energy plc in December 1998). Scottish Nuclear was incorporated into British Energy in 1995.

ScottishPower operates six power stations in Scotland. Scottish and Southern Energy operates a large power station at Peterhead, 56 hydro stations in Scotland, and a diesel backup station in Lerwick, Shetland; it also operates a number of power stations in England and Wales.

The Electricity Association is the electricity industry's main trade association, providing representational and professional services for the electricity companies. EA Technology Ltd provides distribution and utilisation research, development and technology transfer. The Office of Gas and Electricity Markets is the regulatory body for the electricity industry.

ELECTRICITY PRODUCTION IN SCOTLAND 1998
GWh

	Electricity generated 1998	Amount exported to England	From renewable sources
ScottishPower	24,500	c.6,000	c.2%
Scottish and Southern Energy*	14,167	3,260	c.11%

* Scottish and Southern Energy figures are for 1997–8 financial year

NUCLEAR POWER

About half of Scotland's electricity is generated by nuclear power stations. British Energy PLC owns two Advanced Gas-Cooled Reactors (AGRs) at Torness and Hunterston B. British Nuclear Fuels Ltd (BNFL) owns the Magnox nuclear reactor at Chapelcross.

BNFL, which is in public ownership, provides reprocessing, waste management and effluent treatment services. The UK Atomic Energy Authority is responsible for the decommissioning of nuclear reactors and other nuclear facilities used in research and development. UK Nirex, which is owned by the nuclear generating companies and the Government, is responsible for the disposal of intermediate and some low-level nuclear waste. The Nuclear Installations Inspectorate of the Health and Safety Executive is the nuclear industry's regulator.

In 1998 the closure was announced of the nuclear reactor at Dounreay, which started up in 1956.

NUCLEAR POWER GENERATION 1997-8

Terawatt hours

Hunterston B	8.73
Torness	9.27
Total by British Energy	18.0
Chapelcross*	1.40

*1998—9 figure

BNFL
BNFL Risley, Warrington, Cheshire WA3 6AS
Tel: 01925-832000
Chief Executive, J. Taylor

British Energy Plc
10 Lochside Place, Edinburgh EH12 9DF
Tel: 0131-527 2000
Chief Executive (acting), P. Hollins

Scottish and Southern Energy Plc
Dunkeld Road, Perth PH1 5WA
Tel: 01738-455040

ScottishPower Plc
1 Atlantic Quay, Glasgow G2 8SP
Tel: 0141-248 8200
Chief Executive, I. Robinson

Electricity Association Ltd
30 Millbank, London SW1P 4RD
Tel: 020-7963 5700
Chief Executive, P. E. G. Daubeney

EA Technology Ltd
Capenhurst, Chester CH1 6ES
Tel: 0151-339 4181
Managing Director, Dr S. F. Exell

RENEWABLE ENERGY SOURCES

Renewable sources of energy principally include biofuels, hydro, wind, waste and solar.

The UK Government intends to achieve 10 per cent of the UK's electricity needs from renewables by 2010 and to meet the UK's international commitments to future reductions on greenhouse gases. Following the establishment of the Scottish Parliament, decisions on renewable sources of energy have been devolved.

The Scottish Renewables Obligation Orders (SROs) have been the Government's principal mechanism for developing renewable energy sources. They are similar to the Non-Fossil Fuel Obligation Renewables Orders in England and Wales. SRO Orders require ScottishPower and Scottish and Southern Energy to buy specified amounts of electricity from specified renewable sources; the first order was made in 1994 and the latest in March 1999.

Of the 109 projects awarded contracts so far (for about 340 MW), ten projects (27 MW capacity) have been commissioned. Six of these are wind schemes (combined capacity c.21.5 MW), two are hydro schemes (combined capacity c.1.5 MW), and two are waste-to-energy schemes (combined capacity c.3.8 MW). Four wind-farms are now completed. The latest SRO Order included, for the first time, three wave-power projects.

No specific mechanism to support the development of solar energy projects exists, but the Department of Trade and Industry currently funds initiatives and channels European grant funding. There are several small-scale (less than 1 MW) solar projects in operation in various places around Scotland.

THE WATER INDUSTRY

Overall responsibility for national water policy in Scotland rested with the Secretary of State for Scotland until July 1999, when responsibility was devolved to the Scottish Executive. Most aspects of water policy are currently administered through the Scottish Executive Rural Affairs Department.

Water supply and sewerage services were the responsibility of the local authorities and the Central Scotland Water Development Board until 1996. In April 1996 the provision of water and sewerage services became the responsibility of three public water authorities, covering the north, east and west of Scotland, under the terms of the Local Government etc. (Scotland) Act 1994.

The Act also provided for the Scottish Water and Sewerage Customers Council to be established to represent consumer interests. The Council is to be abolished under the provisions of the Water Industries Act 1999, whose provisions have been accepted by the Scottish Executive, and will be replaced in late 1999 by a Water Industry Commissioner, whose role is to promote customers' interests. The Commissioner will make longer-term recommendations about charging and efficiency to the Scottish Executive and will be advised by three water industry consultative committees, one for each water authority.

The Scottish Environment Protection Agency is responsible for promoting the cleanliness of rivers, lochs and coastal waters, and controlling pollution. Scotland has 60 designated bathing waters, and the Scottish Executive is committed to bringing these up to European standards and to improving the quality of rivers, lochs and coastal waters. A £1,800 million programme for modernising the infrastructure and activities of the water industry is planned, based on research carried out during 2000.

WATER RESOURCES 1997

	No.	Yield (Ml/day)
Reservoirs and lochs	287	3,018
Feeder intakes	27	—
River intakes	223	422
Bore-holes	35	77
Underground springs	103	46
Total	*676	3,562

*Including compensation reservoirs

WATER CONSUMPTION 1997

Total (Ml/day)	2,336.3
Potable	2,320.3
Unmetered	1,781.7
Metered	538.5
Non-potable†	16.0
Total (l/head/day)	468.6
Unmetered	357.4
Metered and non-potable†	109.9

† 'Non-potable' supplied for industrial purposes. Metered supplies in general relate to commercial and industrial use and unmetered to domestic use
Source: The Scottish Office

METHODS OF CHARGING
The water authorities set charges for domestic and non-domestic water and sewerage provision through charges schemes which have to be approved by the Scottish Water and Sewerage Customers Council. The authorities are required to publish a summary of their charges schemes.

EAST OF SCOTLAND WATER AUTHORITY

Pentland Gait, 597 Calder Road, Edinburgh EH11 4HJ
Tel: 0131-453 7500
Chief Executive: Dr J. Hargreaves

NORTH OF SCOTLAND WATER AUTHORITY

Cairngorm House, Beechwood Park North, Inverness IV2 3ED
Tel: 0845 743 7437
Chief Executive: A. Findlay

WEST OF SCOTLAND WATER AUTHORITY

419 Balmore Road, Glasgow G22 6NU
Tel: 0141-355 5333
Chief Executive: E. Chambers

WATER INDUSTRY COMMISSIONER FOR SCOTLAND

Ochil House, Springkerse Business Park, Stirling FK7 7XE
Tel: 01786-430200
Fax: 01786 462018
E-mail: enquiries@watercommissioner.co.uk
Web: http://www.watercommissioner.co.uk
Commissioner: D. A. Sutherland

WATER UK

1 Queen Anne's Gate, London, SW1H 9BT
Tel: 020-7344 1844
Water UK is the trade association for almost all the water service companies in the UK, including the three Scottish water authorities.
Chief Executive: Ms P. Taylor

THE FIRE SERVICE

The Scottish Executive Justice Department has overall responsibility for fire services, including the provision of training at the Scottish Fire Service Training School.

Each local council in Scotland is the fire authority for its area. There are six joint fire boards, comprising groups of council areas which have delegated their fire authority responsibilities to the boards. The remaining two councils, Dumfries and Galloway and Fife, each act as the fire authority for their whole council area. Membership of the joint boards comprises elected members of each of the constituent councils. The fire authorities are responsible for setting a budget, making an establishment scheme (which details fire brigade, fire stations and equipment), the 'mutual assistance' scheme for handling major incidents, and hearing disciplinary cases or appeals. Subject to the approval of the Scottish Ministers, fire authorities appoint a firemaster, who is responsible for brigade operations.

Fire brigades are financed by local government, with the exception of some central services (e.g. the Scottish Fire Service Training School) which are financed by the Scottish Executive. Joint fire boards set their budgets and requisition the necessary finance from their constituent councils. The two councils that directly administer their fire brigades set budgets as for their other services. The Scottish Executive pays an annual civil defence grant to each joint board for its role in emergency planning.

HM Inspectorate of Fire Services for Scotland carries out inspections of fire brigades in order to improve the efficiency, effectiveness and standards of the fire service. HM Chief Inspector of Fire Services publishes an annual report and other reports. The interests of fire authorities and members of the fire brigades are considered by the Scottish Central Fire Brigades Advisory Council, which advises Scottish Ministers on matters affecting the service.

JOINT FIRE BOARDS

The Dumfries and Galloway council area and the Fife council area do not have joint boards as a single authority covers the whole of the fire brigade area. The chairman/convenor of the authority for these two brigades is given with the brigade's details.

Central Scotland Fire Board
Municipal Buildings, Falkirk FK1 5RS
Tel: 01324-506070
Fax: 01324-506071
E-mail: bpirie@falkirk-lawadmin.demon.co.uk
Convenor: T. Coll
Clerk to the Board: Ms E. Morton

Grampian Fire Board
Woodhill House, Westburn Road, Aberdeen AB16 5GB
Tel: 01224-665430
Fax: 01224-665445
Chairman: R. Stroud
Clerk to the Board: N. McDowall

Highland and Islands Fire Board
Council Headquarters,Glenurquhart Road Inverness IV3 5NX
Tel: 01463-702103
Fax: 01463-702182
Convener of the Board: A. R. Macfarlane Slack
Clerk to the Board: J. F. P. Black

Lothian and Borders Fire Board
City Chambers, High Street, Edinburgh EH1 1YJ
Tel: 0131-529 4327
Fax: 0131-529 7607
E-mail: dougie.dolan@ediburgh.gov.uk
Convenor: K. Harrold
Clerk to the Board: T. N. Aitchison

Strathclyde Fire Board
Council Offices, Almada Street, Hamilton ML3 0AA
Tel: 01698-454872
Fax: 01698-454407
E-mail: pach.exec@southlanarkshire.gov.uk
Convener: J. Shaw
Clerk to the Board: W. Kirk

Tayside Fire Board
2 High Street, Perth PH1 5PH
Tel: 01738-475102
Fax: 01738-475110
E-mail: j.angus@pkc.gov.uk
Convener: F. Duncan, OBE
Clerk to the Board: J. Angus

FIRE BRIGADES

Central Scotland Fire Brigade
HQ, Main Street, Maddiston, Falkirk FK2 0LG
Tel: 01324-716996
Fax: 01324-715353
Firemaster: vacant

Dumfries and Galloway Fire Brigade
Brigade HQ, Brooms Road, Dumfries DG1 2DZ
Tel: 01387-252222
Fax: 01387-260995
Chairman: B. Conchie
Firemaster: L. Ibbotson

Fife Fire and Rescue Service
HQ, Strathore Road, Thornton, Kirkcaldy
KY1 4DF
Tel: 01592-774451
Fax: 01592-630105
Chairman - Public Protection and Regulation
Committee: A. Keddie
Firemaster: N. Campion

Grampian Fire Brigade
HQ, 19 North Anderson Drive, Aberdeen
AB15 6DW
Tel: 01224-696666
Fax: 01224-692224
E-mail: firemaster@grampianfirebrigade.co.uk
Firemaster: J. Williams

Highland and Islands Fire Brigade
HQ, 16 Harbour road, Longman West, Inverness
IV1 1TB
Tel: 01463-227000
Fax: 01463-236979
E-mail: firemaster@highland.fire-uk.org
Firemaster: B. A. Murray

Lothian and Borders Fire Brigade
HQ, Lauriston Place, Edinburgh EH3 9DE
Tel: 0131-228 2401
Fax: 0131-228 6662
Firemaster: C. Cranston

Strathclyde Fire Brigade
HQ, Bothwell Road, Hamilton ML3 0EA
Tel: 01698-300999
Fax: 01698-338444
Web: http://www.strathclyde.fire-uk.org
Convener: J. Shaw
Firemaster: J. Ord O.St.J., QFSM

Tayside Fire Brigade
Headquarters, Blackness Road, Dundee DD1 5PA
Tel: 01382-322222
Fax: 01382-200791
Firemaster: D. S. Marr OBE, QFSM, FIFireE

STAFF ASSOCIATIONS

**The Chief and Assistant Chief Fire Officers'
Association**
10–11 Pebble Close, Amington, Tamworth
B77 4RD
Tel: 01827-61516
Fax: 01827-61530
E-mail: info@cacfoa.fire-uk.org
Web: http://www.fire-uk.org
Chairman: M. Eastwood, CBE, QFSM
General Manager: K. Rose, MBE

**Scottish Central Fire Brigades Advisory
Council**
Scottish Executive Justice Department,
Room F1–9, Saughton House, Broomhouse
Drive, Edinburgh EH11 3XD
Tel: 0131-244 2166
Fax: 0131-244 2864
E-mail: george.davidson@scotland.gov.uk
Chairman: J. Hamill
Secretary: G. A. Davidson

BRIGADE STRENGTHS MARCH 1999

Wholetime uniformed personnel	4,506
Retained (uniformed on call)	2,547
Volunteer (no retainer fee)	1,215
Control room personnel	213
Non-uniformed personnel	789

HEALTH

Public health policy is a devolved power and is now the responsibility of the Scottish Executive.

Health education in Scotland is the responsibility of the Health Education Board for Scotland. The role of the Board is to provide health information and advice to the public, health professionals, and other organisations, and to advise the Government on health education needs and strategies.

SELECTED CAUSES OF DEATH, BY SEX 1997

	Males	Females
Intestinal infectious disease	7	12
Tuberculosis	38	27
Other infectious and parasitic diseases	167	180
Malignant neoplasms	7,538	7,351
Benign neoplasms	11	18
Other and unspecified neoplasms	61	75
Endocrine and metabolic diseases, immunity disorders	354	366
Nutritional deficiencies	1	6
Diseases of the blood and blood-forming organs	96	104

Mental disorders	657	954
Diseases of the nervous system and sense organs	431	469
Rheumatic fever and rheumatic heart disease	47	138
Hypertensive disease	127	167
Ischaemic heart disease	7,355	6,658
Other heart disease	1,124	1,776
Cerebrovascular disease	2,609	4,350
Other diseases of the circulatory system	757	803
Diseases of the respiratory system	3,528	4,363
Diseases of the digestive system	1,158	1,270
Diseases of the genito-urinary system	371	533
Complications of pregnancy, childbirth and puerperium	—	4
Diseases of the skin, musculo-skeletal system and connective tissue	79	276
Congential anomalies	95	87
Certain conditions originating in the perinatal period	82	58
Signs, symptoms and ill-defined conditions	148	235
Accidents and adverse effects	739	674
Suicide and self-inflicted injury	451	148
Homicide and other violence	274	87
All causes	28,305	31,189

Source: The Stationery Office, Scottish Abstract of Statistics 1998 (Crown copyright)

MOST FREQUENTLY DIAGNOSED CANCERS 1995

By sex, and percentage change in age-standardised incidence rates 1986 to 1995

	Incidence 1995	Change 1986–95
	%	%
Males		
Lung	2,754	23.2 - 15.6
Prostate	1,703	14.3 + 48.8
Colon and rectum	1,604	13.5 + 23.2
Bladder	929	7.8 + 5.1
Stomach	595	5.0 - 25.3
Oesophagus	443	3.7 + 49.0
Non-Hodgkin's lymphoma	396	3.3 + 25.4
Kidney	315	2.7 + 23.2
Leukaemia	268	2.3 + 9.2
Pancreas	251	2.1 - 19.0
All malignant neoplasms*	11,878	100.0 + 7.4
Females		
Breast	3,168	25.2 + 27.4
Lung	1,822	14.5 + 18.1
Colon and rectum	1,647	13.1 + 4.8

Ovary	509	4.1	- 6.1
Bladder	454	3.6	+ 12.5
Stomach	417	3.3	- 26.7
Corpus uteri	400	3.2	+ 14.2
Malignant melanoma of skin	393	3.1	+ 36.2
Non-Hodgkin's lymphoma	367	2.9	+ 31.9
Oesophagus	339	2.7	+ 47.7
All malignant neoplasms*	12,553	100.0	+ 12.9

*Excluding non-melanoma skin cancer
Source: Scottish Office, Health in Scotland 1997 (Crown copyright)

NOTIFICATIONS OF SELECTED INFECTIOUS DISEASES

	1996	1997
All diseases	39,642	42,421
Of which:		
Bacillary dysentery	176	124
Chickenpox	28,509	33,413
Cholera	3	1
Diphtheria	2	1
Food poisoning*	10,234	10,144
Legionellosis	17	21
Malaria	70	57
Measles	1,055	762
Meningococcal infection	201	271
Mumps	368	282
Rubella	2,449	818
Scarlet fever	750	645
Tuberculosis (respiratory)	406	335
Tuberculosis (non-respiratory)	103	98
Viral hepatitis	360	359
Whooping cough	186	545

*Including E.coli 157:H7 outbreak, November 1996
Source: Scottish Office, Health in Scotland 1997 (Crown copyright)

AIDS CASES REGISTERED IN SCOTLAND 1981–97

	Male	Female	Total
Cumulative total to 30 September 1997	715	175	890
Transmission categories			
Intravenous drug user	228	96	324
Sexual intercourse between men*	356	—	356
Sexual intercourse between men and women	74	64	138
Haemophiliac	35	—	35
Recipient of blood or blood product	9	6	15
Mother to child	4	8	12
Other/undetermined	9	1	10

*Figures include several males who are also injecting drug users
Source: The Stationery Office, Scottish Abstract of Statistics 1998 (Crown copyright)

AIDS DEATHS REGISTERED IN SCOTLAND 1981–97

	Male	Female	Total
Cumulative total to 30 September 1997	562	122	684
Transmission categories			
Intravenous drug user	186	75	261
Sexual intercourse between men*	275	—	275
Sexual intercourse between men and women	53	35	88
Haemophiliac	32	—	32
Recipient of blood or blood product	7	6	13
Mother to child	4	5	9
Other/undetermined	5	1	6

Figures include several males who are also injecting drug users
Source: The Stationery Office, Scottish Abstract of Statistics 1998 (Crown copyright)

HIV-INFECTED PERSONS 1981–97

	Male	Female	Total
Cumulative total to 30 September 1997	2,032	644	2,676
Transmission categories			
Intravenous drug user	786	355	1,141
Sexual intercourse between men*	868	—	868
Sexual intercourse between men and women	212	244	456
Haemophiliac	84	—	84
Recipient of blood or blood product	17	15	32
Mother to child	12	14	26
Other/undetermined	53	16	69

Figures include several males who are also injecting drug users
Source: The Stationery Office, Scottish Abstract of Statistics 1998 (Crown copyright)

SEXUALLY TRANSMITTED INFECTIONS*

	1995–6	1996–7
Males	9,303	9,455
Females	8,688	8,918

New cases of syphilis, gonorrhea, chlamydia, genital herpes, genital warts, trichomoniasis, bacterial vaginosis, non-specific genital infections and other sexually transmitted infections seen at genito-urinary clinics
Source: The Stationery Office, Scottish Abstract of Statistics 1998 (Crown copyright)

ADMISSIONS TO MENTAL ILLNESS HOSPITALS AND PSYCHIATRIC UNITS, BY SEX 1996*

	Male No.	Male Rate†	Female No.	Female Rate†
Senile and presenile organic psychotic conditions	2,295	92.3	3,438	130.1
Alcohol psychosis, alcohol dependence syndrome	2,251	90.6	968	36.6
Drug abuse	849	34.2	408	15.4
Schizophrenic psychoses	2,317	93.2	1,268	48.0
Affective psychoses	1,320	53.1	2,179	82.5
Other psychoses	1,241	49.9	1,362	51.5
Disorders of childhood	20	0.8	15	0.6
Neurotic disorders	294	11.8	428	16.2
Depressions (non-psychotic)	2,045	82.3	3,691	139.7
Personality disorders	293	11.8	379	14.3
Mental handicap	30	1.2	29	1.1
Other conditions	1,048	42.2	1,335	50.5
All diagnoses	14,003	563.3	15,500	567.7

Figures for year ending 31 March 1996; figures are provisional
†Rate per 100,000
Source: Scottish Office, Scottish Abstract of Statistics 1998 (Crown copyright)

PREVALENCE OF CIGARETTE SMOKING (SELF-REPORTED) AMONG ADULTS (1995 BASED)

Percentages among adults aged 16–64, by sex

Men: number supplying data	3,902
Current smoker*	34%
Former regular smoker	21%
Never regular smoker/never smoked	45%
Women: number supplying data	3,992
Current smoker	36%
Former regular smoker	16%
Never regular smoker/never smoked	49%

Includes those who smoked less than one cigarette per day on average
Source: Scottish Office, Scottish Health Survey 1995 (Crown copyright)

PEOPLE WHO HAVE EVER TAKEN DRUGS 1996

By type of drug, sex and age (percentage)

	Males						Females						All ages 16–59
	16–19	20–24	25–29	30–39	40–59	Total	16–19	20–24	25–29	30–39	40–59	Total	
Any drug	40.1	49.5	42.3	32.4	11.	26.7	38.2	42.5	27.6	14.2	10.6	19.1	22.5
Cannabis	38.6	45.0	38.3	28.1	8.8	23.3	35.7	38.5	23.9	11.8	5.7	15.3	19.0
Amphetamines	14.2	23.0	20.0	11.4	1.6	9.4	16.3	21.4	9.3	2.4	0.6	5.5	7.3
LSD	15.9	22.8	14.2	7.3	1.7	8.0	11.5	12.2	4.3	1.3	0.7	3.4	5.5
Psilocybin	15.0	25.7	13.3	8.4	0.6	7.9	7.7	5.8	6.5	2.0	0.2	2.6	5.1
Ecstasy	12.7	22.7	7.5	2.9	0.2	5.3	8.8	11.9	3.8	1.1	0.1	2.7	4.0
Temazepam	8.5	16.6	4.5	3.8	1.3	4.6	7.6	9.9	3.2	1.5	1.0	2.9	3.7
Valium	2.9	11.6	3.3	3.5	3.6	4.4	4.2	7.1	3.2	1.5	1.0	4.1	4.2
Solvents	6.6	8.2	6.1	2.7	0.1	2.8	3.2	4.8	3.1	0.7	0.2	1.4	2.1
Cocaine	2.2	12.1	4.4	5.3	0.8	3.7	6.4	5.3	2.5	1.1	0.1	1.7	2.6
Crack	0.0	1.6	2.0	0.8	0.2	0.7	3.4	1.2	0.5	0.8	0.0	0.7	0.7
Heroin	0.0	3.5	2.5	1.7	0.2	1.2	3.4	0.3	0.6	0.7	0.0	0.5	0.8
Methadone	1.0	4.0	2.4	1.5	0.3	1.3	3.6	1.3	0.6	0.7	0.0	0.7	0.9

Source: The Stationery Office, Scottish Crime Survey 1996 (Crown copyright)

CONSUMPTION OF SELECTED FOODS 1995

Men

Butter or hard margarine	24%
Soft margarine	24%
Reduced fat spread	16%
Low fat spread	31%
No spread used	5%
Whole milk	36%
Semi-skimmed milk	57%
Skimmed milk	6%
Other milk	0%
Wholemeal bread	16%
Brown, granary, wheatmeal bread	15%
White or softgrain bread	69%
Eats cereal	68%
Does not eat cereal	32%

Women

Butter or hard margarine	22%
Soft margarine	20%
Reduced fat spread	15%
Low fat spread	35%
No spread used	8%
Whole milk	29%
Semi-skimmed milk	59%
Skimmed milk	11%
Other milk	1%
Wholemeal bread	23%
Brown, granary, wheatmeal bread	19%
White or softgrain bread	58%
Eats cereal	71%
Does not eat cereal	29%

Source: Scottish Office, Scottish Health Survey 1995 (Crown copyright)

FREQUENCY OF CONSUMPTION OF SELECTED FOODS 1995

Men

Eats meat daily	6%
Eats fruit daily	39%
Eats cooked green vegetables daily	26%
Eats chips daily	5%

Women

Eats meat daily	3%
Eats fruit daily	52%
Eats cooked green vegetables daily	30%
Eats chips daily	2%

Source: Scottish Office, Scottish Health Survey 1995 (Crown copyright)

HEALTH TARGETS FOR SCOTLAND

A White Paper on public health in Scotland, *Towards a Healthier Scotland*, was published in February 1999. This announced initiatives to improve the health of people in Scotland, including prevention and early detection of cancer and coronary heart disease and redressing inequalities in health between richer and poorer communities in Scotland, and set targets to measure the impact of these measures by 2010. In certain fields, targets for 2000 already existed. Targets set for 2010 include:

— reducing by 20 per cent the death rate from all cancers of Scots under 75

— reducing by 50 per cent adult deaths from heart disease

— reducing by 50 per cent the death rate from cerebrovascular disease in Scots under 75

— eliminating dental disease in 60 per cent of five-year-olds
— reducing incidence of smoking by pregnant women from 29 to 20 per cent, and by young people by 20 per cent
— reducing the pregnancy rate among 13–15 year olds by 20 per cent
— reducing alcohol consumption exceeding recommended weekly limits from 33 to 29 per cent for men and from 13 to 11 per cent for women
— increasing the proportion of people taking 30 minutes of moderate exercise five or more times a week to 60 per cent of men and 50 per cent of women

Four 'demonstration projects' announced in the White Paper will concentrate on child health, sexual health, cancer and coronary heart disease.

A network of Healthy Living Centres promoting best practice in public health was announced in 1998, with £34.5 million funding over three years from the National Lottery's New Opportunities Fund.

DIET

Government plans to improve the Scottish diet were first outlined in 1991. *The Report on the Scottish Diet* (the James Report) was published in 1993 and, after further consultation, led to the announcement of the Scottish Diet Action Plan. This set targets for healthier eating among people in Scotland by 2005. These targets have now been incorporated into the *Towards a Healthier Scotland* programme, and include:

— increasing average daily intake of non-sugar carbohydrates by 25 per cent through increased consumption of fruit, vegetables, bread (especially wholemeal and brown breads), breakfast cereals, rice, pasta and potato
— reducing average daily intake of fats to no more than 35 per cent, and of saturated fatty acids to no more than 11 per cent, of food energy
— reducing average daily sodium intake (from common salt and other sodium salts such as sodium glutamate) to 100 mmol
— reducing children's average daily intake of NME sugars by half to less than 10 per cent of total food energy
— doubling average weekly consumption of oil-rich fish
— increasing to over 50 per cent the proportion of mothers breastfeeding their babies for the first six weeks

THE NATIONAL HEALTH SERVICE

The National Health Service (NHS) came into being on 5 July 1948. Its function is to provide a comprehensive health service designed to secure improvement in the physical and mental health of the population and to prevent, diagnose and treat illness. It was founded on the principle that treatment should be provided according to clinical need rather than ability to pay, and should be free at the point of delivery. However, prescription charges and charges for some dental and ophthalmic treatment have been introduced over the years.

The NHS covers a comprehensive range of hospital, specialist, family practitioner (medical, dental, ophthalmic and pharmaceutical), artificial limb and appliance, ambulance, and community health services. Everyone normally resident in the UK is entitled to use any of these services.

STRUCTURE

The structure of the NHS underwent a series of reorganisations in the 1970s and, especially, the 1990s. The National Health Service and Community Care Act 1990 introduced the concept of an 'internal market' in health care provision, whereby care was provided through NHS contracts, with health authorities or boards and GP fundholders (the purchasers) being responsible for buying health care from hospitals, non-fundholding GPs, community services and ambulance services (the providers). The Act provided for the establishment of NHS Trusts. These operate as self-governing health care providers independent of health authority control and responsible to the Minister for Health. They derive their income principally from contracts to provide services to health authorities and fund-holding GPs. The community care reforms, introduced in 1993, govern the way care is administered for elderly people, the mentally ill, the physically handicapped and people with learning disabilities.

The Scottish Executive Health Department is responsible for health policy and the administration of the NHS in Scotland. The NHS in Scotland is currently administered by health boards, which are responsible for health services in their areas and also for assessing the health care needs of the local population and developing integrated strategies for meeting these needs in partnership with GPs and in consultation with the public, hospitals and others. The health boards are overseen by the

Management Executive at the Scottish Executive Health Department. There are also local health councils, whose role is to represent the interests of the public to health authorities and boards.

PROPOSED REFORMS

In July 1999, responsibility for administering the NHS in Scotland was devolved from the Secretary of State for Scotland to the Scottish Executive. The White Paper *Designed to Care*, presented to Parliament by the then Secretary of State for Scotland, Donald Dewar, in 1997, lays the foundations for the work of the Scottish Parliament in developing Scotland's devolved health care service provision. The White Paper proposed several reforms, including the establishment of primary care trusts and the replacement of GP fundholding by networks of GPs organised in local health care co-operatives.

The primary health trusts will be responsible for the planning and provision of all primary health care, including mental health services and community hospitals. Their role will include support to general practice in delivering integrated primary health care services, strategic planning and policy development, and promoting improvements in the quality and standards of clinical care. The organisation of GPs into local health care co-operatives emphasises collective health care provision on a community basis. The co-operatives will have the option of holding budgets for providing primary and community services, and the present fundholding management allowance will be redirected towards their development.

Other reforms proposed in the White Paper include:

— a review of acute services, reduction and restructuring of the number of acute hospital trusts
— a single stream of funds to cover both hospital services and drugs
— development of health improvement programmes
— one-stop clinics that will provide tests, results and diagnosis on the same day
— use of new technology to support services, e.g. electronic links between all GP surgeries
— establishment of a Scottish health technology assessment centre
— establishment of a process of quality assurance for clinical services

FINANCE

The NHS is still funded mainly (81.5 per cent) through general taxation, although in recent years greater reliance has been placed on the NHS element of National Insurance contributions, patient charges and other sources of income. Total UK expenditure on the NHS in 1997–8 was £44,719 million, of which £42,787 million derived from public monies and £1,932 million from patient charges and other receipts. NHS expenditure represented 5.7 per cent of GDP.

The Government announced in July 1998 that an additional £21,000 million would be spent on the NHS between 1999 and 2002.

NET COSTS OF THE NATIONAL HEALTH SERVICE IN SCOTLAND 1996–7

Central administration	£8,378,000
Total NHS cost	4,377,923,000
NHS contributions	468,770,000
Net costs to Exchequer	3,909,153,000
Health Board administration	89,282,000
Hospital and community health services	3,108,575,000
Family practitioner services	986,616,000
Central health services	120,586,000
State Hospital*	22,400,000
Training	3,326,000
Research	10,517,000
Disabled services	2,331,000
Welfare foods	13,835,000
Miscellaneous health services	20,455,000
Total	4,386,301,000

Under the direct responsibility of the Scottish Executive Health Department
Source: Scottish Office, Scottish Abstract of Statistics 1998 (Crown copyright)

NET EXPENDITURE 1996-7[1]

| | Revenue expenditure[2] | | Capital expenditure[3] | |
	Total £'000	Per capita	Total £'000	Per capita
Argyll and Clyde	353,509	789	9,355	21
Ayrshire and Arran	292,473	769	11,316	30
Borders	92,403	804	2,293	20
Dumfries and Galloway	128,779	796	2,575	16
Fife	260,858	776	5,968	18
Forth Valley	210,368	794	5,597	21
Grampian	401,386	822	16,123	33
Greater Glasgow	822,428	837	43,778	45
Highland	179,339	817	10,070	46
Lanarkshire	408,409	773	11,962	23
Lothian	599,003	829	18,409	25
Orkney	19,589	970	685	34
Shetland	21,022	862	304	12
Tayside	359,157	859	29,518	71
Western Isles	33,535	909	1,106	30
State Hospital	17,386		5,014	
Central Services Agency	106,380		2,852	
Scottish Ambulance Service	75,756		6,874	
Total	4,381,780	813	183,799	33

1. Data taken from the unaudited accounts of health boards
2. Includes health care purchases and the costs of purchasing and administration
3. Includes expenditure incurred by NHS Trusts in health board areas
Source: Scottish Office, Scottish Abstract of Statistics 1998 (Crown copyright) Employees

NHS EMPLOYEES IN SCOTLAND

Full-time equivalent[1] as at 30 September 1997

Medical[2]	11,214.7
Hospital[3]	7,079.5
General practitioners[4]	3,767.0
Community	368.3
Dental[2]	2,398.6
Hospital[3]	215.7
General practitioners[5]	1,941.0
Community	241.9
Nursing and midwifery[6]	51,468.4
Scientific and professional	1,559.1
Clinical psychologists	463.2
Clinical scientists	487.6
Optometrists[7]	20.3
Pharmacists[7]	588.0
Professions allied to medicine	6,406.7
Technical	5,313.9
Ambulance	2,327.3
Works	358.6
Senior management	2,360.0
Administrative and clerical	16,467.0
Ancillary	10,767.7
Trades	1,610.6
Total staff and practitioners[8]	112,252.7

1. Figures include data for the State Hospital, Carstairs
2. Those holding maximum part-time contracts are counted as one full-time equivalent
3. Includes general medical/dental practitioners employed part-time in hospitals; they may also be counted in general practitioners
4. As at 1 October. Comprises principals, assistants, trainees and associates. Consists of full-time equivalent for unrestricted principals and numbers for all other practitioners
5. Number; comprises principals, assistants and trainees
6. The number of staff employed by the NHS in Scotland is affected by the phased transfer of basic nurse training to the higher education sector. Nurse teachers and nurses in training who are still employed by the NHS are excluded from these totals
7. Excludes high-street pharmacists and optometrists
Source: Scottish Office, Scottish Abstract of Statistics 1998 (Crown copyright)

SALARIES

General practitioners (GPs), dentists, optometrists and pharmacists are self-employed, and work for the NHS under contract. Average salaries as at 1 December 1998 were:

Consultant	£45,740—£59,040
Specialist Registrar	£22,510—£32,830
Registrar	£22,510—£27,310
Senior House Officer	£20,135—£26,910

House Officer	£16,145–£18,225
GP	*£49,030
Nursing Grades G–I (Senior Ward Sister)	£19,240–£26,965
Nursing Grade F (Ward Sister)	£16,310–£19,985
Nursing Grade E (Senior Staff Nurse)	£14,705–£17,030
Nursing Grades C–D (Staff/Enrolled Nurse)	£11,210–£14,705
Nursing Grades A–B (Nursing Auxiliary)	£8,315–£11,210

*Average intended net remuneration

HEALTH SERVICES

PRIMARY AND COMMUNITY HEALTH CARE SERVICES

Primary and community health care services comprise the family health services (i.e. the general medical, personal medical, pharmaceutical, dental, and ophthalmic services) and community services (including family planning and preventive activities such as cytology, vaccination, immunisation and fluoridation) commissioned by health boards and provided by NHS Trusts, health centres and clinics.

The primary and community nursing services include practice nurses based in general practice, district nurses and health visitors, community psychiatric nursing for mentally ill people living outside hospital, and ante- and post-natal care. Pre-school services at GP surgeries or child health clinics monitor children's physical, mental and emotional health and development, and provide advice to parents on their children's health and welfare.

The School Health Service provides for the health monitoring of schoolchildren of all ages, with a focus on prevention. The service includes medical and dental examination and advice to the local education authority, the school, the parents and the pupil of any health factors which may require special consideration during the pupil's school life.

FAMILY DOCTOR SERVICE

Any doctor may take part in the Family Doctor Service (provided the area in which he/she wishes to practise has not already an adequate number of doctors). GPs may also have private fee-paying patients.

GENERAL PRACTITIONER SERVICES 1997

Number of doctors	3,650
Average list size*	1,468
Percentage of patients with doctors in:	
single-handed practice	5.1
partnership	94.9

*Excludes doctors with restricted lists, e.g. residents in homes, schools or other institutions.
Source: Scottish Office, Scottish Abstract of Statistics 1998 (Crown copyright)

PHARMACEUTICAL SERVICE

Patients may obtain medicines, appliances and oral contraceptives prescribed under the NHS from any pharmacy whose owner has entered into arrangements to provide this service, and from specialist suppliers of medical appliances. In rural areas, where access to a pharmacy may be difficult, patients may be able to obtain medicines and other prescribed health care products from their doctor.

Except for contraceptives (for which there is no charge), a charge of £5.90 is payable for each item supplied unless the patient is exempt and a declaration of exemption on the prescription form is completed; booklet HC11, available from main post offices and local social security offices, shows which categories of people are exempt.

GENERAL PHARMACEUTICAL SERVICES 1996–7

Pharmacies open	1,142
Prescriptions dispensed	54,990,000
Average prescriptions per person	10.24
Gross cost of prescriptions	£551,220,000
Average cost per person	£102.70

Source: Scottish Office, Scottish Abstract of Statistics 1998 (Crown copyright)

DENTAL SERVICE

Dentists, like doctors, may take part in the NHS and also have private patients. They are responsible to the health boards in whose areas they provide services.

Patients may go to any dentist who is taking part in the NHS and is willing to accept them. Patients are required to pay 80 per cent of the cost of NHS dental treatment. Since 1 April 1998 the maximum charge for a course of treatment has been £340. As with pharmaceutical services, certain people are exempt from dental charges or have charges remitted; full details are given in booklet HC11.

GENERAL DENTAL SERVICES 1997

Number of dentists	1,798
Number of patients registered	
Adults	2,035,000
Children	710,000
Number of courses of treatment	4,246,000
Cost	
Gross	£154,879,000
Patient charge	£71,617,000
Average per course	£36

Source: Scottish Office, Scottish Abstract of Statistics 1998
(Crown copyright)

GENERAL OPHTHALMIC SERVICES

General ophthalmic services are administered by health boards. Testing of sight may be carried out by any ophthalmic medical practitioner or ophthalmic optician (optometrist). The optician must give the prescription to the patient, who can take this to any supplier of glasses to have them dispensed. Only registered opticians can supply glasses to children and to people registered as blind or partially sighted.

Those on a low income may qualify for help with the cost of NHS sight testing. Certain categories of people qualify for sight testing free of charge or are automatically entitled to help with the purchase of glasses under an NHS voucher scheme; booklet HC11 gives details.

Diagnosis and specialist treatment of eye conditions, and the provision of special glasses, are available through the Hospital Eye Service.

GENERAL OPHTHALMIC SERVICES 1997

Ophthalmic medical practitioners	98
Ophthalmic opticians	1,117
NHS sight tests undertaken	656,000
Voucher claims paid for by health boards	488,000
Total gross costs	£29,588,000

Source: Scottish Office, Scottish Abstract of Statistics 1998
(Crown copyright)

HOSPITALS AND OTHER SERVICES

Hospital, medical, dental, nursing, ophthalmic and ambulance services are provided by the NHS to meet all reasonable requirements. Facilities for the care of expectant and nursing mothers and young children, and other services required for the diagnosis and treatment of illness, are also provided. Rehabilitation services (occupational therapy, physiotherapy and speech therapy) may also be provided, and surgical and medical appliances are supplied where appropriate.

Specialists and consultants who work in NHS hospitals can also engage in private practice, including the treatment of their private patients in NHS hospitals.

CHARGES

Certain hospitals have accommodation in single rooms or small wards which, if not required for patients who need privacy for medical reasons, may be made available to other patients for a small charge. These patients are still NHS patients and are treated as such.

In a number of hospitals, accommodation is available for the treatment of private in-patients who undertake to pay the full commercial-rate costs of hospital accommodation and services and (usually) separate medical fees to a specialist as well.

NHS HOSPITAL ACTIVITY 1997–8[1]
Year ending 31 March

	1997	1998p
Bed complement	41,736	40,783
Average available staffed beds	38,427	36,619
In-patient discharges[2]	964,791	973,325
Mean stay (days)	11.7	11.0
Occupancy (% of beds)	80.3	80.2
In-patient true waiting list[3]	47,717	47,081
Day-case discharges	384,260	419,277
New out-patients[4]	2,675,025	2,708,811
Out-patient attendances	6,271,570	6,327,395

p provisional
1. Excludes NHS activity in joint-user and contractual hospitals
2. Comprises discharges, deaths, transfers out of hospitals and transfers between specialties within same hospital
3. Excludes day-case waiting lists and repeat and deferred waiting lists
4. At consultant clinics, including accident and emergency and genito-urinary medicine
Source: Scottish Office, Scottish Abstract of Statistics 1998
(Crown copyright)

AMBULANCE SERVICE

The NHS provides emergency ambulance services free of charge via the 999 emergency telephone service. The Scottish Ambulance Service is responsible for all ambulance provision, including the air ambulance service. It controls a fleet of dedicated emergency air ambulance helicopters and two non-dedicated fixed-wing aircraft. In 1997–8, 2,412 missions were flown (917 emergency, 652 very urgent, 354 urgent, 489 pre-planned), compared to 2,156 missions in 1996–7.

The Patient's Charter in Scotland requires emergency ambulances to respond to 95 per cent of calls within 14 minutes in areas with a high

AMBULANCE ACTIVITY
Year ending 31 March 1997

Health Board	Road Ambulance Service		Ambulance car service	
	Responses	*Total mileage*	*Patient Journeys*	*Mileage*
Argyll and Clyde	225,727	1,599,498	16,112	218,903
Ayrshire and Arran	179,037	1,649,490	11,839	266,819
Borders	66,246	760,731	5,999	197,311
Dumfries and Galloway	71,313	1,053,711	5,420	273,841
Fife	174,454	1,347,668	23,686	422,619
Forth Valley	118,800	816,400	32,865	577,998
Grampian	193,614	1,854,597	22,222	283,498
Greater Glasgow	354,170	1,820,820	165,816	1,182,437
Highland	69,812	1,592,537	8,731	403,375
Lanarkshire	230,948	1,616,190	79,004	971,388
Lothian	296,804	1,907,680	55,300	663,926
Orkney	3,038	43,779	84	2,941
Shetland	8,197	60,361	—	—
Tayside	185,879	1,635,980	44,898	577,210
Western Isles	12,129	176,639	3,229	78,826
Scotland	2,190,168	17,936,081	475,205	6,121,092

population density (over 3 persons per acre), 18 minutes in areas of medium density (0.5—3 persons per acre), and 21 minutes in areas of low density (fewer than 0.5 persons per acre). In the year ending 31 March 1997, 104,075 responses were made in high-density areas, 105,955 in medium-density areas and 34,386 in low-density areas. The percentages of calls answered within the target times were 91, 96 and 92 per cent respectively.

HOSPICES
Hospice or palliative care for patients with life-threatening illnesses may be provided at the patient's home, in a voluntary or NHS hospice, or in hospital; it is intended to ensure the best possible quality of life for patients during their illness, and to provide help and support to both patients and their families. The Scottish Partnership Agency for Palliative and Cancer Care co-ordinates NHS and voluntary hospice services.

PATIENT'S CHARTERS
The Patient's Charter sets out the rights of patients in relation to the NHS (i.e. the standards of service which all patients will receive at all times) and patients' reasonable expectations (i.e. the standards of service that the NHS aims to provide, even if they cannot in exceptional circumstances be met). The Charter covers issues such as access to services, personal treatment of patients, the provision of information, registering with a doctor, hospital waiting times, care in

hospitals, community services, ambulance waiting times, dental, optical and pharmaceutical services, and maternity services. Under the Charter, patients are guaranteed admission to a hospital within 18 months of being placed on a waiting list.

A new NHS Charter is expected to be introduced in 1999. Further information is available free of charge from the Health Information Service (Tel: 0800-665544).

Health boards, NHS Trusts and GP practices may also have their own local charters setting out the standard of service they aim to provide.

COMPLAINTS
The Patient's Charter includes the right to have any complaint about the service provided by the NHS dealt with quickly, with a full written reply being provided by a relevant chief executive. There are two levels to the NHS complaints procedure: first, resolution of a complaint locally, following a direct approach to the relevant service provider; second, an independent review procedure if the complaint is not resolved locally. As a final resort, patients may approach the Health Service Commissioner if they are dissatisfied with the response of the NHS to a complaint.

NHS TRIBUNALS
The National Health Service Tribunal (Scotland) considers representations that the continued inclusion of a doctor, dentist, optician or pharmacist on the list of a health authority or

health board would be prejudicial to the efficiency of the service concerned.

HEALTH BOARDS

The web site for the health boards is: http://www.show.scot.nhs.uk

Argyll and Clyde
Ross House, Hawkhead Road, Paisley PA2 7BN
Tel: 0141-842 7200
Fax: 0141-848 1414
Chairman, M. D. Jones
General Manager, N. McConachie

Ayrshire and Arran
PO Box 13, Boswell House, 10 Arthur Street,
Ayr KA7 1QJ
Tel: 01292-611040
Fax: 01292-885894
Chairman, Dr J. Morrow
General Manager, Mrs W. Hatton

Borders
Newstead, Melrose, Roxburghshire TD9 OSE
Tel: 01896-825500
Fax: 01896-823401
Chairman, D. A. C. Kilshaw, OBE
General Manager, Dr L. Burley

Dumfries and Galloway
Grierson House, The Crichton Hospital,
Bankend Road, Dumfries DG1 4ZG
Tel: 01387-272700
Fax: 01387-252375
Chairman, J. Ross, CBE
General Manager, N. Campbell

Fife
Springfield House, Cupar KY15 9UP
Tel: 01334-656200
Fax 01334-652210
Chairman, Mrs C. Stenhouse
General Manager, M. Murray

Forth Valley
33 Spittal Street, Stirling FK8 1DX
Tel: 01786-463031
Fax: 01786-451474
Chairman, E. Bell-Scott
General Manager, D. Hird

Grampian
Summerfield House, 2 Eday Road, Aberdeen
AB15 6RE
Tel: 01224-663456
Fax: 01224-404014
Chairman, Dr C. MacLeod, CBE
General Manager, F. E. L. Hartnett, OBE

Greater Glasgow
Dalian House, PO Box 15329, 350 St Vincent
Street, Glasgow G3 8YZ
Tel: 0141-201 4444
Fax: 0141-201 4601
Chairman, Prof. D. Hamblen
General Manager, C. J. Spry

Highland
Beechwood Park, Inverness IV2 3HG
Tel: 01463-717123
Fax: 01463-235189
Chairman, Mrs C. Thomson
General Manager (acting), E. Baigal

Lanarkshire
14 Beckford Street, Hamilton, Lanarkshire
ML3 0TA
Tel: 01698-281313
Fax: 01698-423134
Chairman, I. Livingstone, CBE
General Manager, Prof. T. A. Divers

Lothian
148 Pleasance, Edinburgh EH8 9RS
Tel: 0131-536 9000
Fax 0131-536 9009
Chairman, Mrs M. Ford
General Manager, T. Jones

Orkney
Garden House, New Scapa Road, Kirkwall,
Orkney KW15 1BQ
Tel: 01856-885400
Fax: 01856-885411
Chairman, I. Leslie
General Manager, Mrs J. Wellden

Shetland
Brevik House, South Road, Lerwick ZE1 0TG
Tel: 01595-696767
Fax: 01595-696727
Chairman, J. Telford
General Manager, B. J. Atherton

Tayside
Gateway House, Luna Place, Dundee
Technology Park, Dundee DD2 1TP
Tel: 01382-561818
Fax: 01382-424003
Chairman, Mrs F. Havenga
General Manager, T. Brett

Western Isles
37 South Beach Street, Stornoway, Isle of Lewis
HS1 2BN
Tel: 01851-702997
Fax: 01851-706720
Chairman, A. Matheson
General Manager, M. Maclennan

HEALTH PROMOTION

Health Education Board for Scotland
Woodburn House, Canaan Lane, Edinburgh
EH10 4SG
Tel: 0131-536 5500
Chairman, D. Campbell
Chief Executive, Prof. A. Tannahill

AMBULANCE

Scottish Ambulance Service
National Headquarters, Tipperlinn Road,
Edinburgh EH10 5UU
Tel: 0131-446 7000

BLOOD TRANSFUSION SERVICE

Scottish National Blood Transfusion Service
21 Ellen's Glen Road, Edinburgh EH17 7QT
Tel: 0131-536 5700
National Director, A. McMillan-Douglas

PALLIATIVE CARE

Scottish Partnership Agency for Palliative and Cancer Care
1A Cambridge Street, Edinburgh EH1 2DY
Tel: 0131-229 0538
Director, Mrs M. Stevenson

NHS TRUSTS

Aberdeen Royal Hospitals NHS Trust
Foresterhill House, Ashgrove Road West,
Aberdeen AB9 8AQ
Tel: 01224-681818

Angus NHS Trust
Whitehills Hospital, Forfar, Angus DD8 3DY
Tel: 01307-464551

Argyll and Bute NHS Trust
Aros, Lochgilphead, Argyll PA31 8LB
Tel: 01546-606600

Ayrshire and Arran Community Health Care NHS Trust
1A Hunter's Avenue, Ayr KA8 9DW
Tel: 01292-281821

Borders Community Health Services NHS Trust
Huntlyburn House, Melrose, Roxburghshire
TD6 9BP
Tel: 01896-662300

Borders General Hospital NHS Trust
Melrose, Roxburghshire TD6 9BS
Tel: 01896-754333

Caithness and Sutherland NHS Trust
Caithness General Hospital, Bankhead Road,
Wick, Caithness KW1 5NS
Tel: 01955-605050

Central Scotland Healthcare NHS Trust
Royal Scottish National Hospital, Old Denny
Road, Larbert, Stirlingshire FK5 4SD
Tel: 01324-570700

Dumfries and Galloway Acute and Maternity Hospitals NHS Trust
Bankend Road, Dumfries DG1 4AP
Tel: 01387-246246

Dumfries and Galloway Community Health NHS Trust
Crichton Hall, Crichton Royal Hospital,
Bankend Road, Dumfries DG1 4TG
Tel: 01387-255301

Dundee Healthcare NHS Trust
Royal Dundee Liff Hospital, Dundee DD2 5NF
Tel: 01382-580441

Dundee Teaching Hospitals NHS Trust
Ninewells Hospital and Medical School,
Dundee DD1 9SY
Tel: 01382-660111

East and Midlothian NHS Trust
Edenhall Hospital, Pinkieburn, Musselburgh,
Midlothian EH21 7TZ
Tel: 0131-536 8000

Edinburgh Healthcare NHS Trust
Astley Ainslie Hospital, 133 Grange Loan,
Edinburgh EH9 2HL
Tel: 0131-537 9525

Edinburgh Sick Children's NHS Trust
Royal Hospital for Sick Children, Sciennes
Road, Edinburgh EH9 1LF
Tel: 0131-536 0000

Falkirk and District Royal Infirmary NHS Trust
Major's Loan, Falkirk FK1 5QE
Tel: 01324-624000

Fife Healthcare NHS Trust
Cameron House, Cameron Bridge, Leven, Fife
KY8 5RG
Tel: 01592-712812

Glasgow Dental Hospital and School NHS Trust
378 Sauchiehall Street, Glasgow G2 3JZ
Tel: 0141-211 9600

Glasgow Royal Infirmary University NHS Trust
Glasgow Royal Infirmary, 84 Castle Street,
Glasgow G4 0SF
Tel: 0141-552 4000

Grampian Healthcare NHS Trust
Westholme, Woodend Hospital, Eday Road,
Aberdeen AB2 6LS
Tel: 01224-663131

Greater Glasgow Community and Mental Health Services NHS Trust
Gartnavel Royal Hospital, 1055 Great Western
Road, Glasgow G12 0XH
Tel: 0141-211 3600

Hairmyres and Stonehouse Hospital NHS Trust
Hairmyres Hospital, Eaglesham Road, East
Kilbride, South Lanarkshire G75 8RG
Tel: 01355-220292

Highland Communities NHS Trust
Royal Northern Infirmary, Inverness IV3 5SF
Tel: 01463-242860

Inverclyde Royal NHS Trust
Larkfield Road, Greenock, Renfrewshire
PA16 0ZN
Tel: 01475-633777

Kirkcaldy Acute Hospitals NHS Trusts
Hayfield House, Hayfield Road, Kirkcaldy, Fife
KY2 5AH
Tel: 01592-643355

Lanarkshire Healthcare NHS Trust
Strathclyde Hospital, Airbles Road, Motherwell
ML1 3BW
Tel: 01698-230500

Law Hospital NHS Trust
Carluke ML8 5ER
Tel: 01698-361100

Lomond Healthcare NHS Trust
Vale of Leven District Hospital, Main Street,
Alexandria, Dunbartonshire G83 0UA
Tel: 01389-754121

Monklands and Bellshill Hospitals NHS Trust
Monkscourt Avenue, Airdrie ML6 0JS
Tel: 01236-748748

Moray Health Services
Maryhill House, 317 High Street, Elgin,
Morayshire IV30 1AJ
Tel: 01343-543131

North Ayrshire and Arran NHS Trust
Crosshouse Hospital, Kilmarnock, Ayrshire
KA2 0BE
Tel: 01563-521133

Perth and Kinross Healthcare NHS Trust
Perth Royal Infirmary, Perth PH1 1NX
Tel: 01738-623311

Queen Margaret Hospital NHS Trust
Whitefield Road, Dunfermline, Fife KY12 0SU
Tel: 01383-623623

Raigmore Hospital NHS Trust
Old Perth Road, Inverness IV2 3UJ
Tel: 01463-704000

Renfrewshire Healthcare NHS Trust
Dykebar Hospital, Grahamston Road, Paisley
PA2 7DE
Tel: 0141-884 5122

Royal Alexandra Hospital NHS Trust
Corsebar Road, Paisley PA2 9PN
Tel: 0141-887 9111

Royal Infirmary of Edinburgh NHS Trust
1 Lauriston Place, Edinburgh EH3 9YW
Tel: 0131-536 1000

Scottish Ambulance Service NHS Trust
National Headquarters, Tipperlinn Road,
Edinburgh EH10 5UU
Tel: 0131-447 7711

South Ayrshire Hospitals NHS Trust
Ayr Hospital, Dalmellington Road, Ayr
KA6 6DX
Tel: 01292-610555

Southern General Hospital NHS Trust
Management Office, 1345 Govan Road,
Glasgow G51 4TF
Tel: 0141-201 1100

Stirling Royal Infirmary NHS Trust
Livilands, Stirling FK8 2AU
Tel: 01786-434000

Stobhill NHS Trust
133 Balornock Road, Glasgow G21 3UW
Tel: 0141-201 3000

Victoria Infirmary NHS Trust
Queens Park House, Langside Road, Glasgow
G42 9TY
Tel: 0141-201 6000

West Glasgow Hospitals University NHS Trust
Western Infirmary, Dumbarton Road, Glasgow
G11 6NT
Tel: 0141-211 2000

West Lothian NHS Trust
St John's Hospital at Howden, Howden Road
West, Livingston, West Lothian EH54 6PP
Tel: 01506-419666

Western General Hospitals NHS Trust
Western General Hospital, Crewe Road,
Edinburgh EH4 2XU
Tel: 0131-537 1000

Yorkhill NHS Trust
Royal Hospital for Sick Children, Dalnier
Street, Yorkhill, Glasgow G3 8SJ
Tel: 0141-201 4000

THE POLICE SERVICE

The Scottish Executive is responsible for the organisation, administration and operation of the police service. The Scottish Executive Justice Department works in partnership with chief constables and local police to implement this responsibility, which includes the making of regulations covering matters such as police ranks, discipline, hours of duty, and pay and allowances.

Police authorities are responsible for maintaining an effective and efficient police force in their areas. There are six joint police boards made up of local councillors; the other two police authorities are councils.

A review of the structure of police forces began in April 1998.

Police authorities are financed by central and local government grants and a precept on the council tax. They are responsible for setting a budget, providing the resources necessary to police the area adequately, appointing officers of the rank of Assistant Chief Constable and above, and determining the number of officers and civilian staff in the force.

All police forces in the UK are subject to inspection by HM Inspectors of Constabulary, who report to the Scottish Ministers.

COMPLAINTS
Chief constables are obliged to investigate a complaint against one of their officers; if there is a suggestion of criminal activity, the complaint is investigated by an independent public prosecutor.

THE SPECIAL CONSTABULARY
Each police force has its own special constabulary, made up of volunteers who work in their spare time. Special Constables have full police powers within their force and adjoining force areas, and assist regular officers with routine policing duties.

POLICE STRENGTHS
As at March 1999, there were:

Officers	14,699
men	12,374
women	2,325
Special constables	1,336
Support staff	4,721

PAY
Basic rates of pay since 1 September 1999 have been:

Chief Constable*	
No fixed term	£71,058–£101,613
Fixed term appointment	£74,616–£106,569
Chief Constable, Strathclyde	
No fixed term	£93,297–£105,291
Fixed term appointment	£97,848–£110,430
Assistant Chief Constable	
No fixed term	£59,292–£68,064
Fixed term appointment	£62,259–£71,466
Designated deputies/	The higher of 80%
Assistant Chief Constable	of their Chief
designate	Constable's basic
No fixed term	salary, or £68,064
Fixed term appointment	£71,466
Superintendent	£43,143–£53,556
Chief Inspector	£35,454–£38,307
Inspector	£31,719–£36,918
Sergeant	£24,525–£28,605
Constable	£16,056–£25,410

*Depending on the population of the police force area
Source: Home Office

SCOTTISH CRIME SQUAD

The Scottish Crime Squad investigates organised and serious crime occurring across police force boundaries and abroad. It also supports police forces investigating serious crime.

HQ, Osprey House, Inchinnan Road, Paisley
PA3 2RE
Tel: 0141-302 1000
Commander: D.C.S. Johnstone

JOINT POLICE BOARDS

The Dumfries and Galloway council area and the Fife council area do not have joint boards as a single authority covers the whole of the police area. The chairman of the authority for these two forces is given with the force's details.

Central Scotland Joint Police Board
Municipal Buildings, Falkirk FK1 5RS
Tel: 01324-506070
Fax: 01324-506071
E-mail: bpirie@falkirk-lawadmin.demon.co.uk
Convenor: I. Miller
Clerk to the Board: Ms E. Morton

Covers Clackmannanshire, Falkirk and Stirling area

Grampian Joint Police Board
Town House, Aberdeen AB10 1AQ
Tel: 01224-523010
Fax: 01224-522965
Convenor: Ms M. Stewart
Clerk to the Board: C. Langley

Covers Aberdeen City, Aberdeenshire and Moray areas

Lothian and Borders Police Board
City Chambers, High Street, Edinburgh
EH1 1YJ
Tel: 0131-529 4955
Fax: 0131-529 7607
E-mail: mike.gray@edinburgh.gov.uk
Convenor: Ms L. Hinds
Clerk and Chief Executive to the Board:
   T. N. Aitchison

Covers City of Edinburgh, East Lothian, Midlothian, Scottish Borders and West Lothian areas

Northern Joint Police Board
Council Offices, Glenurquhart Road, Inverness
IV3 5NX
Tel: 01463-702123
Fax: 01463-702182
E-mail: rhona.moir@highland.gov.uk
Convener: Ms J. Home
Clerk to the Board: J. F. P. Black

Covers Highland, Orkney Islands, Shetland Islands and Western Isles areas

Strathclyde Joint Police Board
City Chambers, George Square, Glasgow
G2 1DU
Tel: 0141-287 5894
Fax: 0141-287 4173
Chair: B. Maan
Clerk to the Board: J. Andrews

Covers Argyll and Bute, East Ayrshire, East Dunbartonshire, East Renfrewshire, Glasgow City, Inverclyde, North Ayrshire, North Lanarkshire, Renfrewshire, South Ayrshire, South Lanarkshire and West Dunbartonshire areas

Tayside Joint Police Board
St James House, St James Road, Forfar
DD8 2ZE
Tel: 01307-461460
Fax: 01307-464834
Web: http://www.taysidepolice.uk
Chair: J. Corrigan
Clerk to the Board: Ms C. Coull

Covers Angus, Dundee City, Perth and Kinross areas

POLICE FORCES

Central Scotland Police HQ
Randolphfield, Stirling FK8 2HD
Tel: 01786-456000
Fax: 01786-451177
Web: http://www.centralscotland.police.uk
Chief Constable: A. Cameron

Dumfries and Galloway Constabulary HQ
Conwall Mount, Dumfries, DG1 1PZ
Tel: 01387-252112
Fax: 01387-260501
E-mail: police@dgpcis.demon.co.uk
Web: http://www.dumfriesandgalloway.police.uk
Chief Constable W. Rae, QPM
Chair B. Conchie

Fife Constabulary HQ
Detroit Road, Glenrothes, Fife KY6 2RJ
Tel: 01592-418888
Fax: 01592-418444
E-mail: fifepolice@fife.ac.uk
Web: http://www.fife.police.uk
Chief Constable: J. P. Hamilton, QPM
Chair: A. Keddie

Grampian Police HQ
Queen Street, Aberdeen AB10 1ZA
Tel: 01224-386000
Fax: 01224-643366
Web: http://www.grampian.police.uk
Chief Constable: A. G. Brown, QPM

Lothian and Borders Police HQ
Fettes Avenue, Edinburgh EH4 1RB
Tel: 0131-311 3131
Fax: 0131-311 3038
Web: http://www.lbp.police.uk
Chief Constable Sir Roy Cameron, QPM

Northern Constabulary HQ
Old Perth Road, Inverness IV2 3SY
Tel: 01463-715555
Fax: 01463-720373
Web: http://www.northern.police.uk
Chief Constable: W. A. Robertson, QPM
Clerk: F. Black

Strathclyde Police HQ
173 Pitt Street, Glasgow G2 4JS
Tel: 0141-532 2000
Fax: 0141-532 2618
Web: http://www.strathclyde.police.uk
Chief Constable: J. Orr, OBE, QPM

Tayside Police HQ
PO Box 59, West Bell Street, Dundee DD1 9JU
Tel: 01382-223200
Fax: 01382-225772
E-mail: forcedev@tayside.police.uk
Web: http://www.tayside.police.uk
Chief Constable: W. A. Spence, QPM
Director of Law and Administration:
Ms C. Coull

OTHER POLICE FORCES

British Transport Police Scottish HQ
90 Cowcaddens Road, Glasgow G4 0LU
Tel: 0141-332 3649
Fax: 0141-335 2155
E-mail: russell.elaine.btp@ems.rail.co.uk
Web: http://www.btp.police.uk
Assistant Chief Constable, Scotland: S. Forrest

Ministry of Defence Police
Operational Command Unit HQ Scotland
HMNB Clyde, Helensburgh, Dunbartonshire
G84 8HL
Tel: 01436-674321
Operational Commander, Scotland:
Chief Supt. S. R. Mason

UK Atomic Energy Authority Constabulary
UK HQ: Building E6, Culham Science Centre,
Abingdon, Oxon OX14 3DB
Tel: 01235-463760
Fax: 01235-463764
Chief Constable: W. F. Pryke

STAFF ASSOCIATIONS

Police officers are not permitted to join a trade union or to take strike action. All ranks have their own staff associations.

Association of Chief Police Officers in Scotland
Police Headquarters, Fettes Avenue, Edinburgh
EH4 1RB
Tel: 0131-311 3051
Hon. Secretary: Sir Roy Cameron, QPM

Represents the Chief Constables, Deputy and Assistant Chief Constables of the Scottish police forces

The Association of Scottish Police Superintendents
Secretariat, 173 Pitt Street, Glasgow G2 4JS
Tel: 0141-221 5796
Fax: 0141-532 2489
E-mail: policesupts@hotmail.com
General Secretary: J. Urquhart, QPM

Represents officers of the rank of Superintendent

The Scottish Police Federation
5 Woodside Place, Glasgow, G3 7QF
Tel: 0141-332 5234
Fax: 0141-331 2436
Web: http://www.spf.org.uk
General Secretary: D. J. Keil, QPM

Represents officers up to and including the rank of Chief Inspector

THE PRISON SERVICE

The Scottish Prison Service is an Agency of the Scottish Executive. The chief executive is responsible for operational matters and performance.

There are 16 prison establishments in Scotland, housing about 6,000 prosoners The total budget is £209 million in 2000-1.

Convicted prisoners are classified according to their perceived security risk and are housed in establishments appropriate to that level of security. Female prisoners are housed in women's establishments or in separate wings of mixed prisons. Remand prisoners are, where possible, housed separately from convicted prisoners. Offenders under the age of 21 are usually detained in a young offenders' institution, which may be a separate establishment or part of a prison.

One prison, Kilmarnock, was built, financed and is being run by private contractors.

Her Majesty's Chief Inspector of Prisons is independent and reports annually to the Scottish Executive Justice Department on prison conditions and the treatment of prisoners. Every prison establishment also has an independent visiting committee made up of local volunteers appointed by the Justice Minister. Any prisoner whose complaint is not satisfied by the internal complaints procedures may complain to the Scottish Complaints Commissioner.

Women make up only 3 per cent of the Scottish prison population. Custody is less frequently used as a sanction against female offenders; in 1996, for example, only 4 per cent of women convicted of offences received a custodial sentence, whereas 11.1 per cent of all offenders received such a sentence.

AVERAGE DAILY POPULATION IN SCOTTISH PENAL ESTABLISHMENTS 1993-8

1993-4	5,588
1994-5	5,630
1995-6	5,632
1996-7	5,992
1997-8	6,059

Source: Scottish Prison Service, Annual Report and Accounts 1997-8

AVERAGE DAILY PRISON POPULATION 1997 (BY TYPE OF CUSTODY AND SEX)

	Total	Male	Female
Remand: total	947	901	46
untried	850	816	34
convicted awaiting sentence	98	86	12
Under sentence: total	5,134	4,996	138
young offenders	787	768	19
adult prisoners	4,281	4,163	118
persons recalled from supervision/licence	46	45	1
others	19	19	–
Sentenced by court martial	1	1	–
Civil prisoners	1	1	–
Total	6,083	5,899	184

Source: Scottish Office Statistical Bulletin, December 1998

AVERAGE DAILY SENTENCED POPULATION BY LENGTH OF SENTENCE 1997-8

	Adults	Young Offenders
Less than 4 years	2,141	574
4 years or over (including life)	2,218	200
Total	4,359	774

Source: Scottish Prison Service, Annual Report and Accounts 1997-8

RECEPTIONS TO PENAL ESTABLISHMENTS BY TYPE OF CUSTODY 1997-8

Remand: total	14,723
untried	11,711
convicted awaiting sentence	3,012
Under sentence: total	21,352
young offenders	4,433
adult prisoners	16,906
persons recalled from supervision/licence	13
Persons sentenced by court martial	6
Civil prisoners	21

Total receptions cannot be calculated by adding together receptions in each category because persons received first on remand and then under sentence in relation to the same set of charges are counted in both categories

Source: Scottish Prison Service, Annual Report and Accounts 1997-8

MAIN CRIMES AND OFFENCES OF SENTENCED PRISONERS IN CUSTODY ON 30 JUNE 1997

Main crime/offence	Total	Male	Female
Non-sexual crimes of violence: total	2,188	2,146	42
homicide	644	631	13
robbery	699	697	2
Crimes of indecency: total	354	351	3
sexual assault	161	161	–
Crimes of dishonesty	1,062	1,018	44
Fire-raising, vandalism, etc.	69	68	1
Other crimes: total	788	757	31
drugs offences	702	674	28
Total crimes	4,461	4,340	121
Miscellaneous offences	450	435	15
Motor vehicle offences	231	229	2
Total offences	681	664	17
Unknown charge	8	8	–
Other jurisdiction charge	27	27	–
Total crimes and offences	5,177	5,039	138

Source: Scottish Office Statistical Bulletin, December 1998

PRISON SUICIDES 1997–8

	1996	1997	1998
Male	13	13	12
Female	3	1	1
Total	16	14	13

Source: Scottish Prison Service

OPERATING COSTS OF THE SCOTTISH PRISON SERVICE 1997–8

£	
Total income	1,598,000
Total expenditure	172,071,000
Staff costs	110,874,000
Running costs	47,675,000
Other current expenditure	13,522,000
Operating deficit	(170,473,000)
Interest on capital	(23,199,000)
Interest payable and similar charges	(15,000)
Interest receivable	145,000
Deficit for financial year	(193,542,000)

Average annual cost per prisoner per place 26,170

Source: Scottish Prison Service, Annual Report and Accounts 1997–8

SCOTTISH PRISON SERVICE

Calton House, 5 Redheughs Rigg, Edinburgh
EH12 9HW
Tel: 0131-556 8400

SALARIES
The following pay bands have applied since 1 October 1999:

I £36,725 – £56,700
H £30,600 – £47,275
G £25,600 – £38,925
F £19,550 – £30,050/£33,350
E £15,600 – £24,550/£27,800
D £12,500 – £19,550/£23,350
C £10,200 – £15,600/£17,850
B £8,500 – £12,500
A £8,500 – £10,500

Bands C to F have a normal maximum and an operational maximum rate

STAFF
The number of Scottish Prison Service staff (full-time and part-time) in post at 31 March 1998 was 4,856, of whom 4,069 were male and 787 female.

Chief Executive of Scottish Prison Service: Tony Cameron
Director of Custody: John Durno, OBE
Director, Human Resources: Peter Russell
Director, Finance and Information Systems: Willie Pretswell
Director, Strategy and Corporate Affairs: Ms Jinny Hutchison
Deputy Director, Regime Services and Supplies: John McNeill
Deputy Director, Estates and Buildings: David Bentley
Area Director, South and West: Mike Duffy
Area Director, North and East: Peter Withers
Head of Training, Scottish Prison Service College: Jack Matthews
Head of Communications: vacant

PRISON ESTABLISHMENTS

The figures given here refer to the average number of prisoners/young offenders in 1999–2000.

PRISON ESTABLISHMENTS

The figures given here refer to the average number of prisoners/young offenders in 1998–9.

* **Aberdeen**
Craiginches, Aberdeen AB9 2HN
Prisoners: 181
Governor: I. Gunn

Barlinnie
Barlinnie, Glasgow G33 2QX
Prisoners: 1,124
Governor: R. L. Houchin

Castle Huntly
Castle Huntly, Longforgan, Nr. Dundee DD2 5HL
Prisoners: 106
Governor: K. Rennie

*‡ **Cornton Vale**
Cornton Road, Stirling FK9 5NY
Prisoners and Young Offenders: 180
Governor: Mrs K. Donegan

*‡ **Dumfries**
Terregles Street, Dumfries DG2 9AX
Young Offenders: 137
Governor: G. Taylor

Dungavel
Dungavel House, Strathaven, Lanarkshire ML10 6RF
Prisoners: 113
Governor: T. Pitt

Edinburgh
33 Stenhouse Road, Edinburgh EH1 3LN
Prisoners: 731
Governor: A. Spencer

Friarton
Friarton, Perth PH2 8DW
Prisoners: 77
Governor: Mrs A. Mooney

‡ **Glenochil**
King O'Muir Road, Tullibody,
Clackmannanshire FK10 3AD
Prisoners and Young Offenders: 573
Governor: L. McBain, obe

Greenock
Gateside, Greenock PA16 9AH
Prisoners: 236
Governor: R. MacCowan

* **Inverness**
Porterfield, Inverness IV2 3HH
Prisoners: 122
Governor: H. Ross

Kilmarnock
Bowhouse, Mauchline Road, Kilmarnock KA1 5JH
Prisoners: 500
Director: J. Bywalec

Longriggend
Longriggend, nr Airdrie, Lanarkshire ML6 7TL
Prisoners: 158
Governor: Ms R. Kite

Low Moss
Low Moss, Bishopbriggs, Glasgow G64 2QB
Prisoners: 362
Governor: E. Murch

National Induction Unit
Shotts ML7 4LE
Prisoners: 48
Governor: J. Gerrie

Noranside
Noranside, Fern, by Forfar, Angus DD8 3QY
Prisoners: 102
Governor: A. MacDonald

Penninghame
Penninghame, Newton Stewart DG8 6RG
Prisoners: 89
Governor: S. Swan

Perth
3 Edinburgh Road, Perth PH2 8AT
Prisoners: 477
Governor: W. Millar

Peterhead
Salthouse Head, Peterhead, Aberdeenshire AB4 6YY
Prisoners: 297
Governor: W. Rattray
Governor, Peterhead Unit: B. McConnell

‡ **Polmont**
Brightons, Falkirk, Stirlingshire FK2 0AB
Young Offenders: 443
Governor: D. Gunn

Shotts
Shotts ML7 4LF
Prisoners: 467
Governor: W. McKinlay
Governor, Shotts Unit: G. Storer

* *Women's establishments or establishments with units for women*

‡ *Young Offender Institution or establishment with units for young offenders*

SOCIAL SERVICES

Social work services became a devolved responsibility on 1 July 1999. The children's services functions of the Social Work Services Group have passed to the Children and Young People Group of the Scottish Executive Education Department. The community care functions of the Social Work Services Group have passed to the Scottish Executive Health Department. (The Social Work Services Group within the Scottish Executive Justice Department retains only its criminal justice social work functions.)

Social work services for elderly people, disabled people, families and children, and those with mental disorders are administered by local authorities according to policies and standards set by the Scottish Executive. Each authority has a Director of Social Work and a Social Work Committee responsible for the social services functions placed upon them. Local authorities provide, enable and commission care after assessing the needs of their population. The private and voluntary sectors also play an important role in the delivery of social services.

The community care reforms introduced in 1993 were intended to enable vulnerable groups to live in the community rather than in residential homes wherever possible, and to offer them as independent a lifestyle as possible.

At 31 March 1997 in Scotland, there were 24,000 beds in residential care homes, 37,000 public-sector sheltered houses and 19,000 day care places. A total of 84,000 clients received home care.

FINANCE

The Personal Social Services programme is financed partly by central government, with decisions on expenditure allocations being made at local authority level.

TOTAL PUBLIC EXPENDITURE ON SOCIAL WORK 1995-6

£ million

	Current	Capital	Total
Central government*	46.7	1.3	48.0
Local authority†	1,060.9	32.2	1,093.1
TOTAL	1,107.6	33.5	1,141.1

* Includes grants to former list 'D' schools and to voluntary bodies, and certain specific grants by central government to local authorities
† Includes an allocation of central administration costs
Source: Scottish Office, Scottish Abstract of Statistics 1998 (Crown copyright)

NET REVENUE EXPENDITURE OF LOCAL AUTHORITIES ON SOCIAL WORK 1995-6

£million

Administration and casework	175.0
Residential care of children	102.7
Residential care of older people	153.0
Residential care of people with learning disabilities or mental health problems	42.4
Residential care of physically disabled people	10.7
Day care of children	31.2
Day centres for people with learning disabilities or mental health problems	52.4
Day centres for physically disabled people	11.6
Home help services	130.9
Children's panels	8.1
Other services	234.0
Loan charges	40.7
TOTAL	952.1

Source: The Stationery Office, Scottish Abstract of Statistics 1998 (Crown copyright)

STAFF

STAFF OF LOCAL AUTHORITY SOCIAL WORK DEPARTMENTS 1997*

Central/strategic, fieldwork and special location staff	13,494
Home care staff	10,866
Day centre staff	3,876
Residential care staff	8,160
Secondment	74
Total staff	36,470

*Figures are provisional, and exclude the Scottish Borders
Source: The Stationery Office, Scottish Abstract of Statistics 1998 (Crown copyright)

ELDERLY PEOPLE

Services for elderly people are designed to enable them to remain living in their own homes for as long as possible. Local authority services include advice, domestic help, meals in the home, alterations to the home to aid mobility, emergency alarm systems, day and/or night attendants, laundry services and the provision of day centres and recreational facilities. Charges may be made for these services. Respite care may also be provided in order to allow carers temporary relief from their responsibilities.

Local authorities and the private sector also provide 'sheltered housing' for elderly people, sometimes with resident wardens.

If an elderly person is admitted to a residential home, charges are made according to a means test; if the person cannot afford to pay, the costs are met by the local authority.

RESIDENTIAL CARE HOMES FOR OLDER PEOPLE 1997

	Local authority homes	Registered homes*	All homes
No. homes	246	418	664
No. beds	7,694	8,833	16,527
No. residents†	7,108	7,661	14,769
Ratio of residents/ full-time staff	1.2	1.2	1.2
Average home size	31	22	25

*Private and voluntary
† Includes holiday/respite residents
Source: SOHD, Community Care, Scotland 1997 (Crown copyright)

DISABLED PEOPLE

The group of physically disabled people consists mainly of those who have a disability unrelated to normal ageing. Services for disabled people are designed to enable them to remain living in their own homes wherever possible. Local authority services include advice, adaptations to the home, meals in the home, help with personal care, occupational therapy, educational facilities and recreational facilities. Respite care may also be provided in order to allow carers temporary relief from their responsibilities.

Special housing may be available for disabled people who can live independently, and residential accommodation for those who cannot.

RESIDENTIAL CARE HOMES FOR PEOPLE WITH PHYSICAL DISABILITIES 1997

Number of homes	41
Number of beds	839
Number of residents (including holiday/respite residents)	726
Ratio of residents/full-time staff	0.7
Average home size	20

Source: SOHD, Community Care, Scotland 1997 (Crown copyright)

FAMILIES AND CHILDREN

Local authorities are required to provide services aimed at safeguarding the welfare of children in need and, wherever possible, allowing them to be brought up by their families. Services include advice, counselling, help in the home and the provision of family centres. Many authorities also provide short-term refuge accommodation for women and children.

DAY CARE

In allocating day-care places to children, local authorities give priority to children with special needs, whether in terms of their health, learning abilities or social needs. They also provide a registration and inspection service in relation to childminders, playgroups and private day nurseries in the local authority area.

A national child care strategy is being developed by the Government, under which day care and out-of-school child care facilities will be extended to match more closely the needs of working parents.

A survey in 1997 of 3,540 facilities providing daycare for children in Scotland found that there were about 91,000 term-time places and 49,000 places in school holiday time for children under eight. About 113,500 children attended the facilities, 38 per cent of them for all or part of each day Monday to Friday. Of the different facilities, 46 per cent were playgroups and 28 per cent were nurseries. The largest age group attending these was that of three- and four-year-olds. There were also playschemes, out-of-school care schemes, crèches and family centres. Over 24,000 adults (paid staff and volunteers) were involved in day care, of whom 93 per cent were women, 31 per cent were full-time workers, and 63 per cent were paid staff.

There were also 8,243 childminders registered with local authorities, looking after 34,983 children under eight.

Source: SWSG, Social Work Daycare Services for Children in Scotland, November 1997 (Crown copyright)

CHILD PROTECTION

Children considered to be at risk of physical injury, neglect or sexual abuse are made subject to a case conference and placed on the local authority's child protection register. Local authority social services staff, school nurses, health visitors and other agencies work together to prevent and detect cases of abuse. In Scotland in 1995–6 1,024 boys and 1,083 girls were reported as having been subject to case conferences. Of these, 15.0 per cent were judged to be at risk of neglect, 30.8 per cent of physical injury, 17.5 per cent of sexual abuse and 5.8 per cent of emotional abuse. More boys than girls suffered physical injury, while twice as many girls as boys were victims of sexual abuse.

LOCAL AUTHORITY CARE

The Children in Care (Scotland) Act 1995 governs the provision by local authorities of accommodation for children who have no parent or guardian or whose parents or guardians are unable or unwilling to care for them. A family proceedings court may also issue a care order in cases where a child is being neglected or abused, or is not attending school; the court must be satisfied that this would positively contribute to the well-being of the child.

Children who are being looked after by local authorities may live at home, with friends or relatives, in other community accommodation, with foster carers who receive payments to cover the expenses of caring for the child or children, or in residential care. Children's homes may be run by the local authority or by the private or voluntary sectors; all homes are subject to inspection procedures.

CHILDREN IN CARE/LOOKED AFTER*

As at 31 March

	1997		1998	
	No.	%	No.	%
Male	6,629	58	6,279	58
Female	4,728	42	4,512	42
Total	11,357	100	10,791	100

Figures include estimates for those authorities that were unable to provide data
Source: Scottish Office, Statistical Bulletin (Crown copyright)

At 31 March 1998 a total of 10,791 children (an average of 9.4 children per 1,000 members of the population aged 0–17 years) was being looked after. About 51 per cent of these were living at home; 25 per cent were with foster carers, 17 per cent were in residential care and 7 per cent were living with friends or relatives or in other community accommodation (*Source:* Scottish Office, *Statistical Bulletin* (Crown copyright)).

The number of children being looked after varies considerably from authority to authority, depending on factors such as the size of the authority, the size and age structure of the local population, and the authority's policy and resources.

The implementation of the Children in Care (Scotland) Act 1995 extended the powers and responsibilities of local authorities to look after children who would previously have left care at the age of 16. Also, a number of respite placements which were not hitherto considered as care now fall within the definition of being 'looked after'. Thus, although the number of children being looked after has been falling steadily for some years, the number of older teenagers in care increased between 1997 and 1998. The largest proportion of children being looked after is in the age band 12–16 years (45.7 per cent in 1998). Boys outnumber girls in all age bands.

ADOPTION

Local authorities are required to provide an adoption service, either directly or via approved voluntary societies. The number of adoption applications in Scotland has fallen steadily over the last decade, to only a little over half as many applications in 1998 as in 1988. Applications in 1998 were taken out for 469 children, 211 boys and 257 girls. The largest age group of children for whom adoption applications are made is 5–11 years, with the average age of children for whom applications are made being just under seven years. Less than 10 per cent of applications are made for children less than one year old.

PEOPLE WITH LEARNING DISABILITIES

Services for people with learning disabilities (i.e. mental handicap) are designed to enable them to remain living in the community wherever possible. Local authority services include short-term care, support in the home, the provision of day care centres, and help with other activities outside the home. Residential care is provided for the severely or profoundly disabled, generally in small or group homes. In 1997 more than 75 per cent of homes had ten beds or fewer. Over 20 per cent of the people admitted to this type of home in 1997 were aged 15–20, while only 6 per cent of residents were over 65.

PEOPLE WITH LEARNING DISABILITIES RESIDENT IN HOSPITALS AND HOMES AND ATTENDING DAY CENTRES

As at 31 March

	1996	1997
Hospitals, no. residents	3,218	n/a
Homes, no. residents	4,075	4,491
Daycare centres, persons on register	7,555	8,054

Source: Scottish Office Home Department, Community Care, Scotland 1997 (Crown copyright)

PEOPLE WITH MENTAL HEALTH PROBLEMS

Under the Care Programme Approach, mentally ill people should be assessed by specialist services and receive a care plan, and a key worker should be appointed for each patient. Regular reviews of the patient's progress should be conducted. Local authorities provide help and advice to mentally ill people and their families, and places in day centres and social centres. Social workers can apply for a mentally disturbed person to be compulsorily detained in hospital. Where appropriate, mentally ill people are provided with accommodation in special hospitals or in residential homes. These are generally small homes, most commonly run by voluntary organisations.

Mental Illness Specific Grants assist projects addressing care for people with mental health problems. In 1996–7, 371 such projects were supported by grants.

In July 1998 the Government announced that the system of care for mentally ill people would be reorganised and the Mental Health (Scotland) Act 1984 reviewed. The review committee is to report in summer 2000.

PEOPLE WITH MENTAL HEALTH PROBLEMS RESIDENT IN HOSPITALS AND HOMES AND ATTENDING DAY CENTRES

As at 31 March

	1996	1997
Hospitals, no. residents	10,216	n/a
Homes, no. residents	1,146	1,192
Daycare centres, persons on register	1,350	1,695

Source: SOHD, Community Care, Scotland 1997 (Crown copyright)

TRANSPORT

CIVIL AVIATION

UK airlines are operated entirely by the private sector. Scottish airports are served by several major British airlines, including British Airways, Air UK, Britannia Airways, British Midland, Monarch Airlines and EasyJet; by British Airways franchise Loganair (which operates several inter-island services) and franchised partner British Regional Airlines, and by other airlines such as Highland Airways, Gill-air and Business Air.

Among European airlines, SAS provides links to Scandinavia, KLM with the Netherlands and further afield, and RyanAir and Aer Lingus with Ireland. The Norwegian carrier Ugland Air provides oil industry charters from Sumburgh to Norwegian airports, and Wideroe, also Norwegian, operates scheduled flights in summer on the same route.

The Civil Aviation Authority (CAA) is responsible for the economic regulation of UK airlines and the larger airports, and for the safety regulation of the UK civil aviation industry. Through its wholly-owned subsidiary company National Air Traffic Services Ltd, the CAA is also responsible for the provision of air traffic control services over Britain and its surrounding seas and at most major British airports.

AIRPORTS

Scottish Airports Ltd is a subsidiary of BAA plc, the world's leading commercial aiport operator. It owns and operates Scotland's three principal airports at Glasgow, Edinburgh and Aberdeen which, together currently handle 14 million passengers annually. A total of 250,000 movements of aircraft and helicopters takes place each year and 29,300 metric tonnes of cargo and mail are carried through the airports.

Highlands and Islands Airports Ltd (HIAL) owns and operates ten Scottish airports and receives subsidies for providing links to remote areas of Scotland.

HIAL's airports are Barra, Benbecula, Campbeltown, Inverness, Islay, Kirkwall, Stornoway, Sumburgh, Tiree, and Wick.

A number of airports and small airfields are controlled by local authorities, including Dundee, Orkney and Shetland. Orkney Islands Council has airfields at Eday, North Ronaldsay, Papa Westray, Sanday, Stronsay and Westray. Shetland Islands Council runs Tingwall airport at Lerwick, and gives assistance to airstrips on Foula, Out Skerries and Papa Stour, which are run by local airstrip trusts. Fetlar and Whalsay have airstrips for emergency use, with only occasional other services according to need. Baltasound airstrip on Unst, currently owned and operated by Shetland Islands Council, operates only for about three hours a day and is under review at the time of going to press. Fair Isle airfield is owned, like the whole island, by the National Trust for Scotland. Airports and airfields at Glenrothes, Cumbernauld and Perth (Scone) are privately owned. Scatsta in Shetland and Flotta in Orkney are also privately owned, principally serving the oil industry.

Airport operating hours at Barra are subject to tide variation, since aircraft land on and take off from the beach. Tiree's operating hours are also subject to the variations at Barra, as flights to and from Tiree are via Barra.

Operating hours vary seasonally at several smaller airports and airfields, including Campbeltown, Inverness, Islay and Wick.

BAA PLC

Scottish Airport Division, St Andrew's Drive, Glasgow Airport, Paisley KA9 4DG
Tel: 0141-887 1111; Fax: 0141-887 1699

HIGHLANDS AND ISLANDS AIRPORTS LTD

Head Office, Inverness Airport, Inverness IV2 7JB
Tel: 01667-462445

PASSENGER JOURNEYS

Over 14 million passenger journeys were made through Scottish airports in 1997, including terminal, transit, scheduled and charter passengers. The following list covers BAA, HIAL and local authority controlled airports.

AIR PASSENGERS 1997

Aberdeen (BAA)	2,662,960
Barra (HIAL)	9,045
Benbecula (HIAL)	36,519
Campbeltown (HIAL)	9,595
Dundee	10,583
Edinburgh (BAA)	4,588,507
Glasgow (BAA)	6,566,927
Inverness (HIAL)	340,742
Islay (HIAL)	21,282
Kirkwall (HIAL)	90,610
Lerwick (Tingwall)	4,029
Prestwick (BAA)	564,043
Stornoway (HIAL)	96,070
Sumburgh (HIAL)	305,740
Tiree (HIAL)	4,988
Unst	1,806
Wick (HIAL)	41,057

Source: Civil Aviation Authority

RAILWAYS

Responsibility for legislation on railways will not be devolved to the Scottish Parliament but remains with the UK Government.

Since 1994, responsibility for managing Britain's nationalised railway infrastructure has rested with Railtrack, which was floated on the Stock Exchange in 1996. Railtrack owns all operational track and land pertaining to the railway system, manages the track and charges for access to it, and is responsible for signalling and timetabling. It also owns the stations, and leases most of them out to the train operating companies. Infrastructure support functions are provided by private-sector companies. Railtrack invests in infrastructure principally using finance raised by track charges, and takes investment decisions in consultation with rail operators. It is also responsible for overall safety on the railways.

Railtrack does not operate train services. Since 1994 all passenger services have been franchised to 25 private-sector train-operators, via a competitive tendering process overseen by the Director of the Office of Passenger Rail Franchising. The Government continues to subsidise loss-making but socially necessary rail services. The Franchising Director is responsible for monitoring the performance of the franchisees and allocating and administering government subsidy payments.

The independent Rail Regulator is responsible for the licensing of new railway operators, approving access agreements, promoting the use and development of the network, preventing anti-competitive practices (in conjunction with the Director-General of Fair Trading) and protecting the interests of rail users.

The White Paper *New Deal for Transport*, published in July 1998, announced plans to establish a Strategic Rail Authority which will manage passenger railway franchising, take responsibility for increasing the use of the railways for freight transport, and lead strategic planning of passenger and freight rail services. The Railway Bill published in July 1999 will give effect to these plans once enacted.

Rail Users' Consultative Committees monitor the policies and performance of train and station operators in their area. They are statutory bodies and have a legal right to make recommendations for changes.

OFFICE OF THE RAIL REGULATOR (ORR)

1 Waterhouse Square, 138—142 Holborn, London EC1N 2TQ
Tel: 020-7282 2000
Rail Regulator: Tom Winsor

RAILTRACK

Scottish Office, Buchanan House, 58 Port Dundas Road, Glasgow G4 0LQ
Tel: 0141-335 2424

SCOTRAIL

Caledonian Chambers, 87 Union Street, Glasgow
G1 3TA
Tel: 0141-332 9811

RAIL USERS' CONSULTATIVE COMMITTEE FOR SCOTLAND

5th Floor, Corunna House, 29 Cadogan Street,
Glasgow G2 7AB
Tel: 0141-221 7760

SERVICES

Scotland is served by Great North Eastern
Railway, Scotrail Railways and Virgin Trains
operating companies. There are 335 stations in
passenger service. Railtrack owns all of these with
the exception of the station at Prestwick Airport,
which is privately owned. In 1998 there were
48,895,771 passenger journeys within Scotland,
and 51,185,284 originating in Scotland. The total
ticket revenue for journeys beginning in Scotland
was £162.7 million.

Railtrack publishes a national timetable which
contains details of rail services operated over the
Railtrack network, coastal shipping information
and connections with Ireland, the Isle of Man,
the Isle of Wight, the Channel Islands and some
European destinations.

The national rail enquiries service offers
telephone information about train times and fares
for any part of the country:

NATIONAL RAIL ENQUIRIES

Tel: 0345-484950

EUROSTAR

Tel: 0345-303030

GLASGOW UNDERGROUND RAILWAY

The Glasgow Underground railway system
opened in 1896, was electrified in 1935 and
reopened following modernisation in 1980. It has
15 stations and 6.55 route miles of track.
Strathclyde Passenger Transport is responsible for
the Underground. In 1998-9 there were 14.6
million passenger journeys, of which seven
million were with a season ticket. Total ticket
revenue in 1998-9 was £8.86 million, an increase
of 6.8 per cent on the previous year.

STRATHCLYDE PASSENGER TRANSPORT

Consort House, 12 West George Street, Glasgow
G2 1HN
Tel: 0141-332 6811
Customer enquiries: tel. 0141-332 7133

CHANNEL TUNNEL LINKS

Passenger services operated by Eurostar (UK)
Ltd run from Waterloo station in London and
Ashford, Kent, via the Channel Tunnel to Paris,
Brussels and Lille. Connecting services from
Edinburgh via London began in 1997. The
introduction of through services from Edinburgh,
not stopping in London, is the subject of a
government review which reported in late 1998
and of a subsequent process of investigation.

ROADS

Responsibility for Scotland's road network and
for policy on bus transport now rests with the
Scottish Parliament and Ministers, operating
through the Scottish Executive Development
Department. The highway authority for non-
trunk roads is, in general, the unitary authority in
whose area the roads lie.

The costs of construction, improvement and
maintenance are met by central government.
Total expenditure on building and maintaining
trunk roads in Scotland was estimated at £170
million in 1997-8.

A review of roads policy in Scotland is
currently in progress.

ROAD LENGTHS
as at April 1998

	miles	km
Total roads	32,999	55,266
Trunk roads (including motorways)	2,019	3,266
Motorways	212	344

MOTORWAYS

M8	Edinburgh to Newhouse, Baillieston to West Ferry Interchange
M9	Edinburgh to Dunblane
M73	Maryville to Mollinsburn
M74	Glasgow to Paddy's Rickle Bridge, Cleuchbrae to Gretna
M77	Ayr Road Route
M80	Stirling to Haggs/Glasgow (M8) to Stepps
M90	Inverkeithing to Perth
M876	Dennyloanhead (M80) to Kincardine Bridge

PRINCIPAL ROAD BRIDGES

Tay Road Bridge, over Firth of Tay	- 2,245 m/7,365 ft
Forth Road Bridge, over Firth of Forth	- 1,987 m/6,156 ft
Erskine Bridge, over River Clyde	- 1,321 m/4,336 ft
Kessock Bridge, over Kessock Narrows	- 1,052 m/3,453 ft
Skye Bridge, over Kyle of Lochalsh	- 520 m/1,705 ft

ROAD PASSENGER SERVICES

There is an extensive network of bus and coach services in Scotland, particularly in rural areas. In 1997-8 there were 438 million passenger bus journeys in Scotland.

Until 1988 most road passenger transport services in Great Britain were provided by the public sector; the Scottish Bus Group was the largest operator in Scotland. Since the late 1980s almost all bus and coach services in Great Britain have been privatised; the privatisation of the Scottish Bus Group was completed in 1991. However, local authorities can subsidise the provision of socially necessary services after competitive tendering.

One of the largest bus operators in Great Britain, Stagecoach Holdings, is based in Scotland, at Perth. National Express runs a national network of coach routes, mainly operating through franchises. There is also a large number of smaller private operators.

Information on local bus routes and timetables can be obtained from bus stations and tourist board offices; telephone numbers can be found in local telephone directories.

HIGHLAND SCOTTISH BUSES

Tel: 01463-233371

NATIONAL EXPRESS COACH SERVICES

Tel: 08705-808080/0990-808080

SCOTTISH CITYLINK EXPRESS COACH SERVICES

Tel: 08705-505050/0990-505050

STAGECOACH HOLDINGS

Tel: 01738-629339/442111 (administration)

POSTBUS SERVICES

Since 1968 the Royal Mail has operated a postbus service in Scotland, providing passenger transport in rural areas of the country. There are currently 119 postbuses covering 128 routes throughout Scotland, including the Western Isles, Orkney and Shetland, as well as three routes in Northern Ireland and a similar network in England and Wales. Many of the services receive financial assistance from local councils. A wheelchair-accessible service in Midlothian was introduced in 1998.

The postbus service has its Scottish head office at the Royal Mail headquarters in Edinburgh but is largely administered from Inverness, from where timetables and other information are available.

ROYAL MAIL SCOTLAND AND NORTHERN IRELAND

HQ, 102 West Port, Edinburgh EH3 9HS

POST BUS SUPPORT

Royal Mail, 7 Strothers Lane, Inverness IV1 1AA
Tel: 01463-256228;
customer services: 0345-74074;
Fax: 01463-256392

DRIVING AND VEHICLE LICENCES

The Driver and Vehicle Licensing Agency (DVLA) is responsible for issuing driving licences, registering and licensing vehicles, and collecting excise duty in Great Britain. The Driving Standards Agency is responsible for carrying out driving tests and approving driving instructors.

A leaflet, *What You Need to Know About Driving Licences* (form D100), is available from post offices.

DRIVING LICENCE FEES
as at 1 April 2000

First provisional licence	£23.50
Changing a provisional to a full licence after passing a driving test	£8.50
Renewal of licence	£8.50
Renewal of licence including PCV or LGV entitlements	£28.50
Renewal after disqualification	£24.50
Renewal after drinking and driving disqualification	£33.50
Medical renewal	free
Duplicate Licence	£13.50
Exchange licence	£13.50
Removing endorsements	£13.50
Replacement (change of name or address)	free

DRIVING TEST FEES
(weekday rate/evening and Saturday rate)
as at 1 April 2000

For cars	£36.75/£46
For motor cycles*	£45/£55
For lorries, buses	£73.50/£92
For invalid carriages	free
For cars, after disqualification†	£73.50/£92.50
For motor cycles, after disqualification†	£90/110
Written theory test	£15.50

Before riding on public roads, learner motor cyclists and learner moped riders are required to have completed Compulsory Basic Training, provided by DSA-approved training bodies. The CBT certificate currently costs £8.

†An extended driving test was introduced in 1992 for those convicted of dangerous driving.

MOTOR VEHICLE LICENCES

Registration and first licensing of vehicles is done through local Vehicle Registration Offices of the DVLA. Local facilities for relicensing are available at any post office which deals with vehicle licensing, or by postal application to the post offices shown on form V100, available at any post office. This form also provides guidance on registering and licensing vehicles.

Details of the present duties chargeable on motor vehicles are available at post offices and Vehicle Registration Offices.

VEHICLE EXCISE DUTY RATES
from 22 March 2000

	Twelve months £	Six months £
Motor Cars		
Light vans, cars, taxis, etc.		
Under 1100cc*	100.00	55.00
Over 1100cc*	155.00	85.25
Motor Cycles		
With or without sidecar, not over 150 cc	15.00	–
With or without sidecar, 150—250 cc	40.00	–
Others	60.00	33.00
Electric motorcycles (including tricycles)	15.00	–
Tricycles (not over 450 kg)		
Not over 150 cc	15.00	–
Others	60.00	33.00
Buses†		
Seating 9–16 persons	165.00	(155.00)
	90.75	(85.25)
Seating 17–35 persons	220.00	(155.00)
	121.00	(85.25)
Seating 36–60 persons	330.00	(155.00)
	181.00	(85.25)
Seating over 60 persons	500.00	(155.00)
	275.00	(85.25)

* Rate from 1 June 1999
† Figures in parentheses refer to reduced pollution vehicles

MOT TESTING

Cars, motor cycles, motor caravans, light goods and dual-purpose vehicles more than three years old must be covered by a current MoT test certificate, which must be renewed annually. The MoT testing scheme is administered by the Vehicle Inspectorate.

A fee is payable to MoT testing stations, which must be authorised to carry out tests. The maximum fees, which are prescribed by regulations, are:

For cars and light vans	£32.11
For solo motor cycles	£13.04
For motor cycle combinations	£21.80
For three-wheeled vehicles	£25.63
For non-public service vehicle buses	
13–17 seats	£39.18
17+ seats	£53.36
For light goods vehicles 3,000–3,500 kg	£33.80

SHIPPING AND PORTS

Sea transport, both of passengers and freight, is important in Scotland, particularly between the many islands in the north and west and between the islands and the mainland. Major ferry operators include Stena Line (which runs a service between Stranraer and Belfast), P. & O. Scottish Ferries (serving Orkney and Shetland), and Caledonian MacBrayne (serving the Western Isles). P. & O. Scottish Ferries are also UK agents for Smyril, running services from Lerwick to Norway, Denmark, the Faröe Islands and Iceland. Shetland Islands Council operates an inter-island service in Shetland; inter-island services in Orkney are run by Orkney Ferries Ltd.

FERRY SERVICES

Passenger ferry services within Scotland include the following:

From	To
Aberdeen (P&O)	Lerwick (Shetland)
Aberdeen (P&O)	Stromness
Ardrossan (CM)	Brodick (Arran)
Claonaig (Kintyre) (CM)	Lochranza (Arran)*
Colintraive (Argyll) (CM)	Rhubodach (Bute)
Colonsay (CM)	Port Askaig (Islay)*
Fionnphort (Mull) (CM)	Iona
Gourock (CM)	Dunoon (Cowal)
Gourock (CM)	Kilcreggan, Helensburgh
Kennacraig (CM)	Port Ellen (Islay), Port Askaig
Largs (CM)	Cumbrae Slip (Cumbrae)
Lochaline (Lochaber) (CM)	Fishnish (Mull)
Mallaig (CM)	Armadale (Skye)*
Mallaig (CM)	Castlebay
Mallaig (CM)	Lochboisdale (S. Uist)
Mallaig small isles service (CM)	Eigg, Muck, Rum, Canna
Oban (CM)	Castlebay (Barra)
Oban (CM)	Colonsay
Oban (CM)	Craignure (Mull)
Oban (CM)	Lismore

Oban (CM)	Tobermory (Mull), Coll, Tiree
Otternish (N. Uist) (CM)	Leverburgh (Harris)
Sconser (Skye) (CM)	Raasay
Scrabster (P&O)	Stromness (Orkney)
Tarbert (Kintyre) (CM)	Portavadie (Cowal)*
Tayinloan (CM)	Gigha
Tobermory (CM)	Kilchoan
Uig (Skye) (CM)	Tarbert (Harris)
Uig (CM)	Lochmaddy (N. Uist)
Ullapool (CM)	Stornoway (Lewis)
Wemyss Bay (CM)	Rothesay (Bute)

Summer only
CM Caledonian MacBrayne service
P&O P. & O. Scottish Ferries service

FERRY OPERATORS

CALEDONIAN MACBRAYNE

Tel: 01475-650100 (general enquiries); 01475-650000 (car ferry reservations)
Fax: 01475-637607

HEBRIDEAN CRUISES

Services to Rum, Eigg, Muck and Canna
Tel: 01687-450224; Fax: 01687-450224

ORKNEY FERRIES LTD

Tel: 01856-872044/811397

P. & O. SCOTTISH FERRIES

Offices, Aberdeen, Kirkwall, Lerwick, Stromness
Tel: see local telephone directories

SEACAT

Tel: 0990-523523

STENA LINE

Tel: 0990-707070 (passengers); 0845-0704000 (freight)

VIKING SEA TAXIS

Services to several small Shetland islands
Tel: 01595-692463/859431

PORTS

There are 57 ports of significant size in Scotland. Ports are owned and operated by private companies (including shipping lines), local authorities or trusts. The telephone number given for each port is the number of the port rather than of the port authority; wherever possible, a 24-hour number has been given.

RUN BY THE LOCAL AUTHORITY

Buckie Harbour	01542-831700
Burghead	01343-830371
Campbeltown	01586-552552
Cockenzie Harbour	01620-827282
Dunbar	01620-827282
Dunoon Pier	01369-702652
Flotta	01856-884000
Gairloch	01445-712140
Gigha	01546-602233
Girvan	01292-612302
Kinlochbervie	01971-521235
Kirkwall	01856-873636
Kyle of Lochalsh	01599-534167
Lochinver Harbour	01571-844247
Macduff	01261-832236
Oban (North Pier)	01631-568892
Perth	01738-624056
Rothesay	01700-503842
Scalloway	01806-242551
Stromness	01856-873636
Sullom Voe	01806-242551
Uig	01470-542381

RUN BY TRUSTS

Aberdeen	01224-597000
Fraserburgh	01346-515858
Invergordon	01349-852308
Inverness	01463-715715
Lerwick	01595-692991
Mallaig	01687-462154
Montrose	01674-672302
Peterhead	01779-474281
Scrabster	01847-892779
Stornoway	01851-702688
Tarbert (East Loch Tarbert)	01880-820344
Ullapool	01854-612091
Wick	01955-602030

RUN BY CALEDONIAN MACBRAYNE LTD
(Tel: 01475-650100):

Brodick	01770-302166
Gourock	01475-650100
Kennacraig	01880-730253
Largs	01475-674134
Lochboisdale	01878-700288
Oban (Ferry Terminal)	01631-562285
Port Ellen	01496-302047

RUN BY CLYDEPORT PLC
(Tel: 0141-221 8733)

Ardrossan	0141-221 8733
Glasgow	0141-221 8733
Greenock	0141-221 8733
Hunterston	0141-221 8733

RUN BY FORTH PORTS PLC
(Tel: 0131-554 6473)

Braefoot Bay	0131-555 8750
Burntisland	01592-873708
Dundee	01382-224121
Grangemouth	01324-777432
Granton	0131-554 4343
Leith	0131-554 4343
Methil	01333-426725

RUN BY OTHER OPERATORS

Ardrishaig (British Waterways)	01546-603210
Cairnryan (P.& O. European Ferries)	01581-200663
Stranraer (Stena Line)	01776-802121

MARINE SAFETY

By 1 October 2002 all roll-on, roll-off ferries operating to and from the UK will be required to meet the new international safety standards on stability established by the Stockholm Agreement.

The Maritime and Coastguard Agency was established in 1998 by the merger of the Coastguard Agency and the Marine Safety Agency, and is an executive agency of the Department of the Environment, Transport and the Regions. Its aims are to develop, promote and enforce high standards of marine safety, to minimise loss of life amongst seafarers and coastal users, and to minimise pollution of the sea and coastline from ships.

HM Coastguard in Scotland is divided into two search and rescue regions, one covering the north and east of Scotland and the other covering the west of Scotland and Northern Ireland.

Locations hazardous to shipping in coastal waters are marked by lighthouses and other lights and buoys. The lighthouse authority for Scotland (and the Isle of Man) is the Northern Lighthouse Board. The Board maintains 83 lighthouses, 117 minor lights and many buoys. No Scottish lighthouses are now manned; the last to convert to automated operation was Fair Isle in 1998.

Harbour authorities are responsible for pilotage within their harbour areas; and the Ports Act 1991 provides for the transfer of lights and buoys to harbour authorities where these are used for mainly local navigation.

LEGAL SCOTLAND

INTRODUCTION TO THE SCOTTISH LEGAL SYSTEM
COURTS, JUDGES AND MAGISTRATES
LEGAL NOTES

LEGAL SCOTLAND

THE SCOTTISH JUDICATURE

Scotland has a legal system separate from and differing greatly from the English legal system in enacted law, judicial procedure and the structure of courts.

The system of public prosecution is headed by the Lord Advocate and is independent of the police, who have no say in the decision to prosecute. The Lord Advocate, discharging his functions through the Crown Office in Edinburgh, is responsible for prosecutions in the High Court, sheriff courts and district courts. Prosecutions in the High Court are prepared by the Crown Office and conducted in court by one of the law officers, by an advocate-depute, or by a solicitor advocate. In the inferior courts the decision to prosecute is made and prosecution is preferred by procurators fiscal, who are lawyers and full-time civil servants subject to the directions of the Crown Office. A permanent, legally qualified civil servant known as the Crown Agent is responsible for the running of the Crown Office and the organisation of the Procurator Fiscal Service, of which he is the head.

Scotland is divided into six sheriffdoms, each with a full-time sheriff principal. The sheriffdoms are further divided into sheriff court districts, each of which has a legally qualified resident sheriff or sheriffs, who are the judges of the court.

CRIMINAL COURTS

In criminal cases sheriffs principal and sheriffs have the same powers; sitting with a jury of 15 members, they may try more serious cases on indictment, or, sitting alone, may try lesser cases under summary procedure. Minor summary offences are dealt with in district courts, which are administered by the local government authorities of the districts and the islands and presided over by lay justices of the peace (of whom there are about 4,000) and, in Glasgow only, by stipendiary magistrates. Juvenile offenders (children under 16) may be brought before an informal children's hearing comprising three local lay people.

The superior criminal court is the High Court of Justiciary, which is both a trial and an appeal court. Cases on indictment are tried by a High Court judge, sitting with a jury of 15, in Edinburgh and on circuit in other towns. Appeals from the lower courts against conviction or sentence are heard also by the High Court, which sits as an appeal court only in Edinburgh. There is no further appeal to the House of Lords in criminal cases.

CIVIL COURTS

In civil cases the jurisdiction of the sheriff court extends to most kinds of action. Appeal against decisions of the sheriff may be made to the sheriff principal and thence to the Court of Session, or direct to the Court of Session, which sits only in Edinburgh. The Court of Session is divided into the Inner and the Outer House. The Outer House is a court of first instance in which cases are heard by judges sitting singly, sometimes with a jury of 12. The Inner House, itself subdivided into two divisions of equal status, is mainly an appeal court. Appeals may be made to the Inner House from the Outer House as well as from the sheriff court. An appeal may be made from the Inner House to the House of Lords.

COURT OF SESSION JUDGES

The judges of the Court of Session are the same as those of the High Court of Justiciary, the Lord President of the Court of Session also holding the office of Lord Justice-General in the High Court. Senators of the College of Justice are Lords Commissioners of Justiciary as well as judges of the Court of Session. On appointment, a Senator takes a judicial title, which is retained for life. Although styled 'The Hon./Rt. Hon. Lord —', the Senator is not a peer.

SUDDEN DEATHS

The office of coroner does not exist in Scotland. The local procurator fiscal inquires privately into sudden or suspicious deaths and may report findings to the Crown Agent. In some cases a fatal accident inquiry may be held before the sheriff.

COURT OF SESSION AND HIGH COURT OF JUSTICIARY

The Lord President and Lord Justice-General
The Rt. Hon. the Lord Rodger of Earlsferry, *born* 1944, *apptd* 1996
Secretary: A. Maxwell

INNER HOUSE
Lords of Session

FIRST DIVISION
The Lord President
Rt. Hon. Lord Sutherland (Ranald Sutherland),
  born 1932, apptd 1985
Rt. Hon. Lord Prosser (William Prosser),
  born 1934, apptd 1986
Rt. Hon. Lord Caplan (Philip Caplan),
  born 1929, apptd 1989

SECOND DIVISION
Lord Justice Clerk, The Rt. Hon. Lord Cullen
  (William Cullen), born 1935, apptd 1997
Rt. Hon. Lord Kirkwood (Ian Kirkwood),
  born 1932, apptd 1987
Rt. Hon. Lord Coulsfield (John Cameron),
  born 1934, apptd 1987
Rt. Hon. Lord Milligan (James Milligan),
  born 1934, apptd 1988

OUTER HOUSE
Lords of Session

Hon. Lord Marnoch (Michael Bruce),
  born 1938, apptd 1990
Hon. Lord MacLean (Ranald MacLean),
  born 1938, apptd 1990
Hon. Lord Penrose (George Penrose),
  born 1938, apptd 1990
Hon. Lord Osborne (Kenneth Osborne),
  born 1937, apptd 1990
Hon. Lord Abernethy (Alistair Cameron),
  born 1938, apptd 1992
Hon. Lord Johnston (Alan Johnston),
  born 1942, apptd 1994
Hon. Lord Gill (Brian Gill),
  born 1942, apptd 1994
Hon. Lord Hamilton (Arthur Hamilton),
  born 1942, apptd 1995
Hon. Lord Dawson (Thomas Dawson),
  born 1948, apptd 1995
Hon. Lord Macfadyen (Donald Macfadyen),
  born 1945, apptd 1995
Hon. Lady Cosgrove (Hazel Aronson),
  born 1946, apptd 1996
Hon. Lord Nimmo Smith (William Nimmo
  Smith), born 1942, apptd 1996
Hon. Lord Philip (Alexander Philip),
  born 1942, apptd 1996
Hon. Lord Kingarth (Derek Emslie),
  born 1949, apptd 1997
Hon. Lord Bonomy (Iain Bonomy),
  born 1946, apptd 1997
Hon. Lord Eassie (Ronald Mackay),
  born 1945, apptd 1997

Hon. Lord Reed (Robert Reed),
  born 1956, apptd 1998
Hon. Lord Wheatley (John Wheatley),
  born 1941, apptd 1999
Hon. Lady Paton (Ann Paton), apptd 2000
Hon. Lord Carloway (Colin Sutherland),
  born 1954, apptd 2000
Hon. Lord Clarke (Matthew Clarke), apptd 2000
Rt. Hon. Lord Hardie (Andrew Hardie),
  born 1946, apptd 2000
Rt. Hon. Lord Mackay of Drumadoon (Donald
  Mackay), born 1946, apptd 2000
Hon. Lord McEwan (Robin McEwan),
  born 1943, apptd 2000

COURT OF SESSION AND HIGH COURT OF JUSTICIARY

Parliament   House,   Parliament   Square,
Edinburgh EH1 1RQ
Tel: 0131-225 2595

Principal Clerk of Session and Justiciary
  (£33,391–£55,711): J. L. Anderson
Deputy Principal Clerk of Justiciary and
  Administration (£29,277–£45,365): T.
  Fyffe (presently Deputy Registrar of the
  Scottish Court in the Netherlands)
Acting Deputy Principal Clerk of Justiciary:
  T. Higgins
Acting Deputy Principal Clerk of Session and
  Acting Principal Extractor (£29,277–
  £45,365): A. Finlayson
Keeper of the Rolls (£29,277–£45,365):
  D. Shand
Depute Clerks of Session and Justiciary
  (£22,348–£29,380): M: Weir; N. J. Dowie;
  I. F. Smith; B. Watson; T. B. Cruickshank; Q.
  A. Oliver; F. Shannly; J. McLean; A. S.
  Moffat; G. G. Ellis; W. Dunn; C. C.
  Armstrong; R. M. Sinclair; D. W. Cullen; I.
  D. Martin; N. McGinley; J. Lynn; Mrs E.
  Dickson; K. O. Carter; Miss F. Petrie; Mrs P.
  McFarlane; G. Combe; D. Freaser; A.
  Johnston

SCOTTISH COURT SERVICE

Hayweight House, 23 Lauriston Street,
Edinburgh EH3 9DQ
Tel: 0131-229 9200

The Scottish Court Service became an executive
agency   within   the   Scottish   Courts
Administration in 1995. It is responsible to the
Scottish Ministers for the provision of staff, court
houses and associated services for the Supreme
and Sheriff Courts.
Chief Executive: J. Ewing

SHERIFF COURT OF CHANCERY

27 Chambers Street, Edinburgh EH1 1LB
Tel: 0131-225 2525

The Court deals with service of heirs and completion of title in relation to heritable property.
Sheriff of Chancery: C. G. B. Nicholson, QC

HM COMMISSARY OFFICE

27 Chambers Street, Edinburgh EH1 1LB
Tel: 0131-225 2525

The Office is responsible for issuing confirmation, a legal document entitling a person to execute a deceased person's will, and other related matters.
Commissary Clerk: J. Moyes

SCOTTISH LAND COURT

1 Grosvenor Crescent, Edinburgh EH12 5ER
Tel: 0131-225 3595; Fax: 0131-226 4812

The court deals with disputes relating to agricultural and crofting land in Scotland.
Chairman: The Hon. Lord McGhie (James McGhie), QC
Members: D. J. Houston; D. M. Macdonald; J. Kinloch (part-time)
Principal Clerk: K. H. R. Graham, WS

SHERIFFDOMS

GRAMPIAN, HIGHLANDS AND ISLANDS

Sheriff Court House, Castle Street, Aberdeen AB10 1WP
Tel: 01224-657200
Sheriff Principal: D. J. Risk, QC
Area Director North: J. Robertson

SHERIFFS AND SHERIFF CLERKS
Aberdeen and Stonehaven: D. Kelbie; A. Pollock; Mrs A. M. Cowan; C. J. Harris, QC; I. H. L. Miller; *G. K. Buchanan; *D. J. Cusine; *Sheriff Clerks:* Mrs E. Laing *(Aberdeen);* B. J. McBride *(Stonehaven)*
Peterhead and Banff: K. A. McLernan; *Sheriff Clerk:* A. Hempseed *(Peterhead); Sheriff Clerk Depute:* Mrs F. L. MacPherson *(Banff)*
Elgin, N. McPartlin; *Sheriff Clerk:* W. Cochrane
Inverness, Lochmaddy, Portree, Stornoway, Dingwall, Tain, Wick and Dornoch: W. J. Fulton; D. Booker-Milburn; J. O. A. Fraser; I. A. Cameron; *Sheriff Clerks:* J. Robertson *(Inverness);* M. McBey *(Dingwall); Sheriff Clerks Depute:* Miss M. Campbell *(Lochmaddy and Portree);* Miss S. B. Armstrong *(Stornoway);* L. MacLachlan *(Tain);* Mrs J. McEwan *(Wick);* K. Kerr *(Dornoch)*
Kirkwall and Lerwick: C. S. Mackenzie; *Sheriff Clerks Depute:* Miss A. Moore *(Kirkwall);* M. Flanagan *(Lerwick)*
Fort William: C. G. McKay (also Oban); *Sheriff Clerk Depute:* D. Hood

TAYSIDE, CENTRAL AND FIFE

Sheriff Court House, Tay Street, Perth PH2 8NL
Tel: 01738-620546
Sheriff Principal, R. Alastair Dunlop, QC
Area Director East: M. Bonar

SHERIFFS AND SHERIFF CLERKS
Arbroath: *C. N. R. Stein; *Sheriff Clerk:* M. Herbertson
Dundee: R. A. Davidson; A. L. Stewart, QC; *J. P. Scott; I. D. Dunbar; *Sheriff Clerk:* D. Nicoll
Perth: M. J. Fletcher; Mrs F. L. Reith, QC; *D. W. Pyle; *Sheriff Clerk:* J. Murphy
Falkirk: A. V. Sheehan; A. J. Murphy; *C. Caldwell; *Sheriff Clerk:* R. McMillan
Forfar: K. A. Veal; *Sheriff Clerk:* S, Munro
Stirling: R. E. G. Younger; *A. W. Robertson; *Sheriff Clerk:* Mrs G. McKeand
Alloa: W. M. Reid; *Sheriff Clerk:* Mrs G. McKeand
Cupar: G. J. Evans; *Sheriff Clerk:* R. Hughes
Dunfermline: J. S. Forbes; *G. W. McF. Liddle; *N. C. Stewart; *Sheriff Clerk:* W. McCulloch
Kirkcaldy: F. J. Keane; Mrs L. G. Patrick; *B. G. Donald; *Sheriff Clerk:* W. Jones

LOTHIAN AND BORDERS

Sheriff Court House, 27 Chambers Street, Edinburgh EH1 1LB
Tel: 0131-225 2525
Sheriff Principal: C. G. B. Nicholson, QC
Area Director East: M. Bonar

SHERIFFS AND SHERIFF CLERKS
Edinburgh: R. G. Craik, QC (*also Peebles*); R. J. D. Scott (*also Peebles*); Miss I. A. Poole; A. M. Bell; J. M. S. Horsburgh, QC; J. A. Farrell; *A. Lothian; I. D. Macphail, QC; C. N. Stoddart; A. B. Wilkinson, QC; Mrs D. J. B. Robertson; N. M. P. Morrison, QC; *Miss M. M. Stephen; Mrs M. L. E. Jarvie, QC; N. J. Mackinnon; Mrs K. E. C. Mackie; *Sheriff Clerk:* J. M. Ross

Peebles: R. G. Craik, QC *(also Edinburgh);* R. J.
D. Scott *(also Edinburgh); Sheriff Clerk
Depute:* M. L. Kubeczka
Linlithgow: H. R. MacLean; G. R. Fleming; P.
Gillam; *Sheriff Clerk:* R. D. Sinclair
Haddington: G. W. S. Presslie *(also Edinburgh);
Sheriff Clerk:* J. O'Donnell
Jedburgh and Duns: T. A. K. Drummond, QC;
Sheriff Clerk: I. W. Williamson
Selkirk: T. A. K. Drummond, QC; *Sheriff Clerk
Depute:* L. McFarlane

NORTH STRATHCLYDE

Sheriff Court House, St James's Street, Paisley
PA3 2AW
Tel: 0141-887 5291
Sheriff Principal: B. A. Kerr, QC
Area Director West: I. Scott

SHERIFFS AND SHERIFF CLERKS
Oban: C. G. McKay *(also Fort William); Sheriff
Clerk Depute:* J. G. Whitelaw
Dumbarton: J. T. Fitzsimons; T. Scott; S. W. H.
Fraser; *Sheriff Clerk:* C. Binning
Paisley: J. Spy; C. K. Higgins; N. Douglas; D. J.
Pender; *W. Dunlop *(also Campbeltown);* G.
C. Kavanagh; *I. McColl; *Sheriff Clerk:* Miss
S. Hinder
Greenock: J. Herald *(also Rothesay);* Sir Stephen
Young; *R. Swanney; *Sheriff Clerk:* J.
Tannahill
Kilmarnock: T. M. Croan; D. B. Smith; T. F.
Russell; *Sheriff Clerk:* G. Waddell
Dunoon: Mrs C. M. A. F. Gimblett; *Sheriff
Clerk Depute:* Mrs C. Carson
Campbeltown: *W. Dunlop *(also Paisley); Sheriff
Clerk Depute:* P. G. Hay
Rothesay: J. Herald *(also Greenock); Sheriff Clerk
Depute:* Mrs C. K. McCormick

GLASGOW AND STRATHKELVIN

Sheriff Court House, PO Box 23, 1 Carlton
Place, Glasgow G5 9DA
Tel: 0141-429 8888
Sheriff Principal: E. F. Bowen, QC
Area Director West: I. Scott

SHERIFFS AND SHERIFF CLERKS
Glasgow: B. Kearney; B. A. Lockhart; Mrs A. L.
A. Duncan; A. C. Henry; J. K. Mitchell; A.
G. Johnston; J. P. Murphy; Miss S. A. O.
Raeburn, QC; D. Convery; J. McGowan; I.
A. S. Peebles, QC; C. W. McFarlane, QC; K.
M. Maciver; H. Matthews, QC; J. A. Baird;
Miss R. E. A. Rae, QC; Mrs P. M. M.

Bowman; A. W. Noble; *J. D. Friel; *Mrs D.
M. MacNeill, QC; J. A. Taylor; C. A. L.
Scott; W. J. Totten; S. Cathcart; Miss L. M.
Ruxton; *Sheriff Clerk:* R. Cockburn

SOUTH STRATHCLYDE, DUMFRIES
AND GALLOWAY

Sheriff Court House, Graham Street, Airdrie
ML6 6EE
Tel: 01236-751121
Sheriff Principal: J. C. McInnes, QC
Area Director West: I. Scott

SHERIFFS AND SHERIFF CLERKS
Hamilton: L. Cameron; D. C. Russell; V. J.
Canavan; W. E. Gibson; J. H. Stewart; H. S.
Neilson; S. C. Pender; *Miss J. Paurie; *T.
Welsh; *A. Vannet; *Sheriff Clerk:* P. Feeney
Lanark: J. D. Allan; *Sheriff Clerk:* Mrs M.
McLean
Ayr: N. Gow, QC; R. G. McEwan, QC; *C. B.
Miller; *Sheriff Clerk:* Miss C. D. Cockburn
Stranraer and Kirkcudbright: J. R. Smith *(also
Dumfries); Sheriff Clerks:* W. McIntosh
(Stranraer); B. Lindsay *(Kirkcudbright)*
Dumfries: K. G. Barr; K. Ross
Airdrie: V. J. Canavan R. H. Dickson; I. C.
Simpson; J. C. Morris, QC; *Sheriff Clerk:* D.
Forester

STIPENDIARY MAGISTRATES
GLASGOW

R. Hamilton, *apptd* 1984; J. B. C. Nisbet, *apptd*
1984; R. B. Christie, *apptd* 1985; Mrs J. A.
M. MacLean, *apptd* 1990

**CROWN OFFICE AND PROCURATOR
FISCAL SERVICE**

CROWN OFFICE

25 Chambers Street, Edinburgh EH1 1LA
Tel 0131-226 2626

Crown Agent: A. C. Normand
Deputy Crown Agent: F. R. Crowe

PROCURATORS FISCAL

GRAMPIAN, HIGHLANDS AND
ISLANDS REGION

Regional Procurator Fiscal: Mrs E. Angiolini
(Aberdeen)
Procurators Fiscal: E. K. Barbour *(Stonehaven);*
A. J. M. Colley *(Banff);* G. Aitken
(Peterhead); D. J. Dickson *(Elgin);* J. Bamber

(Portree, Lochmaddy); D. S. Teale
(Stornoway); G. Napier (Inverness); R. W.
Urquhart (Kirkwall, Lerwick); D. J. Buchanan
(Fort William); A. N. MacDonald (Dingwall,
Tain)

TAYSIDE, CENTRAL AND FIFE REGION
Regional Procurator Fiscal: B. K. Heywood
(Dundee)
Procurators Fiscal: J. I. Craigen (Forfar); I. A.
McLeod (Perth); W. J. Gallacher (Falkirk);
C. Ritchie (Stirling and Alloa); E. B. Russell
(Cupar); R. G. Stott (Dunfermline); Miss H.
M. Clark (Kirkcaldy)

LOTHIAN AND BORDERS REGION
Regional Procurator Fiscal: N. McFadyen
(Edinburgh)
Procurators Fiscal: Mrs C. P. Dyer (Linlithgow);
A. J. P. Reith (Haddington); A. R. G. Fraser
(Duns, Jedburgh); Mrs L. Thomson (Selkirk)

NORTH STRATHCLYDE REGION
Regional Procurator Fiscal: W. A. Gilchrist
(Paisley)
Procurators Fiscal: F. Redman (Campbeltown);
C. C. Donnelly (Dumbarton); W. S. Carnegie
(Greenock); D. L. Webster (Dunoon); J. Watt
(Kilmarnock); B. R. Maguire (Oban)

GLASGOW AND STRATHKELVIN REGION
Regional Procurator Fiscal: L. A. Higson
(Glasgow)

SOUTH STRATHCLYDE, DUMFRIES AND GALLOWAY REGION
Regional Procurator Fiscal: D. A. Brown
(Hamilton)
Procurators Fiscal: S. R. Houston (Lanark); J. T.
O'Donnell (Ayr); A. S. Kennedy (Stranraer);
D. J. Howdle (Dumfries); A. S. Kennedy
(Stranraer, Kirkcudbright); D. Spiers (Airdrie)

LEGAL NOTES

These notes outline certain aspects of the law in
Scotland as they might affect the average person.
They focus principally on those aspects of Scots
law which differ from the equivalent law in
England and Wales. They are intended only as a
broad guideline and are by no means definitive.
The information is believed to be correct at the
time of going to press, but the law is constantly
changing, so expert advice should always be
taken. In some cases, sources of further
information are given in these notes.

Timely consultation with a solicitor is always
advisable. Anyone in Scotland who does not have
a solicitor can contact the Citizens' Advice
Bureau (addresses in the telephone directory or at
any post office or town hall) or the Law Society
of Scotland (26 Drumsheugh Gardens,
Edinburgh EH3 7YR) for assistance in finding
one.

The legal aid and legal advice and assistance
schemes exist to make the help of a lawyer
available to those who would not otherwise be
able to afford one. Entitlement depends upon an
individual's means, but a solicitor or Citizens'
Advice Bureau will be able to advise about this.

ADOPTION OF CHILDREN
The adoption of children is mainly governed by
the Adoption (Scotland) Act 1978 (as amended
by the Children (Scotland) Act 1995).

Anyone over 21 who is domiciled in the
United Kingdom, the Channel Islands or the Isle
of Man or has been habitually resident in any of
those places throughout the year immediately
preceding the date of an application, whether
married, single, widowed or divorced, can apply
to adopt a child.

The only organisations allowed to arrange
adoptions are the adoption agencies provided by
local authorities (these agencies are known
collectively as the Scottish Adoption Service) or
voluntary agencies approved as an adoption
society.

Once an adoption has been arranged, a court
order is necessary to make it legal. Petitions for
adoption are made to the Sheriff Court or the
Court of Session.

Each of the child's natural parents (or
guardians) must consent to the adoption, unless
the court dispenses with the consent or the
natural parent does not have parental
responsibilities or parental rights. Once adopted,
the child, for all practical purposes, has the same
legal status as a child born to the adoptive parents
and the natural parents cease to have any rights or
responsibilities where the child is concerned. As
a general rule, the adopted child ceases to have
any rights to the estates of his/her natural parents.

Registration and Certificates
All adoptions in Scotland are registered by the
General Register Office for Scotland. Certificates
from the registers can be obtained in a similar way
to birth certificates.

Further information on qualification to adopt a child, adoption procedures, and tracing natural parents or children who have been adopted can be obtained from:

British Agencies for Adoption and Fostering (BAAF)
Scottish Centre, 40 Shandwick Place, Edinburgh EH2 4RT
Tel: 0131-225 9285

Scottish Adoption Advice Service
16 Sandyford Place, Glasgow G3 7NB
Tel: 0141-339 0772

BIRTHS (REGISTRATION)

The birth of a child must be registered within 21 days at the registration office of either the district in which the baby was born or the district in which the mother was resident at the time of the birth.

If the child is born, either in or out of Scotland, on a ship, aircraft or land vehicle that ends its journey at any place in Scotland, the child, in most cases, will be registered as if born in that place.

Responsibility for registering the birth rests with the parents, except where the father of the child is not married to the mother and has not been married to her since the child's conception, in which case the mother is responsible for registration. Responsibility rests firstly with the parents, but if they fail particulars may be given to the registrar by:
— a relative of either parent
— the occupier of the house in which the baby was born
— a person present at the birth
— a person having charge of the child
Failure to register the birth within 21 days without reasonable cause may lead to a court decree being granted by a sheriff.

Further information is available from local registrars, whose addresses and telephone numbers can be found in local telephone directories.

CERTIFICATES OF BIRTHS, DEATHS OR MARRIAGES

Certificates of births, deaths or marriages that have taken place in Scotland since 1855 can be obtained from the General Register Office for Scotland or from the appropriate local registrar. The General Register Office for Scotland also keeps the Register of Divorces (including decrees of declaration of nullity of marriage), and holds parish registers dating from before 1855.

Fees for certificates are:

Certificates (full or abbreviated) of birth, death, marriage or adoption, £8.00
E-mail application in course of Internet search, £10.00

Particular search for each period of five years or part thereof in the statutory registers, whether specified entry is traced or not:
Personal application, £3.00
Postal application, £5.00
E-mail application, £6.00

Particular search for each period of five years or part thereof in the parochial registers, whether specified entry is traced or not:
Personal application, £5.00
Postal application, £5.00
E-mail application, £6.00

General search in the parochial registers and indexes to the statutory registers, per day or part thereof:
Full day (i.e. 9 a.m. to 4.30 p.m.) search with payment being made not less than 14 days in advance, £13.00
Full day search in any other case, £17.00
Afternoon (i.e. 1 p.m. to 4.30 p.m.) search, £10.00
One week search, £65.00

Further information can be obtained from:

The General Register Office for Scotland
New Register House, Edinburgh EH1 3YT
Tel: 0131-334 0380; Fax: 0131-314 4400

CONSUMER LAW

UK legislation governing the sale and supply of goods applies to Scotland as follows:
— the Sale of Goods Act 1979 applies with some modifications and has been amended by the Sale and Supply of Goods Act 1994
— the Supply of Goods (Implied Terms) Act 1973 applies
— the Supply of Goods and Services Act 1982 does not extend to Scotland but some of its provisions were introduced by the Sale and Supply of Goods Act 1994
— only Parts II and III of the Unfair Contract Terms Act 1977 apply
— the Trade Descriptions Act 1968 applies with minor modifications
— the Consumer Credit Act 1974 applies

DEATHS

When a death occurs, if the death was expected, the doctor who attended the deceased during their final illness should be contacted. If the death was sudden or unexpected, the family doctor (if known) and police should be contacted immediately.

If the cause of death is quite clear the doctor will either:

— issue a certificate of cause of death needed by the registrar, provided that there are no unusual circumstances. If the body is to be cremated, the doctor will arrange for the signature of the second doctor needed to complete the cremation certificate; or

— if the doctor is uncertain as to the cause of death he will report the death to the local procurator fiscal who will make enquiries.

A fatal accident inquiry will be held before a sheriff where the death has resulted from an accident during the course of the employment of the person who has died, or where the person who has died was in legal custody, or where the Lord Advocate deems it in the public interest that an inquiry be held.

A death may be registered in any registration district in which the deceased was ordinarily resident immediately before his/her death or, if different, in the registration district in which the death took place. The death must normally be registered within eight days. If the death has been referred to the local procurator fiscal it cannot be registered until the registrar has received authority from the procurator fiscal to do so. Failure to register a death may lead to a court decree being granted by a sheriff. Whereas in most circumstances in England and Wales a certificate for burial or cremation must be obtained from the registrar before the burial or cremation can take place, in Scotland a body may be buried (but normally not cremated) before the death is registered.

Further information can be obtained from the General Register Office for Scotland.

DIVORCE AND RELATED MATTERS

There are two main types of matrimonial action: those seeking the annulment of a marriage, and those seeking a judicial separation or divorce.

An action for 'declarator of nullity' can be brought only in the Court of Session.

An action for judicial separation or divorce may be raised in the Court of Session. It may also be raised in the Sheriff Court if either party was resident in the sheriffdom for 40 days immediately before the date of the action or for 40 days ending not more than 40 days before the date of the action. The fee for starting a divorce petition in the Sheriff Court is £74.

Nullity of Marriage

A marriage is void (i.e. invalid) from the beginning if:

— the parties were within the prohibited degrees of consanguinity, affinity or adoption

— the parties were not respectively male and female

— either of the parties was already married

— either of the parties was under the age of 16

— either of the parties did not truly consent to marry, e.g. in consequence of mental illness, intoxication, force or fear, or in a sham marriage where the intention was to avoid deportation

— the formalities of the marriage were defective, e.g. each of the parties did not submit a notice of intention to marry (a marriage notice) to the district registrar for the registration district in which the marriage was to be solemnised

A marriage may be voidable (i.e. a decree of nullity may be obtained but in the meantime the marriage remains valid) if either party was unable to consummate the marriage.

Where a spouse is capable of sexual intercourse but refuses to consummate the marriage, this is not a ground of nullity in Scots law, though it could be a ground for divorce.

When a marriage is void, it generally has no legal effect at all, and there is therefore no specific need to seek a declarator of nullity in the Court of Session (although it may be wise to do so, e.g. if one of the parties wishes to marry again). Nevertheless, a child conceived during a valid marriage is presumed to be the child of the 'husband'. A child's mother has parental responsibilities and parental rights in relation to the child whether or not she is or has been married to the father. A child's father has such responsibilities and rights in relation to the child only if married to the mother at the time of the child's conception or subsequently. A father is regarded as having been married to the mother at any time when he was a party to a purported marriage with her which was:

— voidable; or

— void but believed by them in good faith at that time to be valid.

When a marriage has been annulled, both parties are free to marry again.

DIVORCE

Divorce dissolves the marriage and leaves both parties at liberty to marry again. The sole ground for divorce is the irretrievable breakdown of the marriage; this must be proved on one or more of the following grounds:
— the defender has committed adultery; however the pursuer cannot rely on an act of adultery by the other party if, after discovery of the act of adultery, he or she has continued or resumed living together with the defender at any time after the end of a period of three months on which cohabitation has been continued or resumed
— the defender has behaved in such a way that the pursuer cannot reasonably be expected to continue living with him/her
— desertion, which is established by the defender having left the pursuer for a period of two years immediately preceding the action. Irretrievable breakdown is not established if, after the two year desertion period has expired, the parties resume living together at any time after the end of three months from the date when they first resume living together
— the defender and the pursuer have lived separately for two years immediately before the raising of the action and the defender consents to the decree
— the defender and the pursuer have lived separately for five years immediately before the raising of the action
Where a divorce action has been raised, it may be sisted or put on hold for a variety of reasons, including, though rarely, enabling the parties to seek to effect a reconciliation if the court feels that there may be a reasonable prospect of such reconciliation. If the parties do cohabit during such postponement, no account is taken of the cohabitation if the action later proceeds.

A simplified procedure for 'do-it-yourself' divorce was introduced in 1983 for certain divorces. If the action is based on two or five years' separation and will not be opposed, and if there are no children under 16, no financial claims and there is no sign that the applicant's spouse is unable to manage his or her affairs because of mental illness or handicap, the applicant can write directly to the local sheriff court or to the Court of Session for the appropriate forms to enable him or her to proceed. The fee is £57, unless the applicant receives income support, family credit or legal advice and assistance, in which case there is no fee.

The extract decree will be made available fourteen days after the divorce has been granted. The extract decree dissolves or annuls the marriage.

Further information can be obtained from any sheriff court, solicitor or Citizens' Advice Bureau, the Lord Advocate's Office, or the following:

The Court of Session

Parliament House, Parliament Square,
Edinburgh EH1 1RQ
Tel: 0131-225 2595

EMPLOYMENT LAW

Responsibility for employment legislation rests with the UK Parliament and the legislation applies to all parts of Great Britain, with the exception of some separate anti-discrimination legislation for Northern Ireland.

The Employment Rights Act 1996 consolidates the statutory provisions relating to employees' rights. It covers matters such as pay and conditions (including authorised deductions from pay, trade union membership, disputes, and the rights of part-time employees (although the Part-time Employees (Prevention of Less favourable Treatment) Regulations were due to come into force on 1 July 2000) and termination of employment (including redundancy and unfair dismissal). The Working Time Regulations 1998 and the National Minimum Wage Act 1998 now supplement the 1996 Act. Procedure at Employment Tribunals is governed by separate Scottish regulations.

A number of laws protect employees from discrimination in employment on the grounds of sex, race or disability:
— The Equal Pay Act 1970 (as amended)
— The Sex Discrimination Act 1975 (as amended by the Sex Discrimination Act 1986)
— The Race Relations Act 1976
— The Disability Discrimination Act 1995
The Equal Opportunities Commission and the Commission for Racial Equality have the function of eliminating such discriminations in the workplace and can provide further information and assistance. The Disability Rights Commission has been in operation since April 2000 and aims to encourage good practice in the treatment of disabled people and can provide information and assistance.

Equal Opportunities Commission
Stock Exchange House, 7 Nelson Mandela Place,
Glasgow G2 1QW
Tel: 0141-248 5833; Fax: 0141-248 5834

Commision for Racial Equality
45 Hanover Street, Edinburgh EH2 2PJ
Tel: 0131-226 5186; Fax: 0131-226 5243

Disability Rights Commision
1st Floor, Riverside House, Gorgie Road,
Edinburgh EH11 3AF
Tel: 08457 622 63; Fax: 08457 622 688

HOUSE PURCHASE

A contract for the sale of a house in Scotland rarely takes the form of a single document. The purchaser's solicitor issues a formal written offer to purchase. This is usually issued once a survey of the property has been carried out, but can more unusually be issued 'subject to survey'. The seller's solicitor will issue a qualified acceptance of the offer. This is then adjusted between the solicitors until a final concluding letter is issued. At this point the contract is formed and both parties are contractually bound. The letters passing between the solicitors are known as 'missives'.

Some conditions contained within the missives may require the seller to provide information so that the purchaser may be satisfied that the property is unaffected by any statutory notices for repairs or by any planning proposals. Property enquiry reports are obtained by the seller's solicitor from either the local authority or private companies who provide this information. These reports disclose whether the property is adversely affected, if it is served by public water and sewage services and whether the roads adjoining the property are maintained by the local authority.

The purchaser will also examine the title deeds for the property to make sure that there are no flaws in the title to be granted to the purchaser. Searches in the appropriate property register are made. A search is also carried out against both the purchaser and the seller to ensure there is no reason why either party cannot proceed with the transaction.

On the day of settlement the purchaser's solicitor will pass the purchase price to the seller's solicitor who in turn passes over the disposition, title deeds, an obligation to deliver a clear search brought down to disclose the recording of the purchaser's title and keys. The disposition is the deed which transfers ownership of the property from the seller to the purchaser. This deed has to be registered in the appropriate property register in order for the purchaser to have a right to the property — either the Register of Sasines or the newer Land Register which is being phased in by county to replace the old Register of Sasines.

ILLEGITIMACY AND LEGITIMATION

Under the Legitimation (Scotland) Act 1968, which came into operation on 8 June 1968, an illegitimate person automatically becomes legitimate when his/her parents marry, even where one of the parents was married to a third person at the time of the birth.

Illegitimate and legitimate people are given, for all practical purposes, equal status under the Law Reform (Parent and Child) Scotland Act 1986.

The Children (Scotland) Act 1995 gives the mother parental responsibility for her child when she is not married to the child's father. The father has no automatic parental rights when unmarried to the mother, but can acquire parental responsibility by applying to the court. The father of any child, regardless of parental rights, has a duty to aliment that child until he/she is 18 or has completed full-time education, whichever date is later. The Child Support Agency are entitled to make an assessment if this is not done, and the mother of the child can apply to the Child Support Agency for this to be done.

JURY SERVICE

A person charged with any serious crime is tried before a jury. Jury trials in Scottish civil cases in the Court of Session are becoming more common. In Scotland there are 12 members of a jury in a civil case in the Court of Session (the civil jury trial is confined to the Court of Session and a restricted number of actions) and 15 in a criminal trial. Jurors are expected to sit for the duration of the trial.

Every parliamentary or local government elector between the ages of 18 and 65 who has lived in the UK, the Channel Islands or the Isle of Man for any period of at least five years since reaching the age of 13 is qualified to serve on a jury in Scotland, unless ineligible or disqualified.

Those disqualified from jury service include:
— those who have at any time been sentenced by a court in the UK, the Channel Islands and the Isle of Man to a term of imprisonment or custody of five years or more
— those who have within the previous ten years served any part of a sentence of three months or more of imprisonment or detention

Members of the judiciary are ineligible for ten years after ceasing to hold their post, and others concerned with the administration of justice become eligible again only five years after ceasing to hold office. Members and officers of the Houses of Parliament, full time serving members of the armed forces, registered and practising members of the medical, dental, nursing, veterinary and pharmaceutical professions, ministers of religion, persons in holy orders and those who have served on a jury in the previous five years are excusable as of right.

The maximum fine for a person serving on a jury knowing himself/herself to be ineligible is £1,000. The maximum fine for failing to attend without good cause is also £1,000.

Further information can obtained from:

The Clerk of Justiciary
High Court of Justiciary, Parliament House,
Parliament Square, Edinburgh EH1 1RQ
Tel: 0131-225 2595

LANDLORD AND TENANT
When a property is rented to a tenant, the rights and responsibilities of the landlord and the tenant are determined largely by the tenancy agreement but also the general law of Scotland. The main provisions are mentioned below, but it is advisable to contact the Citizens' Advice Bureau or the local authority housing department for detailed information.

Assured and short assured tenancies exist for lettings after 2 January 1989; the relevant legislation is the Housing (Scotland) Act 1988.

If a tenancy was granted on or after 2 January 1989, the tenant may have an assured tenancy giving that tenant greater rights. The tenant could, for example, stay in possession of the dwelling for as long as the tenant observed the terms of the tenancy. The landlord cannot obtain possession from such a tenant unless the landlord can establish a specific ground for possession (the grounds are set out in the 1988 Act) and obtains a court order. The rent payable continues throughout the period of the lease unless the rent has been fixed by the Rent Assessment Committee of the local authority. The Committee also has powers to determine other terms of the lease.

The 1988 Act also introduced short assured tenancies, which are tenancies of not less than six months where a notice has been served to the effect that the tenancy is a short assured tenancy. A landlord in a short assured tenancy has all the rights of a landlord in an ordinary assured tenancy to recover possession and also the right to regain possession on timeously giving notice to quit to the tenant, whether or not the tenant has observed the terms of the tenancy.

Most tenancies created before 2 January 1989 were regulated tenancies and the Rent (Scotland) Act 1984 still applies where these exist. The Act defines, among other things, the circumstances in which a landlord can increase the rent when improvements are made to the property. The provisions of the 1984 Act do not apply to tenancies where the landlord is the Crown, a local authority, the development corporation of a new town or a housing corporation.

The Housing (Scotland) Act 1987 and its provisions relate to local authority responsibilities for housing, the right to buy, and local authority secured tenancies.

Tenancies in agricultural properties are governed by the Agricultural Holdings (Scotland) Act 1991.

Business premises in Scotland are not controlled by statute to the same extent as in England and Wales, although the Shops (Scotland) Act 1949 gives some security to tenants of shops. Tenants of shops can apply to the sheriff for a renewal of tenancy if threatened with eviction. This application may be dismissed on various grounds, including where the landlord has offered to sell the property to the tenant at an agreed price or, in the absence of agreement as to price, at a price fixed by a single arbiter appointed by the parties or the sheriff. The Act extends to properties where the Crown or government departments are the landlords or the tenants.

Under the Leases Act 1449 the landlord's successors (either purchasers or creditors) are bound by the agreement made with any tenants so long as the following conditions are met:
— the lease, if for more than one year, must be in writing
— there must be a rent
— there must be a term of expiry, and
— the tenant must have entered into possession
Many leases contain references to term and quarter days.

LEGAL AID
Under the Legal Aid (Scotland) Act 1986 and subsequent Regulations, people on low or moderate incomes may qualify for help with the costs of legal advice or representation. The scheme is administered by the Scottish Legal Aid Board.

There are three types of legal aid: civil legal aid, legal advice and assistance, and criminal legal aid.

Civil Legal Aid

Applications for legal aid are made through a solicitor; the Citizens' Advice Bureau will have addresses for local solicitors.

Civil legal aid is available for proceedings in the following:

— the House of Lords
— the Court of Session
— the Lands Valuation Appeal Court
— the Scottish Land Court
— Sheriff Courts
— the Lands Tribunal for Scotland
— the Employment Appeal Tribunals
— the Restrictive Practices Court

Eligibility for civil legal aid is assessed and a civil legal aid certificate granted provided that:

— the applicant qualifies financially, and
— the applicant has reasonable grounds for taking or defending the action, and
— it is reasonable to grant legal aid in the circumstances of the case (for example, civil legal aid will not be granted where it appears that the applicant will gain only trivial advantage from the proceedings)

The financial criteria for eligibility are:

— a person is eligible if disposable income is £8,891 or less and disposable capital is £8,560 or less
— if disposable income is between £2,723 and £8,891, contributions are payable
— if disposable capital exceeds £3,000, contributions are payable

Emergency legal aid cover may be granted before a full application has been made and a means test has been carried out. In such cases means testing is carried out later and the applicant is required to meet the cost of any aid received which exceeded their entitlement.

A statutory charge is made if a person is awarded money or property in a case for which they have received legal aid.

Legal Advice and Assistance

The legal advice and assistance scheme covers the costs of getting advice and help from a solicitor and, in some cases, representation in court under the 'assistance by way of representation' scheme (see below).

A person is eligible:

— if disposable income does not exceed £180 a week. If disposable income is between £76 and £180 a week, contributions are payable

— if disposable capital does not exceed £1,000 (£1,335 if the person has one dependant, £1,535 if two dependants, with an additional £100 for every other dependant). There are no contributions from capital

If a person is eligible, an initial amount of authorised expenditure can be incurred without the prior authority of the Scottish Legal Aid Board. The initial limit is £80 in most cases, but a higher initial limit of £150 applies in some circumstances, for example where a civil matter is only likely to be resolved in court, legal aid will be available to the client and the initial work is reasonable. Any increase in authorised expenditure must first be applied for from and granted by the Scottish Legal Aid Board.

Legal advice and assistance covers, for example, giving advice, writing letters, making an application for civil/criminal legal aid and seeking the advice of an advocate. Advice and assistance does not, in general, cover appearance before a court or tribunal other than advice by way of representation.

Assistance by way of representation is available in certain cases such as certain less serious criminal cases, some mental health proceedings and civil proceedings for fine default or breach of a court order.

Criminal Legal Aid

The procedure for application for criminal legal aid depends on the circumstances of each case. In solemn cases (more serious cases, such as homicide) heard before a jury, a person is automatically entitled to criminal legal aid until they are given bail or placed in custody. Thereafter, it is for the court to decide whether to grant legal aid. The court will do this if the person accused cannot meet the expenses of the case without 'undue hardship' on him or his dependants. In summary (less serious) cases the procedure depends on whether the person is in custody:

— anyone taken into custody has the right to free legal aid from the duty solicitor up to and including the first court appearance. Thereafter, if the person has decided to plead guilty, the duty solicitor will continue to act for him/her until the case is finished. If the person pleads not guilty to any charge, they must apply to the Scottish Legal Aid Board so that their solicitor can prepare their defence and represent them at the trial. The duty solicitor may be willing to act for the accused, or they can choose their own solicitor

— if the person is not in custody and wishes to

plead guilty, they are not entitled to criminal legal aid but may be entitled to legal advice and assistance, including assistance by way of representation. The court will not assign the person a solicitor, and they must therefore choose their own if they wish one

— if the person is not in custody and wishes to plead not guilty, they can apply for criminal legal aid. This must be done within 14 days of the first court appearance at which they made the plea. Again, the person must choose their own solicitor

The Scottish Legal Aid Board will grant criminal legal aid if satisfied that the applicant or their family would suffer undue hardship if they had to pay for their own defence and that it is in the interests of justice to grant legal aid (the Board will consider, for example, whether there are difficult legal points to be decided, whether the applicant's job or liberty is at risk, and whether the applicant has a realistic defence).

If criminal legal aid is awarded, no contribution from the person will be required.

Further information may be obtained from:

Scottish Legal Aid Board
44 Drumsheugh Gardens, Edinburgh EH3 7SW
Tel: 0131-226 7061; Fax: 0131-220 4878

MARRIAGE

Regular Marriages
A regular marriage is one which is celebrated by a minister of religion or authorised registrar or other celebrant. Each of the parties must complete a marriage notice form and return it to the district registrar for the area in which they are to be married, irrespective of where they live, at least 15 days before the ceremony is due to take place. The district registrar must then enter the date of receipt and certain details in a marriage book kept for this purpose, and must also enter the names of the parties and the proposed date of the marriage in a list which is displayed in a conspicuous place at the registration office. This entry remains displayed until the date of the marriage has passed. All persons wishing to enter into a regular marriage in Scotland must follow the same preliminary procedure regardless of whether they intend to have a civil or a religious ceremony.

A marriage schedule, which is prepared by the registrar, will be issued to one or both of the parties in person up to seven days before a religious marriage; for a civil marriage the schedule will be available at the ceremony. The schedule must be handed to the celebrant before the ceremony starts; it must be signed immediately after the wedding and the marriage must be registered within three days.

Civil (as opposed to religious) marriage ceremonies are normally conducted by the district registrar in his office. However, if one of the parties cannot attend the registrar's office because of serious illness or serious bodily injury, the registrar may, on application by either party, solemnise the marriage anywhere in his registration district if delay of the wedding is undesirable.

In the case of a religious marriage, the authority to conduct a marriage is deemed to be vested in the authorised celebrant (a minister, priest or other such religious person) conducting the ceremony rather than the building in which it takes place; open-air religious ceremonies are therefore permissible in Scotland.

Marriage by Cohabitation with Habit and Repute
If two people live together constantly as husband and wife and are generally held to be such by the neighbourhood and among their friends and relations, there may arise a presumption from which marriage can be inferred. Before such a marriage can be registered, however, a decree of declarator of marriage must be obtained from the Court of Session.

Civil Fees
The basic statutory fee is £77, comprising a £12 per person fee for a statutory notice of intention to marry, a £45 fee for solemnisation of the marriage in a register office, and an £8.00 fee for a copy of the marriage certificate.

Further information can be obtained from the General Register Office for Scotland.

TOWN AND COUNTRY PLANNING
The principal legislation governing the development of land and buildings is the Town and Country Planning (Scotland) Act 1997. The uses of buildings are classified by the Town and Country Planning (Use Classes) (Scotland) Order 1997. It is advisable in all cases to contact the planning department of the local authority to check whether planning or other permission is needed.

VOTERS' QUALIFICATIONS

All persons registered in the electoral registers (which are compiled on a local basis) and over the age of 18 are entitled to vote at Scottish Parliament, UK Parliament, European Parliament and local government elections. To qualify for registration, a person must be:

— resident in the relevant constituency or ward on 10 October in the year before the electoral register comes into effect
— over 18 years old or will attain the age of 18 during the 12 months following the publication of the annual register on 16 February
— a UK, European Union, Commonwealth or Republic of Ireland citizen

Peers registered in Scotland are entitled to vote in Scottish Parliament, European Parliament and local government elections.

Overseas electors (namely British citizens not resident in the UK on the qualifying date for the electoral register but who were registered as parliamentary electors at some point in the preceding 20 years) are only entitled to vote in UK Parliament and European Parliament elections. Similar provisions apply to enable those who were too young to be registered during the previous 20 years to register provided a parent or guardian was registered.

Peers and European Union citizens are not eligible to vote in UK Parliament elections.

Voters must be entered on an electoral register, which runs from 16 February each year to the following 15 February. Supplementary lists of electors are published throughout the duration of the register.

Further information can be obtained from the local authority's electoral registration officer.

WILLS AND INTESTACY

Wills

In Scotland any person over 12 and of sound mind can make a will. The person making the will can only freely dispose of the heritage and what is known as the 'dead's part' of the estate because:

— the spouse has the right to inherit one-third of the moveable estate if there are children or other descendants, and one-half of it if there are not
— children are entitled to one-third of the moveable estate if there is a surviving spouse, and one-half of it if there is not

The remaining portion is the dead's part, and legacies and bequests are payable from this. Debts are payable out of the whole estate before any division.

From August 1995, wills no longer needed to be 'holographed' and it is now only necessary to have one witness. The person making the will still needs to sign each page. It is better that the will is not witnessed by a beneficiary although the attestation would still be sound and the beneficiary would not have to relinquish the gift.

Subsequent marriage does not revoke a will but the birth of a child who is not provided for may do so. A will may be revoked by a subsequent will, either expressly or by implication, but in so far as the two can be read together both have effect. If a subsequent will is revoked, the earlier will is revived.

Wills may be registered in the sheriff court books of the Sheriffdom in which the deceased lived or in the Books of Council and Session at the Registers of Scotland. If the will has been registered in the Books of Council and Session, the original will can be inspected and a copy obtained for a small fee. On the other hand, if the will has been registered in the sheriff court books, the original will have been returned to the ingiver; however, copies may still be obtained for a small fee from the photographed copy kept in the register.

Confirmation

Confirmation (the Scottish equivalent of English probate) is obtained in the sheriff court of the sheriffdom in which the deceased was resident at the time of death. Executors are either 'nominate' (named by the deceased in the will) or 'dative' (appointed by the court in cases where no executor is named in a will or in cases of intestacy). Applicants for confirmation must first provide an inventory of the deceased's estate and a schedule of debts, with an affidavit. In estates under £25,000 gross, confirmation can be obtained under a simplified procedure at reduced fees. The local sheriff clerk's office can provide assistance.

Further information can be obtained from:

Registers of Scotland
Meadowbank House, 153 London Road,
Edinburgh, EH8 7AU
Tel: 0131-659 6111

Intestacy

Intestacy occurs when someone dies without leaving a will or leaves a will which is invalid or which does not take effect for some reason. In such cases the person's estate (property, possessions, other assets following the payment of debts) passes to certain members of the family.

Under the Succession (Scotland) Act 1964, no distinction is made between 'moveable' and 'heritable' property in intestacy cases.

A surviving spouse is entitled to 'prior rights'. This means that, with effect from 1 April 1999, the spouse has the right to inherit:

— the matrimonial home up to a value of £130,000, or one matrimonial home if there is more than one, or, in certain circumstances, the value of the matrimonial home

— the furnishings and contents of that home, up to the value of £22,000

— a cash sum of £35,000 if the deceased left children or other descendants, or £58,000 if not

These figures are increased from time to time by regulations.

Once prior rights have been satisfied, what remains of the estate is generally divided between the surviving spouse and children (legitimate and illegitimate) according to 'legal' rights. Legal rights are:

Jus relicti (ae) — the right of a surviving spouse to one-half of the net moveable estate, after satisfaction of prior rights, if there are no surviving children; if there are surviving children, the spouse is entitled to one-third of the net moveable estate;

Legitim — the right of surviving children to one-half of the net moveable estate if there is no surviving spouse; if there is a surviving spouse, the children are entitled to one-third of the net moveable estate after the satisfaction of prior rights.

Where there are no surviving spouse or children, half of the estate is taken by the parents and half by the brothers and sisters. Failing that, the lines of succession, in general, are:

— to descendants

— if no descendants, then to collaterals (i.e. brothers and sisters) and parents

— surviving spouse

— if no collaterals or parents or spouse, then to ascendants collaterals (i.e. aunts and uncles), and so on in an ascending scale

If all lines of succession fail, then the estate passes to the Crown.

Relatives of the whole blood are preferred to relatives of the half blood. The right of representation, i.e. the right of the issue of a person who would have succeeded if he/she had survived the intestate, also applies.

BUSINESS

SCOTLAND

INTRODUCTION TO THE SCOTTISH ECONOMY
BANKING
CURRENCY
LOCAL ENTERPRISE COMPANIES
PROFESSIONAL AND TRADE BODIES
TRADE UNIONS
THE VOLUNTARY SECTOR

BUSINESS SCOTLAND

THE SCOTTISH ECONOMY

This review confirms that Scotland is a small, open, regional economy of the UK that has experienced significant structural change. The economy of Scotland is small in relation to that of the UK as a whole (under ten per cent), which in turn is small compared to the EU and world economies. The 'openness' is reflected in Scotland's large trade flows with the rest of the UK, Europe and also with the rest of the World. It is also apparent in the importance of foreign direct investment to the Scottish economy. The regional dimension is evident in the degree of integration of Scottish labour market with that of the rest-of-the UK as reflected, for example, in the historically large net out-migration flows from Scotland. The regional dimension is also reflected in the fact that key policy influences on the national economy, notably monetary and fiscal policies, are reserved to the Westminster Parliament. None of this implies that the economic powers devolved to the Scottish Parliament, established in May 1999, are incapable of significantly influencing the Scottish economy. However, it is undoubtedly true that many of the major influences on the performance of the Scottish economy remain outwith the control of the Scottish (and indeed even the Westminster) Parliaments. The Scottish economy remains heavily dependent on the fortunes of the rest of the UK, the EU and World economies. Furthermore, in line with other developed economies, including that of the UK, Scotland has, over the longer-term become a predominantly service-based economy, where some 75 per cent of employment is accounted for by the service sectors, although aspects of manufacturing activity continue (notably that associated with computers) to exhibit success.

As in any economy total output produced in Scotland can be thought of as reflecting both the scale (or capacity) of the economy, and the rate of utilisation of that capacity. For a given size of labour force, for example, Scottish output is likely to be lower when the unemployment rate is high since the labour force is unlikely to be fully utilised in these circumstances. Considered below is: the scale of the Scottish economy as a whole; the openness of the economy; its regional nature and the implications for public finances; capacity utilisation; the sectoral structure of the Scottish economy and other salient features.

This is necessarily a brief overview, however,

a recent review of the Scottish Economy (Jeremy Peat and Stephen Boyle, *An Illustrated Guide to the Scottish Economy*, Duckworth, London, 1999) provides additional analysis of many of the topics discussed here. The Scottish Executive's new twice-yearly Scottish Economic Report is a valuable source of information and commentary on the Scottish Economy. Further analysis is available in the Fraser of Allander Institute's *Quarterly Economic Commentary*. The principal source for the statistical information presented here is the Scottish Executive, and the Office of National Statistics (ONS), as published in the Scottish Executive's new annual *Scottish Economic Statistics*. In particular, *Scottish Economic Statistics (2000)* and various issues of the publication that preceded this, *Scottish Economic Bulletin (nos. 54, 56 and 58)* are the main data sources employed here. Trade figures are due in part to the Scottish Council Development and Industry. Earnings data are from the New Earnings Survey. Data on household spending and consumption come from the ONS *Family Spending Survey*.

THE SCALE OF THE SCOTTISH ECONOMY

Many aspects of economies are thought to depend on their scale or size. The most commonly employed indicator of an economy's scale is its Gross Domestic Product (GDP), which measures the value of the goods and services produced in an economy over a particular period (usually a single year). Scotland's GDP in 1997 was £56,219 million (at 1997 prices) or 8.1 per cent of UK GDP. These data, however, exclude the oil and gas output from the UK Continental Shelf, which is treated as a separate region in the national accounts. If, say, 80 per cent of this output were attributed to Scotland, estimated GDP would have been increased by over 20 per cent. Other measures of scale include population and employment. Table 1 indicates that Scotland's share of U.K population and employment were 8.7 per cent and 8.5 per cent respectively in 1997. Scotland is therefore a comparatively small region of the UK, except where scale is measured in terms of land area. Scotland accounts for over 32 per cent of the UK's land area and has the lowest population density (average population per square kilometre) of all 11 standard regions of the UK (and just over a tenth of the density of the South East).

TABLE 1. THE SCALE OF THE SCOTTISH REGION IN 1997

Region	Scotland	UK	Scotland per cent of UK
Area (sq km)	77097	240,883	32.0
Population	5,122,500	59,009,000.00	8.7
Population Density (person/sq metre)	66	244	27.0
Total Employment (000's, 1997)	2,278	26,682	8.5
GDP (1997 prices)	56,219	694,435	8.1
GDP per head	10,975	11,488	95.5

Although it is not a measure of scale, the final row of Table 1 shows GDP per head of population. This is the most commonly employed measure of the economic prosperity of regions and nations. Scottish GDP per head, at £10,975 in 1997 is 95.5 per cent of the UK average. Attribution of 20 per cent of the output of oil and gas would increase GDP per head significantly, and raise Scotland from fifth to third position in the rankings of UK regions (after South East England and East Anglia). These most recent estimates of GDP, which are based on the European System of Accounts 1995, have cast doubt on the validity of the earlier view that Scottish GDP per head had effectively converged on that of the UK. These new estimates suggest that while Scottish GDP per head rose to 98.9 per cent of the corresponding UK estimate in 1995, it fell to 96.8 per cent in 1996 and fell again to only 95.5 per cent of UK GDP per head in 1997.

Table 2 indicates that there is considerable variation in GDP per head among the sub-regions of Scotland. In 1996, for example, GDP per head in North Eastern Scotland was 36 per cent higher than in Scotland as a whole, whereas in Highlands and Islands it was over 20 per cent below the Scottish average. The dominance of South Western Scotland is also apparent, since it accounts for some 42 per cent of GDP. Smaller regions naturally show even greater variations in GDP per head, ranging from only 57 per cent of the Scottish figure in East Lothian and Midlothian to 149 per cent in the city of Edinburgh.

TABLE 2. GROSS DOMESTIC PRODUCT AT FACTOR COST (CURRENT PRICES)
FOR LOCAL AREAS IN SCOTLAND, 1996

	£ million	£ per head population	£ per head pop. Scotland=100
Scotland	54,430	10,614	100
North Eastern Scotland (Aberdeen City, Aberdeenshire and North East Moray)	7,347	14,453	136
Eastern Scotland	21,026	11,116	105
Angus and Dundee City	2,642	10,123	96
Clackmannanshire and Fife	3,465	8,704	82
East Lothian and Midlothian	1,009	5,999	57
Scottish Borders	1,000	9,422	89
Edinburgh, City of	7,131	15,888	149
Falkirk	1,580	11,046	104
Perth and Kinross and Stirling	2,168	10,068	95
West Lothian	2,030	13,466	127
South Western Scotland	22,964	9,747	92
East and West Dunbartonshire, Helensburgh and Lomond	1,690	7,211	68
Dumfries and Galloway	1,469	9,955	94
East Ayrshire and North Ayrshire Mainland	1,954	7,637	72
Glasgow City	7,895	12,808	121
Inverclyde, East Renfrewshire and Renfrewshire	3,472	9,814	93
North Lanarkshire	2,594	7,959	75
South Ayrshire	1,294	11,286	106
South Lanarkshire	2,596	8,445	80
Highlands and Islands	3,093	8,308	79
Caithness and Sutherland and Ross and Cromarty	733	8,157	77

Inverness and Nairn and Moray, Badenoch and Strathspey	897	8,152	77
Lochaber, Skye and Lochalsh and Argyll and the Islands	759	7,540	71
Eilean Siar (Western Isles)	233	8,072	76
Orkney Islands	177	8,949	85
Shetland Islands	293	12,748	120

THE OPENNESS OF THE SCOTTISH ECONOMY

Smaller economies tend to be more open than their larger counterparts, often in a number of respects. Scotland has, like many other economies, been affected by increasing 'globalisation', with openness to international trade and capital flows growing through time. A number of dimensions of openness are briefly considered.

Trade

One important feature of the scale of an economy is that smaller economies tend, in general, to be more open to trade. Both exports and imports tend to be relatively more important for small economies. The Scottish input-output tables for 1996 imply that Scotland's total exports amounted to £43,014 million in total. The export to GDP ratio implied is nearly 80 per cent, whereas for the UK as a whole the export to GDP ratio was around 30 per cent in 1997. Admittedly, however, a great deal of Scotland's trade consisted of exports to the other regions of the UK. Scotland's exports to the rest of the world accounted for some 38 per cent of Scottish GDP. Scotland appears to be significantly more open than the UK as a whole (which itself is open relative to the Organisation for Economic Co-operation and Development (OECD)). However, Scotland also imports more, relatively, than the UK as a whole. In 1996 its imports from the rest of the UK, at £22,103 million, exceeded its exports to this region, implying a trade deficit. However, Scotland's imports from the rest of the world were only £16,793 million, implying a trade surplus with the rest of the world.

Manufacturing exports are estimated to account for some 75 per cent of total exports to the rest of the world, and 75 per cent of these were, in turn, attributable in 1996 to only three subsectors: office machinery (including computers, 37.1 per cent), radio, television and communications (16.3 per cent) and whisky (12.4 per cent) (Scottish Council Development and Industry, 1997). Caution is required in interpreting these figures as contributions to the nation's balance of trade, however, since Office machinery, for example, also imports a much larger proportion of its inputs than the whisky industry.

According to the Scottish Council Development and Industry's survey of manufactured exports for 1998, Scotland's main export markets outside of the UK remain the EU (63 per cent) and North America (11.2 per cent). The UK as a whole is less dependent on the EU (56.1 per cent) and more on North America (15.3 per cent) than Scotland. When, as has happened since the launch of European Monetary Union, sterling increases in value against the euro, the implication is that Scottish exporters may be more adversely affected than those in the UK as a whole.

Foreign Ownership

In recent years, foreign ownership has grown more rapidly than international trade, partly as a result of reduced restrictions on international capital flows and the more global perspective of multinational companies. The aggregate stock of foreign owned companies in the world is estimated to have doubled between 1975 and 1994. This important aspect of increasing openness is also a feature of the Scottish economy. Foreign direct investment/ inward investment has been an increasingly important feature of the manufacturing sector, with the number of plants rising from 65 in 1950 to 357 in 1994, by which time foreign-owned plants accounted for over a quarter of manufacturing employment and a third of total sales. The service sector too is increasingly affected. These trends are in part a consequence of a regional policy stance that has sought to encourage inward investment. Inward investors tended to be concentrated in the fastest growing 'high tech' sectors such as electronics, producing computers and workstations or semiconductors. Foreign-owned components of manufacturing tend to have higher productivity, export a higher proportion of their output (but import a larger proportion of inputs) and pay higher wages. There is also the suggestion that they improve efficiency in supplier and customer firms.

Migration and population change

A further feature of the openness of the Scottish economy is the degree of integration of the Scottish and rest of the UK labour markets.

Perhaps the most distinctive manifestation of this in Scotland, as in most regional economies, is the existence of significant migration flows. While in any single year net migration flows have been of a fairly modest scale, these have cumulatively resulted in significant flows of population out of Scotland and into the rest of the UK and overseas, resulting in a lower population than otherwise would have been the case. In 1861, for example, Scotland's share of UK population stood at 12.5 per cent, while by 1997 it had fallen to 8.7 per cent. The population of the UK as a whole increased by around 20 per cent in the 1951–99 period, whereas in Scotland population was broadly static. Over the last thirty years the population of Scotland has in fact fallen by around 1 per cent. During the 1960s net out-migration averaged around 32,000, though this declined in the 1970s and fell to around half that level in the 1980s. In the 1990s population has been fairly stable, with net in-migration in a number of years.

This cumulative net out-migration has reduced the population of working age in Scotland below what it otherwise would have been (to around 3.2 million currently). Of these around 70 per cent actually participate actively in the labour market. Historically male participation rates were much higher than those for females, but these have virtually converged. (In the 1960s male rates were in the high 90 per cent range, and females in the mid 40 per cent range.) Net out-migration therefore reduces the available supply of labour (for a given participation rate), and there is some suggestion too that it is selective in terms of age and skill. However, migration flows are an important means by which regional labour markets function and, with no additional growth in employment, lower net out-migration would have implied much higher unemployment rates.

Significant net out-migration flows can create even greater problems for smaller sub-regions. For example, loss of population from the City of Glasgow has reduced the numbers of households paying taxes to the City, and so creates funding problems.

THE REGIONAL CONTEXT AND PUBLIC SECTOR FINANCES

The scale of a regional economy, particularly in terms of its geographical size and population density, is important in understanding the level of regions' public expenditure per head of population. In particular, where the population of a region is geographically dispersed the provision of a given level of public services becomes more expensive, and this is part of the explanation of the public sector deficit in Scotland.

The devolution debate has tended to focus considerable attention on regional public finances, especially in Scotland. Many elements of government revenues and some elements of government expenditure are not directly measured at the regional level and so have to be estimated somehow. This has given rise to some controversy, although most commentators take the view that Scotland receives more than its population share of public expenditures while contributing roughly its population share to tax revenues. Accordingly, many believe that there is a public sector deficit in Scotland, with public sector expenditures exceeding revenues (even when the unemployment rate in Scotland, and so expenditure on benefits, is low).

Public expenditure in Scotland is divided into three elements: identifiable (Scottish Office spending plus social security); non-identifiable (largely public goods such as defence, foreign affairs etc); other spending (servicing of debt etc). Only the identifiable component is entirely reliably estimated, with Scotland's share of the other expenditures being determined in some more or less mechanical way, normally using population shares. Total expenditure was estimated to be £32.3 billion in 1997–8, of which £24.4 billion was identifiable. This amounted to 10.2 per cent of UK government expenditure, well in excess of Scotland's population share of 8.6 per cent. This could conceivably be justifiable in terms of a greater need for public expenditure given the greater cost of providing comparable public services in Scotland. However, the last 'needs assessment' exercise was conducted in 1976 and suggested that Scottish identified expenditure should be 116 per cent of the corresponding English level, whereas this is currently around 130 per cent. Since there is also some evidence that Scotland has become more affluent relative to the UK as a whole, there is some pressure to reduce Scotland's share of expenditures.

In fact, the Barnett formula, which governs the allocation of expenditures to the Scottish 'block' (or assigned budget under devolution), implies that Scotland receives a fixed share of any change in comparable expenditures in England and Wales. Without any modifications to this formula it would eventually imply a movement towards equal public expenditure per head across all the regions of the UK. This would appear to conflict with the 'principle of equalisation' according to which public expenditures should be such as to provide comparable public services in all parts of the UK. (This would imply higher expenditures where service delivery is more expensive.)

Total public sector revenues in 1997–8 were estimated to be £26.7 billion excluding oil and gas, amounting to 8.6 per cent of total UK revenues, precisely Scotland's population share. This implies a public sector deficit (excess of expenditure over revenues) of £5.6 billion. There is considerable controversy surrounding Scotland's share of oil and gas revenues. If no adjustment at all were made for this, the deficit would amount to nearly 10 per cent of GDP. While this is considerably in excess of the Maastricht requirement of 3 per cent of GDP as indicating a sustainable fiscal deficit, and suitability for membership of the common European currency, this implies that none of the revenues from North Sea oil accrue to Scotland. There are, too, doubts concerning some aspects of the calculations (as well as the rigour with which such criteria are in fact applied), and the controversy will no doubt continue.

CHANGES IN THE SCALE OF THE SCOTTISH ECONOMY OVER TIME

While an appreciation of the absolute and relative scale of the Scottish economy at a particular point in time is useful, it provides only a snapshot of performance. It is also very important to understand the evolution of the Scottish economy through time. While it has already been noted that significant reductions in the Scottish population have occurred most attention tends to be focused on the rate of economic growth (though these are linked).

An economy's rate of economic growth is often measured in terms of its average percentage rate of change of GDP over time. Actual output tends to vary in a cyclical manner, with the level of GDP actually falling in recessions and so generating negative growth rates. The cycles in activity in Scotland and the rest of the UK are broadly in phase, although Scotland did not experience the late 1980s boom, and the last recession was exceptional in that the rest of the UK was more adversely affected than Scotland, a reversal of the historical pattern. It is also clear, however, that the trend rate of growth over the period is positive in both regions. In the rest of the UK the simple average of growth rates over the period was 2.4 per cent, whereas for Scotland it was 1.5 per cent. While the difference may not seem substantial, if such a growth rate differential were to be sustained, the cumulative effect on levels of GDP would be dramatic. Naturally, however, estimates of differential growth depend critically on the period over which they are measured. Over the 1990s, for example, the average annual growth rate in Scotland was, at 1.7 per cent, again less than that in the rest of the UK (2.0 per cent), but from 1991 to 1995 Scotland's growth rate exceeded that of the rest of the UK largely as a consequence of the differential impact of the last recession. Over the long-run, Scotland's average growth rate has been higher, at just over 2 per cent.

Nonetheless, Scottish GDP per head had, at least until recently, been thought to have caught up with that in the UK. This would be possible in a regional economy like Scotland, even with slower GDP growth, since in every decade of this century Scotland has lost population through net out-migration. The factors governing regional and national growth remain little understood, though recently considerable emphasis has been placed on public investment in infrastructure, investment in human resources (through education and training) and research and development activity, as well as population and physical capital growth.

Data on total employment from the Labour Force Survey are available from 1984. These indicate that employment grew by around 12 per cent in both Scotland and the UK over the period to 1998. Employment grew through most of the 1980s, peaking at around 2.3 million in 1992, before contracting substantially and then gradually recovering to the 1992 level. Growth in employees in employment was slightly less (10 per cent over the period), with growth in self-employment accounting for the remainder. Most of the growth in employment over the period, however, is accounted for by an expansion in part-time female employment (which rose by some 87,000 or 17 per cent over the period to 610,000 in 1998). Around 2.3 million people were in work in Scotland in 1999, of whom 2 million (nearly 90 per cent) were employees. There were 213,000 self-employed and 21,000 on training schemes.

REGIONAL UTILISATION OF RESOURCES

The most obvious measure of the regional utilisation of resources is the regional unemployment rate, although at best this measures the utilisation of the labour force. Traditionally, attention has focused on an unemployment rate measured in terms of claimants of the relevant benefit. Since the benefits system has changed considerably through time, so too will this rate of unemployment quite independently of any change in labour utilisation. Some of the difficulties of interpretation are overcome by adoption of the government's new 'headline' rate of unemployment, which is measured through a household survey using the International Labour Organisation (ILO) definition. Recent unemployment rates for Scotland and the UK are presented in Table 2A. Unemployment rates tend to fluctuate with the cycle in GDP: as activity increases, so too does employment, although typically with a lag, and this tends to push unemployment rates down. The unemployment rates peaked in the mid-1980s, and then fell until the beginning of the 1990's when economic activity slowed and unemployment rose. From 1993 unemployment has tended to fall. In the UK context, it has often been argued that there exists a north-south divide, with northern regions (including Scotland) typically experiencing lower growth and higher unemployment. The unemployment differentials did appear to be fairly stable until recently when the Scottish unemployment rate fell below that of the UK. However, the signs are that this disruption to the historical pattern may prove to be a short-lived reflection of the especially severe impact of the last recession on the south.

TABLE 2A. REGIONAL
            UNEMPLOYMENT RATES
            (ILO DEFINITION)

	Scotland	UK
1986	13.9	11.2
1987	14.9	10.8
1988	12	8.8
1989	9.7	7.2
1990	9.3	6.8
1991	9.3	8.4
1992	9.5	9.7
1993	10.2	10.3
1994	10	9.6
1995	8.3	8.6
1996	8.7	8.3
1997	8.5	7.3
1998	7.7	6.8
1999	7	5.9

Source: ONS, Labour Force Survey

Unemployment rates vary significantly among the sub-regions of Scotland, as is apparent from Table 3. In April 1999 claimant counts (typically less than the corresponding ILO measure) varied from 2.3 per cent in Aberdeen city to nearly 11.0 per cent in West Dunbartonshire. Unemployment rates are also systematically higher for men than for women. In the first quarter of 1999, for example, the overall headline rate of unemployment (ILO) was 7.6

per cent (as against 6.3 per cent for the UK). The unemployment rate for men was 8.5 per cent, however, as against 6.4 per cent for women. (The differential is more substantial on the claimant count measure. In October 1999, for example, the claimant count measure of the male unemployment rate was 7.5 per cent and that for females was 2.5 per cent.) The duration of unemployment spells has been tending to fall with the overall unemployment rate, however, men also tend to suffer disproportionately from long spells of unemployment (on a claimant basis).

TABLE 3. CLAIMANT COUNT
           UNEMPLOYMENT RATE
           (PER CENT): BY SCOTTISH
           SUB-REGION, APRIL 1999

Aberdeen City	2.3
Aberdeenshire	3
Angus	6.2
Argyll and Bute	5.2
Clackmannanshire	8.9
Dumfries and Galloway	5.9
Dundee City	7.7
East Ayrshire	9.7
East Dunbartonshire	6.2
East Lothian	4.3
East Renfrewshire	6.7
Edinburgh, City of	3.3
Eilean Siar (Western Isles)	8.7
Falkirk	7.4
Fife	7.6
Glasgow City	6.4
Highland	5.3
Inverclyde	6.9
Midlothian	4.9
Moray	4.5
North Ayrshire	10.2
North Lanarkshire	8.7
Orkney Islands	3.1
Perth and Kinross	3.6
Renfrewshire	5.8
Scottish Borders, The	4.4
Shetland Islands	2.6
South Ayrshire	6.2
South Lanarkshire	6.7
Stirling	4.6
West Dunbartonshire	10.9
West Lothian	5

TABLE 4. GROSS DOMESTIC PRODUCT BY INDUSTRY GROUPS, 1996

	Scotland	% Scotland	UK	%UK
Agriculture, etc.	1,642	3.0	11,790	1.9
Mining, quarrying	1,220	2.2	4,398	0.7
Manufacturing	12,103	22.2	137,006	21.8
Electricity, gas, etc.	1,828	3.4	13,606	2.2
Construction	3,282	6.0	33,746	5.4
Distribution, hotels, etc.	7,237	13.3	93,901	14.8
Transport, etc.	4,181	7.7	54,056	8.6
Financial and business services	10,780	19.8	164,282	26.1
Public administration, etc.	3,709	6.8	38,244	6.1
Education, health, etc.	8,250	15.2	81,876	13.0
Other services	2,160	4.0	24,713	3.9
Adjustment for financial services	-1,962	-3.6	-26,968	-4.3

THE SECTORAL STRUCTURE OF THE SCOTTISH ECONOMY

Gross Domestic Product by Industry Groups

Table 4 presents estimates of Gross Domestic Product by Industry groups in 1996. The traditional notion of Scotland as being characterised by specialisation in heavy industries with shipbuilding as a key activity, as reflected in the proud "Clyde built" label, was true of the first half of the century, but is now outdated. Services now account for over 63 per cent of output (68 per cent in the UK). In employment terms services are even more dominant, accounting for 75 per cent of total employment in Scotland.

Perhaps the most striking feature of Table 4 is the broad similarity between the industrial structure of Scotland's economy and that of the UK as a whole. Both have come to be dominated by services, although there are, of course, some differences in detail. The most noticeable relative specialisation in Scotland is in mining and quarrying where Scotland accounts for nearly 28 per cent of UK GDP. Agriculture, hunting forestry and fishing accounts for 13.9 per cent of the UK total, whereas Scotland as a whole recall contributes 8.6 per cent of UK GDP. There is also comparative specialisation in electricity, gas etc contributes 13.4 per cent of UK GDP. However, each of these sectors is really rather small in terms of their percentage contribution to GDP in each region. Financial and business services is the most important contributor to UK GDP (26.1 per cent), but is second most important in Scotland (accounting for 19.8 per cent of GDP). In Scotland the manufacturing sector is most important (22.2 per cent), but is only slightly more important relatively than in the UK as a whole (21.8 per cent). The rankings of the third and fourth most important sectors in the UK as a

whole, distribution, hotels and catering etc (14.8 per cent) and education, social work and health services (13.0 per cent), are again reversed for Scotland. Scotland has historically enjoyed a higher than average share of education and health expenditures, partly reflecting a perceived greater need here. Transport, public administration and construction feature as the next most important sectors in terms of contribution to GDP, with Scotland comparatively specialised in the latter two sectors. However, the differences in structure are comparatively slight, or concentrated in comparatively small sectors: the predominant impression is of the similarity of the industrial structures of Scotland and the UK.

Of course, a single year's data on industry groups output shares gives no indication of the extent of re-structuring that has occurred over time. In fact the Scottish economy has undergone significant structural change even over the last few decades. Table 4A summarises the structure of the Scottish economy in 1971. One of the most striking features of this table, when contrasted with the current situation, is the decline in importance of manufacturing from 30 per cent to 22 per cent between 1971 and 1996. Equally dramatic is the growth in the importance of financial industries over the same period from 3.1 per cent to 13.9 per cent. The decline in manufacturing reflects the contraction in the heavier industries like steel and shipbuilding, but conceals rapid growth in the electronics sector where substantial inward investment has stimulated the creation of 'Silicon Glen' The growth in the financial sector has been one of Scotland's recent success stories. It is truly international in scope, manages over £200 billion of funds, and is characterised by over 30 major financial institutions, many of which are household names (such as the Bank of Scotland

and the Royal Bank of Scotland). The life and general assurance sector contains a number of world leaders, such as Standard Life. While some part of the apparent shift to services may reflect a shedding of formerly 'in-house' services (reducing measured output in manufacturing and increasing it in services), there is no doubt that a substantial genuine re-structuring has occurred in the Scottish economy over the latter part of the century.

Less dramatic, but nonetheless substantial, changes have occurred in the outputs of other sectors. Thus agriculture's share has fallen from 5 per cent to 3 per cent and construction's from 8 per cent to 6 per cent. The 1990s have proved to be a very mixed decade for Scottish Agriculture, with total income for farming initially rising more than threefold in the first half of the decade to a peak of £737 million, in part due to changes in EU support mechanisms. However, farm incomes then fell by almost 66 per cent in the period to 1998, due in part to the impact of BSE. While the ending of the export ban on beef will improve matters, total income from farming looked set for a modest fall in 1999.

These general comments on structural change are reinforced by inspection of the indices of sectoral Gross Value Added that are reported in Table 5. Thus, for example, manufacturing output grew by only 9 per cent between 1973 and 1995 (in which year all indices are set to equal 100), whereas in total industries averaged around 27 per cent growth. Over this period construction fared worst, with growth of less than 4 per cent over the 26-year period. Business, Financial and

TABLE 4A   THE SECTORAL COMPOSITION OF SCOTTISH GDP, 1971

Sector	%
Agriculture etc.	5
Mining and quarrying	1
Manufacturing	31
Electricity, gas, etc.	3
Construction	8
Distributive trades	11
Transport etc.	8
Insurance, banking, etc.	3
Public administration etc	6
Other	24

TABLE 5. INDICES OF GROSS VALUE ADDED FOR SCOTLAND 1973-98

	Total	Agriculture	Mining & Quarrying	Electricity, Gas and Water Supply	Manufac- turing	Construc- tion	Distribu- tion, Hotels & Catering	Transport, Storage & Communi- cation	Business, Financial, Public & Other Services
1973	72.9	67.8	52.1	66.3	91	96.3	63.5	73.3	59.5
1974	72.8	72.8	52.9	64	90.5	86.5	64	73.9	61.2
1975	71.8	67.9	63.6	64.5	86.1	90.3	61.3	72.9	61.6
1976	73	60.1	62.8	66.6	86.3	87.8	62.9	75.5	65.1
1977	74.3	62.7	60.3	69.6	85.9	91.4	63.2	77.6	67
1978	76.1	64.5	71.5	71.3	86	91.1	67.6	79.5	68.9
1979	76.9	62.2	78.7	75.8	85.7	86.4	69.9	81.9	70.6
1980	75.4	67.1	85.6	72.1	79.9	81.6	66.5	79.9	73
1981	74.4	70.5	88.3	74.3	77.7	71.1	65.9	80.8	73.8
1982	75.5	72	94.6	70.9	78.4	73.2	67.9	79.7	75.3
1983	76.5	70.6	98.2	70.3	78	74.9	69	81.6	77.3
1984	79.4	77.8	89.6	79.5	81.2	74.6	72.2	84.4	80
1985	81.7	76.6	102.8	80.7	83	75.9	74.8	87.1	82.4
1986	82	81.7	96.8	77.1	80.6	77.2	76.2	87.7	84.4
1987	83.6	81	91.7	79.2	80.4	75.7	79.2	92.9	86.9
1988	87	79.4	94.5	83	85.6	79.6	86	93.5	89
1989	89.3	84.9	98	80.6	87.9	82.4	90.5	95.7	90.6
1990	91.3	87.7	104	86.6	89.4	89	90.2	94.6	92.6
1991	91.4	86.5	110.3	91.1	87	91.2	88.7	93.8	94.6
1992	92.7	88	112.9	92	87.3	97.1	90.8	94.2	95.6
1993	95	84.5	110.1	93.2	90.4	100	95.6	95.5	97.2
1994	97	93.4	108.3	94.7	95.9	92.3	97	99	98
1995	100	100	100	100	100	100	100	100	100
1996	102.4	96.8	104.4	103.2	102.8	100.3	106.2	102.1	102.1
1997	105.4	92.3	105.7	111.2	108.4	101.1	108.4	109.6	104.1
1998	108	94.3	108.1	113.8	111.3	98.2	112.6	113.4	107.1

Source: Scottish Executive

TABLE 6 EMPLOYEE JOBS BY SEX AND BROAD INDUSTRY GROUP (DECEMBER 1998, NOT SEASONALLY ADJUSTED)

	Male		Female		Total	Primary	Secondary	Tertiary
	Full-time	Part-time	Full-time	Part-time				
Scotland	898	114	556	462	2030	72	448	1,510
UK	10,646	1,570	6,344	5,448	24,008	513	5,211	18,284

other services grew by some 40 per cent. Since 1995, Agriculture etc has fared particularly badly, followed by construction. Electricity, gas and water supply has registered the greatest growth, followed by the service industries.

There has been little comment so far on the discovery and exploitation of North Sea oil, which now has a history spanning over two decades. The special treatment of North Sea oil production in the national accounts has already been noted, as has the fact that the that attribution of a share of this to the Scottish economy could substantially increase Scottish GDP (though the precise share that can be deemed 'Scottish' remains controversial). Naturally, the offshore activity generated much associated onshore activity. In 1994 some 21,000 people were employed directly by the oil and gas industry, but over 60,000 jobs were attributed to the sector in total, through jobs in supporting activities.

While a prolonged period of low oil prices cast a shadow over the likelihood of further development of the less accessible fields, the impact of this has been mitigated to some degree by technological change. The industry is expected to continue to make a significant contribution to the Scottish economy, although the revenues from oil and gas production are in decline. The real oil price (oil prices divided by an index of retail prices) fell by around 80 per cent between the peak of 1980 and the trough of 1998. While oil prices have more than doubled since the OPEC meeting in early 1999, this has little immediate impact on current activity in the oil and gas industry: investment and subsequent activity depends on the (real) oil price expected to prevail in the medium to longer term.

Another omission from the discussion of structural changes up to this point is the tourism industry. The reason for this is that official statistics do not recognise the existence of a tourism "industry" as such. Many industries are particularly sensitive to tourist expenditures, such as hotels and catering, but they are typically not exclusively devoted to satisfying tourist needs. Accordingly, the importance of tourism is estimated in a variety of ways, stemming from

data collected on the numbers of visits, average duration of visits and average daily tourist expenditures. Spending by tourists is estimated to be in excess of £2 billion per year and estimates of the employment impact range up to 75,000.

Sectoral employment patterns

The sectoral pattern of employment, summarised in Table 6, tells a similar story of a shift to a service economy. The primary industries are here defined as: agriculture, hunting, forestry and fishing; mining and quarrying and electricity, gas and water supply. Inspection of Table 6 reveals that they account for 3.5 per cent of Scottish employee jobs, and only 2.1 per cent of total UK employee jobs, so Scotland is more specialised in these industries than is the UK as a whole. The tertiary industries cover all services and dominate the Scottish economy, accounting for 74 per cent of employment, rather less than their 76 per cent share in the UK. The major part of the production and construction industries make up the secondary sector. Scotland is slightly more specialised in these industries, with 22.1 per cent of its employment concentrated here as against just over 21.4 per cent for the UK as a whole.

The longer-term picture is one of a significant contraction in the secondary sector, concentrated in Scotland's traditional heavy industries, combined with a substantial expansion in the tertiary sector. In 1970, for example, the production industries accounted for over 900 employees or 44 per cent of total employees in employment in Scotland, with the tertiary sector accounting for 1,049 employees or just under 51 per cent of the total.

Table 6 also presents data on the sex composition of employee jobs in Scotland and the UK. In terms simply of numbers of employee jobs the workforce in both regions is now fairly evenly divided between males and females. In Scotland slightly over half of all employees' jobs are now held by females. In fact this reflects the outcome of a sustained increase in female employment and steady contraction in male employment. In 1970, for example, female employment accounted for 38.4 per cent of total employment. However, some 45 per cent of female employment is part-

TABLE 7. EMPLOYEE JOBS BY INDUSTRY (DECEMBER 1998, NOT SEASONALLY ADJUSTED, 000s)

	Scotland	per cent Scot.	UK	per cent UK
Agriculture etc	32	1.6	296	1.2
Mining & Quar.	24	1.2	74	0.3
Manufacturing	315	15.5	4,077	17.0
Elect. Gas etc	16	0.8	143	0.6
Construction	133	6.5	1,133	4.7
Wholesale etc	332	16.3	4,174	17.4
Hotels & rest.	113	5.6	1,300	5.4
Transport etc	110	5.4	1,416	5.9
Financial Inter.	89	4.4	1,029	4.3
Real Estate etc	225	11.1	3,405	14.2
Public admin etc	125	6.2	1,328	5.5
Education	152	7.5	1,931	8.0
Health & Soc. Wrk	266	13.1	2,571	10.7
Other Services	99	4.9	1,128	4.7

time whereas only 11 per cent of male employment is part-time. If part-time employment is taken to be 'third time', then female full-time-equivalent employment is only 42 per cent of the total of such employment. The trends in female employment in part reflect changes in Scotland's industrial structure, in particular the shift to services from heavy manufacturing.

Table 7 provides a more detailed picture of the current sectoral composition of employment in Scotland. The largest concentration of employment is in the wholesale, retail trade and repairs sector which accounts for 16.3 per cent of total employees in Scotland and 17.4 per cent in the UK as a whole. Manufacturing is the second biggest employer with 15.5 per cent of employees in Scotland and 17.0 per cent in the UK. The third most important employer in Scotland is health and social work with 13.1 per cent of employees, and the fourth is real estate, renting and business activities with 11.1 per cent. The positions of these two sectors are reversed in the UK, accounting for 10.7 per cent and 14.2 per cent respectively of total employment there.

The biggest difference in relative specialisation occurs in mining and quarrying, wherein Scotland employs over 32 per cent of total UK employees, as compared to its overall employment share of 8.5 per cent, although the sector accounts for only 1.3 per cent of total Scottish employment. The next biggest specialisations in Scotland relative to the UK are in construction (11.7 per cent of total UK employment in this sector), electricity, gas and water supply (11.1 per cent), agriculture, hunting,

forestry and fishing (10.8 per cent), and health and social work (10.3 per cent). The most under-represented sectors relative to the UK are: real estate, renting and business activities (with 6.6 per cent of total UK employment in this sector), manufacturing (7.7 per cent), education (7.8 per cent) and wholesale, retail trade and repairs (7.9 per cent). The current position, therefore does not offer a clear cut support for the view that Scotland is over-represented in the contracting sectors and under-represented in the expanding sectors, although the data used here remain quite highly aggregated.

It is worth noting that there are some marked differences in sectors relative importance as a source of employment and as a contributor to GDP. These reflect differences in labour productivity, which are considered below.

The historical situation with respect to the sectoral distribution was somewhat different, however, with Scotland specialised in heavy manufacturing. The precise changes are difficult to establish given the various changes in sectoral definitions and other sources of discontinuities in the data, but some orders of magnitude can be established. In 1970, for example, employment in manufacturing industries was 708,000, so it has fallen by 55 per cent of that total to reach its current level. In contrast employment in Services has risen by over 44 per cent since that date.

The structure of Scottish manufacturing
The regional distribution of gross value added by manufacturing sub-sector for 1993 is shown in Table 8. The first line shows the aggregate share of manufacturing gross value-added. Thus

England produced 84.8 per cent of total UK manufacturing value-added while Scotland had 7.9 per cent. Against this overall national share it is interesting to note that Scotland was comparatively specialised in: wood and wood products (13.5 per cent of total UK employment in this sub-sector); food, products, beverages and tobacco (including whisky, 12.2 per cent); and electrical and optical equipment (10.9 per cent). Scotland was comparatively under-represented in: leather and leather products (3.4 per cent); manufactures not elsewhere specified (3.8 per cent); and chemicals etc (4.7 per cent).

TABLE 8 SCOTTISH SHARE OF UK MANUFACTURING GVA AT FACTOR COST BY SECTOR IN 1993

	Scotland	RUK
Food products, bev., tob.	12.2	87.8
Textiles and textile products	12	88
Leather and leather products	3.4	96.6
Wood and wood products	13.5	86.5
Pulp, paper, publishing & print.	7.5	92.5
Chemicals, chem. products	4.7	95.3
Rubber and plastic products	6.8	93.2
Other non-metallic min. prod.	7.2	92.8
Metals & fabricated metal prod.	6.7	93.3
Machinery and equip. n.e.s.	8	92
Electrical and optical equipment	10.9	89.1
Transport equipment	4.8	95.2
Manufactures n.e.s.	3.8	96.2
Total	7.8	92.2

Further detail on the structure of manufacturing in Scotland is presented in Table 9, where total manufacturing has been subdivided into three sub-sectors: food, drink and tobacco; a modern sector and a traditional sector. Naturally, these latter two distinctions are subjective and open to potential objections. A striking feature of this table is Scotland's relative dependence on the food, drink and tobacco sub-sector, and a slightly greater concentration in the more traditional manufacturing activities. Food, drink and tobacco primarily services the domestic economy. While whisky is, as we have seen, a very notable exception to this general rule, it accounts for only 20 per cent of the sub-sector's employment.

TABLE 9. DISTRIBUTION OF MANUFACTURING BY BROAD SECTOR IN 1993

	Scotland	UK
Food, drink and tobacco	21.4	14
Modern	67	75.6
Traditional	11.6	10.4
Total	100	100

Modern	Traditional
Pulp, paper, publishing & print.	Textiles and textile products
Chemicals, chem. products	Leather and leather products
Rubber and plastic products	Wood and wood products
Other non-metallic min. prod.	Manufactures n.e.s.
Metals & fabricated metal prod.	
Machinery and equip. n.e.s.	
Electrical and optical equipment	
Transport equipment	

A longer term perspective on the structure of Scottish manufacturing is provided by Table 10, which presents indices of Gross Value Added by manufacturing sub-sectors for the period 1973–98. Note that the output of four manufacturing sectors actually contracted over the 26 year period. In the case of metals and metal products this decline was particularly dramatic, with output falling by nearly two thirds. However, food, drink and tobacco experienced a contraction of over 20 per cent of output and textiles output fell by nearly 30 per cent. The only comparative success story is in engineering and allied industries, though note that output here fluctuated around a fairly static trend until the late 1980s. This reflects, in part, the experience of electronics.

TABLE 10. INDICES OF GROSS VALUE ADDED FOR SCOTTISH MANUFACTURING INDUSTRIES, 1973-98

	Manufac- turing	Refined Petroleum Products & Nuclear Fuels	Chemicals and Man- made Fibres	Metals & Metal Products	Engineering & Allied Industries	Food, Drink & Tobacco	Textiles, Footwear, Leather & Clothing	Total Other Manufac- turing
1973	91.7	86	92	281	53	122	129	104
1974	91.2	85	102	273	54	127	120	97
1975	86.8	71	89	248	54	123	112	86
1976	87	82	103	225	52	124	117	88
1977	86.6	92	100	216	51	124	122	88
1978	86.7	97	98	205	49	129	121	91
1979	86.4	89	95	198	51	129	114	92
1980	80.5	74	87	161	49	125	102	83
1981	78.3	70	84	174	50	117	95	77
1982	79	76	85	167	53	114	88	76
1983	78.6	98	92	148	51	112	89	79
1984	81.9	81	93	167	55	111	99	80
1985	83.7	85	96	160	57	108	110	82
1986	81.2	86	97	125	56	106	106	84
1987	81.1	62	98	128	54	106	112	88
1988	86.3	70	94	137	61	108	115	95
1989	88.6	87	94	132	65	104	110	102
1990	90.2	94	97	133	66	107	111	103
1991	87.8	94	93	142	64	102	104	98
1992	88	96	92	130	67	101	104	98
1993	91.2	95	93	112	78	104	100	96
1994	95.9	99	97	97	92	100	102	98
1995	100	100	100	100	100	100	100	100
1996	102.8	100	113	101	106	98	103	97
1997	108.4	100	126	104	116	96	105	98
1998	111.3	102	126	119	126	91	94	96

Source: Scottish Executive

Although it is not apparent from the aggregate data presented above, in recent years the experience of manufacturing in Scotland is essentially a tale of two distinct sub-sectors: electronics and the rest of manufacturing. Between the first quarters of 1990 and 1998 electronics grew by 200 per cent as compared to growth of about 29 per cent in the UK. Over the same period manufacturing as a whole grew by some 26 per cent in Scotland but only by around 4 per cent in the UK as a whole. However, the manufacturing sector excluding electronics actually contracted by some 13 per cent in Scotland while remaining fairly constant in the UK as a whole. Silicon Glen is the major success story of Scottish manufacturing.

ADDITIONAL FEATURES OF THE SCOTTISH ECONOMY

Regional competitiveness

The Department of Trade and Industry now produces regular review of regional competitiveness. Considerable emphasis is attached to this concept since it is defined as the ability of regions to generate high income and employment levels while remaining exposed to domestic and international competition. Some indicators, such as GDP per head and unemployment rates discussed above are primarily regarded as the outcome of the competitiveness process. Other indicators, such as labour productivity and the rate of new firm formation are reported as sources of differential competitiveness. Finally, other indicators such as average earnings have a less clear cut status: lower earnings reduce costs and increase competitiveness, but higher earnings also make it easier to sustain higher income levels.

There are two features of regional competitiveness: price competitiveness and non-price competitiveness. Scotland's ability to compete on price depends on the costs of its inputs and the productivity of those inputs. While attention should really focus on all inputs, data on labour are more readily available than on land and capital. In April 1999 the average gross weekly earnings of male employees in Scotland amounted to £378 or about £19,000 per year. Real earnings increased for both males and females over the period from 1986, by some 17 per cent for males and 22 per cent for females. Real wages rose by more in Great Britain, however, by 22 per cent for males and 34 per cent in Great Britain. By April 1999, average male earnings had risen to £406 per week. The average for all employees was £365 about £35 (9 per cent) less than the Great Britain average.

This does not necessarily imply that competitiveness declined in Scotland relative to elsewhere, nor does it imply that Scottish competitiveness improved relative to Great Britain as a whole, because increases in wage costs can be offset by increases in labour productivity. However, aggregate labour productivity (as reflected in GDP per employee) was, until recently thought to have converged on the national average, though doubt has now been cast on this. Evidence on this is mixed. Recent Scottish Executive estimates suggest that aggregate Scottish output per employee is some 5 per cent to 8 per cent below that of the UK, and over 40 per cent below that of the USA. However, data for Gross Value-Added per employee (from the Scottish Production Database) suggest that labour in the production industries as a whole is approximately 12 per cent more productive in Scotland than in England. There were substantial variations in output per head across sectors, however, ranging from a low of £23,876 in food to a high of £111,560 in coke, oil and nuclear processing. This highlights the need for caution in interpreting productivity differentials, since these are clearly heavily influenced by the capital intensity of the industry, among other things.

Firms do not, however, compete on price alone, and rates of new firm formation, expenditures on research and development and innovation rates have all been postulated to contribute to regional competitiveness. However, on these criteria Scotland tends to perform poorly, with the South East tending to dominate. (Ashcroft et al, 1994). Scotland is not favoured either by its 'peripherality'. Although single indices of peripherality are problematic, it may be worth noting that Scotland has been ranked as the second most peripheral economy of the standard regions of the UK, with Northern Ireland the only economy to fare worse in this respect.

Household incomes and consumption expenditures

Average weekly household spending in Scotland in 1997–8 was £297.70 as compared to £328.80 in the UK as a whole. In fact, on average over the last decade average household spending in Scotland has been around 90 per cent of that in the UK, though some caution is required given the comparatively small sample of households on which the data are based. It seems unlikely that this is due to the Scots supposed greater thrift, rather simply due to their lower average household income. In 1995–6 average gross weekly income of Scottish households was £338, only 88 per cent of the UK figure of £381. In fact Scottish average household expenditures tend to be slightly greater than for the UK as a whole.

Figure 1 summarises the distribution of household expenditure for both Scotland and the UK in 1997–8. The spending patterns are broadly similar, although not identical. Scots tend to spend proportionally more on fuel and food, tobacco and alcohol and transport. They spend less on housing, household goods and leisure activities. These no doubt in part reflect the differences in average household incomes, climate and spatial dispersion of the population. However, they may also reflect, to a degree, differences in tastes.

Wages and salaries accounted for some 57 per cent (59 per cent) of household incomes in Scotland/(UK) in 1995–6, with social security payments the next most important source, contributing 27 per cent of the total in Scotland and 26 per cent in the UK. It has already been noted that workers in Scotland received lower average gross weekly earnings than those in the UK as a whole, and have experienced lower real wage growth. If all other things were equal the lower wages would be good news for price-competitiveness, but bad news for living standards and consumption demand. If the higher wages in the UK as a whole are in fact compensated for by higher total factor productivity, then price-competitiveness as well as incomes may be greater in the UK as a whole than in Scotland.

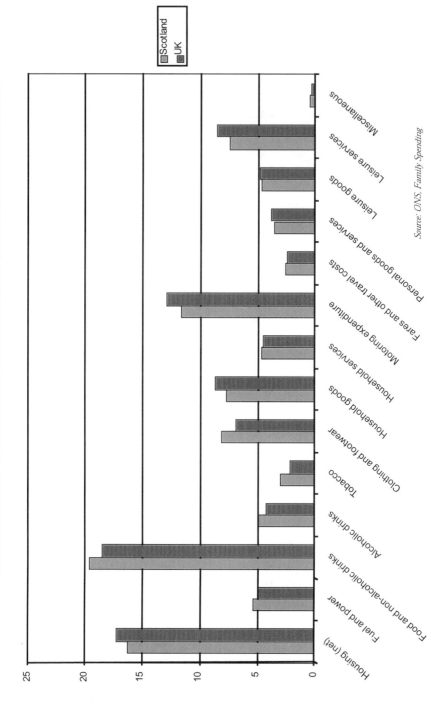

FIGURE 1. PERCENTAGE DISTRIBUTION OF HOUSEHOLD EXPENDITURE IN SCOTLAND AND THE UK 1997–8

Source: ONS, Family Spending

BANKING

Banking in the UK is regulated by the Banking Act 1987 as amended by the European Community's Second Banking Co-ordination Directive, which came into effect on 1 January 1993. The Banking Act 1987 established a single category of banks eligible to carry out banking business; these are known as authorised institutions. Authorisation under the Act is granted by the Bank of England; it is an offence for anyone not on the Bank's list of authorised institutions to conduct deposit-taking business, unless they are exempted from the requirements of the Act (e.g. building societies).

The Government announced in 1997 that it would transfer responsibility for banking supervision to the Financial Services Authority (FSA). The FSA acquired its full range of responsibilities in two stages. The first stage was completed on 1 June 1998 when the FSA acquired responsibility, under the Bank of England Act 1998, for supervising banks, listed money market institutions and related clearing houses. The majority of functions previously carried out by the Insurance Directorate of HM Treasury have also now been taken over by the FSA. The second stage will follow the enactment of the Financial Services and Markets Bill, which received Royal Assent on 14 June 2000. When this Bill is implemented, a date commonly referred to as N2, the FSA will acquire its full range of powers.

The implementation of the Second Banking Co-ordination Directive permits banks incorporated in one EU member state to carry on certain banking activities in another member state without the need for authorisation by that state. Consequently, the Bank of England no longer authorises banks incorporated in other EU states with branches in the UK; the authorisation of their home state supervisor is sufficient provided that certain notification requirements are met.

As at end June 1999, a total of 594 institutions were authorised to carry out banking business in the UK, 335 authorised under the Banking Act 1987 and 259 recognised under the Second Banking Co-ordination Directive as European Authorised Institutions (EAIs).

In the British banking system, the main institutions are the Bank of England (the central bank), the retail banks, the merchant banks and the overseas banks. In its role as the central bank, the Bank of England acts as banker to the Government and as a note-issuing authority; it also oversees the efficient functioning of payment and settlement systems. In Scotland, the Bank of Scotland, the Royal Bank of Scotland and the Clydesdale Bank are also banks of issue.

Since May 1997, the Bank of England has had operational responsibility for monetary policy. At monthly meetings of its monetary policy committee the Bank sets the interest rate at which it will lend to the money markets.

OFFICIAL INTEREST RATES 1999–2000

10 June 1999	5.00%
8 September 1999	5.25%
4 November 1999	5.50%
13 January 2000	5.75%
10 February 2000	6.00%

RETAIL BANKS

The major retail banks are Abbey National, Alliance and Leicester, Bank of Scotland, Barclays, Clydesdale, Halifax, HSBC (formerly Midland), Lloyds/TSB, National Westminster, Northern Rock, Royal Bank of Scotland and the Woolwich. The Clydesdale Bank is also a major retail bank in Scotland.

Retail banks offer a wide variety of financial services to companies and individuals, including current and deposit accounts, loan and overdraft facilities, automated teller (cash dispenser) machines, cheque guarantee cards, credit cards and debit cards.

The Banking Ombudsman scheme provides independent and impartial arbitration in disputes between a bank and its customer.

Banking hours differ throughout the UK. Many banks now open longer hours and some at weekends, and hours vary from branch to branch. Current core opening hours in Scotland are Monday to Friday 9 a.m. to 5 p.m.

PAYMENT CLEARINGS

The Association for Payment Clearing Services (APACS) is an umbrella organisation for payment clearings in the UK. It operates three clearing companies: BACS Ltd, the Cheque and Credit Clearing Company Ltd, and CHAPS Clearing Company Ltd.

ASSOCIATION FOR PAYMENT
CLEARING SERVICES (APACS)

Mercury House, Triton Court, 14 Finsbury Square, London EC2A 1LQ
Tel: 020-7711 6200

BACS LTD

De Havilland Road, Edgware, Middx HA8 5QA
Tel: 0870-165 0019
Bulk clearing of electronic debits and credits (e.g.
direct debits and salary credits)

CHEQUE AND CREDIT CLEARING COMPANY LTD

Mercury House, Triton Court, 14 Finsbury
Square, London EC2A 1LQ
Tel: 020-7711 6200
Bulk clearing systems for inter-bank cheques and
paper credit items in Great Britain

CHAPS CLEARING COMPANY LTD

Mercury House, Triton Court, 14 Finsbury
Square, London EC2A 1LQ
Tel: 020-7711 6200
Same-day clearing for electronic funds transfers
throughout the UK in sterling and globally in
euro

MAJOR RETAIL BANKS: FINANCIAL RESULTS 1999

Bank Group	Profit before taxation £m	Profit after taxation £m	Total assets £m	Number of UK branches
Abbey National	1,783	1,261	180,744	750
Alliance & Leicester	455.2	317.9	27,579	316
Bank of Scotland	1,011.9	580.6	59,796	325
Barclays	1,918	1,380	219,494	1,950
Clydesdale	146.2	99.4	7,861	274
Halifax	1,705	1,171	145,000	814
HSBC*	1,724	1,201	106,468	1,670
Lloyds/TSB Group	3,621	2,520	176,091	2,309
NatWest Group	2,142	1,641	185,993	1,727
Northern Rock	202.6	136.6	18,157	107
Royal Bank of Scotland Group	1,001.0	637.0	79,676	664
Woolwich	495.9	331.3	33,239	406

*Formerly Midland Bank

CURRENCY

The unit of currency is the pound sterling (£) of 100 pence. The decimal system was introduced on 15 February 1971.

Since 1 January 1999, trade within the European Union has been conducted in the single European currency, the euro; euro notes and coins will not enter circulation until 2002.

COIN

	Metal	Standard weight (g)	Standard diameter (cm)
Penny	bronze	3.564	2.032
Penny	copper-plated steel	3.564	2.032
2 pence	bronze	7.128	2.591
2 pence	copper-plated steel	7.128	2.591
5p	cupro-nickel	3.25	1.80
10p	cupro-nickel	6.5	2.45
20p	cupro-nickel	5.0	2.14
25p Crown	cupro-nickel	28.28	3.861
50p	cupro-nickel	13.5	3.0
*50p	cupro-nickel	8.00	2.73
£1	nickel-brass	9.5	2.25
†£2	nickel-brass	15.98	2.84
£2	cupro-nickel, nickel-brass	12.00	2.84
£5 Crown	cupro-nickel	28.28	3.861

New 50p coin introduced on 1 September 1997
† Commemorative coins; not intended for general circulation

LEGAL TENDER

Gold (dated 1838 onwards, if not below least current weight)	to any amount
£5 (Crown since 1990)	to any amount
£2	to any amount
£1	to any amount
50p	up to £10
25p (Crown pre-1990)	up to £10
20p	up to £10
10p	up to £5
5p	up to £5
2p	up to 20p
1p	up to 20p

BANKNOTES

Bank of England notes are currently issued in denominations of £5, £10, £20 and £50 for the amount of the fiduciary note issue, and are legal tender in England and Wales. No £1 notes have been issued since 1984 and in 1998 the outstanding notes were written off.

The current E series of notes was introduced from June 1990. The predominant identifying feature of each note is the portrayal on the back of a prominent British historical figure. The figures portrayed in the current series are:

£5 June 1990–	George Stephenson
£10 April 1992–	Charles Dickens*
£20 June 1991–June 1999	Michael Faraday
£20 June 1999–	Sir Edward Elgar
£50 April 1994–	Sir John Houblon

Although the Bank of England stopped issuing a £1 note in 1983, the Scottish £1 note continues to be issued.

In autumn 2000 a new version of the Bank of England £10 banknote will be issued, bearing a portrait of Charles Darwin.

Legal Tender

Bank of England banknotes which are no longer legal tender are payable when presented at the head office of the Bank of England in London.

Scottish banknotes are not legal tender but they are an authorised currency and enjoy a status comparable to that of Bank of England notes. They are generally accepted by banks irrespective of their place of issue.

Scottish Banknotes

The banks of issue in Scotland are the Bank of Scotland, the Clydesdale Bank and the Royal Bank of Scotland.

BANK OF SCOTLAND

The Mound, Edinburgh EH1 1YZ
Tel: 0131-442 7777
Chief Executive: Peter Burt
Denominations of notes issued: £5, £10, £20, £50, £100

£5	HM The Queen
£10, £20, £50 and £100	Sir Walter Scott

CLYDESDALE BANK

30 St Vincent Place, Glasgow G1 2HL
Tel: 0141-248 7070
Chairman: Lord Sanderson of Bowden
Chief Executive: John R. Wright
Denominations of notes issued: £5, £10, £20, £50, £100

£5	Robert Burns
£10	Mary Slessor
£20	Robert the Bruce
£50	Adam Smith
£100	Lord Kelvin

ROYAL BANK OF SCOTLAND

PO Box 31, 42 St Andrew Square, Edinburgh
EH2 2YE
Tel: 0131-556 8555
Chairman: Rt. Hon. Viscount Younger of
    Leckie, KT, KCVO
Chief Executive: Frederick Goodwin
Denominations of notes issued: £1, £5, £10,
£20, £100

£1	Edinburgh Castle
£5	Culzean Castle
£10	Glamis Castle
£20	Brodick Castle
£100	Balmoral Castle

Earlier Royal Bank of Scotland Banknotes
feature a portrait of Lord Ilay, its first governor

Note Circulation in Scotland

in the four weeks ending 29 May 1999 [†]

	Circulation authorised by certificate £	Average circulation £	Average amount of Bank of England notes and coin held* £
Bank of Scotland	1,289,222 [†]	608,755,847 [†]	618,461,223 [†]
Clydesdale Bank	498,773	399,740,768	403,218,560
Royal Bank of Scotland	888,355	935,807,839	943,362,065

*Includes Bank of England notes deposited at the Bank of England which, by virtue of the Currency and Bank Note Act 1928, are to be treated as gold coin by the Bank
[†] figures as at 14 July 2000

LOCAL ENTERPRISE COMPANIES

Local enterprise companies operate under the aegis of either Highlands and Islands Enterprise (HIE) or Scottish Enterprise (SE). These two statutory bodies were set up in 1991 to further the development of the Scottish economy, working with the private and public sectors. Many of their functions are delegated to the local enterprise companies.

Argyll and the Islands Enterprise (HIE)
The Enterprise Centre, Kilmory Industrial Estate, Lochgilphead, Argyll PA31 8SH
Tel: 01546-602281/602563
Fax: 01546-603964
E-mail: info@aie.co.uk
Web: http://www.aie.co.uk
Chief Executive: K. Abernethy

Caithness and Sutherland Enterprise (HIE)
Tollemache House, High Street, Thurso,
Caithness KW14 8AZ
Tel: 01847-896115
Fax: 01847-893383
E-mail: case@hient.co.uk
Web: http://www.case-lec.co.uk
Chief Executive: N. Money

Scottish Enterprise Dumfries and Galloway
Solway House, Dumfries Business Park, Tinwald Downs Road, Heathhall, Dumfries DG1 3SJ
Tel: 01387-245000
Fax: 01387-246224
Web: http://www.scottish-enterprise.com/
    dumfriesandgalloway
Chief Executive: Ms I. Walker

Scottish Enterprise Dunbartonshire
2nd Floor, Spectrum House, Clydebank Business Park, Clydebank, Glasgow G81 2DR
Tel: 0141-951 2121
Web: http://www.scottish-enterprise.com/
    dunbartonshire
Chief Executive: D. Anderson

Scottish Enterprise Ayrshire (SE)
17—19 Hill Street, Kilmarnock KA3 1HA
Tel: 01563-526623
Fax: 01563-543636
Chief Executive: Ms E. Connolly

Scottish Enterprise Grampian
27 Albyn Place, Aberdeen AB10 1DB
Tel: 01224-252000
Fax: 01224-213417
Chief Executive: E. Gillespie

Inverness and Nairn Enterprise
The Green House, Beechwood Business Park North, Inverness IV2 3BL
Tel: 01463-713504
Fax: 01463-712002
E-mail: ine.general@hient.co.uk
Web: http://www.ine.co.uk
Chief Executive: W. Sylvester

Scottish Enterprise Lanarkshire
New Lanarkshire House, Strathclyde Business Park, Bellshill ML4 3AD
Tel: 01698-745454
Fax: 01698-842211
E-mail: selenquiry@scotent.co.uk
Web: http://www.scottish-enterprise.com/
    lanarkshire
Chief Executive: I. Carmichael

Lochaber Ltd (HIE)
St Mary's House, Gordon Square, Fort William PH33 6DY
Tel: 01397-704326
Fax: 01397-705309
E-mail: locaber@hient.co.uk
Web: http://www.lochaberlimited.co.uk
Chief Executive: Ms J. Wright

Scottish Enterprise Edinburgh and Lothian
Apex House, 99 Haymarket Terrace, Edinburgh EH12 5HD
Tel: 0131-313 4000
Fax: 0131-313 4231
Web: http://www.scottish-enterprise.com/
    edinburghandlothian
Chief Executive: D. Crichton

Orkney Enterprise (HIE)
14 Queen Street, Kirkwall, Orkney KW15 1JE
Tel: 01856-874638
Fax: 01856-872915
E-mail: orkney@bis.uk.com
Chief Executive: K. Grant

Ross and Cromarty Enterprise (HIE)
69–71 High Street, Invergordon, Ross and Cromarty IV18 0AA
Tel: 01349-853666
Fax: 01349-853833
E-mail: info@race.co.uk
Web: http://www.race.co.uk
Chief Executive: G. Cox

Scottish Enterprise Borders
Bridge Street, Galashiels TD1 1SW
Tel: 01896-758991
Fax: 01896-758625
Web: http://www.scottish-enterprise.com/
    borders
Chief Executive: J. McFarlane

Scottish Enterprise Tayside (SE)
45 North Lindsay Street, Dundee DD1 1HT
Tel: 01382-223100
Fax: 01382-322988
E-mail: set.reception@scotent.co.uk
Web: http://www.set.co.uk
Chief Executive: G. McKee

Scottish Enterprise Fife
Kingdom House, Saltire Centre, Glenrothes, Fife
KY6 2AQ
Tel: 01592-623000
Chief Executive: D. Waring

Scottish Enterprise Renfrewshire (SE)
27 Causeyside Street, Paisley PA1 1UL
Tel: 0141-848 0101
Fax: 0141-848 6930
Web: http://www.scottish-enterprise.com/
    renfrewshire
Chief Executive: Mrs L. McMillan

Shetland Enterprise (HIE)
Toll Clock Shopping Centre, 26 North Road,
    Lerwick, Shetland ZE1 0DE
Tel: 01595-693177
Fax: 01595-693208
E-mail: shetland.enterprise@zetnet.co.uk
Chief Executive: D. Finch

Skye and Lochalsh Enterprise (HIE)
Kings House, The Green, Portree, Isle of Skye
IV51 9BS
Tel: 01478-612841
Fax: 01478-612164
E-mail: sale@hient.co.uk
Web: http://www.sale.hie.co.uk
Chief Executive: R. Muir

Western Isles Enterprise (WIE)
James Square, 9 James Street, Stornoway,
    Isle of Lewis HS1 2QN
Tel: 01851-703703
Fax: 01851-704130
E-mail: wie@hient.co.uk
Web: http://www.wie.co.uk
Chief Executive: D. MacAulay

PROFESSIONAL AND TRADE BODIES

The Certification Officer is responsible for receiving and scrutinising annual returns from employers' associations. Many employers' associations are members of the Confederation of British Industry (CBI).

CONFEDERATION OF BRITISH INDUSTRY, SCOTLAND

Beresford House, 5 Claremont Terrace, Glasgow G3 7XT
Tel: 0141-332 8661; Fax: 0141-333 9135
Email: allan.hogarth@cbi.org.uk
Web: http://www.cbi.org.uk

CBI Scotland is part of the Confederation of British Industry, which was founded in 1965. CBI Scotland is an independent non-party political body financed by industry and commerce. It exists primarily to ensure that the Government and Scottish Executive understands the intentions, needs and problems of business in Scotland. It is the recognised voice of business in Scotland and is consulted as such by the Government and Scottish Executive.

CBI Scotland represents the interests of some 26,500 businesses in Scotland of all sizes and across all sectors.

The governing body of CBI Scotland is its elected Council, which meets four times a year in various parts of Scotland. Council is assisted by eight expert Committees which advise on the main aspects of policy. Council and the Committees establish policy in respect of matters devolved to Scotland and contribute their views to the policy formation process of the CBI as a whole on matters reserved to Westminster and in Europe. CBI Scotland has a sister office in Brussels.
Chairman: H. Currie
Director: I. McMillan

PROFESSIONAL AND TRADE BODIES

The following list includes the main professional institutions, employers' associations and trade associations in Scotland, and the Scottish offices of UK institutions.

Aberdeen Fish Curers and Merchants Association
South Esplanade West, Aberdeen AB11 9FJ
Tel: 01224-897744
Fax: 01224-871405
Managing Director: R. H. Milne

Advanced Concrete and Masonry Centre
Department of CSEE, University of Paisley, Paisley PA1 2BE
Tel: 0141-848-3267
Fax: 0141-848 3275
E-mail: peter.bartos@paisley.ac.uk
Chief Executive: Prof. P. J. M. Bartos

Association for Management Education and Training in Scotland (AMETS)
c/o Cottrell Building, University of Stirling, Stirling FK9 4LA
Tel: 01786-467364
Fax: 01786-465070
E-mail: amets@stir.ac.uk
Chairman: Prof. F. Pignatelli

Association of Chartered Certified Accountants
1 Woodside Place, Glasgow G3 7QF
Tel: 0141-309 4050
Fax: 0141-309 4090
Web: http://www.acca.org.uk
Head, ACCA Scotland: vacant

Association of Scottish Colleges
Argyll Court, Castle Business Park, Stirling FK9 4TY
Tel: 01786-892100
Fax: 01786-892109
E-mail: enquiries@ascol.org.uk
Web: http://www.ascol.org.uk
Chief Officer: T. Kelly

Association of Scottish Shellfish Growers
Mountview, Ardvasar, Isle of Skye IV45 8RU
Tel: 01471-844324
Fax: 01471-844324
E-mail: 101723.1376@compuserve.com
Chairman: D. McLeod

Boiler and Radiator Manufacturers Association
Savoy Tower, 77 Renfrew Street, Glasgow G2 3BZ
Tel: 0141-332 0826
Fax: 0141-332 5788
E-mail: barma@metcom.org.uk
Secretary: J. Carruphers

Booksellers Association
Milngavie Bookshop, 37 Douglas Street, Milngavie, Glasgow G62 6PE
Tel: 0141-956 4752
Fax: 0141-956 4819
E-mail: enquiries@scotlandsbooks.co.uk
Web: http://www.scotlandsbooks.co.uk
Hon. Secretary: R. Lane

Brewers and Licensed Retailers Association of Scotland
6 St Colme Street, Edinburgh EH3 6AD
Tel: 0131-225 4681
Fax: 0131-220 1132
Secretary: G. Miller

British Box and Packaging Association
64 High Street, Kirkintilloch, Glasgow G66 1PR
Tel: 0141-777 7272
Fax: 0141-777 7747
E-mail: npcorg@aol.com
Web: http://www.boxpackaging.org.uk
Secretary: T. Bullimore

British Christmas Tree Growers Association
18 Cluny Place, Edinburgh EH10 4RL
Tel: 0131-447 0499
Fax: 0131-447 6443
E-mail: 100553.2161@compuserve.com
Web: http://www.christmastree.org.uk
Secretary: R. M. Hay

British Disposable Products Association
64 High Street, Kirkintilloch, Glasgow G66 1PR
Tel: 0141-777 7272
Fax: 0141-777 7747
E-mail: npcorg@aol.com
Web: http://www.bdpa.co.uk
Secretary T. Bullimre

British Hospitality Association – Scottish Office
Saltire Court, 20 Castle Terrace, Edinburgh EH1 2EN
Tel: 0131-200 7484
Fax: 0131-228 8888
E-mail: john.a.loudon@dundas.wilson.com
Secretary: J. Loudon

British Marine Industries Federation – Scotland
Westgate, Toward, Dunoon, Artyll PA23 7VA
Tel: 01369-870251
Fax: 01369-870251
E-mail: bmif-s@clydemarinepress.co.uk
President: D. Wilkie

British Medical Association – Scottish Office
3 Hill Place, Edinburgh, EH8 9EQ
Tel: 0131-662 4820
Fax: 0131-667 6933
Web: http://www.bma.org.uk
Scottish Secretary: Dr W. O'Neill

British Polyolefin Textiles Association
c/o Priestoun, Edzell, Angus DD9 7UD
Tel: 01356-648521
Fax: 01356-648521
Secretary: R. H. B. Learoyd

British Veterinary Association – Scottish Branch
SAC Veterinary Science Division, Mill of Crabstone, Aberdeen, AB21 9TB
Tel: 01224-711184
Fax: 01224-711177
Hon. Secretary D. Gray

British Wind Energy Association – Scottish Branch
c/o Energy Unlimited, 5 Leighton Avenue, Dunblane, Stirling FK15 0EB
Tel: 01786-825839
Fax: 01786-821133
E-mail: eunlim@aol.com
Web: http://www.bwea.com
Chairman R. Forrest

Business Enterprise Scotland
18 Forth Street, Edinburgh EH1 3LH
Tel: 0131-550 3839
Fax: 0131-550 3839
E-mail: bes@bes.org.uk
Web: http://www.bes.org.uk/bes/
Chief Executive R. Miller

CBS Network
Society Place, West Calder, W. Lothian EH55 8EA
Tel: 01506-871370
Fax: 01506-873079
E-mail: info@cbs-network.org.uk
Web: http://www.cbs-network.org.uk
Company Secretary: J. Pearce

Central Council for Education and Training in Social Work
James Craig Walk, Edinburgh EH1 3BA
Tel: 0131-220 0093
Fax: 0131-220 6717
Head: Ms G. Doherty

Chartered Institutes of Arbitrators (Arbiters) – Scottish Branch
Whittinghame House, 1099 Great Western Road, Glasgow G12 0AA
Tel: 0141-334 7222
Fax: 0141-334 7700
Hon. Secretary and Treasurer: B. L. Smith

Chartered Institute of Bankers in Scotland
Drumsheugh House, 38B Drumsheugh Gardens,
Edinburgh EH3 7SW
Tel: 0131-473 7777
Fax: 0131-473 7788
E-mail: info@ciobs.org.uk
Web: http://www.ciobs.org.uk
Chief Executive: C. W. Munn

Chartered Institute of Housing in Scotland
6 Palmerston Place, Edinburgh EH12 5AA
Tel: 0131-255 4544
Director: A. Ferguson

Chartered Institute of Marketing
3rd Floor, 100 Wellington Street, Glasgow
G2 6DH
Tel: 0141-221 7700
E-mail: glasgow@cim.co.uk
Web: http://www.cim.co.uk
Director, Scotland: vacant

**Chartered Institute of Public Finance and
    Accountancy**
CIPFA Scotland, 8 North West Circus Place,
Edinburgh EH3 6ST
Tel: 0131-220 4316
Fax: 0131-220 4305
E-mail: cipfa.scotland@cipfa.org
Director: I. P. Doig

**Chartered Institution of Water and
    Environmental Management – Scottish
    Branch**
c/o Scottish Environment Protection Agency,
Erskine Court, Castle Business Park, Stirling
FK9 4TR
Tel: 01786-457700
Fax: 01786-446885
Web: http://www.ciwem.org.uk
Chief Executive B. Sargent

Chartered Society of Designers
28 Mansion House Road, Glasgow G41 3DN
Tel: 0141-636 9092
Fax: 0141-649 8146
E-mail: adrian@mephisto.co.uk
Chairman of Scotland: A. Searle

CML Scotland
Royal Bank of Scotland plc, PO Box 123
Cartsdyke Avenue, Cartsbourn East, Greenock
PA15 1EF
Tel: 01475-551036
Fax: 01475-551880
Chairman: K. Foster

Committee of Scottish Clearing Bankers
38 Drumsheugh Gardens, Edinburgh EH3 7SW
Tel: 0131-473 7770
Fax: 0131-473 7799
Chairman: J. Wright

**Confederation of Passenger Transport UK -
    Scotland**
41 Laigh Road, Newton Mearns, Glasgow
G77 5EX
Tel: 0141-577 6455
Fax: 0141-616 0866
Director-General: Mrs V. Palmer OBE

**COSLA (Convention of Scottish Local
    Authorities)**
Rosebery House, 9 Haymarket Terrace,
Edinburgh EH12 5XZ
Tel: 0131-474 9200
Fax: 0131-474 9292
E-mail: caron@cosla.gov.uk
Web: http://www.cosla.gov.uk
Chief Executive: Ms O. Aitken

Dietitians Scotland
Queen Margaret University College, Clerwood
Terrace, Edinburgh EH12 8TS
Tel: 0131-317 3523
Fax: 0131-317 3528
E-mail: fpender@qmuc.ac.uk
Web: http://www.qmuc.ac.uk/dietweb
Senior Lecturer: Dr F. Pender

Direct Marketing Association (UK) Ltd
41 Comely Bank, Edinburgh EH4 1AF
Tel: 0131-315 4422
Fax: 0131-315 4433
Web: http://www.dma.org.uk
Manager: J. Scobie

**Edinburgh Chamber of Commerce and
    Enterprise**
Conference House, The Exchange, 152 Morrison
Street, Edinburgh EH3 8EB
Tel: 0131-477 7000
Fax: 0131-477 7003
E-mail: info@ecce.org
Web: http://www.ecce.org
Chief Executive: W. Furness

Faculty of Actuaries in Scotland
18 Dublin Street, Edinburgh EH1 3PP
Tel: 0131-240 1300
Fax: 0131-240 1313
E-mail: faculty@actuaries.org.uk
Web: http://www.actuaries.org.uk
Secretary: W. Mair

Faculty of Advocates
Advocates Library, Parliament House,Edinburgh
EH1 1RF
Tel: 0131-226 5071
Dean: G. N. H. Emslie QC

Federation of Master Builders
540 Gorgie Road, Edinburgh, EH11 3AL
Tel: 0131-455 7997
Fax: 0131-455 8085
E-mail: ian@fmb.org.uk
Web: http://www.fmb.org.uk
Director-General: I. Davis

Federation of Small Businesses – Scottish Office
74 Berkeley Street, Glasgow G3 7DS
Tel: 0141-221 0775
Fax: 0141-221 5954
E-mail: scotland.policy@fsb.org.uk
Web: http://www.fsb.org.uk
Scottish Policy Convener: J. Torrance

Forestry Contracting Association
Dalfling, Blairdaff, Inverurie, Aberdeenshire
AB51 5LA
Tel: 01467-651368
Fax: 01467-651595
E-mail: members@fcauk.com
Chief Executive: B. Hudson

Forest Industries Development Council
5 Dublin Street, Edinburgh EH1 3PG
Tel: 0131-556 0186
Fax: 0131-556 0190
E-mail: ficgb@aol.com
Executive Director: P. Wilson

Freight Transport Association Ltd
Hermes House, Melville Terrace, Stirling
FK8 2ND
Tel: 01786-457500
Fax: 01786-450412
E-mail: inquiries@fta.org.uk
Web: http://www.fta.co.uk
Director-General: D. C. Green

General Teaching Council for Scotland
Clerwood House, 96 Clermiston Road,
Edinburgh EH12 6UT
Tel: 0131-314 6000
Fax: 0131-314 6001
E-mail: gtcs@gtcs.org.uk
Web: http://www.gtcs.org.uk
Registrar: D. I. M. Sutherland

Glasgow Chamber of Commerce and Manufactures
30 George Square, Glasgow G2 1EQ
Tel: 0141-204 2121
Fax: 0141-221 2336
E-mail: chamber@glasgowchamber.org
Web: http://www.glasgowchamber.org
Chief Executive: P. V. Burdon

Harris Tweed Authority
6 Garden Road, Stornoway, Isle of Lewis
HS1 2QJ
Tel: 01851-702269
Fax: 01851-702600
E-mail: enquiries@harristweed.org
Web: http://www.harristweed.org
Chief Executive and Secretary: I. A. Mackenzie

Headteachers' Association of Scotland
Jordanhill Campus, University of Strathclyde
Southbrae Drive, Glasgow G13 1PP
Tel: 0141-950 3298
Fax: 0141-950 3434
General Secretary: G. S. Ross

Heating and Ventilating Contractors Association
Bush House, Bush Estate, Midlothian EH26 0SB
Tel: 0131-445 5580
Fax: 0131-445 2502
E-mail: hvca.bushhouse@lineone.net
Web: http://www.hvca.org.uk
Regional Officer: B. Dyer

ICFM Scotland (Institute of Charity Fundraising Managers)
c/o Bank of Scotland, 12 Bankhead Crossway
South, Edinburgh EH11 4EN
Tel: 0131-453 6517
E-mail: annemorrison@icfmscotland.freeserve
.co.uk
Web: http://www.icfm.org.uk
Development Officer: Ms A. Morrison

Independent Federation of Nursing in Scotland
Office 5, 18 Crowhill Road, Bishopbriggs
G64 1QY
Tel: 0141-772 9222
Fax: 0141-762 3776
General Secretary: Ms I. F. O'Neill

Institute of Auctioneers and Appraisers in Scotland
The Rural Centre, West Mains, Ingliston
Newbridge, Midlothian EH28 8NZ
Tel: 0131-472 4067
Fax: 0131-472 4067
Secretary: W. Blair

Institute of Chartered Accountants of Scotland
CA House, 21 Haymarket Yards, Edinburgh
EH12 5BH
Tel: 0131-225 5673
E-mail: icas@icas.org.uk
Web: http://www.icas.org.uk
Chief Executive: D. A. Brew

Institute of Chartered Foresters
7A St Colme Street, Edinburgh EH3 6AA
Tel: 0131-225 2705
Faxl: 0131-220 6125
E-mail: icf@charteredforesters.org
Web: http://www.charteredforesters.org
Executive Director: Ms M. Dick

Institute of Energy (Scotland)
Mercaston Campus – School of the Built
Environment, Napier University, 10 Colinton
Road, Edinburgh EH10 5DT
Tel: 0131-455 2253
Chairman: J. Currie

Institute of Enviornmental Management
Welton House, Limekiln Way, Lincoln LN2 4US
Tel: 01522-540069
Fax: 01522-540090
E-mail: info@iema.net
Web: http://www.iema.net
Chief Executive Officer: R. Foster

Institute of Food Science and Technology
Caledonian University, City Campus, Glasgow
G4 0BA
Tel: 0141-331 8514
Fax: 0141-331 3208
E-mail: k.aidoo@gcal.ac.uk
Hon. Secretary: Dr K. Aidoo

**Institute of Information Scientists – Scottish
Branch**
Building Design Partnership, 5 Blythswood
Square, Glasgow G2 4AD
Tel: 0141-226 5291
Fax: 0141-221 0720
E-mail: glasgow@bdp.co.uk
Web: http://www.bdp.co.uk
Chairman: A. Fergusson

**Scottish IPA (Institute of Practitioners in
Advertising)**
c/o Feather Brroksbank, The Old Assembly Hall,
37 Constitution Street, Edinburgh EH6 7BG
Tel: 0777-578 7253
fax: 0131-555 2556
Web: http://www.ipa.co.uk
Chairman: G. Brooksbank

**Institution of Engineers and Shipbuilders in
Scotland**
Clydeport Building, 16 Robertson Street,
Glasgow G2 8DS
Tel: 0141-248 3721
Fax: 0141-221 2698
E-mail: secretary@iesis.org
President: C. Dinardo, CEng.

Institute of Healthcare Management
Netherwyndings Mill, Stonehaven,
Kincardineshire AB39 3UU
Tel: 01569-767458
Fax: 01569-767458
E-mail: deborah.thomson@ihmscotland.co.uk
Web: http://www.ihmscotland.co.uk
Administrator: Mrs D. Thomson

**International Association of Drilling
Contractors (North Sea Chapter)**
Wood International Centre, Craigshaw Drive,
West Tullos, Aberdeen AB12 3AG
Tel: 01224-874800
Fax: 01224-875600
E-mail: dennis.krahn@iadc.org
Web: http://www.iadc.org
Director of European Offshore Affairs:
D. Krahn

Law Society of Scotland
26 Drumsheugh Gardens, Edinburgh EH3 7YR
Tel: 0131-226 7411
Fax: 0131-225 2934
E-mail: lawscot@lawscot.org.uk
Web: http://www.lawscot.org.uk
Chief Executive: D. R. Mill

The Malt Distillers Association of Scotland
1 North Street, Elgin IV30 1UA
Tel: 01343-544077
Fax: 01343-548523
Secretary: Grigor and Young Solicitors

**National Board for Nursing, Midwifery and
Health Visiting for Scotland**
22 Queen Street, Edinburgh EH2 1NT
Tel: 0131-226 7371
Web: http://www.nbs.org.uk
Chief Executive: D. C. Benton

National Farmers' Union of Scotland
Rural Centre, West Mains, Ingliston, Newbridge
Midlothian EH28 8LT
Tel: 0131-472 4000
Fax: 0131-472 4010
Web: http://www.nfus.org.uk
Chief Executive: E. R. Brown

National Federation of Roofing Contractors Ltd, The
PO Box 28011, Edinburgh EH16 6WN
Tel: 0131-467 1998
Fax: 0131-621 7089
E-mail: amckinney@support-services.fsbusiness
    .co.uk
Secretary: A. McKinney

National Specialist Contractors Council
PO Box 28011, Edinburgh, EH16 6WN
Tel: 0131-467 1998
Fax: 0131-621 7089
Web: http://www.scottish-trades.co.uk
Secretary: A. McKinney

Offshore Contractors' Association
12 Queens Road, Aberdeen AB15 4ZT
Tel: 01224-645450
Fax: 01224-645452
E-mail: admin@oca-online.co.uk
Web: http://www.oca-online.co.uk
Chief Executive: I. M. Bell

Procurator Fiscals' Society
Stuart House, 181 High Street, Linlithgow
EH49 7EN
Tel: 01506-844556
Fax: 01506-670102
Procurator Fiscal: Mrs C. Dyer

Producers Alliance for Cinema and Television (PACT) Scotland
249 West George Street, Glasgow, G2 4QE
Tel: 0141-302 1720
Fax: 0141-302 1721
Web: http://www.pact.co.uk
Manager: Ms M. Scott

Professional Association of Teachers
4 – 6 Oak Lane, Edinburgh, EH12 6XH
Tel: 0131-317 8282
Fax: 0131-317 8111
E-mail: pataliba@dial.pipex.com
Web: http://www.pat.org.uk
Secretary for Scotland: R. J. S. Christie

Professional Golfers' Association
Glenbervie Golf Club, Stirling Road, Larbet
Falkirk FK5 4SJ
Tel: 01324-562451
Fax: 01324-562190
Scottish Region Secretary: P. Lloyd

Property Managers Association Scotland Ltd
2 Blythswood Square, Glasgow G2 4AD
Tel: 0141-248 4672
Fax: 0141-221 9270
Secretary: J. Millar

Road Haulage Association Ltd
Roadway House, 17 Royal Terrace, Glasgow
G3 7NY
Tel: 0141-332 9201
Fax: 0141-331 2077
E-mail: scotland-northernireland@rha.net
Web: http://www.rha.net
Regional Director: P. Flanders

Royal College of General Practitioners – Scotland
25 Queen Street, Edinburgh, EH2 1JX
Tel: 0131-260 6800
Fax: 0131-260 6836
E-mail: scottish@rcgp.org.uk
Web: http://www.rcgp.org.uk
Chairman: Dr C. Hunter

Royal College of Nursing of the United Kingdom
42 South Oswald Road, Edinburgh EH9 2HH
Tel: 0131-662 1010
Fax: 0131-662 1032
Scottish Board Secretary: J. Kennedy

Royal College of Physicians and Surgeons of Glasgow
232-242 St Vincent Street, Glasgow G2 5RJ
Tel: 0141-221 6072
Fax: 0141-221 1804
Web: http://www.gla.ac.uk/KXTERNAL/RCPS
Hon. Secretary: Dr C. Semple

Royal College of Physicians of Edinburgh
9 Queen Street, Edinburgh EH2 1JQ
Tel: 0131-225 7324
Secretary: Dr A. C. Parker

Royal College of Surgeons of Edinburgh
Nicholson Street, Edinburgh EH8 9DW
Tel: 0131-527 1600
Fax: 0131-557 6406
Web: http://www.rcsed.ac.uk
Chief Executive: J. R. C. Foster

Royal Environmental Health Institute of Scotland
3 Manor Place, Edinburgh EH3 7DH
Tel: 0131-225 6999
Fax: 0131-225 3993
E-mail: rehis@rehis.org.uk
Web: http://www.rehis.org
Chief Executive: J. Frater

Royal Incorporation of Architects in Scotland
15 Rutland Square, Edinburgh EH1 2BE
Tel: 0131-229 7545
Fax: 0131-228 2188
E-mail: stombs@rias.org.uk
Web: http://www.rias.org.uk
Secretary: S. Tombs

Royal Institution of Chartered Surveyors
9 Manor Place, Edinburgh, EH3 7DN
Tel: 0131-225 7078
Fax: 0131-226 3599
E-mail: emasterman@rics.org.uk
Web: http://www.rics.org.uk
Director: Ms E. Masterman

Royal Pharmaceutical Society of Great Britain
36 York Place, Edinburgh EH1 3HU
Tel: 0131-556 4386
Tel: 0131-558 8850
Secretary: Dr S. Stevens

Royal Scottish Forestry Society
Hagg-on-Esk, Canonbie, Dumfriesshire
DG14 0XE
Tel: 01387-371518
Fax: 01387-371418
E-mail: rsfs@ednet.co.uk
Web: http://www.rsfs.org
Director: A. G. Little

Royal Town Planning Institute
57 Melville Street, Edinburgh EH3 7HL
Tel: 0131-226 1959
Fax: 0131-226 1909
Director: G. U'ren

Scottish and Northern Ireland Plumbing Employers' Federation
2 Walker Street, Edinburgh, EH3 7LB
Tel: 0131-225 2255
Fax: 0131-226 7638
E-mail: info@snipef.org
Web: http://www.snipef.org
Director and Secretary: R. D. Burgon

The Scottish Assessors' Association
Chesser House, 500 Gorgie Road, Edinburgh
EH11 3YJ
Tel: 0131-469 5589
Fax: 0131-469 5599
President: J. A. Cardwell

Scottish Association of Housing Federations
38 York Place, Edinburgh EH1 3HU
Tel: 0131-556 5777
Fax: 0131-557 6028
E-mail: sfha@sfha.co.uk
Director: D. Orr

Scottish Association of Master Bakers
4 Torphichen Street, Edinburgh EH3 8JQ
Tel: 0131-229 1401
Fax: 0131-229 8239
E-mail: master.bakers@samb.co.uk
Web: http://www.samb.co.uk
Chief Executive: I. Hay

Scottish Association of Sign Language Interpreters (SASLI)
54 Queen Street, Edinburgh EH2 3NS
Tel: 0131-225 9995
Fax: 0131-225 9932
E-mail: mail@sasli.org.uk
Web: http://www.sasli.org.uk
Director: Mrs D. Mair

Scottish Building Contractors Association
4 Woodside Place, Glasgow, G3 7QF
Tel: 0141-353 5050
Fax: 0141-332 2928
Association Secretary: N. J. Smith

Scottish Building
Carron Grange, Carrongrange Avenue,
Stenhousemuir FK5 3BQ
Tel: 01324-555550
Fax: 01324-555551
E-mail: info@scottish-building.co.uk
Web: http://www.scottish-building.co.uk
Chief Executive: S. C. Patten, MBA, FRSA

Scottish Chambers of Commerce
Conference House, The Exchange, 152 Morrison
Street, Edinburgh EH3 8EB
Tel: 0131-477 8025
Fax: 0131-477 7002
E-mail: mail@scottishchambers.org.uk
Web: http://www.scottishchambers.org.uk
Director: L. Gold

Scottish Chiropractic Association
St Boswells Chiropractic Clinic, 16 Jenny
Moores Road, St Boswells, Melrose TD6 0AL
Tel: 01835-824026
Fax: 01835-824046
E-mail: sca@scottishborders.co.uk
Secretary: Dr D. Sluce

The Scottish Committee of Optometrists
7 Queens Buildings, Queensferry Road, Rosyth
Fife, KY11 2RA
Tel: 01383-419444
Fax: 01383-416778
E-mail: scoptom@aol.com
Web: http://www.scottishoptometrists.co.uk
Secretary: D. S. Hutton

**Scottish Consortium of Timber Frame
Industries**
TRADA Offices, Office 30, Stirling Business
Centre, Well Green Place, Stirling FK8 2DZ
Tel: 01786-445075
Fax: 01786-474412
E-mail: msmith@stirling-trada.co.uk
Web: http://www.timber-frame.org
Chairman: R. Mackelvie

**Scottish Conveyancing and Executry Services
Board**
Room 426, Mulberry House, 16 – 22 Picardy
Place, Edinburgh EH1 3YT
Tel: 0131-556 1945
Fax: 0131-556 8428
Secretary: E. B. Simmons

Scottish Council Development and Industry
23 Chester Street, Edinburgh EH3 7ET
Tel: 0131-225 7911
Fax: 0131-220 2116
E-mail: edinburgh@scdi.org.uk
Web: http://www.scdi.org.uk
Chief Executive: A. Wilson

Scottish Crofters Union
Old Mill, Broadford, Isle of Skye IV49 9AQ
Tel: 01471-822529
Fax: 01471-822799
E-mail: crofters.union@talk21.com
Web: http://www.scu.co.uk
Director: R. Dutton

Scottish Daily Newspaper Society
48 Palmerston Place, Edinburgh EH12 5DE
Tel: 0131-220 4353
Fax: 0131-220 4344
E-mail: info@sdns.org.uk
Director: J. B. Raeburn

Scottish Dairy Association
46 Underwood Road, Paisley PA3 5TL
Tel: 0141-848 0009
Fax: 0141-848 5559
E-mail: admin@scotdairy.org.uk
Company Secretary: K. Hunter

Scottish Dance Teachers' Alliance
101 Park Road, Glasgow G4 9JE
Tel: 0141-339 8944
Fax: 0141-357 4994
E-mail: Alliance@mcmail.com
President: Ms S. McDonald

**Scottish Employers' Council for the Clay
Industries**
c/o Caradale Brick, Etna Works, Lower
Bathville, Armadale, W. Lothian EH48 2LZ
Tel: 01501-730671
Fax: 01501-732991
Managing Director: V. J. Burgoyne

Scottish Engineering
105 West George Street, Glasgow G2 1QL
Tel: 0141-221 3181
Fax: 0141-204 1202
E-mail: consult@scottishengineering.org.uk
Chief Executive: P. Hughes, OBE, FREng.

Scottish Farm Venison
Balcormo Mains, Leven, Fife, KY8 5QF
Tel: 01333-360229
Fax: 01333-360540
Chairman: J. Gilmour

Scottish Financial Enterprise
91 George Street, Edinburgh EH2 3ES
Tel: 0131-247 7700
Fax: 0131-247 7709
E-mail: info@sfe.org.uk
Web: http://www.sfe.org.uk
Chief Executive: R. Perman

Scottish Fishermen's Organisation Ltd
Braehead, 601 Queensferry Road, Edinburgh
EH4 6EA
Tel: 0131-339 7972
Fax: 0131-339 6682
E-mail: info@scottishfishermen.co.uk
Web: http://www.scottishfishermen.co.uk
Chief Executive: I. MacSween

Scottish Grocers Federation
222 – 224 Queensferry Road, Edinburgh
EH4 2BN
Tel: 0131-343 3300
Fax: 0131-343 6147
Chief Executive: L. Dewar

Scottish House-Builders Association
Carron Grange, Carrongrange Avenue,
Stenhousemuir FK5 3BQ
Tel: 01324-555550
Fax: 01324-555551
E-mail: info@scottish-building.co.uk
Director: S. C. Patten

Scottish Institute for Wood Technology
University of Abertay Dundee, Bell Street,
Dundee DD1 1HG
Tel: 01382-308930
Fax: 01382-308663
E-mail: mltdcrs@tay.ac.uk
Web: http://www.scieng.tay.ac.uk/siwt/
        index.htm
Technical Director: Dr D. Sinclair

Scottish Law Librarians Group
c/o Shepherd and Wedderburn, Saltire Court
20 Castle Terrace, Edinburgh EH1 2ET
Tel: 0131-228 9900
Fax: 0131-228 1222
Secretary of the Group: Ms F. McLaren

Scottish Library and Information Council
1 John Street, Hamilton ML3 7EU
Tel: 01698-458888
Fax: 01698-458899
E-mail: slic@liberator.amlibs.co.uk
Director: R. Craig

Scottish Library Association
1 John Street, Hamilton ML3 7EU
Tel: 01698-458888
Fax: 01698-458899
E-mail: sla@liberator.amlibs.co.uk
Web: http://www.slaine.org.uk
Director: R. Craig

Scottish Local Government Information Unit
Room 507, Baltic Chambers, 50 Wellington
Street, Glasgow G2 6HJ
Tel: 0141-226 4636
Fax: 0141-221 8786
Web: http://www.slgiu.gov.uk
Director: P. Vestri

Scottish Master Wrights' and Builders' Association
98 West George Street, Glasgow G2 1PJ
Tel: 0141-333 1679
Fax: 0141-333 1675
General Secretary: J. F. Lindsay

Scottish Motor Trade Association
3 Palmerston Place, Edinburgh EH12 5AF
Tel: 0131-225 3643
Fax: 0131-220 0446
E-mail: info@smta.co.uk
Web: http://www.smta.co.uk
Director: D. R. W. Robertson

Scottish Museums Council
County House, 20 – 22 Torphichen Street,
Edinburgh EH3 8JB
Tel: 0131-229 7465
Fax: 0131-229 2728
E-mail: inform@scottishmuseums.org.uk
Web: http://www.scottishmuseums.org.uk
Director: Ms J. Ryder

Scottish Newspapers Publishers Association
48 Palmerston Place, Edinburgh EH12 5DE
Tel: 0131-220 4353
Fax: 0131-220 4344
E-mail: info@snpa.org.uk
Web: http://www.snpa.org.uk
Director: J. B. Raeburn

Scottish Pharmaceutical Federation
135 Wellington Street, Glasgow G2 2XD
Tel: 0141-221 1235
Fax: 0141-248 5892
E-mail: secretary@spf.netkonect.co.uk
Secretary: F. E. J. McCrossin

Scottish Pelagic Fishermen's Association Ltd
1 Frithside Street, Fraserburgh, Aberdeenshire
AB43 9AR
Tel: 01346-510714
Fax: 01346-510614
E-mail: spfaltd@btinternet.com
Chairman: A. West

Scottish Plastering and Drylining Association
PO Box 28011, Edinburgh EH16 6WN
Tel: 0131-467 1998
Fax: 0131-621 7089
E-mail: amckinney@support-services.fsbusiness
        .co.uk
Secretary: A. McKinney

Scottish Print Employers Federation
48 Palmerston Place, Edinburgh EH12 5DE
Tel: 0131-220 4353
Tel: 0131-220 4344
E-mail: info@spef.org.uk
Web: http://www.spef.org.uk
Director: J. B. Raeburn

Scottish Public Relations Consultants Association
c/o Harrison Cowley, 62 The Shore, Leith
Edinburgh EH6 6RA
Tel: 0131-553 6000
Fax: 0131-553 4914
E-mail: sues@harrisoncowley.com
Chairman: S. Souter

Scottish Publishers' Association
Scottish Book Centre, 137 Dundee Street
Edinburgh EH11 1BG
Tel: 0131-228 6866
Fax: 0131-228 3220
E-mail: enquiries@scottishbooks.org
Web: http://www.scottishbooks.org
Director: Ms L. Fannin

Scotch Quality Beef and Lamb Association
Rural Centre, West Mains, Ingliston, Newbridge
Midlothian EH28 8NZ
Tel: 0131-472 4040
Fax: 0131-472 4038
E-mail: email@sqbla.co.uk
Web: http://www.sqbla.org.uk
Chief Executive: B. Simpson

Scottish Quality Salmon Ltd
Durn, Isla Road, Perth PH2 7HG
Tel: 01738-587000
Fax: 01738-621454
E-mail: enquiries@scottishsalmon.co.uk
Web: http://www.scottishsalmon.co.uk
Administrator: P. Neame

Scottish Retail Consortium
222–224 Queensferry Road, Edinburgh EH4 2BN
Tel: 0131-332 6619/9298
Fax: 0131-332 6597
Director: P. Browne

Scottish Retail Consortium
222–224 Queensferry Road, Edinburgh EH4 2BN
Tel: 0131-332 6619/9298
Fax: 0131-332 6597
E-mail: info@brc.org.uk
Director-General: Ms A. Robinson

Scottish Software Federation
Innovation Centre, 1 Michaelson Square,
Kirkton Campus, Livingston EH54 7DP
Tel: 01506-472200
Fax: 01506-472209
E-mail: ssf@scotsoft.org.uk
Web: http://www.scotsoft.org.uk
Chairman: E. Robertson

Scottish Timber Trade Association
Office 14, John Player Building, Stirling
Enterprise Park, Springbank Road, Stirling
FK7 7RP
Tel: 01786-451623
Fax: 01786-473112
Secretary: D. J. Sulman

The Scotch Whisky Association
20 Atholl Crescent, Edinburgh EH3 8HF
Tel: 0131-222 9200
Fax: 0131-222 9248
E-mail: enquiries@swa.org.uk
Web: http://www.scotch-whisky.org.uk
Director-General: H. Morison

SELECT
Bush House, Bush Estate, Midlothian EH26 0SB
Tel: 0131-445 5577
Fax: 0131-445 5548
E-mail: admin@select.org.uk
Web: http://www.select.org.uk
Managing Director: M. D. Goodwin, OBE

Skin, Hide and Leather Traders Association Ltd
Douglas House, Douglas Road, Melrose,
Roxburghshire TD6 9QT
Tel: 01896-822233
Fax: 01896-823344
E-mail: offices@andaco.com
Web: http://www.shalta.org
Secretary-General: A. D. Cox, MBE

Society of Indexers – Scottish Group
Bentfield, 3 Marine Terrace, Gullane, E. Lothian
EH31 2AY
Tel: 01620-842247
Fax: 01620-842247
E-mail: annemccarthy@btinternet.com
Web: http://www.socind.demon.co.uk
Group Organiser: Mrs A. McCarthy

The Society of Law Accountants in Scotland
Level 2, Saltire Court, 20 Castle Terrace,
Edinburgh EH1 2ET
E-mail: carol.pike@ledingham-chalmers.co.uk
Web: http://www.solas.co.uk
General Secretary: Mrs C. A. Pike

**Society of Local Authority Chief Executives
and Senior Managers**
c/o Angus Council, The Cross, Forfar, Angus
DD8 1BX
Tel: 01307-473020
Fax: 01307-461874
E-mail: chiefexec@angus.gov.uk
Hon. Secretary: A. Watson

**Society of Messengers-at-Arms and Sheriff
Officers**
11 Alva Street, Edinburgh, EH2 4PH
Tel: 0131-225 9110
Fax: 0131-220 3468
E-mail: admin@smaso.ednet.co.uk
Web: http://www.ednet.co.uk/ssmaso
Administrative Secretary: A. Hogg

Society of Scottish Artists
4 Barony Street, Edinburgh EH3 6PE
Tel: 0131-557 2354
Secretary: Mrs S. Cornish

SPF/NPA
143 Constitution Street, Edinburgh EH6 7AD
Tel: 0131-467 3301
E-mail: secretary@spf.netkonect.co.uk
Public Affairs Executive: B. Cuddihy

**Stone Federation Great Britain – Scottish
Section**
PO Box 28011, Edinburgh EH16 6WN
Tel: 0131-467 1998
Fax: 0131-621 7089
Secretary: A. McKinney

Timber Growers Association Ltd
5 Dublin Street Lane South, Edinburgh
EH1 3PX
Tel: 0131-538 7111
Fax: 0131-538 7222
E-mail: tga@timber-growers.co.uk
Web: http://www.timber-growers.co.uk
Chief Executive: J. Gunn

UK Forest Products Association
John Player Building, Stirling Enterprise Park,
Springbank Road, Stirling FK7 7RP
Tel: 01786-449029
Fax: 01786-473112
E-mail: ukfpa@compuserve.com
Web: http://www.ukfpa.co.uk
Executive Director: D. J. Sulman

UK Offshore Operators Association Ltd
9 Albyn Terrace, Aberdeen AB10 1YP
Tel: 01224-626652
Fax: 01224-626503
E-mail: info@ukooa.co.uk
Web: http://www.oilandgas.org.uk
Director-General: J. May

TRADE UNIONS

The Certification Officer is responsible for certifying the independence of trade unions, receiving and scrutinising annual returns from trade unions, dealing with complaints about trade union elections and ensuring compliance with statutory requirements governing political funds and union mergers.

The Central Arbitration Committee arbitrates on trade disputes; adjudicates on disclosure of information complaints; also determines claims for statutory recognition under the Employment Relations Act 1999 and certain issues relating to the implementation of the European Works Council Directive.

CERTIFICATION OFFICE FOR TRADE
UNIONS AND EMPLOYERS'
ASSOCIATIONS, SCOTLAND

58 Frederick Street, Edinburgh EH2 1LN
Tel: 0131-226 3224
Assistant Certification Officer for Scotland:
J. L. J. Craig

CENTRAL ARBITRATION COMMITTEE

3rd Floor, Discovery House, 28–42 Banner
Street, London EC1Y 8QE
Tel: 020-7251 9747; Fax: 020-7251 3114
Chairman: Prof. Sir Michael Burton
Secretary: C. Johnston

SCOTTISH TRADES UNION CONGRESS
333 Woodlands Road, Glasgow G3 6NG
Tel: 0141-337 8100; Fax: 0141-337 8101;
Email: info@stuc.org.uk

The Congress was formed in 1897 and acts as a national centre for the trade union movement in Scotland. The STUC promotes the rights and welfare of those in work and helps the unemployed. It helps its member unions to promote membership in new areas and industries, and campaigns for rights at work for all employees, including part-time and temporary workers, whether union members or not. It makes representations to government and employers. The Annual Congress in April elects a 38-member General Council on the basis of six industrial sections.

In 2000 the STUC consisted of 46 unions with a membership of 634,797 and 34 directly affiliated Trade Councils.
Chairperson: L. Elkind
General Secretary: B. Speirs

UNIONS AFFILIATED TO THE SCOTTISH TRADES UNION CONGRESS

Amalgamated Engineering and Electrical Union (AEEU)
145–165 West Regent Street, Glasgow G2 4RZ
Tel: 0141-248 7131
Fax: 0141-221 3898
E-mail: glasgow@aeeu.org.uk
Web: http://www.aeeu.org.uk
Scottish Regional Secretary: D. Carrigan

Association of First Division Civil Servants
2 Caxton Street, London SW1H 0QH
Tel: 020-7343 1111
Fax: 020-7343 1105
E-mail: head-office@fda.org.uk
Web: http://www.fda.org.uk
General Secretary: J. Baume

Association of University Teachers
6 Castle Street, Edinburgh EH2 3AT
Tel: 0131-226 6694
Fax: 0131-226 2066
E-mail: scotland&ne@aut.org.uk
Web: http://www.aut.org.uk/auts.html
Assistant General Secretary: D. Bleiman

British Actors' Equity Association
114 Union Street, Glasgow G1 3QQ
Tel: 0141-248 2472
Fax: 0141-248 2473
E-mail: lboswell@glasgow.equity.org.uk
Scottish Organiser and Northern Ireland Secretaries: L. Boswell; D. McFarlane

British Air Line Pilots Association (BALPA)
81 New Road, Harlington, Hayes, Middx UB3 5BG
Tel: 020-8476 4000
Fax: 020-8476 4077
E-mail: balpa@balpa.org
Web: http://www.balpa.org
General Secretary: C. Darke

British Dietetic Association
Department of Dietetics, Raigmore Hospital
Old Perth Road, Inverness IV2 3UJ
Tel: 01463-704000
Scottish Officer: Mrs M. Butters

British Orthoptic Society
Orthoptic Department, Royal Alexandra Hospital, Corsebar Road, Paisley PA2 2PN
Tel: 0141-580 4347

British Orthoptic Society
Orthoptic Department, Perth Royal Infirmary
Taymount Terrace, Perth PH1 1NX
Tel: 01738-623311

Broadcasting, Entertainment, Cinematograph and Theatre Union (BECTU)
114 Union Street, Glasgow G2 3QQ
Tel: 0141-248 9558
Fax: 0141-248 9588
Web: http://www.bectu.org.uk
Scottish Organiser: P. McManus

The Chartered Society of Physiotherapy
14 Bedford Row, London WC1R 4ED
Tel: 020-7306 6666
Fax: 020-7306 6611
E-mail: ceo@csphysio.org.uk
Chief Executive: P. Gray
Policy Officer for Scotland: Ms S. Aitken

Communication Workers Union
Dundee (E) Branch, Room 201, Telephone Exchange, 8 Willisdon Street, Dundee DD1 1DB
Tel: 01382-223612/302385
Fax: 01382-202094
E-mail: dundee@cwu106.freeserve.co.uk
Web: http://www.cwu.org

Communication Workers Union
Granthouse Inn, Duns, Berwickshire TD11 3RW
E-mail: dundee@cwu106.freeserve.co.uk
Web: http://www.cwu.org

Connect
22A Caroline Street, St Paul's Square,
Birmingham B3 1UE
Tel: 0121-236 2637
Fax: 0121-236 2616
E-mail: birmingham@connectuk.com
Web: http://www.connectuk.com
Chief Executive: S. Petch

The Educational Institute of Scotland
46 Moray Place, Edinburgh EH3 6BH
Tel: 0131-225 6244
Fax: 0131-220 3151
E-mail: membership@eis.org.uk
Web: http://www.eis.org.uk
General Secretary: R. A. Smith

Engineers' and Managers' Association
30 New Street, Musselburgh, E. Lothian
EH21 6JP
Tel: 0131-665 4487
Fax: 0131-665 7513
E-mail: scot@ema.org.uk
Web: http://www.ema.org.uk
National Officer: Ms A. Douglas

GMB
Fountain House, 1–3 Woodside Crescent,
Glasgow G3 7UJ
Tel: 0141-332 8641
Fax: 0141-332 4491
E-mail: robert.parker@gmb.org.uk
Regional Secretary: R. Parker

Independent Union of Halifax Staff
Simmons House, 46 Old Bath Road, Charvil
Reading RG10 9QR
Tel: 0118-934 1808
Fax: 0118-932 0208
E-mail: 101670.351@compuserve.com
General Secretary: G. Nichols

**Institution of Professionals, Managers and
    Specialists**
18 Melville Terrace, Stirling FK8 2NQ
Tel: 01786-465999
Fax: 01786-465516
E-mail: DenneyA@ipms.org.uk
Web: http://www.ipms.org.uk
National Officer: A. Denney

Iron and Steel Trades Confederation
20 Quarry Street, Hamilton ML3 7AR
Tel: 01698-422924
Fax: 01698-286332
Senior Organiser: S. McCool

**Manufacturing, Science and Finance union
    (MSF)**
1 Woodlands Terrace, Glasgow G3 6DD
Tel: 0141-331 1216
Fax: 0141-331 1835
E-mail: glasgow@msf.org.uk
Web: http://www.msf.org.uk
National Secretary: J. Wall

Musicians' Union
11 Sandyford Place, Sauchiehall Street, Glasgow
G3 7NB
Tel: 0141-248 3723
Fax: 0141-204 3510
E-mail: info@musiciansunion.org.uk
Web: http://www.musiciansunion.org.uk
Scottish District Organizer: I. Smith

**NASUWT (National Association of
    Schoolmasters/Union of Women Teachers)**
5th Floor, Stock Exchange House, 7 Nelson
Mandela Place, Glasgow G2 1AY
Tel: 0131-523 1110
Fax: 0131-523 1119
E-mail: rc-scotland@mail.nasuwt.org.uk
Web: http://www.nasuwt-scotland.org/
Scottish Official: Ms C. Fox

**National Association of Colliery Overmen,
    Deputies and Shotfirers**
19 Cadzow Street, Hamilton ML3 6EE
Tel: 01698-284981
Fax: 01698-281380
Scottish Area Secretary: R. Letham

National Union of Journalists (NUJ)
114 Union Street, Glasgow G1 3QQ
Tel: 0141-248 6648
Fax: 0141-248 2473
E-mail: nujscot@nuj.org.uk
Scottish Organiser: P. Holleran

**National Union of Knitwear, Footwear and
    Apparel Trades**
Orwell, 6 London Road, Kilmarnock KA3 7AD
Tel: 01563-527476
Fax: 01563-537851
E-mail: kfat@mcr1.poptel.org.uk
Web: http://www.poptel.org.uk/kfat
District Secretary: J. Steele

National Union of Marine, Aviation and Shipping Transport Officers
Oceanair House, 750–760 High Road, London E11 3BB
Tel: 020-8989 6677
Fax: 020-8530 1015
E-mail: info@numust.org
Web: http://www.numast.org
General Secretary: B. D. Orrell
Deputy General Secretary: P. McEwen

National Union of Mineworkers (NUM)
30 New Street, Musselburgh EH21 6JP
Fax: 0131-665 4111
Tel: 0131-665 4104
Scottish Area Secretary: N. Wilson

Public and Commercial Services Union (PCS)
6 Hillside Crescent, Edinburgh EH7 5DY
Tel: 0131-556 0407
Fax: 0131-557 5613
E-mail: pauld@pcs.org.uk
Web: http://www.pcs.org.uk
Scottish Secretary: E. Reilly

Scottish Carpet Workers' Union
Viewfield Business Centre, 62 Viewfield Road Ayr KA8 8HH
Tel: 01292-261676
Fax: 01292-261676
Secrtary: R. Smillie

Scottish Further and Higher Education Association
Suite 2C, Ingram House, 227 Ingram Street
Glasgow G1 1DA
Tel: 0141-221 0118
Fax: 0141-221 2583
E-mail: sfhea@easynet.co.uk
Web: http://www.sfhea.org.uk
General Secretary: E. H. Smith

Scottish Secondary Teachers' Association
15 Dundas Street, Edinburgh EH3 6QG
Tel: 0131-556 5919
Fax: 0131-556 1419
E-mail: info@ssta.org
General Secretary: D. H. Eaglesham

The Society of Chiropodists and Podiatrists
1 Fellmongers Path, London SE1
Tel: 020-7486 3381
Fax: 020-7935 6359
E-mail: enq@scpod.org.uk
Web: http://www.feetforlife.org
Chief Executive: Ms H. B. De Lyon

The Society of Radiographers
6 Victoria Road, Brookfield, Johnstone, Renfrewshire PA5 8TZ
Tel: 01505-382039
Fax: 01505-382039
E-mail: elizabeths@sor.org
Web: http://www.sor-scotland.org
Scotland Officer: Ms E. Stow

Transport and General Workers' Union (TGWU)
290 Bath Street, Glasgow G2 4LD
Tel: 0141-332 7321
Fax: 0141-332 6157
Regional Secretary: A. Baird

UNiFI
146 Argyle Street, Glasgow G2 8BL
Tel: 0141-221 6475/6
Fax: 0141-204 3315
E-mail: info@unifi.org.uk
Web: http://www.unifi.org.uk
Deputy General Secretary: S. Boyle

UNISON
UNISON House, 14 West Campbell Street
Glasgow G2 6RX
Tel: 0141-332 0006
Fax: 0141-331 1203
Web: http://www.unison.org.uk
Scottish Secretary: M. Smith

Union of Construction, Allied Trades and Technicians (UCATT)
20–23 Woodside Place, Glasgow G3 7QF
Tel: 0141-300 0115
Fax: 0141-304 4591
Scottish Secretary: A. S. Ritchie

Union of Shop, Distributive and Allied Workers (USDAW)
Muirfield, 342 Albert Drive, Glasgow G41 5PG
Tel: 0141-427 6561
Fax: 0141-427 3155
Scottish Divisional Officer: F. Whitelaw

THE VOLUNTARY SECTOR IN SCOTLAND

There are around 44,000 voluntary or non-profit organisations in Scotland, of which more than half are registered as charities. It is estimated that four new charities are created in Scotland every working day. Income from public donations is about £500 million a year. Recent research carried out by the Scottish Council for Voluntary Organisations (SCVO) into the size and characteristics of the voluntary workforce found that registered charities in Scotland in 1998–9 employed 59,806 paid staff (equivalent to 49,000 full-time posts), an increase of nearly 9,000 over the 1996 figure. The wider non-profit sector, including Scottish branches of English-registered UK-level charities and voluntary organisations without charity status, employs 100,000 people and generates an annual turnover of as much as £2 billion. Among paid voluntary-sector workers, 68 per cent are women. About 700,000 Scots work on a voluntary basis for non-profit organisations; again, a majority are women.

Voluntary-sector organisations are defined by their independence from the state and by the fact that they are run by unpaid volunteers (although they may employ paid workers), as well as by their non-profit status. However, the sector is increasingly involved in meeting needs and providing services in key areas of government policy such as social inclusion and health, housing and homelessness, and environmental protection. Other fields covered by voluntary organisations include community development; residential care, including care of elderly people; playschemes and other services for children and youth; human rights; peace issues; gender equality and women's rights; racial equality; labour and professional relations; religious interests; mental health; disabilities; racial equality and minorities issues; drugs/alcohol abuse; animal care and wildlife protection; international development and humanitarian aid; and consumers' interests. There are also a great many voluntary organisations promoting arts and culture, sports and outdoor activities (including mountain rescue), and informal education. The sector is very diverse, including organisations of all sizes and ranging from single-issue groups and campaigns to service provision and advocacy. Voluntary groups and organisations play a key role in the economy at the local level and in community well-being.

The fastest growth in the non-profit sector is occurring in the largest charities, those with annual incomes of over £500,000 a year. Many of these are now delivering a range of social care and health services which were previously carried out by central and local government. At the same time, however, smaller charities have experienced a sharp drop in resources owing to reductions both in local authority funding and public donations. Nearly 90 per cent of small non-profit organisations (those with annual incomes of less than £25,000) have no paid staff at all but rely entirely on volunteers.

The significant role played by the voluntary sector in policy development and service provision, as well as at the community level, and its weight as an economic sector complementary to the public and private sectors, are recognised in the Scottish Compact. Launched in 1998, the Compact sets out the principles underlying the relationship of co-operation between the Scottish government and the voluntary sector, and was drawn up by a joint working group consisting of representatives of the Scottish Office (before devolution) and the voluntary sector. As well as promoting good practice and encouraging volunteering as an expression of active citizenship, the Compact enables the voluntary sector to have a voice in policy-making through dialogue with government.

The Scottish Executive is committed to supporting the voluntary sector by creating a more stable funding environment for it, including providing core funding to national voluntary organisations and other funding packages where appropriate.

In June 2000 estimated Scottish Expenditure on the voluntary sector for the next two years was reported to be as follows:

ESTIMATED SCOTTISH EXECUTIVE EXPENDITURE ON THE VOLUNTARY SECTOR FOR 2000–1 AND 2001–2

	2000–1 £ million	2001–2 £ million
Annual Expenditure Report	6.0	5.9
Infrastructure bodies – Scottish Council for Voluntary Organisations, Volunteer Development Scotland	0.6	0.6
Councils for Voluntary Services	1.3	1.3
Local Volunteer Development Agencies	1.0	1.0
Active Communities Initiative	0.6	0.8
Millennium Volunteers	0.7	0.7
Unemployed Voluntary Action Fund	0.9	0.9
Ethnic Minority Grant Scheme	0.3	0.3
Unallocated		

Source: Scottish Parliament, Written Answers for the week 12– 16 June 2000.

RECENT ISSUES

On 29 March 2000, Scottish justice minister Jim Wallace announced the membership and remit of an independent commission to revise charity law in Scotland. The main provisions are in Part I of the Law Reform (Miscellaneous Provisions) (Scotland) Act 1990. Public charitable collections are regulated under section 119 of the Civic Government (Scotland) Act 1982, and educational endowments are governed by the Education (Scotland) Act 1980.

Voluntary organisations which have pressed for such a review for several years welcomed the move, pointing out that charity law in Scotland is in serious need of updating and systematising. Much of it rests on an obsolete definition of charity itself. The current definition of a charitable organisation is unclear, resulting in anomalies; for instance, at present private schools qualify for charity status but self-help groups, credit unions and groups campaigning for equal rights do not. There is no register of charities in Scotland. Also, there is little co-ordination between the existing regulatory bodies: the Inland Revenue grants charitable status, the Scottish Charity Office investigates allegations, and the Scottish Executive funds and works with charities.

Because of its major focus on work with disadvantaged communities and groups, and especially on social inclusion and on training and employment opportunities for unemployed people, the voluntary sector also has an interest in the review of Scotland's two Enterprise Networks (Scottish Enterprise and Highlands and Islands Enterprise), announced by Henry McLeish, Minister for Enterprise and Lifelong Learning, late in 1999. The Enterprise Networks provide a range of training and economic development services in various areas of Scotland.

THE EUROPEAN DIMENSION

Many voluntary organisations in Scotland are involved in activities and projects implementing the European Union's national and regional Structural Fund programmes, which give financial support to measures addressing the needs of less well-off or geographically isolated regions and societal groups in Europe. The European Social Fund (ESF) is the most important Structural Fund for the voluntary sector. In 1999, Scottish voluntary organisations accounted for £60 million in Structural Fund projects. Approximately £14 million of this came through the 1999 ESF Objective 3 programme, which targets long-term unemployment and the integration of young people and others into working life and supports projects in the areas of training and retraining, capacity-building, advice and counselling. The new ESF Objective 3 programme for the period 2000–6 makes over £320 million available for raising employability and addressing social exclusion, including promoting lifelong learning and equal opportunities, much of which will be channelled through the voluntary sector.

SCOTTISH COUNCIL FOR VOLUNTARY ORGANISATIONS

The Scottish Council for Voluntary Organisations (SCVO), established in 1936, is the umbrella body for voluntary organisations in Scotland and aims to promote and advocate the independence, interests and value of the voluntary sector among the major players in Scottish life and the wider community. The SCVO has over 2,000 member organisations which it serves from offices in Edinburgh, Glasgow and Inverness. Its services to the voluntary sector include training, seminars and conferences, advice on funding, legislation and management of voluntary organisations, and research on voluntary sector issues. It has a database of sources of charitable funding, and its European Unit provides an initial point of contact for charities seeking access to European funds. It publishes a weekly newspaper, *Third Force News,* and a variety of other publications addressing practical issues of voluntary organisation management and analysing government policy and other issues affecting the sector. There is also a Parliamentary Information and Advice Service, which has published a *Guide to the Scottish Parliament and a Guide to Parliamentary Lobbying in Scotland* as tools for voluntary organisations with a policy advocacy role.

SCVO has a Racial Equality Unit, which promotes racial equality in Scottish voluntary organisations, gives advice and training on racial equality issues in the sector, and provides support services to the black and minority ethnic sector. The SCVO also has a Scottish Voluntary HIV and AIDS Forum, which is the co-ordinating body for the voluntary sector's response to HIV and AIDS in Scotland, and includes both organisations concerned specifically with HIV and others which include HIV within a broader remit.

COUNCILS FOR VOLUNTARY SERVICE

Councils for Voluntary Service (CVS) are a network of 55 local community development agencies across Scotland. They are co-ordinated by CVS Scotland, which operates within the SCVO and provides training, information, publications and advice to member CVS. The membership of each CVS is drawn from local voluntary and community groups, numbering on average up to 100, and   each CVS plans its activities to meet needs identified by the local voluntary-sector community. CVS develop partnerships with other local organisations (councils, health authorities, enterprise companies, etc.) and act as channels by which local groups can express their views on local decision- and policy-making.

The addresses of CVS and further information on them may be obtained from the Development Officer, CVS Scotland, at the SCVO office in Edinburgh, or from the SCVO website.

ORGANISATIONS

It would be impossible to include here a full list of voluntary-sector organisations in Scotland. SCVO has a database containing details of all its members, which can be consulted on its website.

SCVO (REGISTERED OFFICE):

18/19 Claremont Crescent, Edinburgh EH7 4QD
Tel: 0131-556 3882; Fax: 0131-566 0279
E-mail: enquiries@scvo.org.uk
Web:http://www.scvo.org.uk

SCVO WEST OF SCOTLAND (ALSO RACIAL AND EUROPEAN UNITS)

9th Floor, Fleming House, 134 Renfrew Street, Glasgow G3 6ST
Tel: 0141-332 5660, 0141-332 5667; Fax 0141 332 4225

SCVO NORTH OF SCOTLAND

9 Ardross Terrace, Inverness IV3 5NQ
Tel: 01463-235633; Fax 01463-716003

VOLUNTEER DEVELOPMENT SCOTLAND

72 Murray Place, Stirling FK8 2BX
Tel: 01786-479593

IDEAS

c/o 34—36 Rose Street North Lane, Edinburgh EH2 2NP
Tel: 0131-225 5949; Fax: 0131-225 7618
E-mail: scotdec@aol.com

SCOTTISH COUNCIL FOR CIVIL LIBERTIES

146 Holland Street, Glasgow G2 4NG

SCOTTISH COUNCIL FOR RACIAL EQUALITY

18 Belvedere Park, Edinburgh EH6 4LR

SCOTTISH PENSIONERS' FORUM

333 Woodlands Road, Glasgow G3 6NG
Tel: 0141-337 8100; Fax 0141-337 8101

WOMEN'S FORUM SCOTLAND

102 Earlbank Avenue, Scotstoun, Glasgow G14 9DY
Tel: 0141-579 7355

MEDIA

SCOTLAND

TELEVISION
RADIO
THE PRESS
BOOK PUBLISHERS

MEDIA SCOTLAND

CROSS-MEDIA OWNERSHIP

There are rules on cross-media ownership to prevent undue concentration of ownership. These were amended by the Broadcasting Act 1996. Radio companies are now permitted to own one AM, one FM and one other (AM or FM) service; ownership of the third licence is subject to a public interest test. Local newspapers with a circulation under 20 per cent in an area are also allowed to own one AM, one FM and one other service, and may control a regional Channel 3 television service subject to a public interest test. Local newspapers with a circulation between 20 and 50 per cent in an area may own one AM and one FM service, subject to a public interest test, but may not control a regional Channel 3 service. Those with a circulation over 50 per cent may own one radio service in the area (provided that more than one independent local radio service serves the area) subject to a public interest test.

Ownership controls on the number of television or radio licences have been removed; holdings are now restricted to 15 per cent of the total television audience or 15 per cent of the total points available in the radio points scheme. Ownership controls on cable operators have also been removed. National newspapers with less than 20 per cent of national circulation may apply to control any broadcasting licences, subject to a public interest test. National newspapers with more than 20 per cent of national circulation may not have more than a 20 per cent interest in a licence to provide a Channel 3 service, Channel 5 or national and local analogue radio services.

BROADCASTING

The British Broadcasting Corporation (BBC) is responsible for public service broadcasting in the UK. Its constitution and finances are governed by royal charter and agreement. On 1 May 1996 a new royal charter came into force, establishing the framework for the BBC's activities until 2006.

The Independent Television Commission and the Radio Authority were set up under the terms of the Broadcasting Act 1990. The ITC is the regulator and licensing authority for all commercially-funded television services, including cable and satellite services. The Radio Authority is the regulator and licensing authority for all independent radio services.

COMPLAINTS

The Broadcasting Standards Commission was set up in April 1997 under the Broadcasting Act 1996 and was formed from the merger of the Broadcasting Complaints Commission and the Broadcasting Standards Council. The Commisson is the statutory body for standards and fairness in broadcasting. It is the only organisation in broadcasting to cover all television and radio. This includes BBC and commercial broadcasters as well as text, cable, satellite and digital services. The Commission has three main tasks, set out in the 1996 Broadcasting Act:

— produce codes of practice relating to standards and fairness
— consider and adjudicate on complaints
— monitor, research and report on standards and fairness in broadcasting

BROADCASTING STANDARDS COMMISSION

7 The Sanctuary, London SW1P 3JS
Tel: 020-7233 0544; Fax: 020-7233 0397
E-mail: bsc@bsc.org.uk
Web: http://www.bsc.org.uk
Chairman: Lord Holme of Cheltenham
Director: Stephen Whittle

TELEVISION

All channels are broadcast in colour on 625 lines UHF from a network of transmitting stations. Transmissions are available to more than 99 per cent of the population.

The BBC broadcasts two UK-wide television services, BBC 1 and BBC 2; in Scotland these services are designated BBC Scotland on 1 and BBC Scotland on 2. News 24 is a 24-hour BBC television news service broadcast by cable during the day and on BBC 1 at night.

The ITV Network Centre is wholly owned by the ITV companies and undertakes the commissioning and scheduling of those television programmes which are shown across the ITV network. Through its sister organisation, the ITV Association, it also provides a range of services to the ITV companies where a common approach is required.

The total number of receiving television licences in the UK at July 1999 was 22,274,792, of which 98.8 per cent were for colour televisions. Annual television licence fees are: black and white £34.50; colour £104.00.

British Sky Broadcasting is the UK's

broadband entertainment company, distributing sports, movies, entertainment and news to 8.6 million households throughout the UK (4.1m via digital and analogue satellite, 3.8m via cable and 647,000 via digital terrestrial television). The launch of the UK's first digital television service, Sky digital on 1 October 1998 has been the fastest, most successful digital roll-out in Europe, attracting 3.4m viewers to date. Sky also embraces alternative platforms including interactive TV, WAP telephones, ADLS and the web. British Sky Broadcasting is one of the largest private sector employers in Scotland with more than 6000 individuals, the majority being employed at call centres in Livingston and Dunfermline. Digital television multiplex licences have been awarded, including one to SDN Ltd which guarantees space for Gaelic programmes in Scotland.

BBC TELEVISION

BBC SCOTLAND
BBC Broadcasting House, Queen Margaret Drive, Glasgow G12 8DG
Tel: 0141-339 8844

BBC Broadcasting House, Beechgrove Terrace, Aberdeen AB15 5ZT
Tel: 01224-625233

BBC Broadcasting House, 5 Queen Street, Edinburgh EH2 1JF
Tel: 0131-225 3131

INDEPENDENT TELEVISION

INDEPENDENT TELEVISION NETWORK COMPANIES IN SCOTLAND

Border Television plc
Area: the Borders
The Television Centre, Carlisle CA1 3NT
Tel: 01228-25101

Grampian Television plc
Group, Scottish Media
Area: northern Scotland
Queen's Cross, Aberdeen AB15 2XJ
Tel: 01224-846846

Scottish Television plc
Group, Scottish Media
Area: central Scotland
Cowcaddens, Glasgow G2 3PR
Tel: 0141-300 3000

OTHER INDEPENDENT TELEVISION COMPANIES

Channel 5 Broadcasting Ltd
22 Long Acre, London WC2E 9LY
Tel: 020-7550 5555

Channel Four Television Corporation
227 West George Street, Glasgow G2 2ND
Tel: 0141-568 7100

GMTV Ltd (Breakfast Television)
London Television Centre, Upper Ground, London SE1 9TT
Tel: 020-7827 7000

Independent Television News Ltd
200 Gray's Inn Road, London WC1X 8XZ
Tel: 020-7833 3000

ITN Scottish Bureau
c/o STV, Cowcaddens, Glasgow G2 3PR
Tel: 0141-332 1093

Teletext Ltd (Scottish Editor)
c/o Newstel Information Ltd, Pentagon Centre, 36 Washington Street, Glasgow G3 8AZ
Tel: 0141-243 2716/221 4457

DIRECT BROADCASTING BY SATELLITE TELEVISION

British Sky Broadcasting Ltd
Grant Way, Isleworth, Middx TW7 5QD
Tel: 020-7705 3000

RADIO

UK domestic radio services are broadcast across three wavebands: FM (or VHF), medium wave (also referred to as AM) and long wave (used by BBC Radio 4). In the UK the FM waveband extends in frequency from 87.5 MHz to 108 MHz and the medium wave band extends from 531 kHz to 1602 kHz. Some radios are still calibrated in wavelengths rather than frequency. To convert frequency to wavelength, divide 300,000 by the frequency in kHz.

The frequencies allocated for terrestrial digital radio in the UK are 217.5 to 230 MHz. It is necessary to have a radio set with a digital decoder in order to receive digital radio broadcasts.

BBC RADIO

BBC Radio broadcasts five network services to the UK, Isle of Man and the Channel Islands. There is also a tier of national regional services, including Scotland. The BBC World Service broadcasts over 1,000 hours of programmes a week in 44 languages including English.

BBC NETWORK SERVICES

BBC Radio
Broadcasting House, Portland Place, London W1A 1AA
Tel: 020-7580 4468
Radio 1: frequencies: 97.6–99.8 FM
Radio 2: frequencies: 88–90.2 FM
Radio 3: frequencies: 90.2–92.4 FM
Radio 4: frequencies: 94.6–96.1 FM and 103.5–105 FM; 1449 AM, plus eight local fillers on AM; 5.55a.m.–1.00a.m. daily, with BBC World Service overnight
Radio 5 Live: frequencies: 693 AM and 909 AM, plus one local filler

BBC World Service
Bush House, Strand, London WC2B 4PH
Tel: 020-7240 3456

BBC RADIO SCOTLAND

BBC Scotland
Queen Margaret Drive, Glasgow G12 8DG
Tel: 0141-339 8844

BBC Broadcasting House, Beechgrove Terrace, Aberdeen AB9 2ZT
Tel: 01224-625233

BBC Broadcasting House, 5 Queen Street, Edinburgh EH2 1JF
Tel: 0131-225 3131
Frequencies: 810 AM plus two local fillers; 92.4–94.7 FM
Local programmes on FM as above: Highlands; North-East; Borders; South-West (also 585 AM); Orkney; Shetland

Radio Highland
7 Culduthel Road, Inverness IV2 4AD
Tel: 01463-720720
Frequency: 104.9 FM

Radio nan Gaidheal (Gaelic service)
Rosebank, Church Street, Stornoway, Isle of Lewis HS1 2LS
Tel: 01851-705000
Area: Western Highlands and Islands, Moray Firth and central Scotland

Frequencies: 103.5–105 FM; 990 AM available in Aberdeen

Radio Orkney
Castle Street, Kirkwall, Orkney KW15 1DF
Tel: 01856-873939
Frequency: 93.7 FM

Radio Shetland
Brentham House, Harbour Street, Lerwick, Shetland ZE1 0LR
Tel: 01595-694747
Frequencies: 92–95 FM

Radio Solway
Elmbank, Lover's Walk, Dumfries DG1 1NZ
Tel: 01387-268008
Frequency: 94.7 FM

Radio Tweed
Municipal Buildings, High Street, Selkirk TD7 4BU
Tel: 01750-21884
Frequency: 93.5 FM

INDEPENDENT RADIO

Independent National Radio Stations

Classic FM
Academic House, 24–28 Oval Road, London NW1 7DG
Tel: 020-7343 9000
Frequencies: 99.9–101.9 FM

Talk Radio
76 Oxford Street, London W1N 0TR
Tel: 020-7636 1089
Frequencies: 1053/1089 AM

Virgin Radio
1 Golden Square, London W1R 4DJ
Tel: 020-7434 1215
Frequencies: 1215/1197/1233/1242/1260 AM

INDEPENDENT REGIONAL LOCAL RADIO STATIONS

Scot FM
1 Albert Quay, Leith EH6 7DN
Tel: 0131-554 6677
Area: central Scotland
Frequencies: 100.3/101.1 FM

INDEPENDENT LOCAL RADIO STATIONS

96.3 QFM
26 Lady Lane, Paisley PA1 2LG
Tel: 0141-887 9630
Frequency: 96.3 FM

Argyll FM
27–29 Longrow, Cambeltown, Argyll PA28 6ER
Tel: 01586-551800
Fax: 01586-551888
Chairman: J. Campbell
Frequency: 106.5, 107.1, 107.5

Beat 106
The Four Winds Pavilion, Pacific Quay, Glasgow
G51 1EB
Tel: 0141-566 6106
Fax: 0141-566 6110
E-mail: studio@beat106.com
Web: http://www.beat106.com
Managing Director: B. Hain
Frequencies: 105.7/106.1 FM

Central FM
201 High Street, Falkirk FK1 1DU
Tel: 01324-611164
Frequency: 103.1 FM

Clan FM
Radio House, Rowantree Avenue, Newhouse
Industrial Estate, Newhouse, Lanarkshire
ML1 5RX
Tel: 01698-733107
Fax: 01698-733318
E-mail: studio@clan-fm.co.uk
Web: http://www.clan-fm.co.uk
Managing Director: Ms C. Johnston
Sales Manager: P. T. McCabe
Frequency: 107.5 and 107.9

Clyde 1 (FM) and 2 (AM)
Clydebank Business Park, Clydebank, Glasgow
G81 2RX
Tel: 0141-565 2200
Fax: 0141-565 2265
Web: http://www.clydeonline.co.uk
Managing Director: P. Cooney
Marketing Manager: R. Muir
Frequencies: 102.5 FM; 103.3 FM (Firth of
    Clyde); 97.0 FM (Vale of Leven); 1152 AM

Discovery 102
8 South Tay Street, Dundee DD1 1PA
Tel: 01382-901000
Frequency: 102.0 FM

Forth AM and FM
Forth House, Forth Street, Edinburgh EH1 3LF
Tel: 0131-556 9255
Fax: 0131-558 3277
E-mail: fortham@srh.co.uk or forthfm@srh.co.uk
Web: http://www.forthonline.co.uk
Managing Director: D. Johnston
Frequencies: 1548 AM, 97.3/97.6/102.2 FM

Heartland FM
Atholl Curling Ring, Lower Oakfield, Pitlochry
Perthshire PH16 5HQ
Tel: 01796-474040
Fax: 01796-474007
E-mail: mailbox@heartlandfm.co.uk
Chairman: M. Dobson
Programme Controller: Ms M. Hobson
Frequency: 97.5 FM

Isles FM
PO Box 333, Stornoway, Isle of Lewis HS1 2PU
Tel: 01851-703333
Fax: 01851-703322
E-mail: isles_fm@radiolink.net
Web: http://www.islesfm.co.uk
Managing Director: S. Bennie
Programme Controller: G. Afrin
Frequency: 103.0 FM

Kingdom FM
Haig House, Haig Business Park, Markinch
Fife, KY7 6AQ
Tel: 01592-753753
Fax: 01592-757788
E-mail: kingdomfm@aol.com
Chief Executive: I. Sewell
Programme Controller: K. Brady
Frequencies: 95.2/96.1 FM

Lochbroom FM
Radio House, Mill Street, Ullapool, Wester Ross
IV26 2UN
Tel: 01854-613131
Fax: 01854-613132
E-mail: radio@lochbroomfm.co.uk
Web: http://www.lochbroomfm.co.uk
Chairman: K. Guy
Station Manager: Ms S. Guy
Frequency: 102.2 FM

Moray Firth Radio
Scorguie Place, Inverness, IV3 8UJ
Tel: 01463-224433
Fax: 01463-243224
E-mail: mfr@mfr.co.uk
Web: http://www.morayfirth.co.uk
Managing Director: T. Prag
Frequencies: 97.4 FM, 1107 AM
    Local opt-outs: 96.6 FM (MFR Speysound);
    102.8 FM (MFR Keith Community Radio);
    96.7 FM (MFR Kinnaird Radio); 102.5 FM
    (MFR Caithness)

NECR (North-East Community Radio)
Town House, Kintore, Inverurie, Aberdeenshire
AB51 0US
Tel: 01467-632909
Frequencies: 97.1 FM (Braemaar); 102.1 FM
    (Meldrum and Inverurie); 102.6 FM
    (Kildrummy); 103.2 FM (Colpy)

Nevis Radio
Inverlochy, Fort William, Inverness-shire
PH33 6LU
Tel: 01397-700007
E-mail: studio@nevisradio.co.uk
Web: http://www.nevisradio.co.uk
Station Manager: G. Wright
Frequencies: 96.6 FM (Fort William); 97.0 FM
    (Glencoe); 102.3 FM (Skye); 102.4 FM
    (Loch Leven)

Northsound One (FM) and Two (AM)
45 Kings Gate, Aberdeen AB15 4EL
Tel: 01224-337000
Fax: 01224-400003
Managing Director: R. Webster
Frequencies: 1035 AM, 96.9/97.6/103.9 FM

Oban FM
132 George Street, Oban, Argyll PA34 5NT
Tel: 01631-570057
Fax: 01631-570530
E-mail: us@oban-fm.freeserve.co.uk
Managing Director: J. G. S. Mackay
Studio Manager: I. Mackay
Frequency: 103.3 FM

Radio Borders
Tweedside Park, Galashiels TD1 3TD
Tel: 01896-759444
Frequencies: 96.8/97.5/103.1/103.4 FM

Radio Tay AM and Tay FM
6 North Isla Street, Dundee DD3 7JQ
Tel: 01382-200800
Fax: 01382-423252
E-mail: taynews@srh.co.uk
Managing Director: A. Wilkie
Programme Director: A. Ballingall
Frequencies: 1161 AM, 102.8 FM (Dundee);
    1584 AM, 96.4 FM (Perth)

RNA FM
Arbroath Infirmary, Rosemount Road, Arbroath
Angus DD11 2AT
Tel: 01241-879660
Fax: 01241-439664
Web: http://www.listen.to/rna
Hon. Secretary: M. J. B. Finlayson
Frequency: 96.6 FM

SIBC
Market Street, Lerwick, Shetland ZE1 0JN
Tel: 01595-695299
Fax: 01595-695696
E-mail: info@sibc.co.uk
Web: http://www.sibc.co.uk
Managing Director: Ms I. Walterson
Frequencies: 96.2/102.2 FM

South West Sound
Campbell House, Bankend Road, Dumfries
DG1 4TH
Tel: 01387-250999
Fax: 01387-265629
E-mail: xwestsoundfm@netscapeonline.co.uk
Web: http://www.west.sound.co.uk
Station Director: Ms F. Blackwood
Frequencies: 96.5/97.0/103.0 FM

talkSPORT
18 Hatfields, London SE1 8DJ
Tel: 020-7959 7800
Fax: 020-7959 7805
E-mail: swoodward@talksport.co.uk
Web: http://www.talksport.net
Chief Executive: K. McKenzie
Forward Planning Editor: Ms S. Woodward
Frequencies: 1053/1089 AM

Wave 102
8 South Tay Street, Dundee DD1 1PA
Tel: 01382-901000
Fax: 01382-900999
E-mail: info@wave102.co.uk
Web: http://www.wave102.co.uk
Managing Director: G. Mackenzie
Head of News and Features: Ms G. Lawrie
Frequency: 102.0 FM

Waves Radio Peterhead
Unit 2, Blackhouse Industrial Estate, Peterhead
AB42 1BW
Tel: 01779-491012
Fax: 01779-490802
E-mail: waves@radiophd.freeserve.co.uk
Web: http://www.wavesfm.com
Directors: N Spence; W. McLean
Frequency: 101.2 FM

West Sound AM and West FM
Radio House, 54A Holmston Road, Ayr
KA7 3BE
Tel: 01292-283662
Fax: 01292-283665
E-mail: westsound@srh.co.uk
Web: http://www.west-sound.co.uk
Chief Executive: R. Findlay
Managing Director: Ms S. Borthwick
Frequencies: 1035 AM, 96.7 FM (Ayr); 97.5
    FM (Girvan)

THE PRESS

The press is subject to the laws on publication and the Press Complaints Commission was set up by the industry as a means of self-regulation. It is not state-subsidised and receives few tax concessions. The income of most newspapers and periodicals is derived largely from sales and from advertising; the press is the largest advertising medium in Britain.

COMPLAINTS

The Press Complaints Commission was founded by the newspaper and magazine industry in January 1991 to replace the Press Council (established in 1953). It is a voluntary, non-statutory body set up to operate the press's self-regulation system following the Calcutt report in 1990 on privacy and related matters, when the industry feared that a failure to regulate itself might lead to statutory regulation of the press. The Commission is funded by the industry through the Press Standards Board of Finance.

The Commission's objects are to consider, adjudicate, conciliate, and resolve complaints of unfair treatment by the press; and to ensure that the press maintains the highest professional standards with respect for generally recognised freedoms, including freedom of expression, the public's right to know, and the right of the press to operate free from improper pressure. The Commission judges newspaper and magazine conduct by a code of practice drafted by editors, agreed by the industry and ratified by the Commission.

Seven of the Commission's members are editors of national, regional and local newspapers and magazines, and nine, including the chairman, are drawn from other fields. One member has been appointed Privacy Commissioner with special powers to investigate complaints about invasion of privacy.

PRESS COMPLAINTS COMMISSION

1 Salisbury Square, London EC4Y 8JS
Tel: 020-7353 1248
Chairman: Lord Wakeham, PC
Director: G. Black

NEWSPAPERS

Newspapers are usually financially independent of any political party, though most adopt a political stance in their editorial comments, usually reflecting proprietorial influence. Ownership of the national and regional daily newspapers is concentrated in the hands of large corporations whose interests cover publishing and communications. The rules on cross-media ownership, as amended by the Broadcasting Act 1996, limit the extent to which newspaper organisations may become involved in broadcasting.

Scotland has a number of daily and Sunday newspapers (including Scottish editions of some of the UK national newspapers), as well as local daily and weekly newspapers. The following list shows the main editorial offices of the major newspapers in Scotland, including the Scottish editorial offices of UK national newspapers.

NATIONAL DAILY NEWSPAPERS

Daily Star of Scotland
Park House, Park Circus Place, Glasgow
G3 6AN
Tel: 0141-352 2552

Daily Telegraph
5 Coates Crescent, Edinburgh EH3 7AL
Tel: 0131-225 3313

Financial Times
3rd Floor, 80 George Street, Edinburgh
EH2 2HN
Tel: 0131-220 1420

The Guardian
PO Box 25000, Glasgow G1 5YF
Tel: 0141-553 0875

The Herald
195 Albion Street, Glasgow G1 1QP
Tel: 0141-552 6255

The Independent
Correspondent in Scotland, J. O'Sullivan
Top Left Flat, 8 Cumberland Street, Edinburgh
EH3 6SA
Tel: 0131-557 4904

The Scotsman
20 North Bridge, Edinburgh EH1 1YT
Tel: 0131-243 3207

Scottish Daily Mail
197 Albion Street, Glasgow G1 1QP
Tel: 0141-553 4600

Scottish Express
Park House, Park Circus Place, Glasgow
G3 6AF
Tel: 0141-332 9600

Scottish Mirror
40 Anderston Quay, Glasgow G3 8DA
Tel: 0141-248 7000

The Scottish Sun
124 Portman Street, Glasgow G41 1EJ
Tel: 0141-420 5100

REGIONAL DAILY NEWSPAPERS

Courier and Advertiser
2 Albert Square, Dundee DD1 9QJ
Tel: 01382-223131

Daily Record
40 Anderston Quay, Glasgow G3 8DA
Tel: 0141-248 7000

Edinburgh Evening News
20 North Bridge, Edinburgh EH1 1YT
Tel: 0131-243 3558

Evening Express
PO Box 43, Lang Stracht, Mastrick, Aberdeen
AB15 6DF
Tel: 01224-690222

Evening Times
195 Albion Street, Glasgow G1 1QP
Tel: 0141-552 6255

Greenock Telegraph
Pitreavie Business Park, Dunfermline
KY11 8QS
Tel: 01383-728201

Paisley Daily Express
1 Woodside Terrace, Glasgow G3 7UY
Tel: 0141-353 3366

Press and Journal
PO Box 43, Lang Stracht, Mastrick, Aberdeen
AB15 6DF
Tel: 01224-690222

WEEKLY NEWSPAPERS

The Independent on Sunday
Correspondent in Scotland, J. O'Sullivan
Top Left Flat, 8 Cumberland Street, Edinburgh
EH3 6SA
Tel: 0131-557 4904

Mail on Sunday in Scotland
197 Albion Street, Glasgow G1 1QP
Tel: 0141-553 4600

The Observer
11 Broughton Place, Edinburgh EH1 3RL
Tel: 0131-558 8110

Scotland on Sunday
20 North Bridge, Edinburgh EH1 1YT
Tel: 0131-243 3472

Scottish Sunday Express
Park House, Park Circus Place, Glasgow
G3 6AF
Tel: 0141-332 9600

The Sunday Herald
195 Albion Street, Glasgow G1 1QP
Tel: 0141-552 6255

Sunday Mail
40 Anderston Quay, Glasgow G3 8DA
Tel: 0141-248 7000

Sunday Mirror
40 Anderston Quay, Glasgow G3 8DA
Tel: 0141-248 7000

Sunday Post
Courier Place, Dundee DD1 9QJ
Tel: 01382-223131

Weekly News
Courier Place, Dundee DD1 9QJ
Tel: 01382-223131

CONSUMER PERIODICALS

British Postmark Bulletin
20 Brandon Street, Edinburgh EH3 5TT
Tel: 0131-550 8900
Fax: 0131-550 8501

Scottish Economic & Social History
22 George Square, Edinburgh EH8 9LF
Tel: 0131-650 4220
Fax: 0131-662 0053
E-mail: journals@eup.ed.ac.uk
Web: http://www.eup.ed.ac.uk

Antiques & Art Independent
PO Box 1945, Comely Bank, Edinburgh,
Midlothian EH4 1AB
Tel: 07000-765 263
Fax: 0131-332 4481
E-mail: antiquesnews@hotmail.com
Web: http://www.antiques-uk.co.uk

ArtWork
Mill Business Centre, PO Box 3, Ellon,
Aberdeenshire AB41 9EA
Tel: 01651-842429
Fax: 01651-842180
E-mail: editorial@artwork.co.uk
Web: http://www.artwork.co.uk

Avenue
c/o Publicity Services, 2 The Square, Glasgow
G12 8QQ
Tel: 0141-330 4192
Fax: 0141-330 5643
E-mail: avenue@mis.gla.ac.uk
Web: http://www.gla.ac.uk

Babycare and Pregnancy
80 Kingsway East, Dundee DD4 8SL
Tel: 01382-223131
Fax: 01382-452491
E-mail: baby@dcthomson.co.uk
Web: http://www.dcthomson.co.uk/mags/baby

Boxing News
6th Floor, 195 Albion Street, Glasgow G1 1QQ
Tel: 0141-302 7700
Fax: 0141-302 7799
E-mail: info@calmags.co.uk

Braille Sporting Record
Craigmillar Park, Edinburgh EH16 5NB
Tel: 0131-662 4445
Fax: 0131-662 1968
E-mail: scot.braille@dial.pipex.com
Web: http://www.scottish-braille-press.org

Brig
Robbins Centre, Stirling University, Stirling
FK9 4LA
Tel: 01786-467166
Fax: 01786-467190

British Philatelic Bulletin
20 Brandon Street, Edinburgh EH3 5TT
Tel: 0131-550 8900
Fax: 0131-550 8501

Caledonia
4 Heriot Row, Edinburgh EH3 6HU
Tel: 0131-557 5600
Fax: 0131-557 8665
E-mail: editor@scotthouse.co.uk
Web: http://www.caledonia-magazine.com

Car Mart
Craig O'Loch Road, Forfar, Angus DD8 1BT
Tel: 01307-464899
Fax: 01307-466923
E-mail: anguscountypress@compuserve.com

Celtic View
193 Bath Street, Glasgow G2 4HU
Tel: 0141-226 2200
Fax: 0141-248 1099

Chapman
4 Broughton Place, Edinburgh EH1 3RX
Tel: 0131-557 2207
Fax: 0131-556 9565
E-mail: editor@chapman-pub.co.uk
Web: http://www.airstrip-one.ndirect.co
.uk/chapman

Childminding
Suite 3, 7 Melville Terrace, Stirling FK8 2ND
Tel: 01786-445377
Fax: 01786-449062
E-mail: childminding@dial.pipex.com
Web: http://www.dialspace.dial.pipex.com/
childminding

Classic Stitches
80 Kingsway East, Dundee DD4 8SL
Tel: 01382-223131
Fax: 01382-452491
E-mail: editorial@classicstitches.com
Web: http://www.classicstitches.com

Cornucopia - Turkey for Connoisseurs
48 Castle Street, Edinburgh EH2 3LX
Tel: 01450-880352
Fax: 01450-880352
E-mail: editor@cornucopia.net
Web: http://www.cornucopia.net

Craigmillar Chronicle
Castlebrae Business Centre, Unit 13, Peffer Place
Edinburgh EH16 4NL
Tel: 0131-661 0791
Fax: 0131-661 0791

East Lothian Life
1 Beveridge Row, Belhaven, Dunbar EH42 1TP
Tel: 01368-863593
Tel: 01368-863593

Edinburgh Review
22A Buccleuch Place, Edinburgh EH8 9LF
Tel: 0131-651 1415
Fax: 0131-651 1415
E-mail: Edinburgh.Review@ed.ac.uk
Web: http://www.eup.ed.ac.uk

The Forth Naturalist & Historian
University of Stirling, Stirling, Stirlingshire
FK9 4LA
Tel: 01259-215091
Fax: 01756-464994
E-mail: lindsay.corbett@stir.ac.uk
Web: http://www.stir.ac.uk/theuni/forthnat

Gairm (The Gaelic Magazine)
29 Waterloo Street, Glasgow G2 6BZ
Tel: 0141-221 1971
Fax: 0141-221 1971

Gaudie
Luthuli House, 50–52 College Bounds,
Aberdeen AB24 3DS
Tel: 01224-272968
Fax: 01224-272977

The Great Outdoors
6th Floor, 195 Albion Street, Glasgow G1 1QQ
Tel: 0141-302 7700
Fax: 0141-302 7799
E-mail: info@calmags.co.uk

Heritage Scotland
28 Charlotte Square, Edinburgh EH2 4ET
Tel: 0131-243 9300
Fax: 0131-243 9301
E-mail: information@nts.org.uk
Web: http://www.nts.org.uk

History & Computing
22 George Square, Edinburgh EH8 9LF
Tel: 0131-650 4220
Fax: 0131-662 0053
E-mail: journals@eup.ed.ac.uk
Web: http://www.eup.ed.ac.uk

The Home Show Magazine
6th Floor, 195 Albion Street, Glasgow G1 1QQ
Tel: 0141-302 7700
Fax: 0141-302 7799
E-mail: info@calmags.co.uk

Home Help
Craigmillar Park, Edinburgh EH16 5NB
Tel: 0131-662 4445
Fax: 0131-662 1968
E-mail: scot.braille@dial.pipex.com
Web: http://www.scottish-braille-press.org

Hume Papers on Public Policy
22 George Square, Edinburgh EH8 9LF
Tel: 0131-650 4220
Tel: 0131-662 0053
E-mail: journals@eup.ed.ac.uk
Web: http://www.eup.ed.ac.uk

I Do
40 Anderston Quay, Glasgow G3 8DA
Tel: 0141-242 1414
Fax: 0141-242 1430

Journal of Victorian Culture
22 George Square, Edinburgh EH8 9LF
Tel: 0131-650 4220
Fax: 0131-662 0053
E-mail: journals@eup.ed.ac.uk
Web: http://www.eup.ed.ac.uk

Journal of the Royal College of Surgeons of Edinburgh
22 George Square, Edinburgh EH8 9LF
Tel: 0131-650 4220
Tel: 0131-662 0053
E-mail: journals@eup.ed.ac.uk
Web: http://www.eup.ed.ac.uk

Lallans
A. K. Bell Library, York Place, Perth PH2 8EP
Tel: 01738-440199
Fax: 01738-477010
E-mail: info@aift.co.uk

The List
14 High Street, Edinburgh EH1 1TE
Tel: 0131-558 1191
Fax: 0131-557 8500
E-mail: editor@list.co.uk

Lothian at Leisure
PO Box 6, Haddington, East Lothian
EH41 3NQ
Tel: 01620-822578
Fax: 01620-825079
E-mail: 101324.2142@compuserve.com

M8 Magazine
11 Lynedoch Place, Glasgow G3 6AB
Tel: 0141-353 1118
Fax: 0141-353 1448
Web: http://www.m8magazine.co.uk

Madam
Criagmillar Park, Edinburgh EH16 5NB
Tel: 0131-662 4445
Fax: 0131-662 1968
E-mail: scot.braille@dial.pipex.com
Web: http://www.scottish-braille-press.org

Motor Market Weekly
Cadzow Street, Hamilton, Lanarkshire
ML3 6HB
Tel: 01698-427121

My Weekly
80 Kingsway East, Dundee DD4 8SL
Tel: 01382-223131
Fax: 01382-452491
E-mail: myweekly@dcthomson.co.uk

The New Shetlander
Brentham House, 5 Harbour Street, Lerwick
ZE1 0LR
Tel: 01595-693816
Fax: 01595-696787
E-mail: shetlandcss@zetnet.co.uk

Paragraph
22 George Square, Edinburgh, EH8 9LF
Tel: 0131-650 4220
Fax: 0131-662 0053
E-mail: journals@eup.ed.ac.uk
Web: http://www.eup.ed.ac.uk

Parliamentary History
22 George Square, Edinburgh EH8 9LF
Tel: 0131-650 4220
Fax: 0131-662 0053
E-mail: journals@eup.ed.ac.uk
Web: http://www.eup.ed.ac.uk

People's Friend
80 Kingsway East, Dundee DD4 8SL
Tel: 01382-223131
Fax: 01382-452491

Ranger News
193 Bath Street, Glasgow G2 4HU
Tel: 0141-226 2200
Fax: 0141-248 1099

Romanticism
22 George Square, London EH8 9LF
Tel: 0131-650 4220
Fax: 0131-662 0053
E-mail: journals@eup.ed.ac.uk
Web: http://www.eup.ed.ac.uk

The Saint - Independent Student Newspaper of the University of St Andrews
St Mary's Place, St Andrews, Fife KY16 9HZ
Tel: 01334-477355-462737
Fax: 01334-462716
E-mail: chron@st.and.ac.uk

Scan News
Rosebery House, 9 Haymarket Terrace,
Edinburgh EH12 5EZ
Tel: 0131-313 2488
Fax: 0131-313 6800
E-mail: info@cls.dircon.co.uk
Web: http://www.communitylearning.org

Scenes (Scottish Environment News)
Strome House, North Strome, Lochcarron,
Ross-shire IV54 8YJ
Tel: 01520-722901
Fax: 01520-722902
E-mail: enquiries@scenes.org.uk
Web: http://www.scenes.org.uk

The Scots Magazine
2 Albert Square, Dundee DD1 9QJ
Tel: 01382-223131
Fax: 01382-322214
Web: http://www.scotsmagazine.com

Scottish Auto Trader
Auto Trader House, 14 Dalzell Drive,
Motherwell, Lanarkshire ML1 2DA
Tel: 01698-258811
Fax: 01698-276313
Web: http://www.autotrader.co.uk

Scottish Curler
Pitreavie Business Park, Dunfermline, Fife
KY11 8QS
Tel: 01383-728201
Fax: 01383-737040

Scottish Field
Royston House, Caroline Park, Edinburgh
EH5 1QJ
Tel: 0131-551 2942
Fax: 0131-551 2938
E-mail: editor@scottishfield.co.uk

Scottish Geographical Journal
22 George Square, Edinburgh EH8 9LF
Tel: 0131-650 4220
Fax: 0131-662 0053
E-mail: journals@eup.ac.uk
Web: http://www.eup.ed.ac.uk

Scottish Historical Review
22 George Square, Edinburgh EH8 9LF
Tel: 0131-650 4220
Fax: 0131-662 0053
E-mail: journals@eup.ed.ac.uk
Web: http://www.eup.ed.ac.uk

Scottish Hosteller Magazine
7 Glebe Crescent, Stirling FK8 2JA
Tel: 01786-891400
Fax: 01786-891333
E-mail: syha@syha.org.uk
Web: http://www.syha.org.uk

Scottish Home & Country
42A Heriot Row, Edinburgh EH3 6ES
Tel: 0131-225 1724
Fax: 0131-225 8129
E-mail: magazine@swri.demon.co.uk

The Scottish Review
1/4 Galt House, 31 Bank Street, Irvine, Ayrshire
KA12 0LL
Tel: 01294-311322
Fax: 01294-311322
E-mail: kr@carrickmedia.demon.co.uk

**Scottish Studies (Journal of the School of
Scottish Studies)**
University of Edinburgh, 27 George Square
Edinburgh EH8 9LD
Tel: 0131-650 4167
Fax: 0131-650 4163
E-mail: scottish.studies@ed.ac.uk
Web: http://www.sss.ed.ac.uk

Scottish Transport
PO Box 78, Glasgow G3 6ER

Scottish Wildlife
Cramond House, Kirk Cramond, Cramond
Glebe Road, Edinburgh EH4 6NS
Tel: 0131-312 7765 ext. 253
Fax: 0131-312 8705
E-mail: enquiries@swt.org.uk
Web: http://www.swt.org.uk

Shetland Life
Prince Alfred Street, Lerwick ZE1 0EP
Tel: 01595-693622
Fax: 01595-694637
E-mail: info@shetland-times.co.uk
Web: http://www.shetland-times.co.uk

Shout
2 Albert Square, Dundee DD1 9QJ
Tel: 01382-223131
Fax: 01382-200880
E-mail: shout@dcthomson.co.uk

Spectrum
Craigmillar Park, Edinburgh EH16 5NB
Tel: 0131-662 4445
Fax: 0131-662 1968
E-mail: scot.braille@dial.pipex.com
Web: http://www.scottish-braille-press.org

TGO
6th Floor, 195 Albion Street Glasgow G1 1QQ
Tel: 0141-302 7700
Fax: 0141-302 7799
E-mail: info@calmags.co.uk

Tocher
27 George Square, Edinburgh EH8 9LD
Tel: 0131-650 3056
Fax: 0131-650 4163
E-mail: sssmms@ed.ac.uk

Translation and Literature
22 George Square, Edinburgh EH8 9LF
Tel: 0131-650 4220
Fax: 0131-662 0053
E-mail: journals@eup.ed.ac.uk
Web: http://www.eup.ed.ac.uk

Young Scot
Rosebery House, 9 Haymarket Terrace
Edinburgh EH12 5EZ
Tel: 0131-313 2488
Fax: 0131-313 6800
E-mail: info@youngscot.org
Web: http://www.youngscot.org

Writers News
PO Box 4, Nairn, Nairnshire IV12 4HU
Tel: 01667-454441
Fax: 01667-454401

TRADE PERIODICALS

ACCA Students Newsletter
1 Woodside Place, Glasgow G3 7QF
Tel: 0141-309 4070
Fax: 0141-331 2448
E-mail: newsletter@acca.org.uk

Africa
22 George Square, Edinburgh EH8 9LF
Tel: 0131-650 4220
Fax: 013-662 0053
E-mail: journals@eup.ed.ac.uk
Web: http://www.eup.ed.ac.uk

Agri Business Scotland
Bergius House, 20 Clifton Street, Glasgow
G3 7LA
Tel: 0141-567 6000
Fax: 0141-331 1395
E-mail: agribusiness@peebl.com

Allscot News
PO Box 6, Haddington, East Lothian
EH41 3NQ
Tel: 01620-822578
Fax: 01620-825079
E-mail: 101324.2142@compuserve.com

The Ayrshire Journal
Ayrshire Cattle Society of Great Britain &
Ireland, 1 Racecourse Road, Ayr KA7 2DE
Tel: 01292-267123
Fax: 01272-611973
E-mail: society@ayrshires.org
Web: http://www.ayrshires.org

Ayrshire Dairyman Newsletter
Ayrshire Cattle Society of Great Britain &
Ireland, 1 Racecourse Road, Ayr KA7 2DE
Tel: 01292-267123
Fax: 01292-611973
E-mail: society@ayrshires.org.
Web: http://www.ayrshires.org

BARRA Global Estimates
10—12 Young Street, Edinburgh EH2 4JB
Tel: 0131-473 7070
Fax: 0131-473 7090
E-mail: bge-uk@barra.com
Web: http://www.barra.com

Blood Reviews
Robert Stevenson House, Baxters Place, Leith
Walk, Edinburgh EH1 3AF
Tel: 0131-556 2424
Fax: 0131-558 1278

**The Blue Book: The Directory of the Law
Society of Scotland**
4 Hill Street, Edinburgh, EH2 3JZ
Tel: 0131-225 7828
Fax: 0131-220 1833

Botanical Journal of Scotland
22 George Square, Edinburgh, EH8 9LF
Tel: 0131-650 4220
Fax: 0131-662 0053
E-mail: journals@eup.ed.ac.uk
Web: http://eup.ed.ac.uk

Braille Science Journal
Craigmillar Park, Edinburgh EH16 5NB
Tel: 0131-662 4445
Fax: 0131-662 1968
E-mail: scot.braille@dial.pipex.com
Web: http://scottish-braille-press.org

British Journal of Oral & Maxillofacial Surgery
Robert Stevenson House, Baxters Place, Leith
Walk, Edinburgh EH1 3AF
Tel: 0131-556 2424
Fax: 0131-558 1278

British Journal of Plastic Surgery
Robert Stevenson House, Baxters Place, Leith
Walk, Edinburgh EH1 3AF
Tel: 0131-556 2424
Fax: 0131-558 1278
E-mail: david_dunnachie@harcourtbrace.com
Web: http://www.churchillmed.com/journals/
  bjpj/jhome.html

Building Power Scotland
PO Box 6, Haddington, East Lothian
EH41 3NQ
Tel: 01620-822578
Fax: 01620-825079
E-mail: 101324.2142@compuserve.com

Business & Finance Magazine
Suite 419, The Pentagon Centre, Washington
Street, Glasgow G3 8AZ
Tel: 0141-204 3383
Fax: 0141-204 4967
E-mail: past@businessandfinance.fsnet.co.uk

Businessmatters
The Business Centre, Almondvale Boulevard,
Livingston, West Lothian EH54 6QP
Tel: 01506-777400
Fax: 01506-777909
E-mail: business.centre@westlothian.gov.uk
Web: http://www.westlothian.gov.uk/business

The Business
Chamber of Commerce Buildings, Panmure
Street, Dundee DD1 1ED
Tel: 01382-201122
Fax: 01382-229544
E-mail: dundeechamber@sol.co.uk

Business Bulletin
27 Albyn Place, Aberdeen, AB10 1DB
Tel: 01224-575100
Fax: 01224-213221
E-mail: Lora.Graham@scotent.co.uk
Web: http://www.aberdeenchamber.co.uk

Business News
PO Box 43, Lang Stracht, Mastrick, Aberdeen
AB15 6DF
Tel: 01224-690222
Fax: 01224-694613

Business Power Scotland
PO Box 6, Haddington, East Lothian
EH41 3NQ
Tel: 01620-822578
Fax: 01620-825079
E-mail: 101324.2142@compuserve.com

Business Scotland
Bergius House, Clifton Street, Glasgow
G3 7LA
Tel: 0141-567 6000
Fax: 0141-331 1395
E-mail: businessscotland@peebl.com

Cabletalk
Bush House, Bush Estate, Penicuik, Midlothian
EH26 0SB
Tel: 0131-445 9207
Fax: 0131-445 5548
E-mail: admin@select.org.uk
Web: http://www.select.org.uk

**CA Magazine - Journal of the Institute of
Chartered Accountants in Scotland**
27 Queen Street, Edinburgh, EH2 1LA
Tel: 0131-247 4897
Fax: 0131-247 4830
E-mail: ca.magazine@icas.org.uk
Web: http://www.icas.org.uk

Cartographic Journal
Centre for Remote Sensing and Mapping Science
Department of Geography, University of
Aberdeen, Aberdeen AB24 3UF
Tel: 01224-272324
Fax: 01224-272331
E-mail: d.r.green@abdn.ac.uk
Web: http://www.cartography.org.uk/Pages/
     Publicat/Journal/Journal.html

Catering in Scotland
Sherwood Industrial Estate, Bonnyrigg,
Midlothian EH19 3LW
Tel: 0131-663 2404
Fax: 0131-663 6863

Cell Calcium
Robert Stevenson House, Baxters Place, Leith
Walk, Edinburgh EH1 3AF
Tel: 0131-556 2424
Fax: 0131-558 1278

Clincial Nutrition
Robert Stevenson House, Baxters Place, Leith
Walk, Edinburgh EH1 3AF
Tel: 0131-556 2424
Fax: 0131-558 1278

Comment
Conference House, 152 Morrison Street,
Edinburgh EH3 8EB
Tel: 0131-477 7000
Fax: 0131-477 7702/3
E-mail: mm@ecc.dircon.co.uk
Web: http://www.ecce.org

**Commerce Business Magazine (Scotland
Edition)**
Woodside House Business Centre, 20–21
Woodside Place, Glasgow G3 7QF
Tel: 0141-307 4002
Fax: 0141-307 0288
E-mail: newsdesk@commerce.co.uk
Web: http://www.commerce.co.uk

Components in Electronics
6th Floor, 195 Albion Street, Glasgow G1 1QQ
Tel: 0141-302 7700
Fax: 0141-302 7799
E-mail: adverts-cie@calmags.co.uk

Contrax Weekly
15 Woodlands Terrace, Glasgow G3 6DF
Tel: 0141-332 8247
Fax: 0141-331 2652

The Crofter
Unit One, Industrial Estate, Broadford, Isle of
Skye IV49 9AP
Tel: 01471-822464
Fax: 01471-822694

Current Anaesthesia & Critical Care
Robert Stevenson House, Baxters Place, Leith
Walk, Edinburgh EH1 3AF
Tel: 0131-556 2424
Fax: 0131-558 1278

Current Obstetrics and Gynaecology
Robert Stevenson House, Baxters Place, Leith
Walk, Edinburgh EH1 3AF
Tel: 0131-556 2424
Fax: 0131-558 1278

Current Orthopaedics
Robert Stevenson House, Baxters Place, Leith
Walk, Edinburgh EH1 3AF
Tel: 0131-556 2424
Fax: 0131-558 1278

Current Paediatrics
Robert Stevenson House, Baxters Place, Leith
Walk, Edinburgh EH1 3AF
Tel: 0131-556 2424
Fax: 0131-558 1278

Dance Research
22 George Square, Edinburgh EH8 9LF
Tel: 0131-650 4220
Fax: 0131-662 0053
E-mail: journals@eup.ed.ac.uk
Web: http://www.eup.ed.ac.uk

The Drum
3 Park Street South, Glasgow G3 6BG
Tel: 0141-332 3255
Fax: 0141-332 2012

Edinburgh Gazette
21 South Gyle Crescent, Edinburgh EH12 9EB
Tel: 0131-479 3143
Fax: 0131-479 3311

ENT News
9 Gayfield Square, Edinburgh EH1 3NT
Tel: 0131-557 4184
Fax: 0131-557 4701
E-mail: patricia@pinpoint-scotland.com
Web: http://www.ent-news.com

The Executive Magazine
13 Henderson Road, Longman, Inverness
IV1 1SP
Tel: 01463-710999
Fax: 01463-221251

Eye News
9 Gayfield Square, Edinburgh EH1 3NT
Tel: 0131-557 4184
Fax: 0131-557 4701
E-mail: eyenews@pinpoint-scotland.com
Web: http://www.eye-news.com

Fibrinolysis
Robert Stevenson House, Baxters Place Leith
Walk, Edinburgh EH1 3AF
Tel: 0131-556 2424
Fax: 0131-558 1278

Fife Farmer
Craig O'Loch Road, Forfar, Angus DD8 1BT
Tel: 01307-464899
Fax: 01307-466923

Fish Farming Today
Royston House, Caroline Park, Edinburgh
EH5 1QJ
Tel: 0131-551 2942
Fax: 0131-551 2938

Fishing Monthly
Royston House, Caroline Park, Edinburgh
EH5 1QJ
Tel: 0131-551 2942
Fax: 0131-551 2938

Fish Trader
Royston House, Caroline Park, Edinburgh
EH5 1QJ
Tel: 0131-551 2942
Fax: 0131-551 2938

Foot
Robert Stevenson House, Baxters Place, Leith
Walk, Edinburgh EH1 3AF
Tel: 0131-556 2424
Fax: 0131-524 1790
E-mail: journals@harcourt.com
Web: http://www.harcourt-international.com

Geogscot
Graham Hills Building, 40 George Street,
Glasgow G1 1QL
Tel: 0141-552 3330
Fax: 0141-552 3331

Glasgow Chamber of Commerce Journal
30 George Square, Glasgow G2 1EQ
Tel: 0141-204 2121
Fax: 0141-221 2336
E-mail: marketing@glasgowchamber.org

Health Bulletin
St Andrew's House, Regent Road, Edinburgh
EH1 3DG
Tel: 0131-244 2292
Fax: 0131-244 2835

The Independent Electrical Retailer
6th Floor, 195 Albion Street, Glasgow G1 1QQ
Tel: 0141-302 7700
Fax: 0141-302 7799
E-mail: info@calmags.co.uk

The Independent Community Pharmacist
6th Floor, 195 Albion Street, Glasgow G1 1QQ
Tel: 0141-302 7700
Fax: 0141-302 7799
E-mail: info@calmags.co.uk

The International Journal of Obstetric Anaesthesia
Robert Stevenson House, Baxters Place, Leith
Walk, Edinburgh EH1 3AF
Tel: 0131-556 2424
Fax: 0131-558 1278

Intensive & Critical Care Nursing
Robert Stevenson House, Baxters Place, Leith
Walk, Edinburgh EH1 3AF
Tel: 0131-556 2424
Fax: 0131-558 1278

The Journal of Hand Surgery (British Volume)
Robert Stevenson House, Baxters Place, Leith
Walk, Edinburgh EH1 3AF
Tel: 0131-556 2424
Fax: 0131-459 1177
Web: http://www.churchillmed.com

Journal of Interventional Radiology
Robert Stevenson House, Baxters Place, Leith
Walk, Edinburgh EH1 3AF
Tel: 0131-556 2424
Fax: 0131-558 1278

The Journalist's Handbook
1/4 Galt House, 31 Bank Street, Irvine, Ayrshire
KA12 0LL
Tel: 01294-311322
Fax: 01294-311322
E-mail: fm@carrickmedia.demon.co.uk

Lothian Leader
PO Box 6, Haddington, East Lothian
EH41 3NQ
Tel: 01620-822578
Fax: 01620-825079
E-mail: 101324.2142@compuserve.com

Media Education Journal
c/o Scottish Green, 249 West George Street,
Glasgow G2 4QE
Tel: 01224-481976
E-mail: d@murphy47.freeserve.co.uk
Web: http://www.ames.org.uk

Medical Hypotheses
Robert Stevenson House, Baxters Place, Leith
Walk, Edinburgh, EH1 3AF
Tel: 0131-556 2424
Fax: 0131-558 1278

Nautical Magazine
4–10 Darnley Street, Glasgow G41 2SD
Tel: 0141-429 1234
Fax: 0141-420 1694
E-mail: info@skipper.co.uk
Web: http://www.skipper.co.uk

Neuropeptides
Robert Stevenson House, Baxters Place, Leith
Walk, Edinburgh EH1 3AF
Tel: 0131-556 2424
Fax: 0131-558 1278

Nurse Education Today
Robert Stevenson House, Baxters Place, Leith
Walk, Edinburgh EH1 3AF
Tel: 0131-556 2424
Fax: 0131-558 1278

Oilnews and Gas International
PO Box 6, Haddington, East Lothian
EH41 3NQ
Tel: 01620-822578
Fax: 01620-825079
E-mail: 101324.2142@compuserve.com

Oil News Service Newsletter
Springfield House, Dollar, Clackmannanshire
FK14 7LG
Tel: 01259-743255

Packaging Scotland
Bergius House, Clifton Street, Glasgow G3 7LA
Tel: 0141-567 6000
Fax: 0141-331 1395
E-mail: packscot@peebl.com

Pathfinder UK
3rd Floor, 21 West Nile Street, Glasgow G1 2PS
Tel: 0141-221 5553
Fax: 0141-221 5554
E-mail: sales@pathfinder-one.com
Web: http://www.pathfinder-one.com

Plumb Heat
2 Walker Street, Edinburgh EH3 7LB
Tel: 0131-225 2255
Fax: 0131-226 7638
E-mail: info@snipef.org
Web: http://www.snipef.org

Portfolio - The Catalogue of Contemporary Photography in Britain
43 Candlemaker Row, Edinburgh EH1 2QB
Tel: 0131-220 1911
Fax: 0131-226 4287
E-mail: portfolio@ednet.co.uk
Web: http://www.ednet.co.uk/portfolio

Proceedings of the Royal College of Physicians of Edinburgh
9 Queen Street, Edinburgh
EH2 1JA
Tel: 0131-225 7324
Fax: 0131-220 3939
E-mail: editorial@rcpe.ac.uk
Web: http://www.rcpe.ac.uk

Project Scotland
Bergius House, 20 Clifton Street, Glasgow
G3 7LA
Tel: 0141-331 1022
Fax: 0141-332 2153

Project Plant
Bergius House, Clifton Street, Glasgow
G3 7LA
Tel: 0141-331 1022
Fax: 0141-331 1395

Prostaglandins, Leukotrienes & Essential Fatty Acids
Robert Stevenson House, Baxters Place, Leith Walk, Edinburgh EH1 3AF
Tel: 0131-556 2424
Fax: 0131-558 1278

Roustabout Magazine
Suite 5, International Base, Greenwell Road, East Tullos, Aberdeen AB12 3AX
Tel: 01224-876582
Fax: 01224-879757
E-mail: roustaboutpublications@compuserve.com

Safe Energy
Friends of the Earth Scotland, Edinburgh
EH6 5QG
Tel: 0131-554 9977
Fax: 0131-557 4284

Scottish Affairs
Chisholm House, 1 Surgeon Square, High School Yards, Edinburgh EH1 1LZ
Tel: 0131-650 2456
Fax: 0131-650 6345
E-mail: ladams@ed.ac.uk

The Scottish Banker
43 Queensferry Street Lane, Edinburgh
EH2 4PF
Tel: 0131-535 5555
Fax: 0131-535 5527
E-mail: icp@insider.co.uk
Web: http://www.ciobs.org.uk

Scottish Beekeeper - Journal of the Scottish Beekeepers Association
Brothock printing works, Burnside Drive, Arbroath, Angus DD11 1NS
Tel: 01241-872000
Fax: 01241-870707
E-mail: printing@theheraldpress.fsnet.co.uk

Scottish Business Insider
43 Queensferry Street Lane, Edinburgh
EH2 4PF
Tel: 0131-535 5555
Fax: 0131-220 1203

Scottish Caterer
Bergius House, Clifton Street, Glasgow G3 7LA
Tel: 0141-331 1022
Fax: 0141-331 1395

Scottish Educational Journal
46 Moray Place, Edinburgh EH3 6BH
Tel: 0131-225 6244
Fax: 0131-220 3151
E-mail: kblackwell@eis.org.uk
Web: http://www.eis.org.uk

The Scottish Farmer
6th Floor, 195 Albion Street, Glasgow G1 1QQ
Tel: 0141-302 7700
Fax: 0141-302 7799
E-mail: info@calmags.co.uk

Scottish Forestry
Hag-on-Esk, Canonbie, Dumfriesshire
DG14 0XE
Tel: 01387-371518
Fax: 01318-371418
E-mail: rsfs@ednet.co.uk
Web: http://www.rsfs.org

Scottish Grocer
Bergius House, 20 Clifton Street, Glasgow
G3 7LA
Tel: 0141-567 6000
Fax: 0141-331 1395
E-mail: scottishgrocer@peebl.com

Scottish Licensed Trade Guardian
Bergius House, Clifton Street, Glasgow
G3 7LA
Tel: 0141-331 1022
Fax: 0141-331 1395

Scottish Law Directory & Fees Supplement
59 George Street, Edinburgh EH2 2LQ
Tel: 0131-225 4703
Fax: 0131-220 4260
E-mail: law@tandtclark.co.uk
Web: http://www.tandtclark.co.uk

Scottish Law Gazette
24 Easter Cornton Road, Stirling FK9 5ES
Tel: 01786-472125
Fax: 01786-467308
E-mail: eaml@stir.ac.uk

Scottish Legion News
New Haig House, Logie Green Road, Edinburgh
EH7 4HR
Tel: 0131-557 2782
Fax: 0131-557 5819

Scottish Licensed Trade News
Bergius House, Clifton Street, Glasgow G3 7LA
Tel: 0141-567 6022
Fax: 0141-331 1395

Scottish Planning & Environmental Law
Tontine House, 8 Gordon Street, Glasgow
G1 3PL
Tel: 0141-248 8541
Fax: 0141-248 8277
E-mail: publications@planex.co.uk
Web: http://www.planex.co.uk

Scottish Travel Agents News
71 Henderson Street, Bridge of Allan, Stirling
FK9 4HG
Tel: 01786-834238
Fax: 01786-834295
E-mail: info@stan-news.freeserve.co.uk

Tayside Farmer
Craig O'Loch Road, Forfar, Angus DD8 1BT
Tel: 01307-464899
Fax: 01307-466923

Third Force News
18–19 Claremont Crescent, Edinburgh
EH7 4QD
Tel: 0131-556 3882
Fax: 0131-556 0279
E-mail: george.paterson@scvo.org.uk
Web: http://www.scvo.org.uk

The Times Educational Supplement Scotland
Scott House, 10 South St Andrew Street,
Edinburgh EH2 2AZ
Tel: 0131-557 1133
Fax: 0131-558 1155
E-mail: scoted@tes.co.uk
Web: http://www.tes.co.uk/scotland

The Times Law Reports
59 George Street, Edinburgh EH2 2LQ
Tel: 0131-225 4703
Fax: 0131-220 4260
E-mail: law@tandtclark.co.uk
Web: http://www.tandtclark.co.uk

Tissue & Cell
Robert Stevenson House, Baxters Place, Leith
Walk, Edinburgh EH1 3AF
Tel: 0131-556 2424
Fax: 0131-558 1278

Transactions of the Institution of Engineers & Shipbuilders in Scotland
1 Atlantic Quay, Broomielaw, Glasgow G2 8JE
Tel: 0141-248 3721
Fax: 0141-248 3721

Transport News
Wheatsheaf House, Montgomery Street, East
Kilbride, Glasgow G74 7JS
Tel: 01355-279077
Fax: 01355-279088

Tubercle & Lung Disease
Robert Stevenson House, Baxters Place, Leith
Walk, Edinburgh EH1 3AF
Tel: 0131-556 2424
Fax: 0131-558 1278

Urology News
9 Gayfield Square, Edinburgh EH1 3NT
Tel: 0131-478 8404
Fax: 0131-557 4701
E-mail: katherine@pinpoint-scotland.com
Web: http://www.uronews.com

Utilitas
22 George Square, Edinburgh EH8 9LF
Tel: 0131-650 4220
Fax: 0131-662 0053
E-mail: journals@eup.ed.ac.uk
Web: http://www.eup.ed.ac.uk

The Wire
Strathclyde Police, 173 Pitt Street, Glasgow
G2 4JS
Tel: 0141-532 2659
Fax: 0141-532 2562

Writing Magazine
PO Box 4, Nairn, Nairnshire IV12 4HU
Tel: 01667-454441
Fax: 01667-454401

Yachting Life
Wheatsheaf House, Montgomery Street, East
Kilbride, Glasgow G74 4JS
Tel: 01355-279077
Fax: 01355-279088
Web: http://www.yachtinglife.co.uk

BOOK PUBLISHERS

The following list comprises details for a number
of publishing companies in Scotland.

SCOTTISH PUBLISHERS ASSOCIATION

Scottish Book Centre, 137 Dundee Street,
Edinburgh EH11 1BG
Tel: 0131-228 6866

AA Enterprises
7 Mount Road, Berwick-upon-Tweed

Acair Ltd
7 James Street, Stornoway, Isle of Lewis
HS1 2QN
Tel: 01851-703020

Argyll Publishing
Glendaruel, Argyll PA22 3AE
Tel: 01369-820229

Association for Scottish Literary Studies
c/o Department of Scottish History, University of
Glasgow, 9 University Gardens, Glasgow
G12 8QH
Tel: 0141-330 5309

Atelier Books
6 Dundas Street, Edinburgh EH3 6HZ
Tel: 0131-557 4050

B. & W. Publishing
29 Inverleith Row, Edinburgh EH3 5QH
Tel: 0131-552 5555

Barrington Stoke Ltd
10 Belford Terrace, Edinburgh EH4 3DQ
Tel: 0131-315 4933

A. K. Bell Library
York Place, Perth PH2 8EP
Tel: 01738-444949

Balnain Books
c/o Seol, Unit 8, Canongate Venture, 5 New
Street, Edinburgh EH8 8BH
Tel: 0131-556 6660

Birlinn Ltd
Unit 8, Canongate Venture, 5 New Street,
Edinburgh EH8 8BH
Tel: 0131-556 6660

Black Ace Books
PO Box 6557, Forfar DD8 2YS
Tel: 01307-465096

Brown, Son & Ferguson Ltd
4–10 Darnley Street, Glasgow G41 2SD
Tel: 0141-429 1234

Canongate Books
14 High Street, Edinburgh EH1 1TE
Tel: 0131-557 5111

Chapman
4 Broughton Place, Edinburgh EH1 3RX
Tel: 0131-557 2207

Churchill Livingstone
Robert Stevenson House, 1–3 Baxter's Place,
Edinburgh EH1 3AF
Tel: 0131-556 2424

Citizens Advice Scotland
26 George Square, Edinburgh EH8 9LD
Tel: 0131-667 0156

Clydebank District Libraries
Clydebank Central Library, Dumbarton Road,
Clydebank G81 1XH
Tel: 0141-952 1416

Dionysia Press
20A Montgomery Street, Edinburgh EH7 5JS
Tel: 0131-478 2572

Dudu Nsomba Publications
4 Gailes Park, Bothwell, Glasgow G71 8TS
Tel: 01698-854290

Edinburgh City Libraries
Central Library, George IV Bridge, Edinburgh
EH1 1EG
Tel: 0131-225 5584

Edinburgh University Press
22 George Square, Edinburgh EH8 9LF
Tel: 0131-650 4218

EPER
University of Edinburgh, 21 Hill Place,
Edinburgh EH8 9OP
Tel: 0131-650 6200

Floris Books
15 Harrison Gardens, Edinburgh EH11 1SH
Tel: 0131-337 2372

Forth Naturalist and Historian
The University of Stirling, Stirling FK9 4LA
Tel: 01259-215091

Glasgow City Libraries Publications Board
The Mitchell Library, North Street, Glasgow
G3 7DN
Tel: 0141-287 2846

The Glasgow Royal Concert Hall
2 Sauchiehall Street, Glasgow G2 3NY
Tel: 0141-332 6633

The Gleneil Press
Whittingehame, Haddington, East Lothian
EH41 4QA
Tel: 01620-860292

**Glowworm and The Amaising Publishing
House**
Unit 7, Greendykes Industrial Estate,
Greendykes Road, Broxburn, W. Lothian
EH52 6PG
Tel: 01506-857570

Goblinshead
130B Inveresk Road, Musselburgh, Midlothian
EH21 7AY
Tel: 0131-665 2894

Gordon Wright Publishing Ltd
25 Mayfield Road, Edinburgh EH9 2NQ
Tel: 0131-667 1300

W. Green
21 Alva Street, Edinburgh EH2 4PS
Tel: 0131-225 4879

HarperCollins Publishers
Westerhill Road, Bishopbriggs, Glasgow
G64 2QT
Tel: 0141-772 3200

Health Education Board for Scotland
Woodburn House, Canaan Lane, Edinburgh
EH10 4SG
Tel: 0131-536 5500

House of Lochar
Isle of Colonsay, Argyll PA61 7YP
Tel: 01951-200232

Johnstone Media
55 Melville Street, Edinburgh EH3 7HL
Tel: 0131-220 5380

Keppel Publishing
The Grey House, Kenbridge Road, New
Galloway, Kirkcudbrightshire DG7 3RP
Tel: 01644-420272

Kingfisher Publications plc
7 Hopetoun Crescent, Edinburgh EH7 4AY
Tel: 0131-556 5929

Lomond Books
36 West Shore Road, Granton, Edinburgh
EH5 1QD
Tel: 0131-551 2261

Luath Press Ltd
543/2 Castlehill, Edinburgh EH1 2ND
Tel: 0131-225 4326

Mainstream Publishing Co.
7 Albany Street, Edinburgh EH1 3UG
Tel: 0131-557 2959

Mercat Press
James Thin Ltd, 53-59 South Bridge,
Edinburgh EH1 1YS
Tel: 0131-622 8252

Merchiston Publishing
PMPC Department, Napier University,
Craighouse Road, Edinburgh EH10 5LG
Tel: 0131-445 2227

The National Archives of Scotland
HM General Register House, Edinburgh
EH1 3YY
Tel: 0131-535 1314

National Galleries of Scotland
Belford Road, Edinburgh EH4 3DR
Tel: 0131-556 8921

National Library of Scotland
George IV Bridge, Edinburgh EH1 1EW
Tel: 0131-226 4531

National Museums of Scotland Publishing
Chambers Street, Edinburgh EH1 1JF
Tel: 0131-247 4186

Neil Wilson Publishing Ltd
Suite 303A, The Pentagon Centre,
36 Washington Street, Glasgow G3 8AZ
Tel: 0141-221 1117

The New Iona Press
7 Drynie Terrace, Inverness IV2 4UP
Tel: 01463-242384

The Orcadian Ltd
PO Box 18, Hell's Half Acre, Hatston, Kirkwall,
Orkney KW15 1DW
Tel: 01856-879000

Parish Education
18 Inverleith Terrace, Edinburgh EH3 5NS
Tel: 0131-332 0343

Polygon
22 George Square, Edinburgh EH8 9LF
Tel: 0131-650 4214

The Ramsay Head Press
15 Gloucester Place, Edinburgh EH3 6EE
Tel: 0131-225 5646

Richard Stenlake Publishing
Ochiltree Sawmill, The Lade, Ochiltree, Ayrshire
KA18 2NX
Tel: 01290-423114

Rutland Press
15 Rutland Square, Edinburgh EH1 2BE
Tel: 0131-229 7545

St Andrew Press
121 George Street, Edinburgh EH2 4YN
Tel: 0131-225 5722

The Saltire Society
9 Fountain Close, 22 High Street, Edinburgh
EH1 1TF
Tel: 0131-556 1836

Scottish Council for Research in Education
15 St John Street, Edinburgh EH8 8JR
Tel: 0131-557 2944

**Scottish Cultural Press and Scottish Children's
Press**
Unit 14, Leith Walk Business Centre, 130 Leith
Walk, Edinburgh EH6 5DT
Tel: 0131-555 5950

Scottish Library Association
Scottish Centre for Information and Library
Services, 1 John Street, Hamilton ML3 7EU
Tel: 01698-458888

Scottish Natural Heritage
Publications Section, Battleby, Redgorton, Perth
PH1 3EW
Tel: 01738-627921

Sportscotland
Caledonia House, Redheughs Rigg, South Gyle,
Edinburgh EH12 9DQ
Tel: 0131-317 7200

Scottish Text Society
27 George Street, Edinburgh EH8 9LD

The Shetland Times Ltd
Prince Alfred Street, Lerwick, Shetland
ZE1 0EP
Tel: 01595-695531

Thistle Press
West Bank, Western Road, Insch, Aberdeenshire
AB52 6JR
Tel: 01464-821053

Tuckwell Press Ltd
The Mill House, Phantassie, East Linton, East
Lothian EH40 3DG
Tel: 01620-860164

Unit For The Study of Government in Scotland
Chisholm House, 1 Surgeon Square, High
School Yards, Edinburgh EH1 1LZ
Tel: 0131-650 2456

Whittles Publishing
Roseleigh House, Harbour Road,
Latheronwheel, Caithness KW5 6DW
Tel: 01593-741240

Wild Goose Publications
Unit 15, 6 Harmony Row, Govan, Glasgow
G51 3BA
Tel: 0141-440 0985

The Gaelic Books Council
22 Mansfield Street, Glasgow G11 5QP
Tel: 0141-337 6211

RCAHMS
John Sinclair House, 16 Bernard Terrace,
Edinburgh EH8 9NX
Tel: 0131-662 1456

Scottish Book Trust
Scottish Book Centre, 137 Dundee Street,
Edinburgh EH11 1BG
Tel: 0131-229 3663

Straightline Publishing Ltd
29 Main Street, Bothwell, Glasgow G71 8RD
Tel: 01698-853000

Wigwam Digital Ltd
51 Wren Court, Strathclyde Business Park,
Bellshill, Strathclyde ML4 3NQ
Tel: 01698-844160

Zipo Publishing Ltd
4 Cowan Street, Hillhead, Glasgow G12 8PF
Tel: 0141-339 9729

CULTURAL

SCOTLAND

CULTURAL, HISTORICAL AND RECREATIONAL SCOTLAND

HISTORY

7th-5th millennia BC: Earliest evidence of human settlement in Scotland, by Middle Stone Age hunter-gatherers and fishermen. Radiocarbon dating of large shell mounds on the island of Oronsay suggests that occupation was under way by the middle of the millennium.

4th-3rd millennia BC: New Stone Age farmers began around 4000 BC to cultivate crops and rear livestock on the western and northern coasts and islands and in Orkney. Forests began to be cleared and the making of pottery began. Apart from the Neolithic settlements at Skara Brae in Orkney and Jarlshof in Shetland, however, the principal monuments from this period, most of which date from c. 3000 BC, are religious. Communal burial took place in massive chambered cairns, such as those at Maeshowe and Isbister (Orkney) and Nether Largie South (Kilmartin, Argyll); while stone circles and other monuments, e.g. the Calanais (Callanish) standing stones (Lewis) and the Ring of Brodgar (Orkney), served ritual purposes.

c.2000 BC onwards: Metalworking and use of bronze artefacts began. Settlement by the Early Bronze Age 'Beaker people', so called from the distinctive style of their drinking vessels, mainly in eastern Scotland, although quantities of Beaker ware have also been found in the west, dating back perhaps to the mid–third millennium. There is evidence that the largest of the hilltop forts previously attributed to the Iron Age, such as Traprain Law (East Lothian) and Eildon Hill (Roxburghshire), may belong to the Bronze Age. Similar types of artefact found in widely separated locations are evidence of networks of exchange across Europe, in which Scotland participated.

From about 1300 BC the climate became colder and wetter, a trend which was possibly exacerbated by the effect of intense volcanic activity in Iceland (1159). Bronze Age communities gradually retreated from the uplands and marginal farming areas.

c.700 BC - AD 200: Further settlement as tribes were displaced from further south by new incursions from the Continent. This movement was accompanied by the development of Iron Age tools and weapons such as the sword and the rotary quern for grinding grain. In this period communities became more self-contained and competition and conflict between them increased. The building efforts previously put into ritual and mortuary structures was diverted into strong and imposing fortified dwellings and settlements.

Many hillforts of different types were built throughout Scotland during the first millennium BC. The huge drystone broch towers, such as those of Mousa (Shetland), Midhowe (Orkney) and Dun Carloway (Lewis), were at their peak in the latter half of the millennium and the first century AD, and other forms, such as wheelhouses, roundhouses and crannogs, were common, with regional variations. It is possible that these large buildings also reflected growing material prosperity and served a political purpose as symbols of the power of local and tribal leaders.

AD 43 onwards: Julius Agricola, the Roman governor of Britain AD 77–84, advanced deep into Caledonia, culminating with a victory at Mons Graupius in the north-east, probably in AD 84; however, he was recalled to Rome shortly afterwards and his forward policy was not pursued.

AD 122-410: Hadrian set the northern boundary of the Roman empire in Britain and ordered the construction of a wall to defend it. Hadrian's Wall marked the frontier until the Roman troops withdrew, except AD c. 144–90, when the frontier moved north to the Forth-Clyde isthmus and a turf-built curtain wall, the Antonine Wall, was manned and policed, tolls and the surrender of weapons being demanded of anyone wishing to cross it. There were frequent invasions and counter-invasions by Romans and Picts in the following centuries, though the last major Roman campaign north of the Forth, carried out under the emperor Severus in 210, was a muted success and after Severus's death in 211 the Roman legions fell back to merely defending the border. The Picts, on the other hand, became much bolder in the fourth century, uniting against Rome with other peoples not only in Scotland but Ireland and the continent and at one point (AD 367) reaching as far south as London.

Although the Roman hold on the territory

north of Hadrian's Wall was never more than tenuous, some Roman influence in parts of Scotland persisted until the fourth century, the legions finally being withdrawn from Britain altogether around 407–10.

2nd-9th centuries: This period is marked by the gradual coalescing of the many small tribes existing in the Roman period into larger and more definable kingdoms, and continual warfare between them. The Picts, a loose confederation of a dozen or so tribes occupying the territory north of the Forth, appear to have dominated the north and east by the fifth century. The Scots, a Gaelic-speaking people of northern Ireland, colonised the area of Argyll and Bute from about AD 500, establishing the kingdom of Dalriada centred on Dunadd, and then expanded eastwards and northwards. The Britons, speaking a Brythonic Celtic language, colonised Scotland from the south from the first century BC; they lost control of south-eastern Scotland (incorporated into the kingdom of Northumbria) to the Angles in the early seventh century but retained south-western Scotland and Cumbria.

However, it was the arrival of the Vikings in the eighth century that constituted the next major influence on Scotland. Viking raids from the late eighth century were consolidated into a permanent Norse presence by settlement on the mainland and islands of the north and west from the early ninth century onwards.

397: First Christian church in Scotland established by St Ninian at Whithorn.

c.563: Arrival of St Columba (d. 597), with 12 companions, on Iona from Ireland and establishment there of a monastery and a missionary base from which Columba and his monks accomplished the conversion to Christianity of the Picts as far afield as Fife. The island became a place of pilgrimage and a centre of Christian scholarship: the eighth-century Book of Kells, now in the library of Trinity College, Dublin, was probably largely produced at the abbey of Iona and was moved to Ireland, with Columba's remains, by monks fleeing Viking raids aound 800.

612: Death of St Kentigern (also known as St Mungo), reputedly founder and first bishop of the city of Glasgow.

685: Northward incursions by Northumbrian Angles halted by Picts at Battle of Nechtansmere,

near Forfar. This defeat for the Northumbrians effectively checked their northward expansion into Scotland.

Scotland's first law?
In 697 St Adomnán, an abbot of Iona and biographer of St Columba, drew up a Law of the Innocents, which aimed to protect non-combatants - women, children and members of religious communities - from violence in war. Written on Iona, the law was promulgated and enforced in Ireland, Scotland and Pictland.

---

c.736: King Aengus of the Picts captured Dunadd, royal centre of Dalriada, thus acquiring overlordship of the Scots. In 756, in league with the Northumbrians, he defeated the north Britons at Dumbarton.

c.794 onwards: Viking raids and Norse settlement in Argyll, Caithness and Sutherland, Orkney, Shetland, and the Western Isles. By 890 Orkney, Shetland, the Hebrides and Caithness had become part of the kingdom of Norway under Harald Fairhair and in 987 Earl Sigurd of Orkney annexed Sutherland, Ross and Moray.

843: Unification of the areas which now comprise Scotland began, when Kenneth mac Alpin, king of the Scots from c.834, became also king of the Picts, joining the two lands to form the kingdom of Alba (comprising Scotland north of a line between the Forth and Clyde rivers). Kenneth mac Alpin was helped in this enterprise by the severe defeat inflicted on the mainland Picts by the Danes in 839, weakening their resistance.

890: Orkney, Shetland, Caithness and the Hebrides became part of the Norwegian kingdom of Harald Fairhair.

903: St Andrews became the religious capital of Scotland after Kenneth mac Alpin's new religious centre at Dunkeld was destroyed by the Vikings.

c.973–4: Lothian, the eastern part of the area between the Forth and the Tweed, ceded or leased to Kenneth II of Alba by Edgar of England.

1010: Malcolm II defeated a Norse army at Dufftown and further secured his northern border by marriage of his daughter to the Earl of Orkney.

c.1018: Malcolm II's victory over a Northumbrian army at Carham restored Scottish possession of Lothian, lost earlier in his reign. At about this time Malcolm placed his grandson Duncan on the throne of the British kingdom of Strathclyde, bringing under Scots rule virtually all of what is now Scotland. The hybrid name 'Scotland' began to supplant the Gaelic name 'Alba' (still the name of the country in Gaelic).

1040: Duncan I slain in battle by Macbeth, who ruled until 1057. Macbeth fell at the battle of Lumphanan to Malcolm Canmore, who was aided by Earl Siward of Northumbria and Edward the Confessor of England.

1098: Magnus III of Norway devastated the Western Isles; but an uprising in the mid twelfth century drove the Norse from most of mainland Argyll. From then onwards the Norse possessions were gradually incorporated into the kingdom of Scotland.

Late 11th century onwards: Frequent conflict continued between Scotland and England over territory and the extent of England's political influence, and between the Scottish crown and rebellious Highland leaders such as Somerled, who became Lord of the Isles in 1156. At the same time Scotland was developing as a fully-fledged medieval society. Towns and burghs developed, encouraged by contact with the Normans, who brought trade and the marketplace, and by the court's increasing sophistication. David I granted the status of burgh, with special trading privileges, to numerous towns. Many had become royal burghs by the end of the 12th century. In return they paid rents and customs. As well as centres of trade and crafsmanship, royal burghs were centres of justice where the king's sheriffs held courts.

In the same period (roughly 1113–78) many of the great Scottish abbeys were founded under Alexander I, David I and William I (who founded Arbroath Abbey, 1178).

The number of burghs increased sharply in the reign of Alexander III. By 1283 most of the towns in Scotland, with exception of a few in the West Highlands and the Hebrides, had acquired the status of either royal or baronial burghs.

1237: Treaty of York, establishing Scotland's border with England.

1266: Treaty of Perth, by which Magnus IV of Norway ceded the Hebrides and the Isle of Man to Scotland after an unsuccessful Norwegian expedition in 1263 by Haakon IV.

1296–1328: Wars of Independence. The failure of the Scottish royal line with the death of Margaret of Norway in 1290 led to disputes over the throne which were resolved by the adjudication of Edward I of England. He awarded the throne to John Balliol in 1292, but Balliol's refusal to be a puppet king led to war.

A Parliament held in Stirling in 1295 overturned Balliol's government and appointed a ruling Council, which made an alliance with Philip IV of France against England, formalising a relationship which had already existed for 200 years. (The treaty has become known as 'the Auld Alliance', and was the basis for Scottish military support for France in the following centuries. Scots fought in the army of Joan of Arc.)

Balliol surrendered to Edward I and Edward attempted to rule Scotland himself. Resistance was led by William Wallace, who defeated the English under Hugh de Cressingham, Edward's Lord High Treasurer, at Stirling Bridge in 1297 but was later defeated by a large force under Edward himself at Falkirk the following year, and Robert Bruce, who seized the throne in 1306. Bruce had regained most of Scotland by 1311 and, famously, routed Edward II's army at Bannockburn in 1314, following up the victory by incursions deep into northern England and even into Ireland in the succeeding years.

Edward did not renounce his claim to Scotland, however, and when Bruce rejected a papal truce in 1317 Pope John XXII excommunicated him and placed Scotland under interdict. The bishops' reply, in a letter dated 6 April 1320 and probably written by Bernard Linton, abbot of Arbroath and Chancellor of Scotland, passionately defended Scotland's independence, and has become known as the Declaration of Arbroath.

England finally recognised Scotland's independence of in the Treaty of Northampton in 1328. However, this was not the end of the story. By 1336 the forces of Edward III had penetrated Scotland again as far as Elgin; and although David II imposed a degree of stability and order in the 1360s, the conflict between Scotland and England was by no means settled when he died.

The journeying Stone of Destiny

Reputedly been brought to Scotland from Ireland by King Fergus in the sixth century, Scotland's ancient symbol of kingship graced the coronation ceremonies of generations of Scottish monarchs. The Dalriadic kings were enthroned upon it at Iona, Dunadd and finally Scone, which became its supposedly permanent home c. 840. However, in 1296, the English king Edward I sealed his defeat of John Balliol by removing the Stone to London and placing it in Westminster Abbey, where - although the treaty of Northampton granted its return to the Scots - it stayed for the next six-and-a-half centuries, being incorporated into the coronation ceremonies of English and then British monarchs.

In 1950 the Stone nearly succeeded in going home when a group of Nationalist students took it from Westminster Abbey early on Christmas morning; but it stayed in Scotland for only a few months, being placed symbolically in Arbroath Abbey, and was back in London for the coronation of Queen Elizabeth II. It was not until 1996, the 700th anniversary of its first removal, that the Stone was finally formally returned to Scotland.

1349: Bubonic plague, the 'Black Death' which had swept England in 1347, reached Scotland and spread throughout the country.

1371 onwards: The first Stewart kings, Robert II and Robert III, were weak administrators, and the power of the barons and rivalries between them resulted in vendettas and lawlessness on which parliamentary attempts at legislation had little practical effect. In particular, the throne had little control of the Highlands or the Western Isles. Although David II had subdued the Lord of the Isles in 1369, the Western Isles were for practical purposes independent

The Highlands and Lowlands were in many respects becoming two nations. Predating and underlying the basically Norman feudal system which functioned in the lowlands was the clan system, based on attachment to the land and loyalty to the clan chieftain, and this continued to exist in the Highlands in an undiluted form and to pose continual challenges to the king's power in the north and west.

1390: Burning of Elgin cathedral and town by the 'Wolf of Badenoch' - Alexander Stewart, Earl of Buchan and youngest brother of Robert III. Though in part an act of reprisal for opposition from the Bishop of Moray, this was also part of a wider campaign of terror waged by the Wolf to maintain Stewart control in the north - and to enrich himself.

1407: City of Bruges gave Scots trading rights, opening the way for trade with the Continent; these were later suspended (1412–15) by the Hanseatic League because of Scottish piracy.

1414: Scotland's first university founded at St Andrews. Teaching had begun in 1410 and the papal bull giving formal recognition was issued in 1414. The foundation of the universities of Glasgow and Aberdeen followed later in the century, in 1451 and 1495 respectively. Edinburgh University, founded in 1583, is Britain's oldest secular university foundation.

1411: Outbreak of open war in the Highlands. Donald, Lord of the Isles, defeated at Battle of Harlaw near Inverurie by the Earl of Mar (the Wolf's son) and a local army including burgesses of Aberdeen. Donald retreated to the west, but with his local power intact.

1424: James I set in motion a series of legislative reforms aimed at controlling the nobles, creating a fair and efficient judiciary, and raising national revenue. In 1426 parliament abolished all laws other than the king's. James backed this up by force in 1428 by arresting and in some cases executing about 50 Highland chiefs. Their resentment was instrumental in his death.

1468–9: Orkney and Shetland ceded to Scotland as a pledge for the unpaid dowry of Margaret of Denmark, wife of James III, though Danish claims of suzerainty persisted, to be relinquished only in 1590 with the marriage of Anne of Denmark to James VI.

1493: After continual strife in the reign of James III, James IV annexed the lands and titles of John, Lord of the Isles, to the crown, and made a series of expeditions to the west between 1493 and 1498. However, he was soon (1504–7) faced with rebellion from John's son Donald Dubh. The integration of the west into the kingdom remained fragile, and James's granting of governorships to the Earls of Argyll and Huntly in 1500–1 bolstered the power of the Campbells and Gordons and provoked long-standing resentment from other clans.

1507: Establishment of Scotland's first printing press, licensed to Andrew Myllar and Walter Chepman by James IV, whose court promoted literature, learning and music. Their first book contained poems by William Dunbar.

1511–13: In 1511, reviving the Auld Alliance, James signed a new treaty with Louis XII of France in which Scotland pledged to make war on England if France did so. He found himself almost at once drawn into a war of little direct relevance to Scotland, supporting the French against the Holy League of Pope Julius II, of which England, under Henry VIII, was a member. In 1513 James took on an English army at Flodden; although it was the largest and best-armed Scottish force ever to have entered England, the result was a disastrous defeat for the Scots, in which James IV, many of his nobles, and thousands of soldiers died.

1532: Creation of the Court of Session by an Act of Parliament which established a permanent 15-man College of Justice. A central criminal court, the High Court of Justiciary, was later founded. The present-day court system is based on these institutions.

1544–50: Renewed hostilities with England. The 'Rough Wooing' was a savage campaign waged by Henry VIII on the Catholic, pro-French Scottish monarchy in retaliation for the breaking of a treaty by which Mary (later Queen of Scots) was to marry his son Edward. The whole of the south-east was ravaged and the great Border abbeys sacked.

1555–60: The doctrines of Luther and Calvin, introduced into Scotland by John Knox, a priest disaffected by the growing secularity and wealth of the Catholic church, quickly became popular among the local clergy and the lesser nobility. The outlawing of Knox and his followers in 1559 provoked riots by Protestants which flared briefly into war. The 'Reformation Parliament', held on 1 August 1560 in the name of Queen Mary but without a royal presence, abolished the Latin Mass and rejected the jurisdiction of the Pope. Only a month earlier, the Treaty of Leith effectively ended the Auld Alliance and French troops withdrew from Scotland. The Protestant majority in government was established, and sufficiently secure to force Mary's abdication in 1567.

1603: James VI of Scotland succeeded Elizabeth I on the throne of England (his mother, Mary Queen of Scots, was the great-granddaughter of Henry VII), his successors reigning as sovereigns of Great Britain. James became an absentee monarch, and England and Scotland remained distinct in important ways, each retaining its own parliament and legal system.

The Union improved the physical links between Scotland and England and reduced much of the cross-border bickering and raiding. However, Scotland was in many respects not treated as England's equal: it could not trade with England or the colonies England later acquired without paying duties.

1608: Emigration of thousands of Border families to the province of Ulster, which James VI was colonising.

1614: Publication of the logarithmic tables of Edinburgh scholar and inventor John Napier.

1618: James VI attempted to bring the Church in Scotland into line with English practice in the Five Articles of Perth, passed by a General Assembly of the Church in August.

1632–40: Building of Parliament House in Edinburgh, confirming its status as capital city of Scotland. Glasgow, meanwhile, was growing rapidly as a centre of industry, commerce and foreign trade. The building of a deep-water harbour at Port Glasgow began in 1667.

1638: Signing of the National Covenant, overturning the Five Articles and reasserting the people's right to keep the reformed church. The Covenant overturned the Articles, sacked the Scottish bishops and proscribed the use of the Book of Common Prayer.

1666: The Pentland Rising, a popular revolt - unsupported by landowners - against the repression of Covenanters which followed the Restoration, and in particular the prohibition of conventicles (outdoor religious meetings). It failed when a poorly armed force of a few thousand Covenanters was defeated by government troops at Rullion Green.

1681: Publication by James Dalrymple, *Viscount of Stair* (1619–95), of the Institutions of the Law of Scotland, establishing Scots law as an independent and coherent system distinct from English law.

1688–9: After the abdication (by flight) in 1688 of James VII and II, the crown devolved upon William III (grandson of Charles I) and Mary II (elder daughter of James VII and II). In April 1689 the Convention of the Estates issued the Claim of Right and the Articles of Grievances, which asserted the independence of the Scottish parliament and Presbyterianism as the established Church. William and Mary were offered the Scottish crown on condition that they accepted these proposals.

From April 1689 Graham of Claverhouse roused the Highlands on behalf of James, but died after a military success at Killiecrankie in July.

1692: The Massacre of Glencoe. The clan chiefs who had opposed William were offered pardon if they took an oath of allegiance before 1 January 1692 and threatened with persecution if they did not. The small clan of MacDonald of Glencoe missed the deadline by a few days, news that the chief had taken the oath was kept from the Privy Council, and a detachment of Campbell soldiers was sent to Glencoe and billeted with the MacDonalds with secret orders to destroy them. Thirty-eight people were killed. The violation of the tradition of hospitality and the Government's implication in the massacre turned Glencoe into a Jacobite rallying banner.

1695: Establishment of the Bank of Scotland in Edinburgh, Scotland's first bank. It had a monopoly until around the time of the Act of Union, when the financial settlement required by the Union and the losses sustained by the collapse of the Darien scheme led to the foundation, also in Edinburgh, of the Royal Bank of Scotland in 1727. The Clydesdale Bank, Scotland's third major bank today, was founded in Glasgow in 1838, around the same time as three other Glasgow-based banks (the Union Bank of Scotland, the Western Bank of Scotland, and the City of Glasgow Bank), in a bid to challenge the financial power of Edinburgh and service the ever-growing industrial and commercial needs of Glasgow.

1698–1700: The Darien Venture. In 1695, an Act of Parliament was passed establishing the Company of Scotland Trading to Africa and the Indies, modelled on the London East India Company and intended to revive Scotland's depressed overseas trade. Darien, in Panama, was chosen as the site for a Scottish colony which would be a crossroads for world trade. Large amounts of money were invested in the scheme, but three successive attempts at settling in Darien and trading, between 1698 and 1700, failed miserably through inability to cope with the tropical climate, attacks from the Spanish, and a complete absence of trade. About 2,000 people died and the disaster not only crippled individual investors financially but dealt further blows to the already weak Scottish economy.

1707: Act of Union, joining Scotland and England politically under one Parliament in London, in which Scotland would have 45 seats (in both Houses).

Recognition of Scottish law was an integral part of the settlement, and, although certain laws have been superseded or nullified subsequently, the Scottish legal system today remains based on that in force at the time of the Union.

1714–15: After the death of Anne (younger daughter of James VII and II), the throne devolved upon George I (great-grandson of James VI and I). In 1715, armed risings on behalf of James Stuart (the Old Pretender, son of James VII and II) led to the indecisive battle of Sheriffmuir, and the Jacobite movement died down until 1745.

1723: Society for Improvement in the Knowledge of Agriculture formed in Edinburgh. In 1727 the Commissioners and Trustees for Improving Manufactures and Fisheries were established. New ideas and technology were being developed by Scots farmers and manufacturers. Some heads of clans became increasingly concerned with making profit from their lands, either by selling land or by adopting the methods of improvement, which often involved turning large areas over to cattle and sheep at the expense of small tenants. The depopulation of the Highlands began.

From 1723 to 1725 there were outbreaks of protest by the Galloway Levellers, dispossessed tenants who had been evicted by lairds in Galloway in order to enclose pastures for fattening cattle.

The clans and the land

While political and social relations in lowland Scotland gradually became largely formalised and institutionalised during the Middle Ages, Highland society, isolated by geography and language, continued to be organised in the clan system, which originated in - and still retained many features of - the tribal organisation of early Gaelic society, based on strong but informal bonds of loyalty and trust and occupation of land. Clan members were those people, including non-relatives, living on the lands owned by the chieftain, and for whom chieftains assumed a patriarchal responsibility in return, particularly, for the loyal support of fighting men. Clan territory boundaries were broadly established by the 16th century.

Chiefs leased tracts (or 'tacks') of land to clan members (originally relatives) or allies to guarantee their security and also their allegiance. The traditional tack carried with it the requirement to provide military service. The tacksmen, in turn, sublet their land to tenants who worked for them on the land in return. Highland cattle were the principal source of wealth, and the tacksmen's power over the poorer tenants was potentially almost absolute.

Over time, the clan chiefs became members of the national aristocracy; they spent time in England and abroad and became part of European society. This was not the case with ordinary Highlanders, who at the beginning of the eighteenth century still spoke only Gaelic and were largely illiterate. By this time, however, some heads of clans were beginning to see themselves as landowners (and landlords) rather than chiefs. The leading chiefs were largely absentees. The bonds of responsibility to their tenants began to loosen as land began to signify money rather than ancestral tradition. This shift was an important facilitator of the Highland Clearances.

1745: Charles Stuart (the Young Pretender) defeated the Royalist troops at Prestonpans and advanced as far as Derby (1746). From Derby, the adherents of 'James VIII and III' (the title claimed for his father by Charles Stuart) fell back on the defensive. The Highland army of 5,000, exhausted and outnumbered by the Duke of Cumberland's 9,000-strong force, was finally crushed catastrophically at Culloden on 16 April 1746. Prince Charles fled the country, and retaliation against the Jacobites by the victorious army was unprecedentedly savage.

1747-8: Anxious to prevent the rise of any form of social and cultural organisation which could become a rallying point for further rebellion, the Government passed legislation intended to annihilate the clan system. The Abolition of Heritable Jurisdictions Act of 1747 confiscated the lands of those chiefs who had rebelled (the forfeited estates were later returned, in 1784), and the Disarming Act of 1748 proscribed the bearing of weapons and the playing of the Great Pipes. The wearing of Highland dress was also outlawed from 1746–82, although it made a comeback, in a somewhat romanticised form, in the early 19th century.

c.1750 onwards: Import of tobacco and cotton were established as mainstays of the non-agrarian economy. Revenue from the processing and re-export of these commodities financed the development of Scottish merchant banking and further industry.

1754: Foundation of the 'Royal and Ancient Golf Club' at St Andrews.

1759: Birth of Robert Burns at Alloway, Ayrshire (d. 1796)

1767: Building of Edinburgh New Town (designed by James Craig) began, with the draining and clearing of land to the north of the Castle and the laying out of Princes Street, George Street and Queen Street. Building continued in phases until 1840.

Elsewhere, from the 1770s onward, a new model of village planning, stone-built and based on a central market square or high street, was applied by landowners, businessmen and government bodies in over a hundred villages, with the specific aim of economic development.

1770: An Act of Parliament created the Clyde Trust, authorising plans to deepen the Clyde. This initiated a process of development which led to the building of the great shipyards and docks in Glasgow in the following century.

Other technological and industrial developments around this time (e.g. the opening of the Carron Ironworks in 1759; James Watt's patenting of an improved steam engine in 1769; the introduction of large water-powered spinning mills from 1779) laid the basis for Scotland's industrial economy in the 19th and 20th centuries.

1771: Birth of Sir Walter Scott, Edinburgh (d. 1832)

1776: Adam Smith (1723–90) published *The Wealth of Nations*. David Hume (b. 1711) died. Cutoff of tobacco imports by American War of Independence caused financial crisis in Glasgow, but the Glasgow merchants had other commodities, including exports of their own - coal, linen and ale, for instance - which ensured their survival.

1785–1820: First period of the Highland Clearances. As the majority of Highland estates were reorganised for sheep-farming, thousands of tenants were evicted or 'cleared' from land they had farmed for generations with no security of tenure other than the unwritten contract of clan loyalty. Clearances took place across Sutherland in 1785–6, 1800, 1807, 1809, 1812–14 and 1819–20, one of the harshest being the clearance of Strathnaver on the northern coast in 1814. Some of the evicted tenants were encouraged to emigrate to the Lowlands and overseas, and a great many did so; others were moved forcibly to the coast where they were expected to survive as fishermen. The Clearances were the principal impetus for the mass diaspora of Scots to North America and the Antipodes.

New Lanark, a model community

In 1785, David Dale, a Glasgow merchant, built a new industrial village near the old market town of Lanark. Built in a valley near the Falls of Clyde and using the river as a power source for its cotton mills, New Lanark became one of the largest cotton-manufacturing centres in Scotland, and continued in operation until 1968.

New Lanark was most renowned, however, as the place where the pioneering and enlightened ideas of Robert Owen were put into practice. Between 1800 and 1825 Owen ploughed much of the profits from the industry into improving life for the workers and their families, outlawing child labour, founding schools whose curriculum and disciplinary regime were far ahead of their time, and providing free medical care for workers and subsidised food at the village shop.

1790: Opening of the Forth-Clyde Canal, Britain's first sea-to-sea canal. The 250 miles of military road-building by General Wade in the early 18th century had improved communications in the Highlands, and from 1802 onwards Thomas Telford, engineer to the Commission for Highland Roads and Bridges, oversaw the construction of nearly 1,000 miles of roads. The Caledonian Canal was built between 1804 and 1822.

1793: Beginning of war with France and formation of Highland regiments (e.g. Cameron Highlanders, Argyll Highlanders, Gordon Highlanders). Lairds recruited energetically in the Highlands, and the Scottish regiments played a significant part in the creation and defence of the British Empire, and in all Britain's wars of the 19th and 20th centuries.

1799: Emancipation of coal-miners and salt workers from serfdom. An Act of Parliament in 1606 had allowed for serfdom of these workers on the grounds that they were 'necessary servants'.

1820: Following years of economic depression and discontent among workers, exacerbated by rising grain prices after the Corn Laws of 1815, a series of riots and a widespread strike in the west culminated in a march from Glasgow to Falkirk and an attempt by a small band of radicals to seize the Carron ironworks. Both actions were crushed by government forces and the leaders executed or transported. The incidents became known as the 'Radical War'.

1830 onwards: New smelting processes enabled the development of the iron industry and related industries, such as coal-mining, also flourished. In the 1830s Scotland boasted the largest chemical works in the world.

1832: The First Reform Bill increased Scotland's representation at Westminster to 53 seats and extended the franchise to over 60,000 voters. The population of Scotland at the time was 2,364,000 (1831 census).

1838–9: Scottish Chartists' organisation formed in the wake of the Reform Bill. By 1839 there were 80 local Chartist Associations. Although their aims were modest and limited exclusively to electoral reform, they were viewed with alarm by the authorities. In 1848 10,000 Chartists demonstrated on Calton Hill in Edinburgh and caused riots in Glasgow; but the movement became overshadowed by trade unionism.

1840–54: Second wave of Highland Clearances, from Ross-shire and the Isles. The Highland and Island Emigration Society was formed in 1853 under the patronage of Prince Albert, offering ships and assistance to emigrants. Large-scale emigration was increased by severe famine in 1846–7.

1841: Govan shipyard founded by Robert Napier. Aided by a fast-growing local steel industry, by the 1870s and 1880s Scotland had become the world leader in shipbuilding, particularly with the introduction of the large steel-hulled steamships that supplanted the tea clippers.

1842: First visit to Scotland by Queen Victoria and Prince Albert. The royal family bought Balmoral Castle in 1853.
Opening of Edinburgh-Glasgow railway.

1850s onward: Development of the herring fishing industry on the east coast. New net technology and later the use of steamboats increased catches vastly, and the development of the railways enabled efficient transport of the processed fish.

1855: Foundation of the United Coal and Iron Miners' Association, Scotland's first effective labour organisation.

1867: Franchise extended to all males; Scottish Women's Suffrage Society formed. In 1869 women gained the right to vote in municipal elections, but they were not to win the right to vote in parliamentary elections on the same terms as men until 1928.

1872: The Education (Scotland) Act, bringing burgh and parish schools under state control; but education was not provided free until 1892. The Scottish Leaving Certificate was introduced in 1888.

1873: Foundation of Scottish Football Association; and of Glasgow Rangers football club. Celtic was founded in 1887.

1882: Formation of the Highland Land Leagues, and 'Battle of the Braes' in Skye, when crofters defied police and landlords in defence of their grazing rights. Continuing trouble with crofters forced the government to set up a Royal Commission of enquiry, leading to the adoption of the Crofters' (Holdings) Act in 1886, which gave crofters security of tenure, fixed rents and other rights.

1882: Formation of the Scottish Labour Party, with James Keir Hardie as a founder member. However, Labour did not win the largest share of either votes or parliamentary seats in Scotland until 1922.

1885: Establishment of the Scottish Office in Whitehall, and post of Secretary for Scotland. In 1928 the post was upgraded to Secretary of State for Scotland, thus reinstating a post which had been abolished in 1745.

1886: Scottish Home Rule Association founded, with both Labour and Liberal support. The concept of Home Rule was limited to Scotland's management of Scottish affairs, leaving wider areas such as foreign policy to Westminster, which would retain Scottish MPs.

1897: Formation of the Scottish Trades Union Congress, at least partly in opposition to the British TUC, which was felt to represent the smaller Scottish unions inadequately. Organised labour was to achieve considerable strength during the Great War and its aftermath, for instance in the 1919 strike for a 40-hour working week, and was particularly militant during the inter-war period.

1909: Construction of naval dockyard at Rosyth began.

1910: Twenty Liberal MPs set up a Scottish National Committee to promote self-government, but the issue was shelved until after World War I, when the Scottish Home Rule Association was refounded (1918) and the Scots National League, with its roots in radical politics, was formed in (1921). This was renamed the National Party of Scotland in 1927.

1924: James Ramsay MacDonald elected Prime Minister and Secretary of State for Foreign Affairs in Britain's first Labour government. He returned as Prime Minister in 1929–31 and 1931–5 (in a coalition government with the Conservatives).

Successive draft Home Rule Bills presented to Parliament in 1924, 1926, 1927 and 1928 failed.

1934: Founding of the Scottish National Party through a merger of the National Party of Scotland and the Scottish Party (formed 1932). The diverse nature of its components and their points of view, added to indifferent or unfavourable attitudes towards Home Rule on the part of government and large sections of the public, meant that the party was slow to cohere. In 1946 it produced its statement of aims and policy, and in 1967 it won its first seat in Parliament when Winifred Ewing won the Hamilton by-election.

1930s: Scottish literary renaissance.

1937: Scottish Gaelic Text Society established.

1939–45: Industrial decline, which had already begun to steepen with the Depression (1929–31), was temporarily reversed by the need for production in the war effort. There was full employment and women workers were particularly active both in industry and on the land, as they had been in the Great War.

1948: East Kilbride and Glenrothes become Scotland's first New Towns.

1959 onwards: Large oil and gas reserves discovered in North Sea. In 1974 Highland One, the world's largest oil platform, was launched from Nigg on the Cromarty Firth. The first oil was pumped ashore in 1975. The oil industry has become an important, if insecure, source of revenue and employment particularly for the north-east. In particular, the installation of the large Sullom Voe terminal in Shetland, based on agreements between the oil companies and the Island Council, has brought economic benefits to the islands.

1971 onwards: By the beginning of the 1970s the once industrially vibrant Upper Clyde was reduced to five shipyards, linked in the Upper Clyde Shipbuilders consortium. Under Edward Heath's Conservative government there was a series of sell-offs and liquidations of part of the consortium. The workers responded by organising a 'work-in' by 300 men. In February 1972 the government agreed to allow three shipyards to continue.

Nonetheless, the long, slow attrition of Scotland's industrial base was only momentarily halted, and in the next two decades mines, shipyards, iron and steel works and factories continued to be closed down and dismantled, a process accelerated with the emergence of the globalised economy. The fishing industry also contracted severely.

To some extent the heavy industries have been replaced by energy supply (oil and gas, hydroelectric power), manufacturing (computers, office machinery, television, radio and communications equipment), chemicals, tourism and related industries, and whisky. Membership of the European Union has also benefited agriculture, urban regeneration and small-scale industry in the Highlands and Islands.

1975: Major changes in local government introduced by the Local Government (Scotland) Act 1973. The structure was reorganised again in 1994.

1976: Crofting Reform Act enabled crofters to buy their land.

1979: Referendum on the Scotland and Wales Act, which was introduced by the Labour government of James Callaghan to give some degree of devolution to Scotland and Wales. The referendum failed to reach the requisite 40 per cent of affirmative votes, partly because of a high level of abstention, and the Act was abandoned.

1988: 166 people killed in a fire on the Piper Alpha oil rig, 6 July. On 21 December a bomb placed by Libyan terrorists caused a PanAm jumbo jet to explode over Lockerbie, killing 259 passengers and 11 townspeople.

1990: Glasgow held the title of European City of Culture.

1994 onwards: Contamination of British cattle herds by BSE (bovine spongiform encephalitis) depressed the Scottish beef industry. Confidence in British beef was not fully restored until early 2000.

1997: Referendum on the reinstatement of a separate Scottish Parliament. This time the people voted Yes, by a considerable majority, for a Scottish Parliament with powers to raise or lower taxes.

1999: Elections for Scottish Parliament, 6 May, carried out using a partial proportional representation system of voting for the first time in Britain. On 12 May the Parliament met for the first time since 1709. The official date of devolution was 1 July 1999.

A lost parliamentary manuscript found
In 1999, the year in which the Scottish Parliament was restored, a lost 17th-century manuscript, recording activities of the pre-Union Scottish government which have been missing since the council was abolished in 1708, was rediscovered. The book contains notes taken from the records of the Scottish Parliament, 1424–1621, and the Scottish privy council, 1561–1633. Written by an Edinburgh lawyer, Sir George Mackenzie of Rosehaugh, who was Lord Advocate 1677–86, the book is believed to have been lost some time after the national historian Cosmo Innes, put in a request to consult it to its owner, the Marquess of Bute, in 1842. The MS has been returned to the archives of Bute House, now the official residence of the First Minister.

KINGS AND QUEENS OF SCOTS, 834 TO 1603

c.834–860	Kenneth mac Alpin, king of Scots, and also of Picts from 843; Kenneth I of Alba
860–63	Donald I
863–77	Constantine I
877–78	Aed
878–89	Giric
889–900	Donald II
900–43	Constantine II (abdicated)
944–54	Malcolm I
954–63	Indulf
963–67	Dubh (Duff)
967–71	Culain
971–95	Kenneth II
995–97	Constantine III
997	Kenneth III
997–1005	Grig
1005–34	Malcolm II (c.954–1034)

THE HOUSE OF ATHOLL

1034–40	Duncan I
1040–57	Macbeth (c.1005–57)
1057–58	Lulach (c.1032–58)
1058–93	Malcolm III (Canmore) (c.1031–93)
1093–97	Donald III Ban (c.1033–1100) Deposed May 1094, restored November 1094
1094	Duncan II (c.1060–94)
1097–1107	Edgar (c.1074–1107)
1107–24	Alexander I (The Fierce) (c.1077–1124)
1124–53	David I (The Saint) (c.1085–1153)
1153–65	Malcolm IV (The Maiden) (c.1141–65)
1165–1214	William I (The Lion) (c.1142–1214)
1214–49	Alexander II (1198–1249)
1249–86	Alexander III (1241–86)
1286–90	Margaret (The Maid of Norway) (1283–90)

First Interregnum 1290–92
Throne disputed by 13 competitors. Crown awarded to John Balliol by adjudication of Edward I of England

THE HOUSE OF BALLIOL

1292–96	John (Balliol) (c.1250–1313)

Second Interregnum 1296–1306
Edward I of England declared John Balliol to have forfeited the throne for contumacy in 1296 and took the government of Scotland into his own hands

THE HOUSE OF BRUCE

1306–29	Robert I (Bruce) (1274–1329)
1329–71	David II (1324–71)
1332	Edward Balliol, son of John Balliol, crowned King of Scots September, expelled December
1333–36	Edward Balliol restored as King of Scots

THE HOUSE OF STEWART

1371–90	Robert II (Stewart) (1316–90)
1390–1406	Robert III (c.1337–1406)
1406–37	James I (1394–1437)
1437–60	James II (1430–60)
1460–88	James III (1452–88)
1488–1513	James IV (1473–1513)
1513–42	James V (1512–42)
1542–67	Mary (1542–87)
1567–1625	James VI (and I of England) (1566–1625) Succeeded 1603 to the English throne, so joining the English and Scottish crowns

BRITISH KINGS AND QUEENS SINCE 1603

THE HOUSE OF STUART

1603–25	James I (and VI of Scotland) (1566–1625)
1625–49	Charles I (1600–49)

Commonwealth declared 19 May 1649

1649–53	Government by a council of state
1653–58	Oliver Cromwell, Lord Protector
1658–59	Richard Cromwell, Lord Protector
1660–85	Charles II (1630–85)
1685–88	James II (and VII) (1633–1701)

Interregnum 11 December 1688 to 12 February 1689

1689–1702 and	William III (1650–1702)
1689–94	Mary II (1662–94)
1702–14	Anne (1665–1714)

THE HOUSE OF HANOVER

1714–27	George I (Elector of Hanover) (1660–1727)
1727–60	George II (1683–1760)
1760–1820	George III (1738–1820)

Regency 1811–20
Prince of Wales regent owing to the insanity of George III

1820–30	George IV (1762–1830)
1830–37	William IV (1765–1837)
1837–1901	Victoria (1819–1901)

THE HOUSE OF SAXE-COBURG AND GOTHA

1901–10	Edward VII (1841–1910)

THE HOUSE OF WINDSOR

1910–36	George V (1865–1936)
1936	Edward VIII (1894–1972)
1936–52	George VI (1895–1952)
1952–	Elizabeth II (1926–)

CITIES

EDINBURGH

Edinburgh is the capital of and seat of government in Scotland. The city is built on a group of hills and contains in Princes Street one of the most beautiful thoroughfares in the world. In 1995 UNESCO designated Edinburgh Old and New Towns a World Heritage Site. There are three universities: Edinburgh (1583), Heriot-Watt (1966), and Napier (1992). The Edinburgh International Festival, held in August each year, has become one of the world's principal festivals of the performing arts.

The principal buildings include: the Castle, which now houses the Stone of Scone and also contains St Margaret's Chapel (12th century), the oldest building in Edinburgh, and the Scottish National War Memorial (1923); the Palace of Holyroodhouse (begun 1501 by James IV, rebuilding completed 1679); Parliament House (1632–40), the present seat of the judicature; St Giles' Cathedral (15th century, but the site of a church since AD 854); St Mary's (Scottish Episcopal) Cathedral (Sir George Gilbert Scott); the General Register House (Robert Adam, 1774); the National and the Signet Libraries (founded 1682 and 1722); the National Gallery (1859); the Royal Scottish Academy; the National Portrait Gallery (1889); the Royal Museum of Scotland (1861); the New Royal Observatory (1896); St Cecilia's Hall (1762), the first purpose-built concert hall in Scotland; the Usher Hall; and the Edinburgh International Conference Centre, opened in 1995. The Museum of Scotland opened 1998. The new Scottish Parliament building is due to open in 2001.

Other places of interest include Arthur's Seat (a volcanic hill 251 m/823 ft high overlooking the city), Calton Hill, the Royal Botanic Garden Edinburgh, the Physic Garden (1676), and the Firth of Forth road bridge (1964) and rail bridge (1890).

OTHER PRINCIPAL CITIES

ABERDEEN

Aberdeen, 130 miles north-east of Edinburgh, received its charter as a royal burgh in 1179. Scotland's third largest city, Aberdeen is the second largest Scottish fishing port and the main centre for offshore oil exploration and production. It is also an ancient university town (Aberdeen University, founded 1495; Robert Gordon University, 1992) and a distinguished research centre. Other industries include engineering, food processing, textiles, paper manufacturing and chemicals.

Places of interest include: King's College (from 1500); St Machar's Cathedral (1370–1424); Brig o' Balgownie (1314–18), Duthie Park (1881) and Winter Gardens (1972); Hazlehead Park; the Kirk of St Nicholas (from 12th century); the Mercat Cross (1686); Marischal College (founded 1593, present building 1891), the second largest granite building in Europe, and Marischal Museum; Provost Skene's House (from 1545); the Art Gallery (1884); Robert Gordon's College (begun by William Adam, 1731) and Robert Gordon University; the Gordon Highlanders Museum; the Satrosphere Hands-On Discovery Centre, and the Aberdeen Maritime Museum, which incorporates Provost Ross's House (1593) and the former Trinity Church.

DUNDEE

Dundee, which received its charter as a royal burgh in 1327, is situated on the north bank of the Tay estuary. The city's port and dock installations are important to the offshore oil industry and the airport also provides servicing facilities. Principal industries include textiles, computers and other electronic industries, lasers, printing, tyre manufacture, food processing, carpets, engineering, clothing manufacture and tourism. There are two universities, Dundee (1967) and Abertay Dundee (1994).

The unique City Churches – three churches under one roof, together with the 15th-century St Mary's Tower – are the city's most prominent architectural feature. Dundee has two historic ships: the Dundee-built RRS Discovery (built 1901), which took Captain Scott to the Antarctic, lies alongside Discovery Quay, and the frigate Unicorn (built 1825), the only British-built wooden warship still afloat, is moored in Victoria Dock. Places of interest include Mills Public Observatory, the Tay road and rail bridges, the Dundee Museum and Art Gallery (1872), McManus Galleries, the new Contemporary Arts Centre, Barrack Street Museum, Claypotts Castle (a town house built 1569–88), Broughty Castle (1454), Caledon Shipyard (1874), and Verdant Works (Textile Heritage Centre).

GLASGOW

Glasgow, a royal burgh (1611), is Scotland's principal commercial and industrial centre. The city occupies the north and south banks of the river Clyde, formerly one of the chief commercial estuaries in the world. The main industries include engineering, electronics, finance, chemicals and printing. The city has also developed recently as a cultural, tourism and conference centre. It was designated European City of Culture in 1990 and City of Architecture and Design in 1999. There are two universities: Glasgow (1451) and Strathclyde (1964). The city was raised to an archdiocese in 1492.

Among the chief buildings are the 13th-century Gothic Cathedral, the only mainland Scottish cathedral to have survived the Reformation intact; the University (Sir George Gilbert Scott); the City Chambers; the Royal Exchange (1829); the Royal Concert Hall; St Mungo Museum of Religious Life and Art; Pollok House; the Hunterian Museum (1805); the People's Palace (1898); the New Glasgow School of Art (Charles Rennie Mackintosh, 1896); Glasgow Art Gallery and Museum, Kelvingrove (1893); the Gallery of Modern Art; the Burrell Collection museum and the Mitchell Library (1911). The city is home to the Scottish National Orchestra (founded 1950), Scottish Opera (founded 1962) and Scottish Ballet.

INVERNESS

Inverness, a royal burgh, is the largest town in the Highlands and their administrative centre. It is situated at the northern end of the Great Glen, where the River Ness flows into the Beauly Firth, now spanned by the Kessock Bridge across to the Black Isle. Originally built on the axis between the medieval castle and the Old High Church, the town now has a population of 50,000. Inverness Castle was occupied and then destroyed by the Jacobites in 1746 and in the 19th century replaced by a courthouse and prison. The battlefield at Culloden, where the Jacobites were finally defeated on 16 April 1746, lies to the east of the town.

Other important buildings include the late Victorian Town House (1882), the Highland Council Buildings (1876), the episcopal St Andrew's Cathedral (1869), and the modern Eden Court Theatre (1976). Industries include light engineering, biotechnology, electronics, service industries and tourism. Nearby is the oil platform construction yard at Ardersier.

PERTH

Perth is situated in north-central Scotland, on the right bank of the Tay. It became a burgh in 1106 and a royal burgh in 1210, and was one of the cities which fulfilled the function of Scottish capital until the mid-15th century, a number of Parliaments and Council meetings being held there in the medieval period. The Blackfriars monastery was a favoured residence of James I, who founded Charterhouse, the last monastery to be established in Scotland, in Perth in 1425.

Little now remains to indicate Perth's former position as one of the chief towns of medieval Scotland, the ancient monasteries and castles having fallen victim to floods and conflict. The main buildings are St John's Kirk (founded by David I c.1125; Perth was also known as St John's Town until the 16th century); Perth Bridge; the King James VI Hospital; the Old Academy; the Sheriff Court buildings; Huntingtower Castle (16th century); Scone Palace (built 1802–13 on the site of the medieval palace); and Balhousie Castle (present building, 1862).

The city lies between two large areas of open parkland and has a wealth of fine Georgian buildings. The principal industries are now tourism, agriculture, insurance, whisky and transport.

STIRLING

Stirling, a royal burgh since c.1124, lies on the River Forth in the centre of Scotland. It was one of the chief cities to serve as the Scottish capital between the 13th and the 16th centuries, and the castle was a royal residence from c.1226. Stirling was the site of the Parliament which took over the government from John Balliol in 1295, the birthplace of James IV and the site of the coronations of Mary and of James VI.

Stirling's strategic situation led to its being the site of several battles. English armies were defeated at the Battle of Stirling Bridge in 1297 by Scots led by William Wallace, and at Bannockburn in 1314 by forces led by Robert Bruce.

The local economy comprises mainly service industries with some manufacturing. The city houses the headquarters of Scottish Amicable, the Bank of Bermuda and Scottish Natural Heritage. Stirling is also an important tourist centre.

Places of interest include Stirling Castle; Argyll's Lodgings; the National Wallace Monument (1887); the Bannockburn Heritage Centre; Rob Roy Centre; Old Town Jail; Inchmahome Priory (1238); Cambuskenneth Abbey (1147); the Church of the Holy Rood (16th and 17th centuries); the Smith Art Gallery and Museum; and the Changing Room contemporary art gallery.

LANGUAGES

The main language of Scotland is English. Gaelic is a recognised minority language and the various Scots dialects are widely spoken. Language is one of the aspects in which Orkney and Shetland are distinct from the rest of Scotland. Having been under Norse and Nordic influence and actual dominion until the fifteenth century, much longer than any other part of the country, they manifest a strong Norse influence in their place-names and dialect. Norn, an old Norse language, was commonly spoken in many of the islands until the eighteenth century, long after English had become the official language. Norse colonisation also influenced language and place-names in the Hebrides, but to a lesser extent.

GAELIC

The Gaelic language was introduced into Scotland from Ireland in the fifth century or before, and was at its strongest from the ninth to the 12th centuries. Despite the steady advance of English from the Middle Ages onwards, Gaelic remained the main language in much of rural Scotland until the early 17th century. However, in 1616 James VI and I passed an Act proscribing Gaelic, and with the suppression of Highland culture following the Jacobite rising of 1745 and the depopulation of Gaelic-speaking areas by the Highland clearances in the 19th century, the language declined.

The movement for the revival of Gaelic grew in the late 19th and early 20th centuries. A clause was inserted in the Education Act 1918 allowing Gaelic to be taught in Gaelic-speaking areas, although it was not until 1958 that a local education authority (Inverness-shire) first adopted a bilingual policy, teaching Gaelic in primary schools in Gaelic-speaking areas.

At the time of the 1991 census, 1.4 per cent of the population of Scotland, mainly in the Highlands and the Western Isles, were able to speak Gaelic. This represents a fall of 0.2 per cent since the 1981 census. The percentage of Gaelic speakers was highest among people aged 65 and over (2.2 per cent), and lowest among people aged three to 15 (0.9 per cent). Geographically, by far the highest proportion of Gaelic speakers to total population occurred in the Western Isles area, where over 68 per cent of people speak Gaelic.

The following table shows the total number of persons aged three and over who speak Gaelic, by region and as a percentage of the total population, at the 1991 census.

Region	Total persons	% of population
Borders	103,881	0.5
Central	267,492	0.6
Dumfries and Galloway	147,805	0.4
Fife	341,199	0.5
Grampian	503,888	0.5
Highland	204,004	7.5
Lothian	726,010	0.6
Strathclyde	2,248,706	0.8
Tayside	383,848	0.7
Orkney Islands	19,612	0.5
Shetland Islands	22,522	0.5
Western Isles	29,600	68.4
Total	4,998,567	1.4

The following table shows Gaelic speakers as a percentage of the total population, by age group, at the 1981 and 1991 censuses.

Age	1981	1991
3–15	1.0	0.9
16–44	1.4	1.1
45–64	2.0	1.6
65+	2.7	2.2
Total	1.6	1.4

Source: General Register Office (Scotland), 1991 Census Monitor for Scotland (Crown copyright)

PROMOTION OF GAELIC

In recent years, more official measures have been taken to promote the revival of Gaelic, and the Scottish Executive includes a junior minister for Gaelic.

Gaelic is taught as an academic subject at universities including Aberdeen, Edinburgh and Glasgow, at numerous colleges of education, and in some schools, principally in Gaelic-speaking areas. Fifty-nine primary schools in Scotland offer Gaelic-medium education, and the Scottish Executive is committed to increasing the supply of Gaelic-medium teachers and locating training for them in the Highlands. Sàbhal Mor Ostaig is the Gaelic-medium further and higher education college.

BBC programmes in Gaelic are broadcast throughout the country. BBC Scotland delivered 116 hours of Gaelic television programmes in 1997–8 and an average of 45 hours of Gaelic radio programmes per week. The Scottish and Grampian independent stations also broadcast regular Gaelic television programmes. The Gaelic-language radio station BBC Radio nan Gaidheal is now available to 90 per cent of the audience in Scotland. There are local community radio stations in Stornoway, Ullapool, Portree and Fort William.

In 1992 the Gaelic Television Committee/ Comataidh Telebhisein Gàidhlig (now the Gaelic Broadcasting Committee/Comataidh Craolaidh Gàidhlig) was established to fund up to 200 additional hours of Gaelic-medium television. The committee's remit was extended to radio programmes by the Broadcasting Act 1996. The Scottish Executive provides £8.5 million a year to the Committee, which is based in Stornaway.

A number of institutions for the promotion of the Gaelic language and culture exist. Comunn na Gàidhlig is the national development agency for Scottish Gaelic. It promotes the use of the Gaelic language, the continuance of Gaelic culture in education and the arts, and the integration of Gaelic into social and economic development, including the promotion of Gaelic businesses. An Comunn Gaidhealach promotes Gaelic culture through everyday use of the language and encourages the traditions of music, literature and folklore.

LOWLAND SCOTTISH

Several dialects, known collectively as Lowland Scots, Lallans or Doric, are widely spoken in the south, east and extreme north of the country. 'Scots' is the term commonly used in Scotland itself and in the European Charter for Minority and Regional Languages, which recognises Scots as a minority language. In the last 20 years the term 'Doric' has come to be used locally in the north-east to refer exclusively to the group of dialects in that area.

Although the UK government ratified the European Charter in 1998, no official recognition or encouragement has yet been given to Scots. The General Register Office (Scotland) has estimated that 1.5 million, or 30 per cent of the population, are Scots speakers.

PROMOTION OF SCOTS

Courses in Scots language and literature are taught at several universities, further and higher education colleges and community colleges. The Scots Language Resource Centre is the lead agency for the promotion of Scots and supports other bodies engaged in the promotion and study of Scots language and culture, including the Scottish National Dictionary Association, the Scots Language Society, the Scots Leid Associe, the Scots Speakers' Curn and Scots Tung

CHIEFS OF CLANS AND NAMES

The word 'clan', derived from the Gaelic 'clann', meaning children, originally referred to an extended family or tribe occupying a certain area of land. This was the early form of Gaelic society. After the Jacobean rebellion in 1745–6, the clan system was suppressed by the Government in order to forestall further rebellion, and gradually declined as an organising force in Scottish society. However, the clans continue to be one of the strongest social and emotional links between Scots in Scotland and abroad and a potent symbol of what it means to be Scottish. Their links with the land are not entirely severed either: many clan chiefs still live on the land, and in the buildings, which have been the clan seat for centuries.

The title of chief is usually hereditary, passing to the nearest heir. However, a chief may nominate a successor, subject to the confirmation of the Lord Lyon King of Arms. If a title is dormant, the Lord Lyon can award it to a person bearing the clan name, although this decision may be revoked if a proven heir is found within 20 years.

The style 'of that Ilk' began to be used by some chiefs in the late 16th century. More recently, chiefs who do not have an estate have been recognised as 'of that Ilk.' Certain chiefs use the prefix 'The'. The duplication of surnames by chiefs (e.g. Macdonald of Macdonald) is a feature that became common after the Act of Union 1707.

Only chiefs of whole names or clans are included here, except certain special instances (marked *) who, though not chiefs of a whole name, were or are for some reason (e.g. the Macdonald forfeiture) independent. Under decision (Campbell-Gray, 1950) that a bearer of a 'double- or triple-barrelled' surname cannot be held chief of a part of such, several others cannot be included in the list at present.

STANDING COUNCIL OF SCOTTISH CHIEFS

Hope Chambers, 52 Leith Walk, Edinburgh, EH6 5HW
Tel: 0131-554 6321

STYLES

There are a number of different styles for chiefs of clans and names; the appropriate use depends on the title and designation of the person, and for exact guidance a specialist source should be consulted. The following examples show the more common styles:

F – represents forename
S – represents surname
D – represents designation

Examples:
The S –
The S – of D –
F – S – of D –
Sir F – S – of D –, Bt.
F – S – of that Ilk
Madam/Mrs/Miss S – of D – (according to preference)
Dame F – S – of D –, DBE

For forms of address, see page 270

CLAN CHIEFS

THE ROYAL HOUSE
HM The Queen

AGNEW
Sir Crispin Agnew of Lochnaw, Bt., QC
6 Palmerston Road, Edinburgh EH9 1TN

ANSTRUTHER
Sir Ralph Anstruther of that Ilk, Bt., GCVO, MC
Balcaskie, Pittenweem, Fife KY10 2RD

ARBUTHNOTT
The Viscount of Arbuthnott, KT, CBE, DSC
Arbuthnott House, Laurencekirk, Kincardineshire AB30 1PA

BARCLAY
Peter C. Barclay of Towie Barclay and of that Ilk
28A Gordon Place, London W8 4JE

BORTHWICK
The Lord Borthwick
Crookston, Heriot, Midlothian EH38 5YS

BOYD
The Lord Kilmarnock
194 Regent's Park Road, London NW1 8XP

BOYLE
The Earl of Glasgow
Kelburn, Fairlie, Ayrshire KA29 0BE

BRODIE
Ninian Brodie of Brodie
Brodie Castle, Forres, Morayshire IV36 0TE

BRUCE
The Earl of Elgin and Kincardine, KT
Broomhall, Dunfermline, Fife KY11 3DU

BUCHAN
David S. Buchan of Auchmacoy
Auchmacoy House, Ellon, Aberdeenshire

BURNETT
J. C. A. Burnett of Leys
Crathes Castle, Banchory, Kincardineshire

CAMERON
Sir Donald Cameron of Lochiel, KT, CVO, TD
Achnacarry, Spean Bridge, Inverness-shire

CAMPBELL
The Duke of Argyll
Inveraray, Argyll PA32 8XF

CARMICHAEL
Richard J. Carmichael of Carmichael
Carmichael, Thankerton, Biggar, Lanarkshire

CARNEGIE
The Duke of Fife
Elsick House, Stonehaven, Kincardineshire
AB3 2NT

CATHCART
Maj.-Gen. The Earl Cathcart
Gately Hall, Dereham, Norfolk

CHARTERIS
The Earl of Wemyss and March, KT
Gosford House, Longniddry, East Lothian
EH32 0PX

CLAN CHATTAN
M. K. Mackintosh of Clan Chattan
Maxwell Park, Gwelo, Zimbabwe

CHISHOLM
Hamish Chisholm of Chisholm (The Chisholm)
Elmpine, Beck Row, Bury St Edmunds, Suffolk

COCHRANE
The Earl of Dundonald
Lochnell Castle, Ledaig, Argyllshire

COLQUHOUN
Sir Ivar Colquhoun of Luss, Bt.
Camstraddan, Luss, Dunbartonshire G83 8NX

CRANSTOUN
David A. S. Cranstoun of that Ilk
Corehouse, Lanark

CRICHTON
vacant

CUMMING
Sir William Cumming of Altyre, Bt.
Altyre, Forres, Moray

DARROCH
Capt. Duncan Darroch of Gourock
The Red House, Branksome Park Road,
Camberley, Surrey

DAVIDSON
Alister G. Davidson of Davidston
21 Winscombe Street, Takapuna, Auckland, New
Zealand

DEWAR
Kenneth Dewar of that Ilk and Vogrie
The Dower House, Grayshott, nr Hindhead,
Surrey

DRUMMOND
The Earl of Perth, PC
Stobhall, Perth PH2 6DR

DUNBAR
Sir James Dunbar of Mochrum, Bt.
211 Gardenville Drive, Yorktown, Virginia
23693 USA

DUNDAS
David D. Dundas of Dundas
8 Derna Road, Kenwyn 7700 South Africa

DURIE
Andrew Durie of Durie, CBE
Finnich Malise, Croftamie, Stirlingshire
G63 0HA

ELIOTT
Mrs Margaret Eliott of Redheugh
Redheugh, Newcastleton, Roxburghshire

ERSKINE
The Earl of Mar and Kellie
Erskine House, Kirk Wynd, Clackmannan
FK10 4JF

FARQUHARSON
Capt. A. Farquharson of Invercauld, MC
Invercauld, Braemar, Aberdeenshire AB35 5TT

FERGUSSON
Sir Charles Fergusson of Kilkerran, Bt.
Kilkerran, Maybole, Ayrshire

FORBES
The Lord Forbes, KBE
Balforbes, Alford, Aberdeenshire AB33 8DR

FORSYTH
Alistair Forsyth of that Ilk
Ethie Castle, by Arbroath, Angus DD11 5SP

FRASER
The Lady Saltoun
Inverey House, Braemar, Aberdeenshire
AB35 5YB

FRASER (OF LOVAT)*
The Lord Lovat
Beaufort Lodge, Beauly, Inverness-shire
IV4 7AZ

GAYRE
R. Gayre of Gayre and Nigg
Minard Castle, Minard, Inverary, Argyll
PA32 8YB

GORDON
The Marquess of Huntly
Aboyne Castle, Aberdeenshire AB34 5JP

GRAHAM
The Duke of Montrose
Buchanan Auld House, Drymen, Stirlingshire

GRANT
The Lord Strathspey
The School House, Lochbuie, Mull, Argyllshire
PA62 6AA

GRIERSON
Sir Michael Grierson of Lag, Bt.
40C Palace Road, London SW2 3NJ

HAIG
The Earl Haig, OBE
Bemersyde, Melrose, Roxburghshire TD6 9DP

HALDANE
Martin Haldane of Gleneagles
Gleneagles, Auchterarder, Perthshire

HANNAY
Ramsey Hannay of Kirkdale and of that Ilk
Cardoness House, Gatehouse-of-Fleet,
Kirkcudbrightshire

HAY
The Earl of Erroll
Woodbury Hall, Sandy, Beds

HENDERSON
John Henderson of Fordell
7 Owen Street, Toowoomba, Queensland,
Australia

HUNTER
Pauline Hunter of Hunterston
Plovers Ridge, Lon Cecrist, Treaddur Bay,
Holyhead, Gwynedd

IRVINE OF DRUM
David C. Irvine of Drum
Holly Leaf Cottage, Inchmarlo, Banchory
AB31 4BR

JARDINE
Sir Alexander Jardine of Applegirth, Bt.
Ash House, Thwaites, Millom, Cumbria
LA18 5HY

JOHNSTONE
The Earl of Annandale and Hartfell
Raehills, Lockerbie, Dumfriesshire

KEITH
The Earl of Kintore
The Stables, Keith Hall, Inverurie,
Aberdeenshire AB51 0LD

KENNEDY
The Marquess of Ailsa
Cassillis House, Maybole, Ayrshire

KERR
The Marquess of Lothian, KCVO
Ferniehurst Castle, Jedburgh, Roxburghshire
TN8 6NX

KINCAID
vacant

LAMONT
Revd Peter N. Lamont of that Ilk
309 Bungarribee Road, Blacktown, NSW 2148
Australia

LEASK
Madam Leask of Leask
1 Vincent Road, Sheringham, Norfolk

LENNOX
Edward J. H. Lennox of that Ilk
Tods Top Farm, Downton on the Rock, Ludlow,
Shropshire

LESLIE
The Earl of Rothes
Tanglewood, West Tytherley, Salisbury, Wilts
SP5 1LX

LINDSAY
The Earl of Crawford and Balcarres, KT, PC
Balcarres, Colinsburgh, Fife

LOCKHART
Angus H. Lockhart of the Lee
Newholme, Dunsyre, Lanark

LUMSDEN
Gillem Lumsden of that Ilk and Blanerne
Stapely Howe, Hoe Benham, Newbury, Berks

MACALESTER
William St J. S. McAlester of Loup and Kennox
Dun Skeig, 27 Burnham Road, Burton,
Christchurch, Dorset BH23 7ND

MCBAIN
J. H. McBain of McBain
7025 North Finger Rock Place, Tucson, Arizona
USA

MACDONALD
The Lord Macdonald (The Macdonald of
Macdonald)
Kinloch Lodge, Sleat, Isle of Skye

MACDONALD OF CLANRANALD*
Ranald A. Macdonald of Clanranald
Mornish House, Killin, Perthshire FK21 8TX

MACDONALD OF SLEAT (CLAN HUSTEAIN)*
Sir Ian Macdonald of Sleat, Bt.
Thorpe Hall, Rudston, Driffield, N. Humberside
YO25 0JE

MACDONELL OF GLENGARRY*
Ranald MacDonell of Glengarry
Elonbank, Castle Street, Fortrose, Ross-shire
IV10 8TH

MACDOUGALL
vacant

MACDOWALL
Fergus D. H. Macdowall of Garthland
16 Rowe Road, Ottawa, Ontario K2G 2ZS
Canada

MACGREGOR
Brig. Sir Gregor MacGregor of MacGregor, Bt.
Bannatyne, Newtyle, Blairgowrie, Perthshire
PH12 8TR

MACINTYRE
James W. MacIntyre of Glenoe
15301 Pine Orchard Drive, Apartment 3H,
Silver Spring, Maryland USA

MACKAY
The Lord Reay
98 Oakley Street, London SW3

MACKENZIE
The Earl of Cromartie
Castle Leod, Strathpeffer, Ross-shire IV14 9AA

MACKINNON
Madam Anne Mackinnon of Mackinnon
16 Purleigh Road, Bridgwater, Somerset

MACKINTOSH
The Mackintosh of Mackintosh
Moy Hall, Inverness IV13 7YQ

MACLACHLAN
vacant

MACLAREN
Donald MacLaren of MacLaren and Achleskine
Achleskine, Kirkton, Balquhidder, Lochearnhead

MACLEAN
The Hon. Sir Lachlan Maclean of Duart, Bt.,
CVO
Arngask House, Glenfarg, Perthshire PH2 9QA

MACLENNAN
vacant

MACLEOD
John MacLeod of MacLeod
Dunvegan Castle, Isle of Skye

MACMILLAN
George MacMillan of MacMillan
Finlaystone, Langbank, Renfrewshire

MACNAB
J. C. Macnab of Macnab (The Macnab)
Leuchars Castle Farmhouse, Leuchars, Fife
KY16 0EY

MACNAGHTEN
Sir Patrick Macnaghten of Macnaghten and
Dundarave, Bt.
Dundarave, Bushmills, Co. Antrim

MACNEACAIL
Iain Macneacail of Macneacail and Scorrybreac
12 Fox Street, Ballina, NSW Australia

MACNEIL OF BARRA
Ian R. Macneil of Barra (The Macneil of Barra)
95/6 Grange Loan, Edinburgh

MACPHERSON
The Hon. Sir William Macpherson of Cluny, TD
Newtown Castle, Blairgowrie, Perthshire

MACTAVISH
E. S. Dugald MacTavish of Dunardry
c/o 2519 Vivaldi Avenue, Four Seasons Estates,
Gambrills, MD 21054 USA

MACTHOMAS
Andrew P. C. MacThomas of Finegand
c/o Roslin Cottage, Pitmedden, Aberdeenshire
AB41 7NY

MAITLAND
The Earl of Lauderdale
12 St Vincent Street, Edinburgh

MAKGILL
The Viscount of Oxfuird
Kemback, Stoke, nr. Andover, Hants SP11 0NP

MALCOLM (MACCALLUM)
Robin N. L. Malcolm of Poltalloch
Duntrune Castle, Lochgilphead, Argyll

MAR
The Countess of Mar
St Michael's Farm, Great Witley, Worcs
WR6 6JB

MARJORIBANKS
Andrew Marjoribanks of that Ilk
10 Newark Street, Greenock

MATHESON
Maj. Sir Fergus Matheson of Matheson, Bt.
Old Rectory, Hedenham, Bungay, Suffolk
NR35 2LD

MENZIES
David R. Menzies of Menzies
Wester Auchnagallin Farmhouse, Braes of Castle
Grant, Grantown on Spey PH26 3PL

MOFFAT
Madam Moffat of that Ilk
St Jasual, Bullocks Farm Lane, Wheeler End
Common, High Wycombe

MONCREIFFE
vacant

MONTGOMERIE
The Earl of Eglinton and Winton
Balhomie, Cargill, Perth PH2 6DS

MORRISON
Dr Iain M. Morrison of Ruchdi
Magnolia Cottage, The Street, Walberton, Sussex

MUNRO
Hector W. Munro of Foulis
Foulis Castle, Evanton, Ross-shire IV16 9UX

MURRAY
The Duke of Atholl
Blair Castle, Blair Atholl, Perthshire

NESBITT (OR NISBET)
Robert Nesbitt of that Ilk
Upper Roundhurst Farm, Roundhurst,
Haslemere, Surrey

NICOLSON
The Lord Carnock
90 Whitehall Court, London SW1A 2EL

OGILVY
The Earl of Airlie, KT, GCVO, PC
Cortachy Castle, Kirriemuir, Angus

RAMSAY
The Earl of Dalhousie, KT, GCVO, GBE, MC
Brechin Castle, Brechin, Angus DD7 6SH

RATTRAY
James S. Rattray of Rattray
Craighall, Rattray, Perthshire

RIDDELL
Sir John Riddell of Riddell, CB, CVO, Hepple,
Morpeth, Northumberland

ROBERTSON
Alexander G. H. Robertson of Struan (Struan-Robertson)
The Breach Farm, Goudhurst Road, Cranbrook, Kent

ROLLO
The Lord Rollo
Pitcairns, Dunning, Perthshire

ROSE
Miss Elizabeth Rose of Kilravock
Kilravock Castle, Croy, Inverness

ROSS
David C. Ross of that Ilk and Balnagowan
Shandwick, Perth Road, Stanley, Perthshire

RUTHVEN
The Earl of Gowrie, PC
34 King Street, London WC2

SCOTT
The Duke of Buccleuch and Queensberry, KT, VRD
Bowhill, Selkirk

SCRYMGEOUR
The Earl of Dundee
Birkhill, Cupar, Fife

SEMPILL
The Lord Sempill
3 Vanburgh Place, Edinburgh EH6 8AE

SHAW
John Shaw of Tordarroch
East Gaig an Ron, 22 Academy Street, Fortrose IV10 8TW

SINCLAIR
The Earl of Caithness
137 Claxton Grove, London W6 8HB

SKENE
Danus Skene of Skene
Nether Pitlour, Strathmiglo, Fife

STIRLING
Fraser J. Stirling of Cader
44A Oakley Street, London SW3 5HA

STRANGE
Maj. Timothy Strange of Balcaskie
Little Holme, Porton Road, Amesbury, Wilts

SUTHERLAND
The Countess of Sutherland
House of Tongue, Brora, Sutherland

SWINTON
John Swinton of that Ilk
123 Superior Avenue SW, Calgary, Alberta Canada

TROTTER
Alexander Trotter of Mortonhall
Charterhall, Duns, Berwickshire

URQUHART
Kenneth T. Urquhart of Urquhart
507 Jefferson Park Avenue, Jefferson, New Orleans, Louisiana 70121 USA

WALLACE
Ian F. Wallace of that Ilk
5 Lennox Street, Edinburgh EH4 1QB

WEDDERBURN OF THAT ILK
The Master of Dundee
Birkhill, Cupar, Fife

WEMYSS
David Wemyss of that Ilk
Invermay, Forteviot, Perthshire

THE NATIONAL FLAGS

THE SCOTTISH FLAG

The flag of Scotland is known as the Saltire. It is a white diagonal cross on a blue field (saltire argent in a field azure) and symbolises St Andrew, the patron saint of Scotland.

A traditional explanation for the adoption of the St Andrew's cross as the symbol of Scotland is that the Saltire appeared in the sky to the Pictish king Hungus as an omen of victory over the Anglo-Saxons at the battle of Aethelstaneford. The Saltire was adopted as a national symbol at about the same time as St Andrew was adopted as Scotland's patron saint, and by the mid 14th century it was being used on coins. From about that time also, it has been used as a symbol of the struggle for independence.

In Scotland, HM The Queen and her representatives (The First Minister, The Lord Lyon, The Lord High Commissioner to the General Assembly and the Lord Lieutenants) use a flag called the Royal Lion Rampant (Scotland). The flag features a red lion rampant on a yellow field. George V granted permission for Scots to use the flag as a sign of loyalty.

THE NATIONAL FLAG

The national flag of the United Kingdom is the Union Flag, generally known as the Union Jack.

The Union Flag is a combination of the cross of St George, patron saint of England, the cross of St Andrew, patron saint of Scotland, and a cross similar to that of St Patrick, patron saint of Ireland.

The Union Flag was first introduced in 1606 after the union of the kingdoms of England and Scotland under one sovereign. The cross of St Patrick was added in 1801 after the union of Great Britain and Ireland.

DAYS FOR FLYING FLAGS

It is the practice to fly the Union Flag daily on some customs houses. In all other cases, flags are flown on government buildings by command of The Queen.

Days for hoisting the Union Flag are notified to the Department for Culture, Media and Sport by The Queen's command and communicated by the department to other government departments. On the days appointed, the Union Flag is flown on government buildings in the UK from 8 a.m. to sunset.

Both the Union Flag and the Saltire are flown in Scotland. The Saltire is flown from government buildings alongside, but not superior to, the Union Flag on the flag-flying days, which are the same days as those announced by the Department for Culture, Media and Sport. On Europe Day only, the EU flag flies alongside the Union Flag and the Saltire.

The Queen's Accession	6 February
Birthday of The Duke of York	19 February
Birthday of The Earl of Wessex	10 March
Commonwealth Day (2001)	12 March
Birthday of The Queen	21 April
*Europe Day	9 May
Coronation Day	2 June
The Queen's Official Birthday (2001)	16 June
Birthday of The Duke of Edinburgh	10 June
Birthday of Queen Elizabeth the Queen Mother	4 August
Birthday of The Princess Royal	15 August
Birthday of The Princess Margaret	21 August
Remembrance Sunday (2001)	11 November
Birthday of The Prince Charles, Duke of Rothesay	14 November
The Queen's Wedding Day	20 November
St Andrew's Day	30 November

The Union Flag should fly alongside the EU flag. On government buildings that have only one flagpole, the Union Flag should take precedence

FLAGS AT HALF-MAST

Flags are flown at half-mast (e.g. two-thirds up between the top and bottom of the flagstaff) on the following occasions:

(a) From the announcement of the death up to the funeral of the Sovereign, except on Proclamation Day, when flags are hoisted right up from 11a.m. to sunset
(b) The funerals of members of the royal family, subject to special commands from The Queen in each case
(c) The funerals of foreign rulers, subject to special commands from The Queen in each case
(d) The funerals of prime ministers and ex-prime ministers of the UK, subject to special commands from The Queen in each case
(e) Other occasions by special command of The Queen

On occasions when days for flying flags coincide with days for flying flags at half-mast, the following rules are observed. Flags are flown:

(a) although a member of the royal family, or a near relative of the royal family, may be lying dead, unless special commands are received from The Queen to the contrary

(b) although it may be the day of the funeral of a foreign ruler

If the body of a very distinguished subject is lying at a government office, the flag may fly at half-mast on that office until the body has left (provided it is a day on which the flag would fly) and then the flag is to be hoisted right up. On all other government buildings the flag will fly as usual.

THE ROYAL STANDARD

The Royal Standard is hoisted only when the Queen is actually present in the building, and never when Her Majesty is passing in procession.

NATIONAL ANTHEM

The official national anthem throughout the UK is God Save The Queen.

At national events and international competitions (primarily sporting), Scottish songs are sometimes used, including Scotland the Brave at the Commonwealth Games and Flower of Scotland for international rugby matches.

In 1998 the Herald newspaper ran a competition for a new Scottish anthem and the winner, announced in January 1999, was William Jackson's Land of Light.

NATIONAL DAY

The national day is 30 November, the festival of St Andrew, the patron saint of Scotland.

St Andrew, one of the apostles and brother of Simon Peter, was born at Bethsaida on the Sea of Galilee and lived at Capernaum. He preached the gospel in Asia Minor and in Scythia along the shores of the Black Sea and became the patron saint of Russia. It is believed that he suffered crucifixion at Patras in Achaea, on a crux decussata (now known as St Andrew's Cross) and that his relics were removed from Patras to Constantinople and thence to Scotland, probably in the eighth century, since which time he has been the patron saint of Scotland. The church and settlement founded at the place where the relics were brought ashore became the town of St Andrews.

THE HEAD OF STATE

ELIZABETH II, by the Grace of God, of the United Kingdom of Great Britain and Northern Ireland and of her other Realms and Territories Queen, Head of the Commonwealth, Defender of the Faith

Her Majesty Elizabeth Alexandra Mary of Windsor, elder daughter of King George VI and of HM Queen Elizabeth the Queen Mother
Born 21 April 1926, at 17 Bruton Street, London W1
Ascended the throne 6 February 1952
Crowned 2 June 1953, at Westminster Abbey
Married 20 November 1947, in Westminster Abbey, HRH The Prince Philip, Duke of Edinburgh, KG, KT, OM, GBE, AC, QSO, PC (born 10 June 1921, son of Prince and Princess Andrew of Greece and Denmark, naturalised a British subject 1947, created Duke of Edinburgh, Earl of Merioneth and Baron Greenwich 1947)
Official residences: Buckingham Palace, London SW1A 1AA; Palace of Holyroodhouse, Edinburgh; Windsor Castle, Berks
Private residences: Balmoral Castle, Aberdeenshire; Sandringham, Norfolk

THE HEIR TO THE THRONE

HRH THE PRINCE CHARLES, DUKE OF ROTHESAY (Prince Charles Philip Arthur George), KG, KT, GCB and Great Master of the Order of the Bath, AK, QSO, PC, ADC(P)
Born 14 November 1948, created Prince of Wales and Earl of Chester 1958, succeeded as Duke of Cornwall, Duke of Rothesay, Earl of Carrick and Baron Renfrew, Lord of the Isles and Prince and Great Steward of Scotland 1952
Married 29 July 1981 Lady Diana Frances Spencer (Diana, Princess of Wales (1961—97), youngest daughter of the 8th Earl Spencer and the Hon. Mrs Shand Kydd), marriage dissolved 1996
Issue:
HRH Prince William of Wales (Prince William Arthur Philip Louis), born 21 June 1982
HRH Prince Henry of Wales (Prince Henry Charles Albert David), born 15 September 1984
Residences: St James's Palace, London SW1A 1BS; Highgrove, Doughton, Tetbury, Glos GL8 8TN
Office: St James's Palace, London SW1A 1BS. Tel: 020-7930 4832

ORDER OF SUCCESSION TO THE THRONE

1   HRH The Prince Charles, Duke of Rothesay
2   HRH Prince William of Wales
3   HRH Prince Henry of Wales
4   HRH The Duke of York
5   HRH Princess Beatrice of York
6   HRH Princess Eugenie of York
7   HRH The Earl of Wessex
8   HRH The Princess Royal
9   Peter Phillips
10   Zara Phillips
11   HRH The Princess Margaret, Countess of Snowdon
12   Viscount Linley
13   Hon. Charles Linley
14   Lady Sarah Chatto
15   Samuel Chatto
16   Arthur Chatto
17   HRH The Duke of Gloucester
18   Earl of Ulster
19   Lady Davina Windsor
20   Lady Rose Windsor
21   HRH The Duke of Kent
22   Baron Downpatrick
23   Lady Marina Charlotte Windsor
24   Lady Amelia Windsor
25   Lord Nicholas Windsor
26   Lady Helen Taylor
27   Columbus Taylor
28   Cassius Taylor
29   Lord Frederick Windsor
30   Lady Gabriella Windsor
31   HRH Princess Alexandra, the Hon. Lady Ogilvy
32   James Ogilvy
33   Alexander Ogilvy
34   Flora Ogilvy
35   Marina, Mrs Paul Mowatt
36   Christian Mowatt
37   Zenouska Mowatt
38   The Earl of Harewood

The Earl of St Andrews and HRH Prince Michael of Kent lost the right of succession to the throne through marriage to a Roman Catholic. Their children remain in succession provided that they are in communion with the Church of England.

THE QUEEN'S HOUSEHOLD

Office: Buckingham Palace, London SW1A
   1AA
Tel: 020-7930 4832
Web: http://www.royal.gov.uk

The Lord Chamberlain is the most senior
member of The Queen's Household and under
him come the heads of the six departments: the
Private Secretary, the Keeper of the Privy Purse,
the Comptroller of the Lord Chamberlain's
Office, the Master of the Household, the Crown
Equerry, and the Director of the Royal
Collection. Positions in these departments are
full-time salaried posts.
   There are also a number of honorary or now
largely ceremonial appointments which carry no
remuneration or a small honorarium. In the
following list, honorary appointments are
indicated by an asterisk.

GREAT OFFICERS OF STATE
Lord Chamberlain, The Lord Camoys, GCVO,
   PC
*Lord Steward, The Viscount Ridley, KG,
   GCVO, TD
*Master of the Horse, The Lord Vestey

LADIES-IN-WAITING AND EQUERRIES
*Mistress of the Robes, The Duchess of Grafton,
   GCVO
*Ladies of the Bedchamber, The Countess of
   Airlie, DCVO; The Lady Farnham, CVO
Women of the Bedchamber, Hon. Mary
   Morrison, DCVO; Lady Dugdale, DCVO;
   Mrs Robert de Pass; Mrs Christian Adams
   (temp.)
Equerries, Lt.-Col. Sir Guy Acland, Bt., MVO;
   Sqn. Ldr. S. Brailsford

THE PRIVATE SECRETARY'S OFFICE
Private Secretary to The Queen, Sir Robin
   Janvrin, KCVO, CB
Deputy Private Secretary, vacant
Communications Secretary, S. Lewis

PRESS OFFICE
Press Secretary, G. Crawford, LVO
Deputy Press Secretary, Miss P. Russell-Smith

THE PRIVY PURSE AND TREASURER'S
OFFICE
Keeper of the Privy Purse and Treasurer to The
   Queen, Sir Michael Peat, KCVO
Chief Accountant and Paymaster, I. McGregor

Personnel Officer, Miss P. Lloyd
Resident Factor, Balmoral, P. Ord, FRICS

THE LORD CHAMBERLAIN'S OFFICE
Comptroller, Lt.-Col. W. H. M. Ross, CVO,
   OBE
Assistant Comptroller, Lt.-Col. R.
   Cartwright
State Invitations Assistant, J. O. Hope

Marshal of the Diplomatic Corps, Vice-Adm. Sir
   James Weatherall, KBE
Vice-Marshal, P. Astley, LVO

MASTER OF THE HOUSEHOLD'S DEPARTMENT
Master of the Household, Maj.-Gen. Sir Simon
   Cooper, KCVO
Deputy Master of the Household, Lt.-Col. C.
   Richards
Superintendent, The Palace of Holyroodhouse,
   Lt.-Col. D. Anderson, OBE

ROYAL MEWS DEPARTMENT
Crown Equerry, Lt.-Col. S. Gilbart-Denham,
   CVO

THE ROYAL COLLECTION
Director of Royal Collection and Surveyor of The
   Queen's Works of Art, H. Roberts, CVO,
   FSA
Surveyor of The Queen's Pictures, C. Lloyd,
   LVO
Director of Media Affairs, R. Arbiter, LVO
Financial Director, M. Stevens

ROYAL COLLECTION ENTERPRISES LTD
Managing Director, M. E. K. Hewlett, LVO

THE QUEEN'S HOUSEHOLD IN SCOTLAND
*Hereditary Lord High Constable of Scotland,
   The Earl of Erroll
*Hereditary Master of the Household in
   Scotland, The Duke of Argyll
Lord Lyon King of Arms, Sir Malcolm Innes of
   Edingight, KCVO, WS
*Hereditary Banner-Bearer for Scotland, The
   Earl of Dundee
*Hereditary Bearer of the National Flag of
   Scotland, The Earl of Lauderdale
*Hereditary Keeper of the Palace of
   Holyroodhouse, The Duke of Hamilton and
   Brandon
*Governor of Edinburgh Castle, Maj.-Gen. R. D.
   S. Gordon, CBE

*Historiographer, Prof. T. C. Smout, CBE, FBA, FRSE, FSA Scot.
*Botanist, Prof. D. Henderson, CBE, FRSE
*Painter and Limner, vacant
*Sculptor in Ordinary, Prof. Sir Eduardo Paolozzi, CBE, RA
*Astronomer, Prof. J. Brown, Ph.D, FRSE
*Heralds and Pursuivants, see page 000

ECCLESIASTICAL HOUSEHOLD
*Dean of the Chapel Royal, Very Revd J. Harkness, CB, OBE
*Dean of the Order of the Thistle, Very Revd G. I. Macmillan, CVO
*Chaplains in Ordinary: 10
Domestic Chaplain, Balmoral, Revd R. P. Sloan

MEDICAL HOUSEHOLD
*Physicians in Scotland, P. Brunt, OBE, MD, FRCP; A. Toft, CBE, FRCPE
*Surgeons in Scotland, J. Engeset, FRCS; I. Macintyre
Apothecary to the Household at Balmoral, D. J. A. Glass
Apothecary to the Household at the Palace of Holyroodhouse, Dr J. Cormack, MD, FRCPE, FRCGP

*ROYAL COMPANY OF ARCHERS (QUEEN'S BODYGUARD FOR SCOTLAND)
Captain-General and Gold Stick for Scotland, Maj. Sir Hew Hamilton-Dalrymple, Bt., KCVO
President of the Council and Silver Stick for Scotland, The Duke of Buccleuch and Queensberry, KT, VRD
Adjutant, Maj. the Hon. Sir Lachlan Maclean, Bt., CVO
Secretary, Capt. J. D. B. Younger
Treasurer, J. M. Haldane of Gleneagles
Members on the active list: c.400

OTHER HONORARY APPOINTMENTS
Master of The Queen's Music, M. Williamson, CBE, AO
Poet Laureate (1999–2009), A. Motion

ROYAL SALUTES

Royal salutes are authorised at Edinburgh Castle and Stirling Castle, although in practice Edinburgh Castle is the only operating saluting station in Scotland.
A salute of 21 guns is fired on the following occasions:
(a) the anniversaries of the birth, accession and

coronation of The Queen
(b) the anniversary of the birth of HM Queen Elizabeth the Queen Mother
(c) the anniversary of the birth of HRH Prince Philip, Duke of Edinburgh
A salute of 21 guns is fired in Edinburgh on the occasion of the opening of the General Assembly of the Church of Scotland.
A salute of 21 guns may also be fired in Edinburgh on the arrival of HM The Queen, HM Queen Elizabeth the Queen Mother, or a member of the royal family who is a Royal Highness on an official visit.

THE ROYAL ARMS

SHIELD
1st and 4th quarters (representing Scotland) – Or, a lion rampant within a double tressure flory counterflory Gules
2nd quarter (representing England) – Gules, three lions passant guardant in pale Or
3rd quarter (representing Ireland) – Azure, a harp Or, stringed Argent
The whole shield is encircled with the Thistle

SUPPORTERS
Dexter (right) – a unicorn Argent, armed, crined, imperially crowned and unguled Or, gorged with a coronet composed of crosses patées and fleurs-de-lis, a chain affixed, passing between the forelegs, and reflexed

over the back
Sinister (left) – a lion rampant guardant Or,
imperially crowned

CREST
Upon an imperial crown Proper a lion sejant
affrontée Gules imperially crowned Or, holding
in the dexter paw a sword and in the sinister a
sceptre erect, also Proper

BADGE
A thistle, slipped and leaved proper

Flags bearing an earlier version of the royal arms
of Scotland – Or, a lion rampant Gules, armed
and langued Azure, within a double tressure flory
counter-flory of fleur-de-lis of the second – are
often flourished by supporters of the Scottish
team at football and rugby matches.

THE MOST ANCIENT AND MOST
NOBLE ORDER OF THE THISTLE

Postnominal initials, KT (Knights); LT (Ladies)
Ribbon, Green
Motto, Nemo me impune lacessit (No one
provokes me with impunity)

The Order of the Thistle is an exclusively
Scottish order of knighthood. There is evidence
of an order of chivalry in Scotland from at least
the Middle Ages; James II created an order of
knighthood in 1452, and James III (1460–88)
may also have created an order and certainly used
the thistle as the royal emblem. However, the
present Order of the Thistle was founded by
James VII and II in 1687, comprising the
sovereign and eight knights. Following James's
exile, the Order fell into abeyance until 1703
when it was revived by Queen Anne, who
increased the number of knights to 12; since 1827
the maximum number of knights has been 16.
Conferment of the Order also confers a
knighthood on the recipient.
    The Order's motto, Nemo me impune lacessit,
is the motto of all Scottish regiments; it is usually
translated into Scots as 'Wha daur meddle wi'
me?'.

SOVEREIGN OF THE ORDER
The Queen

ROYAL KNIGHTS AND LADY
HM Queen Elizabeth the Queen Mother, 1937
HRH The Prince Philip, Duke of Edinburgh,
  1952
HRH The Prince Charles, Duke of Rothesay,
  1977

KNIGHTS BRETHREN AND LADIES
The Earl of Wemyss and March, 1966
Sir Donald Cameron of Lochiel, 1973
The Duke of Buccleuch and Queensberry, 1978
The Earl of Elgin and Kincardine, 1981
The Lord Thomson of Monifieth, 1981
The Lord MacLehose of Beoch, 1983
The Earl of Airlie, 1985
Capt. Sir Iain Tennant, 1986
The Viscount Younger of Leckie, 1995
The Viscount of Arbuthnott, 1996
The Earl of Crawford and Balcarres, 1996
Lady Marion Fraser, 1996
The Lord Macfarlane of Bearsden, 1996
The Lord Mackay of Clashfern, 1997

Chancellor, The Duke of Buccleuch and
  Queensberry, KT, VRD
Dean, The Very Revd G. I. Macmillan, CVO
Secretary and Lord Lyon King of Arms, Sir
  Malcolm Innes of Edingight, KCVO, WS
Usher of the Green Rod, Rear-Adm. C. H.
  Layman, CB, DSO, LVO
Chapel, The Thistle Chapel, St Giles's Cathedral,
  Edinburgh

PRECEDENCE IN SCOTLAND

The Sovereign
The Prince Philip, Duke of Edinburgh
The Lord High Commissioner to the General
   Assembly of the Church of Scotland (while
   the Assembly is sitting)
The Duke of Rothesay (eldest son of the
   Sovereign)
The Sovereign's younger sons
The Sovereign's cousins
Lord-Lieutenants*
Lord Provosts of cities being *ex officio*
   Lord-Lieutenants of those cities*
Sheriffs Principal*
Lord Chancellor of Great Britain
Moderator of the General Assembly of the
   Church of Scotland
Keeper of the Great Seal (The First Minister)
Presiding Officer of the Scottish Parliament
Secretary of State for Scotland
Hereditary High Constable of Scotland
Hereditary Master of the Household
Dukes, according to their patent of creation:
   (1) of England
   (2) of Scotland
   (3) of Great Britain
   (4) of the United Kingdom
   (5) those of Ireland created since the Union
      between Great Britain and Ireland
Eldest sons of Dukes of the Blood Royal
Marquesses, according to their patent of creation:
   (1) of England
   (2) of Scotland
   (3) of Great Britain
   (4) of the United Kingdom
   (5) those of Ireland created since the Union
      between Great Britain and Ireland
Dukes' eldest sons
Earls, according to their patent of creation:
   (1) of England
   (2) of Scotland
   (3) of Great Britain
   (4) of the United Kingdom
   (5) those of Ireland created since the Union
      between Great Britain and Ireland
Younger sons of Dukes of Blood Royal
Marquesses' eldest sons
Dukes' younger sons
Lord Justice-General
Lord Clerk Register
Lord Advocate
Advocate-General
Lord Justice-Clerk
Viscounts, according to their patent of creation

(1) of England
(2) of Scotland
(3) of Great Britain
(4) of the United Kingdom
(5) those of Ireland created since the Union
   between Great Britain and Ireland
Earls' eldest sons
Marquesses' younger sons
Lord-Barons, according to their patent of
   creation:
   (1) of England
   (2) of Scotland
   (3) of Great Britain
   (4) of the United Kingdom
   (5) those of Ireland created since the Union
      between Great Britain and Ireland
Viscounts' eldest sons
Earls' younger sons
Lord-Barons' eldest sons
Knights of the Garter
Knights of the Thistle
Privy Counsellors
Senators of College of Justice (Lords of Session)
Viscounts' younger sons
Lord-Barons' younger sons
Sons of Life Peers
Baronets
Knights Grand Cross of the Order of the Bath
Knights Grand Commanders of the Order of the
   Star of India
Knights Grand Cross of the Order of St Michael
   and St George
Knights Grand Commanders of the Order of the
   Indian Empire
Knights Grand Cross of the Royal Victorian
   Order
Knights Commanders of the Order of the Bath
Knights Commanders of the Order of the Star of
   India
Knights Commanders of the Order of St Michael
   and St George
Knights Commanders of the Order of the Indian
   Empire
Knights Commanders of the Royal Victorian
   Order
Solicitor-General for Scotland
Lyon King of Arms
Sheriffs Principal, except as shown above
Knights Bachelor
Sheriffs
Commanders of the Royal Victorian Order
Companions of the Order of the Bath
Companions of the Order of the Star of India
Companions of the Order of St Michael and St
   George
Companions of the Order of the Indian Empire

Lieutenants of the Royal Victorian Order
Companions of the Distinguished Service Order
Eldest sons of younger sons of Peers
Baronets' eldest sons
Knights' eldest sons, in the same order as their
     fathers
Members of the Royal Victorian Order
Baronets' younger sons
Knights' younger sons, in the same order as their
     fathers
Queen's Counsel
Esquires
Gentlemen

* *During term of office and within their own
counties/cities/sheriffdoms*

FORMS OF ADDRESS

It is only possible to cover here the forms of address for peers, baronets and knights, their wife and children, Privy Counsellors, and holders of certain political, legal and civic posts; for chiefs of clans, see pages 256 and 261. Greater detail should be sought in one of the publications devoted to the subject.

Both formal and social forms of address are given where usage differs; nowadays, the social form is generally preferred to the formal, which increasingly is used only for official documents and on very formal occasions.

The form of address for a woman holding office is given if different from that of a man holding the same position, but only where a woman holds or has held that particular office, as new styles tend to be adopted only when circumstances require it.

F – represents forename
S – represents surname
D – represents a designation, e.g. a title (peer) or city (convenor)

BARON
see Lord of Parliament

BARON'S WIFE
see Lord of Parliament's wife

BARON'S CHILDREN
see Lord of Parliament's children

BARONESS IN OWN RIGHT
see Lady of Parliament in own right

BARONESS (WOMAN LIFE PEER)
Envelope, may be addressed in same way as for a Lord of Parliament's wife, or, if she prefers (formal), The Right Hon. the Baroness D – ; (social), The Baroness D –
Letter (formal), My Lady; (social), Dear Lady D –
Spoken, Lady D –

BARONET
Envelope, Sir F – S – , Bt.
Letter (formal), Dear Sir; (social), Dear Sir F –
Spoken, Sir F –

BARONET'S WIFE
Envelope, Lady S –
Letter (formal), Dear Madam; (social), Dear Lady S–
Spoken, Lady S –

CHAIRMAN OF SCOTTISH LAND COURT
As for Lords of Session

CONVENER OF COUNCIL
Envelope, The Convener of D –
Letter, Dear Convener
Spoken, Convener

COUNTESS IN OWN RIGHT
As for an Earl's wife

COURTESY TITLES
The heir apparent to a Duke, Marquess or Earl uses the highest of his father's other titles as a courtesy title. The holder of a courtesy title is not styled The Most Hon. or The Right Hon., and in correspondence 'The' is omitted before the title. The heir apparent to a Scottish title may use the title 'Master'.

DAME
Envelope, Dame F – S – , followed by appropriate post-nominal letters
Letter (formal), Dear Madam; (social), Dear Dame F –
Spoken, Dame F –

DUKE
Envelope (formal), His Grace the Duke of D – ; (social), The Duke of D –
Letter (formal), My Lord Duke; (social), Dear Duke
Spoken (formal), Your Grace; (social), Duke

DUKE'S WIFE
Envelope (formal), Her Grace the Duchess of D – ; (social), The Duchess of D –
Letter (formal), Dear Madam; (social), Dear Duchess
Spoken, Duchess

DUKE'S ELDEST SON
see Courtesy titles

DUKE'S YOUNGER SONS
Envelope, Lord F – S –
Letter (formal), My Lord; (social), Dear Lord F –
Spoken (formal), My Lord; (social), Lord F –

DUKE'S DAUGHTER
Envelope, Lady F – S –
Letter (formal), Dear Madam; (social), Dear Lady F –
Spoken, Lady F –

EARL
Envelope (formal), The Right Hon. the Earl (of) D – ; (social), The Earl (of) D –
Letter (formal), My Lord; (social), Dear Lord D –
Spoken (formal), My Lord; (social), Lord D –

EARL'S WIFE
Envelope (formal), The Right Hon. the Countess (of) D – ; (social), The Countess (of) D –
Letter (formal), Madam; (social), Lady D –
Spoken (formal), Madam; (social), Lady D –

EARL'S CHILDREN
Eldest son, *see* Courtesy titles
Younger sons, The Hon. F – S – (for forms of address, *see* Lord of Parliament's children)
Daughters, Lady F – S – (for forms of address, *see* Duke's daughter)

KNIGHT (BACHELOR)
Envelope, Sir F – S –
Letter (formal), Dear Sir; (social), Dear Sir F –
Spoken, Sir F –

KNIGHT (ORDERS OF CHIVALRY)
Envelope, Sir F – S – , followed by appropriate post-nominal letters. Otherwise as for Knight Bachelor

KNIGHT'S WIFE
As for Baronet's wife

LADY OF PARLIAMENT IN OWN RIGHT
As for Lord of Parliament's wife

LIFE PEER
As for Lord of Parliament/Baroness in own right

LIFE PEER'S WIFE
As for Lord of Parliament's wife

LIFE PEER'S CHILDREN
As for Lord of Parliament's children

LORD ADVOCATE
Usually admitted a member of the Privy Council on appointment.
Envelope, The Right (Rt.) Hon. the Lord Advocate, or The Right (Rt.) Hon. F – S –
Letter (formal), My Lord (if a peer), or Dear Sir; (social), Dear Lord Advocate, or Dear Lord D – /Mr S –
Spoken, Lord D – /Mr S –

LORD HIGH COMMISSIONER TO THE GENERAL ASSEMBLY
Envelope, His/Her Grace the Lord High Commissioner
Letter, Your Grace
Spoken, Your Grace

LORD JUSTICE-CLERK
Envelope, The Hon. the Lord Justice-Clerk; if a Privy Counsellor, The Right (Rt.) Hon. the Lord Justice-Clerk
Letter (formal), My Lord; (social), Dear Lord Justice-Clerk
Spoken (formal), My Lord; (social), Lord Justice-Clerk

LORD JUSTICE-GENERAL
Usually admitted a member of the Privy Council on appointment
Envelope, The Right (Rt.) Hon. the Lord Justice-General
Letter (formal), My Lord; (social), Dear Lord Justice-General
Spoken (formal), My Lord; (social), Lord Justice-General

LORD OF PARLIAMENT
Envelope (formal), The Right Hon. Lord D – ; (social), The Lord D –
Letter (formal), My Lord; (social), Dear Lord D –
Spoken, Lord D –

LORD OF PARLIAMENT'S WIFE
Envelope (formal), The Right Hon. Lady D – ; (social), The Lady D –
Letter (formal), My Lady; (social), Dear Lady D –
Spoken, Lady D –

LORD OF PARLIAMENT'S CHILDREN
Envelope, The Hon. F – S –
Letter, Dear Mr/Miss/Mrs S –
Spoken, Mr/Miss/Mrs S –

LORD/LADY OF SESSION
Envelope, The Hon. Lord/Lady D – ; if a Privy Counsellor, The Right (Rt.) Hon. Lord/Lady D –
Letter (formal), My Lord/Lady; (social), Dear Lord/Lady D –
Spoken (formal), My Lord/Lady; (social), Lord/Lady D –

LORD OF SESSION'S WIFE
As for the wife of a Lord of Parliament, except that there is no prefix before 'Lady'

LORD PROVOSTS — ABERDEEN AND DUNDEE
Envelope, The Lord Provost of Aberdeen/Dundee
Letter (formal), My Lord Provost; (social), Dear Lord Provost
Spoken, My Lord Provost

LORD PROVOSTS — EDINBURGH AND GLASGOW
Envelope, The Right (Rt.) Hon. the Lord Provost of Edinburgh/Glasgow; or (Edinburgh only) The Right (Rt.) Hon. F – S – , Lord Provost of Edinburgh
Letter (formal), My Lord Provost; (social), Dear Lord Provost
Spoken, My Lord Provost

LORD PROVOST'S WIFE/CONSORT
Envelope, The Lady Provost of D – (may be followed by her name)
Letter (formal), My Lady Provost; (social), Dear Lady Provost
Spoken, My Lady Provost/ Lady Provost

MARQUESS
Envelope (formal), The Most Hon. the Marquess of D – ; (social), The Marquess of D –
Letter (formal), My Lord; (social), Dear Lord D –
Spoken (formal), My Lord; (social), Lord D –

MARQUESS'S WIFE
Envelope (formal), The Most Hon. the Marchioness of D – ; (social), The Marchioness of D –
Letter (formal), Madam; (social), Dear Lady D –
Spoken, Lady D –

MARQUESS'S CHILDREN
Eldest son, *see* Courtesy titles
Younger sons, Lord F – S – (for forms of address, *see* Duke's younger sons)
Daughters, Lady F – S – (for forms of address, *see* Duke's daughter)

MARQUIS
see Marquess; 'Marquis' is sometimes used for titles predating the Union

MASTER
The title is used by the heir apparent to a Scottish peerage, though usually the heir apparent to a Duke, Marquess or Earl uses his courtesy title rather than 'Master'.
Envelope, The Master of D –
Letter (formal), Dear Sir; (social), Dear Master of D –
Spoken (formal), Master, or Sir; (social), Master, or Mr S –

MASTER'S WIFE
Addressed as for the wife of the appropriate peerage style, otherwise as Mrs S –

MEMBER OF SCOTTISH PARLIAMENT
Envelope, Mr/Miss/Mrs S – , MSP
Letter, Dear Mr/Miss/Mrs S –
Spoken, Mr/Miss/Mrs S –

MODERATOR OF THE GENERAL ASSEMBLY
Envelope, The Rt. Revd the Moderator of the General Assembly of the Church of Scotland
Letter (formal), Dear Moderator/Dear Sir; (social), Dear Dr/Mr S – /Dear Moderator
Spoken, Moderator
After their year in office, former Moderators are styled The Very Reverend

PRESIDING OFFICER
Style/title used before the Scottish Parliament elections, e.g. if a minister is a privy counsellor, he is styled Rt. Hon.
Envelope (ministerial business), addressed by his appointment; (personal), Sir F – /Mr/ Miss/Mrs S – , The Presiding Officer
Letter, Dear Sir F – /Mr/Miss/Mrs S –
Spoken, addressed by his appointment or name

PRIVY COUNSELLOR
Envelope, The Right (or Rt.) Hon. F – S –
Letter, Dear Mr/Miss/Mrs S –
Spoken, Mr/Miss/Mrs S –
It is incorrect to use the letters PC after the name in conjunction with the prefix The Right Hon., unless the Privy Counsellor is a peer below the rank of Marquess and so is styled The Right Hon. because of his rank. In this case only, the post-nominal letters may be used in conjunction with the prefix The Right Hon.

PROVOST
Envelope, The Provost of D – , or F – S – , Esq., Provost of D – /Mrs F – S – , Provost of D –
Letter, Dear Provost
Spoken, Provost

SCOTTISH MINISTER
Style/title used before the Scottish Parliament elections, e.g. if a minister is a privy counsellor, he/she is styled Rt. Hon.

Envelope (ministerial business), minister addressed by his/her appointment; (personal), Mr/Miss/Mrs S – , followed by the minister's appointment

Letter, Dear Mr/Miss/Mrs S –

Spoken, addressed by his/her appointment or name

SHERIFF PRINCIPAL AND SHERIFF
Envelope, Sheriff F – S –

Letter, Dear Sheriff S –

Spoken (formal), My Lord/Lady (in court); (social), Sheriff S –

VISCOUNT
Envelope (formal), The Right Hon. the Viscount D – ; (social), The Viscount D –

Letter (formal), My Lord; (social), Dear Lord D –

Spoken, Lord D –

VISCOUNT'S WIFE
Envelope (formal), The Right Hon. the Viscountess D – ; (social), The Viscountess D –

Letter (formal), Madam; (social), Dear Lady D –

Spoken, Lady D –

VISCOUNT'S CHILDREN
As for Lord of Parliament's children

Chiefs of Clans and Names
As there are a number of different styles for chiefs of clans and names, forms of address vary widely. Male chiefs are styled by their designation or estate rather than their surname; 'Esquire' is not added. A female chief is styled Madam or Mrs/Miss (according to her preference) in addition to her estate. Envelope, chief's designation

Letter (formal), Dear Chief (if writer is a member of the clan or name); Dear Sir/Madam; (social), 'Dear' followed by chief's designation

CHIEF'S WIFE
As for her husband, with the addition of 'Mrs'.

CHIEF'S HEIR APPARENT
As for the chief, with the addition of 'younger' (yr), e.g.

F – S – of D – , yr

F – S – , yr. of D –

HISTORIC BUILDINGS AND MONUMENTS

Scotland is rich in buildings of historical and architectural value. They date from all periods from the Middle Ages to the 20th-century, and include castles, strongholds and keeps, palaces, tower houses, historic houses and mansions, churches, cathedrals, chapels, abbeys and priories, formal gardens, industrial buildings and military installations.

There are about 2,000 castles and towers in Scotland. Among the oldest castles still visible are Castle Sween, in Knapdale, Argyll, whose oldest parts may date from the 11th-century, and Cubbie Roo's Castle, built in 1145 by the Norseman Kolbein Hruga on the island of Wyre, Orkney, where there is also a later twelfth-century chapel. Dunvegan Castle in Skye is the oldest continuously inhabited castle in Scotland, having been occupied by the MacLeods for 700 years, although its present appearance is the result of massive 19th-century remodelling. Many castles were subject to frequent rebuilding over the centuries, and new castles were still being built as late as the nineteenth-century, the most famous example being Balmoral, built in 1855 for Prince Albert. The north-east of Scotland is particularly rich in castles, and the Aberdeen and Grampian Tourist Board together with the Scottish Tourist Board promote exploration of this heritage by sign-posting a Castle Trail in the region.

Tower houses, which became popular from the 15th-century and were the major form of secular building in the sixteenth, were a peculiarly (though not exclusively) Scottish type of fortified dwelling for the local nobility. Good examples are Claypotts Castle, near Dundee, and Craigievar and Crathes Castles, Aberdeenshire.

Ecclesiastical buildings have an equally long and chequered history and many of the oldest buildings, such as St Ninian's Chapel, Isle of Whithorn, and the abbey buildings on the island of Iona, replace even earlier structures. The ruined Orphir church near Kirkwall, Orkney, is Scotland's only surviving round church, probably dating from before 1122. The monastery foundations of King Alexander I (reigned 1107–24) and his brother David I (1124-53) resulted in the building of St Margaret's Chapel in Edinburgh Castle, Inchcolm Abbey, on a small island in the Firth of Forth, and a string of great abbeys in the Borders (Dryburgh, Jedburgh, Melrose, Kelso, Sweetheart, Glenluce, etc.) in the twelfth and thirteenth centuries. The Border abbeys suffered severely in the conflicts of the 14th-century, however, and much of what is visible today reflects fifteenth-century rebuilding.

Scotland's built heritage from later centuries spans a wide variety of structures. From the late seventeenth and eighteenth centuries there are great houses such as Hopetoun House, Edinburgh, Duff House, Banff, and other buildings by William and Robert Adam, and the military bridges built by General Wade in the Highlands. The Industrial Revolution produced mills, factories, built harbours and shipyards, and the unique industrial village of New Lanark, purpose-built in 1785 as a cotton-manufacturing centre and made famous by the social ideas of Robert Owen in the 1820s. From the early 20th-century, the Hill House, Helensburgh, is a fine example of the work of Charles Rennie Mackintosh, Scotland's best-known architect. Coming almost up to the present day, the state of military structures around the Scottish coasts from both world wars is the subject of a recent review by Historic Scotland.

Under the Planning (Listed Buildings and Conservation Areas) (Scotland) Act 1997 and the Ancient Monuments and Archaeological Areas Act 1979, the Scottish Executive is responsible for listing buildings and scheduling monuments in Scotland on the advice of Historic Scotland, the Historic Buildings Council for Scotland and the Ancient Monuments Board for Scotland .

Listed buildings are classified into Grade A, Grade B and Grade C. All buildings of interest erected before 1840 which are in use and are still largely in their original condition, are listed. More recent buildings are selected according to their individual character and quality. The main purpose of listing is to ensure that care is taken in deciding the future of a building. No changes which affect the architectural or historic character of a listed building can be made without listed building consent (in addition to planning permission where relevant). It is a criminal offence to demolish a listed building, or alter it in such a way as to affect its character, without consent. There are currently about 44,462 listed buildings in Scotland.

All monuments proposed for scheduling are considered to be of national importance. Where buildings are both scheduled and listed, ancient monuments legislation takes precedence. The main purpose of scheduling a monument is to preserve it for the future and to protect it from damage, destruction or any unnecessary interference. Once a monument has been scheduled, scheduled monument consent is required before any works are carried out. The scope of the control is more extensive and more detailed than that applied to listed buildings, but certain minor works may be carried out without consent. It is a criminal offence to carry out unauthorised work to scheduled monuments. There are currently about 7,035 scheduled monuments in Scotland, but the full number of buildings which meet scheduling standards is probably twice this. Both scheduling and listing are ongoing processes.

Whereas most listed buildings are currently in use or could be returned to use (even if it is not their original use), monuments that are scheduled have usually fallen into disuse and are unlikely to be used again in anything like their original form. In fact, a structure used as a dwelling house or in ecclesiastical use cannot be scheduled. Thus houses, bridges, factories, public buildings, war memorials and so on are more likely to be listed than scheduled, and terms of public access differ from those of access to scheduled monuments. The Forth Bridge, for instance, is a listed building – the largest in Scotland – and so are some traditional blue police boxes and red telephone boxes.

Historic Scotland, the government agency responsible for scheduling and listing, has around 330 monuments in its care. It provides financial assistance to financial assistance to private owners towards the costs of conserving and repairing important monuments and buildings. It also undertakes research into building conservation and published educational material on Scotland's built heritage.

The National Trust for Scotland, an independent trust, also cares for many castles, historic buildings and sites. A number of councils also care for historic buildings, while others are privately owned or cared for by independent conservation trusts.

OPENING TO THE PUBLIC

The following is a selection of the many historic buildings and monuments open to the public. Opening hours vary. Many properties are closed in winter and some are also closed in the mornings. Most properties are closed on Christmas Eve, Christmas Day, Boxing Day and New Year's Day, and many are closed on Good Friday. Information about a specific property should be checked by telephone.

Closed in winter (usually October to March)
†*Closed in winter, and in mornings in summer*
HS Historic Scotland property
NTS National Trust for Scotland property

Abbot House, Dunfermline. Tel: 01383-733266. Dates from 16th-century. Owners have included Anne of Denmark, wife of James VI

***Abbotsford House,** Melrose, Borders. Tel: 01896-752043. Sir Walter Scott's house

Aberdour Castle (HS), Aberdour, Burntisland, Fife. Tel: 01383-860519. Closed Sun. mornings, Thurs. afternoons, and Fri. in winter. A 14th-century castle built by the Douglas family

Abernethy Round Tower (HS), nr Perth. Site of a Culdee Celtic Christian establishment. Built by the Culdees in 9th-or 10th-century, one of only two examples in Scotland

†**Aikwood Tower,** nr Selkirk, Borders. Open Apr. - Sep., only Tues., Thurs. and Sun. afternoons. Tel: 01750-52253. A 16th-century fortified tower house. Home of Sir David Steel

***Alloa Tower (NTS),** Alloa. Tel: 01259-211701. Closed mornings. Ancestral home of Earls of Mar for 400 years

Arbroath Abbey (HS), Arbroath, Angus. Tel: 01241-878756. Site of Declaration of Arbroath 1320. Founded 1178, completed 1233, granted abbey status 1285

Ardchattan Priory (HS), Loch Etive, nr Oban. Ruins of a Valliscaulian priory founded 1231 by Duncan MacDougall. Burnt by Cromwell's troops in 1654

Argyll's Lodging (HS), Stirling. Tel: 01786-461146. Fine example of a 17th-century town residence. Built by Sir William Alexander of Menstrie, first Earl of Stirling

***Armadale Castle,** Ardvasar, Skye. Tel: 01471-844227. The seat of the Macdonalds since 1790

†**Arniston House,** Gorebridge. Tel: 01875-830515. Open Jul. - Sep. on Sun., Tues. and Thurs. afternoons only. Designed by William Adam for Robert Dundas, judge who dented the Campbell monopoly of Scottish patronage

†**Ayton Castle,** Eyemouth, Berwickshire. Tel: 01890 781212. Neo-baronial red sandstone castle built 1845-8

†**Balfour Castle,** Shapinsay, Orkney. Tel: 01865-711282. Completed 1848 by the Balfour family of Westray

Balgonie Castle, nr Glenrothes. Tel: 01592-750119. 14th-century keep and courtyard. Occupied by Rob Roy and 200 clansmen in 1716

Balhousie Castle, Perth. Tel: 01738-621281. Neo-baronial mansion of 1862, built for the Earl of Kinnoull

Ballindalloch Castle, Bridge of Avon, Aberlour. Tel: 01807–500206. Begun 1546, historically a Grant seat

Balmerino Abbey (NTS), Balmerino, nr Leuchars. Remains of a Cistercian abbey founded 1229 by Alexander II and built by the religious house of Melrose

Balmoral Castle, nr Braemar. Tel: 013397-42334. Open mid-April to end July. Baronial-style castle built for Victoria and Albert. The Queen's private residence

Balvaird Castle (HS), Balvaird, Abernethy. Tel: 0131-668 8800. Tower house on the Ochil Hills. Built 1500 by Sir Andrew Murray

*Balvenie Castle (HS), Dufftown, Keith, Banffshire. Tel: 01340-820121. 13th-century castle owned by the Comyns

*Barcaldine Castle, Peninsula of Benderloch. Tel: 01631 720598. Early 17th century Campbell tower house

*Barrie's Birthplace (NTS), Kirriemuir. Birthplace of author of Peter Pan, J.M. Barrie

Beauly Priory (HS), Beauly. Ruins of priory founded 1230 by the Bisset family for the Valliscaulian order, later Cistercian

*The Binns (NTS), nr Linlithgow. Closed Fridays. Castellated mansion built between 1612 and 1630. Originally property of the Livingstones of Kilsyth but sold to the Dalziels

*Bishop's and Earl's Palaces (HS), Kirkwall, Orkney. Tel: 01856-871918. A 12th-century hall-house and an early 17th-century palace

Black House, Arnol (HS), Lewis, Western Isles. Tel: 01851-710395. Closed Sun.; also Fri. in winter. Traditional Lewis thatched house

Blackness Castle (HS), nr Linlithgow, W. Lothian. Tel: 01506-834807. Following the Treaty of Union 1707, one of only four castles in Scotland to be garrisoned

*Blair Castle, Blair Atholl. Tel: 01796-481207. Mid 18th-century mansion with 13th-century tower; seat of the Dukes of Atholl

*Bod of Germista, Lerwick, Shetland. Closed Mon. and Tues. Birthplace of Arthur Anderson, first MP of Shetland

*Bonawe Iron Furnace (HS), Argyll and Bute. Tel: 01866-822432. Charcoal-fuelled ironworks founded in 1753

Bothwell Castle (HS), Uddingston, Glasgow. Tel: 01698-816894. Closed Sun. mornings, Thurs. afternoons, and Fri. in winter. Largest 13th-century castle in Scotland. Built by Moray family as protection against Edward I of England

†Bowhill, Selkirk. Tel: 01750-22204. House open July only; grounds open April–une, Aug. except Fri., daily in July. Seat of the Dukes of Buccleuch and Queensberry; fine collection of paintings, including portrait miniatures. Includes Newark Castle, a ruined 15th-century keep and courtyard within grounds of Bowhill

*Braemar Castle, Braemar. Closed Fridays. Tel: 01339-741219. Built 1628 by John Erskine, Earl of Mar. Used as a garrison following Jacobite rising

Brechin Cathedral, Brechin. Religious building here since 900 AD. Current building restored 1900-2. Adjacent 11th-century round tower, one of only two which survive in Scotland

*Brodick Castle (NTS), Isle of Arran. Tel: 01770-302202. Gardens open all year. Site of the ancient seat of the Dukes of Hamilton

*Brodie Castle (NTS), Forres, Moray. Tel: 01309-641371; Grounds open all year. A 16th-century castle with later additions

Brough of Birsay (HS), Orkney. Remains of Norse church and village on the tidal island of Birsay

†Broughton House (NTS), Kirkcudbright, Galloway. Tel: 01557-330437. Home of Edward Hornel, member of late 19th century Scottish art establishment. Japanese garden

Broughty Castle (HS), Broughty Ferry, Dundee. Tel: 01382 76121. Tower house built around 1454 to guard the Firth of Tay

Burleigh Castle (HS), Milnathort. Tel: 0131-668 8800. Red-sandstone tower built around 1500. Home of the Balfours of Burleigh.

Burns Cottage and Museum, Alloway, Ayrshire. Tel: 01292-441215. Birthplace of Robert Burns

Caerlaverock Castle (HS), nr Dumfries. Tel: 01387-770244. Fine early classical Renaissance building. Built c.1270

Callendar House, Falkirk. Closed Sun. mornings Tel: 01324 503770. Large ornate mansion of 1870s incorporating towers and turrets of a 14th and 15th-century castle

*Cambuskenneth Abbey, (HS) Stirling. Grounds open all year. Ruins of 12th-century abbey founded by David I on site of an Augustinian settlement

*Cardoness Castle (HS), Gatehouse of Fleet. Closed Sun. mornings Tel: 01557-814427. Late 15th-century stronghold

*Carlyle's Birthplace (NTS), Ecclefechan, Lockerbie, Dumfriesshire. Tel: 01576-300666. Closed October - April and Saturday mornings. Birthplace of Thomas Carlyle

Carnasserie Castle (HS), nr Kilmartin. Tel: 0131-668 8800. Built by John Corsewell in 1560s, who published first ever book in Gaelic, *Knox's Liturgy*, 1567

Carrick House, Eday, Orkney. Tel: 01857-622260. Built by Laird of Eday, 1633. Associated with pirate John Gow, on whom Sir Walter Scott's *The Pirate* is based

Carsluith Castle (HS), Carsluith, Creetown. Tel: 0131-668 8800. 16th-century tower house built by Richard Brown. Abandoned 1748

Castle Campbell (HS) (NTS), Dollar Glen, nr Stirling. Tel: 01259-742408. Closed Sun. mornings, Thurs. afternoons, and Fri. in winter. A 15th-century castle with parapet walk. John Knox preached here in 1556

***Castle Fraser (NTS),** Sauchen, Inverurie, Aberdeenshire. Tel: 01330-833463. Garden and grounds open all year. Castle built between 1575 and 1636

Castle Menzies, nr Aberfeldy. Tel: 01887-820982. Closed Sun. mornings. A 16th-century tower house. Occupied by Oliver Cromwell's force in 1650s

Castle of Old Wick (HS), Wick. Tel: 0131-668 8800. Ruins of one of oldest castles in Scotland. Built 12th-century, when this part of Scotland was ruled from Orkney by the Norsemen

***Castle Stalker,** nr Port Appin. Open by appointment. Tel: 01631-730234. Built on tiny rock island by the Stewarts of Appin in 16th-century and gifted to King James IV

***Castle Stuart,** Petty. Tel: 01463-790745. Built between 1621–5 by James Stuart, 3rd Earl of Moray. Visited by Bonny Prince Charlie prior to Culloden

Castle Sween, (HS) Kilmichael. Tel: 0131-668 8800. Ruins of 11th-century castle. Earliest stone castle in Scotland

***Cawdor Castle, (HS)** Inverness. Tel: 01667-404615. A 14th-century keep with 15th- and 17th-century additions. Setting of Shakespeare's *Macbeth*

***Claypotts Castle, (HS)** Broughty Ferry. Open only Sat. and Sun., July–Sept. Tel: 01786-450000. Z-shaped tower house built 1569–88 for the Strachans, then the Grahams

Corgarff Castle (HS), Strathdon, Aberdeenshire. Tel: 01975-651460. Closed weekdays in winter. Former 16th-century tower house converted into barracks

†**Craigievar Castle (NTS),** nr Alford. Tel: 01339-883635. Built by a Baltic trader, 'Willy the Merchant', in 1626

Craigmillar Castle (HS), Edinburgh. Tel: 0131-661 4445. Closed Sun. mornings, Thurs. afternoons, and Fri. in winter. Where the murder of Lord Darnley, second husband of Mary Queen of Scots, was plotted

***Craignethan Castle (HS),** nr Lanark. Tel: 01555-860364. Castle dating from the 16th century, with Britain's only stone vaulted artillery chamber. Last major castle built in Scotland

***Crathes Castle (NTS),** nr Banchory. Tel: 01330-844525. Garden and grounds open all year. A 16th-century baronial castle in woodland, fields and gardens

***Crichton Castle (HS),** nr Pathhead, Midlothian. Tel: 01875-320017. Castle with Italian-style faceted stonework facade

Crookston Castle (NTS), Pollok, Glasgow. Tel: 0141-226 4826. Built 12th-century by Robert de Croc. Visited by Mary, Queen of Scots. Became first property of NTS, in 1931

Cross Kirk (HS), Peebles. Ruins of Trinitarian Friary founded 1474, dedicated to St Nicholas

***Crossraguel Abbey (HS),** nr Maybole, Ayrshire. Tel: 01655-883113. Remains of 13th-century abbey

Culross Abbey (HS), Culross. Remains of Cistercian abbey founded 1217 by Malcolm, Earl of Fife

***Culross Palace,** Town House and Study (NTS), Culross, Dunfermline. Tel: 01383-880359. Town House and Study closed mornings. Refurbished 16th and 17th-century buildings

***Culzean Castle (NTS),** S. Ayrshire. Tel: 01655-760274. Country park open all year. An 18th-century Adam castle with oval staircase and circular saloon

†**Dalmeny House,** South Queensferry, Edinburgh. Open only July-August, Mon., Tue. and Sun. afternoons. Tel: 0131-331 1888 Seat of the Earls of Rosebery

***Darnaway Castle,** Darnaway, Forres. Open only July-Aug. Tel: 01309-641469. Now a gothic mansion of 1802–12. Original castle acquired by the Stuarts in 1562

Dean Castle, Kilmarnock. Tel: 01563-522702. Keep dates from 1350. Castle burnt 1735, now restored. Originally owned by the Boyd family

***Delgatie Castle,** Delgatie, Turriff. Tel: 01888-562750. Original castle dates to 1030, current building 1570. Taken from Earl of Buchan 1314 and granted to the Hays

Dirleton Castle (HS), Dirleton, North Berwick, E. Lothian. Tel: 01620-850330. Twelfth-century castle with 16th-century gardens

Dornoch Cathedral, Dornoch. Founded 1224. Cathedral of Bishops of Caithness. Restored 19th-century

Doune Castle (HS), Doune, Perthshire. Tel: 01786-841742. Closed Sun. mornings, Thurs. afternoons, and Fri. in winter. A 14th-century castle built for the Regent Albany

†**Drum Castle (NTS),** Drumoak, by Banchory, Aberdeenshire. Tel: 01330-811204. Grounds open all year. Late 13th-century tower house

Drumcoltran Tower (HS), Dalbeattie. Tel: 0131–668 8800. Built around 1550 for the Maxwell family. Still inhabited in 1890s

*****Drumlanrig Castle,** nr Thornhill, Dumfriesshire. Open May-August only. Tel: 01848 330248. A 17th-century courtyard mansion. Home of Duke of Buccleuch and Queensberry

*****Drumlanrig's Tower,** Hawick, Borders. Closed Sun. mornings. Tel: 01450–372457. Only building left unburnt after burning of Hawick by English in 1570

Dryburgh Abbey (HS), Scottish Borders. Tel: 01835-822381. Closed Sun. mornings in winter. A 12th-century abbey containing tomb of Sir Walter Scott

*****Duart Castle,** nr Craignure, Mull. Tel: 01680-812309. Headquarters of MacLean Clan from 13th century

Duff House (HS), Banff. Tel: 01261-818181. Closed Mon.–Wed. in winter. Georgian mansion housing part of National Galleries of Scotland collection. Built by William Adam

Duffus Castle (HS), Old Duffus, Elgin. Tel: 0131-668 8800. Dates in part to 1151. Originally a royal stronghold. Abandoned in late 17th-century

Dumbarton Castle (HS), Dumbarton. Tel: 01389-732167. Closed Sun. mornings, Thurs. afternoons, and Fri. in winter. Castle overlooking River Clyde. A royal seat from where Mary, Queen of Scots sailed to France in 1548

Dunblane Cathedral (HS), Dunblane. Closed Sun. mornings. Tel: 01786-823338. Dates from 13th-century, in Gothic style

*****Dundonald Castle (HS),** Dundonald, Kilmarnock, Ayrshire. Tel: 01563-851489. Castle built by the Stewart royal dynasty

Dundrennan Abbey (HS), nr Kirkcudbright. Tel: 01557-500262. Closed weekdays in winter. Remote 12th-century abbey. Where Mary, Queen of Scots spent her last night on Scottish soil

Dunfermline Palace and Abbey (HS), Dunfermline, Fife. Tel: 01383-739026. Closed Sun. mornings, Thurs. afternoons, and Fri. in winter. Remains of palace and Benedictine abbey

Dunnottar Castle, Stonehaven. Closed Sun. mornings and weekends November-Easter. Tel: 01569–762173. A 12th to 17th-century fortress on a sheer cliff jutting into the sea. One of Scotland's finest ruined castles

*****Dunrobin Castle,** Golspie, Sutherland. Tel: 01408-633177. Closed Sun. mornings. The most northerly of Scotland's great castles, seat of the Earls of Sutherland

Dunstaffnage Castle and Chapel (HS), nr Oban. Tel: 01631-562465. Closed Sun. mornings, Thurs. afternoons, and Fri. in winter. Fine 13th-century castle, briefly the prison of Flora Macdonald

*****Dunvegan Castle,** Skye. Tel: 01470-521206. A 13th-century castle with later additions; home of the chiefs of the Clan MacLeod; trips to seal colony

Earl's Palace (HS), Birsay, Orkney. Ruins of 16th-century courtyard castle, started by Robert Stewart, Earl of Orkney

*****Earl's Palace (HS),** Kirkwall, Orkney. Tel: 01856-875461. Ruins of 17th-century palace, built by Patrick Stewart, Earl of Orkney, illegitimate half-brother of Mary Queen of Scots

Edinburgh Castle (HS). Tel: 0131-225 9846. Includes the Scottish National War Memorial, Scottish United Services Museum and historic apartments

Edzell Castle (HS), nr Brechin. Tel: 01356-648631. Closed Sun. mornings, Thurs. afternoons and Fri. in winter. Medieval tower house; unique walled garden. Gardens by Sir David Lindsay in 1604

*****Eilean Donan Castle,** Wester Ross. Tel: 01599-555202. A 13th-century castle with Jacobite relics. Established by Alexander II to protect the area from the vikings

*****Elcho Castle (HS),** nr Perth. Tel: 01738-639998. 16th-century fortified mansion

Elgin Cathedral (HS), Moray. Tel: 01343-547171. Closed Sun. mornings, Thurs. afternoons and Fri. in winter. A 13th-century cathedral with fine chapterhouse

*****Falkland Palace (NTS),** Falkland, Cupar, Fife. Tel: 01337-857397. Country residence of the Stewart kings and queens, built between 1502 and 1541

*****Fasque House,** nr Fettercairn. Tel: 01561-340202. Family home of Prime Minister William Gladstone 1789-1809

***Fearn Abbey,** Fearn. Open May-Sep. Sat. and Sun. only. A 14th-century church, one of the oldest pre-Reformation Scottish churches still used for worship

†**Finlaystone House,** nr Port Glasgow. Only open Sun. afternoons April–August. Tel: 01475-540285. Mansion dating from 1760, incorporating 15th-century castle of the Cunningham Earls of Glencairn, where John Knox preached in 1556

***Floors Castle,** Kelso. Tel: 01573-223333. Largest inhabited castle in Scotland; seat of the Dukes of Roxburghe

Fort Charlotte, Lerwick, Shetland. Begun by Charles II in 1665 during war against Dutch. Named in honour of George III's queen in 1780s

Fort George (HS), Highland. Tel: 01667-462800. Closed Sunday mornings in winter. An 18th-century fort

***Fyvie Castle (NTS),** nr Turriff, Grampian. Tel: 01651-891266. Closed mornings May–June and September, grounds open all year. 15th-century castle with finest wheel stair in Scotland

***Georgian House (NTS),** Edinburgh. Tel: 0131-226 3318. Closed Sun. mornings. Fine example of 18th-century New Town architecture

***Gladstone's Land (NTS),** Edinburgh. Tel: 0131-226 5856. Closed Sun. mornings. Typical 17th-century Old Town tenement building with remarkable painted ceilings

***Glamis Castle,** Angus. Tel: 01307-840393. Seat of the Lyon family (later Earls of Strathmore and Kinghorne) since 1372. Scene of the murder of Duncan in Shakespeare's Macbeth

Glasgow Cathedral (HS). Tel: 0141-552 6891. Closed Sun. mornings. Medieval cathedral with elaborately vaulted crypt

Glenbuchat Castle (HS), Glenbuchat, Strathdon. Tel: 0131-668 8800. Ruins of tower house built 1590 by John Gordon and Helen Carnegie. Owned by Gordons until 1738

Glenfinnan Monument (NTS), Glenfinnan, Highland. Tel: 01397-722250. Visitor centre closed in winter. Monument erected by Alexander Macdonald of Glenaladale in 1815 in tribute to the clansmen who fought and died in the cause of Prince Charles Edward Stuart

†**Glenluce Abbey (HS),** Glenluce, Dumfries and Galloway. Tel: 01581-300541, Ruins of Cistercian abbey of the Blessed Virgin Mary, dating from 1192

Greenknowe Tower (HS), Gordon. Tel: 0131-668 8800. Built 1581 by James Seton of Touch and Janet Edmonstone. Owned late 17th-century by Walter Pringle of Stichel, writer and Covenanter

†**Haddo House (NTS),** nr Tarves, Ellon, Aberdeenshire. Tel: 01651-851440. Garden and country park open all year. Georgian mansion house, home to Earls of Gordon and Marquesses of Aberdeen

Hailes Castle (HS), East Linton. Adm. free. Tel: 0131-668 8800. Oldest parts date from 13th-century. Built by the Dunbars, Earls of the March. Destroyed in 1650 by Cromwell's troops

***Hermitage Castle (HS),** nr Newcastleton, Roxburghshire. Tel: 01387-376222. Closed on Sun. mornings. Open through winter. Fortress in the Scottish Borders

***The Hill House (NTS),** Helensburgh. Tel: 01436-673900. Designed by Charles Rennie Mackintosh

***Hill of Tarvit Mansion house (NTS),** nr Cupar, Fife. Tel: 01334-653127. Mansion house closed mornings; grounds open all year. Rebuilt in 1906, with collection of paintings, furniture and Chinese porcelain. Former home of geographer and cartographer Sir John Scott

***Holmwood House (NTS),** Glasgow. Tel: 0141-637 2129. Closed mornings. House designed by Alexander 'Greek' Thomson

Holyroodhouse and Holyrood Abbey (HS) Edinburgh. Open all year except when monarch in residence. Tel: 0131-556 1096. Official residence of monarch of Scotland. Range of buildings dating from 16th-century. Remodelled and extended for Charles II 1671–8

***Hopetoun House,** nr Edinburgh. Tel: 0131-331 2451. House designed by Sir William Bruce, enlarged by William Adam

***House of Dun (NTS),** nr Montrose. Tel: 01674-810264. Closed mornings; grounds open all year. Georgian house with walled garden. Built in 1730 for David Erskine, Laird of Dun

***House of the Binns (NTS),** nr Edinburgh. Tel: 01506-834255. Closed Fri.; parkland open daily. Home of Dalyell family since 1612

Huntingtower Castle (HS), nr Perth. Tel: 01738-627231. Closed Sun. mornings, Thurs. afternoons, and Fri. in winter. Castle with painted ceilings. James VI held captive here

Huntly Castle (HS). Tel: 01466-793191. Closed Sun. mornings, Thurs. afternoons and Fri. in winter. Ruin of a 16th- and 17th-century house. Centre of the Gordon family. Sheltered Robert the Bruce

*****Inchcolm Abbey (HS),** Firth of Forth. Tel: 01383-823332. Abbey founded in 1192 on island in Firth of Forth

*****Inchmahome Priory (HS),** nr Aberfoyle. Tel: 01877-385294. A 13th-century Augustinian priory on an island in the Lake of Menteith. Mary, Queen of Scots, as a five-year old, was hidden here before being taken to France

Innerpeffray Chapel and Library (HS), nr Crieff. Closed December-January, Thurs., and Sun. mornings. Chapel founded by Lord Drummond 1508, although site of a church since 1342. Adjoining building houses the oldest library in Scotland, founded 1691

*****Inveraray Castle,** Argyll. Tel: 01499-302203. Gothic-style 18th-century castle; seat of the Dukes of Argyll

*****Inverness Castle,** Inverness. Closed Sunday. 19th-century red-sandstone edifice on site of earlier castles. Currently houses the Sheriff Court

Iona Abbey, Inner Hebrides. Tel: 01828-640411. Monastery founded by St Columba in AD 563

Italian Chapel, Lamb Holm, Orkney. Tel: 01856-781268. Two Nissan huts painted in the style of an Italian chapel

Jedburgh Abbey (HS), Scottish Borders. Tel: 01835-863925. Romanesque and early Gothic church founded c.1138

*****Kelburn Castle,** Fairlie, Largs. Open only July and Aug. Tel: 01475-568685. Tower house built 1581. Home of the Boyle family, the Earls of Glasgow from 1703

*****Kellie Castle (NTS),** nr Pittenweem, Anstruther. Tel: 01333-720271. Closed mornings; grounds open all year. Restored 14th-century castle

Kelso Abbey (HS), Scottish Borders. Remains of great abbey church founded 1128

Kilchurn Castle (HS), nr Dalmally. Closed Oct-Mar. Ruins of 15th-century castle on a rocky spit. Campbell stronghold.

Kildalton Chapel (HS), nr Port Ellen, Islay. Ruined 12th- or 13th-century chapel dedicated to St John the Beloved. Grounds have the finest surviving intact High Cross in Scotland, dating from eighth century

*****Kildrummy Castle (HS),** nr Alford, Aberdeenshire. Tel: 01975-571331. A 13th-century castle, from where the 1715 Jacobite Rising was organised

†**Kilravock Castle,** nr Nairn. Open only Wed afternoons April-Oct. Tel: 01667-493258. Stately home dating from 15th-century. Bonnie Prince Charlie was entertained here on eve of Culloden, 1745

Kings College Chapel, Aberdeen. Closed Sat and Sun.. College building completed 1495 in honour of James IV

Kinloch Castle, Rum. Open Tues. and Thurs. afternoons only. Built 1900 as a base for a few weeks each autumn for Sir George Bullough who brought the island as a sporting estate 1888

Kinnaird Head Castle Lighthouse and Museum (HS), Fraserburgh, Aberdeenshire. Tel: 01346-511022. Northern Lighthouse Company's first lighthouse, still in working order

†**Kisimul Castle,** Castlebay, Barra. Open May-Sep. Mon., Wed. and Sat. afternoons. Tel: 01871-810336. Islet fortress of the MacNeil clan. Original castle dates from 1120

Lauriston Castle, Edinburgh. Tel: 0131-336 1921. Closed Fri., and weekdays in winter. A 1590s tower house set in 30 acres of parkland

*****Leighton Library,** Dunblane. Closed weekends in summer. Oldest private library in Scotland, housing 4,500 books in 90 languages, printed 1500 to 1840

*****Leith Hall (NTS),** nr Kennethmont, Huntly. Tel: 01464-831216. Closed mornings; grounds open all year. Mansion house with semicircular stables, in 286-acre estate. Home of the Leith family since 1650

*****Lennoxlove House,** Haddington. Closed Mon., Tues. and Thurs. Tel: 01620-823720. Art collection belonging to Duke of Hamilton

Lincluden Collegiate Church (HS), Dumfries. Nunnery founded here by Uchtred, son of Fergus, Lord of Galloway. Present ruins date from 15th-century

Linlithgow Palace (HS). Tel: 01506-842896. Closed Sun. mornings Oct.-March. Ruin of royal palace in park setting. Birthplace of Mary, Queen of Scots

Loch Doon Castle (HS), Craigmalloch, Loch Doon. Tel: 0131-668 8800. Ruins of 13th-century castle built by Earls of Carrick

*****Lochleven Castle (HS),** on an island in Loch Leven. Tel: 01388-040483. Closed Sun. mornings, Thurs. afternoons, and Fri. in winter. Scene of Mary, Queen of Scots' imprisonment

Lochmaben Castle (HS), Castle Mains, Lochmaben. Tel: 0131-668 8800. Extensive ruins. Originally the seat of the Bruces. Mary Queen of Scots visited in 1656 with Darnley

*__Lochranza Castle (HS),__ Isle of Arran. Tel: 0131-668 8800. Acquired by the Montgomeries in 1452, lost to the Hamiltons 1705

MacLellan's Castle (HS), Kirkcudbright, Galloway. Closed Sun. mornings Oct. – March. Tel: 01557-331856. Built 1577 for Sir Thoam Maclellan of Bombie

*__Manderston House,__ nr Duns, Berwickshire. Open Thurs. and Sun. afternoons. Tel: 01361-883450. Edwardian country house of Miller family

*__Maxwelton House,__ nr Moniaive, Dumfriesshire. Closed Sat. Tel: 01848-200385. A 17th-century tower house. Home of the Laurie family

†**Mellerstain House,** nr Earlston, Borders. Tel: 01573 410225. Work of William and Robert Adam dating from 1725. Formal Edwardian gardens

Melrose Abbey (HS), Scottish Borders. Tel: 01896-822562. Ruin of Cistercian abbey founded c.1136. Founded by David I

†**Menstrie Castle,** Menstrie. Open only Sat. and Sun. afternoons May–September. Tel: 01259-213131. Restored 16th-century mansion, birthplace of Sir William Alexander, first Earl of Stirling

*__Miller's Birthplace (NTS),__ Cromarty. Closed Sun. mornings. Birthplace of author, geologist and folklorist Hugh Miller (1802–56)

Morton Castle (HS), Morton Mains, Carronbridge. Tel: 0131-668 8800. Ruins of late 13th-century castle at foot of Lowther Hills. Principal seat of the Douglas Earls of Morton

*__Mount Stuart House,__ Isle of Bute. Tel: 01700-503877. Closed Tues. and Thurs. Spectacular Victorian Gothic house with stained glass and marble

Muness Castle (HS), Unst, Shetland. Adm. free. Tel: 0131-668 8800. Ruins of 16th-century tower house built by Lawrence Bruce of Cultmolindie, Chamberlain of the Lordship of Shetland

*__Neidpath Castle,__ nr Peebles. Closed Sun. mornings Tel: 01721-720333. Wall hangings depicting life of Mary Queen of Scots

New Abbey Corn Mill (HS), nr Dumfries. Tel: 01387-850260. Closed Sun. mornings, Thurs. afternoons and Fri. in winter. Water-powered mill

New Lanark, nr Lanark. Open all year with full programme of educational and touristic events. Tel: 01555-661345; Industrial village built in 1785 by David Dale for the manufacture of cotton; became famous under enlightened management (1800–25) of Robert Owen

*__Newark Castle (HS),__ Port Glasgow, Renfrewshire. Tel: 01475-741858. Virtually intact 15th-century castle

Noltland Castle (HS), Westray, Orkney. Tel: 0131-668 8800. Ruined 16th-century tower house. Built by Gilbert Balfour, Master of the Household of Mary Queen of Scots

Orchardton Tower (HS), Old Orchardton, Palnackie. Tel: 0131-668 8800. Only cylindrical tower house in Scotland. Built for John Carnys around 1456

Orphir Church (HS), nr Kirkwall, Orkney. Ruined remains of only surviving round church in Scotland, dating from 12th century

Paisley Abbey, Paisley. Closed Sun. Tel: 0141-889 7654. Built on site of town's original settlement, 1163 by Walter, son of Alan, Steward of Scotland. became an abbey in 1219

Palace of Holyroodhouse, Edinburgh. Tel: 0131-556 7371. Closed when the Queen is in residence. The Queen's official Scottish residence. Main part of the palace built 1671–9

Parliament House, Edinburgh. Closed Sat. and Sun. Tel: 0131-25-2595. Stronghold of the independent Scots Parliament 1639 until Treaty of Union 1707

*__Paxton House,__ near Berwick upon Tweed, Borders. Tel: 01289-386291. A Palladian country house built in 1758

*__Pitmedden Great Garden (NTS),__ Pitmedden, Aberdeenshire. Tel: 01651-842352. Formal 17th-century garden

Pittencrieff House, Dunfermline. Estate house, 1610. Exhibits of local history. A 76-acre park

Pluscarden Abbey, nr Elgin. Founded by Alexander II in 1230. One of only two abbeys in Scotland with permanent community of monks

Pollok House (NTS), Glasgow. Tel: 0141-649 7151. An 18th-century house with collection of paintings, porcelain and furnishings, set in Pollok Country Park

Preston Tower, Prestonpans. Tel: 0131-226 5922. A 15th-century tower house, enlarged in 17th-century. Residence of the Hamiltons of Preston. Burned by Cromwell in 1650

Provost Skene's House, Aberdeen. Tel: 01224-641086. Closed Sun. mornings. A 16th-century house with period room settings. Aberdeen's oldest surviving private house, dating from 1545

*Queen Mary's House, Jedburgh. Closed Dec.-Feb. Tel: 01835863331. Altered 16th-century tower house. Belonged to Scotts of Ancrum. Mary Queen of Scots lay very ill here for many days in 1566

Ravenscraig Castle (HS), Kirkcaldy. Ruins of 15th-century castle and courtyard. Nearby steps inspiration for John Buchan's novel '*The 39 Steps*'

Restenneth Priory, nr Forfar. Site of 8th-century priory built by King Nechtan of the Picts; adapted as Augustinian priory in 12-thcentury. Remains 12th-15th centuries

Rothesay Castle (HS), Isle of Bute. Tel: 01700-502691. Closed Sun. mornings, Thurs. afternoons, and Fri. in winter. A 13th-century circular castle

Ruthven Barracks (HS), Kingussie. Garrison built after the 1715 rebellion, taken by Jacobites 1744. Blown up following battle of Culloden

Scalloway Castle (HS), Scalloway, Shetland. Tel: 0131-668 8800. Ruins of 17th-century tower house built by Patrick Stewart, Earl of Orkney, 1600

*Scone Palace, Perth. Tel: 01738-552300. House built 1802–13 on the site of a medieval palace. Once the site of the Stone of Destiny

*Scotstarvit Tower (NTS), Craigrothie, Cupar. Closed Nov.- Easter and Mon.- Fri. in Oct. Tel: 01334-653127. Erected between 1550 and 1579 for the Inglis family

Scott Monument, Edinburgh. Tel: 0131-529 4068. Monument affording fine views of the city

Seton Collegiate Church (HS), nr Tranent, East Lothian. Founded 1492 by the fourth Lord Seton. Monuments survive within church

Skipness Castle, (HS) Tarbert, Argyll. Tel: 0131-668 8800. Ruins of 13th-century castle and chapel overlooking Kilbrannon Sound. Probably built by the Macdonald Lord of the Isles

*Smailholm Tower (HS), Scottish Borders. Tel: 01573-460365. Well-preserved tower-house

Spynie Palace (HS), Elgin, Moray. Tel: 01343-546358. Closed weekdays in winter. Residence of Bishops of Moray from 14th to 17th centuries

St Giles Cathedral, Edinburgh. Church on site since 854, existing building dates from 15th-century following sacking by the English in 1385

St Andrews Castle and Cathedral (HS), Fife. Tel: 01334-477196 (castle); 01334-472563 (cathedral). Ruins of 13th-century castle and remains of the largest cathedral in Scotland

St Blane's Church (HS) Kingarth, Bute. Site of Celtic community of 6th-century. In centre of site is a 12th-century chapel

St Clement's Church (HS) Rodel, Harris. A 16th-century cruciform-plan church. Built by Alasdair Crotach MacLeod

St John's Kirk, Perth. Founded by David I, 1126. Present building dates from 15th-century. John Knox preached here.

St Machar's Cathedral, Aberdeen. Medieval cathedral of Bishops of Aberdeen. Reputedly founded 580 by Machar, follower of Columba

St Magnus Cathedral, Kirkwall, Orkney. Closed Sun. mornings. Founded 1137 by Orkney Earl Rognvald. Dedicated to St Magnus the Martyr. Completed 1500 and one of finest in Scotland

St Ninian's Chapel (HS), Isle of Whithorn, Galloway. Ruins of 13th-century chapel on site associated with St Ninian

Stirling Castle and Argyll's Lodging (HS). Tel: 01786-450000. 17th-century town house, seat of the Campbell Earls of Argyll

*Stranraer Castle, Stranraer. Closed Sun. Tel: 01776-705088. Castle of St John. Built c.1511. Exhibitions trace history of castle

Strome Castle (NTS), Stromemore, Lochcarron. Ruins of 15th-century castle built for Alan Macdonald Dubh, 12th chief of the Camerons. Destroyed 1602 by Colin McKenzie of Kintail

Sweetheart Abbey (HS), New Abbey Village, Dumfries. Tel: 01387-850397. Closed Sun. mornings, Thurs. afternoons, and Fri. in winter. Remains of 13th and early 14th-century abbey; burial site of John Balliol's heart

Tantallon Castle (HS), E. Lothian. Tel: 01620-892727. Closed Sun. mornings, Thurs. afternoons and Fri. in winter. Fortification with earthwork defences and a 14th-century curtain wall with towers

*Thirlstane Castle, Lauder, Berwickshire. Closed Sat. Tel: 01578-722430. One of finest castles in Scotland owned by Maitland family since 16th-century

*Threave Castle (HS),** Dumfries and Galloway. Tel: 0411-223101. Late 14th-century tower on an island

Tolquhon Castle (HS), nr Aberdeen. Tel: 01651-851286. Closed weekdays in winter. Mansion house with 15th-century tower

Torosay Castle, Craignure, Mull. Tel: 01680-812421. Castellated mansion of 1858 built for the Campbells of Possel. 18th-century Venetian statues and Japanese garden

*Traquair House,** Innerleithen, Peeblesshire. Tel: 01896-830323. Scotland's oldest inhabited house. Bonnie Prince Charlie stayed here in 1745. Working 18th-century brewery. Gardens and maze

Tullibardine Chapel (HS), nr Crieff. Medieval church founded 1446, rebuilt 1500. One of most complete small collegiate churches in Scotland

Urquhart Castle (HS), Loch Ness. Tel: 01456-450551. Ruins of 13th to 17th-century castle built as a base to guard the Great Glen. Taken by Edward I of England

Wallace Monument, Stirling. Tel: 01786-472140. Closed Jan. and Feb. Exhibitions about Sir William Wallace and others, and a diorama showing the view from the top of the monument

*Whithorn Priory (HS),** nr Newton Stewart, Dumfries and Galloway. Tel: 01988-500700. Site of first Christian church in Scotland, dedicated to St Ninian in 5th-century. Popular place of pilgrimage in medieval times

ARCHAEOLOGICAL SITES AND MONUMENTS

Many visible traces remain throughout Scotland of prehistoric and early historic (to end of first millennium AD) settlement. Mesolithic sites well over 6,000 years old have been found in many parts of Scotland, generally in coastal areas and along rivers. Stone, Bronze and Iron Age settlement and the Pictish period of the early Christian era are extensively represented. Archaeological sites can be found and visited in all parts of Scotland, but the north and west and the islands are particularly rich in them, partly because the stone that was used in construction there is more durable than the wood and turf commonly used for building in the south of Scotland, and partly also because the disturbance due to modern agriculture has been less intensive in the Highlands and Islands. However, the north-east also has a good number of ancient sites.

THE NEOLITHIC PERIOD

The Neolithic period, c.4000-2000 BC, was characterised by communal monuments serving both the living and the dead, such as stone circles, henges and domestic settlements as well as chambered cairns and other massive communal burial places. Among the best-preserved chambered cairns are the 'Tomb of the Eagles' at Isbister, South Ronaldsay, and Maes Howe on Mainland, both in Orkney. Neolithic communities include Skara Brae on Orkney and the first layers of the large Jarlshof site in Shetland. The Neolithic period also produced many of the best-known standing stones and stone circles, which had ritual and perhaps astronomical functions. Examples are the standing stone circle at Callanish (Calanais) on Lewis, the Twelve Apostles in Dumfries, Scotland's largest stone circle, and the Ring of Brodgar (Brogar) on Orkney. However, standing stones continued to be erected right through to the early Middle Ages, and can be found throughout Scotland, often in spectacular settings.

THE BRONZE AGE

During the Bronze Age, c.2000-700 BC, burial took place in individual cairns and tombs, sometimes arranged in 'cemeteries' and sometimes located within existing stone monuments, as at Cairnpapple, West Lothian. Although they are not as numerous as Iron Age settlements, traces of Bronze Age domestic settlements exist, for instance, on the island of Whalsay, Shetland, and at Lairg, Sutherland.

Towards the end of the Bronze Age the building of enclosed and fortified settlements increased. Some of the largest hillforts in the south of Scotland show evidence of having been built in the later Bronze Age (e.g. Traprain Law, East Lothian, and Eildon Hill, Borders), and they appear to have continued in occupation for many centuries, as the important hoard of Roman silver found at Traprain Law suggests.

THE IRON AGE

The different forms of Iron Age dwelling vary widely with time and place, and include several different kinds of roundhouse of timber or stone, massive hilltop forts or enclosures sheltering a number of small roundhouses, drystone broch towers and broch villages, and crannogs – artificial islet dwellings built in lochs and joined to the shore by defended causeways. The wide regional variations are partly – but not entirely – accounted for by the geography of the country, which posed different defensive problems in different places: small dispersed settlements grew up in the broken landscapes of the north and west, where arable land was interrupted and access made difficult by deep sea-lochs and high, steep mountains, while large hillforts were more characteristic of the more open, rolling country of the east and the lowlands with its broad, flat upland summits.

Probably the best known of these structures, being the best preserved, are the brochs. These are concentrated particularly in the north and west and in Orkney and Shetland, although a group of lowland brochs was built in Angus, Perthshire and the Borders, most probably in the first century AD. Stone hut circles and roundhouses predominate in the north and east; traces of similar timber buildings are found in the lowlands; crannogs belong particularly to the Highlands and the south-west (and to Ireland). A group of Iron Age wheelhouses comprises one of the many layers of settlement at Jarlshof in Shetland.

THE ROMANS AND AFTER

While traces of the first Roman invasion of Scotland under Agricola (AD 81–83) can be seen in the remains of a string of forts thrown up to block the Forth-Clyde isthmus, and later forts, signal stations and roads built to consolidate the Roman gains, the most visible sign of the troubled Roman presence in what is now Scotland is the Antonine Wall.

From the seventh to ninth centuries - the so-called Dark Ages - symbol stones and cross-slabs were erected by the Picts, who by the seventh century had mostly been converted to Christianity. These stones occur throughout Scotland, with concentrations in the Pictish territory along the east coast and the Moray Firth and in the far north. While there are some Pictish stones in the West Highlands, the great carved crosses characteristic of the area ruled by the Lords of the Isles until the end of the 15th-century illustrate a later artistic tradition dating from the middle ages and centred upon Iona.

The Pictish symbol stones from the seventh and early eighth centuries, usually carved only on one face and most often with the figures of animals, are probably gravestones. Examples are at Aberlemno, Forfar (Angus), Papil (Shetland), and a collection of most of the Pictish stones found in Sutherland is now in the grounds of Dunrobin Castle Museum, near Golspie.

A slightly later introduction in the eighth and ninth centuries was the more intricately carved and more obviously Christian cross-slab, in which ornamented crosses on one face are often combined with Pictish symbols on the other. The decoration of these slabs shows the influence of the Dalriadic (originally Irish) style that also produced Book of Kells on Iona. Some of them may have served as landmarks where people might gather for worship or private prayer, or as the focus of religious processions. A battle scene on one of the stones at Aberlemno may depict the victory of the Picts over the Northumbrians at Nechtansmere (685). Other excellent examples are at Shandwick, Rosemarkie and Nigg (Ross and Cromarty); but many of the slabs are no longer in their original positions and have been re-erected (or even incorporated) inside churches and other buildings.

Aberlemno Sculptured Stones (HS), nr Forfar, Angus. Cross-slab with Pictish symbols and four other sculptured Pictish stones.

Achavanich Stone Setting, nr Latheron, Caithness. 36 small standing stones arranged in shape of a horseshoe. Nearby cairn dates to Neolithic period.

Achnabreck Cup and Ring Marks (HS), nr Lochgilphead, Kilmartin Glen, Argyll. Among the most impressive and largest ring marks in Scotland, dating over a long period of time.

Aiky Brae Recumbent Stone Circle, Old Deer, Aberdeenshire. Hilltop circle dating from third or second millennium BC.

Antonine Wall (HS), between the Clyde and the Forth. Built c. AD 142, consists of ditch, turf rampart and road, with forts every two miles.

Arbory Hill Fort, Abington, Lanarkshire. Stone fort with earlier ditches and ramparts. Includes hut circles.

Ardestie, Carlungie and Tealing Souterrains (HS), nr Monifieth, Angus. Iron age food cellars, the first two 80 feet and 150 feet in length respectively. Probably in use between AD 150 and AD 450. Nearby stone huts. Sites approximately 1 mile apart.

Auchagallon Cairn (HS), nr Blackwaterfoot, Arran. Stone cairn surrounded by stone circle. Balfarg Henge, nr Glenrothes, Fife. Timber circle built around 3000 BC. Stone circle - only two stones remain. Possible ritual site in fourth millennium BC.

Ballinaby Standing Stones, nr Bruichladdich, Islay. Originally three standing stones of second millennium BC, two remain. The tallest at 5 metres is one of the tallest standing stones in western Scotland.

Ballochmyle Cup and Ring Marks, nr Mauchline, Ayrshire. As well as cup and rings, motifs include geometric shapes. Discovered 1986. One of the largest in Britain.

Ballymeanoch Standing Stones, nr Kilmartin, Kilmartin Glen, Argyll. Four stones lying parallel to two others. Nearby fallen stone has a hole through it. Possibly used to seal marriage vows, hands would be joined through the hole in the stone.

Barnhouse Settlement, nr Stromness, Orkney. Reconstructed foundations of a Neolithic village. Fifteen houses, similar to those found at Skara Brae.

Barpa Langass Chambered Cairn, nr Lochmaddy, North Uist. Chambered burial cairn, 25 metres in diameter and 4 metres in height. Chamber has collapsed and is too dangerous to enter but can be viewed from outside.

Ben Freiceadain, nr Dorrery, Caithness. Extensive fort of first millennium BC, known as Buaile Oscar. Occupies the summit of the hill. Within the fort is the remains of a Neolithic chambered cairn. Close-by are Neolithic and Bronze Age cairns.

Benie Hoose, Whalsay, Shetland. Bronze Age house, over 1,800 tools discovered here. Nearby chambered tomb.

Blackhammer Chambered Cairn (HS), Rousay, Orkney. Chambered tomb with seven burial compartments.

Brough of Birsay (HS), Mainland, Orkney. Pictish settlement on a small tidal island. Remains of Norse church and village.

Burghead Fort and Well (HS), Burghead, Moray. Promontory fort dating from first millennium AD, one of the main centres of Pictish power.

Burgi Geos (HS), Yell, Shetland. Iron Age Fort and field system.

Cairn of Get (HS), nr Ulbster, Caithness. Chambered cairn dating from fourth or third millennium BC. Excavations in 1866 revealed bones of at least seven people along with animal bone, flint and pottery fragments. Nearby cairn maybe a Bronze Age cairn or a Pictish grave of first millennium AD.

Cairnholy Chambered Cairns (HS), nr Creetown, Dumfries and Galloway. remains of two chambered cairns overlooking Wigtown Bay. Traces of fires and pottery suggest possible sites for ceremonies connected with burials.

Cairnbaan Cup and Ring Marks (HS), nr Lochgilphead, Argyll. Two rock outcrops carved with cups and rings.

Cairnpapple Hill (HS), nr Bathgate, West Lothian. Closed October-March. Tel: 01506-634622. Burial site dating from 3000 BC to 1400 BC. Three standing stones in centre surrounded by a henge. Used for burials and held sacred into the Iron Age.

Caisteal Grugaig Broch, Totaig, Inverness-shire. Late first-millennium broch on hillside overlooking the junction of Loch Alsh, Loch Duich and Loch Long.

Calanais (Callanish) Standing Stones (HS). Callanish, Lewis. Visitor centred closed Sundays. Tel: 01851-621422; Slabs of gneiss up to 4.7 metres in height, arranged in the shape of a Celtic Cross. Transported here between 3000 BC and 1500 BC. Many stones aligned with the sun and stars; possible lunar observatory.

Capo Long Barrow, nr Brechin, Kincardine and Deeside. Situated in clearing in Inglislmaldie Forest. Neolithic earthen long mound measuring 80 metres in length and 28 metres in width. Probable burials and mortuary structures.

Carn Liath (HS), nr Golspie, Sutherland. Iron Age broch. Excavations in late 19th-century uncovered beads, rings and bangles.

Castle Haven, nr Borgue, Dumfries and Galloway. Galleried dun. Restored early 20th century.

Castlelaw Hill Fort (HS), nr Glencorse, Midlothian. Iron Age fort in Pentland Hills. Includes fenced enclosure dating to first millennium BC and 20-metre long souterrain dug into silted-up ditch of fort, probably of Roman origin.

Caterthuns Forts (HS), nr Menmuir, Angus. Iron Age fort and settlements sat on top of neighbouring hills, Brown Caterthun and White Caterthun. Excavations suggest dates 700 BC to 300 BC for stoneworks.

Catpund Quarries, nr Cunningsburgh, Shetland. In Norse times, the biggest soapstone quarry in the world.

Chesters Hill Fort (HS), nr Drem, East Lothian. Oval Iron Age fort. Within hill fort are at least 20 hut circles.

Clach a' Charridh, nr Shandwick, Ross and Cromarty. Late 8th or early 9th-century cross-slab and one of the most impressive of all Pictish monuments standing in original position on hill overlooking Shandwick. Covered by glass for protection.

Clach an Trushal Standing Stone, nr Barvas, Lewis. At over 6 metres in height, is one of the tallest in Scotland.

Clava Cairns (NTS), nr Inverness, Highlands. A.k.a. Balnuaran of Clava. Burial chambers clustered on bank of River Nairn, near site of **Culloden.** Erected some time around 2000 BC and encircled by standing stones. Cremated remains have been found.

Cleaven Dyke, nr Blairgowrie, Perthshire. Long bank over 2 km in length and flanked by ditches. Probably the route along which communal ritual of funerary ceremonies would have passed.

Clickhimin Broch (HS), nr Lerwick, Shetland. Broch tower and Iron Age outbuildings on what was once a small island in Clickhimin Loch. Settlement began around 700 BC.

Cnoc Freiceadain Chambered Cairns (HS), nr Thurso, Caithness. Two long cairns now covered in grass. One which measures 78 metres in length, is one of the largest in Scotland.

Corrimony Chambered Cairn (HS), nr Drumnadrochit, Glen Urquhart, Highlands. Circular cairn similar to the Clava Cairns near Inverness dating to third millennium BC. Excavations have found that the chamber contained a crouched body.

Craig Phadrig Fort, nr Inverness. Dates from millennium BC with additions 6th-7th centuries AD. Occupies summit of wooded hill owned by Forestry Commission.

Cullerlie Stone Circle (HS), nr Westhill, Aberdeenshire. Circle of eight boulders surrounding eight cairns dating to second millennium BC. Excavations revealed circular pit containing cremated human bone.

Culsh Souterrain (HS), nr Tarland, Aberdeenshire. Iron age underground passage and food-cellar, 12 metres long and 2 metres wide and high.

Cuween Hill Chambered Cairn (HS), nr Finstown, Orkney. Chambered tomb which contained the skulls of 24 dogs and the skeletal remains of eight humans.

Dreva Craig Fort, nr Biggar, Borders. Fort, hut circles and field systems dating to the late Iron Age. Round houses inside the fort.

Dun-Da-Lamh Fort, nr Laggan, Inverness-shire. Dating to first millennium AD, built on ridge known as the Black Craig.

Dun Ardtreck, nr Corbost, Ardtreck Point, Skye. Dun or fort. Ruins lie on stack of rock 20 metres above the shore. Walls up to 3 metres thick with traces of a gallery.

Dun Beag Broch (HS), nr Dunvegan, Struanmore, Skye. One of the best preserved brochs on Skye. Excavations have found a variety of artefacts including pottery, beads, rings, numerous tools and bone and horn objects.

Dun Bharpa Chambered Cairn, nr Castlebay, Barra. Impressive chambered cairn measuring 25 metres in diameter and 5 metres in height. No longer possible to enter cairn.

Dun Charlabhaig (Carloway) Broch (HS), Carloway, Lewis. One of the best preserved brochs on Scotland's Atlantic coast. Measures up to 9 metres at its tallest point. Nearby Doune Broch Centre, closed November to March and Sundays. Tel: 01851 643338. Fax: 01851 621446. Email: calanais.centre@btinternet.com

Dun Dornaigil Broch (HS), nr south end of Loch Hope, Caithness. A.k.a. Dun Dornadilla. One section almost 7 metres high. Interior full of rubble. Broch tower which may have housed local nobility.

Dun Fiadhairt Broch, nr Dunvegan, Skye. A.k.a Dun of Iardhard. On shores of Camalig Bay. Excavated in 1914. Objects found include pottery, an amber necklace and a terracotta model of a bale of goods of Roman origin.

Dun Gerashader Fort, Portree, Skye. A once-powerful fort with walls 4 metres thick. Most of the dun has gone to make dry walls on nearby farms, but traces of walls still recognisable.

Dun Lagaidh, Loch Broom, Ross and Cromarty. Three successive fortifications built on a ridge on western shore of Loch Broom. Vitrified fort dates to first millennium BC, the dun to the early centuries AD; also medieval castle, probably built 12th-century AD.

Dun Mor Broch, Vaul, nr Scarinish, Tiree. Constructed first century BC, continued in use until the Norse period. Broch survives up to 2 metres in height.

Dun Ringill, Kilmarie, Skye. Galleried dun. Foundations of two medieval buildings inside the dun.

Dun Telve Broch (HS), nr Glenelg, Lochalsh. One of the best preserved Iron Age broch towers in Scotland, although much of the wall is missing. Built around 2000 years ago to protect surrounding settlements from raiders. Excavations have found pottery and stone cups which may have been used as lamps.

Dun Troddan Broch (HS), nr Glenelg, Lochalsh. Lies less than 1 mile from Dun Telve. A section of the wall and staircase survive.

Dun an Sticar Broch, nr Lochmaddy, North Uist. One of best preserved brochs in the Western Isles, surviving to a height of 3 metres. Medieval rectangular house inside dun. Nearby causeway is also medieval in date. Can only be viewed from the outside.

Dunfallandy Stone (HS), nr Pitlochry, Perthshire. Pictish sculptured cross-slab, dating from 9th-century.

Dwarfie Stane Rock (HS), Hoy, Orkney. Chambered tomb cut from a solid block of sandstone, dating to 3000 BC. Named "Dvergasteinn" by the Norse settlers who believed it to be the home of dwarfs.

Easter Aquorthies Stone Circle (HS), nr Inverurie, Aberdeenshire. Dating from third millennium BC. Circle measures almost 20 metres in diameter. Raised in centre, indicative of a burial cairn. Different stone types include pink porphyry, red and grey granite and red jasper.

Edin's Hall Broch (HS), nr Preston, Borders. Oval Iron Age fort with ditches and a broch built in a corner of the fort. Internal diameter of 17 metres and walls 5 metres thick.

Eildon Hill Fort, nr Melrose, Borders. Summit of Eildon Hill North. Occupied since Bronze Age. Included some 300 houses dating to Bronze and Iron Ages. Also traces of a Roman signal station.

Eileach an Naoimh (HS), island in Garvellach group, north of Jura. Ruins of beehive cells from an early Christian community. Small underground cell. Supposedly traditional burial place of Eithne, Columba's mother.

Embo Chambered Cairn, Embo, Sutherland. Dating to between fourth and second millennium BC. Remains of stone cairn containing two Neolithic burial chambers and also Bronze Age graves

Finavon Fort, nr Forfar, Angus. Pictish or Roman fort on the ridge of Finavon Hill. Destroyed by fire and vitrified by the heat.

Glassel Stone Setting, nr Banchory, Aberdeenshire. Oval setting of five granite pillars dating to second millennium BC.

Grain Souterrain (HS), Kirkwall, Orkney. Now in centre of an industrial site. Iron Age food cellar almost 2 metres below the ground dating to the first millennium BC. Excavations have found a hearth, animal bones and shells.

Grey Cairns of Camster (HS), nr Lybster, Caithness. Burial chambers built 4000–5000 years ago. Includes a massive round cairn 18 metres in diameter and a long cairn 70 metres in length covered with two separate round cairns.

Gurness Broch (HS), nr Evie, Orkney. Closed Oct.-March. Best preserved broch in the area, surrounded by a complex of later buildings. Some houses date to late Iron Age. Iron Age house has been reconstructed next to the visitors' centre.

High Banks Cup and Ring Marks, nr Kirkcudbright, Dumfries and Galloway. Over 350 cup and cup and ring marks, some of the most impressive of south-west Scotland.

Hill o' Many Stanes (HS), nr Lybster, Caithness. A.k.a. the Mid Clyth stone rows. Consists of 200 boulders forming 22 parallel rows down the side of the hill. Purpose unknown but possibly an astronomical observatory.

Holm of Papa Westray Chambered Cairns (HS), Island and Holm of Papa Westray, Orkney. Two chambered tombs, one at either end of the island, the one to the north being part of an earlier tomb.

Holyrood Park Settlements (HS), Edinburgh. Natural wilderness in heart of Edinburgh containing four forts and several settlements dating from late Bronze Age and Iron Age. Forts on Arthur's Seat, above Samson's Rib and beside Dunsapie Loch. Hut circles near Hunter's Bog.

Isbister Chambered Cairn, nr St Margaret's Hope, South Ronaldsay, Orkney. Closed afternoons Nov.-March. Tel: 01856-831339. A.k.a. 'Tomb of the Eagles', as bones and talons from white-tailed sea eagles were uncovered here. Ancient chambered burial cairn. Remains of 340 people recovered during excavations in 1970s.

Jarlshof Settlement (HS), Sumburgh Head, Shetland. Closed Oct.-March. Tel/fax: 01950-460112. Largest and most impressive archaeological site in Scotland. Covers three acres, with more than 4000 years of continuous occupation. Earliest buildings date to Neolithic period. Iron Age buildings include a broch, roundhouses and wheelhouses. Norse farmhouses. Latest building dates to the 17th-century laird's house.

Kemp's Walk Fort, nr Stranraer, Dumfries and Galloway. The largest of Galloway's promontory forts, overlooking Broadsea Bay and measuring 83 metres by 44 metres.

Kildonan Dun, nr Campbeltown, Kintyre. Drystone-walled dun dating to first or second century AD. Re-occupied 9th–12th-centuries. Occupied into medieval times.

Kilphedir Broch and Hut Circles, Kilphedir, Sutherland. Broch and hut circles dating to the late Bronze Age. Pottery, stone and flint tools have been unearthed during excavations.

Kintraw Cairns and Standing Stone, nr Kilmartin, Argyll. Cairns excavated 1956–60 and unearthed cremated bone, shells and jet beads. Site possibly marks the sunset at mid-winter solstice as the sun set through notch in Paps of Jura.

Knap of Howe (HS), Papa Westray, Orkney. The island's prime prehistoric site dating from 3500 BC. Neolithic farm-building lays claims to be the oldest standing house in Europe. Bone and stone implements have been uncovered during excavations in the 1930s and 1970s.

Knock Farril Fort, nr Dingwall, Ross and Cromarty. Date from late second or first millennium BC. Occupies summit of ridge overlooking Strath Peffer.

Knowe of Yarsar, Rousay, Orkney. Chambered cairn dating to 3500 BC. Remains of 29 humans discovered here along with deer bones.

Liddle Burnt Mound, nr St Margaret's Hope, Orkney. Probably Bronze Age in date. One of very few to have been excavated. Consists of a central stone-built trough, surrounded by paving and a stone wall, possibly a windbreak. Served as a cooking area or sauna.

Loanhead of Daviot Stone Circle (HS), nr Inverurie, Aberdeenshire. Dated to third or second millennia BC. Recumbent stone circle over 20 metres in diameter consisting of eight standing stones, the recumbent and flankers. Ring cairn later constructed within circle. Beside circle is a Bronze Age cremation cemetery. Excavations uncovered remains of 30 humans in urns and pits.

Lochbuie Stone Circle, Lochbuie, Mull. Circle containing nine stones, one replaced by a boulder, and three outliers. Possibly used for astronomical observations.

Lundin Links Standing Stones, Lundin Links golf course, Fife. Three standing stones remaining of a stone circle, the tallest 5 metres in height. According to legend the gravestones of three Danish warriors defeated by Macbeth.

Machrie Moor Stone Circles (HS), nr Blackwaterfoot, Arran. The area of Machrie Moor contains hut circles, chambered cairns, round cairns and six Bronze Age stone circles, the most impressive has three sandstone pillars over 5 metres in height.

Maes Howe Chambered Cairn (HS), West Mainland, Orkney. Closed Thurs. afternoons, Fri. and Sun. mornings Nov.-March. Tel: 01856-76106. Probably the most impressive Neolithic burial chamber in Europe dating from around 3000 BC. Original capping destroyed in 12th-century.

Maiden Stone (HS), Chapel of Garioch, Aberdeenshire. One of the finest Pictish stones in Grampian dating from 9th-century AD.

Meigle Sculptured Stones (HS), Meigle, Angus. Exhibition in museum, closed Oct.-March. Tel: 01828-640612. Collection of 25 sculptured stones. Early Christian and Dark Age sculpture.

Memsie Round Cairn (HS), Rathen, Aberdeenshire. Dating to Bronze Age, great cairn of bare stones, 24 metres in diameter and over 4 metres in height. Only survivor of a cemetery of three large cairns on the low ridge of Cairn Muir.

Midhowe Broch (HS), Rousay, Orkney. Originally built as fortified family house. Continuously occupied until second century AD. A number of houses surround the broch.

Midhowe Chambered Cairn (HS), Rousay, Orkney. A 100 foot communal burial chamber dating to 3500 BC. Chamber divided into 12 compartments where remains of 25 people were found in a crouched position.

Mither Tap o' Bennachie, nr Inverurie, Aberdeenshire. Granite tor, the summit of which is flanked by stone-walled hillfort dating to first millennium AD. Excavations in 1870s revealed 10 hut foundations. Area north of Bennachie may be site of battle of Mons Graupius in AD 84.

Mousa Broch (HS), Mousa, Shetland. The best preserved prehistoric broch in Scotland standing over 13 metres in height. Thought to be around 2000 years old. In the courtyard are remains of a wheelhouse, built around third century AD.

Mutiny Stones Long Cairn, nr Longformacus, Borders. About 80 metres long and 20 metres wide, one of very few long cairns in the Borders.

Na Fir Bhreige, nr Lochmaddy, North Uist. A.k.a. 'The Three False Men'. Three standing stones which according to legend represent three spies buried alive or three men who deserted their wives and were turned to stone by a witch.

Ness of Burgi Fort (HS), nr Sumburgh, Shetland. Blockhouse positioned across the neck of the Scatness Peninsula.

Nether Largie Cairns (HS), Kilmartin, Kilmartin Glen, Argyll. Bronze Age and Neolithic cairns. Three cairns forming part of a large complex of stones and tombs in the Kilmartin Glen. Nether Largie South is a chambered cairn. Carved with cupmarks.

New and Old Kinord Settlement, nr Ballater, Kincardine and Deeside. Probably dates from latter part of first millennium BC. Hut circles in an enclosure, the largest 19 metres in diameter. Settlement also contains a souterrain.

Ord Archaeological Trail, The Ord, Lairg, Sutherland. Tel: 01549-402638. Hill overlooking Loch Shin containing a number of structures dating from Neolithic to post-Medieval period. Two chambered cairns near summit. Hut circles date from 1500 BC.

Pobull Fhinn Stone Circle, nr Lochmaddy, North Uist. Originally 48 stones of which 30 remain. Occupies amphitheatre cut into hillside.

Quoyness Chambered Cairn (HS), nr Kettletoft, Sanday, Orkney. Megalithic tomb dating from around 2000 BC. Partially re-constructed. Human bones found during excavations in 1860s.

Raedykes Ring Cairns, nr Stonehaven, Aberdeenshire. Strung out along the crest of Campstone Hill, an important group of early ritual sites dating to the third or second millennium BC.

Rennibister Souterrain (HS), nr Kirkwall, Orkney. Iron Age semi-underground structure used to store grain and produce dating to first millennium BC. Excavations uncovered remains of 18 people – rare to fine human bones in an earth-house, so possibly converted to a burial vault.

Ring of Brodgar Circle and Henge (HS), nr Stromness, Orkney. Neolithic circle and one of the largest stone circles in Scotland. originally 60 stones of which just 36 remain. Only the ditch remains of the henge. Possibly part of a ritual complex which included Maes Howe and the Stones of Stenness.

Rubh' an Dunain Cairn and Dun, nr Glenbrittle, Skye. When cairn was excavated in 1930s pottery and flints artefacts were uncovered as well as bones of several people. Near the cairn are the remains of an Iron Age fort, one of best preserved galleried duns in Skye.

Scatness Broch and Settlement, Sumburgh, Shetland. Accessible July and August. Tel: 01595-694688. Excavations currently taking place west of the airport. Ancient broch and Iron Age village which may include Norse occupation. One of the buildings was reused by the Vikings as a smithy.

St Vigeans Sculptured Stones (HS), nr Arbroath, Angus. Exhibition closed Oct.-March. Early Christian and Pictish stones housed in cottages.

Scord of Brouster Settlement, nr Bridge of Walls, Shetland. Ruined houses and field boundaries occupied between 3000 and 1500 BC.

Skara Brae Settlement (HS), nr Stromness, Orkney. Closed Sun. morning Oct.-March. Tel: 01856-841815; Fax: 01856-841885. One of the best preserved Stone Age settlements in Europe, dating back to 3000 BC. Excavated by V.G. Childe in 1920s. Reconstructed house next to visitor centre. Visitor centre displays stone and bone artefacts as well as pottery discovered during excavations.

Staneydale Settlement (HS), nr Bridge of Walls, Shetland. Shattered Neolithic structure. Surrounding oval-shaped houses in ruins. Probably once an important community meeting-place.

Stone of Settar, Eday, Orkney. Orkney's most distinctive standing stone.

Stones of Stenness and Henge (HS), nr
Stromness, Orkney. Originally a circle of 12
rock slabs, just four remain. Dates back to the
same time as the nearby Neolithic village, the
Barnhouse Settlement.

Strathpeffer Symbol Stone, Strathpeffer, Ross
and Cromarty. Pictish symbol stone dating
from 7th or 8th-century AD. Often called The
eagle Stone.

Strontoiller Cairn and Standing Stones, nr
Oban, Argyll. Standing stone stands 4 metres
high. According to legend it is said to mark
the grave of Diarmid, a mythical hero of
Ireland. Excavations of the cairn have found
cremated bone along with quartz chips and
pebbles.

Sueno's Stone (HS), Forres, Moray. Probably the
most remarkable sculptured stone in Scotland.
Dating from 9th-century and over 22 feet in
height. Protected by glass enclosure.

Sunhoney Stone Circle, nr Banchory,
Aberdeenshire. Consists of 11 standing stones
of red granite and a recumbent stone of grey
granite carved with cupmarks. Within the
circle is a ring cairn.

Tap o' Noth Fort, nr Rhynie, Aberdeenshire.
Timber-laced stone rampart, originally 8
metres thick, on top of a high hill. Up to 150
hut platforms within fort.

Taversoe Tuick Chambered Cairn (HS),
Rousay, Orkney. Two-storeyed chambered
cairn dating to 3500 BC. Piles of bones found
in lower chamber, cremated remains in upper
chamber. Pottery bowls also recovered.

Temple Wood Stone Circles (HS), nr Kilmartin,
Kilmartin Glen, Argyll. Stone circle 12 metres
in diameter. One stone is decorated with two
concentric circles and another with a double
spiral. Excavations have revealed an earlier
timber and stone circles.

Tinto Hill Cairn, nr Biggar, Lanarkshire. One of
largest Bronze Age round cairns in Scotland,
situated on top of Tinto Hill. Measures 45
metres in diameter and 6 metres in height.

Tirefour Broch, nr Achnacroish, Lismore. Iron
Age broch. Stands up to 5 metres in height on
one side.

Tomnaverie Stone Circle (HS), nr Aboyne,
Aberdeenshire. Dating from third or second
millennium BC. Red granite circle, 18 metres
in diameter. Four uprights and the recumbent
remain in place. Ring of smaller stones within
the circle.

Torhouse Stone Circle (HS), nr Wigtown,
Dumfries and Galloway. Circle of 19 granite
boulders. Three stones in middle of the circle.

Torwoodlee Fort and Broch, nr Galashiels,
Borders. Ruins of broch now less than 1 metre
in height. Built on site of an earlier fort.
Probably demolished by the Romans.

Traprain Law Fort, nr East Linton, East
Lothian. Two ramparts on summit of Traprain
Law. Artefacts dating back to the Neolithic
period have been unearthed. Collection of late
Roman silver found under floor of one of the
many houses around the summit.

Tullos Hill Round Cairns, Loirston, nr
Aberdeen. Four cairns, the remains of an
important cairn cemetery of the Bronze Age.

Twelve Apostles Stone Circle, nr Dumfries,
Dumfries and Galloway. The largest stone
circle in Scotland and one of the largest in
Britain, measuring 87 metres at widest point.
11 stones remain. Originally thought to have
consisted of 18 stones.

Tynron Doon, nr Moniavie, Achengibbert Hill,
Dumfries and Galloway. Iron Age fort on
summit of the hill. Used until relatively
recently with tower house built in late 16th-
century. Outlines of hut circles.

Unival Chambered Cairn, nr Claddach Illeray,
North Uist. Square cairn now robbed of much
of its stone.

Unstan Chambered Cairn (HS), nr Stromness,
Orkney. Situated on promontory in the Loch
of Stenness. Concentric rings of drystone
walling. Skeletal remains found in chambers
along with animal and bird bones and shards
of pottery known as Unstan Ware.

Vinquay Chambered Cairn, Eday, Orkney.
Neolithic burial chamber dating from around
3000 BC.

Wag of Forse Broch and Settlement, nr
Latheron, Caithness. Turf-walled enclosure
and remains of a number of houses including
roundhouses and brochs. Also rectangular
buildings known as 'wags'. Best preserved
dwelling is 12 metres long with two rows of
stone pillars.

Wideford Hill Chambered Cairn, nr Kirkwall,
Orkney. Neolithic burial chamber, similar to
chambered cairn at Maes Howe.

Yoxie Biggins, Whalsay, Shetland. Bronze Age
house a.k.a. The Standing Stones of Yoxie as
the megaliths were used to form the walls,
many still standing. Excavations have
unearthed stone tools and pottery.

MUSEUMS AND GALLERIES

There are some 296 museums and galleries in Scotland, of which 288 are fully or provisionally registered with the Museums and Galleries Commission. Registration indicates that they have an appropriate constitution, are soundly financed, have satisfactory collection management standards and public services, and have access to professional curatorial advice. Museums should achieve full or provisional registration status in order to be eligible for grants from the Museums and Galleries Commission and from the Scottish Museums Council. Of the registered museums in Scotland, 136 are run by a local authority and 111 are independently run.

The national collections in Scotland are the National Galleries of Scotland and the National Museums of Scotland, which are funded by direct government grant-in-aid. An online art museum (Web: http://www.24hourmuseum.org.uk) has also been awarded national collection status.

Local authority museums are funded by the local authority and may also receive grants from the Museums and Galleries Commission. Independent museums and galleries mainly rely on their own resources but are also eligible for grants from the Museums and Galleries Commission.

The Scottish Museums Council is one of ten area museum councils in the UK. It is an independent charity that receives an annual grant from the Scottish Executive, and gives advice and support to museums in Scotland. It may offer improvement grants and also assists with training and marketing.

OPENING TO THE PUBLIC

The following is a selection of the museums and art galleries in Scotland. Opening hours vary. Most museums are closed on Christmas Eve, Christmas Day, Boxing Day and New Year's Day; some are closed on Good Friday or the May Day Bank Holiday. Some smaller museums close at lunchtimes. Information about a specific museum or gallery should be checked by telephone.

Local authority museum/gallery

ABERDEEN

*Aberdeen Art Gallery, Schoolhill. Tel: 01224-523700. Closed Sun. mornings. Art from the 18th to 20th-century

*Aberdeen Maritime Museum, Shiprow. Tel: 01224-337700. Maritime history, including shipbuilding and North Sea oil

*Arts Centre Gallery, King Street. Tel: 01224-635208. Exhibitions of contemporary art

Gordon Highlanders Museum, St Luke's, Viewfield Road. Tel: 01224-311200

Marischal Museum, University of Aberdeen, Broad Street. Tel: 01224-274301. Foreign ethnography, local history and archaeology

*Tolbooth Museum of Civic History, Castle Street. Tel: 01224-621167. The history of Aberdeen, housed in what was originally the city's prison

ALFORD

Grampian Transport Museum. Tel: 01975-562292. Large collection of road transport vehicles

ANSTRUTHER

Scottish Fisheries Museum, St Ayles, Harbourhead. Tel: 01333-310628. Marine aquarium, fishing boats, period interior and other fishing artefacts

ARBROATH

*Arbroath Museum, Ladyloan. Tel: 01241-875598. Local history museum

BLANTYRE

David Livingstone Centre, Station Road. Tel: 01698-823140. Museum relating the life of David Livingstone

CREETOWN

Creetown Gem Rock Museum and Gallery, Chain Road. Tel: 01671-820357. Minerals, crystals and gemstones from around the world

DUMFRIES

*Burns House, Burns Street. Tel: 01387-255297. The house where Robert Burns died

Robert Burns Centre, Mill Road. Tel: 01387-264808. Displays and exhibitions relating to Robert Burns and to Dumfries during his lifetime

*Dumfries Museum and Camera Obscura, The Observatory. Tel: 01387-253374. Natural history, archaeology and folk collections

Shambellie House Museum of Costume, New Abbey. Tel: 01387-850375. Costumes from the 1850s to the 1920s

DUNDEE

*Broughty Castle Museum, Broughty Ferry. Tel: 01382-436916. A former estuary fort housing a museum of local history, arms and armour, seashore life and whaling

Discovery Point, Riverside. Tel: 01382-201245. Visitor centre telling the story of Scott's voyage to Antarctica; incorporates the Discovery

*McManus Galleries, Albert Square. Tel: 01382-432084. Local history museum and gallery showing temporary art exhibitions

EDINBURGH

Britannia, Leith docks. Tel: 0131-555 5566. Former royal yacht with royal barge and royal family picture gallery. Tickets must be pre-booked

*City Art Centre, Market Street. Tel: 0131-529 3993. Closed Sun. Late 19th and 20th-century art and temporary exhibitions

*Fruit Market Gallery, Market Street. Tel: 0131-225 2383. Contemporary art gallery

*Huntly House Museum, Canongate. Tel: 0131-529 4143. Closed Sun. Local history, silver, glass and Scottish pottery

*Museum of Childhood, High Street. Tel: 0131-529 4142. Closed Sun. Toys, games, clothes and exhibits relating to the social history of childhood

Museum of Flight, East Fortune Airfield, nr North Berwick. Tel: 01620-880308. Display of aircraft

Museum of Scotland, Chambers Street. Tel: 0131-247 4422. Closed Sun mornings. Scottish history from prehistoric times to the present

National Gallery of Scotland, The Mound. Tel: 0131-624 6200. Closed Sun. mornings. Paintings, drawings and prints from the 16th to 20th-century, and the national collection of Scottish art

*The People's Story, Canongate. Tel: 0131-529 4057. Closed Sun. Edinburgh life since the 18th-century

Royal Museum of Scotland, Chambers Street. Tel: 0131-225 7534. Closed Sun. mornings. Scottish and international collections from prehistoric times to the present

Royal Scots Regimental Museum, Edinburgh Castle. Tel: 0131-310 5016

Scottish Agricultural Museum, Ingliston. Tel: 0131-333 2674. Closed Sat. and Sun. in winter. History of agriculture in Scotland

Scottish National Gallery of Modern Art, Belford Road. Tel: 0131-624 6200. Closed Sun. mornings. Twentieth-century painting, sculpture and graphic art

Scottish National Portrait Gallery, Queen Street. Tel: 0131-624 6200. Closed Sun. mornings. Portraits of eminent people in Scottish history, and the national collection of photography

Scottish United Services Museum, Edinburgh Castle. Tel: 0131-225 7534. Collections connected to the Scottish armed forces since the 17th-century

*The Writers' Museum, Lawnmarket. Tel: 0131-529 4901. Closed Sun. Robert Louis Stevenson, Walter Scott and Robert Burns exhibits

FORT WILLIAM

West Highland Museum, Cameron Square. Tel: 01397-702169. Closed Sun. Includes tartan collections and exhibits relating to 1745 uprising

FRASERBURGH

*Museum of Scottish Lighthouses, Kinnaird Head. Tel: 01346-511022. Lighthouse artefacts, including the original Kinnaird Head lighthouse

GLASGOW

*Burrell Collection, Pollokshaws Road. Tel: 0141-649 7151. Paintings, textiles, furniture, ceramics, stained glass and silver from classical times to the 19th-century

Collins Gallery, University of Strathclyde, Richmond Street. Tel: 0141-552 4400 ext. 2558. Touring exhibitions of contemporary work by Scottish artists

*Gallery of Modern Art, Queen Street. Tel: 0141-229 1996. Collection of contemporary Scottish and world art

*Glasgow Art Gallery and Museum, Kelvingrove. Tel: 0141-287 2699. Includes Old Masters, 19th-century French paintings and armour collection

Glasgow School of Art, Renfrew Street. Tel: 0141-353 4500. Exhibitions, mainly of contemporary art, in Rennie Mackintosh building

*House for an Art Lover, Bellahouston Park, Dumbreck Road. Tel: 0141-353 4770. Based on Rennie Mackintosh designs

Hunterian Art Gallery, Hillhead Street. Tel: 0141-330 5431. Closed Sun. Rennie Mackintosh and Whistler collections; Old Masters, Scottish paintings and modern paintings, sculpture and prints

*McLellan Galleries,** Sauchiehall Street. Tel: 0141-332 7521. Temporary exhibitions

*Museum of Transport,** Bunhouse Road. Tel: 0141-287 2720. Includes a reproduction of a 1938 Glasgow street, cars since the 1930s, trams and a Glasgow subway station

*People's Palace Museum,** Glasgow Green. Tel: 0141-554 0223. History of Glasgow since 1175

*Pollok House,** Pollokshaws Road. Tel: 0141-616 6410. Palladian house containing the Stirling Maxwell art collection

*Provand's Lordship,** Castle Street. Tel: 0141-553 2557. Exhibition of period displays housed in medieval buildings

Royal Highland Fusiliers Museum, Sauchiehall Street. Tel: 0141-332 5639

*St Mungo Museum of Religious Life and Art,** Castle Street. Tel: 0141-553 2557. Explores universal themes through objects of all the main world religions

*Scotland Street School Museum of Education,** Scotland Street. Tel: 0141-429 1202. The history of education in Scotland, in a building designed by Rennie Mackintosh

GLENCOE
Glencoe and North Lorn Folk Museum, Glencoe. No telephone. Closed in winter. Restored cottage with local and natural history exhibits

GREENOCK
*McLean Museum and Art Gallery,** Kelly Street. Tel: 01475-715624. Local and natural history museum and temporary art exhibitions

INVERARAY
Inveraray Jail, Church Square. Tel: 01499-302381. A 19th-century courthouse with two prisons

Inveraray Maritime Museum and Arctic Penguin, Maritime Heritage Centre, Inveraray Pier. Tel: 01499-302213. Museum of Clyde ships and shipyards

INVERNESS
*Inverness Museum and Art Gallery,** Castle Wynd. Tel: 01463-237114. The history of the Highlands

Queen's Own Highlanders Regimental Museum, Fort George, nr Inverness. Tel: 01463-224380

IRVINE
Scottish Maritime Museum, Laird Forge, Gottries Road. Tel: 01294-278283. Full-size ships, an exhibition gallery, an educational centre and a restored tenement flat

JOHN O'GROATS
Last House Museum. Tel: 01955-611250. Local history museum in a restored 18th-century house

KILMARTIN
Kilmartin House Museum. Tel: 01546-510278. Landscape and archaeology of Argyll

KINGUSSIE
*Highland Folk Museum,** Duke Street. Tel: 01540-661307. Highland artefacts

KIRKCALDY
*Kirkcaldy Museum and Art Gallery,** War Memorial Gardens. Tel: 01592-412860. Historical displays and collection of paintings including works by the Scottish Colourists and Camden Town group

KIRKWALL
*Tankerness House Museum,** Broad Street. Tel: 01856-873191. Closed Sundays in winter. Two restored farmsteads

LERWICK
*Shetland Museum,** Lower Hillhead. Tel: 01595-695057. Museum depicting all aspects of island life

LOCHMADDY
Taigh Chearsabhagh. Tel: 01876-500293. Local history museum

MOTHERWELL
*Motherwell Heritage Centre,** High Road. Tel: 01698-251000. Includes Technopolis, a multi-media local history exhibition

NEWTONGRANGE
Scottish Mining Museum, Lady Victoria Colliery. Tel: 0131-663 7519. Museum of mining history

PAISLEY
*Paisley Museum and Art Galleries, High
Street. Tel: 0141-889 3151. Local and natural
history and a collection of Paisley shawls

PEEBLES
*Tweeddale Museum and Art Gallery,
Chambers Institute, High Street. Tel: 01721-
724820. Local history museum and
contemporary art gallery

PERTH
Black Watch Regimental Museum, Balhousie
Castle, Hay Street. Tel: 01738-621281 ext.
8530
*Perth Museum and Art Gallery, George Street.
Tel: 01738-632488. Local history museum
and art exhibitions

ST ANDREWS
British Golf Museum, Bruce Embankment. Tel:
01334-478880. Museum of the history and
development of golf
*St Andrews Museum, Kinburn Park, Double
Dykes Road. Tel: 01334-412690. Local
history and temporary exhibitions

STIRLING
Argyll and Sutherland Highlanders Museum,
Stirling Castle. Tel: 01786-475165
Smith Art Gallery and Museum, Dumbarton
Road. Tel: 01786-471917. Scottish paintings
and artefacts

STORNOWAY
*An Lanntair Gallery, Town Hall, South Beach.
Tel: 01851-703307. Contemporary art
exhibitions

STRANRAER
*Stranraer Museum, George Street. Tel: 01776-
705088. Exhibition on farming, archaeology
and polar explorers

WANLOCKHEAD, VIA BIGGAR
Museum of Leadmining. Tel: 01659-74387.
The history of leadmining in Scotland

GARDENS

Scotland's varied climate allows for a very wide range of plants to be grown. Particularly on the west coast and in the islands of the west and south-west, mild weather caused by the Gulf Stream makes it possible to grow palms, tender perennials, and plants from the southern hemisphere; while acid, peaty soil and the frequency of rain and low cloud provide a suitable climate for plants usually thought of as typically Scottish, such as rhododendrons and heathers. Several national collections of plants are housed in Scotland.

The National Trust for Scotland is the country's largest garden owner, with just over 700 acres under intensive cultivation supporting over 13,500 different sorts of plants. The Trust acquired its first garden in 1945 when it accepted Culzean Castle. Several years later Inverewe, Brodik, Falkland Palace and Pitmedden Gardens were added. The Trust now has in its care 34 major gardens and designed landscapes and another 30 smaller gardens. It plays an important role in promoting the conservation of the art and craft of horticulture, through its School of Practical Gardening at Threave.

Each year some 400 Scottish gardens, most privately owned, open their gates to the public for one or more weekends under the banner of Scotland's Gardens Scheme. Founded in 1931, the Scheme is an independent charity and the money raised from garden visitors supports the Queen's Nursing Institute (Scotland) and the gardens fund of the National Trust for Scotland. In addition garden owners may donate up to 40 per cent of their takings to a charity of their choice. The National Scotland's Gardens Scheme Handbook is available from any National Trust for Scotland shop or by post from the Trust's headquarters.

Historic Scotland and Scottish Natural Heritage jointly maintain an Inventory of Gardens and Designed Landscapes in Scotland. The Inventory provides a representative sample of historic gardens and landscapes of special interest, and includes botanic gardens, parks, private gardens and policies in country estates. The Inventory is currently being extended.

The following is a list of gardens in Scotland which are regularly open to the public, including botanic gardens and historical gardens. Also included are gardens in the grounds of castles and houses which are open to public, and in some cases gardens which are open to the public although the buildings are not.

Closed in winter (usually October or November to March)
† Also appears in Historic Buildings and Monuments list
NTS National Trust for Scotland property
HS Historic Scotland property

Achamore, Isle of Gigha, Argyll and Bute. Tel: 01583-505267. Established by Sir James Horlick of the hot drink fame. Rhododendrons and azaleas.

*****Achnacloich,** Connel, Oban, Argyll and Bute. Tel: 01631-710221. Spring bulbs, azaleas, Japanese maples.

*****An Cala,** Easdale, Isle of Seil, Argyll. Tel: 01852-300237. Created in 1930s. Water features.

Arbuthnott House, Laurencekirk, Kincardineshire. Tel: 01561-361226. Late 17th-century herbaceous borders, roses, rhododendrons, hostas.

*****Ardencraig Rothesay,** Isle of Bute. Closed Sat. and Sun. mornings. Victorian hothouses.

Ardkinglas Woodland Garden, Cairndow, Loch Fyne. Rhododendrons, azaleas, conifers.

*****Ardtornish,** Lochaline, Morvern, Oban, Highland. Tel: 01967-421288. Shrubs, deciduous trees, conifers, rhododendrons.

Arduaine (NTS). Oban, Argyll and Bute. Tel: 01852-200366. Originally planted early 1900s. Restored after 1971. Lawns, lily ponds, mature woods, rhododendrons and magnolias.

†**Armadale Castle and Museum of the Isles.** Armadale, Sleat, Isle of Skye. Tel: 01471-844305. Pond gardens, herbaceous border, lawns and ornamental trees.

*****Ascog Fernery and Garden,** nr Rothesay, Bute. Closed Mon. Tues. Victorian fernery. Boasts a fern reputed to be 1,000 years old.

*****Attadale,** Strathcarron, Highland. Tel: 01520-722217. Water features, rhododendron walk, herb plot.

†**Ballindalloch Castle,** Grantown-on-Spey, Highland. Tel: 01807-500205. 1937 rock garden, rose and fountain garden.

*†**Balmoral Castle,** Ballater, Aberdeenshire. Tel: 013397-42334. A 3-acre garden; rare coniferous forest trees, sunken rose garden, water garden.

*****Bell's Cherrybank Gardens,** Cherrybank, Perth. Tel: 01738-621111. Two 18-acre gardens; includes 830 varieties of heather, largest collection of heathers in Britain.

*****Bolfracks,** Aberfeldy, Perth and Kinross. Tel: 01887-820207. A 3-acre garden. Spring bulbs, shrub roses, gentians.

*Branklyn (NTS), 116 Dundee Road, Perth. Tel: 01738-625535. Alpine plants and rhododendrons on 2-acre hillside.

†Brodick Castle (NTS), Isle of Arran, North Ayrshire. Tel: 01770-302202. Plants from Himalayas, China and South America, bog garden.

*†Broughton House (NTS), 12 High Street, Kirkcudbright, Dunfries and Galloway. Tel: 01557-330437. Open afternoons only April–Oct. Created by artist E. A. Hornel. Sunken courtyard, Japanese garden, rose parterre.

*Broughton Place, Broughton, Biggar, Scottish Borders. Tel: 01899-830234. Closed Wed. An 18th-century beech avenue. National collections of thalictrums and tropaeolums.

Cambo, Kingsbarns, St.Andrews, Fife. Tel: 01333-450054. Walled garden. Ornamental garden, lilac walk.

*Candacraig, Dinnet, Aberdeenshire. Tel: 01975-651226. Closed Sat. and Sun. mornings. An 1820s garden, cottage-garden flowers, mecanopsis, primulas.

†Castle Fraser (NTS), Sauchen, Inverurie, Aberdeenshire. Tel: 01330-833463. 17th/18th-century designed landscape, herbaceous border, walled garden.

*Castle Kennedy, Stranraer, Wigtownshire, Dumfries and Galloway. Tel: 01776-702024. Laid out 1730. A 75-acre garden noted for monkey-puzzle trees, magnolias, rhododendrons, spring bulbs.

*†Cawdor Castle, Cawdor, Nairn, Highland. Tel: 01667-404615. Herbaceous borders, peony border, rose tunnel, thistle garden, holly maze.

*Cluny House, Aberfeldy, Perth and Kinross. Tel: 01887-820795. Wild garden. National Collection of Asiatic primulas; meconopsis, rhododendrons.

Crarae, Minard, Inveraray, Argyll and Bute. Tel: 01546-886614. Laid out early 20th-century as a 'Himalayan ravine'. 400 rhododendrons, azaleas, eucalyptus and conifers.

†Crathes Castle (NTS) Banchory, Aberdeenshire. Tel: 01330-844525. 8 themed gardens, rare shrubs, herbaceous borders. National Collection of Malmaison carnations.

Cruickshank Botanic Garden, University of Aberdeen, St.Machar Drive, Aberdeen. Tel: 01224-272704. Closed weekends Oct.-April. 11 acres; arboretum, rose garden, water gardens. Essentially for research.

*†Culzean Castle (NTS) Maybole, South Ayrshire. Tel: 01655-884400. Camelia house and orangery, 563-acre country park, 30-acre garden, walled garden, herbaceous borders.

*Dawyck Botanic, Stobo, Peebleshire, Scottish Borders. Tel: 01721-760254. Branch of Royal Botanic Garden Edinburgh. 300 years of tree-planting. Fine arboretum, beech walk, azalea terrace.

*†Drum Castle (NTS) Drumoak, by Banchory, Aberdeenshire. Tel: 01330-811204. Closed weekdays in Oct. Garden of historic roses. Herbaceous borders, plants of 17th–20th centuries.

*†Drummond Castle, Muthill, Crieff, Perth and Kinross. Tel: 01764-681257. Open afternoons only May-Oct. Laid out by John Drummond, 2nd Earl of Perth, 1630. French and Italian influence. A 17th-century Scottish garden.

*†Dunrobin Castle, Golspie, Sutherland, Highlands. Tel: 01408-633177. Closed Sun. mornings. Victorian formal gardens in French style, laid out 1850. Water features, roses, clematis, sweet peas.

†Dunvegan Castle, Isle of Skye. Tel: 01470-521206. Closed weekends Nov.-Feb. Box-wood parterre, mixed borders, fern houses, woodland waterfall dell, walled garden.

†Edzell Castle (HS) Edzell, Brechin, Angus. Tel: 01356-648631. Closed Sun. mornings Oct.-March. Walled garden dating from 1930s but laid out as it may have looked in early 1600s.

*†Falkland Palace (NTS), Falkland, Fife. Tel: 01337 857397. Closed Sun. mornings. Shrub island borders, herbaceous borders, delphiniums, orchard.

Finlaystone, Langbank, Renfrewshire. Tel: 01475-540285. A 10-acre garden and 70-acre woodland laid out 1900. Herbaceous borders, copper beeches, Celtic paving maze, bog garden.

*†Floors Castle, Kelso, Roxburghshire. Tel: 01573-223333. Herbaceous borders, walled kitchen garden.

*†Glamis Castle, Glamis, Forfar, Angus. Tel: 01307-840393. Landscaped 1790s by designer influenced by 'Capability' Brown. 2-acre Italian garden, herbaceous borders, gazebos.

Glasgow Botanic Gardens, 730 Great Western Road, Glasgow. Tel: 0141-334 2422 Glasshouses contain orchids, cacti and ferns. Paths alongside wooded banks of River Kelvin.

*Glenarn, Rhu, Dunbartonshire. Tel: 01436-820493. Woodland garden established 1920s. Rhododendrons, magnolias, olearias, pieris.

*Glenwhan, Dunragit, Stranraer, Dumfries and Galloway. Tel: 01581-400222. 12-acre hillside garden laid out 1979. Exotic plants, trees and shrubs, lakes and bog gardens, rhododendrons, primula.

Greenbank (NTS), Flenders Road, Clarkston, Glasgow. Tel: 0141-639 3281. Walled garden, water features, woodland walks, herb garden.

†Haddo House (NTS), nr Tarves, Ellon, Aberdeenshire. Tel: 01651-851440. 177 acres of woodland, lakes and ponds, home to otters, red squirrel, pheasants and deer.

†Hill of Tarvit (NTS), Cupar, Fife. Tel: 01334-653127. Rose garden, perennials and annuals, ornamental trees.

Hirsel, Coldstream, Berwickshire. Tel: 01890-882834. Spring bulbs, rhododendrons, rose beds, herbaceous borders.

*House of Pitmuies, Guthrie, by Forfar, Angus. Tel: 01241-828245. Walled gardens, rhododendrons, semi-formal gardens with old fashioned roses and delphiniums.

Inveresk Lodge (NTS), Musselburgh, East Lothian. Tel: 0131-665 1855. Closed Sat. Oct.–March and Sat. and Sun. mornings April–September. Semi-formal gardens, shrub roses, conservatory.

Inverewe (NTS), Poolewe, Highlands. Tel: 01445-781200. Brainchild of Osgood Mackenzie; created from 1865 covering the Am Ploc Ard peninsula. Wild garden, rock gardens, rhododendrons, vegetable garden and orchard. Species from around the world. National collections of olearias and ourisias. Hydroponicum.

Jura House, Ardfin, Isle of Jura, Argyll and Bute. Tel: 01496-820315. Walled garden. Fuchsias, ferns and lichens. Antipodean plants. Organic walled garden.

Kailzie, Peebles, Peebleshire, Scottish Borders. Tel: 01721-720007. April–October, free November–March free (honesty box). A 17-acre walled-garden. Spring bulbs, secret gardens, laburnum, rhododendrons, azaleas, mecanopsis, primulas. Trout pond.

†Kellie Castle (NTS), Pittenweem, Fife. Tel: 01333-720271. Lawn edged with box-hedges and borders, roses, vegetable garden, woodland walks.

*†Kildrummy Castle (HS), Alford, Aberdeenshire. Tel: 01975-571203. Rock garden, water garden, Japanese garden, maples, rhododendrons, acers, mecanopsis.

Kilmory Woodland Park, nr Lochgilphead. Gardens laid out in 1830 around Kilmory Castle.

*Kinross House, Kinross, Perth and Kinross. A 4-acre formal walled garden designed 1680s. Herbaceous borders, rose borders, ornamental yew hedges.

*Leckmelm Shrubbery and Arboretum, Little Leckmelm House, Lochbroom, Ullapool, Highland. A 10-acre arboretum.

†Leith Hall (NTS), Huntly, Aberdeenshire. Tel: 01464-831216. Rock garden, perennial borders, catmint border, water features.

*Logan Botanic Garden, Port Logan, Stranraer, Dumfries and Galloway. Tel: 01776-860231. Outpost of Edinburgh's Royal Botanic Garden. Exotic plants from around the world. Excellent collection of Scottish tender perennials. A 100 year old walled garden. Water garden, palms and ferns. Eucalyptus, magnolias.

Malleny (NTS), Balerno, Edinburgh. Tel: 0131-449 2283. A 3-acre walled garden with Deodar cedar. 17th-century clipped yews. Herbaceous borders, herb and ornamental vegetable garden. National Collection of 19th-century shrub roses.

*†Manderston, Duns, Scottish Borders. Tel: 01361-883450. Open May–Sept. Thurs. and Sun. afternoons only. With 56 acres including formal terraces, woodland garden, formal walled garden, water features.

*Megginch Castle, Errol, Perthshire. Tel: 01821-642222. Gardens and Gothic courtyard of 1806. Yew and holly topiary, 1000 year old yews, 18th-century walled garden and annual border

*†Mellerstain House, nr Earlston, Borders. Tel: 01573 410225. Parkland and formal Edwardian gardens, rose garden laid out by Sarah, 12th Countess of Haddington.

*Mertoun, St Boswell's, Roxburghshire, Scottish Borders. Open April–Sept. weekends, public holidays and Monday afternoons. A 26-acre flower garden beside the Tweed. Azaleas, herbaceous border, ornamental pond. A 3-acre walled garden.

*Monteviot, Jedburgh, Scottish Borders. Open afternoons only, April–Oct. River garden with herbaceous perennials and shrubs. Rose gardens, water garden.

*†Mount Stuart House, Rothesay, Isle of Bute. Closed Tues. and Thurs. A 300-acre designed landscape. Mature pinetum, lime tree avenue, conifers, rock gardens, kitchen and herb garden, exotic southern hemisphere plants

*Pitmedden (NTS) Pitmedden, Ellon, Aberdeenshire. Tel: 01651 842352. A 17th-century patterned garden, box hedging and annuals. Herbaceous borders.

Priorwood Garden (NTS) Melrose. Closed
Jan.–Mar and Sun. morning. Orchard;
flowers suitable for drying.
Royal Botanic Garden, Edinburgh. Inverleith
Row, Edinburgh. Tel: 0131-552 7171.
Established 17th century, now a 75-acre site.
Noted for rhododendrons and azaleas. Rock
garden, peat and woodland gardens,
herbaceous borders. Arboretum. Glasshouses
display orchids, giant water-lilies and 200-
year-old West Indian palm tree. Chinese
Garden.
St Andrews Botanic Garden, Canongate,
St. Andrews. Tel: 01334-477178. Peat, rock
and water gardens.
*****Sea View,** Durnamuck, Dundonnell, Highlands.
Tel: 01854-633317. Began 1990 on shores of
Little Loch Broom. Heather bed, rock garden,
orchard, bog garden.
*****Teviot Water Garden,** Kirkbank House,
Eckford, Kelso, Scottish Borders. Tel: 01835-
850734. Adm. free. Waterfalls, aquatic plants,
perennials, grasses, ferns, bamboos.
Threave (NTS), Stewartry,Castle Douglas,
Dumfries and Galloway. Tel: 01556-502575.
A 65-acre garden used as school of
horticulture since 1960. Perennials and
annuals.Walled garden, vegetable garden and
orchard. Woodland and rock gardens.
Specialty rose garden and rhododendrons.
Arboretum.
†**Torosay Castle,** Craignure, Isle of Mull, Argyll
and Bute. Tel: 01680-812421. Formal Italian
garden with Italian rococo statues. Water
garden, Japanese garden, rhododendrons,
azaleas. Australian and New Zealand trees
and shrubs.
University of Dundee Botanic Garden,
Riverside Drive, Dundee. Tel: 01382-566939.
A 23-acre garden, glasshouses.
*****Younger Botanic Gardens,** Dunoon, Argyll and
Bute. Tel: 01369-706261. Offshoot of
Edinburgh's Royal Botanic Gardens.
Flowering trees and shrubs. 250 species of
rhododendrons and Great Redwoods planted
in 1863; magnolias; arboretum.

THE ARTS IN SCOTLAND

The distinctive character of the arts in Scotland is recognised worldwide. While the country is perhaps most widely known for the works of certain writers (Scott, Burns, MacGonagall) and for its traditional music and dance, and the popular concepts of 'Scottishness' that depend – rightly or wrongly – on them, Scotland has produced, and continues to produce, internationally important works of art, architecture, literature, classical music, and cinema. Scotland has 152 art galleries and 180 performing arts venues. In the performing arts, Scottish musicians and actors are outstanding in many fields.

Crafts, too, are thriving. A significant percentage (14 per cent) of the total population involved in crafts in Britain works in Scotland, a proportion which rose sharply during the 1980s, possibly under the influence of rapidly expanding tourism.

Around 46,000 people in Scotland, about two per cent of the workforce, work in cultural institutions or have culture-related occupations. Glasgow's designation as European City and Culture in 1990 is widely held to have given a big stimulus to its wider regeneration in the 1990s, and this was boosted by its being City of Architecture and Design in 1999.

ARTS FESTIVALS IN SCOTLAND

Founded in 1947, the Edinburgh International Festival (EIF) was the first major festival of the arts to be established in Europe as it recovered from the cataclysm of World War II. It was the initiative of Rudolph Byng, director of the Glyndebourne Festival Opera. Ironically, London, Oxford and Cambridge all turned down Byng's proposals for a festival in the style of Salzburg or Bayreuth, and the Edinburgh Festival quickly expanded and is now one of the world's major festivals of the arts, attracting world-class performers in music, opera and drama each August and surrounded by a flotilla of other events. In 1999 an estimated 400,000 people attended Festival events. Simultaneously with the EIF, the Festival Fringe and the Edinburgh International Film, Jazz and Book Festivals are held. The Fringe in particular has grown exponentially in recent years and now features thousands of events at hundreds of venues. In 1998 it decided to shift its dates to a week before the opening of the EIF; the decision proved controversial but has been sustained.

Edinburgh is the largest but by no means the only arts festival held regularly in Scotland. The annual St Magnus Festival in Orkney (June) is an important event, particularly for classical music, with a strong focus on new music and on involving the local community. There are big festivals at Glasgow (Celtic Connections, January; Glasgow International Jazz Festival, July; World Pipe Band Championship, August); Aberdeen (Aberdeen International Youth Festival, July; Aberdeen Alternative Festival, October; Bon Accord Festival, June), Perth (Perth Festival of the Arts, May), Dundee (Dundee City Festival, June), and many other places. There is even an annual Mendelssohn festival on the Isle of Mull.

Scotland's Voice is a new traditional music festival in Edinburgh, held for the first time in July 2000. Festivals focusing chiefly on traditional music and jazz are held in many towns and regions throughout the country. A large pop music festival, 'T in the Park', is held annually in Perth in July.

Detailed information on festivals can be obtained from the Scottish Arts Council, tourist boards, and the Scottish Music Information Centre.

THE SCOTTISH ARTS COUNCIL

The Scottish Arts Council (SAC) is the principal channel for government funding of the contemporary arts and crafts in Scotland. It receives an annual grant from the Scottish Executive, most of which is distributed to arts organisations and individual artists and craftspeople across Scotland, and is the channel for distributing National Lottery funds to the arts in Scotland. It also does important work in the promotion of arts education in schools.

However, despite the support of the SAC, arts funding is a perennial problem, particularly for many of the larger institutions. Because Scotland has a small population relative to its size, expected audiences outwith the Edinburgh-Glasgow 'central belt' and the major arts festivals are inevitably lower than in, for instance, the south-east of England, and it is not always easy to attract funding or sponsorship, particularly for permanent entities such as galleries and performance spaces or the national performing companies. For example, ambitious plans by the National Galleries of Scotland to locate a new National Gallery of Scottish Art and Design in Glasgow, first in the former Post Office buildings in George Square and then in the old sheriff courts in Ingram Street, were rejected by the Heritage Lottery Fund.

SUMMARY OF SAC BUDGET FOR 2000-1

Department	Budget
Visual arts	£2,240,531
Crafts	£363,363
Combined arts	£3,002,499
Dance	£3,156,916
Drama	£5,706,331
Literature	£1,247,169
Music	£11,399,455
Central funds	£656,319
Total	£27,772,583
Source: Scottish Arts Council	

Arts Council Grants
Grant to SAC from Scottish Office/Scottish Executive:
1999–2000:   £28.097 million
2000–1:   £27.772 million

LOTTERY FUNDING TO THE ARTS

The SAC has distributed well over £100 million in National Lottery funds to Scottish artists and arts organisations since 1994. As elsewhere in Britain, the bulk of Lottery funding tends to go to building projects, and some of these have been impressive, e.g. the Hub, Edinburgh (an all-year-round base for the Edinburgh Festival, opened in June 1999, containing an auditorium, rehearsal space, café-bar, and ticket office); and Dundee Contemporary Arts Centre (opened in March 1999, containing two art cinema screens, galleries, a printmaking studio, and a café-bar). However, funding is also available for creative activities; for instance, since 1995 the SAC lottery fund has also provided about £1 million in finance for the production of films in Scotland.

On 28 March 2000 the SAC announced the latest round of Lottery awards, totalling £6.6 million.

Awards
The SAC issues a number of awards for excellence in the different arts. A new set of awards begun only in 2000 are the Creative Scotland Awards, 14 of which, each worth £25,000, will be given each year to established artists living in Scotland and working in architecture, crafts, dance, design, digital media, drama/theatre, film/video, literature, music, photography, visual arts, and other artforms. The 2001 awards will be made on Burns Night (25 January) 2001.

All SAC Council meetings are now held in public, at different venues around the country.

Information on the Scottish Arts Council, its funding policies, and the arts in Scotland can be obtained from the SAC Helpdesk Tel: 0131-240 2443/4.

LITERATURE

It is impossible here to survey the whole wealth of Scottish literature; but we can mention a few of the best-known authors, beginning with William Dunbar and Robert Henryson, two of the 'Scottish Chaucerians' of the 15th and 16th centuries. These poets were all clearly influenced by Chaucer, but by no means slavish imitators of him. Writing in Scots, Dunbar, court poet to James IV, wrote celebratory poetry for the king but also mordant satire with equal virtuosity. Henryson returned several times to classical themes such as the tales of Orpheus and Eurydice, Troilus and Cressida (his most overt nod to Chaucer, but with an alternative ending), and his Morall Fabillis, which look back to Aesop.

The 18th and early 19th centuries produced the two most famous figures in Scottish literature: Robert Burns and Sir Walter Scott. The immense popularity of both authors has turned them into icons of 'Scottishness', though from very different perspectives. Both were immensely prolific, and both confronted the enormous changes taking place in Scottish society and governance after the suppression of Jacobitisim. But whereas Burns, the son of an Ayrshire tenant farmer, is loved for his celebration of ordinary people and democratic values and for his ability to express personal feelings, particularly love, in vivid and apparently simple verse and song, the novels and poems of Scott (who came from a more prosperous farming family in the Borders and had a successful career as a lawyer) reflect a vision of history that, while romantic and mythologising, also helped to revive and sustain an idea of Scottish identity and nation.

From the late Victorian era and the turn of the 20th century come several well-known authors such as Robert Louis Stevenson, J. M. Barrie, and John Buchan. Then, from the 1920s onward, there was a fresh flowering of Scottish literature which has become known as the 'Scottish Renaissance'. One of its instigators, and its main poet, was Hugh McDiarmid, possibly most famous for A drunk man looks at the thistle (1926). The novels of Neil M. Gunn, Sir Compton Mackenzie, Lewis Grassic Gibbon and others deal in different ways with social change and social conditions of the time - and, in the case of Gunn, of other times in Scotland's history. The poems and novels of George Mackay Brown are also steeped in history, that of his native Orkney.

The last two decades have seen a new generation of Scottish novelists and a shift of attention towards often uncompromising realism and urban themes. These writers include James Kelman, Janice Galloway, Candia McWilliam, Irvine Welsh, and others.

GAELIC LITERATURE

Alongside literature in English and Scots stands a strong tradition of poetry and prose in Gaelic reaching back to at least the early Middle Ages and encompassing heroic ballads narrating the deeds of legendary figures; an oral tradition of prose sagas; poems of praise written by professional bards in the services of clan chiefs and the nobility; songs and love poems, many of them anonymous, from the 16th and 17th centuries; poems of satire and nostalgia expressing a specifically Gaelic consciousness in response to the slow disintegration of Highland culture after the Jacobite rebellion and, later, the Clearances; and religious prose works. Much of the oral tradition in both prose and poetry was collected and written down in the 18th and 19th centuries. An Comunn Gaidhealach, founded in 1891 to promote Gaelic language and culture, increased interest in Gaelic writing in Gaelic-language periodicals which published stories and essays. Contemporary issues began to be written about in Gaelic.

Iain Crichton Smith (1928–98) was among those instrumental in maintaining and enriching the tradition of Gaelic prose writing after World War II, with novels and collections of stories. Sorley Maclean (1911–96) is a seminal figure in 20th-century Gaelic poetry; and he has been followed by a generation of young writers, particularly poets, carrying writing in Gaelic strongly into the new millennium.

CURRENT INSTITUTIONS

Several organisations of different kinds exist for the promotion of Scottish literature. The Association for Scottish Literary Studies, based at the University of Glasgow, promotes the study, teaching and writing of Scotland's literature and languages. Founded in 1970, it is now an international organisation with members in over 20 countries. It publishes a variety of periodicals (e.g. Scottish Studies Review), and in addition publishes each year an edition of a Scottish work which has either gone out of print or needs to be reintroduced to a contemporary readership, and an anthology of new writing.

The Scottish Poetry Library is a reference and lending library promoting Scottish and other poetry. Among other services, it has a computerised index to its collection called INSPIRE (International and Scottish Poetry Information Resrouce). The Society of Authors in Scotland is an independent trade union representing writers' interests in all areas of the profession.

The literary journal and magazine scene in Scotland is also lively, with old and new periodicals including the *Edinburgh Review, Cencrastus* (Edinburgh), *Cutting Teeth* (Glasgow), *Dark Horse* (Glasgow), *Inscotland* (Edinburgh, formerly *Books in Scotland*), *Markings* (Kirkcudbright), *Northwords* (Inverness), *Poetry Scotland* (Edinburgh), and *Scottish Studies* (Edinburgh). *Gairm*, the only all-Gaelic quarterly in existence, has been published since 1952; *Lallans*, the journal of the Scots Language Society, publishes work in Scots.

In addition, many of the major Scottish publishers specialise in Scottish literature, e.g. Canongate, Polygon, Chapman, and a number of small and locally focused presses.

EVENTS AND AWARDS

Coinciding with the Edinburgh International Festival, the annual Edinburgh International Book Festival holds readings, meetings and interviews with writers and publishers, and sells a wide range of modern and antiquarian books.

The Scottish Arts Council issues Spring and Autumn Book Awards and has recently instituted annual Children's Book Awards. Other awards include the Dundee Book Prize (University of Dundee), the Fidler Award for children's literature (c/o Scottish Book Trust), the James Tait Black Memorial Prize (Department of English Literature at the University of Edinburgh), the Macallan/*Scotland on Sunday* Short Story Competition, the RLS Memorial Award (National Library of Scotland), the Scottish International Open Poetry Competition, the Saltire Society Scottish Literary Awards, and the Scottish Writer of the Year (c/o Scottish Book Trust).

MUSIC

CLASSICAL MUSIC

There is archaeological evidence of music-making in Scotland as far back as the eighth century BC, in finds such as a fragment of a bronze horn of that date, a carnyx (a long bronze war trumpet) from about 200 BC–AD 200, and representations of musical instruments on Pictish stone carvings of the eighth to tenth centuries AD.

The first music manuscripts containing Scottish music date from the 13th century, although some of the music in them, such as the chants for St Columba, may be older. They bear witness to a highly developed tradition of church music in Scotland, which seems to have reached its peak in the early 16th century with the work of Robert Carver, Scotland's greatest pre-Reformation composer and one of its greatest of any period. The manuscript containing all his extant work is one of the few music books to have survived the destruction wrought by the Reformation. Choral music from the late 16th century shows how radically the style of music permitted in church changed from the complex polyphony of Carver to unornamented hymn tunes and psalm settings, in Scots rather than Latin. Instrumental music, such as the keyboard works of William Kinloche, dating from c. 1610, shows a continuing secular tradition with some distinct echoes of contemporary French styles. However, the Union of the Crowns in 1603 and the removal of the court to London and its patronage of the arts was a severe blow to classical musicians.

From the late 17th century a flow of composers and performers between Scotland and Italy began, stimulated in part by the fast-growing popularity of the violin in Scotland. One of the first to travel was John Clerk of Penicuik, who studied with Corelli. Among his many cantatas was one celebrating the ill-fated Darien venture of 1689; like its subject, it was abandoned unfinished.

In the late 18th and the 19th centuries, political and social turbulence and a shortage of resources limited the production of composed music. In fact it was not until the late 20th century, with the foundation of the Edinburgh International Festival and the establishment of the major orchestras and Scottish Opera and Ballet, that a new wave of outstanding Scottish composers arose. These include Thea Musgrave, Ronald Stevenson, James Macmillan, Judith Weir, Sally Beamish and William Sweeney.

TRADITIONAL MUSIC

Alongside – and intertwined with – the history of composed classical music runs a strong double strand of Gaelic and Scots traditional music, unbroken for centuries. It is basically an oral tradition, and although many of the old songs and tunes have been written down since the 17th

century and have been the subject for much scholarship, the tradition is passionately alive today and continually developing. The Gaelic tradition is the oldest of all, and was probably brought to Scotland with the early settlers from Ireland. Its characteristic instrument is the clàrsach, or Celtic harp. A well-known form of Gaelic song is the waulking song, a strongly rhythmic work song which accompanied the hand-treatment of linen or tweed cloth. The tradition of Scots-language songs and ballads began later, in about the 13th century, and included epic narrative ballads as well as work songs and dance forms. The industrial revolution, the Clearances, and emigration were later ballad themes.

The 17th century, while something of a fallow period for large-scale classical compositions, was one of the richest times for the ballad tradition and especially for Gaelic music. In was in this period that the music of the pipes and the uniquely Scottish *piobaireachd* or *pibroch* form were developed. Similarly, in the 19th century, perhaps the strongest area of musical activity, in part inspired by romantic views of Scottish history, was the collection, notation and arrangement of folk-songs, ballads and fiddle tunes. In fact, people had been writing ballads down since the 16th century, and Robert Burns was an avid collector and writer of songs (many of which were recorded by the traditional singer Jean Redpath in the 1970s). The National Mod, an annual, competitive festival of performing arts in Gaelic, was instituted in 1892 and remains an important instrument for the promotion of Gaelic culture.

The last 20 years have seen a big upsurge in traditional music and popular music with strong folk elements, building upon the pioneering work of Ewan McColl and his recordings of Scottish popular ballads in the 1950s and 1960s. A few key figures of the many musicians in this movement are the Boys of the Lough with the Shetland fiddle player Aly Bain, the Whistlebinkies, fiddler Alasdair Fraser, singers Cathy-Ann McPhee and Sheena Wellington, and bands singing in Gaelic such as Runrig and Capercaillie.

CURRENT MUSICAL INSTITUTIONS

Scotland's contemporary musical life is underpinned by several national performing companies: the Royal Scottish National Orchestra (RNSO; founded 1890), Scottish Opera (founded 1962 under Alexander Gibson), and the Scottish Chamber Orchestra (SCO;

founded 1974). Each of these has an associated chorus, and there is also an Edinburgh Festival Chorus which performs specifically for the Festival. There are also a number of smaller professional orchestras and vocal groups of international status.

The National Youth Orchestras of Scotland (NYOS), formed in 1979, comprises four orchestras: the National Youth Orchestra of Scotland (symphony orchestra), Camerata Scotland (a pre-professional chamber orchestra), the National Children's Orchestra of Scotland, and the National Youth Jazz Orchestra of Scotland. Together, they aim to provide a continuous sequence of practical music education and playing experience from nursery-school age to the professional level.

The Royal Scottish Academy of Music and Drama, in Glasgow, is the chief higher education institution for music, theatre and opera. It began in 1928 as the Scottish National Academy of Music, becoming the Royal Scottish Academy of Music in 1944 and adding the drama school the following year.

For traditional music, the Traditional Music and Song Association of Scotland, founded in 1966, is a valuable resource centre. Also in Glasgow, the Piping Centre is a national centre for the promotion of the bagpipes and their music.

DANCE

CLASSICAL DANCE

Scottish Ballet is Scotland's national classical dance company. Originally formed in Bristol in 1957 as Western Theatre Ballet, it moved to Glasgow in 1969, and on 3 May that year had a famous debut together with Scottish Opera in Berlioz's *The Trojans*. The company's arrival to take on the role of Scotland's national ballet company followed a series of unsuccessful attempts to establish such a company from about 1940 onwards, one candidate for which had been the Glasgow-based Celtic Ballet Company run by Margaret Morris, wife of the Colourist painter J. D. Fergusson.

Scottish Ballet performs both large-scale classics with a full dance company and orchestra in major theatres such as the Edinburgh Festival Theatre and chamber works for much smaller forces in spaces as small as a village hall or school gym. Its Education Unit carries out an extensive programme of education and outreach work in schools from nursery to secondary level (both mainstream and special education), universities

and colleges of further education, community groups and hospitals, and with senior citizens' groups and sight- and hearing-impaired adults. It organises summer schools and courses, and can tailor projects to meet the needs of specific groups.

In recent years Dundee has become a focus for dance and dance education, with its own full-time professional dance company, Scottish Dance Theatre, based at the Dundee Repertory Theatre, and Scotland's only contemporary dance school, Scottish School of Contemporary Dance, which was founded in 1999 and is based at Dundee College. An aim of the school was to enable students to pursue their training for the profession in Scotland rather than having to travel elsewhere. A new multi-purpose venue, The Space, is being built to accommodate dance and drama classes, workshops and master classes for the local community and college students, and other facilities for the community and business.

The Dance School of Scotland, at Knightswood Secondary School in Glasgow, is Scotland's first full-time dance course for secondary-level students offering dance, singing and drama training within the state comprehensive school system

TRADITIONAL DANCE

Traditional Scottish dance encompasses various forms: sets or dances for groups of four of more people, dances for couples, and solo dances. Strictly speaking, 'Highland dancing' refers to the dancing which has its roots in the creation of the Highland regiments in the 18th and 19th centuries and the development of Highland Games, which always included dancing. The solo Sword Dance, for instance, is certainly as old as the 18th century and possibly older. In that context the pipes would have provided the music, but as Highland dancing became fashionable with Queen Victoria's patronage of Highland Games, other instruments, especially the violin, became associated with dancing. Dances for couples became popular in the 19th century under the influence of dances from England and further afield. Scottish country dancing seems always to have been a democratic affair; much the same dances were performed at balls and at village gatherings. No doubt the steps were familiar to most people; in the 19th century dances would often be taught by dancing masters at village schools.

Modern Scottish country dancing or 'ceilidh dancing' generally means set dancing. The term 'country dance' is a corruption of the French 'contredanse', referring to the fact that in these dances two lines of dancers typically stand facing ('opposite') each other. Ceilidhs (literally, the Gaelic word *céilidh* means 'visit') were an essential feature of social life in the Highlands, accompanying most celebrations, particularly weddings, and dancing is still a standard ingredient of weddings today, as well as Christmas and other celebrations. However, ceilidh dancing nowadays is most often performed by non-experts. As dancing became more popular among people who were not necessarily skilled at it, the practice of having a caller to call out the steps was adopted, and this still occurs sometimes. Formal Scottish country dances are also still held, where the dancers are expected to know the steps.

From quite early in the 20th century a movement to record and preserve traditional dances arose. The Scottish Country Dance Society was formed in 1923 (later adding 'Royal' to its title); it has published a large amount of dance music. Thirty years later, the Scottish Official Board of Highland Dancing was founded to preserve the traditional forms. Also concerned with researching and conserving Scotland's dance traditions is the Scottish Traditions of Dance Trust.

Traditional dance has a competitive as well as a social side, and several Highland dancing competitions are held each year. Dunoon hosts the World Highland Dancing championships, attracting competitors from around not only Scotland but also the world.

FILM

Until the 1990s, the film industry in Scotland was small. Scottish directors and actors tended to migrate to London or Hollywood and few feature directors derived their thematic material from their own country and culture before the 1980s, when Bill Douglas and Bill Forsyth began to make feature films showing a picture of Scotland that reached beyond the folkloric to address issues such as city life, poverty, or growing up . Yet Scots have been involved in moving pictures for many decades, ever since Queen Victoria was filmed at Balmoral in 1895. Among the most notable figures is John Grierson, founding father of the British documentary.

Scotland's rollcall of well-known and highly regarded film actors is long. Current stars such as Ewan McGregor, Robert Carlyle, John Hannah, Douglas Henshall, and others are just the latest in a long line including Dame Flora Robson (1902-

84), James Robertson Justice (1905–75), Deborah Kerr CBE (1921–), Gordon Jackson (1923–90), Ian Bannen (1928–99), Sir Sean Connery (1930), Phyllida Law (1932–), Tom Conti (1941), Bill Paterson (1946–), Billy Connolly (1942–), and Phyllis Logan (1956–).

But it is since 1994, the year in which Danny Boyle's *Shallow Grave* appeared, that the film industry in Scotland has been experiencing a boom. The unexpected success of that film, the immense popularity of Mel Gibson's *Braveheart* (1995), and particularly the runaway success in 1996 of Boyle's next film, *Trainspotting* (the most profitable British film ever, making £45 million in global box-office earnings), made the mid-1990s a watershed for Scottish film. Since then a stream of successful and well-received Scottish features has appeared, including *Small Faces* (Gillies MacKinnon, 1996), *Mrs Brown* (John Madden, 1997), *Carla's song* and *My Name is Joe* (Ken Loach, 1995 and 1998), *Orphans* (Peter Mullan, 1999), *Ratcatcher* (Lynne Ramsay, 1999), *Women Talking Dirty* (Coky Giedroyc, 1999), and *Complicity* (Gavin Millar, 2000).

On the small screen, whereas representations of Scotland once tended to be synonymous with *Dr Finlay's Casebook*, Scottish themes as well as Scottish locations, from the gritty (*Roughnecks, Rebus*) to the whimsical (*Monarch of the Glen, Hamish McBeth*) and the outrageous (*Rab C. Nesbit*), are now more and more frequently seen on British television. Much of this growth in the film and television industry is due to the development of an institutional infrastructure and the increased availability of funding from the SAC (particularly via the National Lottery), Scottish Screen, Channel 4, the BBC, and the Glasgow Film Fund.

SCOTLAND THE PHOTOGENIC

The 'Braveheart factor' has also caused interest in Scotland's potential as a source of film locations. Over 40 feature films were shot entirely or partly in Scotland in the 1990s by directors as varied as Franco Zeffirelli, Brian de Palma, Ken Loach, Lars von Trier and Mel Gibson, as well as by Scottish directors. Even 'Bollywood', the Indian commercial film industry, seeking ever more exotic locations for its popular spectaculars, has used Scottish castles as a backdrop. The connection between more Scottish locations appearing on screen and more tourists appearing in Scotland has not passed unnoticed, either. In April 2000 Scottish Screen joined forces with the Scottish Tourist Board, Scottish Trade International and Historic Scotland to publish a brochure promoting Scottish film locations to the industry.

EXHIBITIONS
Developments in commercial distribution and exhibition in Scotland parallel those elsewhere in Britain, with a trend towards big-chain multiplexes and a corresponding reduction in other cinemas. The principal chains operating in Scotland are UCI, Odeon, Virgin, ABC, Warner Village and Showcase. There are still some cinemas in smaller communities run by the Scottish chain Caledonian Cinemas, and a few family-run enterprises such the Pavilion, Galashiels, and the Dominion in Edinburgh.

Outside the major conurbations, however, permanent commercial cinemas are rare. The SAC has identified a cinema shortage, and National Lottery funding has recently been awarded to cinema development projects in Newton Stewart, Thurso, Portree, Stornoway, and Stranraer, and to Britain's first mobile cinema. The Screen Machine, a lorry trailer which converts to a 110-seat cinema, tours the Highlands and Islands showing mainstream and other films. It is administratively based in Inverness.

The Edinburgh International Film Festival is Scotland's largest annual film event and is now a world-class festival, premiering both British and international films. In 2000 it showed the world première of Terence Davies' House of Mirth, which uses Glasgow as a location (standing in for turn-of-the-century New York!), and UK premières of Lars von Trier's *Dancing in the Dark* and Wong Kar-Wai's *In the Mood for Love*.

A pioneer of television
The inventor John Logie Baird (1888–1946), a pioneer of television and radio, was a native of Helensburgh. His achievements in sending images by telephone wire from London to Glasgow and then across the Atlantic enabled the BBC to show its first television picture in 1929. However, his technological innovations were overtaken by those of IBM in the mid-1930s, although he continued to experiment with colour, 3-D and other developments, and radar.

SCOTTISH SCREEN
Scottish Screen is the public body responsible for promoting and developing all aspects of film, television and multimedia in Scotland, through

the support of industrial and cultural initiatives. It took over the Scottish Film Production Fund in 1996 and is a major funder of films in Scotland. It supports and facilitates the production of films by Scottish film-makers, the use of Scottish locations by national and international film-makers, the preservation of Scotland's film heritage, and increased cinema-going and understanding of film in Scotland. It runs a variety of long and short training courses, industry-related initiatives and educational activities, and is a first port of call for both Scottish film-makers developing a project and foreign film-makers looking for locations and facilities. It is a member of the Cinema Exhibitors' Association, the trade association for the cinema industry, and works with the commercial sector where appropriate.

The Scottish Film and Television Archive preserves Scotland's heritage of films from the past, both professional and amateur. It holds some 20,000 reels of film from 1897 onwards, mostly non-fiction, including thousands of old feature films, home movies, newsreels, government information films and early advertisements for local businesses, unearthed and donated by members of the public. Film researchers have been sifting through these and in June 2000 Glasgow Film Theatre hosted a special screening of a selection of them.

Scottish Screen provides support to seven art cinemas, which in 1998–9 recorded 400,000 admissions. They are:

- Eden Court Theatre, Inverness
- Dundee Contemporary Arts, Dundee
- MacRobert Arts Centre, Stirling
- Adam Smith Theatre, Kirkcaldy
- Filmhouse, Edinburgh
- Glasgow Film Theatre, Glasgow
- Robert Burns Centre, Dumfries

Oscar-winning tartan shorts
Seawards the Great Ships was made for Films of Scotland and the Clyde Shipbuilders Association in 1960. An evocative testimony to the achievements of the shipbuilders on the Clyde and to the men of the "black squads", it was directed by Hilary Harris from a treatment by John Grierson. It won an Oscar for best live-action short film 1961.
Thirty-five years later, the 1995 Oscar for best live-action short film went to Peter Capaldi's Franz Kafka's It's a Wonderful Life.

VISUAL ARTS

ART IN EARLY SCOTLAND

Evidence of artistic skill in Scotland from the earliest times survives in finely wrought gold jewellery and bronze weapons; in the bronze boar's head from the Deskford carnyx (*see* Classical Music); in the early Christian stones and slabs which combine Pictish spirals and stylised animal motifs with ornamented crosses and other motifs of Irish origin, visible also in the great illuminated books such as that of Kells. The seventh to ninth centuries were a high point for Celtic art.

Though the arrival of the Vikings is often thought of merely as a time of destruction, their long occupation of parts of Scotland did make a cultural contribution, reflected most strongly in the 12th-century Lewis chess pieces, whether these were locally made or imported from Norway.

REFORMATION AND RECOVERY

Far more thoroughgoing destruction was inflicted by the Reformation. The double blow of the Reformation and the departure of the court to London in 1603 was devastating. Only a few tantalising fragments – remnants of wall paintings (Dunkeld cathedral), textile fragments, maps – give clues to the flourishing visual culture under James IV and James V that was lost in this period and the mid-17th century Bishops' Wars.

It was not until the 1640s that Scottish artists appeared again in their own country. The portraits painted by George Jameson of Aberdeen, including his self-portrait against a background of other paintings, establish him as the first Scottish painter in the modern sense. The Scottish School of Portraiture was to find its highest expression in the works of Allan Ramsay and Henry Raeburn in the following century. But before them came a series of painters including John Michael Wright, Jameson's most distinguished pupil. Wright's portrait of Lord Mungo Murray in Highland dress, echoed both in costume and pose by Raeburn's famous picture of Alasdair Macdonell of Glengarry over a century later, created an image of 'Scottishness' that was to become persistent.

THE SCOTTISH ENLIGHTENMENT

The neoclassicism of the 18th century was mainly expressed through architecture, but as the century progressed landscape paintings began to be produced which show the influence of Continental neoclassicists such as Claude Lorrain. A circle of intellectuals and artists grew up in Edinburgh, and Scotland's first art school, the Academy of St Luke, was established in 1729. Portraitists like William Aikman (1682–1731) found it easier to get commissions in London than in Scotland, though some, such as Aberdonians John Alexander (1686–c.1766) and William Mosman (1700–71) spent most of their careers in Scotland after studying in Rome.

The second half of the 18th century was marked by the interaction of art and philosophy – Allan Ramsay, together with his friends the philosopher David Hume and the economist Adam Smith, formed the Select Society – and further development of art training institutions, such as the Foulis Academy in Glasgow (1754) and the Trustees' Academy in Edinburgh (1766). Ramsay is the outstanding figure of this period. His genius lay in his empathetic interpretation of the sitter in either formal or intimate portraits, and in his delicate luminosity of style.

Alongside the classical themes favoured by several painters of this period (e.g. the six huge canvases by Gavin Hamilton (1723–98)) depicting scenes from Homer's *Iliad*, there grew up a romantic interest in the Celtic past, a pioneer in this respect being Alexander Runciman (1736–85), who chose the harper Ossian and other themes from Celtic legend for his etchings and some sketches for a set of murals (now lost) for the house of Sir James Clerk of Penicuik. This began a process of Celtic revival and reclamation of the Scottish past which is some respects is still going on, and a duality between classicism and Celticism that was to continue throughout the century.

Henry Raeburn was the second great portraitist of the Scottish Enlightenment, and probably the best-known painter of the century, not least because of his famous Rev. *Robert Walker Skating* in Edinburgh's National Gallery. His major portraits date from the early 1790s and are works of great humanity and perception as well as masterly essays in the study of light.

After its zenith with Raeburn, portraiture became less central to Scottish painting (although an active school of portrait sculpture developed in the early 19th century), and landscape and genre painting came to the fore. Alexander Nasmyth was the seminal figure in landscape painting. To the usual art education in London and Rome he added an acquaintance with northern European – particularly Dutch – landscape painting and an interest in the relationship between human beings and landscape, nature and culture; this can be seen in his two canvases of Edinburgh, which juxtapose the wild natural forms of Calton Hill and Arthur's Seat with the perspectives of human construction. Nasmyth was also an influential teacher.

In genre painting, David Wilkie became the master of paintings depicting daily life. His paintings 'tell a story' and assert the dignity of ordinary people; some of them implicitly comment on the social and economic reality of the time.

WILDERNESS AND DISPOSSESSION
In 1826 a group of 11 artists formed themselves into the Scottish Academy as a representative body for Scottish artists. The academy was modelled loosely on the Royal Academy in London. It obtained its royal charter in 1837, and its members were instrumental in founding the National Gallery of Scotland, which opened in 1859.

As the 19th century progressed, a school of painting emerged which could lay claim to be distinctively Scottish. Many of its members had studied at the Trustees' Academy, which became the principal art school in the country under Robert Scott Lauder (1803–61). Lauder painted scenes from Scott's Waverley novels, among other subjects, and was one of a diverse circle including David Octavius Hill (1802–70), also a pioneering photographer, Horatio McCulloch (1805–67), Thomas Faed (1826–1900) and William Dyce (1806–64). These artists painted the Highlands as uninhabited wilderness and spectacle, while at the same time depicting themes of emigration and exile from the land, for instance in Faed's Highland Mary (1857) and his famous The Last of the Clan (1865), or McCulloch's The Emigrant's Dream of his Highland Home (1860).

At this time there was a vogue for large public sculptures of important Scottish and British figures. Outstanding here is John Steell (1804–91), whose figure of Sir Walter Scott forms the central element of the Scott Memorial in East Princes Street Garden, Edinburgh.

THE RISE OF GLASGOW AS AN ART CENTRE
Toward the end of the century, a new approach to landscape painting was introduced by William McTaggart, who used a freer, almost impressionist technique, particularly noticeable in his coastal scenes and seascapes. He too took up the theme of the Highland Clearances and emigration in a series of 'Emigrant Ship' canvases of the 1890s.

In the 1880s Glasgow took over from Edinburgh as the epicentre of Scottish painting.

The Glasgow Institute of the Fine Arts had been set up in 1861 as a counterpart – and in part a challenge – to Edinburgh's Royal Scottish Academy, and a sizeable group of artists, nicknamed the 'Glasgow Boys' (although one at least was a woman) coalesced around a reaction to the Victorian concept of landscape and a tendency to look to France for inspiration. Following McTaggart's lead, this as the first group of Scottish painters who regularly painted in the open air, and this led to a change in landscape subject matter from mountain and moor to rivers, coasts and villages. The 'Boys' also returned to subjects from ordinary life, such as John Lavery's Tennis party of 1885 or James Guthrie's more down-to-earth A Hind's Daughter (1883), with hints of Cézanne in its brushwork. It is possible to discern a line of descent from these works, via the jewel-like watercolours of Arthur Melville (1855–1904), to the treatment of colour and paint characteristic of the Colourists a few decades later.

Also in the early 1890s, Charles Rennie Mackintosh was at the centre of a group of artists, fellow-students at the Glasgow School of Art: Margaret Macdonald (1863–1933), who became Mackintosh's wife, her sister Frances (1874–1921), and Herbert MacNair (1868–1955). The decorative style they developed, close to Art Nouveau but identifiably their own, has become very famous, and inspired the work of a wider circle of graphic and applied artists. Mackintosh's own landscape paintings, however, overshadowed by the popularity of his design, have not fully received the appreciation they deserve. In Edinburgh, the clear thematic and stylistic links between the Arts and Crafts movement and the Celtic Revival are illustrated in the work of Phoebe Anna Traquair (1852–1936), which encompasses a vast range of crafts from metalwork to murals. Her murals for the Catholic Apostolic Church are an impressive example.

THE 20TH CENTURY
The four Colourists – Samuel Peploe, J. D. Fergusson, F. C. B. Cadell and G. L. Hunter – are distinguished by their freshness and spontaneity and the brilliance of light and colour in their paintings. All four spent considerable time in France and it is likely the Fauves were an influence on them and, later, Matisse.

By the 1930s, Modernism was firmly established in Scottish painting in the works of William Crozier (1897–1930), Anne Redpath (1895–1965), William Johnstone (1897–1981), James Cowie (1880–1956) and others. The continental influence (Matisse, Klee, Cubism) remained strong, but landscape continued to be a principal source of subject matter. The influence of the Colourists continued to be felt after World War II and to show up in Scottish interpretations of newer styles. But great diversity characterises artists of the 1950s and after, such as Robert MacBryde (1913–66), Robert Colquhoun (1914–62), Joan Eardley (1921–63), and the sculptors Eduardo Paolozzi (1924–) and Ian Hamilton Finlay. Among yet more recent work are large projects working in the landscape by George Wyllie, Kate Whiteford and Will Maclean; Maclean's three large works on Lewis (1996), commemorating the struggle between landlords and tenants at the turn of the 20th century, raise again questions of national history and identity. Calum Colvin, a winner of one of the SAC's Creative Scotland Awards, is taking up the Celtic thread with an exhibition of digital and analog photographic works based on James Macpherson's *The Poems of Ossian and Related Works*. A resurgence of figurative art has informed the work of the new generation of Glasgow painters such as Alexander Moffat; and the opening of the Glasgow Gallery of Modern Art in 1996 has made a new space available for the work of Scotland's new generation of artists.

CURRENT INSTITUTIONS

Most of the art institutions set up in the last century continue in existence, though they have all undergone changes and sometimes crisis over the years. Bodies existing today include the following.

The Royal Scottish Academy (RSA) is the main exhibiting body promoting the works of living Scottish professional artists. It has about 40 full members and 50 associate members, elected from the disciplines of architecture, painting, printmaking and sculpture, and holds a large annual exhibition.

The Royal Glasgow Institute of the Fine Arts, established in 1861 also has a gallery and exhibition space, and holds lectures.

Royal Society of Painters in Watercolours promotes the status of watercolour as a major art. It holds an annual exhibition at the RSA galleries, and also issues financial awards.

The principal remit of the Royal Fine Art Commission for Scotland is to advise government on the visual impact of new constructions.

Among institutions for art education and training, many are part of universities. Glasgow School of Art is one of the very few remaining independent art schools in the United Kingdom.

It was founded in 1845 as a Government School of Design and added the study and practice of the fine arts and architecture to its curriculum in the late 19th century. The present building, commissioned in 1896, is one of Charles Rennie Mackintosh's masterpieces. The School's degrees are accredited by the University of Glasgow.

At Aberdeen, Gray's School of Art, which is part of the Robert Gordon University, has almost as long a history as the Glasgow School of Art. It was founded in 1850, gifted to Robert Gordon's College by John Gray, an engineer and philanthropist. A new Gray's School was built at its current location in 1966.

Other art schools include the Edinburgh College of Art and the Duncan of Jordanstone College of Art in Dundee.

ARCHITECTURE

A HERITAGE IN STONE

Stone has always been a characteristic material of Scottish architecture, and this has ensured a very large and varied built heritage from all periods, with buildings more likely to have been destroyed by conflict than just to have fallen into decay. The prevailing styles of the Middle Ages, except in the Highlands and Islands, were very similar to those found in England and France, since it was to these countries that the kings responsible for the upsurge in building from the 12th century onwards looked. Norman-style churches such as Dalmeny church, near South Queensferry, and Dunfermline Abbey date from the early part of this period. The Gothic style which followed can be seen at its best in what survives of the Border abbeys, of which Melrose is both one of the latest (having been completely destroyed in the 14th century and rebuilt in the 15th) and most elaborate.

Over the medieval period, the typical form of the castle settled into that of a keep with a courtyard defended by a heavy curtain wall. Many castles dating from the 14th and 15th centuries survive: some well-known examples are Glamis, Dunvegan and the much-photographed Eilean Donan. Smaller castles of the period, such as Smailholm (Borders), show the features that were to evolve into the tower house, the typical dwelling of the Scottish lairds from the 15th to the 17th centuries. Here the jewel in the crown is widely held to be Craigievar Castle (Aberdeenshire), largely because its elegant original lines escaped Victorian remodelling. Meanwhile, beauty as much as strength was the principle governing the creation of the great palaces of the Stewart kings, such as Linlithgow, Falkland and Stirling, which show strong French Renaissance influences; while in the crowded city of Edinburgh (now the Old Town), confined within the city wall, a jigsaw of closes and wynds with six- and seven-storey tenements proliferated, becoming ever more cramped and jumbled.

CLASSICISM AND ROMANTICISM
The first Scottish buildings whose architects are known date from the early 17th century. The names of William Wallace, William Ayton, and John and Robert Mylne are associated with the building of George Heriot's Hospital (now a school) in Edinburgh, begun in 1628, while the palace of Holyroodhouse was rebuilt, after a fire in 1650, to a design by Sir William Bruce, assisted by Robert·Mylne (1633–1710). Mylne was one of a dynasty of master masons and architects, spanning 200 years from the late 16th century and based in Dundee.

In the late 18th century, a more flourishing economy fuelled a boom in building and a flowering of the English Classical style, which is best illustrated by Edinburgh's New Town, designed by James Craig in 1767 and with later contributions by Robert Adam (Charlotte Square, 1791). Robert and his father William Adam, probably Scotland's greatest classicists, designed Mellerstain House (Borders), and were responsible for both the interior and exterior of a large extension to Hopetoun House (South Queensferry), originally built by William Bruce. This was also the period of construction of new towns and villages, part of the policy of Improvement.

Victorian architecture was heavily influenced by retrospection and a romantic idea of Scotland, but innovative in its eclectic borrowing from any and every style of the past. In a revival of the Scottish baronial style, the turrets and crenellations of 16th century tower houses reappeared not only on country mansions but suburban villas. As the cities mushroomed, the tenement, at varying levels of luxury, became the typical urban dwelling. Church-building took off again and neo-Gothic churches are to be seen in every Scottish town. Gilbert Scott's Glasgow University Building of 1867 is a fine example of this style, as is St John's Tolbooth on the High Street, Edinburgh, originally built as General Assembly Rooms by James Gillespie Graham in 1842, later transformed by Augustus Pugin, and converted in 1999 to a new administrative and social centre for the Edinburgh Festival, the Hub.

Looking even further back to classical models, but also forward in his use of them, was Alexander 'Greek' Thomson in Glasgow. His churches at St Vincent Street (1859), and Caledonian Road (1856) are particularly important examples of neoclassical architecture; while in his use of Egyptian-inspired decoration and severely horizontal composition, for instance in the Egyptian Halls, Union Street (1871–3), he was well ahead of his time. A major exhibition of his work as part of Glasgow's year as City of Architecture and Design (1999) has contributed to a revaluation of Thomson.

MACKINTOSH AND AFTER
Glasgow's other major architect, and probably Scotland's best known architect and designer ever, is, of course, Charles Rennie Mackintosh, whose greatest work was carried out at the turn of the 20th century. One of the greatest exponents of the British Arts and Crafts movement, Mackintosh was also a designer of furniture and textiles and a painter, and his elegant Art Nouveau decoration, which has been overly imitated in recent years, has perhaps distracted attention from architecture such as the Glasgow School of Art (1897), his most famous building, the Willow Tea Rooms in Sauchiehall Street, and Hill House (Helensburgh, 1902), a Scottish tower house for the 20th century with an exquisitely detailed interior.

Glasgow continues to produce innovative buildings at the end of the 20th century, such as Sir Norman Foster's Clyde Auditorium, nicknamed 'the Armadillo' because of its use of overlapping shells reminiscent of the Sydney Opera House. In Dundee, Richard Murphy's Contemporary Arts Centre, converted from a former garage and car showroom, combines a spacious, clean-lined interior with a sweeping, curvilinear frontage.

Meanwhile, in Edinburgh, the new National Museum of Scotland (1996–8), built mostly of sandstone, has been widely acclaimed. At the time of writing, the most controversial architectural project in Scotland must be the new Scottish Parliament Building in Edinburgh. An architectural competition in 1997 awarded the design contract to the Catalan architect Enric Miralles, who submitted an imaginative and elegant design; but progress has been dogged by budget problems and the project has been dealt a further blow by Miralles' untimely death, at the age of 45, in early July 2000.

SOME KEY FIGURES IN THE ARTS

Writers

Barrie, Sir James M. (1860–1937). Playwright and novelist. *Quality Street* (1902), *The Admirable Crichton* (1902), *Peter Pan* (1904)

Brown, George Mackay (1921–), poet, novelist and short-story writer. Poetry: *Loaves and Fishes* (1959), *Fishermen with Ploughs* (1971), *Stone: Poems* (1987): novels: *Greenvoe* (1972), *Magnus*(1973), *Time in a Red Coat* (1984). Short stories: *The Masked !   'erman and Other Stories* (1989)

Buchan, John (1   )–1940), novelist, biographer, historian, essayists, journalist, editor, poet and publisher. Wrote 100 books, including *The Thirty-Nine Steps* (1915), *Witch Wood* (1927), *Castle Gay* (1930); biographies of Montrose, Cromwell, and Scott

Burns, Robert (1759–96), poet and songwriter. *Poems Chiefly in the Scottish Dialect* (1786); poems include 'Auld lang syne', 'O my luve is like a red, red rose', *Tam O'Shanter*

Carlyle, Thomas (1795–1881), essayist, historian, philosopher, and critic. *The French Revolution* (1837), *On Heroes, Hero-worship and the Heroic in History* (1841), *Past and Present* (1843), *Oliver Cromwell's Letters and Speeches* (1845), *The History of Frederick the Great* (1858–65)

Dunbar, William (1460–c.1513), poet. *Lament for the Makaris, The Thrissil and the Rois* (nuptial song for marriage of James IV and Margaret Tudor in 1503), *The Flyting of Dunbar and Kennedie, Dance of the Sevin Deidly Synnes*

Galloway, Janice (1956–), novelist and short-story writer. *The Trick is to Keep Breathing* (1989), *Blood* (1992), *Foreign Parts* (1994)

Gibbon, Lewis Grassic (James Leslie Mitchell, 1901–35), novelist, journalist, historian and archaeologist. *A Scots Quair* (trilogy, 1932–4), *Stained Radiance* (1930), *Scots Scene: or, The Intelligent Man's Guide to Albyn* (1934, with Hugh MacDiarmid)

Gunn, Neil M. (1891–1973), novelist. *Morning Tide* (1930), *Highland River* (1937), *The Silver Darlings* (1941)

Gray, Alasdair (1934–), novelist. *Lanark* (1981), *Janine* (1982), *Poor Things* (1992)

Henryson, Robert (c.1420–c.1490), poet. *The Testament of Cresseid, The Morall Fabillis of Esope the Phrygian, Robene and Makyne*

Kelman, James (1946–), novelist and short-story writer. *Greyhound for Breakfast* (1987), *A Disaffection* (1989), *How Late It Was, How Late* (1994, Booker Prize)

Lindsay, Sir David (1490–1555), playwright. *Ane Satyre of the Thrie Estaits*

Lochhead, Liz (1947–), poet and playwright. Poetry: *Memo for Spring* (1972), *The Grimm Sisters* (1981), *True Confessions and New Clichés* (1985); plays: *Blood and Ice* (1982), *Mary Queen of Scots Got Her Head Chopped Off* (1989), *Perfect Days* (1998)

Macbeth, George (1932–92), poet. *The Broken Places* (1963), *Shrapnel* (1973), *Anatomy of a Divorce* (1988)

MacDiarmid, Hugh (Christopher Murray Grieve, 1892–1978). Poet and critic. *Sangschaw* (1925), *A Drunk Man Looks at the Thistle* (1926), *In Memoriam James Joyce* (1954), 'On a raised beach' (1934)

MacGonagall, William (1825–1902), affectionately hailed as 'the world's worst poet'. *Poetic Gems* (1890); 'Railway bridge of the silv'ry Tay', 'The Tay Bridge disaster', 'The death of Lord and Lady Dalhousie'

Mackenzie, Sir Compton (1883–1972), novelist, playwright, journalist and broadcaster. *Sinister Street* (1918), *The Four Winds of Love* (6 vols., 1937–45), *Whisky Galore* (1947)

Ramsay, Allan (1684–1758), poet and editor. Collections of verse 1721, 1728; editor of *The Ever Green* (anthology of Middle Scots poetry) and *Tea-Table Miscellany* (traditional songs and ballads plus some compositions of his own).

Scott, Sir Walter (1771–1832), novelist, poet, editor and critic. Poems include *The Lay of the Last Minstrel* (1805), *The Lady of the Lake* (1810); novels include *Waverley* (1814), *Rob Roy* (1817), *The Heart of Midlothian* (1818), *St Ronan's Well* (1823)

Stevenson, Robert Louis (1850–94), novelist, poet, playwright, essayist, travel writer. Novels include *Treasure Island* (1883), *The Strange Case of Dr Jekyll and Mr Hyde* (1886), *Kidnapped* (1886); poetry: *A Child's Garden of Verses* (1885)

Welsh, Irvine (1958–), novelist. *Trainspotting* (1994), *Marabou Stork Nightmares* (1996), *Filth* (1998)

Composers

Carver, Robert (1487–1566), motets: *O bone Jesu, Gaude flore virginali;* 5 masses

Clarke, Sir John of Penicuik (1676–1755), cantatas: *Leo Scotiae irritatus, Dic mihi, saeve puer* (1690s); *violin sonata* (c.1705)

Davies, Sir Peter Maxwell (1934–), founder of St Magnus festival; *The martyrdom of St Magnus; Eight songs for a mad king;* 10 Strathclyde Concertos

MacMillan, James (1959–), *The confession of Isabel Gowdie* (1990), *Seven last words* (1994); *Inés de Castro* (opera, (1996) *Musgrave,* Thea (1928–), *Journey through a Japanese landscape* (marimba and wind orchestra, 1994); *Helios* (oboe concerto, 1995); *Autumn Sonata (A concerto for bass clarinet and orchestra) Peebles,* David (c.1510–79), *Si quis diligit me;* harmoinsations of tunes from *The Scottish Psalter*

Stevenson, Ronald (1928–), *Passacaglia on DSCH* (1963); violin concerto 1992; cello concerto *In memoriam Jacqueline du Pré*

Sweeney, William (1950–), *Salm an fhearainn/Psalm of the land* (1987), *An rathad ur/The new road* (1988), *Coilltean Ratharsair/The woods of Raasay* (1993)

Weir, Judith (1954–), operas: *A night at the Chinese opera* (1987), *The vanishing bridegroom* (1990); *Moon and star* (chorus/orchestra, 1995)

Dancers

Clark, Michael (1962–), dancer
Kemp, Lindsay (1939–), dancer and mime artist
MacMillan, Kenneth (1929–92), choreographer
Morris, Margaret (1891–1980), dancer and teacher. Celtic Ballet in 1940

Film-Makers

Boyle, Danny (1956–), *Shallow Grave* (1994), *Trainspotting* (1996)
Douglas, Bill (1937–91), trilogy: *My Childhood* (1972), *My ain folk* (1973), *My Way Home* (1978)
Forsyth, Bill (1946–), *Gregory's Girl* (1981), *Local Hero* (1983), *Gregory's 2 Girls*
Grierson, John (1898–1972), *Industrial Britain* (1933), *Song of Ceylon* (1934), *Night Mail* (1936)
MacKinnon, Gillies (1948–), *Small Faces* (1996), *Regeneration* (1997), *Hideous Kinky* (1998)
Mullan, Peter, *Orphans* (1997)
Ramsay, Lynne, *Ratcatcher* (1999)

Visual Artists

Cowie, James (1880–1956), *Two schoolgirls* (c. 1937), *Self-portrait* (1945–50)
Crozier, William (1897–1930), *Edinburgh from Salisbury Crags* (1927)
Davie, Alan (1920–), *Playing card adventure no. 4* (1964), *Jingling space* (1950)

Dyce, William (1806–1864), *Titian's first essay in colour* (1857), *Christ as the Man of Sorrows* (1860)
Jameson, George (c.1589–1644). *Portraits of Mary Erskine, Countess Marischal* (1626), self-portrait (c. 1637–40)
Johnstone, William (1897–1981), *A point in time* (1929–8), *Celebration of earth, air, fire and water* (1974)
McTaggart, William (1835–1910), *A ground swell, Carradale* (1883), *Sailing of the emigrant ship* (1895), *The coming of St Columba* (1895)
Nasmyth, Alexander (1758–1840), 'father of Scottish landscape'. *Edinburgh from Calton Hill* (1825), *Princes Street with the commencement of the building of the Royal Institution* (1825); *portrait of Robert Burns* (1787)
Raeburn, Henry (1756–1823). Portraits of the fiddler Niel Gow (1793), Colonel Alasdair Macdonell of Glengarry (1811); *The Rev. Robert Walker Skating*
Ramsay, Allan (1713–84). Portraits of John Stuart, 3rd Earl of Bute, Flora Macdonald, Anne Bayne, his first wife (1740), Margaret Lindsay, his second (early 1760s)
Read, Catherine (1723–78), pastellist. One of the earliest women artists in Scotland
Redpath, Anne (1895-1965), *The Indian rug* (c. 1942), *The white cyclamen*
Traquair, Phoebe Anna (1852–1936), murallist and other crafts. Embroidered panels, The progress of a soul
Wilkie, David (1785–1841). Scenes of village life and Scottish history, including *The village politicians* (1806), *The blind fiddler* (1806), *Distraining for rent* (1815)
Wright, John Michael (1617–94). Portraits of Sir William Bruce (1664), Lord Mungo Murray (c.1680)

THE COLOURISTS:
Cadell, Francis (1883–1937), *Lunga from Iona, Still life (the grey fan)* (c.1920-5)
Fergusson, J. D. Fergusson (1974–61), *Les Eus* (c.1910–13), *In the sunlight*
Hunter, Leslie (1877–1931), *Houseboats, Balloch* (c.1924), *Village in Fife*
Peploe, Samuel (1871–1935), *Ben More from Iona* (1925), *Palm trees, Antibes* (1928), *many still lives*

Architects

Adam, Robert (1728–1792), Register House, Charlotte Square (Edinburgh, 1791), Culzean Castle (Ayrshire, from 1777)

Adam, William (1684–1748), father of Robert and James, both also architects. Hopetoun House (South Queensferry, Edinburgh, from 1721), Duff House (Banff, 1735); Robert Gordon's College, Aberdeen (1739)

Bruce, Sir William (c.1630–1710), Holyroodhouse (1671–9), Hopetoun House (1699–1702); Kinross House (1685–93)

Graham, James Gillespie (1776–1855), St John's Tolbooth (Edinburgh, 1842), St Mary's Cathedral (Edinburgh, 1813–14)

Mackintosh, Charles Rennie (1868–1928), Glasgow School of Art, Hill House (Helensburgh), Willow Tea Rooms (Glasgow). Many designs for furniture and textiles; also landscape paintings and flower paintings

Thomson, Alexander 'Greek' (1817–75), Moray Place (Glasgow), United Presbyterian Churches at Caledonian Road (1856) and St Vincent Street (1859), Glasgow

ARTS

The following list of arts organisations includes those organisations and institutions which are in receipt of revenue grants or three-year funding from the Scottish Arts Council.

7:84 Theatre Company

333 Woodlands Road, Glasgow G3 6NG
Tel: 0141-334 6686
Fax: 0141-334 3369
E-mail: 7.84-theatre.btinternet.com
Artistic Director: G. Laird

An Lanntair

Town Hall, South Beach, Stornoway, Isle of Lewis
Tel: 01851-703307
Director: R. Murray

An Tuireann

Arts Centre, Struan Road, Portree, Isle of Skye IV51 9EG
Tel: 01478-613306
Fax: 01478-613156
E-mail: norah@antuireann.demon.co.uk
Director: Ms N. Campbell

art.tm (Highland Printmakers Workshop)

20 Bank Street, Inverness IV1 1QU
Tel: 01463-712240
Fax: 01463-239991
E-mail: info@arttm.org.uk
Web: http://www.arttm.org.uk
Director: G. Rogers

Artlink (Edinburgh and the Lothians)

13A Spittal Street, Edinburgh EH3 9DY
Tel: 0131-229 3555
Fax: 0131-228 5257
E-mail: artlink@easynet.co.uk
Web: http://easyweb.easynet.co.uk/artlink
Director: J.B. van den Berg

Art in Partnership

233 Cowgate, Edinburgh EH1 JQ
Tel: 0131-225 4463
Fax: 0131-225 6879
E-mail: info@art-in-partnership.org.uk
Web: http://www.art-in-partnership.org.uk/aip/
Executive Director: R. Breen

Assembly Direct

2nd Floor, 89 Giles Street, Edinburgh EH6 6BZ
Tel: 0131-553 4000
Director: R. Spence

Association for Scottish Literary Studies
Department of Scottish History, University of
Glasgow, 9 University Gardens, Glasgow
G12 8QH
Tel: 0141-330 5309
Fax: 0141-330 5309
E-mail: d.jones@scothist-arts.gla.ac.uk
Web: http://www.arts.gla.ac.uk/ScotLit/ASLS
General Manager: D. Jones

Borderline Theatre Company
North Harbour Street, Ayr KA8 8AA
Tel: 01292-281010
Fax: 01292-263825
E-mail: enquiries@borderlinetheatre.co.uk
Web: http://www.borderlinetheatre.co.uk
Chief Executive: E. Jackson

BT Scottish Ensemble
5 Newton Terrace Lane, Glasgow G3 7PB
Tel: 0141-221 2222
Fax: 0141-221 4444
E-mail: scottishensemble@yahoo.com
General Manager: Ms H. Duncan

Byre Theatre
36 South Street, St Andrews KY16 9JT
Tel: 01334-476288
Fax: 01334-475370
E-mail: byretheatre@btinternet.com
General Manager: T. Gardner

Cappella Nova
172 Hyndland Road, Glasgow G12 9HZ
Tel: 0141-552 0634
Fax: 0141-552 4053
E-mail: alan.tavener@strath.ac.uk
Chief Executive: Ms R. Tavener

Citizens' Theatre
Gorbals, Glasgow G5 9DS
Tel: 0141-429 5561
Fax: 0141-429 7374
E-mail: info@citz.co.uk
Web: http://www.citz.co.uk
General Manager: Ms A. Stapleton

Crawford Arts Centre
93 North Street, St Andrews KY16 9AL
Tel: 01334-474610
Fax: 01334-479880
E-mail: crawfordarts@crawfordarts.free-online
   .co.uk
Web: http://www.crawfordarts.free-online.co.uk
Director: D. Sykes

Cumbernauld Theatre
Kildrum, Cumbernauld, G67 2BN
Tel: 01236-737235
Fax: 01236-738408
Artistic Director: S. Sharkey

Dumfries and Galloway Arts Association
28 Edinburgh Road, Dumfries DG1 1JQ
Tel: 01387-253383
Fax: 01387-253303
Director: Ms J. Wilson

Dundee Contemporary Arts
152 Nethergate, Dundee DD1 4DY
Tel: 01382-432000
Fax: 01382-432294
E-mail: dca@dundeecity.gov.uk
Web: http://www.dca.org.uk
Communications Officer: Ms A. McIntyre

Dundee Repertory Theatre
Tay Square, Dundee DD1 1PB
Tel: 01382-227684
Fax: 01382-228609
Web: http://www.dundeereptheatre.co.uk
General Manager: J. Reid

Eden Court Theatre
Bishop's Road, Inverness IV3 5SA
Tel: 01463-234234
Fax: 01463-713810
Director: C. Marr

Edinburgh International Book Festival
Scottish Book Centre, 137 Dundee Street
Edinburgh EH11 1BG
Tel: 0131-228 5444
Director: Ms F. Liddell

Edinburgh Contemporary Arts Trust
16 Clerwood Gardens, Edinburgh, EH12 8PT
Tel: 0131-539 8877
Fax: 0131-539 2211
E-mail: bsheppard@compuserve.com
Administrator: Ms H. Sheppard

Edinburgh Festival Fringe Society
The Fringe Office, 180 High Office, Edinburgh
EH1 1QS
Tel: 0131-226 5257
Fax: 0131-220 4205
E-mail: admin@edfringe.com
Web: http://www.edfringe.com
Director: P. Gungin

Edinburgh International Festival
The Hub, Castlehill, Edinburgh EH1 2NE
Tel: 0131-473 2000
Fax: 0131-473 2002
E-mail: info@eif.co.uk
Web: http://www.eif.co.uk
Administrative Director: N. Dodds

Edinburgh Printmakers
23 Union Street, Edinburgh EH1 3LR
Tel: 0131-557 2479
Fax: 0131-558 8418
E-mail: printmakers@ednet.co.uk
Web: http://www.edinburgh-printmakers.co.uk
Director: D. Watt

Edinburgh Sculpture Workshop
25 Hawthornvale, Edinburgh EH6 4JT
Tel: 0131-551 4490
Fax: 0131-551 4491

Enterprise Music Scotland
37 Dee Street, Aberdeen AB11 6DY
Tel: 01224-574422
Fax: 01224-572315
E-mail: emusicscotland@btclick.com
Director: R. Rae

Fèisan nan Gàidheal
Nicholson Buildings, Wentworth Street, Portree
Isle of Skye IV51 9EJ
Tel: 01478-613355
Fax: 01478-613399
E-mail: feisean@dircon.co.uk
Web: http://www.feisean.org
Director: A. Cormack

Fruitmarket Gallery
45 Market Street, Edinburgh EH1 1DF
Tel: 0131-225 2383
Director: G. Murray

The Gaelic Books Council (Comhairle nan Leabhraichean)
22 Mansfield Street, Glasgow G11 5QP
Tel: 0141-337 6211
Fax: 0141-341 0515
E-mail: fios@gaelicbooks.net
Web: http://www.gaelicbooks.net
Director: I. MacDonald

Glasgow Print Studio
22 King Street, Glasgow G1 5QP
Tel: 0141-552 0704
Fax: 0141-552 2919
E-mail: gallery@gpsart.co.uk
Web: http://www.gpsart.co.uk
Chief Executive: J. McKechnie

Hebrides Ensemble
11 Palmerston Place, Edinburgh EH12 5AF
Tel: 0131-225 2006
Fax: 0131-225 2006
Chief Executive: F. J. Carroll

HI Arts (Highland and Islands Arts)
Bridge House, Bridge Street, Inverness IV1 1QR
Tel: 01463-244223
Fax: 01463-244331
E-mail: r.livingston@hieut.co.uk
Web: http://www.scot-highlands.com
Development Director: R. Livingston

The Lemon Tree
5 West North Street, Aberdeen AB24 5AT
Box office: 01224-642230;
Admin: 01224-647999
Tel: 01224-630888
E-mail: info@lemontree.org
Web: http://www.lemontree.org
Director: Ms S. Powell

Moniack Mohr
Teavarran, Kiltarlity, Beauly, Inverness-shire
IV4 7HT
Tel: 01463-741675
Fax: 01463-741733
E-mail: m-mhor@arvonfoundation.org
Web: http://www.arvonfoundation.org
Director: C. Aldridge

National Federation of Music Societies Scotland
63 Threestanes Road, Strathaven, Lanarkshire
ML10 6EB
Tel: 01357-522138
Fax: 01357-522138
E-mail: l.young@nfms.org.uk
Web: http://www.nfms.org.uk/scotland
Secretary: Ms L. Young

NVA
128 Elderslie Street, Glasgow G3 7AW
Tel: 0141-353 3223
General Manager: Ms E. Gibbons

Paragon Ensemble Scotland
1 Bowmont Gardens, Glasgow G12 9LR
Tel: 0141-342 4242
Fax: 0141-342 4442
E-mail: admin@paragonensemble.org.uk
Web: http://www.paragonensemble.org.uk
Artistic Director: D. Davies

Peacock
21 Castle Street, Aberdeen AB11 5BQ
Tel: 01224-639539
Fax: 01224-627094
E-mail: peacockprint.co.uk@virgin.net
Chief Executive: L. Gordon

Perth Repertory Theatre
185 High Street, Perth PH1 5UW
Tel: 01783-472700
Fax: 01738-624576
E-mail: theatre@perth.org.uk
Web: http://www.perth.org.uk/perth/theatre.htm
General Manager: P. Hackett

Pier Arts Centre
Victoria Street, Stromness, Orkney KW16 3AA
Tel: 01856-850209
Fax: 01856-851462
E-mail: pierartscentre@stromnessorkney.fsnet
            .co.uk
Director: N. Firth

Pitlochry Festival Theatre
Pitlochry, PH16 5DR
Tel: 01796-484600
Fax: 01796-484616
E-mail: admin@pitlochty.org.uk
Web: http://www.pitlochry.org.uk
Administrator: S. Harborth

Proiseact nan Ealan/National Gaelic Arts Agency
10 Shell Street, Stornoway HS1 2BS
Tel: 01851-704493
Fax: 01851-704734
E-mail: pne@gaelic-arts.com
Web: http://www.gaelic-arts.com
Director: M. MacLean

Project Ability
Centre for Developmental Arts, 18 Albion Street
Glasgow G1 1LH
Tel: 0141-552 2822
Fax: 0141-552 3490
E-mail: info@project-ability.co.uk
Web: http://www.project-ability.co.uk
General Manager: Ms A. Knowles

Puppet and Animation Festival
Netherbow Arts Centre, 43-45 High Street,
Edinburgh EH1 1SR
Tel: 0131-557 5724
Director: S. Hart

Royal Lyceum Theatre Company
Grindlay Street, Edinburgh EH3 9AX
Tel: 0131-248-4800
Fax: 0131-228 3955
Artistic Director: K. Ireland

Royal Scottish National Orchestra
73 Claremont Street, Glasgow G3 7JB
Tel: 0141-226 3868
Fax: 0141-221 4317
E-mail: admin@rsno.org.uk
Web: http://www.rsmo.org.uk
Chief Executive: S. Crookall

St Magnus Festival
60 Victoria Street, Kirkwall, Orkney KW15 1DN
Tel: 01856-871445
Fax: 01856-871170
Web: http://www.orkneyislands.com
Director: Mrs G. Hughes

Scottish Ballet
261 West Princes Street, Glasgow G4 9EE
Tel: 0141-331 2931
Fax: 0141-331 2629
Web: http://www.scottishballet.co.uk
Managing Director: N. L. Quirk

Scottish Chamber Orchestra
4 Royal Terrace, Edinburgh EH7 5AB
Tel: 0131-557 6800
Fax: 0131-557 6933
E-mail: info@sco.org.uk
Web: http://www.sco.org.uk
Managing Director: R. McEwan

Scottish Dance Theatre
Dundee Repertory Theatre, Tay Square, Dundee
DD1 1PB
Tel: 01382-342600
Fax: 01382-228609
E-mail: aroberts@dundeereptheatre.co.uk
Web: http://www.sdt.co.uk
Senior Administrator: Ms A. Chinn

Scottish International Children's Festival
45A George Street, Edinburgh EH2 2HT
Tel: 0131-225 8050
Fax: 0131-225 6440
E-mail: info@imaginate.org.uk
Web: http://www.imaginate.org.uk
Communications Director: Ms A. Carney

Scottish Music Information Centre
1 Bowmont Gardens, Glasgow G12 9LR
Tel: 0141-334 6393
Fax: 0141-337 1161
E-mail: info@smic.org.uk
Web: http://www.smic.org.uk
Chief Executive: M. Brooksbank

Scottish Opera
39 Elmbank Crescent, Glasgow G2
0141-248 4567
Fax: 0141-221 8812
Web: http://www.scottishopera.org.uk
Chief Executive: C. Barron

The Scottish Poetry Library
5 Crichton's Close, Edinburgh EH8 8DT
Tel: 0131-557 2876
Fax: 0131-557 8393
E-mail: inquiries@spl.org.uk
Web: http://www.spl.org.uk
Chief Executive: Dr R. Marsack

Scottish Publishers Association
Scottish Book Centre, 137 Dundee Street,
Edinburgh, EH11 1BG
Tel: 0131-228 6866
Fax: 0131-228 3220
E-mail: enquiries@scottishbooks.org
Web: http://www.scottishbooks.org
Chief Executive: L. Fannin

Scottish Storytelling Centre
The Netherbow Arts Centre, 43–45 High Street
Edinburgh EH1 1SR
Tel: 0131-556 9579
Fax: 0131-557 5224
Web: http://www.storytellingcentre.org.uk
Co-ordinator: J. Bremner

Scottish Youth Dance
69 Dublin Street, Edinburgh EH3 6NS
Tel: 0131-556 8844
Fax: 0131-556 7766
E-mail: info@scottishyouthdance.org
Web: http://www.scottishyouthdance.org
Director: Ms J. Savin

Shetland Arts Trust
Pitt Lane, Lerwick, Shetland ZE1 0DN
Tel: 01595-694001
Fax: 01595-692941
E-mail: admin@shetland-arts-trust.co.uk
Web: http://www.shetland-music.com
Chief Executive: A. Watt

Stills Gallery
23 Cockburn Street, Edinburgh EH1 1BP
Tel: 0131-622 6200
Director: K. Tregaskis

Street Level
26 King Street, Glasgow G1 5QP
Tel: 0141-552 2151
Fax: 0141-552 2323
E-mail: info@sl-photoworks.demon.co.uk
Director: M. Dickson

Suspect Culture
128 Elderslie Street, Glasgow G3 7AW
Tel: 0141-248 8052
Fax: 0141-221 4470
E-mail: suspectculture@btinternet.com
Artistic Director: G. Eatough

TAG Theatre Company
18 Albion Street, Glasgow G1 1LH
Tel: 0141-552 4949
Fax: 0141-552 0666
E-mail: info@tag-theatre.co.uk
Web: http://www.tag-theatre.co.uk
General Manager: J. Morgan

Talbot Rice Gallery
Old College, South Bridge, Edinburgh
EH8 9YL
Tel: 0131-650 2211
Fax: 0131-650 2211
E-mail: valeriefiddes@ed.ac.uk
Curator: Prof. D. Macmillan

Theatre Workshop
34 Hamilton Place, Edinburgh EH3 5AX
Tel: 0131-226 5425
Fax: 0131-220 0112
E-mail: info@live.co.uk
Director: R. Rae

Tosg Theatre Company
Sàbhal Mor Ostaig, Sleat, Isle of Skye IV44 8RQ
Tel: 01471-888542
Fax: 01471-888541
E-mail: tosg@tosg.org
Web: http://www.tosg.org
Artistic Director: S. Mackenzie

The Traditional Music and Song Association of Scotland
95–97 St Leonard's Street, Edinburgh
EH8 9QY
Tel: 0131-667 5587
Fax: 0131-662 9153
E-mail: tmsa@tmsa.demon.co.uk
Web: http://www.tmsa.demon.co.uk/tmsa/home
    /tmsa.html
National Organiser: E. Cowie

Tramway
c/o Cultural and Leisure Services, Glasgow City Council, 3rd Floor, 20 Trongate, Glasgow
G1 5ES
Tel: 0141-287 8960
Fax: 0141-287 8909
E-mail: stephen.slater@cls.glasgow.gov.uk
Web: http://www.tramway.org
Senior Producer: S. Slater

Transmission Gallery
28 King Street, Trongate, Glasgow G1 5QP
Tel: 0141-552 4813
Fax: 0141-552 1577
E-mail: transmission@compuserve.com
Web: http://www.transmissiongallery.com
The Committee of Six Artists

Traverse Theatre
Cambridge Street, Edinburgh EH1 2ED
Tel: 0131-228 3223
Fax: 0131-229 8443
Web: http://www.traverse.co.uk
Chief Executive: P. Howard

WASPS
256 Alexandra Parade, Glasgow G31 3AJ
Tel: 0141-554 2499
Fax: 0141-556 5340
E-mail: info@waspsstudios.org.uk
Web: http://www.waspsstudios.org.uk
Property Manager: D. Cook

SPORT AND PHYSICAL RECREATION

AMERICAN FOOTBALL
Britain's only professional American football team is the Scottish Claymores, a team established in 1995 and named after the two-edged sword formerly used by warriors of the Scottish clans. They play their home games at Murrayfield and Hampden Park.

The team competes in the NFL Europe League, comprising of six teams and the regular season is 11 weeks followed by the post-season leading up to the World Bowl. The NFL Europe League is affiliated with the National Football League (NFL) in the USA and is a joint venture between the NFL and Fox Sports, a division of News Corporation.

The Claymores hosted the 1996 World Bowl and defeated the Frankfurt Galaxy 33–27 in front of a home crowd of 32,982 spectators. In 2000 the World Bowl was won by Rhein Fire who beat the Claymores 13–10 at Frankfurt.

ANGLING
Fishing as a sport can be dated to the early 17th-century. Rod fishing for food probably existed in the Highlands much earlier, but most of the clan chiefs and tacksmen (leaseholders or tenants) would have had ghillies to provide them with fish. By the latter half of the 18th-century the Duke of Gordon was letting salmon fishing for sport on the Spey. By then, much of the country, especially the Highlands had become a playground for the rich with sporting estates and hunting and fishing lodges springing up across the country.

The oldest angling club is the Ellem Fishing Club, founded in 1829 by gentlemen from Edinburgh and Berwickshire. The influential sporting writer William Scrope, helped to boost interest in fly-fishing in the late 1800s. Victorian anglers fished with huge 18-foot rods of split cane and green heart wood imported from the colonies.

The protection of salmon was the subject of legislation probably before the 11th-century and was first recorded by the Scottish Parliament in 1318. In 1862 Scotland was divided into 101 salmon fishery districts, each with a catchment area consisting of a river or a system of rivers. District Salmon Fishery Boards were created by owners of the salmon rivers fishings and they form the basis of the present-day organisation of the sport. Almost all river fishings are in private ownership and the fishing policy is determined by the owner.

Today, salmon and trout fishing are enormously popular. Thousands of anglers compete in annual events such as the Worldwide Trout Open fly-fishing competition. However, the industry, estimated at a value of £140 million a year, is now threatened by shrinking numbers of salmon and sea trout in the rivers and increased danger of disease spread by fish escaping from salmon farms.

The largest authenticated salmon ever caught by rod and line in Scotland was a fish weighing 29kg (64lbs) by Miss G. W. Ballantine on the Tay in 1922. The sea trout record was set in 1989 by Mr S. Burgoyne was 10kg (22 1/2lbs) on the River Leven, which flows out of Loch Lomond.

BOXING

The rules of boxing were first drawn up by Sir John Shalto Douglas, 8th Marquess of Queensberry (1844–1900). In 1866 he published a code of 12 rules, the first being that gloves had to be worn. There has been a gradual modification of the rules over the years, but the Queensberry Rules laid the foundations of modern boxing.

Amateur boxing is administrated by the Scottish Amateur Boxing Association, founded in 1909. Tournaments are regularly held with England, Wales and Ireland and at the Commonwealth and Olympic Games. The best Scottish performance was that by Dick McTaggart, winning gold at the 1956 Melbourne Olympic Games.

Scotland has produced six world champions. Benny Lynch, Jackie Paterson, Walter McGown and Clinton all were flyweight champions, along with Kenny Buchanan and Jim Watt in the lightweight class.

The record attendance for a Scottish boxing match was 32,000 for a fight between Tommy Milligan and Frank Moody at the Carntyne Stadium in 1928. Milligan was the welterweight champion of Great Britain and Europe in 1924.

CRICKET

Cricket was introduced to Scotland by English soldiers garrisoned in the country in the years following the Jacobite rising of 1745 and by immigrant English workers in the paper, textile and iron industries. Records exist of Scottish immigrants playing cricket in Savannah, Georgia USA in the 1730s. A match involving English officers is believed to have been played at Perth as early as 1750, but the first cricket match in the country for which records exist was played in September 1785 at Shaw Park, Alloa between the Duke of Atholl's XI and a Colonel Tabot's teams.

Scotland's oldest known cricket club is that of Kelso, dating back to 1820, but the Perthshire club claims the longest continuous existence from 1826. The governing body for cricket is the Scottish Cricket Union (SCU). It was orignally set up in 1879, but then disbanded in 1883. Grange Club in Edinburgh acted as the Scottish equivalent of the Marylebone Cricket Club (MCC) until the SCU was re-formed in 1908. The Western Division Union and Border Leagues date from the 1890s and the county championship from 1902.

Since 1980, Scotland has taken part, by invitation, in England's Benson and Hedges Cup and NatWest Trophy one-day test matches. There are annual three-day matches against Ireland and MCC with regular games against overseas touring sides. The Triple Crown Tournament, inaugurated in 1993 and involving the England Amateur XI, Wales, Ireland and Scotland was won by Scotland in 1994 and again in 1995. In 1992 Scotland resigned from the UK Cricket Council and in 1994 was elected for associated membership of the International Cricket Council (ICC). This gave them autonomy in world cricket and the team competed for the first time in the ICC Trophy in Kuala Lumpur, Malaysia in March–April 1997 reaching the semi-finals.

CURLING

The origins of curling have been made by rival claims from Scotland and the Netherlands. The Dutch claim that 16th-century paintings by Pieter Bruegel (1530–69) show a game similar to curling being played on frozen canals. While claims by Scotland are more valid with a varied collection of old stones which have been salvaged from lochs and ponds over the centuries. While the controversy goes on, one thing is certain and that is that the Scots have nurtured the game, provided the rules of play and exported it throughout the world.

The early curling stones called loofies (lof being the old Scots world for the palm of the hand) resembled this shape and had grooves for fingers and the thumb and were thrown with a quoiting action

Over 300 years ago strong-arm curling was introduced. Channel stones were used and they were given this name because they taken from channels of rivers and were worn smooth. The stones had rough handles inserted and became bigger and bigger. The object was to hurl them into the house where it would be difficult to dislodge them.

Spherical stones replaced rough and irregularly shaped stones towards the end of the 18th-century and with the introduction of these stones came a whole new aspect to curling. Skill and accuracy took over from brute strength, with the turning of the hand on delivery, the round stones 'curled' consistently on the ice.

Solid iron crampits were used as footholds during delivery, thus replacing the old 'cramps' and 'tramps' (iron or steel pads) with prongs underneath which were attached to the boots with straps. Nowadays the modern hack is used throughout the curling world.

The famous Duddingston Club in Edinburgh formulated the first curling rules in 1804 and 12 of the Duddingston regulations for play for the basis of the much-enlarged modern rulebook.

The Grand Caledonian Curling Club was established in Edinburgh in 1838 and became the Royal Caledonian Curling Club (RCCC) in 1843 after a visit by Queen Victoria (1819–1901) to Scone Palace where the Earl of Mansfield demonstrated the game to her on a polished ballroom floor.

The Scots made their first tour to Canada in 1902–3 with a team of 28 members who toured the country for three months. In 1909 was the Canadians first tour in Scotland and 500 curlers attended a welcoming banquet in Edinburgh. As a result of these tours came the Strathcona Cup (first presented by RCCC president Lord Strathcona and Mount Royal) which is played every five years on a home-and-away basis.

Scottish women began touring with the men in the 1950s on exchange tours to Canada and the USA and play against European countries was arranged on a regular basis.

The formation of the International Curling Federation (ICF) was initiated by the RCCC in 1965 during the World Championship for the Scotch Cup. A meeting was attended by officebearers and representatives from Scotland, Canada, the USA, Norway, Sweden and Switzerland to consider setting up an international committee.

The following year the Scotch Cup was held at Vancouver, British Columbia Canada and the six countries that attended the previous meeting along with a representative from France met again. The end result was the start of the International Curling Federation, which was officially established on 1 April 1966. Major Allan Cameron, President of the RCCC became the first president. In 1991 the ICF became the World Curling Federation (WCF). The headquarters of the WCF are based at 81 King Street, Edinburgh EH3 6RN. Tel: 0131-333 3003; Fax: 0131-333 3323.

The Scotch Cup was launched in Scotland in 1959 and sponsored by The Scotch Whisky Association. It was originally played between the champion teams from Scotland and Canada, but the competition quickly grew into the men's World Championship.

The Ladies World Championship was established in Scotland in 1979 and sponsored by the Royal Bank of Scotland. The first three years this tournament was played in Scotland, but is now played in a different country each year.

In February–March 2000 the world championships were held at Glasgow, with the Canadian men and women both taking top honours. It should be noted however that Canada is not only the largest curling nation in the world, but have produced the top players for many years.

DEERSTALKING

Deerstalking became established in the Highlands during the 19th century and marked a change in practice from earlier methods of deer hunting, in which the deer were driven into an enclosed space, either a natural pass or a built enclosure and shot by waiting riflemen. The new sport was based on approaching the deer as closely as possible and killing it with a single shot. In the early days deerhounds were used as a back-up to the rifle, which often wounded the deer without killing it outright. The introduction of telescopic sights in the 1880s was at first considered unsporting, as it gave the stalker an unfair advantage.

The 19th century fashion for deerstalking, fuelled by the creation of deer forests, lodges, bothies and improved access into the hills, was even further promoted when Queen Victoria and Prince Albert took a long lease on the Balmoral estate in 1848. Deerstalking inspired the work of Sir Edwin Landseer, painter of the famous Monarch of the Glen and himself a keen stalker. The growth of the sport gave rise to the professional stalker, or gamekeeper. The gamekeeper looked after the sporting estate all year round and acted as a guide to stalkers in the open season.

Paradoxically, the organised pursuit of deer helped to increase their chances of survival, by reducing poaching and the numbers of deer steadily increased through the 19th century. By the end of the century over seven million acres were given over to deer forest.

Today deer face competition from many sources – hikers, climbers, skiers and tourists, as well as foresters. New forestry plantations deny the deer low ground. Poaching has made a comeback. Nonetheless, deer and the sport of deerstalking continue to flourish.

EQUESTRIAN SPORTS

In the 12th-century, William the Lion organised a horse race, known as the Lanark Silver Bell, on Lanark Moor making Scotland the birthplace of British horse racing.

The Scottish Grand National is held at Ayr. It moved from Bellesisle, where racing had taken place since 1576, to today's site in 1907. The largest crowd for a race was 20,000 at the Grand National in 1969.

Scotland has produced a number of racing celebrities over the years. Matt Dawson was a trainer who won the Derby in 1860 and on five subsequent occasions, as well as 23 other major classics. Charlie Cunningham rode and trained his own horses with great success between 1865 and 1891 and despite his height (6ft 3in), he was champion amateur jockey in 1852. In the 1950s George Boyd produced 700 winners from his east-coast stables. Willie Carson is the most successful Scottish jockey, being five times champion jockey and having ridden almost 4,000 winners in Great Britain during his career.

Peaty Sandy was Scotland's most famous horse, winning the Coral Welsh National in 1981. He won 20 of the 74 races entered and never missed a fence until his last race. Throughout his career he won his owners £100,000.

Pony trekking was introduced by the late Lieutenant Commander Jock Kerr Hunter, who opened the first riding school in the 1940s. There are now around 60 riding centres throughout the country and are approved by either the Trekking and Riding Society of Scotland or the British Horse Society.

FOOTBALL

The Scottish Football Association (SFA) came into being in 1873 and is the second oldest football association in the world. The original eight clubs belonging to the SFA were Queen's Park, Clydesdale, Vale of Leven, Dumbreck, Third Lanarkshire Rifle Volunteers, Eastern, Granville and Kilmarnock.

The Queen's Park Football Club was formed in 1867 and with this football saw a rapid growth. However with no formal structure, matches were often irregular and organised in a casual manner.

The Queen's Park FC proposed a meeting to be held at the Dewar Hotel, 11 Bridge Street,

Glasgow in the evening of Thursday, 13 March 1873 at 8pm with teams that played Scotch Club Association rules being invited. Seven of the original eight clubs (Kilmarnock sent a letter stating their willingness to join) accepted the invitation. The purpose of the meeting was to form an Association, with the member clubs taking part in a challenge cup starting the following season and being played annually and to propose the laws of the competition.

From this date forward, the SFA became the governing body of football in Scotland and has the ultimate responsibility for the control and development of football.

The first official international match was played on 30 November 1872 in Glasgow between England and Scotland (drawing 0–0) in front of roughly 4,000 spectators.

The football associations from Scotland, England, Wales and Ireland set up the International Football Association Board in 1886, to control the laws of the game.

The SFA joined the Fédération Internationale de Football Association (FIFA) in 1910 and was also a founding member of the Union des Associations Européennes de Football (UEFA) in 1954.

The national stadium for Scotland games is Hampden Park. It officially opened in 1903 and recent development has made it into one of the finest stadiums in the world, capable of holding 52,000 spectators.

Scotland's international teams lost only 3 of their first 43 international matches and first participated in the World Cup in 1954, having previously turned down a chance to appear in 1950. The first official international match against a continental team was in 1929 when they beat Norway 7–3 in Olso. The current manager Craig Brown is the 13th manager of the national team.

Scottish Gas sponsors all Scotland home matches, including the international teams (both home and away) for the 'A', 'B' and Under 21's.

In 1972 came the formation of the Scottish Women's Football Association, which now has over 4,000 registered players and is the fastest growing sport for women in the country.

On Sunday, 25 October 1998 a special dinner was held in Glasgow to commemorate the 125th anniversary of the Scottish Football Association.

PREMIER DIVISION TEAMS

(foundation date in brackets)

Aberdeen Football Club (1903)
Pittodrie Stadium
Pittodrie Street
Aberdeen AB2 1QH
Tel: 01224-650400; Fax: 01224-644173/650469;
Ticket Office: 01224-631903
Email: feedback@afc.co.uk
Web: http://www.afc.co.uk
Manager: Ebbe Skovdahl; Shirt sponsor: Atlantic

Celtic Football Club (1888)
Celtic Park
95 Kerrydale Street
Glasgow G40 3RE
Tel: 0141-556 2611; Fax: 0141-551 8106; Ticket
Office: 0141-551 8653
Email: celtic.view@celticfc.btinternet.com
Web: http://www.celticfc.co.uk
Manager: Martin O'Neill; Shirt sponsor: ntl

Dundee Football Club (1893)
Dens Park Stadium
Sandeman Street
Dundee DD3 7JY
Tel: 01382-826104; Fax: 01382-832284; Ticket
Office: 01382-204777
Email: dundeefc@dfc.co.uk
Web: http://www.dundeefc.co.uk
Manager: Ivano Bonetti; Shirt sponsor: Ceramic
Tile Warehouse

Dundee United Football Club (1909)
Tannadice Park
Tannadice Street
Dundee DD3 7JW
Tel: 01382-833166; Fax: 01382-389398
Email: dundee.united.fc@cableinet.co.uk
Web: http://www.dundeeunitedfc.co.uk
Manager: Paul Sturrock; Shirt sponsor: Telewest

Glasgow Rangers Football Club (1872)
Ibrox Stadium
Edminston Drive
Glasgow G51 2XD
Tel: 0870-600 1972; Fax: 0870-600 1978
Web-site: http://www.rangers.co.uk
Manager: Dick Advocaat; Shirt sponsor: ntl

Heart of Midlothian Football Club (1874)
Tynecastle Stadium
Gorgie Road
Edinburgh EH11 2NL
Tel: 0131-200 7200; Fax: 0131-200 7222; Ticket
Office: 0131-200 7201/9
Web: http://www.heartsfc.co.uk
Manager: Jim Jefferies; Shirt sponsor: Strongbow

Hibernian Football Club (1875)
Easter Road Stadium
12 Albion Place
Edinburgh EH7 5QG
Tel: 0131-661 2159; Fax: 0131-659 6488
Email: club@hibernianfc.co.uk
Web: http://www.hibernianfc.co.uk
Manager: Alex McLeish; Shirt sponsor: Le Coq
Sportif

Kilmarnock Football Club (1869)
Rugby Park
Kilmarnock KA1 2DP
Tel: 01563-545300; Fax: 01563-522181; Ticket
Office: 01563-545300
Email: kfc@sol.co.uk or kilmarnockfc@sol.co.uk
Manager: Bobby Williamson; Shirt sponsor:
Scotland Online

Motherwell Football Club
Fir Park Stadium
Motherwell ML1 2QN
Tel: 01698-333333; Fax: 01698-338001; Ticket
Office: 01698-338033
Email: mfc@motherwellfc.co.uk
Web: http://www.motherwellfc.co.uk
Manager: Billy Davies; Shirt sponsor: Motorola

St Johnstone Football Club (1884)
McDiarmid Park
Crieff Road
Perth PH1 2SJ
Tel: 01738-459090; Fax: 01738-625771; Ticket
Office: 01738-455000
Email: paul.fraser@huntingtower.sol.co.uk
Web: http://www.stjohnstonefc.co.uk
Manager: Sandy Clark; Shirt sponsor: Scottish
Hydro-Electric

GOLF

In 1457 a Scottish Act of Parliament by James II
(1430–60) banned both golf and football as it
interfered with his subjects' archery practice.
James III (1452–88) in 1471 and James IV (1473
–1513) in 1491 also adopted this act.

The Gentlemen Golfers of Edinburgh (now
the Honourable Company of Edinburgh Golfers)

was founded in 1744 and is generally considered to be the first golf club, with Edinburgh Town Council granting a Silver Club to the 'Gentlemen', which became the first golf trophy. From this event came the first known rules of golf.

The Society of St Andrews Golfers was formed in 1754 and drew up a set of 13 rules for their annual golfing competition. In 1834, they changed the name to The Royal & Ancient Golf Club of St Andrews (R & A) after receiving royal patronage through William IV (1765–1837). The standard round of golf at St Andrews was 22 holes (11 holes to the shoreline and 11 back) and in 1764 this was reduced to 18 holes as the first four holes were combined into two.

At St Andrews in 1819 the first known professional tournament was played. In 1821 James Cheape, Laird of Strathtyrum purchased the St Andrews Links to preserve it for the game of golf. The Links were re-purchased by St Andrews Town Council in 1894 for £5,000 and run by the Green Committee of St Andrews Link.

The first club house at St Andrews was built in 1835 by the Union Club offering facilities to sportsmen. By 1854 a new clubhouse was opened behind the first tee on the Old Course.

At Prestwick Golf Club the first Open Championship was held in 1860 with the winner receiving the Challenge Belt, which was won by Willie Park. Ten years later in 1870 the Challenge Belt would become the property of the player who won the Open three years in succession. This was achieved by Tom Morris, Jnr, whose father became keeper of the green at St Andrews in 1864.

Leading golf clubs of Britain asked the R & A to take charge of setting up and administrating a universal code of rules in 1897 and since then every new golfing nation with connections to the R & A have agreed to abide by them. The United States however, have set their own rules and are responsible for their own country. The rules set up by the R & A were freely available to all by 1908 and a sponsorship deal was struck with Royal Insurance for publication of all English language copies.

The R & A and United States Golf Association (USGA) have worked together since 1952 to create a common set rules that apply to all golfing nations. These supreme authorities of the game meet every four years to agree any revisions that are required.

KEY HISTORICAL EVENTS

1922 - The Walker Cup is first played.
1927 - The Ryder Cup is played for the first time.
1931 - The USGA sets the legal ball limits as a maximum weight of 1.62 ounces and a minimum diameter of 1.68 inches.
1932 - The Curtis Cup started.
1938 - The USGA limit the clubs a golfer can carry to 14.
1939 - The R & A follow suit and limit the number of clubs to 14.
1952 - The first unified code of rules came into force world-wide.
1955 - Television coverage of the Open is provided live from St Andrews for the first time.
1957 - Leader of the Open go last after 36 holes due to the influence of television.
1969 - The first colour television images of the Open are broadcast.
1974 - St Andrews Town Council passed control of the Links courses to the St Andrews Links Trust and Management Committee.
1980 - The Open Championship is played from Thursday to Sunday for the first time.
1987 - Laura Davies became the first Briton to win the US Ladies' Open.
1990 - The 1.68 inch ball comes the only legal ball for all golfers. The British Golf Museum opens at St Andrews
1992 - Nick Faldo wins the Open for the third time.

Events for 2001
The Open Championship – Royal Liytham St Anne's 19–22 July
Ryder Cup – Belfry 28–30 September

British Golf Museum
Bruce Embankment
St Andrews
Fife KY16 9AB
Tel: 01334-478880; Fax: 01334-473306
Web: http://www.britishgolfmuseum.co.uk

HIGHLAND AND BORDER GAMES
The origins of these competitions were arranged by ancient kings and clan chiefs to help them select the strongest men as their champions, the fastest cross-country runners as their couriers, the best pipers and dancers to entertain both themselves and their guests.

The first Games took place in Ceres, Fife in 1314 with victorious soldiers upon returning from the Battle of Bannockburn discovered an outlet for their high spirits by taking part in athletic competitions.

The wearing to the kilt and playing of the bagpipes was banned following the Jacobite Rising in 1745. In fact any expression of Scottish culture and large gatherings were forbidden, so competition in sports came to a virtual standstill.

Queen Victoria's (1819–1901) love for Scottish things and her patronage of the Braemar Gathering started a revival of interest and involvement in the Games.

The Games are organised and run by their own committees under the rules of the Scottish Games Association (SGA) that was established in 1946. These annual events cover a full range of running and cycle track events, light field and heavy field events along with highland dancing and piping. The Border Games however have more emphasis in track competitions.

All competitors in heavy field events must wear a kilt. Some Games use stones in the putting events and the Scottish hammer has a rigid wooden or bamboo handle, with the throwers wearing special boots fitted to the sole and extended beyond the toe so that they can 'dig in' and throw without turning their whole body.

Weights of 28lbs and 56lbs are thrown for distance with weights of 56lbs thrown for height over a bar. The famous Scottish Caber events have athletes attempting to toss heavy tree trunks, with some over 20ft in length.

Tug-o-War takes place at the more traditional Highland Games and involves teams of five or eight men plus a coach. Draws take place prior to the start of competitions with the judge tossing a coin to decide the direction of the pull. The length of the pull is 12 feet and the team with the best of three pulls is declared the winner.

The objectives of the SGA are to encourage and foster the highest standards of ethics and performance, lay down and enforce rules and regulations covering all aspects of traditional Highland Games activities and to assist committees in the improvement of their events. All competitors must register with the SGA prior to participating in any events.

As Scots have moved and settled throughout the world they have taken with them their love of the Games and today there are events in Europe, America and Asia to Australia. Many of the overseas venues have attracted large numbers of exiled Scots, their descendants and friends.

For more information about the Highland Games, please contact the local Tourist Board in that area.

MOTOR RALLYING AND RACING

The RSAC Scottish Rally was established in 1932, but was born out of a series of reliability trials in 1903 by the Scottish Automobile Club, form in 1899 and the forerunner of the Royal Scottish Automobile Club (RSAC). The rally is held in June and covers 700 miles. At the UK level, the RAC Lombard Rally includes some Scottish stages. The first Scot to win the RAC Rally was Colin McRae in 1994.

Scots have made a major contribution to motor-racing since the 1950s. Ecurie Ecosse was formed in 1952 as a non-profit making syndicate of Scottish racing enthusiasts. In 1956 and 1957 the team won the Le Mans 24-hour race.

RUGBY

A game similar to rugby was played in Scotland during Roman times, by playing harpastum. It involved two teams running, passing and throwing a small round ball with an end result of crossing the opponents' line at the far end of a rectangular field.

By the middle of the 19th-century some private schools, colleges and universities throughout the country played a game that involved kicking and handling of the ball. In 1846 rules were formally introduced, which brought much need consistency to this new sport.

Captains from five Scottish rugby clubs got together in 1870 and discussed challenging English clubs to represent their respective countries in the first international rugby match. The game took place on Monday, 27 March 1871 at Raeburn Place (a cricket field) at Edinburgh Academy, with Scotland winning. This gave Scotland the distinction of being both the first hosts and first winners ever in an international rugby match.

The Scottish Football Union (SFU) was formed in 1873 and one of its main objectives was to find a pitch for international matches. Previously international fixtures had been played at Old Hampden Park in Glasgow, Powderhall in Edinburgh and the West of Scotland Cricket Club's ground in Hamilton. The SFU (later to become the Scottish Rugby Union – SRU) purchased a ground at Inverleith in Edinburgh, thus becoming its first home union to own and run its own rugby ground. The first international match at the new location was in 1899 against Ireland.

A Scotsman named Ned Haig suggested a seven-a-side tournament in order to raise cash for his club, Melrose. On 25 April 1883 the first tournament took place at The Greenyards with

Melrose defeating their close neighbours (and rivals) Gala in the final.

The popularity of the sport continued to grow and after World War I, Inverleith could no longer hold the large crowds that flocked to see Scottish games. The SFU purchased 19 acres of land at Murrayfield in 1922, which had previously been the home of the Edinburgh Polo Club. Funds were raised for the new stadium by an issue of debentures and on 21 March 1925 it officially opened with an international match against England and 70,000 spectators cheering throughout the immensely exciting game. Scotland once again defeated England by a score of 14–11.

Most of the rugby club grounds were used to grow potatoes during World War II and the Armed Forces arranged a game between England and Scotland Services Internationals that took place at Inverleith as Murrayfield was used as a supply depot.

In 1955 Scotland's defeat of Wales at Murrayfield ended a 17-game winless streak, which started when the Fourth Springboks from South Africa visited the UK in 1950–1. In 1960 Scotland became the first of the home unions to tour foreign countries when they went to South Africa. This tradition continues to this day. In 1984 Scotland won their second Grand Slam (the first one was in 1925) by defeating Wales at Cardiff, England at Murrayfield, Ireland in Dublin and after a slow start in the first half – finally beat France at Murrayfield 21–12.

In 1986 the HRH the Princess Royal accepted an invitation to become patron of the SRU. A year later they reached the quarter-finals of the first Rugby World Cup in New Zealand, but lost to the mighty All Blacks, who became the eventual winners.

In 1996, it was the 125th anniversary of the first international rugby match, followed by the 125th anniversary of the SRU in 1998 and Murrayfield celebrates its 75th birthday in 2000.

There are approximately 300 clubs that belong to the SRU and 200 affiliated schools. Member clubs account for some 13,500 people currently playing the game and around 32,000 are non-playing members of clubs.

RUGBY CLUBS — DIVISION I

Boroughmuir Rugby Club (1919)
Meggetland
Colinton Road
Edinburgh EH14 1AS
Tel: 0131-443 7571;
Ticket Office: 0131-443 7571
E-mail: admin@brfc.co.uk
Web: http://www.boroughmuirrfc.co.uk
Director of Rugby: Bruce Hay;
Shirt sponsor: Gilbert

Currie R.F.C. (1970)
5 Malleny
Malleny Park
Balerno
Midlothian EH14 7AF
Tel: 0131-449 2432; Fax: 0131-449 7688
Web: http://www.currierfc.freeserve.co.uk
Head coach: Bruce MacNaughton

George Heriot's FP (1890)
Goldenacre
Bangholm Terrace
Edinburgh EH3 5QN
Tel: 0131-552 5925; Fax: 0131-551 4519
E-mail: douglas_bruce@talk21.com
Director of Rugby: Fraser Dall; Shirt sponsor: Warners, Solicitors and Estate Agents

Glasgow Hawks Rugby Club (Glasgow Accies 1866; GHK 1888 merged 1997)
The Pavilion
Old Anniesland - Crow Road
Glasgow G13 1PL
Tel: 0141-959 115; Fax: 0141-959 9972
Coaches: Bill McDonald and Shade Munro;
Shirt sponsor: Britannic Asset Management

Hawick Rugby Football Club (1873)
Mansfield Park
Hawick TD9 8AL
Tel: 01450-370687
E-mail: enquiries@hawickrfc.co.uk
Web: http://www.hawickrfc.co.uk
Coach: Ian Barnes; Shirt sponsor: Callaghan's Irish Bar and Pringle of Scotland

Jed-Forest Football Club (1884)
Riverside Park
Jedburgh TD8 6UE
Tel: 01835-862855;
Ticket Office: 01835-864092
E-mail: david@jedforest.freeserve.co.uk
Director of Rugby: Gordon Hume

Melrose (1877)
The Greenyards
Melrose TD6 9SA
Tel: 01896-822993; Fax: 01896-822993
E-mail: rugby@melrose.bordernet.co.uk
Web-site: http://www.melrose.bordernet.co.uk
Coach: Gary Parker; Shirt sponsor: Calders

Stirling County (1904)
Bridgehaugh Park
Causewayhead Road
Stirling FK9 5AP
Tel: 01786-833543; Fax: 01786-447767
Director of Rugby: Eddie Pollock
Shirt sponsor: Simpson Donald

West of Scotland Football Club (1865)
Bumbrae
Glasgow Road
Milngavie
Glasgow G62 6HX
Tel: 0141-956 3116; Fax: 0141-956 3116;
Ticket Office: 0141-956 3116
Email: westrugby@btinternet.com
Web: http://www.btinternet.com/~westrugby
Coach: Ivan Torby;
Shirt sponsor: Cullen Packaging

SHINTY

The Gaelic name for shinty, camanachd, identifies the sport as possibly the oldest organised team game in western Europe. Many of the ancient Irish heroes were said to have played shinty. Cu Chulainn, the hero of the Ulster cycle of tales, is said to have attended an ancient training school for young heroes, where camanachd was part of the curriculum. In 563 Columba left Ireland for Scotland because of a quarrel that had supposedly broken out during a game of camanachd, so tradition says the game was brought to Scotland in that year, if not before. Its roots were shared with Irish hurling until the mid-fourteenth century.

The first written records mentioning shinty date from the 14th and 15th centuries. A 15th century memorial stone on the island of Iona depicts not only the owner's broadsword beneath his name in the old Lombard script, but also a caman (stick) with a ball beside it. The following description of the game is from Jamieson's Dictionary of the Scottish Lanaguage (1821):

Shinty has remained popular in the Highlands, although Lowland law was against it and the enforced observation of the Sabbath in many places affected the game, as it was customarily played on Sundays. The custom of playing on Sundays

eventually faded away, but the games survived Culloden, the Highland Clearances and later waves of migration out of the Highlands and is still played according to virtually the same rules as it was centuries ago.

By the mid-nineteenth century the popularity of the game had declined until it was played only in the glens of Lochaber, Strathglass and Badenoch. Captain Chisholm of Glassburn published a code of rules for the Strathglass Club in 1880 and in Feburary 1887 Strathglass (led by Chisholm) played against Glen-Urquhart in a 15-a-side game at Inverness. Strathglass won the game, but the following year they were defeated. Following the loss, Chisholm revised the rules he had published earlier.

Celtic Club rules drawn up in Glasgow were played in the south of the country. The lack of set rules prompted a meeting of representatives from all the leading clubs on 10 October 1893 at Kingussie, which lead to the formation of the Camanachd Association. This became the governing body of the game and drew up rules to control play and competitions which are still followed today.

The Challenge Trophy was set up in 1895 and Kingussie defeated Glasgow Cowal 2–0 at Inverness in 1896 in the first final. The trophy has been contested annually, except during the two world wars. Shinty's premier competition is now known as the Glenmorangie Camanachd Cup and is played each year at one of five regular venues.

SKIING

Compared with other sports, skiing in Scotland is a relatively recent introduction. It dates back to 1890, when W. W. Naismith, founder of the Scottish Mountaineering Club, ventured into the hills on a wooden Nordic-style skis to test the efficiency of the skis as a form of cross-country transport. However, Nordic skiing did not catch on because snow conditions were – as they remain – too unpredictable, there were few dependable routes and the equipment was heavy and cumbersome.

Scotland offered more potential for the development of Alpine or downhill skiing and the Scottish Ski Club was founded in 1907, shortly after the Ski Club of Great Britain (founded in 1903). The founding members of the club were all mountaineers and included Naismith.

Alpine skiing was just becoming popular in Scotland when World War I broke out. The Scottish Ski Club did not reconvene until 1929. By that time equipment had improved and this, plus easier access to the hills and a string of cold, snowy winters all generated a surge in popularity of skiing in the 1930s and 1940s. Powered ski-tows were introduced on Ben Lawers, Glen Clunie and Glenshee in the late 1940s and the first permanent ski-lift in Scotland was installed at Glencoe in 1956. The development of Aviemore as Scotland's first snow sports centre began in the early 1960s and it is still the principal centre for snow sports.

Skiing and snowboarding now take place at five major resorts. National and international events are staged, weather permitting. The uncertainty of weather conditions is the greatest obstacle faced by snow sports and the resort facilities that depend on them. A succession of mild winters in the 1990s has seriously threatened the viability of the companies who run the resorts.

However, there are artificial slopes at some of the major resorts and elsewhere in Scotland. The biggest dry ski slope in Europe is at Edinburgh's Hillend Park.

The Scottish National Ski Council (SNSC) was formed in 1963. It was renamed Snowsport Scotland in 1998 and is the national governing body for all sports that take place on snow and artificial slopes in the country.

WALKING AND MOUNTAINEERING

Scotland is a walker's paradise. It has thousands of walks and climbs on coastal footpaths, nature trails, woodland trails, long-distance footpaths and hundreds of mountain peaks. It is known worldwide for its rock climbs.

The earliest recorded rock climb in the UK took place in 1698, on Stac na Biorrach, St Kilda by Sir Robert Murray. The first recorded ascent of Ben Nevis was that of James Robertson in 1771; Ben MacDui and Braeriach were both climbed in 1810 by the Revd George Keith.

There are 284 mountains over 914 metres (3,000ft) high and these have become known as Munros, after Sir Hugh Munro, who first scaled them in 1891. Sir Hugh's list has undergone several revisions over the years, most recently in 1998 when a number of peaks increased from 277 to 284. Munro himself died in 1909 just before climbing the last of the 238 summits he had identified. However, they had already been conquered by the Revd A. E. Robertson in 1901, who achieved the feat over a period of 10 years. In 1974, Hamish Brown completed the challenge of the 277 Munros, covering 1,639 miles and 136,855 metres (449,000ft) of ascent in just 112 days. Kathy Murgatroyd repeated this feat in

1982. George Keeping was the first to complete the entire round on foot in 1984. Hugh Symonds climbed all the Munros in 66 days and 22 hours in 1990. Munro-bagging, as it has become known, is a popular pastime, especially since most of the Munros are reasonably accessible and within easy reach of public roads.

Peaks between 762 and 914 metres (2,500 and 3,000 ft) in height, with a drop of at least 152.4 metres (500 ft) between each listed hill and any adjacent higher one, are called Corbetts. They are name after J. Rooke Corbett, who listed them in 1930. Currently 222 mountains are classed as Corbetts. The current record for completing all the Munros and Corbetts was set by Craig Caldwell in 1985–6, when he achieved the feat in 377 days. A further list of hills in the Lowlands of 609 to 762 metres (2,000 to 2,500 ft) was produced by Percy Donald, giving these hills the nickname of Donalds.

WRESTLING

Scottish wrestling is known as 'backhold' and has a style and rules which are different from those of standard wrestling. The Scottish Amateur Wrestling Association organises and registers wrestlers. The sport is still quite widespread and is most commonly practised at the Highland Games. In backhold, the wrestlers take hold of each other's waist with the right hand under the left arm. Both men then close their hands and when the referee shouts 'Hold', the bout commences. If any part of a wrestler's body, except the soles of his feet, touches the ground, he loses the bout. The wrestlers are not permitted to break their grip until the opponent is on the ground. Bouts are normally the best three or five.

The earliest depiction of wrestling in Scotland is to be found on two carved Pictish stones dating from the 6th and 7th centuries, which are housed in the National Museum of Antiquities in Edinburgh.

In the Western Isles, wrestling was made popular by the men of a Highland regiment known as the Lovat Scouts, formed in 1900. The Highlanders practised two forms of wrestling, one using the same rules as the rest of the country and an alternative form that did not allow tripping of opponents, which developed in Europe into the 'classical' style. An ancient Norse style of wrestling known as Hryggspenna is still practised in the Hebrides.

YACHTING

Pioneered in the Netherlands during the 17th-century, modern yachting offered a ways and means of travelling along the waterways throughout the country. The word 'yacht' also comes from the Dutch word *jaght*, which means a small cargo or passenger carrier.

Charles II (1630–85) was given a Dutch pleasure boat named Mary three months after his return from an almost 10-year exile in the Low Countries, until the Restoration in 1660. She had originally been built for the Dutch East India Company. He also received another gift from the Dutch – the yacht Bezan and added another the Surprise to his ever-increasing fleet.

In the early 18th-century yachting was considered a rather eccentric occupation because of the certain discomforts associated to it.

However, sailing off the west coast of Scotland and among the western and northern islands is now a very popular pastime and sport, although the weather and currents can be tricky. Several yachting events take place each year. Yacht races of the famous Scottish Series off the west coast and the Round Mull Three-Day Yacht Race, held in June, are the largest events. During May there is also an annual race between Bergen in Norway and Shetland. The Scottish Hebridean Islands Peak Race is the biggest combined sailing and fell-running competition in the world.

FAMOUS SCOTTISH SPORTING PERSONALITIES

Jim Clark, OBE - Formula 1 Driver
b. 4 March 1936 in Kilmany

Career - Jim won a total of 25 Formula 1 races throughout his illustrious career. He became the F1 world champion on two occasions in 1963 and again in 1965. After F1 he went to the USA became an Indy Car driver and won the Indy 500 at Indianapolis in 1965.

He was awarded an OBE in 1964. Tragically, he was killed at Hockenheim during the German Grand Prix on 7 April 1968.

David Coulthard - Formula 1 Driver
b. 27 March 1971 in Twynholm

Career - David was three times Scottish Junior Kart Champion between 1982–85. He joined Paul Stewart Racing (PRS) in 1990 driving for the GM Lotus team and was runner-up in the British F3 Championships in 1991. Moving into Formula 1 David began testing for Benetton-Ford in 1992, then moved to Williams-Renault in 1993 as a test driver. Also in 1993 David and PSR won the GT Class at Le Mans 24-hour Race with Jaguar. He made his F1 debut with Williams-Renault at the Spanish Grand Prix in 1994 following the tragic death of Ayrton Senna at Imola.

He was voted both Scottish Sports Personality of the Year and ITV Young Sports Personality of the Year in 1994. In his first full season as a Formula 1 driver in 1995, he won his first race in Portugal and finished third in the drivers championship. David moved to McLaren-Mercedes in 1997 and won the first race of the season in Australia. For the past two years he has taken the top step of the podium at the British Grand Prix at Silverstone.

Throughout David's F1 career he has obtained over 235 points, had eight grand prix wins and has been in pole position eight times.

Kenny Dalglish, MBE - Footballer
b. 4 March 1951 in Glasgow

Career - After signing with Celtic on 29 April 1968 at the age of 17, Kenny made his first league appearance on 4 October 1969. In August 1977, Dalglish was transferred to Liverpool for £440,000. Eleven years later in May 1985 he was named the new player-manager, a mere 24-hours after the Heysel Stadium tragedy in Brussels (where 39 fans died) in which Juventus defeated Liverpool 1–0. The 1985–6 season saw Kenny name as manager of the year.

Kenny resigned as Liverpool's manager on the 22 February 1991 and eight months later he was appointed the new manager of Blackburn Rovers. He stayed on at Blackburn until the 25 June 1995 when he relinquished his managerial duties to become their Director of Football, a role he held until he resigned in August 1996.

During his playing and managerial career, Kenny was part of nine championship teams –five as a player, three as a player-manager and one as manager.

His international debut came against Belgium at Aberdeen in November 1971. Following his 102nd appearance for the national team (a 3–0 defeat of Luxembourg at Hampden Park) he retired from the international stage on 12 November.

He was awarded a MBE in the New Years Honours List for services to football in 1985 and in March 1986 at a ceremony in Glasgow was made a Freeman of the City by the Lord Provost, Robert Gray.

Sir Alex Ferguson, CBE - Football Manager
b. 31 December 1941 in Govan

Career - Alex made his league debut in November 1957 at Stranraer in the 2nd division. Three years later he joined St Johnstone on a part-time basis while he completed his apprenticeship as a toolmaker for the typewriter manufacturer, Remington Rand. In 1967 he represented the Scottish League against the Football League and scored 10 goals in seven matches on a Scotland tour of the USA and Australia.

His career wound down in September 1973 when he played part-time for Ayr United, which allowed him to spend time at his public house 'Fergie's Bar' in Glasgow.

His managerial role started when he was appointed by East Stirling in July 1974 and in October of that same year he took over at St Mirren, guiding them to the First Division Championship. Following his successful campaign at St Mirren, he was soon had offers from Scotland's bigger clubs and in 1978 he joined Aberdeen. During his stay at Aberdeen, he guided them to three Premier League titles, four Scottish Cup victories, one League Cup win and in 1983 won the European Cup Winners Cup over Spain's Real Madrid.

Ferguson temporarily took over the national team in 1986 after the untimely death of Jock Stein and stayed until after the World Cup Finals in Mexico. He declined not only the opportunity to stay on as Scotland's national manager, but also turned down many other lucrative offers from clubs both north and south of the border.

On 6 November 1986, he took control of Manchester United and in his first full season guided them into the league runners-up position. Since his time at Man U, they have been at or near the top of the Premiership and in 1999 won an amazing treble – the FA Cup, The European Champions' Cup and top of the Premiership.

In 1995 Alex was awarded a CBE in the New Years Honours list and became Sir Alex in the 1999 Queen's Birthday Honours. He has also been made a Freeman of Aberdeen and in November 1999 was given the Freedom of his home city of Glasgow.

Dario Franchitti - CART Driver
b. 19 May 1993 in Edinburgh

Career - Dario took up carting in 1984 and became the Scottish Junior Champion. The following year he was the British Junior Champion and by 1987 he had reached the World Championship finals.

In 1992 he was voted the 'Autosport McLaren Young Driver of the Year' and was fourth overall as part of the Formula Vauxhall Lotus, Paul Stewart Racing Team. The following year he was Champion of Formula Vauxhall Lotus, amassing six victories along the way and was voted the 'British Club Driver of the Year'.

He moved to the CART World Series racing in 1997, joining Hogan Racing and was runner-up 'Rookie of the Year' with 10 points and one pole position. In 1998 he joined the CART Champ Car Series with Team Kool Green and finished third in the championship. That same year he was voted 'Autosport British Driver of the Year'. Last year Dario was tied with Columbia's Juan Pablo Montoya on points, but ended up in second place as Montoya had won more races. There was talk in the paddock of Formula 1 that Franchitti could be tested as Jaguar's new driver in July for the 2001 campaign.

Stephen Hendry, MBE - Snooker Player
b. 13 January 1969 in Edinburgh

Career - After becoming the British Under 16 Champion in 1983 and the Scottish Amateur Champion in 1984-5, Stephen turned professional in 1985. Since then he has become the best snooker player the world has ever seen.

In 1999 he won the Embassy World Championship for the seventh time. His first world championship came in 1990, followed by a five-year repeat performance between 1992 and 1996. Stephen has also won the Benson & Hedges Masters at Wembley from 1989-93 and again 1996. His success on the snooker table is so vast it is impossible to list all his accomplishments.

He was the BBC Scotland's Sports Personality of the Year in 1987 and 1996 and voted the World Professional Billiards and Snooker Association (WPBSA) Player of the Year between 1990 and 1993 and 1995 to 1997.

Stephen was awarded the MBE in 1994 in recognition of his pre-eminence in the game. Currently, he is ranked number three in the world and still puts in 4–6 hours of practice six days a week at the Spencer Leisure in Stirling.

John Higgins - Snooker Player
b. 18 May 1975 in Wishaw

Career - John turned professional in 1992 and since that time has went on to win 13 ranking tournaments with the first victory coming in 1994 at the Grand Prix in Preston and again in 1999. Along the way he has also won the British

Open twice, German Open twice, European Open, Embassy World Champions, Liverpool Victoria UK Championship, Regal China International and Regal Welsh.

He is known throughout the snooker world as the 'Wizard of Wishaw' and is currently ranked number two in the world behind Welshman Mark J. Williams. John stands third on the all-time winners' list behind fellow Scotsman Stephen Hendry and England's Steve Davis.

Paul Lawrie - Golfer
b. 1 January 1969 in Aberdeen

Career - Being backed by a consortium of local businessmen, Paul won the 1992 UAP under-25s Championship by eight stokes. In 1993 he finished The Open in sixth place and went on to win it in 1999 after a spectacular final round of 67 and a four-hole play-off against Frenchman Jean Van de Velde and the 1997 Open champion Justin Leonard of the USA. In 1999 he also won the Qatar Masters and went on to make his Ryder Cup debut that same year. He reached the last eight of the WGC-Andersen Consulting Match Play and eventually lost to Tiger Woods.

He is now coached by former European Tour player Adam Hunter. Paul was awarded an honorary law doctorate from Robert Gordon University and was made an Honorary Life Member of the European Tour.

Colin McRae, MBE – Rally Driver
b. 5 August 1968 in Lanark

Career - At the age of 21, Colin has become the youngest rally champion in the history of the sport. He comes from a family of well-known rally drivers including his father Jimmy, who won the British Rally a record of five times and his younger brother Alistair has carried on the family tradition.

He made is debut in 1986 and won his first world rally in 1987. Since then he has started in 92 races, winning 19 of them. He has won the British Rally Championship Title in 1991, 1992 and 1998. From 1991–8 he drove for the 555 Subaru World Rally Team and joined Ford Martini World Rally Team in 1999. In 1995 he became the Rally World Champion.

So far in 2000 he has won the Catalunya Rally and the Acropolis (Greece) Rally. Currently Colin is second in the overall standings, 14 points behind Richard Burns.

David Millar - Professional cyclist
b. 4 January 1977 in Malta

Career - The Malta born Scottish cyclist turned professional in 1997 and since then has been part of the French Cofidis team. David is one of the most promising cyclists today and since his professional debut has won the Tour de l'avenir's first stage and has won various stages in different competitions including Route de Sud and Dauphiné-Libéeé. He won the silver medal at the 1999 British Chrono championships.

David won the first stage of the world's most prestigious cycling race - The Tour de France - this year by fending off last years overall winner Lance Armstrong of USA. After taking control the yellow jersey (awarded to the overall leader) he said he couldn't believe it and was going to sleep with the jersey on and not take if off for years!

Colin Montgomerie - Golfer
b. 23 June 1963 in Glasgow

Career - Colin attended Houston Baptist University on a golf scholarship and graduated in business studies. He turned professional in 1987 and since then has accumulated 23 international victories. In 1999 he won the Benson & Hedges International, British PGA Championship, Loch Lomond, Scandinavian Masters, BMW International Open and the World Match Play Championship.

On five occasions he has represented Great Britain in the Ryder Cup, with his first appearance in 1991 and has been on the team every year that the bi-annual event takes place.

Colin has won an unprecedented six straight European Order of Merit thanks to a third-place finish in the final event.

John (Jackie) Stewart, OBE - Formula 1 Driver
b. 11 June 1939 in Dumbarton

Career - Jackie's was an Olympic-class shot before becoming one of the top five Formula 1 drivers of all time. His Grand Prix career began in 1965 when he partnered Graham Hill at BRM and won that same year at Monza. His second victory came in 1966 at the world famous street circuit in Monaco. In 1968 he teamed up with the incomparable Ken Tyrell, which saw the formation of one of the most successful alliances in World Championship history. He won 27 races out of 99 starts and was on pole position 17 times. Jackie was crowned World Champion on three occasions 1969, 1971 and 1973.

In 1996 Jackie and his son Paul created the Stewart Grand Prix team. With the help of dedicated designers, mechanics, technicians and drivers (Rubens Barrichello and Jan Magnussen), the first year saw amazing results with Barrichello taking second place at Monaco in 1997. Johnny Herbert joined the team in 1999 and won Stewart-Ford's first race – the European Grand Prix at the Nurburgring with Barrichello taking third spot on the podium and the team clinched fourth place in the constructors' championship.

In 1999 Jackie sold Stewart Grand Prix to the Ford Motor Company and was appointed Chairman and Chief Executive Officer for the new team. Six months later he informed them that he was stepping down as Chairman and CEO, but is still plays an avid role within the team.

Jackie was awarded with an OBE in 1972 as a recognised sportsman and as an inspirational speaker and motivator by honorary doctorates from as far afield as University of Michigan, Glasgow Caledonian University and most recently Heriot-Watt University.

Jim Watt - Boxer
b. 1948 in Glasgow

Career - Jim turned professional in 1968 and was the British Lightweight Champion on two separate occasions and the European Lightweight Champion from 1977–9. He was the World Lightweight Boxing Champion between 1979 and 1981 and successfully defended his title on four occasions.

Watt was awarded an MBE in 1980 and the Freedom of the City of Glasgow in 1981.

THE COMMONWEALTH GAMES COUNCIL FOR SCOTLAND

Moray House Institute of Education, Cramund Campus, Cramond Road North, Edinburgh EH4 6JD
Tel: 0131-336 1924
E-mail: info@cgcs.org.uk
Hon. Secretary: D. C. J. Braun

SPORTSCOTLAND

Caledonia House, South Gyle, Edinburgh EH12 9DQ
Tel: 0131-317 7200
Chief Executive, F. A. L. Alstead, CBE

SPORTSCOTLAND NATIONAL CENTRES

Cumbrae, Millport, Isle of Cumbrae KA28 0HQ
Tel: 01475-530757; Fax: 01475-674720
Web: http://www.nationalcentrecumbrae.org.uk
Principal: R. Smith

Glenmore Lodge, Aviemore, Inverness-shire PH22 1QU
Tel: 01479-861256; Fax: 01479-861212
Web: http://www.glenmorelodge.org.uk
Principal: T. Walker

Inverclyde, Burnside Road, Largs, Ayrshire KA30 8RW
Tel: 01475-674666; Fax: 01475-674720
Web:
   http://www.nationalcentreinverclyde.org.uk
Principal: J. Kent

The following list includes the main organisations concerned with sports and physical recreation in Scotland.

AEROMODELLING

Scottish Aeromodellers Association
49 Houston Gardens, Uphall, W. Lothian EH53 5SH
Tel: 01506-857455
Secretary: T. Laird

ANGLING

The Salmon and Trout Association Scotland
The Caledonia Club, Abercromby Place, Edinburgh EH3 6QE
Tel: 0131-558 3644
Fax: 0131-557 6269
Director: P. Fothringham

Scottish Anglers National Association
Caledonia House, South Gyle, Edinburgh
EH12 9DQ
Tel: 0131-339 8808
Fax: 0131-317 7202
E-mail: admin@sana.org.uk
Web: http://www.sana.org.uk
Administrator: Mrs H. Bull

Scottish Federation for Coarse Angling
8 Longbraes Gardens, Kirkcaldy, Fife KY2 5YJ
Tel: 01592-642242
E-mail: stephen.clerkin@uk.sun.com
Web: http://www.sfca.co.uk
Secretary: S. Clerkin

Scottish Federation of Sea Anglers
Caledonia House, South Gyle, Edinburgh
EH12 9DQ
Tel: 0131-317 7192
Fax: 0131-317 7192
Secretary/Administrator: D. Wilkie

ARCHERY

Scottish Archery Association
4 Howard Street, Falkirk FK1 5JG
Tel: 01324-624363
E-mail: moi.taylor@ukonline.co.uk
Secretary: Miss M. C. Taylor

Scottish Field Archery Association
c/o 65 Napier Avenue, Bathcate, W. Lothian
EH48 1DF
E-mail: sfaa-archery@hotmail.com
Liaison Officer: I. Oldershaw
President: P. A. Sutherland

ASSOCIATION FOOTBALL

Scottish Amateur Football Association
6 Park Gardens, Glasgow G3 7YF
Tel: 0141-333 0839
Secretary: H. Knapp

Scottish Football Association
6 Park Gardens, Glasgow G3 7YF
Tel: 0141-332 6372
Fax: 0141-332 7559
E-mail: info@scottishfa.co.uk
Web: http://www.scottishfa.co.uk
Chief Executive: D. Taylor
President: J. McGinn

Scottish Football League
188 West Regent Street, Glasgow G2 4RY
Tel: 0141-248 3844
Fax: 0141-221 7450
E-mail: sfl@sol.co.uk
Web: http://www.scottishfootball.com
Secretary: P. Donald

Scottish Schools Football Association
6 Park Gardens, Glasgow G3 7YF
Tel: 0141-353 3215
Fax: 0141-353 3815
General Secretary: J. C. Watson

Scottish Women's Football Association
4 Park Gardens, Glasgow G3 7YE
Tel: 0141-353 1162
Fax: 0141-353 1823
E-mail: swfa@supanet.com
Executive Administrator: Mrs M. McGonigle

ATHLETICS

Scottish Athletics Federation
Caledonia House, South Gyle, Edinburgh
EH12 9DQ
Tel: 0131-317 7320
Fax: 0131-317 7321
Web: http://www.saf.org.uk
General Manager: N. F. Park
President: Mrs J. Watt

The Thistle Awards Scheme
Caledonia House, South Gyle, Edinburgh
EH12 9DQ
Tel: 0131-317 7320
Fax: 0131-317 7321
Administrator: Ms W. Dalziel

BADMINTON

Scottish Badminton Union
Cockburn Centre, 40 Bogmoor Place, Glasgow
G51 4TQ
Tel: 0141-445 1218
Fax: 0141-425 1218
E-mail: enquiries@scotbadminton.demon.co.uk
Web: http://www.scotbadminton.demon.co.uk
Hon. Secretary: I. E. Brown
Chief Executive: Miss A. Smillie

Scottish Schools Badminton Union
The Sheiling, Browsburn Road, Airdrie
ML6 9QG
Tel: 01236-760943
Fax: 01236-621320
E-mail: h.ainsley@cableinet.co.uk
Secretary: H. Ainsley

BASKETBALL

Basketball Scotland
Caledonia House, South Gyle, Edinburgh
EH12 9DQ
Tel: 0131-317 7260
Fax: 0131-317 7489
E-mail: sba@basketballscotland.com
Web: http://www.basketballscotland.com
Chief Executive Officer: Mrs S. F. E. Mason
Chairman: W. D. McInnes

Scottish Schools Basketball Association
Caledonia House, South Gyle, Edinburgh
EH12 9DQ
Tel: 0131-317 7260
Fax: 0131-317 7489
Chairman: T. Hardie

BOWLS

Scottish Bowling Association
50 Wellington Street, Glasgow G2 6EF
Tel: 0141-221 8999/2004
Fax: 0141-221 8999
E-mail: scottishbowling@aol.com
Secretary: R. Black

Scottish Indoor Bowling Association
41 Montfode Court, Ardrossan, Ayrshire
KA22 7NJ
Tel: 01294-468372
Fax: 01294-605937
Secretary: J. Barclay

Scottish Women's Indoor Bowling Association
39/7 Murray Burn Park, Edinburgh EH14 2PQ
Tel: 0131-453 2305
Fax: 0131-453 2305
Hon. Secretary: Mrs M. Old

CANOEING

Scottish Canoe Association
Caledonia House, South Gyle, Edinburgh
EH12 9DQ
Tel: 0131-317 7314
Fax: 0131-317 7319
E-mail: scaadmin@dircon.co.uk
Web: http://www.scot-canoe.org
Administrators: Mrs M. Winter; Miss R. Todd
General Secretary: B. Chapman

CAVING

Grampian Speleological Group
8 Scone Gardens, Edinburgh EH8 7DQ
Tel: 0131-661 1123
Fax: 0131-661 1123
E-mail: goon90@hotmail.com
Web: http://www.sat.dundee.ac.uk/~arb/gsg
Recorder: A. Jeffreys

CRICKET

Scottish Cricket Union
Caledonia House, South Gyle, Edinburgh
EH12 9DQ
Tel: 0131-317 7247
Fax: 0131-317 7103
E-mail: postmaster@scu-u-net.com
Web: http://www.scu.org.uk
Acting General Manager: D. Hayes

CROQUET

Scottish Croquet Association
14 Greenbank Crescent, Edinburgh EH10 5SG
Tel: 0131-222 4185
E-mail: sca@tonyfoster.co.uk
Web: http://www.grue.demon.co.uk/sca/
Treasurer: T. Foster

CURLING

Royal Caledonian Curling Club
Cairnie House, Ingliston Showground,
Newbridge, Midlothian EH28 2NB
Tel: 0131-333 3003
Fax: 0131-333 3323
Secretary: W. J. Duthie Thomson

CYCLING

CTC Scotland
10 Woodhall Terrace, Edinburgh EH14 5BR
Tel: 0131-453 3366
Secretary: P. Hawkins

Scottish Cyclists Union
The Velodrome, London Road, Edinburgh
EH7 6AD
Tel: 0131-652 0187
Fax: 0131-661 0474
E-mail: scottish.cycling@btinternet.com
Web: http://www.btinternet.com/~scottish
.cycling
Executive Development Officer: J. Riach
Administrator: Ms L. Dickson

DANCE AND KEEP FIT

The British Association of Teachers of Dancing
23 Marywood Square, Glasgow G41 2BP
Tel: 0141-423 4029
Fax: 0141-423 0677
Secretary: Mrs K. Allan

Fitness Scotland
Caledonia House, South Gyle, Edinburgh
EH12 9DQ
Tel: 0131-317 7243
Fax: 0131-317 1998
E-mail: fitscot@talk21.com
Web: http://www.fitness-scotland.com
Manager: Ms J. Small

The Fitness League
Ashgrove, 23 Carrick Road, Ayr KA7 2RD
Tel: 01292-262299
Fax: 01292-290290
Organiser: Ms F. Gillanders

**The Medau Society of Great Britain and
Northern Ireland**
Shieling of Blebo, Pitscottie, Fife KY15 5TX
Tel: 01334-828623
E-mail: medau@nascr.net
Scottish Representative: Ms R. Garton

Royal Scottish Country Dance Society
12 Coates Crescent, Edinburgh EH3 7AF
Tel: 0131-225 3854
Fax: 0131-225 7783
E-mail: info@rscdshq.freeserve.co.uk
Web: http://www.rscds.org
Secretary: Ms E. Gray

Scottish Dancesport
93 Hillfoot Drive, Bearsden, Glasgow G61 3QG
Tel: 0141-563 2001
Fax: 0141-563 2001
General Secretary and Administrator:
   Mrs M. Fraser

Scottish Official Board of Highland Dancing
32 Grange Loan, Edinburgh EH9 2NR
Tel: 0131-668 3965
Fax: 0131-662 0404
Director of Administration: Miss M. Rowan

EQUESTRIANISM

Scottish Equestrian Association
c/o Grange Cottage, Station Road, Langbank
Renfrewshire PA14 6YB
Tel: 01475-540687
Development Officer: I. M. Menzies

The Trekking and Riding Society of Scotland
Steadingfield, Wolfhill by Perth PH2 6DA
Tel: 01821-650210
Secretary: Mrs M. Sraham

FENCING

Scottish Fencing
Cockburn Centre, 40 Bogmoor Place, Glasgow
G51 4TQ
Tel: 0141-445 1602
Fax: 0141-445 1602
E-mail: scottishfencing@msn.com
Web: http://www.britsport.com/fencing
Executive Administrator: Ms R. Crawford

FIELD SPORTS

Scottish Countryside Alliance
Redden, Kelso TD5 8HS
Tel: 01890-830333
Fax: 01890-830222
E-mail: AllanMurray@scotca.freeserve.co.uk
Director: A. Murray

GLIDING

Scottish Gliding Association
48 McIntosh Drive, Elgin, Moray IV30 6AW
Tel: 01343-547701
Fax: 01343-547701
E-mail: ray@dalfaber.globalnet.co.uk
Web: http://www.gliding.org
Secretary: R. M. Lambert
Chairman: G. Douglas

GOLF

The Golf Foundation
Foundation House, Hanbury Manor, Ware, Herts
SG12 0UH
Tel: 01920-484044
Fax: 01920-484055
Web: http://www.golf-foundation.org
Executive Director: M. Round

Ladies' Golf Union
The Scores, St Andrews, Fife KY16 9AT
Tel: 01334-475811
Fax: 01334-472818
Web: http://www.lgu.org
Secretary: Mrs J. Hall

The Royal and Ancient Golf Club of St Andrews
Golf Place, St Andrews, Fife KY16 9JD
Tel: 01334-472112
Fax: 01334-477580
E-mail: thesecretary@randagc.org
Web: http://www.randa.org
Secretary: P. Dawson

Scottish Golf Union
Scottish National Golf Centre, Drumoig,
Leuchars, St Andrews KY16 0DW
Tel: 01382-549500
Fax: 01382-459510
E-mail: sgu@scottishgolf.com
Web: http://www.scottishgolf.com
Chief Executive: H. Grey

Scottish Ladies Golfing Association
Scottish National Golf Centre, Drumoig,
Leuchars, St Andrews, Fife KY16 0DW
Tel: 01382-549502
E-mail: slga@scottishgolf.com
Web: http://www.scottishgolf.com
Secretary: Mrs S. Simpson

Scottish Schools Golf Association
The Waid Academy, St Andrews Road,
Anstruther, Fife KY10 3HD
Tel: 01333-592000
Fax: 01334-592049
Secretary: Mrs D. Scott

GYMNASTICS

Scottish Gymnastics
Woodhall Mill, Lanark Road, Edinburgh
EH14 5DL
Tel: 0131-458 5657
Fax: 0131-458 5659
E-mail: info@scottishgymnastics.com
Web: http://www.scottishgymnastics.com
President: Mrs L. Milne

HANG GLIDING

Scottish Hang Gliding and Paragliding Federation
16 Johnston Street, Menstrie, Clackmannanshire
FK11 7DB
Tel: 01259-762055
Secretary: Mrs L. Wilson Wallace

HIGHLAND AND BORDER GAMES

Scottish Games Association
24 Florence Place, Perth PH1 5BH
Tel: 01738-627782
Fax: 01738-639622
E-mail: s.g.a@cableinet.co.uk
Web: http://www.st-and.ac.uk/~ig2/sga/
   agahomepage.html
Secretary: A. Rettie

HOCKEY

Scottish Hockey Union
34 Cramond Road North, Edinburgh EH4 6JD
Tel: 0131-312 8870
Fax: 0131-312 7829
E-mail: info@scottish-hockey.org.uk
Web: http://www.scottish-hockey.org.uk
Chairman: P. Monaghan
General Manager: C. Grahamslaw

ICE HOCKEY

Scottish Ice Hockey Association
9 Merton Avenue, Clement Park, Dundee
DD2 3NA
Tel: 01382-610890
Secretary: J. Guilcher

ICE SKATING

Scottish Ice Skating Association
c/o The Ice Sports Centre, Riversdale Crescent
Edinburgh EH12 5XN
Tel: 0131-337 3976
Fax: 0131-337 9239
Administrator: J. Macdonald

JU-JITSU

Scottish Ju-Jitsu Association
3 Dens Street, Dundee DD4 6BU
Tel: 01382-458262
Fax: 01382-458262
E-mail: 106146.2127@compuserve.com
Web: http://www.scottish-jujitsu.org.uk
General Secretary: R. G. Ross

JUDO

Scottish Judo Federation
Caledonia House, South Gyle, Edinburgh
EH12 9DQ
Tel: 0131-317 7270
Fax: 0131-317 7050
E-mail: info@scotjudo.org
Web: http://www.scotjudo.org
Chief Executive: C. McIver
Hon. Secretary: G. Campbell

KARATE

Scottish Karate Board
2 Strathdee Road, Netherlee, Glasgow G44 3TJ
Tel: 0141-633 1116
Fax: 0141-633 1116
E-mail: scottishkarateboard@btinternet.com
Secretary: J. A. Miller

LACROSSE

Scottish Lacrosse Association
Scottish Lacrosse Administration Office, St
Leonards School, St Andrews, Fife KY16 9QU
Tel: 01334-472126
Fax: 01334-476152
E-mail: stleonards@fife.org
Secretary: Mrs J. Caithness

LAWN TENNIS

Scottish Lawn Tennis Association
Craiglockhart Tennis and Sports Centre, 177
Colinton Road, Edinburgh EH14 1BZ
Tel: 0131-444 1984
Fax: 0131-444 1973
E-mail: gduncan@slta.org.uk
Secretary and Director of Administration:
   Ms G. Duncan
Director of Tennis: M. Hulbert

MOTOR SPORT

Scottish Auto Cycle Union Ltd
28 West Main Street, Uphall, W. Lothian
EH52 5DW
Tel: 01506-858354
Fax: 01506-855792
Office Manager: E. W. Jones
Administrator: Ms Y. Kelly

**Royal Scottish Automobile Club (Motor Sport)
Ltd**
11 Blythswood Square, Glasgow G2 4AG
Tel: 0141-204 4999
Fax: 0141-204 4949
E-mail: rsac_motorsport@compuserve.com
Web: http://www.motorsport.co.uk
Secretary: J. C. Lord

MOUNTAINEERING

Mountain Bothies Association
18 Castle View, Airth, Stirlingshire FK2 8GE
Tel: 01324-832700
Web: http://www.ma.hw.ac.uk/mba
General Secretary: Mrs L. Woods

Mountain Rescue Committee of Scotland
31 Craigfern Drive, Blanefield, Glasgow
G63 9DP
Tel: 01360-770431
Fax: 0141-950 3132
E-mail: R.H.Sharp@strath.ac.uk
Web: http://www.bluedome.co.uk/assoc/mrcscot
   /mrcsteam.htm
Secretary: Dr R. H. Sharp

Mountaineering Council of Scotland
Ground Floor, The Old Granary, West Mill
Street, Perth PH1 5QP
Tel: 01738-638227
Fax: 01738-442095
Web: http://www.mountaineering-scotland
   .org.uk
National Officer: K. Howett

Scottish Mountain Leader Training Board
Glenmore, Aviemore, Inverness-shire
PH22 1QU
Tel: 01479-861248
Fax: 01479-861249
E-mail: smltb@aol.com
Secretary: A. Fyffe

MULTI-SPORT BODIES

Scottish Disability Sport
Fife Institute of Physical and Recreational
Education, Viewfield Road, Glenrothes Fife
KY6 2RB
Tel: 01592-415700
Fax: 01592-415710
E-mail: ssadsds@aol.com
Web: http://www.scottishdisabilitysport.com
Administrator: Mrs M. MacPhee
Chairman: R. Brickley

NETBALL

Netball Scotland
Hillington Business Park, 24 Ainslie Road
   Hillington, Glasgow G52 4RU
Tel: 0141-570 4016
Fax: 0141-570 4017
E-mail: netballscotland@btinternet.com
Administrator: D. McLaughlan
Director: K. Halliday-Brown

ORIENTEERING

Scottish Orienteering Association
10 Neuk Crescent, Houston, Johnstone
PA6 7DW
Tel: 01505-613094
E-mail: donald@soa.almac.co.uk
Web: http://www.scottish-orienteering.org
Development Officer: D. Petrie

PARACHUTING

Scottish Sport Parachute Association
Strathallan Airfield, Nr Auchterarder, Perthshire
PH3 1LA
Tel: 01764-662572
E-mail: info@sspa.co.uk
Web: http://www.sspa.co.uk
Chairman: Ms A. Johnson

POLO

Scottish Bicycle Polo Association
16 Edmiston Drive, Linwood, Paisley PA3 3TD
Tel: 01505-328105
Secretary: A. McGee

Scottish Polo Association
The Grange, Cupar, Fife KY15 4QH
Tel: 01382-330234
Fax: 01382-223135
Vice-Chairman: Capt. M. Fox-Pitt

Scottish Pool Association
3 Strath Gardens, Dores, Inverness IV2 6TT
Tel: 01463-751282
Fax: 01463-751396
Hon. General Secretary: N. A. Donald

ROWING

Scottish Schools Rowing Council
1 Kirkhill Gardens, Edinburgh EH16 5DF
Tel: 0131-667 5389
Fax: 0131-229 6363
Secretary: R. H. C. Neill

RUGBY UNION

Scottish Rugby Union
Murrayfield, Roseburn Street, Edinburgh
EH12 5PJ
Tel: 0131-346 5000
Fax: 0131-346 5001
E-mail: feedback@sru.org.uk
Web: http://www.sru.org.uk
Chief Executive: W. S. Watson
Secretary: I. A. L. Hogg

Scottish Schools Rugby Union
59 Lochinver Crescent, Dundee DD2 4TY
Tel: 01382-660907
Fax: 01382-435701
E-mail: headteacher@harris-academy.dundeecity
.sch.uk
Hon. Secretary: D. C. M. Stibbles

Scottish Women's Rugby Union
108 (3F3) Comiston Road, Edinburgh
EH10 5QL
Tel: 0131-557 5663
Fax: 0131-556 7379
E-mail: barb@shawltd.demon.co.uk
Chairwoman: Miss B. Wilson
Secretary: Ms S. Kinnear

SHINTY

The Camanachd Association
Algarve, Badabrie, Banavie, Fort William
Inverness-shire PH33 7LX
Tel: 01397-772772
Fax: 01397-772255
E-mail: executive@camanachd.freeserve.co.uk
Web: http://www.shinty.com
Executive Officer: A. MacIntyre

SHOOTING

Scottish Air Rifle and Pistol Association
45 Glenartney Court, Glenrothes, Fife KY7 6YF
Tel: 01592-743929
Secretary: E. B. Wallace

Scottish Association for Country Sports
River Lodge, Trochry, Dunkeld PH8 0DY
Tel: 01350-723259
Fax: 01350-723259
Director: D. Cant

Scottish Pistol Association
Sandhole, Furance, Inveraray, Argyll PA32 8XU
Tel: 01499-500640
Fax: 01499-500640
Joint Secretaries: Mrs M. McCarthy;
    T. McCarthy

Scottish Small-Bore Rifle Association
128 Easton Drive, Shield Hill, Falkirk FK1 2DW
Tel: 01324-720440
E-mail: secretary@ssra.co.uk
Secretary: S. J. McIntosh MBE

Scottish Target Shooting Federation
1 Mortonhall Park Terrace, Edinburgh
EH17 8SU
Tel: 0131-664 9674
Fax: 0131-664 9674
Hon. Secretary: C. R. Aitken

SKATEBOARDING

Skateboard Contact/Federation of Scottish Skateboarders
16 Northwood Par, Livingston EH54 8BD
Tel: 01506-415308
E-mail: kenny_omond@agilent.com
Secretary: K. Omond
Treasurer: M. French

SKIING

British Association of Snowsport Instructors
Glenmore, Aviemore, Inverness-shire
PH22 1QU
Tel: 01479-861717
Fax: 01479-861718
E-mail: basi@basi.org.uk
Web: http://www.basi.org.uk
Chief Executive: R. Kinnaird

British Ski and Snowboard Federation
Hillend, Biggar Road, Midlothian EH10 7EF
Tel: 0131-445 7676
Fax: 0131-445 7722
E-mail: britski@easynet.co.uk
Web: http://www.complete-skier.com
Operations Director: Ms F. McLean

Scottish School Ski Association
Dollar Academy, Dollar FK14 7DU
Tel: 01259-742511
Fax: 01259-742867
Chairman: Mrs L. Hutchison

SKIING AND SNOWBOARDING

Snowsport Scotland
Hillend, Biggar Road, Midlothian EH10 7EF
Tel: 0131-445 4151
Fax: 0131-445 4949
E-mail: admin@snsc.demon.co.uk
Web: http://www.snsc.demon.co.uk
Development Manager: B. Crawford

SQUASH RACKETS

Scottish Squash
Caledonia House, South Gyle, Edinburgh
EH12 9DQ
Tel: 0131-317 7343
Fax: 0131-317 7734
E-mail: norman@brydon.safc.net
Web: http://www.scottishsquash.com
Secretary: N. Brydon
President: A. McCue

SUB AQUA

Scottish Sub Aqua Club
Cockburn Centre, 40 Bogmoor place, Glasgow
G51 4TQ
Tel: 0141-425 1021
Fax: 0141-425 1021
E-mail: ab@hqssac.demon.co.uk
Web: http://www.scotsac.com
Administrative Secretary: Mrs A. Bannon
General Secretary: Ms M. Galloway

SURFING

Scottish Surfing Federation
13 Eton Terrace, Edinburgh EH4 1QD
Tel: 0131-332 8388
President: S. Christopherson

SWIMMING

Scottish Amateur Swimming Association
Holmhills Farm, Greenlees Road, Cambuslang
Glasgow G72 8DT
Tel: 0141-641 8818
Fax: 0141-641 4443
E-mail: scotswim@aol.com
Chief Executive: P. Bush

Scottish Schools Swimming Association
55 Dalgety Gardens, Dalgety Bay, Dunfermline
KY11 9LF
Tel: 01383-825428
Hon. Secretary: Mrs C. Rees

Scottish Swimming Awards Office
Holmhills Farm, Greenlees Road, Cambuslang
G72 8DT
Tel: 0141-646 0490
Fax: 0141-646 0491
Manager: Ms S. Birrell

**The Swimming Teachers Association –
Scottish Division**
Anchor House, Birch Street, Walsall WS2 8HZ
Tel: 01922-645097
Regional Organiser – Aberdeen Area:
Ms D. Patterson
Regional Organiser – Ayrshire Area: H. Hall

TABLE TENNIS

Scottish Table Tennis Association
Caledonia House, South Gyle, Edinburgh
EH12 9DQ
Tel: 0131-317 8077
Fax: 0131-317 8224
E-mail: ralph@stta.freeserve.co.uk
Web: http://www.sol.co.uk/t/tabletennis/
Chairman: D. Clifford
Administration Secretary: R. Knowles

TEN-PIN BOWLING

Scottish Tenpin Bowling Association
Bower Cottage, Fountainhall, Galashiels
TD1 2TD
Tel: 01578-760209
Fax: 01578-760209
E-mail: admin@stba.org.uk
Web: http://www.stba.org.uk
National Secretary: D. Johnston

TRIATHLON

Scottish Triathlon Association
Glenearn Cottage, Edinburgh Road, Port Seton
E. Lothian EH32 0HQ
Tel: 01875-811344
Fax: 01875-811344
E-mail: Jacqui.Dunlop@btinternet.com
Web: http://www.tri-scotland.org
Secretary: Ms J. Dunlop

TUG-OF-WAR

Scottish Tug of War Association
47 Finlay Avenue, East Calder, W. Lothian
EH53 0RP
Tel: 01506-881650
Fax: 01506-881650
E-mail: garygillespie@stowa47.freeserve
      .co.uk
Secretary: G. Gillespie

VOLLEYBALL

Scottish Volleyball Association
48 The Pleasance, Edinburgh EH8 9TJ
Tel: 0131-556 4633
Fax: 0131-557 4314
E-mail: sva@callnetuk.com
Director: N. S. Moody
Executive Officer: Ms K. Benney

WALKING

Ramblers' Association Scotland
Kingfisher House, Auld Mart Business Park,
Milnathort, Kinross KY13 9DA
Tel: 01577-861222
Fax: 01577-861333
E-mail: enquiries@scotland.ramblers.org.uk
Web: http://www.ramblers.org.uk
Director: D. Morris

WRESTLING

Scottish Amateur Wrestling Association
Kelvin Hall, Argyle Street, Glasgow G3 8AW
Tel: 0141-334 3843
Fax: 0141-334 3843
Web: http://www.britishwrestling.org
Secretary C. Marshall

YACHTING

Royal Yachting Association Scotland
Caledonia House, South Gyle, Edinburgh
EH12 9DQ
Tel: 0131-317 7388
Fax: 0131-317 8566
E-mail: ryascotland@freeserve.co.uk
Web: http://www.scotsport.co.uk/sail/
Hon. Secretary: S. Boyd
Chairman: O. Ludlow

ENVIRONMENTAL

SCOTLAND

THE LAND

AREA

As at March 1981

	Scotland		UK	
	sq. km	sq. miles	sq. km	sq. miles
Land	77,097	29,767	240,883	93,006
Inland water*	1,692	653	3,218	1,242
Total	78,789	30,420	244,101	94,248

Excluding tidal water
Source: The Stationery Office, Annual Abstract of Statistics 1999 (Crown Copyright)

GEOGRAPHY

Scotland occupies the northern portion of the main island of Great Britain and includes the Inner and Outer Hebrides, and the Orkney, Shetland, and many other islands. It lies between 60° 51´; 30´´; and 54° 38´; N. latitude and between 1° 45´; 32´´; and 6° 14´; W. longitude, with England to the south, the Atlantic Ocean on the north and west, and the North Sea on the east.

The greatest length of the mainland (Cape Wrath to the Mull of Galloway) is 274 miles, and the greatest breadth (Buchan Ness to Applecross) is 154 miles. The customary measurement of the island of Great Britain is from the site of John o' Groats house, near Duncansby Head, Caithness, to Land's End, Cornwall, a total distance of 603 miles (965 km) in a straight line and approximately 900 miles (1,440 km) by road.

RELIEF

The highest parts of the United Kingdom lie in Scotland. As part of Highland Britain, 65 per cent of Scottish landscape lies above 120m (400ft), of which 6 per cent is above 600m (2,000ft), while 20 per cent lies below 60m (200ft).

There are three natural orographic divisions of mainland Scotland. The southern uplands have their highest points in Merrick (2,764 ft/814 m), Rhinns of Kells (2,669 ft/814 m), and Cairnsmuir of Carsphairn (2,614 ft/796 m), in the west; and the Tweedsmuir Hills in the east (Broad Law 2,756 ft/830 m, Dollar Law 2,682 ft/817 m, Hartfell 2,651 ft/808 m).

The central lowlands, formed by the valleys of the Clyde, Forth and Tay, divide the southern uplands from the northern Highlands, which extend almost from the extreme north of the mainland to the central lowlands, and are divided into a northern and a southern system by the Great Glen.

The Grampian Mountains, which entirely cover the southern Highland area, include in the west Ben Nevis (4,406ft/1,343m), the highest point in the British Isles, and in the east the Cairngorm Mountains (Ben Macdui 4,296ft/1,309m, Braeriach 4,248ft/1,295m, Cairn Gorm 4,084ft/1,246m). The north-western Highland area contains the mountains of Wester and Easter Ross (Carn Eighe 3,880 ft/1,183m, Sgurr na Lapaich 3,775ft/1,150m).

Created, like the central lowlands, by a major geological fault, the Great Glen (60 miles/96 km long) runs between Inverness and Fort William, and contains Loch Ness, Loch Oich and Loch Lochy. These are linked to each other and to the north-east and south-west coasts of Scotland by the Caledonian Canal, the River Lochy and the long sea-loch Loch Linnhe, providing a navigable passage between the Moray Firth and the Inner Hebrides.

HYDROGRAPHY

The western coast is fragmented by peninsulas and islands and deeply indented by sea-lochs (fjords), the longest of which is Loch Fyne (42 miles long) in Argyll. Although the east coast tends to be less fractured and lower, there are several great drowned inlets (firths), for instance the Firth of Forth, the Firth of Tay and the Moray Firth. The Firth of Clyde is the chief example of this feature in the west.

The lochs are the principal hydrographic feature. The largest in Scotland and in Britain is Loch Lomond (27.46 sq. miles/71.12 sq. km), in the Grampian valleys; the longest and deepest is Loch Ness (24 miles/38 km long and 800ft/244m deep), in the Great Glen. Loch Shin (20 miles/32 km long) and Loch Maree in the Highlands are the longest lochs in the north-west Highlands

The longest river is the Tay (117 miles/188 km), noted for its salmon. It flows into the North Sea, with Dundee on the estuary, which is spanned by the Tay Bridge (10,289ft/3,137m), opened in 1887, and the Tay Road Bridge (7,365ft/2,245m), opened in 1966. The present Tay rail bridge is the second to have been built; the original collapsed in 1879, only a year after completion, with the loss of 150 lives.

Other noted salmon rivers are the Dee (90 miles/144 km) which flows into the North Sea at Aberdeen, and the Spey (110 miles/172 km), the swiftest flowing river in the British Isles, which flows into the Moray Firth. The Tweed, which gave its name to the woollen cloth produced along its banks, marks in the lower stretches of its 96-mile (155 km) course the border between Scotland and England.

The most important river commercially is the Clyde (106 miles/171m), formed by the junction of the Daer and Portrail water, which flows through the city of Glasgow to the Firth of Clyde. During its course it passes over the picturesque Falls of Clyde, Bonnington Linn (30ft/9m), Corra Linn (84ft/26m), Dundaff Linn (10ft/3m) and Stonebyres Linn (80ft/24m), above and below Lanark. The Forth (66 miles/106 km), upon which stands Edinburgh, is spanned by the Forth (Railway) Bridge (1890), which is 5,330ft (1,625m) long, and the Forth (Road) Bridge (1964), which has a total length of 6,156 feet (1,987m) (over water) and a single span of 3,300 feet (1,006m).

The highest waterfall in Scotland, and the British Isles, is Eas a'Chùal Aluinn with a total height of 658 feet (200m), which falls from Glas Bheinn in Sutherland. The Falls of Glomach, on a head-stream of the Elchaig in Wester Ross, have a drop of 370 feet (113m).

THE ISLANDS

Scotland's northern and western coasts are fringed by 790 islands and islets, products of the same geological forces that have shaped its deeply indented coastlines. They fall into four main groups: Orkney, Shetland, and the Inner and Outer Hebrides. There are also some offshore islands, which lie in the North Atlantic well outwith the main Outer Hebrides group but are still part of the Outer Hebrides. Rockall, 184 miles west of St Kilda, was annexed in 1955 and added to the territories of the UK by an Act of Parliament in 1972.

Only 130 of the islands are inhabited today, although some of them became uninhabited only in the last century or so, some after many centuries of habitation, such as Mousa, site of one of the major Iron Age brochs but uninhabited since the mid 19th century. The last families to leave the St Kilda group were evacuated in 1930 (a military base and missile-tracking station were installed on Hirta in 1957, but the island is not permanently occupied). A number of the uninhabited islands are, or contain, nature reserves, principally for the protection of birds.

ORKNEY

The Orkney Islands lie about six miles north of the mainland, separated from it by the Pentland Firth. Of the 90 islands and islets (holms and skerries) in the group, about one-third are inhabited.

The principal islands and their areas are:

Mainland (with Burray, South Ronaldsay, and Hunda)	58,308 ha/144,079 acres
Hoy	14,381 ha/35,380 acres
Graemsay	409 ha/1,011 acres
Flotta	876 ha/2,165 acres
Rousay	4,860 ha/12,009 acres
Shapinsay	2,948 ha/7,285 acres
Stronsay	3,275 ha/8,093 acres
Eday	2,745 ha/6,783 acres
Sanday	5,043 ha/12,461 acres
Westray	4,713 ha/11,646 acres
Papa Westray	918 ha/2,268 acres
North Ronaldsay	690 ha/1,705 acres

Most of the inhabited islands are low-lying and fertile owing to the geological underlay of Old Red Sandstone, and farming, principally of beef cattle, is the main economic activity. Flotta is the site of a large oil terminal.

Hoy is the highest of the islands (highest point Ward Hill, 479m/1,571ft) and has the most dramatic landscape. Although most of the Orkney Islands are low-lying, St John's Head on Hoy (350m/1,148ft) is one of the highest sea-cliffs in the British Isles.

Several of the islands contain rare flora – e.g. Hoy, where rare alpine plants are to be found – and several contain nature reserves specialising in birds. Mainland boasts over 600 species of flowering plant, some of which are extremely rare.

North Ronaldsay, the northernmost island, is very isolated but also sufficiently fertile to support a small farming population. It has been cotinuously populated since prehistoric times. A species of small sheep, descendants of the original Orkney sheep, is unique to the island.

SHETLAND

The Shetland Islands lie about 50 miles north of Orkney, with Fair Isle about half-way between the two groups. Out Stack, off Muckle Flugga, one mile north of Unst, is the most northerly point in the British Isles (60° 51′ 30″ N. lat.). Lerwick, the capital, is in fact almost equidistant from Aberdeen and Bergen in Norway. Foula, the most westerly of the Shetland Islands, is the most isolated inhabited island in the British Isles. The group contains over 100 islands, of which 16 are populated.

The principal islands and their areas are:

Mainland (with Muckle Roe, West and East Burra, and Trondra)	100,230 ha/247,668 acres
Bressay	2,805 ha/6,932 acres
Fair Isle	768 ha/1,898 acres
Fetlar	4,078 ha/10,077 acres
Foula	1,265 ha/3,126 acres
Housay (with Bruray and Grunay)	218 ha/539 acres
Unst	12,068 ha/29,820 acres
Whalsay	1,970 ha/4,868 acres
Yell	21,211 ha/52,412 acres

Shetland's geology is different from that of Orkney, resulting in a harsher, more dramatic landscape, with impressive sea cliffs (e.g. the Kame of Foula, 376m/1,233 ft) and also in poorer soil, which has made fishing traditionally more important than agriculture as a livelihood. The islands are largely treeless, and peat bog, grass and heather moorland are characteristic. The North Atlantic Drift, an extension of the Gulf Stream, keeps Shetland's climate milder than its northern latitude would suggest.

THE HEBRIDES
The Inner and Outer Hebrides, stretching from Lewis, the most northerly island, to Ailsa Craig, the most southerly, comprise over 500 islands and islets, of which about 100 are inhabited, although mountainous terrain and extensive peat bogs and heather mean that only a fraction of the total land area is under cultivation.

THE INNER HEBRIDES
The Inner Hebrides lie off the west coast of Scotland, relatively close to the mainland. The largest and best known of the islands is Skye (1,648 sq. km/ 643 sq. m), which contains the spectacular Cuillin Hills (highest peak Sgurr Alasdair 993m/3,257ft), the more smoothly shaped Red Cuillin (highest peak Beinn na Caillich, 732m/2,403ft), Bla Bheinn (928m/3,046ft), and, in the north if the island, the strange formations of the Quiraing and the Storr (719m/2,358ft). Skye is itself surrounded by several small islands, and not far to the south-west are the Small Isles, Rum, Eigg, Muck, and Canna. Muck is low-lying and is the most fertile

of the Small Isles; Eigg and Rum are craggier. Some of the rock formations on Rum are geologically unique. Further north, off the north-west coast, lie a few small islands of which the principal group is the Summer Isles, about a dozen islands lying off the Coigach peninsula. Tanera Mór, the largest of the group, has tourist facilities. Still further north, Handa is famous for its rich bird life.

Major islands in the southern Inner Hebridean islands include:
- Arran – area 43.201 ha/106,750 acres; highest points Goat Fell (874m/2,868ft) Caisteal Abhail (834m/2,735ft); geologically very complex, it was described by Scottish geologist Sir Archibald Geikie (1835-1924) as 'a complete synopsis of Scottish geology';
- Bute – area 12,217 ha/30,188 acres; undulating and relatively fertile, hence much of its land is cultivated, with some woodland, although it is today chiefly geared up for tourism;
- Colonsay and Oronsay – area 4,617 ha/11,409 acres; a wide stretch of shell sand between them may be crossed on foot at low tide;
- Islay – 61,956 ha/151,093 acres; its large peat deposits colour the water used in its famous whiskies;
- Jura – 36,692 ha/90,666 acres; highest points the picturesque Paps of Jura (Beinn an Oir, 785m/2,575ft, Beinn Shiantaidh, 755m/2,476ft, and Beinn a' Chaolais, 734m/2,408ft); poor soils mean that much of the land is now used only for deerstalking;
- Mull – area 941 sq. km/367 sq. m; highest point Ben More, 966 m/3,168ft, the highest example of volcanic Tertiary basalt in Britain; some natural woodland remains and there is relatively little heather; sea lochs cut deeply into the coastline;
- Iona – area 877 ha/2,167 acres; best known for its religious aspects, it attracts visitors from all over the world;
- Coll and Tiree – areas 7,685 ha/18,989 acres and 7,834 ha/19,358 acres respectively; a single island until relatively recently in geological time, they are flattish in profile; their rock contains quartz and marble (which was briefly mined at Tiree in the late eighteenth century); the coasts are fringed with dunes and machair, and on Tiree are favourable for surfing and windsurfing. Tiree is also much more fertile than Coll and supports crofting.

THE OUTER HEBRIDES

The Outer Hebrides are separated from the mainland by the Minch

The main islands are:

- Lewis and Harris with Great Bernera – total area 220,020 ha/5,389,369 acres; highest point Clisham, 799m/2,621ft; Great Bernera is joined to Lewis by a bridge; much of Lewis is ancient, deep peat bog, while its south-western end and Harris are more mountainous;
- Barra with Vatersay – area 6,385 ha/16,889 acres; highest point Heaval (383 m/ 1,256 ft); the two islands are linked by a causeway completed in 1990;
- North and South Uist with Benbecula, Baleshare, Grimsay, Vallay, Kirkibost, and Oronsay – total area 72,827 ha/179,956 acres; highest point Beinn Mhór (620m/2,034ft), on South Uist; North Uist is very low-lying, with half its total area under water; all one long island until the Ice Age; Vallay, Kirkibost and Oronsay are now uninhabited;
- Berneray – located in the Sound of Harris, this island is now joined to North Uist by a causeway built in 1999;
- Eriskay – area 703 ha/1,737 acres; famed as the spot where, in 1745, Bonnie Prince Charlie first set foot in Scotland, and for its traditional music; however, the island itself is rather barren;
- Scalpay – now part of Lewis and Harris, joined to Harria by a bridge completed in 1998.

THE OFFSHORE ISLANDS

The offshore Hebridean islands are:

- Flannan Isles (seven islands known as the Seven Hunters), 21 miles west of Butt of Lewis;
- Sula Sgeir, 41 miles north of Butt of Lewis;
- Rona, 10 miles east of Sula Sgeir;
- St Kilda archipelago, 100 miles WSW of Butt of Lewis, consisting of Hirta (main island), Soay, Boreray and Dun.

GEOLOGY

The geology of Scotland is extremely complex. Its rugged mountains, hundreds of rocky islands, fjord-like lochs, moorlands and glens are the result of a gradual modification by weather, erosion, the work of ice and water and, most recently, human intervention. The British Geological Survey (BGS) is the nation's laboratory concerned with understanding onshire and offshire geology, geochemistry and groundwater. Its activities cover geological resources such as minerals and oil, environmental pollution and hazards from abandoned mines, waste, landslips, earthquakes and magnetic storms. There is a strong environmental interface where the ecosystem meets the ground and the landscape and where geochemistry impacts in human and animal health.

British Geological Survey (Scotland), Murchison House, West Mains Road, Edinburgh EH9 3LA
Tel: 0131-667 1000; Fax: 0131-667 1877;
Email: c.browitt@bgs.ac.uk
Web: http://www.bgs.ac.uk
Director, BGS Scotland: Dr Chris Browitt
Onshore Geology: Dr Martin Smith
Offshore Geology: Dr Nigel Fannin
Earthquakes and Geomagnetism:
  Dr David Kerridge

YEARS BP	EVENT
c. 2,500 – 3,000 million	Metamorphic Lewisian gneiss, found in north-western Scotland and the Outer Hebrides, is formed
c. 1,000 million	These rocks uplifted to form the mountain ranges of north-west Scotland, at the time linked to what are now Greenland and Canada. In the Inner Hebrides, Coll and Tiree form part of the Lewisian landform of the far north-west
c. 900 million	Torridonian sandstone, the oldest sedimentary rock in Britain, is deposited by rivers from Greenland in north-west Scotland, forming Torridonian mountains, e.g. Liathach (1054m/3,436ft) and An Teallach (1,062m/3,484ft), once over 10,000 feet high. Further north, sand fills an old valley in Assynt, leaving relict mountains, e.g. Suilven (731m/2,399ft), rising abruptly from barren moorland
from c. 800 million	The formation of the rocks that make up most of the Highlands we now see begins, when the area is an ocean trough. River deposits pour into this trough for some 400–500 million years

c. 670 million	Scotland (at the time 30° south of the Equator) is covered by huge ice-sheet, resulting in glacial deposits which form Inner Hebrides south if Coll and Tiree
c. 500 million	Caledonian Mountains are thrust up and folded as the American and European tectonic plates start to converge. Subsequent glaciation and weathering mould the rocks into what are now the Grampians and Cairngorms. These rocks, mostly granites, lavas and schists, make up the largest outcrop of granite in the United Kingdom, covering 410 sq. km (160 sq. miles) and its most extensive area above 3,000 feet, including Britain's highest mountain, Ben Nevis (1,343m / 4,406ft).
c. 400 million	Scotland lies 20° south of the Equator. Collisions of the crustal plates cause cracks or fault lines (e.g. the Great Glen). Highland Boundary Fault (Firth of Clyde to Stonehaven) and Southern Upland Fault (Stranraer to Dunbar) form boundaries of a great central rift valley into which Old Red Sandstone, debris from Caledonian Mountains to the north, pours for 50 million years. Widespread volcanic activity, especially in what is now Central Lowlands, producing Ochil Hills, Pentland Hills, also Glencoe
340 million	Arthur's Seat (251m/833ft), in Edinburgh, Scotland's best preserved extinct volcano, active. The igneous rocks of this area, a mixture of lavas and granite, extend to the Cheviot Hills on the English border
350–300 million	Carboniferous period: Scotland lies at Equator. Volcanic activity ceases; warm seawater floods central rift valley. Tropical swamps and deltas result, laying down rock types which give rise to limestone, coal, oil-shale and ironstone. East and north of the Caledonian Mountains, sedimentary Old Red Sandstone, deposited in shallow seas, is eventually uplifted, producing the sandstone lowlands of the Moray Firth area, Caithness and Orkney. Erosion after this uplift can

	now be seen in cliffs and sea stacks, e.g. the Old Man of Hoy
300–200 million	Permian and Triassic periods: New Red Sandstone formed. Much of this is now under water, notably under the North Sea, providing the basis for North Sea oil reserves
70–50 million	Jurassic period: American and European continents begin to pull apart; faults develop, forming the North Atlantic. Major volcanic upheaval affects Inner Hebrides, parts of Argyll and Arran. Extensive lava flows from massive volcanoes bury the older rocks; there is further faulting and uplift. Ben More (966m/3,169ft), the highest mountain on Mull, consists entirely of lava. Lava flows result in the contorted landscape of northern Skye. Erosion of these volcanic rocks produces the gabbro of the Cuillin ridge, Skye. Small Isles also a product of volcanic activity
from 50 million	Scotland gradually attains its present shape
from 3 million	Three periods of glaciation occur, each lasting thousands of years. Scotland's ice-cap is centred in the Grampians. Intense glaciation produces the characteristic U-shaped valleys, some filled with water (e.g. Loch Lomond). Glacial erosion can also be seen in the mountain areas as corries and troughs, and in the lowlands and plateaux. Large areas of Lewis and Sutherland are moulded down into the characteristic knob and lochan terrain. Lowland areas accumulate layers of glacial deposits, such as those on which Glasgow is built
c. 10,000	End of the Ice Age: glacial deposits result in the white sands found on Barra, the Uists and parts of the west coast. As the ice recedes, the sea-level rises, leading to formation of the fjord-like coastline of western Scotland; post-glacial drowning in Shetland produces a similar effect
8,000 to present	Human activity, e.g. deforestation, mining, quarrying, dumping, is the greatest cause of change in the shape and structure of the land

CLIMATE

Scotland's temperate climate owes much to the warm ocean current known as the Gulf Stream. In the same latitude in the northern hemisphere, only the west coast of Canada, close to the border of Alaska, enjoys a similar climate. Pressure systems rolling in off the Atlantic control Scotland's climate, especially on the west coast, which is significantly wetter than the rest of the country, but milder in winter, due to the influence of the Gulf Stream. The climate of some of the Western Isles is sufficiently mild to allow introduced subtropical plant species to grow.

RAINFALL

Rainfall varies markedly from west to east across Scotland. The rugged scenic areas are very wet: the Western Highlands, especially around Loch Quoich, average 4000mm (157 inches) a year, falling on average over 250 days per annum. By contrast the east coast averages less than 800mm (31 inches) falling on an average of 175 days per annum, with Dunbar, at 555mm (22 inches), being the driest. It is the heavy rainfall which provides the natural resource for the generation of hydro-electricity. There is a marked seasonal variation in average monthly rainfall in the west of Scotland, the wettest months being September to January; this seasonal variation is less marked in the east. There is a much greater chance of enjoying dry, settled weather in spring and early summer.

The wettest day on record was 17 January 1974, when 238.4mm (9.39 inches) fell at Sloy Main Adit on Loch Lomond. A local storm produced 254mm in just over 24 hours at Cruadach on Loch Quoich in December 1954.

The most damaging floods in the last 200 years include the Moray floods of August 1829, when record levels were reached on the Spey and Dee. Massive floods occurred on 5–6 February 1989 in widespread storms from Loch Shin to Loch Lomond. Kinlochhourn registered 306mm (inches), the highest two-day total ever recorded in Britain. The floods of April 2000 caused millions of pounds of damage to parts of eastern Scotland, and more especially central Scotland and Edinburgh.

SUNSHINE

Monthly averages of mean daily sunshine show a strong bias in favour of late spring and early summer, especially on the west coast and the Western Isles, where May is the sunniest month of the year, closely followed by June. April on the west coast is often more sunny than July or August. The sunniest parts of Scotland are in Angus, Fife, the Lothians, Ayrshire, Dumfries and Galloway, and the western coastal fringes from the Uists to the Firth of Clyde and the Solway Firth. In any given year, Dunbar, on average, is the sunniest place in Scotland with 1,523 hours. The dullest parts of Scotland are the mountain regions of the Highlands, with an average of less than 1,100 hours of sunshine a year. The sunniest months on record were May 1946 and May 1975, when 329 hours of bright sunshine were registered at Tiree. Conversely, the dullest month on record was January 1983 with just 0.6 hours (36 minutes) recorded at Cape Wrath.

Scotland's relatively high latitude means that winter days are very short, but in compensation, summer days are long with extended twilight. Around the longest day of the year darkness is never complete in the north of Scotland. In Shetland this is called the 'simmer dim'. Lerwick has about four hours more daylight, including twilight, at mid-summer than London. The least sunshine in Britain is at Lochhranza on the Isle of Arran, where the south-east end of the village is in continuous shadow from 18 November to 8 February each year.

TEMPERATURE

In winter the temperature in Scotland is influenced by the surface temperature of the surrounding sea. The North Sea is cooler than the waters off the west coast, thus the temperature decrease across the country is from west to east. The average winter daytime maximum varies from 6.5 to 7.5 Celsius on the west coast to 5.5 to 6.0 Celsius on the east coast. At night, the average minimum temperature ranges from 1.5 to 2.5 Celsius on the west coast to a little below 0 Celsius over low ground in Central Scotland. The coldest nights occur when skies are clear, winds are light and there is a covering of snow on the ground. The lowest temperature reading recorded in Britain was -27.2 Celsius at Braemar in upper Deeside on 11 February 1895, repeated on 10 January 1982.

In spring, summer and autumn the effect of latitude on the heat received from the sun is a dominant factor; hence Scotland is cooler than England, with the greatest difference in the summer. The mid-summer daily maximum varies from 16 to 18 Celsius on the west coast to 19 Celsius in the east central highlands. The night minimum averages out at around 10-10.5 Celsius across the bulk of Scotland. The extreme south-west, Arran, southern Kintyre peninsula, and Mull and Islay, as well as the Berwick-on-Tweed area, are all about a degree warmer. There are few excessively hot days or nights. The hottest day in Scotland was at Dumfries on 2 July 1908, when the temperature soared to 32.8 Celsius. This temperature was equalled on a few other occasions between 1868 and 1908, namely at Selkirk, Swinton in Berwickshire and Stenton near Dunbar.

Warm or even hot weather can occur in inland Scotland, but it is often accompanied by a large daily range of temperature in the glens, especially in spring and early summer. Occasionally the temperature will fall below freezing at night and rise to the mid-twenties during the day. The greatest range of temperature in one day occurred at Tummel Bridge, Tayside on 9 May 1978. At night the temperature dipped to -7 Celsius, the following afternoon soaring to 22 Celsius giving a range of 29 degrees.

WIND
Many of the major Atlantic depressions pass close to or over Scotland, making strong winds and gales frequent. The windiest areas are the Western Isles, the north-west coast, Orkney and Shetland. Even in these extreme western and northern parts of Scotland the highest frequency of gales occurs during the winter months and prolonged spells of strong winds are unusual between May and August. An exceptional storm occurring during the second week of June 2000 gave the strongest summer winds for more than 30 years over much of the country.

A day with a gale is defined as one on which the mean wind speed at the standard measuring height of 10 metres above ground reaches a value of 34 knots (39 mph) or more over any period of 10 minutes during the 24 hours. The frequency of gales of a year varies from 4 at Glasgow to 47 in Lerwick. The gale of January 1968 was probably the most destructive, causing extensive damage especially to forestry plantations in west and central Scotland. The strongest gust recorded at a low-level site is 123 knots (142 mph) at Fraserburgh, Grampian on 13 February 1989. The strongest gust recorded at high-level is 150 knots (173 mph) at Cairngorm Automatic Weather Station on 20 March 1986.

The frequency of winds from different directions also varies with the seasons. Winds from an easterly component are much more frequent from April through early June than they are during the autumn and winter, when westerlies are predominant. The lowest

barometric pressure measured in Britain is 925.5 millibars (27.33 inches) at Ochtertyre on 26 January 1884.

SNOW
The frequency of snow cover varies considerably from place to place and year to year. On low ground in the Western Isles and in most coastal areas of Scotland, snow lies on average for less than 10 days in a year. This increases to around 20 days in the north and north-east and up to 70 days inland at Braemar. Temperature generally falls with height, and rain which reaches the ground at low levels may fall as snow over high ground. As a result there is a marked increase with height in the number of days with snow falling and lying. Snow cover can exceed 100 days in the Cairngorm mountains.

The windiness of Scotland's winter months determines the pattern of snow cover. When snowfall is accompanied by strong winds the snow is mostly deposited on leeward slopes, exposed areas often being left bare. Natural hollows become filled to a considerable depth. It is the existence of these high-level corries which has enabled the development of the skiing industry in Scotland. It is rare for complete snow cover to persist for long except near the summits of the highest mountains. On average snow lies for six to seven months on the tops of Ben Nevis and Ben Macdui, but snow bed are even more persistent and many survive well into the summer, some semi-permanent and only disappear in very occasional summers. The oldest snow bed in Britain has persisted for 50 years, and is on Braeriach, the third highest mountain in Scotland.

VISIBILITY
In contrast to popular clichés about Scotland's mistiness, the general visibility over Scotland is very good. The greater part of the country is remote from the industrial and populous areas of Britain and continental Europe. Smoke fogs are now rare even in industrial areas of central Scotland, and the growing obsolescence of open fires for domestic heating has greatly reduced pollution.

Inland fogs on calm, clear nights usually clear quickly the following morning except possibly in the glens. When poor visibility occurs on or near the east coast or in the Northern Isles the cause is, more often than not, a sea fog from the North Sea known locally as haar. Haar occurs from time to time from April to September, often accompanied by glorious sunshine just a few miles inland. It is caused by warmer air flowing over colder sea, which causes evaporation from the sea surface.

Moist south-west winds can result in very low cloud which can be quite dense and reduce visibility to under 100 metres. The west is more prone to this type of fog, which tends to shroud all high ground in cloud and is a potential hazard to hillwalkers. One of the longest-lasting fogs in the world is at the summit of Ben Nevis, which is cloaked in low cloud for around 300 days a year.

THE HISTORICAL PERSPECTIVE

At a time when global warming is high on climatologists' agendas, there is ample historical and archaeological evidence that the changes in Scotland's climate observable today are not unique. Scotland has undergone, and is still undergoing, considerable climate change and variability.

There was a significant increase in warmth, for instance, from c. AD 800 to 1300, when the treeline and limits of cultivation were higher compared to today. Climatic upheavals towards the end of this period, including severe storms, flooding along low coasts, and droughts, affected vegetation and animals, and therefore also the lives of the people of Scotland. A protracted run of wet summers between 1313 and 1320 resulted in crop failure, starvation and disease.

A period of gradual cooling set in from the fourteenth century onward. The 1430s especially were noted for a series of extremely severe winters. The history of clan raids and cattle stealing from the Lowlands shows the impact of a deteriorating climate. During the 'Little Ice Age' of the 16th to 18th centuries, sea temperatures off the north and east coasts of Scotland were some 5°C cooler than today, and snow was permanent on the Cairngorms. Frosts, a short growing season and low summer temperatures resulted repeatedly in famine and loss of livestock, occurring with increasing frequency and severity. The 1740s witnessed probably the most severe winter weather on record.

The 19th and 20th-centuries have seen a gradual improvement in Scotland's climate, although with occasional regressions. The last decade of the 20th century witnessed a significant rise in average temperature and weather events, especially storms and flooding, have become more extreme.

THE FUTURE

What will be the impact and consequences of global warming on the climate of Scotland? In short, the climate is likely to become warmer, wetter and windier. An overall increase in world temperature would mean more moisture. Storms thrive on available moisture, hence Atlantic storms would become even more frequent and destructive. Increased storminess is likely to be accompanied by increased rainfall and the melting of the polar ice-cap will result in a rise in sea-level. As a result, flooding, including flooding of coastal areas, has been identified as one of the main impacts of climate change for Scotland. This has implications for the design standards of existing river flood prevention schemes.

LAND USE

USES OF LAND
Percentage of total area

	Scotland	UK
Agricultural Land		
Crops and bare fallow	8	20
Grasses and rough grazing[1]	65	51
Other[2]	2	3
Forest and Woodland[3]	15	10
Urban land not otherwise specified[4]	11	15

1. Includes grasses over and under five years old, and sole right and common grazing
2. Set-aside and other land on agricultural holdings. Excludes woodland on agricultural holdings
3. Forestry Commission data; covers both private and state-owned land. Includes woodland on agricultural holdings
4. Land used for uran and other purposes, e.g. transport and recreation, and for non-agricultural, semi-natural environments, e.g. grouse moors, sand dunes, inland waters.
Source: The Stationery Office, Digest of Environmental Statistics 20, 1998 (Crown Copyright)

Much of Scotland is open hill and moorland; less than 30 per cent is developed farmland or woodland and only 3 per cent is urban land (1996 figures). The Caithness and Sutherland peatlands constitute Europe's largest area of blanket bog, extending over about 400,000 hectares. The following table gives the distribution of different kinds of land cover at the end of the 1980s:

SCOTLAND'S LAND COVER IN THE 1980S

Land cover	Area covered (%)
Grassland	28
Mire	23
Heather moorland	15
Arable land	11
Woodland	14
Fresh water	3
Built and bare ground	4
Bracken	2

Source: Adapted from E.C. Mackey, M.C. Shewry and G.J. Taylor, Land cover change in Scotland from the 1940s to the 1980s. TSO/SNH.

FORESTS AND FORESTRY

Forests and woodlands cover about 16 per cent of Scotland, and nearly half of these are less than 30 years old. While very little remains of Scotland's old broad-leaved woodland, large tracts of land have been taken over by productive and commercial forestry. One of the most visible, and most debated, current features of the Scottish landscape, particularly – but not exclusively – in the Highlands, is the presence of large swathes of non-native species of conifer. Although the practice of planting exotic conifer species had been pioneered in the nineteenth century by some landowners, much of this planting was introduced after the second world war. In particular the Dedication Scheme, aimed at restoring what was seen as the Highlands' lost fertility and at bringing employment to the region, allowed private landowners tax exemptions for timber production. More recently, in the 1980s, individual buyers from business and media circles acquired big tracts of northern Scotland and began planting conifers there, the choice of tree depending more on quick returns on investment than on use of native tree species. This loophole was closed by the 1988 Finance Act, and although quite a number of individuals and companies still invest heavily in forestry in Scotland, production-oriented forestry is now balanced by a concept and a policy driven by the twin concerns of conservation and access, the result of a recognition of the poor economic return to the community from the forest industry and pressure from environmentalists from the 1980s onward.

Scotland's state-owned forests are managed by the Forestry Commission, which is responsible for their production and amenities and also acts as an advisory and implementing body for UK government forestry policy towards both public and private sectors. Although its remit is UK-wide, the Commission is based in Edinburgh in recognition of the fact that Scotland accounts for about half the nation's publicly-owned forestry. Since 1992 the Commission has been reorganised into two units: Forest Enterprise, which is responsible for the management of state-owned forests, and the Forest Authority, which implements government policy on privately-owned woodland and carries out research. Privately-owned forestry also owes much to Forestry Commission expertise and financial assistance in the form of grants and tax incentives. Forestry is a major source of rural employment.

The Scottish Executive intends to restore or create a further 15,000 hectares (c. 37,000 acres) of native woodland by 2003.

LAND OWNERSHIP

In 1996 there were 1,500 private landowners in Scotland. Three per cent of Scotland's land area was covered by cities and towns; 12 per cent was owned by public bodies, such as the Forestry Commission. Among the institutional and individual private owners who account for the rest, the National Trust for Scotland is one of the largest. The pattern of private ownership is dominated by fewer and larger landowners. In 1996:

50% of the 19 million acres in private ownership was owned by 608 people
40% was owned by 283 people
30% was owned by 136 people
20% was owned by 58 people
10% was owned by 18 people[1]

1. Robin Callender, How Scotland is Owned. Edinbiurgh: Canongate, 1997

THE TOP FIVE NON-PUBLIC LANDOWNERS IN SCOTLAND
- Buccleuch Estates Ltd
- National Trust for Scotland
- Blair Trust and Sarah Broughton
- Invercauld and Torloisk Trusts
- Alcan Highland Estates Ltd

Land changes hands faster in the Highlands than elsewhere in Scotland. Research carried out in 1983 showed that about 6 per cent of Highland estates changed hands every year compared with 2 per cent for the rest of Scotland, and only four estates had remained in the same hands for over a century. Estates are owned by individuals and entities other than individuals – joint owners, trusts, non-governmental organisations (NGOs) and companies, including investment forestry companies. Some owners are resident all year round and make a living from their estates; some use them as holiday homes; others, particularly owners of land under forestry, exploit them commercially but live elsewhere. Recent figures produced by Highland Council show that foreign owners now control 365,000 hectares (about 900,000 acres) in the Highlands, while other research suggests that overseas buyers now control as much as 18 per cent of all land in Scotland.

The agility of turnover has also been beneficial for the non-profit sector, whose holdings in Scotland have doubled in size since 1980 and are expected to double again by 2010. About 30 non-profit organisations, including 'green charities' such as the National Trust for Scotland (NTS), the John Muir Trust (JMT), the Royal Society for the Protection of Birds (RSPB) and the Scottish Wildlife Trust, own or lease about 21,800 hectares (about 540,000) acres in the Highlands. The RSPB now holds 30,358 hectares (75,015 acres) in the Highlands and Islands, compared to 16,000 hectares (nearly 40,000 acres) 10 years ago; while the John Muir Trust is now one of the biggest landowners on Skye. In spring 2000 JMT purchased 1,694 hectares (4,185 acres) including Ben Nevis, together with two neighbouring mountains and the upper Glen Nevis nature reserve, from the Fairfax-Lucy family, who had owned the land for the past 150 years.

At the same time, some crofting communities are acquiring the land on which they live and work. In 1993 the Assynt Crofters' Trust accomplished the first ever community buy-out of estate land in Scotland, and are now developing projects there to strengthen the local economy and conserve the environment. Following this pioneering example, Eigg, one of the small isles south of Skye, was sold in 1997 for £1.5 million to the Isle of Eigg Heritage Trust, which is jointly controlled by the island's 75 residents, Highland Council and Scottish Wildlife Trust. (Two other islands of the group, Rum and Canna, already belong to national conservation agencies.) In Knoydart, one of Scotland's most isolated inhabited peninsulas, crofters won control over the land they lived on in a community buy-out in 1998. Several other land takeovers or buy-outs by crofters or local trusts have occurred in the last few years. Scottish land reform legislation currently under way will be accompanied by the establishment of an £11 million Scottish Land Fund to aid local buy-outs.

ACCESS

With the growth in large-scale and mechanised agriculture and forestry, tourism, and the popularity of outdoor pursuits, public access to the countryside has become an increasingly urgent question, especially in the Highlands and other areas of great natural beauty. Changes in the pattern of land ownership are also generating more challenges to the long-standing but contested 'right to roam'.

A total of 9,315 miles (14,904 km) of known public rights of way in Scotland has been mapped by the Scottish Rights of Way Society (see below). However, only 3 per cent of this total has legally secure status as a public right of way. The status of much of the rest is open to challenge, and while many of these rights of way are well used and not at risk, many others are blocked, not in regular use, or not known about by the public. Little information is available about these routes, or about the extent of the network of other paths and tracks which are used by the public but which cannot be claimed as rights of way.

The government's commitment to access legislation followed publication in November 1998 of recommendations by the Access Forum and their endorsement by Scottish Natural Heritage. The January 1999 conclusions of the Land Reform Policy Group recognised the importance of public access to the countryside as part of the wider land reform agenda and the need for change in the current access arrangements in Scotland and for a law which would cover a right of responsible access to land for purposes of informal recreation and passage, on enclosed land as well as open ground and hills. Legislation for a right of access for informal recreation on all land and water in Scotland is therefore included in the forthcoming Land Reform Bill.

THE ACCESS FORUM

The creation of a multisectorial Access Forum was among the results of a review of access to the countryside carried out by SNH in 1994. The Forum brings together representative bodies for land management and public and private agencies with a role in facilitating open-air recreation and enjoyment in landscape and the countryside in Scotland. It aims to promote greater understanding of countryside access issues and improved arrangements for access, while minimising the impact of greater access on land management and conservation. The Forum does not attempt to resolve specific local access issues: its role is to foster debate and work towards solutions to the main problems at a general level. An early achievement was the agreement of a Concordat on Access to Scotland's Hills and Mountains. A separate group has been established to review arrangements for access over water.

Members of the Access Forum
Association of Deer Management Groups (L*)
Convention of Scottish Local Authorities (L& W)
Forestry Commission (L)
Mountaineering Council of Scotland (L)
National Farmers' Union of Scotland (L & W)
Ramblers' Association Scotland (L)
Scottish Countryside Activities Council (L)
Scottish Crofters' Union (L)
Scottish Landowners' Federation (L & W)
Scottish Natural Heritage (L& W)
Scottish Rights of Way Society (L)
Scottish Sports Association (L & W)
SportScotland (L & W)
Scottish Tourist Board (L & W)
Association of District Salmon Fisheries Board (W)
Royal Yachting Association Scotland (W)
Scottish Anglers' National Association (W)
Scottish Canoe Association (W)
Water Authorities (represented by East of Scotland Water Authority) (W)

L = concerned with access over land; W = concerned with access over water

THE SCOTTISH RIGHTS OF WAY SOCIETY

The Scottish Rights of Way Society is the successor to the Scottish Rights of Way and Recreation Society Ltd, formed in 1845 for the preservation, maintenance and defence of public rights of way in Scotland. It gives advice on matters relating to rights of way and, where practicable, seeks to secure the recognition of rights of way by agreement. It also signposts the major rights of way in Scotland and maintains a national *Catalogue of Rights of Way.*

LAND REFORM

Land reform in Scotland has been regarded as a high priority for the Scottish government since well before devolution. In preparation for the advent of the Scottish Parliament, a Land Reform Policy Group was set up in October 1997

to identify and assess proposals for reform in rural Scotland. The Group issued two consultation papers in 1998 and published its final recommendations in January 1999, setting out a comprehensive Land Reform Action Plan, covering ownership, tenure and access, which has been adopted by the Scottish Executive. This was followed by a White Paper in July 1999.

The Action Plan is an integrated package of legislative and non-legislative measures, which include:

(a) Legislation to reform and modernise existing property laws, including legislation to abolish the feudal system and to replace it with a system of outright ownership of land;

(b) Legislation on land reform, including legislation to allow time to assess the public interest when major properties change hands, giving a community the right to buy such land when it changes hands, and increasing powers of compulsory purchase in the public interest;

(c) Legislation on the countryside and natural heritage, including reform of access arrangements and creation of National Parks;

(d) Legislation on agricultural holdings, including provisions for more flexible tenancy arrangements, extension of the role of the Scottish Land Court and greater protection for tenants against eviction, legislation to permit wider diversification and part-time farming by farm tenants;

(e) Legislation on crofting, including legislation to give all crofting communities the right to buy their croft land, to allow the creation of new crofts and the extension of crofting to new areas, to devolve regulatory decisions to local bodies, to remove the link between crofting grants and agricultural production, and to clarify the law on crofter forestry;

(f) Non-legislative changes, e.g. increasing the involvement of local communities in the management of publicly-owned land, developing codes of good practice for rural land ownership and land use, and setting up a substantially enhanced lottery-funded Scottish Land Fund.

On 24 November 1999 it was announced that crofting 'right-to-buy' legislation would be brought forward and included in the Land Reform Bill, instead of in a later Bill specifically on crofting.

The third Progress Report on the Action Plan, published in June 2000, summarised achievements up to the end of May. These include:

- Abolition of Feudal Tenure Bill (section A) completed its third stage in Parliament on 3 May;
- Bill to reform leasehold casualties introduced to Parliament on 11 May;
- National Parks Bill introduced into Parliament on 27 March;
- White Paper on agricultural holdings legislation (section D) published on 17 May, with consultation due to be completed by 9 August

Targets for introducing land reform legislation (section B) and legislation on access arrangements (in section C) were put back to early 2001, owing to the complexity of the issues involved and the large number and variety of stakeholders.

Key non-legislative measures (section F) achieved so far include the setting up of the Scottish Land Fund; commitments from a number of public bodies with landholdings to increasing local community involvement in the management of their land; issuing of guidance on use of existing compulsory purchase powers. Many other new measures, such as developing a code of good practice for rural land ownership by individuals and organisations, are at various stages of development.

THE ENVIRONMENT

The UK government is committed to sustainable development under the terms of the 1992 Rio Declaration, and to meeting internationally agreed targets with regard to the reduction of greenhouse gases, improving air and water quality, protecting the sea, increasing and protecting forest and woodland areas, making energy savings, reducing and recycling waste, reducing empty housing, and so on. While these targets apply to Scotland as part of the UK, policy on sustainable development and the environment has been devolved to the Scottish Parliament and Executive, which is free to adopt a separate approach to sustainable development in accordance with Scottish circumstances and priorities.

SUSTAINABLE DEVELOPMENT

A series of policy documents dating from before devolution outline the Scottish government's approach to sustainable development. *Down to earth: A Scottish perspective on sustainable development (February 1999)* covers planning for sustainability in energy, industry, waste management, housing, transport, and other areas. Two strategic documents under the general title *Scotland the sustainable?*, published by the Secretary of State for Scotland's Advisory Group on Sustainable Development (March 1999) recommended the setting of objectives, activities, targets, and timescales, the establishment of a Sustainable Development Commission, and support for innovation in sustainable development initiatives, and laid out an action plan for the Scottish Parliament and Executive.

Since devolution, the Scottish Parliament and Executive have reiterated this commitment to sustainable development. Rural Scotland is a particular priority. The rural areas of the country constitute 89 per cent of its landmass and 29 per cent of the population, and, despite a low population density of 0.21 persons per hectare, 29 per cent of employment. Twelve per cent of all rural Scottish employees are engaged in agriculture.

Average population density in rural Scotland, Scotland and the European Union

Rural Scotland	All Scotland	EU
0.21	0.66	1.1

Source: Scottish Executive, Rural Scotland: A new approach, appendix 1: A profile of rural Scotland.
http://www.scotland.gov.uk/library2/doc15/rsna-07.asp

Rural Scotland: A new approach (May 2000) sets out the Scottish Executive's commitments as regards support for rural life and the natural environment and promotion of their sustainability. The Rural Stewardship Scheme, to be launched later in 2000, aims to promote a viable and environmentally friendly farming industry and support farmers' management of natural resources.

Resources to be devoted by SE to agri-environment schemes, 1999–2002

1999–2000	2000–2001	2001–2002
£18.9m	£20.2m	£21.5m

Source: Scottish Executive, Rural Scotland: A new approach, chap.5, 'Sustaining and asking the most of its natural and cultural heritage'.

Scottish Natural Heritage (SNH) and the Scottish Environment Protection Agency (SEPA) have a statutory duty to take sustainable development into account in all their overall environmental functions. SNH's budget has been increased from £39 million in 1999-2000 to £46.5 million in 2001–2.

More generally, the Executive established in February 2000 a Ministerial Group on Sustainable Scotland, chaired by Sarah Boyack, the Environment Minister. The Group is working with representatives of the business and environment sectors to identify practical ways of integrating sustainability considerations into areas such as waste, energy and transport.

In the European context, the Scottish Executive is committed, like the UK as a whole, to sustainable development as policy underpinning its overall policies and programmes in the environmental, social and economic areas. A long-term strategic view is seen as vital, and sustainability is defined as being not only about the environment but also about social and economic progress. In line with the definition of sustainable development in the Treaty of Amsterdam (1997), the Scottish Executive's approach links the promotion of environmental sustainability firmly with its existing commitments to economic growth with social cohesion and inclusion. Environmental sustainability is being included together with economic growth and social cohesion in the ambit of European Structural Funds programmes for the period 2000–6.

LOCAL AGENDA 21

As elsewhere in the world, local government and organisations seek to promote sustainable development through the Local Agenda 21 programme, under which local authorities draw up a sustainable development strategy for their area, to protect and enhance the local environment while meeting social needs and promoting economic success. The programme is managed by the Local Agenda 21 Steering Group, made up of representatives from the Local Government Association, the Convention of Scottish Local Authorities, the Association of Local Authorities of Northern Ireland, the TUC, the Advisory Committee on Business and the Environment, the World-Wide Fund for Nature, and other organisations.

Although local authorities are under no statutory obligation to take part in Local Agenda 21, most local authorities are engaged in or committed to the programme, and have a Local Agenda 21 officer or responsible staff member. They can contribute to a wide variety of activities related to planning, transport, waste management and pollution control, an so on, depending on local circumstances and needs. There is also LA21 involvement in Local Biodiversity Action Plans, which aim to contribute to local public awareness of biodiversity issues and the contribution local action can make to preserving biodiversity at the national and global levels.

For Local Agenda 21 officers and contacts at each council, *see* Council Directory. The government web-site about sustainable development in Scotland is at http://www.sustainable.scotland.gov.uk

Advisory Committee on Business and the Environment
Floor 6/D9, Ashdown House, 123 Victoria Street, London SW1E 6DE
Tel: 020-7890 6624

Education for Sustainable Development Group
Saltcoats, Gullane, East Lothian EH31 2AG
Tel/fax: 01620-843565

Environmental Technology Best Practice Programme
Environment and Energy helpline:
   0800-585794
Web: http://www.environment.detr.gov.uk/bpp/
   helpline.htm

Government Panel on Sustainable Development
Zone 4/D9 Ashdown House, 123 Victoria Street, London SW1E 6DE
Tel: 020-7890 4962
Web: http://www.detr.gov.uk/environment

Improvement and Development Agency (Local Agenda 21)
Layden House, 76-78 Turnmill Street, London EC1M 5QU
Tel: 020-7296 6599
Web: http://www.la21-uk.org.uk

Scottish Environment Protection Agency

Sustainable Development Team
Scottish Executive Rural Affairs Department, Victoria Quay, Edinburgh EH6 6QQ
Tel: 0131-244 0395; Fax: 0131-244 0195
E-mail: sustainable@scotland.gov.uk

UK Biodiversity Group
c/o Biodiversity Action Plan Secretariat, European Wildlife Division, Department of the Environment, Transport and the Regions, Room 902D, Tollgate House, Houlton Street, Bristol BS2 9DJ
Tel: 0117-987 8974
Web: http://www.jncc.gov.uk/ukbg

ENVIRONMENTAL PROTECTION AND CONSERVATION

THE CHANGING COUNTRYSIDE

Particularly in the Highlands, changes in land ownership and use over the past 50 years have been far-reaching. Among the factors involved are grazing pressure from greatly increased numbers of sheep and deer, the loss of land around lochs and rivers to hydro-electric schemes, the rapid expansion of commercial forestry, and a growing tendency for land to be purchased by new owners who are not experienced in the sustainable management of rural and forested estates.

The process of change on the land in Scotland is practically as old as its human habitation. There is evidence that much forest was cleared in prehistoric times as the first farming communities became established. Up to the early 18th - century, agricultural life was dominated by seasonal farming cycles. Change accelerated sharply particularly after the suppression of the Jacobite rebellion of 1745, with the disintegration of the old clan society, a marked growth in population (not fully offset at first by emigration), and most of all by agricultural improvement and the introduction of sheep farming into the Highlands, aimed at pacifying the Highlands and exploiting them economically. Also, throughout the late eighteenth, nineteenth, and early twentieth centuries, much of the Highlands was developed and managed by large landowners as productive forests and sporting estates, including deer forests,[1] grouse moors, and angling reaches.

Later, the development of hydro-electric schemes from the 1930s required the damming of rivers, resulting in increases in the area of lochs and reducing the grazing land available to both domestic animals and deer.

The Hill Farming Act of 1946 and subsequent legislation on agriculture ensured subsidies that underpinned the hill farming sector until the UK joined the European Economic Community (now the European Union) in 1973 and British agriculture of all kinds became subject to the European Common Agricultural Policy. These developments have further shaped patterns of land use across Scotland. The new legislation currently in progress will constitute the next landmark in the shaping of Scotland's countryside.

1 *Since the Middle Ages, the word 'forest' has been used in Scotland to describe a hunting reserve, especially of deer. A deer forest does not necessarily contain trees.*

SCOTTISH NATURAL HERITAGE

Scottish Natural Heritage (SNH) is the government's statutory adviser on the conservation and enhancement of Scotland's natural heritage and on its enjoyment and understanding by the public. It was formed in 1992 under the Natural Heritage (Scotland) Act of 1991, through a merger of the Countryside Commission for Scotland with the Nature Conservancy Council for Scotland. As well as its advisory function to government and others, it carries out certain executive tasks on behalf of government, working in partnership with a range of other bodies in conservation and sustainable management projects in environmentally fragile areas of Scotland, particularly focusing on Sites of Special Scientific Interest (SSSIs). It is involved in managing the Natura 2000 programme. SNH also engages extensively in environmental education activities.

NATURAL HERITAGE DESIGNATIONS

Natural heritage designations are given to areas of land or water which it is considered important to preserve or manage sensitively in the interests of scientific knowledge, preservation of flora or fauna, or enhancement of the natural landscape. There is no strict definition of a designations, and they cover a very wide variety of landscape and conservation scenarios. Designated areas can be of many different sizes, again according to the situation they address. Nowadays designated land is being managed more frequently in the context of a working countryside, laying emphasis on sustainability and a harmonious interaction between human intervention and natural processes rather than on preservation for its own sake.

The system of designations has evolved over about 50 years according to perceived need. Some, but by no means all, are supported by Acts of Parliament: this will be the case, for instance, with Scottish National Parks. Since designation also tends to respond to particular conservation needs, such as the protection of a specific kind of landscape or of particular flora or fauna, a single area of land or water may have more than one designation. National designations can also overlap with European designations or those emanating from international conventions.

Scottish Natural Heritage is the principal body responsible for implementing the provisions of different natural heritage designations, but several other public and non-governmental bodies, including local authorities, the Forestry

356   Environmental Scotland

Commission/Forest Enterprise, the National Trust for Scotland, Historic Scotland, the Royal Society for the Protection of Birds and other wildlife protection organisations, and the John Muir Trust, also own, lease or manage extensive areas in the interests of conserving and promoting Scotland's natural or cultural heritage.

NATIONAL PARKS
Legislation setting the framework for National Parks in Scotland was introduced to the Scottish Parliament on 27 March 2000. The first National Parks to be established will be in Loch Lomond and the Trossachs (summer 2001), followed by the Cairngorms.

SITES OF SPECIAL SCIENTIFIC INTEREST (SSSIs)
Sites of Special Scientific Interest (SSSI) is a legal notification applied to land which Scottish Natural Heritage (SNH) identifies as being of special interest because of its flora, fauna, geological or physiographical features. As well as land they can include rivers, freshwater areas, and inter-tidal areas, including mudflats, as far as the mean low water of spring tides. In some cases, SSSIs are managed as nature reserves.

SNH must notify the designation of a SSSI to the local planning authority, every owner/occupier of the land, and the Scottish Executive. Forestry and agricultural departments and a number of other bodies are also informed of this notification.

Objections to the notification of a SSSI are delat with by the appropriate regional board or the main board of SNH, depending on the nature of the objection. Unresolved objections on scientific grounds must be referred to the Advisory Committee for SSSI. The protection of these sites depends on the co-operation of individual landowners and occupiers. Owner/occupiers must consult SNH and gain written consent before they can undertake certain listed activities on the site. Funds are available through management agreements and grants to assist owners and occupiers in conserving sites' interests. As a last resort a site can be purchased. At 31 March 1999 there were 1,448 SSSIs in Scotland with and area of 919,597 ha/2,272,324 acres, almost 12 per cent of the country. Many large sites are in the north and west of the country; the largest complex, in the Flow Country of Caithness and Sutherland, totalling over 150,000 hectares (370,650 acres).

The forthcoming Land Reform Bill includes legislation to revise the SSSI system; part of the aim of this is to make the arrangements for SSSIs more user-friendly and involve local communities more in their management. SNH is already increasingly entering into agreements with landowners to manage SSSIs on their land postively in addition to their normal practices.

NATIONAL NATURE RESERVES (NNRs)
National Nature Reserves are defined in the National Parks and Access to the Countryside Act 1949 and the Wildlife and Countryside Act 1981 as land designated for the study and preservation of flora and fauna, or of geological or physiographical features. They have four main functions:
* habitat management, such as fencing, controlled grazing by sheep, and tree-planting;
* research;
* historical and other interpretation of the landscape;
* access and amenity.

SNH allows access to all reserves provided this is compatible with the wildlife conservation interests of the area. In practice this means that there is open public access to most NNRs.

SNH can designate as a NNR land which is being managed as a nature reserve under an agreement with one of the statutory nature conservation agencies. This arrangement applies to 67 per cent of the current NNRs. NNRs may also be designated on land already held and managed by SNH 30 per cent or land held and managed as a nature reserve by another approved body. SNH can make by-laws to protect reserves from undesirable activities, subject to confirmation by the SE.

There are 71 NNRs in Scotland, occupying 114,277 hectares/282,378 acres, about 1.4 per cent of the country. All NNRs are also SSSIs. They cover a wide range of habitats:

Habitat	Percentage of total NNRs
Uplands	68
Coastlands	12
Woodlands	10
Peatlands	6
Open water	3
Lowlands	1

Scotland was the first part of Britain to acquire an NNR, with the designation of Beinn Eighe (4,758 ha/11,757 acres) in Wester Ross in 1951. The largest NNR in Scotland and indeed the whole of Britain is the Cairngorms National Nature Reserve (25,949ha/64,120 acres). Other well-known NNRs are Ben Lawers, Isle of Rum, Creag Meagaidh, Spey Valley, Loch Lomond, Inverpolly (north of Ullapool), and Sands of Forvie (north of Aberdeen).

NATIONAL NATURE RESERVES

National Nature Reserve	SSSI within which the Nature Reserve lies	Local Authority	Area (ha)
Abernethy Forest	Abernethy (inc. Dell Woods)	Highland	2,296
Achanarras Quarry	Achanarras Quarry	Highland	43
Allt Nan Carnan	Allt Nan Carnan	Highland	7
Ariundle Oakwood	Ariundle	Highland	70
Beinn Eighe	Beinn Eighe	Highland	4,758
Ben Lawers	Ben Lawers	Perthshire and Kinross	4,035
Ben Lui	Ben Lui	Argyll and Bute/Stirling	2,104
Ben Wyvis	Ben Wyvis	Highland	5,673
Blar Nam Faoileag	Blar Nam Faoileag	Highland	2,126
Blawhorn Moss	Blawhorn Moss	West Lothian	69
Braehead Moss	Braehead Moss	South Lanarkshire	87
Caenlochan	Caenlochan	Angus	1,680
Caerlaverock	Upper Solway Flats & Marshes	Dumfries and Galloway	7,706
Cairngorms	Cairngorms	Highland/Aberdeenshire/Moray	25,949
Cairnsmore of Fleet	Cairnsmore of Fleet	Dumfries and Galloway	1,922
Claish Moss	Claish Moss	Highland	563
Clyde Valley Woodlands	Cartland Craigs	South Lanarkshire	51
	Cleghorn Glen	South Lanarkshire	
Corrieshalloch Gorge	Corrieshalloch Gorge	Highland	5
Cragbank Wood	Cragbank & Wolfhopelee Woods	Scottish Borders	9
Craigellachie	Craigellachie	Highland	257
Creag Meagaidh	Creag Meagaidh	Highland	3,948
Den of Airlie	Den of Airlie	Angus/Perthshire and Kinross	87
Dinnet Oakwood	Dinnet Oakwood	Aberdeenshire	13
Dunnet Links	Dunnet Links	Highland	465
Eilean Na Muice Duibhe	Eilean Na Muice Duibhe	Argyll and Bute	360
Flanders Moss	Flanders Moss	Stirling	210
Forvie	Sands of Forvie & Ythan Estuary	Aberdeenshire	973
Glasdrum Wood	Glasdrum	Argyll and Bute	169
Glen Diomhan	Arran Northern Mountains	North Ayrshire	10
Glen Nant	Glen Nant	Argyll and Bute	59
Glen Roy	Parallel Roads of Lochaber	Highland	1,168
Glen Tanar	Glen Tanar	Aberdeenshire	4,185
Glencripesdale	Glencripesdale	Highland	609
Gualin	Foinaven	Highland	2,522
Hermaness	Hermaness	Shetland Isles Council	964
Inchnadamph	Ben More Assynt	Highland	1,295
Invernaver	Invernaver	Highland	552
Inverpolly	Inverpolly	Highland	10,857
Isle of May	Isle of May	Fife	57
Keen of Hamar	Keen of Hamar	Shetland Isles Council	30
Kirkconnell Flow	Kirkconnell Flow	Dumfries and Galloway	142
Loch a'Mhuilinn	Loch a'Mhuilinn	Highland	67
Loch Druidibeg	Loch Druidibeg	Western Isles	1,677
Loch Fleet	Loch Fleet	Highland	1,058
Loch Leven	Loch Leven	Perthshire and Kinross	1,597
Loch Lomond	Aber Bog, Gartocharn Bog & Bell Moss	WestDumbarton/Stirling	428
	Endrick Mouth & Islands	WestDumbarton	

Loch Maree Islands	Loch Maree	Highland	200
Mealdarroch	Tarbert to Skipness Coast	Argyll and Bute	205
Milton Wood	Milton Wood	Perthshire and Kinross	24
Moine Mhor	Moine Mhor	Argyll and Bute	493
Monach Isles	Monach Isles	Western Isles	577
Morrone Birkwood	Morrone Birkwood	Aberdeenshire	225
Morton Lochs	Morton Lochs	Fife	24
Mound Alderwoods	Mound Alderwoods	Highland	267
Muir of Dinnet	Muir of Dinnet	Aberdeenshire	1,415
Nigg and Udale Bays	Cromarty Firth	Highland	640
North Rona and Sula Sgeir	North Rona and Sula Sgeir	Western Isles	130
Noss	Noss	Shetland Isles Council	313
Rannoch Moor	Rannoch Moor	Perthshire and Kinross	1,499
Rassal Ashwood	Rassal	Highland	85
Rum	Rum	Highland	10,684
St Abb's Head	St Abb's Head to Fast Castle Head	Scottish Borders	77
St Cyrus	St Cyrus & Kinnaber Links	Aberdeenshire	92
St Kilda	St Kilda	Western Isles	853
Silver Flowe	Merrick Kells	Dumfries and Galloway	191
Strathfarrar	Glen Strathfarrar	Highland	2,189
Strathy Bogs	Strathy Bogs	Highland	281
Taynish	Taynish Woods	Argyll and Bute	362
Tentsmuir Point	Tayport Tentsmuir Coast	Fife	515
Tynron Juniper Wood	Tynron Juniper Wood	Dumfries and Galloway	5
Whitlaw Mosses	Whitlaw Mosses	Scottish Borders	19

TOTAL: 114,277

NATIONAL SCENIC AREAS (NSAs)

National Scenic Areas have a broadly equivalent status to the Areas of Outstanding Natural Beauty in England and Wales. They were identified by the Countryside Commission for Scotland (now part of SNH) and introduced by the government under town and country planning legislation in 1980. The NSA is the main landscape designation in Scotland and is unique to Scotland. At mid-1999 there were 40 of these, covering a total area of 1,001,800 hectares (2,475,448 acres).

National Scenic Areas would continue to exist after the designation of National Parks. A review is in progress to determine whether any areas should be added to or removed from the current list.

Development within National Scenic Areas is dealt with by the local planning authority, which is required to consult Scottish Natural Heritage concerning certain categories of development. Land management uses can also be modified in the interest of scenic conservation.

Assynt-Coigach (Highland), 90,200 ha/222,884 acres

Ben Nevis and Glen Coe (Highland/Argyll and Bute/Perth and Kinross), 101,600 ha/251,053 acres

Cairngorm Mountains (Highland/Aberdeenshire/ Moray), 67,200 ha/166,051 acres

Cuillin Hills (Highland), 21,900 ha/54,115 acres

Deeside and Lochnagar (Aberdeenshire/Angus), 40,000 ha/98,840 acres

Dornoch Firth (Highland), 7,500 ha/18,532 acres

East Stewartry Coast (Dumfries and Galloway), 4,500 ha/11,119 acres

Eildon and Leaderfoot (Scottish Borders), 3,600 ha/8,896 acres

Fleet Valley (Dumfries and Galloway), 5,300 ha/13,096 acres

Glen Affric (Highland), 19,300 ha/47,690 acres

Glen Strathfarrar (Highland), 3,800 ha/9,390 acres

Hoy and West Mainland (Orkney Islands), 14,800 ha/36,571 acres

Jura (Argyll and Bute), 21,800 ha/53,868 acres

Kintail (Highland), 15,500 ha/38,300 acres

Knapdale (Argyll and Bute), 19,800 ha/48,926 acres

Knoydart (Highland), 39,500 ha/97,604 acres

Kyle of Tongue (Highland), 18,500 ha/45,713 acres

Kyles of Bute (Argyll and Bute), 4,400 ha/10,872 acres

Loch na Keal, Mull (Argyll and Bute), 12,700 ha/31,382 acres

Loch Lomond (Argyll and Bute/Stirling/West Dunbartonshire), 27,400 ha/67,705 acres

Loch Rannoch and Glen Lyon (Perth and Kinross/Stirling), 48,400 ha/119,596 acres

Loch Shiel (Highland), 13,400 ha/33,111 acres

Loch Tummel (Perth and Kinross), 9,200 ha/22,733 acres

Lynn of Lorn (Argyll and Bute), 4,800 ha/11,861 acres

Morar, Moidart and Ardnamurchan (Highland), 13,500 ha/33,358 acres

North-west Sutherland (Highland), 20,500 ha/50,655 acres

Nith Estuary (Dumfries and Galloway), 9,300 ha/22,980 acres

North Arran (North Ayrshire), 23,800 ha/58,810 acres

River Earn (Perth and Kinross), 3,000 ha/7,413 acres

River Tay (Perth and Kinross), 5,600 ha/13,838 acres

St Kilda (Western Isles), 900 ha/2,224 acres

Scarba, Lunga and the Garvellachs (Argyll and Bute), 1,900 ha/4,695 acres

Shetland (Shetland Islands), 11,600 ha/28,664 acres

Small Isles (Highland), 15,500 ha/38,300 acres

South Lewis, Harris and North Uist (Western Isles), 109,600 ha/270,822 acres

South Uist Machair (Western Isles), 6,100 ha/15,073 acres

The Trossachs (Stirling), 4,600 ha/11,367 acres

Trotternish (Highland), 5,000 ha/12,355 acres

Upper Tweeddale (Scottish Borders), 10,500 ha/25,945 acres

Wester Ross (Highland), 145,300 ha/359,036 acres

LOCAL NATURE RESERVES (LNRs)

The 1949 National Parks and Access to the Countryside Act gives local authorities the power to designate local nature reserves, where they own or lease the land and have an agreement with the landowner. They are managed in consultation with SNH. Conservation trusts can also own and manage non-statutory LNRs. LNRs have an educational as well as a conservation purpose and should have facilities to enable people both to enjoy and to understand them.

The acquisition in June 2000 of two new LNRs in Dundee brings the total number of LNRs in Scotland to 33, covering a total of about 9,343 hectares (23,086 acres). Many LNRs are located in or on the edge of cities, for instance Kincorth Hill, Aberdeen, and Corstorphine Hill, Edinburgh; but large areas of countryside such as Findhorn Bay in Moray, Wigtown Bay, Dumfries and Galloway, and Montrose Basin, Angus, are also LNRs.

Other designations which local authorities can make are:

- Regional Parks: large areas, principally in private ownership and not dedicated exclusively to conservation, landscape or heritage purposes, but where initatives can be taken by local authorities to increase informal recreation land uses. There are four Regional Parks in Scotland, of between 6,500 and 44,000 hectares: Clyde-Muirsheil, Fife, the Pentland Hills, and Loch Lomond;

- Country Parks: also in multiple use, though here recreation is the main use of the land. Close to, or within, urban areas and smaller than Regional Parks (40–600 hectares), they are mostly owned and managed by local authorities. There are 36 in Scotland.

LOCAL NATURE RESERVES

Local Nature Reserve	Unitary Authority	Area (ha)
Aberlady Bay	East Lothian	582.0
Arnhall Moss	Aberdeenshire	9.6
Balquidderock Wood	Stirling	6.0
Birnie and Gaddon Lochs, Collessie	Fife	28.2
Bishop Loch	Glasgow City	24.3
Broughty Ferry	Dundee City	3.9
Castle & Hightae Lochs	Dumfries & Galloway	109.4
Corstophine Hill	Edinburgh	67.3
Coul Den, Glenrothes	Fife	10.7
Coves Community Park	Inverclyde	44.0
Den of Maidencraig	Aberdeen City	15.0
Donmouth	Aberdeen City	36.0
Duchess Wood	Argyll & Bute	22.0
Dumbreck Marsh	North Lanarkshire	18.6
Eden Estuary	Fife	891.0
Findhorn Bay	Moray	1,200.0
Gartmorn Dam	Clackmannan	44.0
Hermitage of Braid / Blackford Hill	Edinburgh	59.4
Hogganfield Park	Glasgow City	46.0
Inner Tay	Dundee City	1,176.0
Jennys Well	Renfrewshire	6.0
Kincorth Hill	Aberdeen City	41.0
Langlands Moss	South Lanarkshire	20.0
Montrose Basin	Angus	1,024.0
Mull Head	Orkney	243.5
Paisley Moss	Renfrewshire	4.0

Perchy Pond	North Lanarkshire	40.7
Scotstown Moor	Aberdeen City	34.0
Straiton Pond	Midlothian	5.2
Torry Bay	Fife	683.0
Trottick Mill Ponds	Dundee City	3.0
Waters of Philorth	Aberdeenshire	0.3
Wigtown Bay	Dumfries & Galloway	2,844.7
	TOTAL	9,342.8

FOREST NATURE RESERVES (FNRs)

Forest Enterprise (an executive agency of the Forestry Commission) is responsible for the management of the Commission's forests. It has created 46 Forest Nature Reserves with the aim of protecting and conserving special forms of natural habitat, flora and fauna. There are about 300 SSSIs on the estates, some of which are also Nature Reserves.

Forest Nature Reserves extend in size from under 50 hectares (124 acres) to over 500 hectares (1,236 acres). Several of the largest are in Scotland, including the Black Wood of Rannoch, by Loch Rannoch; Culbin Forest, near Forres; Glen Affric, near Fort Augustus; Kylerhea, Isle of Skye; and Starr Forest, in Galloway Forest Park.

Other forest areas managed by the Forestry Commission are:
- Forest Parks: large tracts of Forestry Commission land, often containing areas of scenic importance, and managed by Forestry Enterrpise as multi-purpose forestry. The first Forest Park in Britain was in Scotland, Argyll Forest Park, established 1935;
- Caledonian Forest Reserves: like FNRs, established by Forestry Enterprise as representing the best of the Forestry Commission's conservation areas. There are 18 of these, covering 16,000 hectares of native oak and pine woods in the Highlands;
- Woodland Parks: smaller versions of Forest Parks, usually located nearer to population centres.

The following list of Forest Nature reserves described as being the very best of their kind has been supplied by the Forestry Commission and derives from a much bigger list, space for which is precluded here.

Black Burn – nr Hawick. Wetlands. Scottish small reed, fibrous tussock sedge
Black Wood of Rannoch – Loch Rannoch. Native pinewood. Insects, fungi, lichens, otter, pine marten

Culbin Forest – near Forres. Pine forest on sand dunes. Red squirrel; capercaillie; osprey
Eilean Ruairidh Mor – Loch Awe. Semi-natural oakwood, 42 lichens, 67 plants, butterflies
Glenan – nr Tighnabruaich. Range of habitats – coastal, woodland, moorland. Nightjar, bryophytes
Glen Affric – nr Fort Augustus. Native pinewood. Pine marten, diver, dragonflies
Glen Nant – nr Taynuilt. Native deciduous woodland. 151 mosses, lichens, 175 moths and butterflies
Knockman Wood – nr Newton Stewart. Semi-natural oakwood. Fallow deer, butterflies, barn owl; 126 lichens
Kylerhea – Skye. Ancient birchwood, ashwood, oakwood. Otter, seal, golden eagle
Leiterfearn – nr Fort Augustus. Ashwood, hazel coppice. Loch flora, butterflies
Lochaber Loch – nr Dumfries. Ancient oak coppice. Loch flora, butterflies
Loch Lomond Oakwood – Loch Lomond. Ancient broadleaved woods. Wood warbler, pied flycatcher
Redmyre – nr Auchtermuchty. Loch with rich flora including slender sedge; bats
Retreat Wood – nr Castle Douglas. Oald oaks, epiphyte flora, redstart
Ryovan Pass – nr Aviemore. Caledonian pine; red deer, roe deer, wildcat
Starr Forest – Galloway Forest Park. Forest lochs. Black-throated diver, peregrine falcon, golden eagle

MARINE RESERVES

There is statutory provision for Marine Nature Reserves analogous to NNRs, covering the management of marine sites in British waters, but it is has never been used in Scotland.

However, SNH has published a list of possible marine Special Areas for Conservation under the EC Habitats Directive, which identifies certain marine species found in Scottish waters as rare, endangered or vulnerable. Consultation on these possible sites is in progress.

ENVIRONMENTALLY SENSITIVE AREAS (ESAs)

Ten large areas of Scotland, totalling 1.4 million hectares in area, are designated under the Agriculture Act 1986 as Environmentally Sensitive Areas. These are areas where traditional farming practices have been important in maintaining the conservation, landscape or heritage aspects of the land. Farmers and crofters living in these areas can qualify for agricultural support payments, which enable them to manage their land in environmentally sensitive ways and contribute to maintaining features of natural of cultural heritage, including improving public access. The scheme is managed by the Scottish Executive.

EUROPEAN UNION NATURAL HERITAGE DESIGNATIONS

Two pieces of EU legislation in particular apply to the conservation of the natural environment in Scotland:

- Council Directive 92/43/EEC on the conservation of natural habitats and of wild fauna and flora, commonly known as the EC Habitats Directive (1992);
- Council Directive 79/409/EEC on the conservation of wild birds, commonly known as the EC Birds Directive (1979).

The implementation of these two Directives was brought into UK law by the Conservation (Natural Habitats, &c.) Regulations (1994).

SPECIAL AREAS OF CONSERVATION (SACs)

SACs are areas designated to safeguard rare or endangered fauna and flora under the terms of the EC Habitats Directive. SACs on land are normally also SSSIs.

In June 2000 the Scottish Environment Minister, Sarah Boyack, announced that 90 possible candidates SACs had been identified, including Cape Wrath, Fair Isle, the Monadhliath mountains, and the Sound of Barra. Following consultation and the selection of a definitive list, these will be proposed to the European Commission for SAC status.

SPECIAL PROTECTION AREAS (SPAs)

SPAs are land and marine sites devoted to the protection of birds under the terms of the EC Wild Birds Directive. Following the publication in July 1999 of selection guidelines for SPAs by the Joint Nature Conservation Committees, the Scottish Executive has developed a programme to classify appropriate sites as SPAs. SPAs on land are normally also SSSIs.

In May 2000 SPA status was announced for three areas providing habitat for some of Scotland's most important birds: an extension to Glenmore Forest in the existing Cairngorms SPA (Scottish crossbill, capercaillie); Fiacaill a' Choire Chais, to the west of the Cairn Gorm summit (dotterel and various raptors); and Loch Urigill and six other lochs around Inverpolly NNR in

south-west Sutherland (black-throated diver). These new sites bring the total number of Scottish SPAs to 117.

NATURA 2000

The Habitats Directive introduced the idea of 'Natura 2000', symbolising the conservation of precious natural resources into the new millennium; and this name has been given to a European network consisting of SACs and SPAs, aiming to maintain rare, endangered or vulnerable species and conserve their habitats throughout Europe.

INTERNATIONAL CONVENTIONS

The UK is party to a number of international conventions protecting wildlife and its habitats including:

- the Ramsar Convention on Wetlands of International Importance (ratified 1976)
- the Bonn Convention on the Conservation of Migratory Species of Wild Animals (ratified 1979)
- the Bern Convention on the Conservation of European Wildlife and Natural Habitats (ratified 1972)
- the Convention on Trade in Endangered Species of Wild Fauna and Flora (CITES) (ratified 1975)

WORLD HERITAGE SITES

These are areas of outstanding natural or cultural value identified and listed by the World Heritage Committee of UNESCO under the Convention on World Cultural and Natural Heritage (1972). They may be urban or rural.

St Kilda is listed as a World Heritage Site. It was the first such site awarded in Scotland and the first for a wildlife area in Britain.

Edinburgh Old and New Towns were accorded World Heritage Site status in 1995.

The Heart of Neolithic Orkney is also a World Heritage Site.

WILDLIFE CONSERVATION

The Wildlife and Countryside Act 1981 gives legal protection to a wide range of wild animals and plants. Subject to parliamentary approval, the Secretary of State for the Environment, Transport and the Regions may vary the animals and plants given legal protection. The most recent variation of Schedules 5 and 8 came into effect in March and April 1998.

Under Section 9 and Schedule 5 of the Act it is illegal without a licence to kill, injure, take, possess or sell any of the listed animals (whether alive or dead) and to disturb its place of shelter and protection or to destroy that place.

Under Section 13 and Schedule 8 of the Act it is illegal without a licence to pick, uproot, sell or destroy any of the listed plants and, unless authorised, to uproot any wild plant.

The Act lays down a close season for wild birds (other than game birds) from 1 February to 31 August inclusive, each year. Exceptions to these dates are made for:

Capercaillie –   1 February to 30 September
Snipe –   1 February to 11 August
Wild Duck and Wild Goose (below high water mark) –   21 February to 31 August

Birds which may be killed or taken in Scotland outside the close season (except on Sundays and on Christmas Day) are the above-named, plus coot, certain wild duck (gadwall, goldeneye, mallard, pintail, pochard, shoveler, teal, tufted duck, wigeon), certain wild geese (Canada, greylag, pink-footed), moorhen, golden plover and woodcock.

Certain wild birds may be killed or taken subject to the conditions of a general licence at any time by authorised persons: crow, collared dove, gull (great and lesser black-backed or herring), jackdaw, jay, magpie, pigeon (feral or wood), rook, sparrow (house) and starling. Conditions usually apply where the birds pose a threat to agriculture, public health, air safety, other bird species, and to prevent the spread of disease.

All other British birds are fully protected by law throughout the year.

A Private Member's Bill on the protection of wild mammals, seeking to ban hunting of wild mammals with dogs, has been introduced to the Scottish Parliament. An independent report commissioned by the Scottish Executive, assessing the possible economic impacts of this Bill on fox hunting with hounds and on gamekeepers employed on Scottish sporting estates, was published on 26 June 2000.

PROTECTED SPECIES

The lists below contain details of protected species of bird, animal and plant in the UK. Degrees of protection for certain species are determined statutorily. For further information please contact Scottish Natural Heritage.

BIRDS

(At All Times)

Common name	Scientific name
Avocet	*Recurvirostra avosetta*
Bee-eater	*Merops apiaster*
Bittern	*Botaurus stellaris*
Bittern, Little	*Ixobrychus minutus*
Bluethroat	*Luscinia svecica*
Brambling	*Fringilla montifringilla*
Bunting, Cirl	*Emberisa cirlus*
Bunting, Lapland	*Calcarius lapponicus*
Bunting, Snow	*Plectrophenax nivalis*
Buzzard, Honey	*Pernis apivorus*
Chough	*Pyrrhocorax pyrrhocorax*
Corncrake	*Crex crex*
Crake, Spotted	*Porzana porzana*
Crossbills (all species)	*Loxia*
Curlew, Stone	*Burhinus oedicnemus*
Divers (all species)	*Gavia*
Dotterel	*Charadrius morinellus*
Duck, Long-tailed	*Clangula hyemalis*
Eagle, Golden	*Aquila chrysaetos*
Eagle, White-tailed	*Haliaetus albicilla*
Falcon, Gyr	*Falco rusticolus*
Fieldfare	*Turdus pilaris*
Firecrest	*Regulus ignicapillus*
Garganey	*Anas querquedula*
Godwit, Black-tailed	*Limosa limosa*
Goshawk	*Accipiter gentilis*
Grebe, Black-necked	*Podiceps nigricollis*
Grebe, Slavonian	*Podiceps auritus*
Greenshank	*Tringa nebularia*
Gull, Little	*Larus minutus*
Gull, Mediterranean	*Larus melanocephalus*
Harriers (all species)	*Circus*
Heron, Purple	*Ardea purpurea*
Hobby	*Falco subbuteo*
Hoopoe	*Upupa epops*
Kingfisher	*Alcedo atthis*
Kite, Red	*Milvus milvus*
Merlin	*Falco columbarius*
Oriole, Golden	*Oriolus oriolus*
Osprey	*Pandion haliaetus*
Owl, Barn	*Tyto alba*
Owl, Snowy	*Nyctea scandiaca*
Peregrine	*Falco peregrinus*
Petrel, Leach's	*Oceanodroma leucorhoa*

Phalarope, Red-necked	*Phalaropus lobatus*
Plover, Kentish	*Charadrius alexandrinus*
Plover, Little Ringed	*Charadrius dubius*
Quail, Common	*Coturnix coturnix*
Redstart, Black	*Phoenicurus ochruros*
Redwing	*Turdus iliacus*
Rosefinch, Scarlet	*Carpodacus erythrinus*
Ruff	*Philomachus pugnax*
Sandpiper, Green	*Tringa ochropus*
Sandpiper, Purple	*Calidris maritima*
Sandpiper, Wood	*Tringa glareola*
Scaup	*Aythya marila*
Scoter, Common	*Melanitta nigra*
Scoter, Velvet	*Melanitta fusca*
Serin	*Serinus serinus*
Shorelark	*Eremophila alpestris*
Shrike, Red-backed	*Lanius collurio*
Spoonbill	*Platalea leucorodia*
Stilt, Black-winged	*Himantopus himantopus*
Stint, Temminck's	*Calidris temminckii*
Swan, Bewick's	*Cygnus bewickii*
Swan, Whooper	*Cygnus cygnus*
Tern, Black	*Chlidonias niger*
Tern, Little	*Sterna albifrons*
Tern, Roseate	*Sterna dougallii*
Tit, Bearded	*Panurus biarmicus*
Tit, Crested	*Parus cristatus*
Treecreeper, Short-toed	*Certhia brachydactyla*
Warbler, Cetti's	*Cettia cetti*
Warbler, Dartford	*Sylvia undata*
Warbler, Marsh	*Acrocephalus palustris*
Warbler, Savi's	*Locustella luscinioides*
Whimbrel	*Numenius phaeopus*
Woodlark	*Lullula arborea*
Wryneck	*Jynx torquilla*

(During the Close Season)

Common name	Scientific name
Goldeneye	*Bucephala clangula*
Goose, Greylag (in Outer Hebrides, Caithness, Sutherland and Wester Ross only)	*Anser anser*
Pintail	*Anas acuta*

ANIMALS

Common name	Scientific name
Adder	*Vipera berus*
Anemone, Ivell's Sea	*Edwardsia ivelli*
Anemone, Startlet Sea	*Nematosella vectensis*
Apus	*Triops cancriformis*
Bats, Horseshoe (all species)	*Rhinolophidae*
Bats, Typical (all species)	*Vespertilionidae*
Beetle	*Graphoderus zonatus*
Beetle	*Hypebaeus flavipes*
Beetle	*Paracymus aeneus*
Beetle, Lesser Silver Water	*Hydrochara caraboides*
Beetle, Mire Pill	*Curimopsis nigrita*
Beetle, Rainbow Leaf	*Chrysolina cerealis*
Beetle, Stag	*Lucanus cervus*
Beetle, Violet Click	*Limoniscus violaceus*
Burbot	*Lota lota*
Butterfly, Northern Brown Argus	*Aricia artaxerxes*
Butterfly, Adonis Blue	*Lysandra bellargus*
Butterfly, Chalkhill Blue	*Lysandra coridon*
Butterfly, Large Blue	*Maculinea arion*
Butterfly, Silver-studded Blue	*Plebejus argus*
Butterfly, Small Blue	*Cupido minimus*
Butterfly, Large Copper	*Lycaena dispar*
Butterfly, Purple Emperor	*Apatura iris*
Butterfly, Duke of Burgundy Fritillary	*Hamearis lucina*
Butterfly, Glanville Fritillary	*Melitaea cinxia*
Butterfly, Heath	*Mellicta athalia Fritillary (otherwise known as Melitaea athalia)*
Butterfly, High Brown Fritillary	*Argynnis adippe*
Butterfly, Marsh Fritillary	*Eurodryas aurinia*
Butterfly, Pearl-bordered Fritillary	*Boloria euphrosyne*
Butterfly, Black Hairstreak	*Strymonidia pruni*
Butterfly, Brown Hairstreak	*Thecla betulae*
Butterfly, White Letter Hairstreak	*Stymonida w-album*
Butterfly, Large Heath	*Coenonympha tullia*
Butterfly, Mountain Ringlet	*Erebia epiphron*
Butterfly, Chequered Skipper	*Carterocephalus palaemon*
Butterfly, Lulworth Skipper	*Thymelicus acteon*
Butterfly, Silver Spotted Skipper	*Hesperia comma*
Butterfly, Swallowtail	*Papilio machaon*
Butterfly, Large Tortoiseshell	*Nymphalis polychloros*

Common name	Scientific name
Butterfly, Wood White	*Leptidea sinapis*
Cat, Wild	*Felis silvestris*
Cicada, New Forest	*Cicadetta montana*
Crayfish, Atlantic Stream	*Austropotamobius pallipes*
Cricket, Field	*Gryllus campestris*
Cricket, Mole	*Gryllotalpa gryllotalpa*
Damselfly, Southern	*Coenagrion mercuriale*
Dolphin (all species)	*Cetacea*
Dormouse	*Muscardinus avellanarius*
Dragonfly, Norfolk Aeshna	*Aeshna isosceles*
Frog, Common	*Rana temporaria*
Goby, Couch's	*Gobius couchii*
Goby, Giant	*Gobius cobitis*
Grasshopper, Wart-biter	*Decticus verrucivorus*
Hatchet Shell, Northern	*Thyasira gouldi*
Hydroid, Marine	*Clavopsella navis*
Lagoon Snail	*Paludinella littorina*
Lagoon Snail, De Folin's	*Caecum armoricum*
Lagoon Worm, Tentacled	*Alkmaria romijni*
Leech, Medicinal	*Hirudo medicinalis*
Lisard, Sand	*Lacerta agilis*
Lisard, Viviparous	*Lacerta vivipara*
Marten, Pine	*Martes martes*
Moth, Barberry Carpet	*Pareulype berberata*
Moth, Black-veined	*Siona lineata (otherwise known as Idaea lineata)*
Moth, Essex Emerald	*Thetidia smaragdaria*
Moth, Fiery Clearwing	*Bembecia chrysidiformis*
Moth, Fisher's Estuarine	*Gortyna borelii*
Moth, New Forest Burnet	*Zygaena viciae*
Moth, Reddish Buff	*Acosmetia caliginosa*
Moth, Sussex Emerald	*Thalera fimbrialis*
Mussell, Fan	*Atrina fragilis*
Mussell, Freshwater Pearl	*Margaritifera margaritifera*
Newt, Great Crested (otherwise known as Warty newt)	*Triturus cristatus*
Newt, Palmate	*Triturus helveticus*
Newt, Smooth	*Triturus vulgaris*
Otter, Common	*Lutra lutra*
Porpoise (all species)	*Cetacea*
Sandworm, Lagoon	*Armandia cirrhosa*
Sea Fan, Pink	*Eunicella verrucosa*
Sea Mat, Trembling	*Victorella pavida*
Sea Slug, Lagoon	*Tenellia adspersa*
Shad, Allis	*Alosa alosa*
Shad, Twaite	*Alosa fallax*
Shark, Basking	*Cetorhinus maximus*
Shrimp, Fairy	*Chirocephalus diaphanus*
Shrimp, Lagoon Sand	*Gammarus insensibilis*
Slow-worm	*Anguis fragilis*
Snail, Glutinous	*Myxas glutinosa*
Snail, Sandbowl	*Catinella arenaria*
Snake, Grass	*Natrix helvetica (otherwise known as Natrix natrix)*
Snake, Smooth	*Coronella austriaca*
Spider, Fen Raft	*Dolomedes plantarius*
Spider, Ladybird	*Eresus niger*
Squirrel, Red	*Sciurus vulgaris*
Sturgeon	*Acipenser sturio*
Toad, Common	*Bufo bufo*
Toad, Natterjack	*Bufo calamita*
Turtles, Marine (all species)	*Dermochelyidae and Cheloniidae*
Vendace	*Coregonus albula*
Vole, Water	*Arvicola terrestris*
Walrus	*Odobenus rosmarus*
Whale (all species)	*Cetacea*
Whitefish	*Coregonus lavaretus*

PLANTS

Common name	Scientific name
Adder's-tongue, Least	*Ophioglossum lusitanicum*
Alison, Small	*Alyssum alyssoides*
Anomodon, Long-leaved	*Anomodon longifolius*
Beech-lichen, New Forest	*Enterographa elaborata*
Blackwort	*Southbya nigrella*
Bluebell	*Hyacinthoides non-scripta*
Bolete, Royal	*Boletus regius*
Broomrape, Bedstraw	*Orobanche caryophyllacea*
Broomrape, Oxtongue	*Orobanche loricata*
Broomrape, Thistle	*Orobanche reticulata*
Cabbage, Lundy	*Rhynchosinapis wrightii*
Calamint, Wood	*Calamintha sylvatica*
Caloplaca, Snow	*Caloplaca nivalis*
Catapyrenium, Tree	*Catapyrenium psoromoides*
Catchfly, Alpine	*Lychnis alpina*
Catillaria, Laurer's	*Catellaria laureri*
Centaury, Slender	*Centaurium tenuiflorum*
Cinquefoil, Rock	*Potentilla rupestris*
Cladonia, Convoluted	*Cladonia convoluta*
Cladonia, Upright Mountain	*Cladonia stricta*
Clary, Meadow	*Salvia pratensis*
Club-rush, Triangular	*Scirpus triquetrus*
Colt's-foot, Purple	*Homogyne alpina*
Cotoneaster, Wild	*Cotoneaster integerrimus*
Cottongrass, Slender	*Eriophorum gracile*
Cow-wheat, Field	*Melampyrum arvense*

Crocus, Sand	*Romulea columnae*	Lecanora, Tarn	*Lecanora archariana*
Crystalwort, Lisard	*Riccia bifurca*	Lecidea, Copper	*Lecidea inops*
Cudweed, Broad-leaved	*Filago pyramidata*	Leek, Round-headed	*Allium sphaerocephalon*
Cudweed, Jersey	*Gnaphalium luteoalbum*	Lettuce, Least	*Lactuca saligna*
Cudweed, Red-tipped	*Filago lutescens*	Lichen, Arctic Kidney	*Nephroma arcticum*
Cut-grass	*Leersia oryzoides*	Lichen, Ciliate Strap	*Heterodermia leucomelos*
Deptford Pink (in respect of England and Wales only)	*Dianthus armeria*	Lichen, Coralloid Rosette	*Heterodermia propagulifera*
		Lichen, Ear-lobed Dog	*Peltigera lepidophora*
Diapensia	*Diapensia lapponica*	Lichen, Forked Hair	*Bryoria furcellata*
Dock, Shore	*Rumex rupestris*	Lichen, Golden Hair	*Teloschistes flavicans*
Earwort, Marsh	*Jamesoniella undulifolia*	Lichen, Orange Fruited Elm	*Caloplaca luteoalba*
Eryngo, Field	*Eryngium campestre*		
Feather-moss, Polar	*Hygrohypnum polare*	Lichen, River Jelly	*Collema dichotomum*
Fern, Dickie's Bladder	*Cystopteris dickieana*	Lichen, Scaly Breck	*Squamarina lentigera*
Fern, Killarney	*Trichomanes speciosum*	Lichen, Stary Breck	*Buellia asterella*
Flapwort, Norfolk	*Lieocolea rutheana*	Lily, Snowden	*Lloydia serotina*
Fleabane, Alpine	*Erigeron borealis*	Liverwort	*Petallophyllum ralfsi*
Fleabane, Small	*Pulicaria vulgaris*	Liverwort, Lindenberg's Leafy	*Adelanthus lindenbergianus*
Fleawort, South Stack	*Tephroseris integrifolia (ssp maritima)*	Marsh-mallow, Rough	*Althaea hirsuta*
		Marshwort, Creeping	*Apium repens*
Frostwort, Pointed	*Gymnomitrion apiculatum*	Milk-Parsley, Cambridge	*Selinum carvifolia*
Fungus, Hedgehog	*Hericium erinaceum*	Moss	*Drepanocladius vernicosus*
Galingale, Brown	*Cyperus fuscus*		
Gentian, Alpine	*Gentiana nivalis*	Moss, Alpine Copper	*Mielichoferia mielichoferi*
Gentian, Dune	*Gentianella uliginosa*		
Gentian, Early	*Gentianella anglica*	Moss, Baltic Bog	*Sphagnum balticum*
Gentian, Fringed	*Gentianella ciliata*	Moss, Blue Dew	*Saelania glaucescens*
Gentian, Spring	*Gentiana verna*	Moss, Blunt-leaved Bristle	*Orthotrichum obtusifolium*
Germander, Cut-leaved	*Teucrium botrys*		
Germander, Water	*Teucrium scordium*	Moss, Bright Green Cave	*Cyclodictyon laetevirens*
Gladiolus, Wild	*Gladiolus illyricus*		
Goblin Lights	*Catolechia wahlenbergii*	Moss, Cordate Beard	*Barbula cordata*
Goosefoot, Stinking	*Chenopodium vulvaria*	Moss, Cornish Path	*Ditrichum cornubicum*
Grass-poly	*Lythrum hyssopifolia*	Moss, Derbyshire Feather	*Thamnobryum angustifolium*
Grimmia, Blunt-leaved	*Grimmia unicolor*		
Gyalecta, Elm	*Gyalecta ulmi*	Moss, Dune Thread	*Bryum mamillatum*
Hare's-ear, Sickle-leaved	*Bupleurum falcatum*	Moss, Flamingo	*Desmatodon cernuus*
Hare's-ear, Small	*Bupleurum baldense*	Moss, Glaucous Beard	*Barbula glauca*
Hawk's-beard, Stinking	*Crepis foetida*	Moss, Green Shield	*Buxbaumia viridis*
Hawkweed, Northroe	*Hieracium northroense*	Moss, Hair Silk	*Plagiothecium piliferum*
Hawkweed, Shetland	*Hieracium zetlandicum*	Moss, Knothole	*Zygodon forsteri*
Hawkweed, Weak-leaved	*Hieracium attenuatifolium*	Moss, Large Yellow Feather	*Scorpidium turgescens*
Heath, Blue	*Phyllodoce caerulea*	Moss, Millimetre	*Micromitrium tenerum*
Helleborine, Red	*Cephalanthera rubra*	Moss, Multifruited River	*Cryphaea lamyana*
Helleborine, Young's	*Epipactis youngiana*		
Horsetail, Branched	*Equisetum ramosissimum*	Moss, Nowell's Limestone	*Zygodon gracilis*
Hound's-tongue, Green	*Cynoglossum germanicum*	Moss, Rigid Apple	*Bartramia stricta*
		Moss, Round-leaved Feather	*Rhyncostegium rotundifolium*
Knawel, Perennial	*Scleranthus perennis*		
Knotgrass, Sea	*Polygonum maritimum*	Moss, Schleicher's Thread	*Bryum schleicheri*
Lady's-slipper	*Cypripedium calceolus*		
Lecanactis, Churchyard	*Lecanactis hemisphaerica*	Moss, Triangular Pygmy	*Acaulon triquetrum*

CLOSE SEASONS AND RESTRICTIONS ON GAME

Shooting game or hares at night is prohibited, with certain exceptions. Although there are no legal restrictions, it is not customary to kill game on a Sunday or Christmas Day. If shooting is to take place on a Sunday, it should begin after noon.

All dates are inclusive.

GAME BIRDS

Black game (heathfowl)	11 December to 19 August
Grouse (muirfowl)	11 December to 11 August
Partridge	2 February to 31 August
Pheasant	2 February to 30 September
Ptarmigan	11 December to 11 August

HUNTING AND GROUND GAME

There is no statutory close time for fox-hunting or rabbit-shooting, nor for hares. However, under the Hares Preservation Act 1892 the sale of hares (except imported ones) or leverets in Great Britain is prohibited from 1 March to 31 July inclusive. The recognised date for the opening of the fox-hunting season is 1 November, and it continues until the following April.

Deer

The statutory close seasons for deer are:

Fallow deer

Male	1 May to 31 July
Female	16 February to 20 October

Red deer

Male	21 October to 30 June
Female	16 February to 20 October

Roe deer

Male	21 October to 31 March
Female	1 April to 20 October

Sika Deer

Male	21 October to 30 June
Female	16 February to 20 October

Red/Sika Hybrids

Male	21 Octboer to 20 June
Female	16 February to 20 October

ANGLING

BROWN TROUT

The statutory close time for fishing for brown trout is from 7 October to 14 March inclusive.

SALMON

The Scottish Parliament is responsible for the regulation of salmon fishing, through the Scottish Executive Rural Affairs Department. Local management is devolved to district salmon and fishery boards. The annual close time for salmon fishing in each salmon fishery is set by law. District salmon fishery boards may apply to change the annual close time for their district. Weekly close time for nets is 6 p.m. on Friday to 6 a.m. on Monday. Weekly close time for salmon angling is Sunday. Details of regulations may be obtained from the Inspector of Salmon and Freshwater Fisheries.

INSPECTOR OF SALMON AND FRESHWATER FISHERIES

Pentland House, 47 Robb's Loan, Edinburgh EH14 1TY
Tel: 0131-244 6227
Fax: 0131-244 6313

ASSOCIATION OF DISTRICT SALMON FISHERY BOARDS

5A Lennox Street, Edinburgh EH4 1QB
Tel: 0131-343 2433

SEA TROUT

The regulations on fishing for sea trout are the same as those on fishing for salmon.

COARSE FISHING

The Scottish Parliament is responsible for the regulation of coarse fishing, through the Scottish Executive Rural Affairs Department.Information may be obtained from the Inspector of Salmon and Freshwater Fisheries.

LICENCES

No licence is required to fish in Scotland. In the case of salmon fishing, a person must have a legal right to fish or written permission from a person having such right. To fish for freshwater fish, including trout, permission should be obtained from the riparian owner. Where a protection order is in force, it is an offence to fish for freshwater fish in inland waters without a permit.

THE PEOPLE

POPULATION

The first official census of population in Great Britain was taken in 1801 and a census has been taken every ten years since, except in 1941 when there was no census because of war. The next official census in the UK is due in April 2001.

CENSUS RESULTS (SCOTLAND) 1801–1991

	Total	Male	Female
1801	1,608,000	739,000	869,000
1811	1,806,000	826,000	980,000
1821	2,092,000	983,000	1,109,000
1831	2,364,000	1,114,000	1,250,000
1841	2,620,000	1,242,000	1,378,000
1851	2,889,000	1,376,000	1,513,000
1861	3,062,000	1,450,000	1,612,000
1871	3,360,000	1,603,000	1,757,000
1881	3,736,000	1,799,000	1,936,000
1891	4,026,000	1,943,000	2,083,000
1901	4,472,000	2,174,000	2,298,000
1911	4,761,000	2,309,000	2,452,000
1921	4,882,000	2,348,000	2,535,000
1931	4,843,000	2,326,000	2,517,000
1951	5,096,000	2,434,000	2,662,000
1961	5,179,000	2,483,000	2,697,000
1971	5,229,000	2,515,000	2,714,000
1981	5,131,000	2,466,000	2,664,000
1991	4,998,567	2,391,961	2,606,606

POPULATION BY AGE AND SEX 1997

The estimated population at 30 June 1997 was 5,122,500, which represented a decrease of 5,500 since 1996 but an overall increase of about 123,000 since the 1991 census. In 1997 the population of Scotland was 8.6 per cent of the total population of the UK (59,009,000).

Age	Total	Male	Female
0—14	955,859	489,247	466,612
15—29	1,042,991	530,872	512,119
30—44	1,162,155	579,365	582,790
45—59	924,214	453,024	471,190
60—74	698,361	316,967	381,394
75	338,920	114,832	224,088
Total	5,122,500	2,484,307	2,638,193
% of total	100	48.5	51.5

Source: The Stationery Office, Annual Report of the Registrar-General for Scotland 1997 (Crown copyright)

PROJECTED POPULATION 2001–21 (MID-YEAR)

Age	2001	2011	2021
0 — 14	924,000	837,000	801,000
15—29	975,000	959,000	877,000
30—44	1,195,000	1,008,000	905,000
45—59	967,000	1,100,000	1,085,000
60—74	695,000	778,000	902,000
75+	351,000	375,000	423,000
Total	5,107,000	5,057,000	4,993,000

Source: The Stationery Office, Annual Report of the Registrar-General for Scotland 1997 (Crown copyright)

RESIDENT POPULATION BY ETHNIC GROUP (1991 CENSUS)

Ethnic group	Total	Male	Female
Caribbean	934	490	444
African	2,773	1,588	1,185
Other black	2,646	1,415	1,231
Indian	10,050	5,295	4,755
Pakistani	21,192	10,810	10,382
Bangladeshi	1,134	634	500
Chinese	10,476	5,482	4,994
Other Asian	4,604	2,162	2,442
Other	8,825	4,848	3,577
White	4,935,933	2,359,237	2,576,696
All ethnic groups	4,998,567	2,391,961	2,606,606

Source: General Register Office (Scotland) (Crown copyright)

AVERAGE POPULATION DENSITY

The average density of population at the 1991 census was 0.65 persons per hectare. For population density by council area, *see* Council Directory.

BIRTHS

In 1997 there were 59,440 live births in Scotland. The birth rate (live births per 1,000 members of the population) was 11.6, a little below the rate of 12.3 for the UK as a whole. Of the total number of live births, 62.3 per cent were to married parents. While the birth rate overall has fallen since 1987, and especially since 1991, the proportion of births outside marriage has increased markedly, from 22.8 per cent to 37.6 per cent.

LIVE BIRTHS 1997

	Number	Percentage
All live births	59,440	100
To married parents	37,052	62.3
To unmarried parents		
Joint registration	18,163	30.5
Sole registration	4,225	7.1

LIVE BIRTHS OUTSIDE MARRIAGE 1997 BY AGE OF MOTHER AND TYPE OF REGISTRATION

Age	Total	Joint registration %	Sole registration %
Under 20	4,529	70.8	29.2
20—24	6,884	80.4	19.6
25—29	5,710	84.8	15.2
30—34	3,643	87.5	12.5
35 and over	1,802	86.0	14.0
All ages	22,388	81.1	18.9

Source: The Stationery Office, Annual Report of Registrar-General for Scotland 1997 (Crown copyright)

ABORTIONS

A total of 12,080 legal pregnancy terminations were performed in Scotland in 1997 (an increase of about 9 per cent since 1990), of which women aged between 20 and 34 accounted for over half. The number of girls under 16 undergoing abortions in 1997 was 289, 2.4 per cent of the total; but the percentage of under-16s undergoing abortions rose by 16 per cent between 1990 and 1997.

LEGAL ABORTIONS 1997p

By age of mother

Under 16	289
16—19	2,428
20—34	7,929
35—44	1,410
45 and over	24
Total	12,080

p provisional
Source: The Stationery Office, Annual Abstract of Statistics 1999 (Crown copyright)

LIFE EXPECTANCY

LIFE TABLES 1994–6

(interim figures)

Age	Male	Female
0	72.1	77.6
5	67.7	73.2
10	62.7	68.2
15	57.8	63.2
20	53.1	58.3
25	48.3	53.4
30	43.6	48.6
35	38.9	43.7
40	34.2	38.9
45	29.6	34.2
50	25.2	29.6
55	21.0	25.2
60	17.2	21.0
65	13.7	17.2
70	10.8	13.7
75	8.3	10.6
80	6.2	7.9
85	4.6	5.7

Source: The Stationery Office, Annual Abstract of Statistics 1999 (Crown copyright)

DEATHS

There were 59,494 deaths in 1997; the death rate was 11.6, slightly above the UK average. Infant mortality (deaths under one year of age) was 5.3 per 1,000 live births (UK average 5.8).

DEATHS AND DEATH RATES 1997p

	Deaths	Death rate*
Males	28,305	11.4
Females	31,189	11.8
Total	59,494	11.6

p provisional
*Deaths per 1,000 population
Sources: The Stationery Office, Annual Abstract of Statistics 1999; General Register Office for Scotland

MARRIAGE AND DIVORCE

At just under 30,000, the number of marriages in 1997 reflects a gradual but steady decline over the past decade. At the same time, the divorce rate (11 per thousand population members in 1997), has remained relatively stable.

Year	Marriages No.	Marriages Rate*	Divorces No.	Divorces Rate*
1987	35,813	14.0	12,133	10.2
1988	35,599	14.0	11,472	9.8
1989	35,326	13.9	11,659	10.0
1990	34,672	13.6	12,272	10.5
1991	33,762	13.2	12,399	10.6
1992	35,057	13.7	12,479	10.8
1993	33,366	13.0	12,787	11.1
1994	31,480	12.3	13,133	11.5
1995	30,663	11.9	12,249	10.8
1996	30,242	11.8	12,308	10.9
1997	29,811	11.6	12,222	11.0

*Per 1,000 members of population.
Source: The Stationery Office, Annual Abstract of Statistics 1999 (Crown copyright)

FORECAST SERVICES

Localised forecasts can be obtained by telephone or fax by dialing the prefix code followed by (+) the appropriate area code given below.

WEATHERCALL SERVICE
Prefix codes:
For local seven-day forecast Tel: 09068-500 4+
For local same-day forecast Fax: 09065-300 1+

Area numbers:

South-west Scotland	20
West and central Scotland	21
Edinburgh, Fife, Lothian, Borders	22
East and central Scotland	23
Grampian and east Highlands	24
North-west Scotland	25
Caithness, Orkney and Shetland	26

For national ten-day forecast Tel: 09068-575575
                                Fax: 09065-200200

Weathercall helpdesk   Tel: 0870-600 4242

MetFAX helpline   Tel: 08700-750075
                        Fax: 08700-750076

MARINECALL SERVICE
Prefix codes:
For inshore conditions (up to 12 miles off the coast) for same and next day Tel: 09068-11010
For data by fax   Fax: 09060-100+

Area codes:

Cape Wrath to Rattray Head, including Orkney	451
Rattray Head to Berwick-upon-Tweed	452
Berwick-upon-Tweed to Whitby	453
Colwyn Bay to Mull of Galloway	461
Mull of Galloway to Mull of Kintyre, including the North Channel and Firth of Clyde	462
Mull of Kintyre to Ardnamurchan Point	463
Ardnamurchan Point to Cape Wrath, including the Western Isles	464

For four-day offshore forecasts Fax: 09060-100+

Area codes:

Rockall, Malin, Bailey, Hebrides and Faröes	468
Fair Isle, Viking, Cromarty, Forth, Forties and Fisher	469

For 24-hour shipping forecasts
                        Tel: 09060-100441

SPECIALIST FORECASTING SERVICES
The Met Office provides a variety of national and local weather forecast services. Information about the full range can be obtained from its web-site at http://www.met-office.gov.uk or the helpline: 08700-750077.

AIRMET AVIATION FORECASTS
A specialised forecast for pilots, updated three times daily. Calls are charged at 50p a minute.
For Scottish region   Tel: 09068-771342
                       Fax: 09060-700509

GRAMPIAN AND HIGHLAND ROADLINE
For weather conditions on roads in these areas:

Grampian	Tel: 0336-401199
Highland	Tel: 0336-401363

MOUNTAINCALL
Prefix code   0891-500+

Area codes:

West Highlands	441
East Highlands	442

SCOTTISH SKICALL
Prefix code   0891-500+

Area codes:

All resorts	777
Glencoe	771
The Lecht	772
Cairngorm	773
Glenshee	774
Nevis Range	775

SCOTTISH AVALANCHE SERVICE
For forecasts of avalanche risk in Scottish ski resorts Tel: 0800-096 0007

RELIGIOUS

SCOTLAND

INTRODUCTION TO RELIGION IN SCOTLAND
INTER CHURCH AND FAITH CO-OPERATION
CHRISTIAN CHURCHES
NON-CHRISTIAN FAITHS
THE CHURCH OF SCOTLAND
THE SCOTTISH EPISCOPAL CHURCH
THE ROMAN CATHOLIC CHURCH
PRESBYTARIAN CHURCHES
OTHER CHURCHES

RELIGIOUS SCOTLAND

About 24 per cent of the population of Scotland (about 1.2 million people) professes active membership of a religious faith. Of this number, the overwhelming majority (92.9 per cent) is Christian (in the Trinitarian sense); 65 per cent of Christians (725,494 people) adhere to the Church of Scotland and other Presbyterian churches, 22 per cent (249,180) to the Roman Catholic Church, just under 5 per cent (54,382) to the Scottish Episcopal Church, 2 per cent (23,732) to Orthodox churches, and 6 per cent (71,550) to other Christian churches, including Methodists, Baptists, Pentecostal churches, Congregational churches, assemblies of Brethren, the Religious Society of Friends (Quakers) and the Salvation Army. About 14 per cent of the adult population regularly attends a Christian church.

About 0.75 per cent of the population (37,271 people) is affiliated to non-Trinitarian churches, e.g. Jehovah's Witnesses, the Church of Jesus Christ of Latter-Day Saints (Mormons), the Church of Christ, Scientist and the Unitarian churches.

Just under 1 per cent of the population (47,971 people) are adherents of other faiths, including Buddhism, Hinduism, Islam, Judaism, Sikhism and a number of new religious movements. There are sizeable Islamic communities in Glasgow and Edinburgh, and a significant Jewish community, particularly in Glasgow. The Samye Ling Tibetan Buddhist Centre, based in Eskdalemuir, Dumfriesshire, is building a Buddhist retreat centre on Holy Island, a small island off the Isle of Arran.

Over the past decade adherence to religion has been falling overall, but a steady decline in membership of the Trinitarian Christian churches and Judaism has been offset by a growth in non-Trinitarian churches, Islam and other faiths. By the first years of the new century a projected 22 per cent of Scotland's population will be adherents of a religion, of whom 91 per cent will be members of Christian churches.

ADHERENTS TO RELIGIONS IN SCOTLAND

	1990	1995	2000 (projected estimate)
Christianity (Trinitarian)	1,255,268	1,125,092	1,032,013
Non-Trinitarian churches	34,704	37,271	42,258
Buddhism	1,370	1,950	2,270
Hinduism	3,550*	3,950*	4,275
Judaism	3,274	2,341†	1,700
Islam	21,000	24,600*	30,275
Sikhism	8,400*	12,000*	13,650
Other	3,092	3,888	3,967
Total	1,330,658	1,211,092	1,130,408

*Estimate
† Heads of households, male or female, affiliated to synagogues. The figures represent about one-third of the Jewish community
Source: Based on tables from UK Christian Handbook Religious Trends No. 1 1998–9 (Christian Research/Paternoster Publishing, 1998); figures in text are for 1995

ADULT CHURCH ATTENDANCE IN SCOTLAND

	1990	1995	2000 (projected estimate)
Church of Scotland	236,200	216,300	196,200
Other Presbyterian	21,100	17,900	15,000
Baptist	19,900	18,300	16,900
Episcopal	16,100	16,600	17,100
Roman Catholic	283,600	248,900	233,300
Independent	31,700	35,100	37,000
Other churches	20,500	22,600	24,300
Total	629,100	575,700	539,800
% of adult population	15.2	13.8	13.3

Source: UK Christian Handbook Religious Trends No. 1 1998–9

INTER-CHURCH AND INTER-FAITH CO-OPERATION

The main umbrella body for the Christian churches in the UK is the Council of Churches for Britain and Ireland (formerly the British Council of Churches). Ecumenical bodies in Scotland are Action of Churches Together in Scotland (ACTS) and the Churches Agency for Inter-Faith Relations in Scotland. The Church of Scotland, the Methodist Church, the Religious Society of Friends (Quakers), the Roman Catholic Church, the Salvation Army, the Scottish Episcopal Church and the United Reformed Church belong to both. ACTS also includes the Congregational Federation, the Scottish Congregational Church and the United Free Church; the Eastern Orthodox Church has associate membership. The Evangelical Alliance, representing evangelical Christians, has an office in Scotland.

The Scottish Inter-Faith Council is composed of Christians, Buddhists, Hindus, Jews, Muslims, Sikhs and representatives from other inter-faith groups. Churches Together in Britain and Ireland also has a Commission on Inter-Faith Relations.

Several of the UK-wide inter-church and inter-faith bodies do not have offices in Scotland; in these cases the contact details for the UK office are given.

ACTION OF CHURCHES TOGETHER IN SCOTLAND

Scottish Churches House, Kirk Street, Dunblane, Perthshire FK15 0AJ
Tel: 01786-823588
Fax: 01786 825844
E-mail: acts.ecum@dial.pipex.com
Web: http://www.acts.dial.pipex.com
General Secretary: Dr K. Franz

CHURCHES AGENCY FOR INTER-FAITH RELATIONS IN SCOTLAND

Flat 1/1, 326 West Princes Street, Glasgow G4 9HA
Tel: 0141-339 8174
E-mail: ismyth@bigfoot.com
Secretary: Sr I. Smyth

CHURCHES TOGETHER IN BRITAIN AND IRELAND

Inter-Church House, 35–41 Lower Marsh, London SE1 7SA
Tel: 020-7523 2121
Fax: 020-7928 0010
E-mail: gensec@ctbi.org.uk
Web: http://www.ctbi.org.uk
General Secretary: Dr D. Goodbourn

COUNCIL OF CHRISTIANS AND JEWS

5th Floor, Camelford House, 87–89 Albert Embankment London, SE1
Tel: 020-7820 0090
Fax: 020-7820 0504
E-mail: ccjuk@aol.com
Web: http://www.ccj.org.uk
Director: Sr M. Shepherd

EVANGELICAL ALLIANCE SCOTLAND

Challenge House, 29 Canal Street, Glasgow G4 0AD
Tel: 0141-332 8700
Fax: 0141-332 8704
E-mail: scotland@eauk.org
Web: http://www.eauk.org
General Secretary: Revd D. Anderson

FREE CHURCHES' COUNCIL

27 Tavistock Square, London WC1H 9HH
Tel: 020-7387 8413
General Secretary: Revd G. H. Roper

INTER FAITH NETWORK FOR THE UNITED KINGDOM

5–7 Tavistock Place, London WC1H 9SN
Tel: 020-7388 0008
Fax: 020-7387 7968
E-mail: ifnet@interfaith.org.uk
Web: http://www.interfaith.org.uk
Director: B. Pearce

SCOTTISH INTER-FAITH COUNCIL

St Mungo's Museum, 2 Castle Street, Glasgow, G4 ORH
Tel: 0141-553-2557
Fax: 0141-552-4744
E-mail: sifc@freeuk.com
Secretary: Sr I. Smyth

THE CHRISTIAN CHURCHES

Christianity is believed to have reached the Roman province of Britain from Gaul in the third century or slightly earlier, but spread no further northwards than the limits of Roman rule, leaving the northern part of Britain to be evangelised by Celtic missionaries. The first Christian church in Scotland, at Whithorn, was established by St Ninian in AD 397. But it was with the arrival c. AD 563 of St Columba from Ireland on the island of Iona, and his creation there of an abbey and missionary centre, that Christianity in Scotland took firm root. It was slow to spread, however, despite the work of missionaries such as St Kentigern (also known as St Mungo), the patron saint of Glasgow. Iona remained the religious centre until the time of the Viking raids, in the early ninth century.

After the Synod of Whitby (AD 663) asserted the practices of the Roman Church over those of the Celtic, the Roman Church gradually became dominant throughout Scotland. In c. AD 850 the Pictish king Kenneth mac Alpin established a new religious centre at Dunkeld, but this too was destroyed by the Vikings and the religious centre shifted to St Andrews, where the cult of that saint was growing.

Malcolm III (1058–93) introduced a number of reforms in the Church, including the banning of Gaelic from use in church services. His wife Margaret encouraged monastic foundations and revived the monastery at Iona. In the reign of David I (1124–53), a full episcopal structure with nine bishoprics was established, with St Andrews as the leading see.

THE REFORMATION

By the late 15th-century the church was the largest and richest institution in the country, with revenues far exceeding those of the state. However, the widening gap between the higher clergy, who often combined religious and secular functions, and the underpaid parish priests provided fertile ground for dissent among the lower clergy when the new Reform doctrines of Luther and Calvin were introduced in the mid 16th-century from the continent by John Knox, a disaffected priest.

The Reformers' ideas quickly became popular, particularly in the east and among the lesser nobility. In 1555 nobles who favoured the Protestant cause were organised, with the help of Knox, into the Lords of the Congregation; in 1557, these reforming nobles signed the 'First Bond', in which they declared their intention to overthrow the Roman church. The regent, Mary of Guise, outlawed Knox and his followers, provoking riots by Protestants and a brief war in 1559.

A Parliament (the 'Reformation Parliament') called on 1 August 1560 in the name of Queen Mary but without a royal presence, abolished the Latin Mass and rejected the jurisdiction of the Pope; the first assembly of the Church of Scotland ratified the Confession of Faith, drawn up by a committee including John Knox.

In 1578, the Second Book of Discipline provided for the establishment of the kirk session as the governing body for each church and set out the overall organisation of the Kirk into presbyteries, provinces and a general assembly.

THE BISHOPS' WARS

In 1592 Parliament passed an Act guaranteeing the liberties of the Kirk and its Presbyterian government, although James VI and I and later Stewart monarchs made several attempts to restore episcopacy. Scottish fears that Charles I would reinstate Roman Catholicism led to the signing in 1638 of the National Covenant, which reasserted the right of the people to keep the reformed church. At the end of 1638 the General Assembly abolished the episcopacy and proscribed the use of the Book of Common Prayer. In the ensuing Bishops' Wars of 1639–40, an army of Covenanters took Durham and Newcastle before peace was restored in 1641. When the civil war broke out in 1644, the Scottish Covenanters sided with Cromwell's army, concluding the Solemn League and Covenant with the English Parliament on condition that England would adopt a Presbyterian church.

The restoration of Charles II in 1660 brought a reinstatement of episcopacy and intolerance of presbyterianism. Covenanters were persecuted and the Covenant declared illegal. Several waves of protest and repression followed. James VII and II issued decrees in 1687–8 allowing Catholics and Quakers, and later Presbyterians, to hold meetings in private houses; the various Presbyterian factions reunited, fearing a return to Catholicism. A Presbyterian church was restored in 1690 and secured by the Act of Settlement 1690 and the Act of Union 1707.

The 18th, 19th and early 20th centuries saw a series of divergent and convergent movements in the Kirk and the formation of successive splinter groups, which subsequently regrouped. Five smaller Presbyterian churches exist today.

MEMBERSHIP OF INSTITUTIONAL CHURCHES IN SCOTLAND 1995

	Membership	Churches	Ministers/ priests
Total membership of institutional churches	1,053,542	2,757	2,573
Presbyterian*	725,494	1,958	1,382
Roman Catholic (mass attendance)	249,180	464	936
Anglican of which	55,136	320	244
Scottish Episcopal	54,382	316	230
Orthodox	23,732	15	11

Including Church of Scotland and other Presbyterian churches

MEMBERSHIP OF FREE CHURCHES IN SCOTLAND 1995

	Membership	Churches	Ministers/ priests
Total free church membership	71,550	1,087	593
Baptist	18,083	208	180
Independent[1] of which	27,572	470	146
Scottish Congregational	8,673	62	38
Brethren assemblies	12,826	323	50
Methodist	6,312	76	31
New Churches	3,460	40	29
Pentecostal[2]	6,681	112	89
Other[3] of which	9,442	200	269
Quakers	705	31	–
Lutherans	775	7	4
Salvation Army	5,187	112	178

1. Total of Brethren, Congregational and other independent churches
2. Total of mainstream Afro-Caribbean and Overseas Apostolic
3. Total of Central, Holiness, Lutheran and overseas nationals churches and denominations
Source: UK Christian Handbook Religious Trends No. 1 1998–9

THE CHURCH OF SCOTLAND

The Church of Scotland is the established (e.g. national) church of Scotland. It was established in 1567, and its contractual relation with the state is expressed in a series of statutes from that year onward, concluding with an Act of 1921 setting out the constitution of the new Church and one of 1925 handing over the state endowments to the Church.

The Church is Reformed and Evangelical in doctrine, and Presbyterian in constitution, e.g. based on a hierarchy of councils of ministers and elders and, since 1990, of members of a diaconate. At local level the kirk session consists of the parish minister and ruling elders. At district level the presbyteries, of which there are 47, consist of all the ministers in the district, one ruling elder from each congregation, and those members of the diaconate who qualify for membership. The General Assembly is the supreme authority, and is presided over by a Moderator chosen annually by the Assembly. The Sovereign, if not present in person, is represented by a Lord High Commissioner who is appointed each year by the Crown.

The Church of Scotland has about 700,000 members, 1,200 ministers and 1,600 churches. There are about 100 ministers and other personnel working overseas.

Lord High Commissioner (2000):
Prince Charles, Duke of Rothesay
Moderator of the General Assembly (2000):
The Rt. Revd A. R. C. McLennan
Principal Clerk: Revd F. A. J. Macdonald
Depute Clerk: Revd Marjory MacLean
Procurator: P. S. Hodge, QC
Law Agent and Solicitor of the Church:
Mrs J. S. Wilson
Parliamentary Agent: Revd G. Blant
General Treasurer: D. F. Ross

CHURCH OFFICE

121 George Street, Edinburgh EH2 4YN.
Tel: 0131-225 5722

PRESBYTERIES AND CLERKS
Edinburgh: Revd W. P. Graham
West Lothian: Revd D. Shaw
Lothian: J. D. McCulloch

Melrose and Peebles: Revd J. H. Brown
Duns: Revd James Cutler
Jedburgh: Revd A. D. Reid

Annandale and Eskdale: Revd C. B. Haston

Dumfries and Kirkcudbright:
Revd G. M. A. Savage
Wigtown and Stranraer: Revd D. Dutton

Ayr: Revd J. Crichton
Irvine and Kilmarnock: Revd C. G. F. Brockie
Ardrossan: Revd D. Broster

Lanark: Revd I. D. Cunningham
Paisley: Revd D. Kay
Greenock: Revd D. Mill
Glasgow: Revd A. Cunningham
Hamilton: Revd J. H. Wilson
Dumbarton: Revd D. P. Munro

South Argyll: Revd M. A. J. Gossip
Dunoon: Revd R. Samuel
Lorn and Mull: Revd W. Hogg

Falkirk: Revd Ian W. Black
Stirling: Revd B. W. Dunsmore

Dunfermline: Revd W. E. Farquhar
Kirkcaldy: Revd B. L. Tomlinson
St Andrews: Revd P. Meager

Dunkeld and Meigle: Revd A. B. Reid
Perth: Revd A. M. Millar
Dundee: Revd J. A. Roy
Angus: Revd M. I. G. Rooney

Aberdeen: Revd A. Douglas
Kincardine and Deeside: Revd J. W. S. Brown
Gordon: Revd I. U. Thomson
Buchan: Revd R. Neilson
Moray: Revd G. Melvyn Wood

Abernethy: Revd J. A. I. MacEwan
Inverness: Revd A. S. Younger
Lochaber: Revd A. Ramsay

Ross: Revd R. M. MacKinnon
Sutherland: Revd J. L. Goskirk
Caithness: Revd M. G. Mappin
Lochcarron/Skye: Revd A. I. Macarthur
Uist: Revd M. Smith
Lewis: Revd T. S. Sinclair

Orkney (Finstown): Revd T. Hunt
Shetland (Lerwick): Revd N. R. Whyte
England (London): Revd W. A. Cairns

Europe (Geneva): Revd J. W. McLeod

THE SCOTTISH EPISCOPAL CHURCH

The Scottish Episcopal Church was founded after the Act of Settlement (1690) established the presbyterian nature of the Church of Scotland. The Scottish Episcopal Church is in full communion with the Church of England but is autonomous. The governing authority is the

General Synod, an elected body of approximately 170 members which meets once a year. The diocesan bishop who convenes and presides at meetings of the General Synod is called the Primus and is elected by his fellow bishops.

There are 49,995 members of the Scottish Episcopal Church, of whom 31,247 are communicants. There are seven bishops, 315 serving clergy, and 310 churches and places of worship.

THE GENERAL SYNOD OF THE SCOTTISH EPISCOPAL CHURCH

21 Grosvenor Crescent, Edinburgh EH12 5EE
Tel: 0131-225 6357
Secretary General: J. F. Stuart

PRIMUS OF THE SCOTTISH EPISCOPAL CHURCH
Most Revd Richard F. Holloway (Bishop of Edinburgh), elected 1992

DIOCESES

ABERDEEN AND ORKNEY
Bishop, Rt. Revd A. Bruce Cameron, b. 1941, cons. 1992, elected 1992
Clergy, 40

ARGYLL AND THE ISLES
Bishop, Rt. Revd Douglas M. Cameron, b. 1935, cons. 1993, elected 1992
Clergy, 16

BRECHIN
Bishop, Rt. Revd Neville Chamberlain, b. 1939, cons. 1997, elected 1997
Clergy, 24

EDINBURGH
Bishop, Rt. Revd Richard F. Holloway, b. 1933, cons. 1986, elected 1986
Clergy, 90

GLASGOW AND GALLOWAY
Bishop, Rt. Revd Idris Jones, b. 1943, cons. 1998, elected 1998
Clergy, 68

MORAY, ROSS AND CAITHNESS
Bishop, Rt. Revd John Crook, b. 1940, cons. 1999, elected 1999
Clergy, 25

ST ANDREWS, DUNKELD AND DUNBLANE
Bishop, Rt. Revd Michael H. G. Henley, b. 1938, cons. 1995, elected 1995
Clergy, 52

The minimum stipend of a diocesan bishop of the Scottish Episcopal Church iss £23,355 in 2000 (e.g. 1.5 x the minimum clergy stipend of £15,570).

THE ROMAN CATHOLIC CHURCH

The Roman Catholic Church is one world wide Christian church, with an estimated 890.9 million adherents, acknowledging as its head the Bishop of Rome, known as the Pope (Father). The Pope is held to be the successor of St Peter and a direct line of succession is therefore claimed from the earliest Christian communities. The Pope exercises spiritual authority over the Church with the advice and assistance of the Sacred College of Cardinals, the supreme council of the Church. He is also advised about the concerns of the Church locally by his ambassadors, who liaise with the Bishops' Conference in each country.

The Roman Catholic Church universally and the Vatican City State are run by the Curia, which is made up of the Secretariat of State, the Sacred Council for the Public Affairs of the Church, and various congregations, secretariats and tribunals assisted by commissions and offices. The Vatican State has its own diplomatic service, with representatives known as nuncios and apostolic delegates.

THE BISHOPS' CONFERENCE
The Bishops' Conference of Scotland is the permanently constituted assembly of the Bishops of Scotland. To promote its work, the Conference establishes various agencies which have an advisory function in relation to the Conference. The more important of these agencies are called Commissions and each one has a Bishop President who, with the other members of the Commissions, is appointed by the Conference.

The Roman Catholic Church in Scotland has around 705,650 baptised members, two archbishops, six bishops, 907 priests and 464 parishes.

SECRETARIAT OF THE BISHOPS' CONFERENCE OF SCOTLAND

64 Aitken Street, Airdrie, ML6 6LT
Tel: 01236-764061;
Fax: 01236-762489

President: HE Cardinal Thomas J. Winning
General Secretary: Very Revd Mgr Henry
  Docherty
Episcopal Secretary: Rt. Revd Maurice Taylor

ARCHDIOCESES

ST ANDREWS AND EDINBURGH
Archbishop: Most Revd Keith Patrick O'Brien,
Con. 1985
Clergy: 192
Diocesan Curia: 113 Whitehouse Loan,
Edinburgh EH9 1BD.
Tel: 0131-452 8244

GLASGOW
Archbishop: HE Cardinal Thomas J. Winning,
cons. 1971, apptd. 1974
Clergy: 253
Diocesan Curia: 196 Clyde Street, Glasgow
G1 4JY.
Tel: 0141-226 5898

DIOCESES

ABERDEEN
Bishop: Rt. Revd Mario Conti, cons. 1977
Clergy: 58
Bishop's Residence: 3 Queen's Cross, Aberdeen
AB2 6BR.
Tel: 01224-319154

ARGYLL AND THE ISLES
Bishop: Rt. Revd Ian Murray, con. 1999
Clergy: 33
Diocesan Curia: St Columba's Cathedral,
Esplanade, Oban PA34 5AB.
Tel: 01631-571003

DUNKELD
Bishop: Rt. Revd Vincent Logan, cons. 1981
Clergy: 51
Diocesan Curia: 29 Roseangle, Dundee
DD1 4LR.
Tel: 01382-25453

GALLOWAY
Bishop: Rt. Revd Maurice Taylor, cons. 1981
Clergy: 66
Diocesan Curia: 8 Corsehill Road, Ayr KA7 2ST.
Tel: 01292-266750

MOTHERWELL
Bishop: Rt. Revd Joseph Devine, cons. 1977,
apptd.1983
Clergy: 168

Diocesan Curia: Coursington Road, Motherwell
ML1 1PW.
Tel: 01698-269114

PAISLEY
Bishop: Rt. Revd John A. Mone, cons. 1984,
apptd. 1988
Clergy: 86
Diocesan Curia: c/o St Lawrence's, 6 Kilmacolm
Road, Greenock PA16 7UH.
Tel: 01475-892143
Bishop Emeritus: Rt. Revd. Stephen McGill,
cons. 1960, apptd. 1968
13 Newmarket Street, Greenock PA16 7UH.
Tel: 01475-783696

PRESBYTERIAN CHURCHES

THE FREE CHURCH OF SCOTLAND
The Free Church of Scotland was formed in
1843, when over 400 ministers withdrew from
the Church of Scotland as a result of interference
in the internal affairs of the church by the civil
authorities. In 1900, all but 26 ministers joined
with others to form the United Free Church
(most of which rejoined the Church of Scotland
in 1929). In 1904 the remaining 26 ministers
were recognised by the House of Lords as
continuing the Free Church of Scotland. This
Church is also known as the 'Wee Frees'.
   The Church maintains strict adherence to the
Westminster Confession of Faith of 1648 and
accepts the Bible as the sole rule of faith and
conduct. Its General Assembly meets annually. It
also has links with Reformed Churches overseas.
The Free Church of Scotland has 6,000
members, 90 ministers and 140 churches.
General Treasurer: I. D. Gill,
The Mound, Edinburgh EH1 2LS.
Tel: 0131-226 5286

UNITED FREE CHURCH OF SCOTLAND
The United Free Church of Scotland has existed
in its present form since 1929, but has its origins
in divisions in the Church of Scotland in the
18th-century. The Secession Church broke away
from the Church of Scotland in 1733, and the
Relief Church in 1761. In 1847 the Secession and
Relief Churches united, becoming the United
Presbyterian Church of Scotland. In 1900 this
church united with a majority of the Free Church
of Scotland to become the United Free Church of
Scotland. The majority of members rejoined the
Church of Scotland in 1929, with the minority
continuing as the United Free Church.
   The Church accepts the Bible as the supreme

standard of faith and conduct and adheres to the Westminster Confession of Faith. It is opposed to the state establishment of religion. The system of government is presbyterian. It has approximately 6,000 members, 41 ministers and 70 churches.
Moderator: Revd A. D. Scrimgeour
General Secretary: Revd J. O. Fulton, 11 Newton Place, Glasgow G3 7PR.
Tel: 0141-332 3435

THE FREE PRESBYTERIAN CHURCH OF SCOTLAND

The Free Presbyterian Church of Scotland was formed in 1893 by two ministers of the Free Church of Scotland who refused to accept a Declaratory Act passed by the Free Church General Assembly in 1892. The Free Presbyterian Church of Scotland is Calvinistic in doctrine and emphasises observance of the Sabbath. It adheres strictly to the Westminster Confession of Faith.

The Church has about 3,000 members in Scotland and about 4,000 in overseas congregations. It has 23 ministers and 50 churches.
Moderator: Revd G. G. Hutton, Free Presbyterian Manse, Broadford, Isle of Skye IV49 9AQ
Clerk of Synod: Revd J. MacLeod, 16 Matheson Road, Stornoway, Isle of Lewis HS1 2LA.
Tel: 01851-702755

ASSOCIATED PRESBYTERIAN CHURCHES OF SCOTLAND

The Associated Presbyterian Churches came into being in 1989 as a result of a division within the Free Presbyterian Church of Scotland. Following two controversial disciplinary cases, the culmination of deepening differences within the Church, a presbytery was formed calling itself the Associated Presbyterian Churches (APC). The Associated Presbyterian Churches has about 1,000 members, 15 ministers and 20 churches.
Clerk of the Scottish Presbytery:
Revd A. MacPhail, Fernhill, Polvinster Road, Oban, PA34 5TN
Tel: 01631-567076

REFORMED PRESBYTERIAN CHURCH OF SCOTLAND

The Reformed Presbyterian Church of Scotland has its origins in the Covenanter movement. After the 'Glorious Revolution' of 1688, a minority of Presbyterians in southern Scotland did not accept the religious settlement and remained outside the Church of Scotland. Known

as 'Cameronians', they met in 'Societies' and formed the Reformed Presbyterian Church of Scotland in 1743. In 1872 the majority of the church joined the Free Church of Scotland.

The Church regards the Bible as its sole standard and adheres strictly to the Westminster Confession of Faith. The Church is Presbyterian in structure, with the Synod the supreme court. At present there are four congregations and approximately 150 members and adherents.
Clerk of Synod (pro tem), Revd A. Sinclair Horne, 17 George IV Bridge, Edinburgh EH1 1EE.
Tel: 0131-220 1450

OTHER CHURCHES

Afro-West Indian United Council of Churches
c/o New Testament Church of God, Arcadian Gardens, High Road, London N22 5AA
Tel: 020-8888 9427
Secretary, Bishop E. Brown

Council of African and Afro-Caribbean Churches UK
31 Norton House, Sidney Road, London SW9 0UJ
Tel: 020-7274 5589
Chairman, His Grace The Most Revd Father Olu A. Abiola

Baptist Union of Scotland
14 Aytoun Road, Glasgow G41 5RT

Eastern Orthodox Church (Patriarchate of Constantinople)
Archbishop of Constantinople, New Rome and Oecumenical Patriarch, Bartholomew, elected 1991
Representative in Great Britain, Archbishop Gregorios of Thyateira and Great Britain, 5 Craven Hill, London W2 3EN.
Tel: 020-7723 4787

Lutheran Church
Lutheran Council of Great Britain, 30 Thanet Street, London WC1H 9QH
Tel: 020-7383 3081
General Secretary, Revd T. Bruch
Methodist Church
20 Inglewood Crescent, East Kilbride, Glasgow G75 8QD

Pentecostal Churches
Assemblies of God in Great Britain and Ireland, 3 Cypress Grove, Denmore, Aberdeen AB23 8LB

Elim Pentecostal Church, 146 Wishaw Road,
Waterloo, Wishaw, Lanarkshire ML2 8EN

The Religeous Society of Friends (Quakers)
Friends House, Euston Road, London NW1 2BJ
Tel: 020-7663 1000

The Salvation Army
Territorial HQ, 101 Newington Causeway,
London SE1 6BN
Tel: 020-7332 0022
General, J. Gowans
UK Territorial Commander, A. Hughes

Scottish Congregational Church
PO Box 189, Glasgow GL 2BX
Tel: 0141-332 7667
President, Dr J. Merrilees
General Secretary, Revd J. Arthur

The Seventh-Day Adventist Church
Stanborough Park, Watford WD2 6JP
Tel: 01923-672251
President of the British Union Conference,
    Pastor C. R. Perry

NON-TRINITARIAN CHURCHES

The Church of Christ, Scientist
2 Elysium Gate, 126 New Kings Road,
London SW6 4LZ
Tel: 020-7371 0600
District Manager for Great Britain and Ireland,
    H. Joynes

The Church of Jesus Christ of Latter-Day Saints
751 Warwick Road, Solihull, W. Midlands
B91 3DQ
Tel: 0121-712 1202
President of the Europe North Area, Elder S. J.
    Condie

Jehovah's Witnesses
Watch Tower House, The Ridgeway, London
NW7 1RN
Tel: 020-8906 2211

General Assembly of Unitarian and Free Christian Churches
Essex Hall, 1–6 Essex Street, Strand, London
WC2R 3HY
Tel: 020-7240 2384
General Secretary, J. J. Teagle

NON-CHRISTIAN FAITHS

Several non-Christian religions with significant membership in Scotland do not have representative bodies specific to Scotland. In the following list, contact details for the UK body, or bodies, are given where no Scottish representative body has been identified.

BUDDHISM

THE BUDDHIST SOCIETY

58 Eccleston Square, London SW1V 1PH
Tel: 020-7834 5858 Fax: 020-7976 5238
Web: http://www.buddsoc.org.uk
Registrar: Margaret Connan

SAMYE LING MONASTERY AND TIBETAN CENTRE

Eskdalemuir, Langholm, Dumfriesshire
DG13 0QL
Tel: 01387-373232 Fax: 01387-373223
E-mail: scotland@samyeling.org
Abbot: Lama Yeshe Losal

HINDUISM

ARYA PRATINIDHI SABHA (UK) AND ARYA SAMAJ LONDON

69A Argyle Road, London W13 0LY
Tel: 020-8991 1732
President: Prof. S. N. Bharadwaj

INTERNATIONAL SOCIETY FOR KRISHNA CONSCIOUSNESS (ISKCON)

Bhaktivedanta Manor, Dharam Marg, Hilfield
Lane, Aldenham, Watford, Herts WD2 8EZ
Tel: 01923-856173
Governing Body Commissioner:
    Sivarama Swami

NATIONAL COUNCIL OF HINDU TEMPLES (UK)

Bhaktivedanta Manor, Dharam Marg, Hilfield
Lane, Aldenham, Watford WD2 8EZ
Tel: 01923-856269 Fax: 01923-856269
E-mail: bimal.krnsa.bcs@pamtio.net
President: Mr O. P. Sherma

SWAMINARAYAN HINDU MISSION

105–119 Brentfield Road, London NW10 8JB
Tel: 020-8-965 2651 Fax: 020-8965 6313
E-mail: shm@swaminarayan-baps.org.uk
Web: http://www.swaminarayn-baps.org.uk
Chairman: Sadhu Atmaswarup Das

VISHWA HINDU PARISHAD (UK)

48 Wharfedale Gardens, Thornton Heath, Surrey CR7 6LB
Tel: 020-8684 9716
General Secretary: K. Ruparelia

ISLAM

ISLAMIC COUNCIL OF SCOTLAND

30 Clyde Place, Glasgow G5 8AA
Director: B. Man

IMAMS AND MOSQUES COUNCIL

20–22 Creffield Road, London W5 3RP
Tel: 020-8992 6636; Fax: 020-8993 3946
Chairman: Dr M. A. Z. Badawi

MUSLIM WORLD LEAGUE

46 Goodge Street, London W1P 1FJ
Tel: 020-7636 7568; Fax: 020-7637 5034
E-mail: mwl@webstar.co.uk
Web: http://www.mwl@aol.com
Secretary: G. Rahman

UNION OF MUSLIM ORGANISATIONS OF THE UK AND EIRE

109 Campden Hill Road, London W8 7TL
Tel: 020-7221 6608
General Secretary: Dr S. A. Pasha

JUDAISM

CHIEF RABBINATE

735 High Road, London N12 0US
Tel: 020-8343 6301
Chief Rabbi: Prof. Jonathan Sacks
Executive Director: Mrs S. Weinberg

BETH DIN (COURT OF THE CHIEF RABBI)

735 High Road, London N12 0US
Tel: 020-8343 6280; Fax: 020-83436257
Registrar: Mr D. Frei
Dayanim: Rabbi C. Ehrentreu; Rabbi I. Binstock; Rabbi C. D. Kaplin; Rabbi M. Gelley

BOARD OF DEPUTIES OF BRITISH JEWS

Commonwealth House, 1–19 New Oxford Street, London WC1A 1NU
Tel: 020-7543 5400; Fax: 020-7543 0010
E-mail: info@bod.org.uk
Web: http://www.bod.org.uk
Director External Issues: Mr J. Sacker

ASSEMBLY OF MASORTI SYNAGOGUES

1097 Finchley Road, London NW11 0PU
Tel: 020-8201 8772
Director: H. Freedman

FEDERATION OF SYNAGOGUES

65 Watford Way, London NW4 3AQ
Tel: 020-8201 8772; Fax: 020-8201 8917
E-mail: office@masorti.org.uk
Web: http://www.masorti.org.uk
Director: H. Freedman

REFORM SYNAGOGUES OF GREAT BRITAIN

The Sternberg Centre for Judaism, 80 East End Road, London N3 2SY
Tel: 020-8349 5640; Fax: 020-8349 5699
E-mail: admin@reformjudaism.org.uk
Web: http://www.refsyn.org.uk
Chief Executive: Rabbi A. Bayfield

SPANISH AND PORTUGUESE JEWS' CONGREGATION

2 Ashworth Road, London W9 1JY
Tel: 020-7289 2573; Fax: 020 7289 2709
Chief Administrator and Secretary: H. Miller

UNION OF LIBERAL AND PROGRESSIVE SYNAGOGUES

The Montagu Centre, 21 Maple Street, London W1P 6DS
Tel: 020-7580 1663; Fax: 020-7436 4184
E-mail: montaguculps.org
Executive Director: Rabbi Dr C. H. Middleburgh

UNION OF ORTHODOX HEBREW CONGREGATIONS

140 Stamford Hill, London N16 6QT
Tel: 020-8802 6226

UNITED SYNAGOGUE

Adler House, 735 High Road, London N12 0US
Tel: 020-8343 8989; Fax: 020-8343 6262
Web: http://www.unitedsynagogue.org.uk
Chief Executive: G. Willman

SIKHISM

SIKH MISSIONARY SOCIETY UK

10 Featherstone Road, Southall, Middx UB2 5AA
Tel: 020-8574 1902 Fax: 020-85741912
Hon. General Secretary: K. Singh Rai

WORLD SIKH FOUNDATION

33 Wargrave Road, South Harrow, Middx HA2 8LL
Tel: 020-8864 9228 Fax: 020-8864 9228
Secretary: Mrs H. Bharara

SCOTLAND AND

THE WORLD

TIME ZONES
INTERNATIONAL DIRECT DIALING
CONSULATES

SCOTLAND AND THE WORLD

TIME ZONES

Standard time differences from the Greenwich meridian

+ hours ahead of GMT
_ hours behind GMT
* may vary from standard time at some part of the year (Summer Time or Daylight Saving Time)

h hours
m minutes

	h	m
Afghanistan	+4	30
* Albania	+1	
Algeria	+1	
* Andorra	+1	
Angola	+1	
Anguilla	- 4	
Antigua and Barbuda	- 4	
Argentina	- 3	
* Armenia	+ 4	
Aruba	- 4	
Ascension Island		
Australia	+10	
ACT, NSW (except Broken Hill area), Qld, Tas., Vic, Whitsunday Islands		
* Broken Hill area (NSW)	+ 9	30
* Lord Howe Island	+10	30
Northern Territory	+ 9	30
* South Australia	+ 9	30
Western Australia	+ 8	
* Austria	+ 1	
* Azerbaijan	+ 4	
* Bahamas	- 5	
Bahrain	+ 3	
Bangladesh	+ 6	
Barbados	- 4	
* Belarus	+ 2	
* Belgium	+ 1	
Belize	- 6	
Benin	+1	
Bermuda	- 4	
Bhutan	+ 6	
Bolivia	- 4	
Bosnia-Hercegovina	+ 1	
Botswana	+ 2	
Brazil		
Acre	- 5	
central states	- 4	
N. and NE coastal states	- 3	
* S. and E. coastal states, including Brasilia	- 3	

	h	m
Fernando de Noronha Island	- 2	
western states	- 5	
British Antarctic Territory	- 3	
British Indian Ocean Territory	+ 5	
Diego Garcia	+ 6	
British Virgin Islands	- 4	
Brunei	+ 8	
* Bulgaria	+ 2	
Burkina Faso	0	
Burundi	+ 2	
Cambodia	+ 7	
Cameroon	+ 1	
Canada		
* Alberta	- 7	
* British Columbia	- 8	
* Labrador	- 4	
* Manitoba	- 6	
* New Brunswick	- 4	
* Newfoundland	- 3	30
* Northwest Territories		
east of 85° W.	- 5	
85° W.–102° W.	- 6	
* Nunavut	- 7	
* Nova Scotia	- 4	
* Ontario		
east of 90° W.	- 5	
west of 90° W.	- 6	
* Prince Edward Island	- 4	
Québec		
east of 63° W.	- 4	
* west of 63° W.	- 5	
Saskatchewan	- 6	
* Yukon	- 8	
Cape Verde	- 1	
Cayman Islands	- 5	
Central African Republic	+ 1	
Chad	+1	
* Chatham Islands	+12	45
* Chile	- 4	
China (inc. Hong Kong and Macao)	+ 8	
Christmas Island (Indian Ocean)	+ 7	
Cocos (Keeling) Islands	+ 6	30
Colombia	- 5	
Comoros	+ 3	
Congo (Dem. Rep.)		
east	+ 2	
west	+ 1	
Congo-Brazzaville	+ 1	
Cook Islands	- 10	
Costa Rica	- 6	
Côte d'Ivoire		
* Croatia	+ 1	

	h	m		h	m
* Cuba	- 5		Bali,		
* Cyprus	+ 2		Flores,		
* Czech Republic	+ 1		Kalimantan (south and east),		
* Denmark	+ 1		Sulawesi, Sumbawa, West Timor	+ 8	
* Farøe Islands	0		Irian Jaya, Maluku, Tanimbar	+ 9	
* Greenland	- 3		* Iran	+ 3	30
Danmarkshavn	0		* Iraq	+ 3	
Mesters Vig	0		* Ireland, Republic of	0	
* Scoresby Sound	- 1		* Israel	+ 2	
* Thule area	- 4		* Italy	+ 1	
Djibouti	+ 3		Jamaica	- 5	
Dominica	- 4		Japan	+ 9	
Dominican Republic	- 4		* Jordan	+ 2	
East Timor	+ 8		* Kazakhstan		
Ecuador	- 5		western (Aktau)	+ 4	
Galápagos Islands	- 6		central (Atyrau)	+ 5	
* Egypt	+ 2		eastern	+ 6	
El Salvador	- 6		Kenya	+ 3	
Equatorial Guinea	+ 1		Kiribati	+12	
Eritrea	+ 3		Line Islands	+14	
* Estonia	+ 2		Phoenix Islands	+13	
Ethiopia	+ 3		Korea, North	+ 9	
* Falkland Islands	- 4		Korea, South	+ 9	
Fiji	+12		Kuwait	+ 3	
* Finland	+ 2		* Kyrgyzstan	+ 5	
* France	+ 1		Laos	+ 7	
French Guiana	- 3		* Latvia	+ 2	
French Polynesia	- 10		* Lebanon	+ 2	
Guadeloupe	- 4		Lesotho	+ 2	
Martinique	- 4		Liberia	0	
Réunion	+ 4		* Libya	+ 2	
Marquesas Islands	- 9	30	* Liechtenstein	+ 1	
Gabon	+ 1		Line Islands not part of Kiribati	- 10	
The Gambia	0		* Lithuania	+ 1	
* Georgia	+ 3		* Luxembourg	+ 1	
* Germany	+ 1		* Macedonia	+ 1	
Ghana	0		Madagascar	+ 3	
* Gibraltar	+ 1		* Madeira	0	
* Greece	+ 2		Malawi	+ 2	
Grenada	- 4		Malaysia	+ 8	
Guam	+10		Maldives	+ 5	
Guatemala	- 6		Mali	0	
Guinea	0		* Malta	+ 1	
Guinea-Bissau	0		Marshall Islands	+12	
Guyana	- 4		Ebon Atoll	- 12	
* Haiti	- 5		Mauritania	0	
Honduras	- 6		Mauritius	+ 4	
* Hungary	+ 1		* Mexico	- 6	
Iceland	0		Nayarit, Sinaloa, Sonora,		
India	+ 5	30	S. Baja California	- 7	
Indonesia			N. Baja California	- 8	
Java,			Micronesia		
Kalimantan (west and central),			Caroline Islands	+10	
Sumatra	+ 7		Kosrae	+11	
			Pingelap	+11	

	h	m		h	m
Pohnpei	+11		Samoa	- 11	
* Moldova	+ 2		Samoa, American	- 11	
* Monaco	+ 1		* San Marino	+ 1	
* Mongolia	+ 8		São Tomé and Princípe	0	
Montserrat	- 4		Saudi Arabia	+ 3	
Morocco	0		Senegal	0	
Mozambique	+ 2		Seychelles	+ 4	
Myanmar	+ 6	30	Sierra Leone	0	
* Namibia	+ 1		Singapore	+ 8	
Nauru	+12		* Slovakia	+ 1	
Nepal	+ 5	45	* Slovenia	+ 1	
* Netherlands	+ 1		Solomon Islands	+11	
Netherlands Antilles	- 4		Somalia	+ 3	
New Caledonia	+11		South Africa	+ 2	
* New Zealand	+12		South Georgia	- 2	
Nicaragua	- 6		* Spain	+ 1	
Niger	+ 1		* Canary Islands	0	
Nigeria	+ 1		Sri Lanka	+ 6	
Niue	- 11		Sudan	+ 2	
Norfolk Island	+11	30	Suriname	- 3	
Northern Mariana Islands	+10		Swaziland	+ 2	
* Norway	+ 1		* Sweden	+ 1	
Oman	+ 4		* Switzerland	+ 1	
Pakistan	+ 5		* Syria	+ 2	
Palau	+ 9		Taiwan	+ 8	
Panama	- 5		Tajikistan	+ 5	
Papua New Guinea	+10		Tanzania	+ 3	
* Paraguay	- 4		Thailand	+ 7	
Peru	- 5		Togo	0	
Philippines	+ 8		Tonga	+13	
* Poland	+ 1		Trinidad and Tobago	- 4	
* Portugal	0		Tristan da Cunha	0	
* Azores	- 1		Tunisia	+ 1	
Puerto Rico	- 4		* Turkey	+ 2	
Qatar	+ 3		Turkmenistan	+ 5	
Réunion	+ 4		Turks and Caicos Islands	- 5	
* Romania	+ 2		Tuvalu	+12	
* Russia			Uganda	+ 3	
Zone 1	+ 2		* Ukraine	+ 2	
Zone 2	+ 3		United Arab Emirates	+ 4	
Zone 3	+ 4		* United Kingdom	0	
Zone 4	+ 5		* United States of America		
Zone 5	+ 6		Alaska	- 9	
Zone 6	+ 7		Aleutian Islands, east of 169° 30 W.	- 9	
Zone 7	+ 8		Aleutian Islands, west of 169° 30 W.	- 10	
Zone 8	+ 9		eastern time	- 5	
Zone 9	+10		central time	- 6	
Zone 10	+11		Hawaii	- 10	
Zone 11	+12		mountain time	- 7	
Rwanda	+ 2		Pacific time	- 8	
St Helena	0		Uruguay	- 3	
St Christopher and Nevis	- 4		Uzbekistan	+ 5	
St Lucia	- 4		Vanuatu	+11	
* St Pierre and Miquelon	- 3		* Vatican City State	+ 1	
St Vincent and the			Venezuela	- 4	
Grenadines	- 4				

Vietnam	+ 7
Virgin Islands (US)	- 4
Yemen	+ 3
* Yugoslavia (Fed. Rep. of)	+ 1
Zambia	+ 2
Zimbabwe	+ 2

Source: reproduced with permission from data produced by HM Nautical Almanac Office

INTERNATIONAL DIRECT DIALLING (IDD)

International dialling codes are composed of four elements which are dialled in sequence:

(i)   the international code
(ii) the country code (see below)
(iii) the area code
(iv) the customer's telephone number

Calls to some countries must be made via the international operator. (*Source:* BT)

† Connection is currently unavailable
‡ Calls must be made via the international operator
p A pause in dialling is necessary whilst waiting for a second tone
* Varies in some areas
** Varies depending on carrier

Country	IDD from UK	IDD to UK
Afghanistan	†	†
Albania	00 355	00 44
Algeria	00 213	00p44
Andorra	00 376	00 44
Angola	00 244	00 44
Anguilla	00 1 264	011 44
Antigua and Barbuda	00 1 268	011 44
Argentina	00 54	00 44
Armenia	00 374	810 44
Aruba	00 297	00 44
Ascension Island	00 247	00 44
Australia	00 61	00 11 44
Austria	00 43	00 44
Azerbaijan	00 994	810 44
Azores	00 351	00 44
Bahamas	00 1 242	011 44
Bahrain	00 973	0 44
Bangladesh	00 880	00 44
Barbados	00 1 246	011 44
Belarus	00 375	810 44
Belgium	00 32	00 44
Belize	00 501	00 44
Benin	00 229	00p44
Bermuda	00 1 441	011 44
Bhutan	00 975	00 44
Bolivia	00 591	00 44
Bosnia-Hercegovina	00 387	00 44
Botswana	00 267	00 44
Brazil	00 55	00 44
British Virgin Islands	00 1 284	011 44
Brunei	00 673	00 44
Bulgaria	00 359	00 44
Burkina Faso	00 226	00 44
Burundi	00 257	90 44
Cambodia	00 855	00 44
Cameroon	00 237	00 44
Canada	00 1	011 44
Canary Islands	00 34	00 44
Cape Verde	00 238	0 44
Cayman Islands	00 1 345	011 44
Central African Republic	00 236	19 44
Chad	00 235	15 44
Chile	00 56	00 44
China	00 86	00 44
Hong Kong	00 852	001 44
Colombia	00 57	009 44
Comoros	00 269	00 44
Congo, Dem. Rep. of	00 243	00 44
Congo, Republic of	00 242	00 44
Cook Islands	00 682	00 44
Costa Rica	00 506	00 44
Cote d'Ivoire	00 225	00 44
Croatia	00 385	00 44
Cuba	00 53	119 44
Cyprus	00 357	00 44
Czech Republic	00 420	00 44
Denmark	00 45	00 44
Djibouti	00 253	00 44
Dominica	00 1 767	011 44
Dominican Republic	00 1 809	011 44
Ecuador	00 593	00 44
Egypt	00 20	00 44
El Salvador	00 503	0 44
Equatorial Guinea	00 240	00 44
Eritrea	00 291	00 44
Estonia	00 372	800 44
Ethiopia	00 251	00 44
Falkland Islands	00 500	0 44
Faroe Islands	00 298	009 44
Fiji	00 679	05 44
Finland	00 358	00 44**
France	00 33	00 44
French Guiana	00 594	00 44
French Polynesia	00 689	00 44
Gabon	00 241	00 44
The Gambia	00 220	00 44
Georgia	00 995	810 44
Germany	00 49	00 44
Ghana	00 233	00 44
Gibraltar	00 350	00 44
Greece	00 30	00 44
Greenland	00 299	009 44
Grenada	00 1 473	011 44
Guadeloupe	00 590	00 44
Guam	00 1 671	001 44
Guatemala	00 502	00 44

Guinea	00 224	00 44
Guinea-Bissau	00 245	099 44
Guyana	00 592	001 44
Haiti	00 509	00 44
Honduras	00 504	00 44
Hungary	00 36	00 44
Iceland	00 354	00 44
India	00 91	00 44
Indonesia	00 62	001 44**
		00844**
Iran	00 98	00 44
Iraq	00 964	00 44
Ireland, Republic of	00 353	00 44
Israel	00 972	00 44**
Italy	00 39	00 44
Jamaica	00 1 876	011 44
Japan	00 81	001 44**
		004144**
		006144**
Jordan	00 962	00 44*
Kazakhstan	00 7	810 44
Kenya	00 254	00 44
Kiribati	00 686	00 44
Korea, North	00 850	00 44
Korea, South	00 82	001 44**
		00244**
Kuwait	00 965	00 44
Kyrgystan	00 996	00 44
Laos	00 856	00 44
Latvia	00 371	00 44
Lebanon	00 961	00 44
Lesotho	00 266	00 44
Liberia	00 231	00 44
Libya	00 218	00 44
Liechtenstein	00 423	00 44
Lithuania	00 370	810 44
Luxembourg	00 352	00 44
Macao	00 853	00 44
Macedonia	00 389	99 44
Madagascar	00 261	00 44
Madeira	00 351 91	00 44*
Malawi	00 265	101 44
Malaysia	00 60	00 44
Maldives	00 960	00 44
Mali	00 223	00 44
Malta	00 356	00 44
Mariana Islands, Northern	00 1 670	011 44
Marshall Islands	00 692	011 44
Martinique	00 596	00 44
Mauritania	00 222	00 44
Mauritius	00 230	00 44
Mayotte	00 269	10 44
Mexico	00 52	98 44
Micronesia, Federated States of	00 691	011 44
Moldova	00 373	810 44
Monaco	00 377	00 44
Mongolia	00 976	00 44
Montenegro	00 381	99 44
Montserrat	00 1 664	011 44
Morocco	00 212	00p44
Mozambique	00 258	00 44
Myanmar	00 95	00 44
Namibia	00 264	00 44
Nauru	00 674	00 44
Nepal	00 977	00 44
Netherlands	00 31	00 44
Netherlands Antilles	00 599	00 44
New Caledonia	00 687	00 44
New Zealand	00 64	00 44
Nicaragua	00 505	00 44
Niger	00 227	00 44
Nigeria	00 234	009 44
Niue	00 683	00 44
Norfolk Island	00 672	0101 44
Norway	00 47	00 44
Oman	00 968	00 44
Pakistan	00 92	00 44
Palau	00 680	011 44
Panama	00 507	00 44
Papua New Guinea	00 675	05 44
Paraguay	00 595	00 44**
		003 44**
Peru	00 51	00 44
Philippines	00 63	00 44
Poland	00 48	00 44
Portugal	00 351	00 44
Puerto Rico	00 1 787	011 44
Qatar	00 974	00 44
Réunion	00 262	00 44
Romania	00 40	00 44
Russia	00 7	810 44
Rwanda	00 250	00 44
St Christopher and Nevis	00 1 869	011 44
St Helena	00 290	0 44
St Lucia	00 1 758	011 44
St Pierre and Miquelon	00 508	00 44
St Vincent and the Grenadines	00 1 784	001 44
Samoa	00 685	0 44
Samoa, American	00 684	00 44
San Marino	00 378	00 44
Sao Tomé and Principe	00 239	00 44
Saudi Arabia	00 966	00 44
Senegal	00 221	00p44
Serbia	00 381	99 44
Seychelles	00 248	00 44
Sierra Leone	00 232	00 44

Singapore	00 65	001 44
Slovak Republic	00 421	00 44
Slovenia	00 386	00 44
Solomon Islands	00 677	00 44
Somalia	00 252	16 44
South Africa	00 27	09 44
Spain	00 34	00 44
Sri Lanka	00 94	00 44
Sudan	00 249	00 44
Suriname	00 597	00 44
Swaziland	00 268	00 44
Sweden	00 46	007 44**
		00944**
		008744**
Switzerland	00 41	00 44
Syria	00 963	00 44
Taiwan	00 886	002 44
Tajikistan	00 7	810 44
Tanzania	00 255	00 44
Thailand	00 66	001 44
Tibet	00 86	00 44
Togo	00 228	00 44
Tonga	00 676	00 44
Trinidad and Tobago	00 1 868	011 44
Tristan da Cunha	00 2 897	‡
Tunisia	00 216	00 44
Turkey	00 90	00 44
Turkmenistan	00 993	810 44
Turks and Caicos		
Islands	00 1 649	0 44
Tuvalu	00 688	00 44
Uganda	00 256	00 44
Ukraine	00 380	810 44
United Arab Emirates	00 971	00 44
Uruguay	00 598	00 44
USA	00 1	011 44
Uzbekistan	00 998	810 44
Vanuatu	00 678	00 44
Vatican City State	00 390 66982	00 44
Venezuela	00 58	00 44
Vietnam	00 84	00 44
Virgin Islands (US)	00 1 340	011 44
Yemen	00 967	00 44
Yugoslav Fed. Rep.	00 381	99 44
Zambia	00 260	00 44
Zimbabwe	00 263	00 44

CONSULATES

The list below is of Consulates based in Scotland.

Austrian Consulate
Alderwood, 49 Craigcrook Road, Edinburgh
EH4 3PH
Tel: 0131-332 3344; Fax: 0131-332 1777

Consulate General of The People's Republic of China
Romano House, 43 Station Road Edinburgh
EH12 7AF
Tel: 0131-316 4789
E-mail: cgprc@talk21.com
Web: http://www.chinese-embassy.org.uk

The Danish Consulate
Eadie House, 74 Kirkintilloch Road,
Bishopbriggs, Glasgow G64 2AH
Tel: 0141-762 2288; Fax: 0141-772 3554

4 Royal Terrace, Edinburgh EH7 5AB
Tel: 0131-556 4263

The Federal Republic of Germany
16 Eglinton Crescent, Edinburgh, Midlothian
EH12 5DG
Tel: 0131-337 2323
E-mail: 106071.2110@compuserve.com

Pentagon Centre, 36 Washington Street,
Glasgow G3 8AZ
Tel: 0141-226 8443; Fax: 0141-226 8441
E-mail: 106071.2110@compuserve.com

12 Albert Street, Aberdeen, AB25 1XQ
Tel: 01330-844414
E-mail: 106071.2110@compuserve.com

Greek Consulate
19 Walker Street, Edinburgh EH3 7HX
Tel: 0131-226 1309; Fax: 0131-220 4281

Consulate General of India
17 Rutland Square, Edinburgh EH1 2BB
Tel: 0131-229 2144; Fax: 0131-229 2155
E-mail: indian@consulate.fsnet.co.uk

Irish Consulate General
16 Randolph Crescent, Edinburgh EH3 7TT
Tel: 0131-226 7711; Fax: 0131-226 7704
E-mail: info@congenirl.totalserve.co.uk

Italian Consulate
32 Melville Street, Edinburgh EH3 7PG
Tel: 0131-226 3631
Fax: 01224-627406

Italian Vice-Consulate
Brebner Court, Castle Street, Aberdeen
AB11 5BQ
Tel: 01224-647135; Fax: 01224-627406

Japanese Consulate General
2 Melville Crescent, Edinburgh EH3 7HW
Tel: 0131-225 4777; Fax: 0131-225 4828

Monaco Consul
39 North Castle Street, Edinburgh EH2 3BH
Tel: 0131-225 1200; Fax: 0131-225 4412

The Netherlands Consulate
3 Annandale Terrace, Dalnottar Avenue,
Old Kilpatrick, Glasgow G60 5DJ
Tel: 01389-875744; Fax: 01839-875744

100 Union Street, Aberdeen AB10 1QR
Tel: 01224-561616

53 George Street, Edinburgh EH2 2HT
Tel: 0131-220 3226

The Royal Norwegian Consulate
86 George Street, Edinburgh EH2 3BU
Tel: 0131-226 5701

80 Oswald Street, Glasgow G1 4PX
Tel: 0141-204 1353; Fax: 0141-248 5647

Philippines Consulate
1 Bankhead Medway, Edinburgh EH11 4BY
Tel: 0131-453 3222; Fax: 0131-453 6444
E-mail: ian@shapesfurniture.co.uk

Consulate General of the Russian Federation
58 Melville Street, Edinburgh EH3 7HF
Tel: 0131-225 7098; Fax: 0131-225 9587
E-mail: visa@edconsul.demon.co.uk
Web: http://www.sol.co.uk/c/consulate

Spanish Consulate General
63 North Castle Street, Edinburgh EH2 3LJ
Tel: 0131-220 1843; Fax: 0131-226 4568

Swedish Consulate General
22 Hanover Street, Edinburgh EH2 2EP
Tel: 0131-220 6050; Fax: 0131-220 6006

Swiss Consular Agency
66 Hanover Street, Edinburgh EH2 1HH
Tel: 0131-226 5660; Fax: 0131-226 5332

Taipei Respresentative Office in the UK
1 Melville Street, Edinburgh EH3 7PE
Tel: 0131-220 6886; Fax: 0131-226 6884
E-mail: troed@dial.pipex.com

SOCIETIES AND
INSTITUTIONS

SOCIETIES AND INSTITUTIONS

The listing below includes major charities, think tanks, special interest groups and recreational groups in Scotland, and the Scottish offices of UK organisations.

Adoption Advice Service
16 Sandyford Place, Glasgow G3 7NB
Tel: 0141-339 0772
Fax: 0141-248 8032
Joint Team Leaders: Mrs J. Atherton;
   Mrs R. McMillan

Advocates for Animals
Queensferry Chambers, 10 Queensferry Street, Edinburgh EH2 4PG
Tel: 0131-225 6039
Fax: 0131-220 6377
E-mail: advocates.animals@virgin.net
Web: http://www.advocatesforanimals.org.uk
Director: L. Ward

Age Concern Scotland
113 Rose Street, Edinburgh EH2 3DT
Tel: 0131-220 3345
Fax: 0131-220 2779
E-mail: enquiries@acsinfo3.freeserve.co.uk
Director: Ms M. O'Neill

Alzheimer Scotland - Action on Dementia
22 Drumsheugh Gardens, Edinburgh EH3 7RN
Tel: 0131-243 1453
Fax: 0131-243 1450
E-mail: alzscot@alzscot.org
Web: http://www.alzscot.org
Chief Executive: J. Jackson

Amnesty International Scotland
11 Jeffrey Street, Edinburgh EH1 1DR
0131-557 2957
Fax: 0131-557 8501
Fundraising Manager: G. Pope
Development Manager: R. Burnett

An Comunn Gàidhealach
109 Church Street, Inverness IV1 1EY
Tel: 01463-231226
Fax: 01463-715557
Chief Executive: D. J. MacSween

Apex Trust Scotland
9 Great Stuart Street, Edinburgh EH3 7TP
Tel: 0131-220 0130
Fax: 0131-220 6796
E-mail: apex-hq@sol.co.uk
Web: http://www.apexscotland.org.uk
Director: Ms J. Freeman
Deputy Director: P. Dunion

Army Benevolent Fund
The Castle, Edinburgh EH1 2YT
Tel: 0131-310 5132
Fax: 0131-310 5075
Director - Scotland: Lt.-Col. I. Shepherd

Arthritis Care in Scotland
68 Woodvale Avenue, Bearsden, Glasgow G61 2NZ
Tel: 0141-942 2322
Fax: 0141-942 2322
Director - Scotland: Ms P. Wallace
Administrator - Scotland: Ms K. Green

Arts and Business Scotland
13 Abercromby Place, Edinburgh EH3 6LB
Tel: 0131-558 1277
Fax: 0131-558 3370
E-mail: scotland@AandB.org.uk
Web: http://www.AandB.org.uk
Chief Executive: C. Tweedy
Director: Ms A. Hogg

Association for Mental Health
Cumbrae House, 15 Carlton Court, Glasgow G5 9JP
Tel: 0141-568 7000
Fax: 0141-568 7001
E-mail: enquire@samh.org.uk
Chief Executive: Ms S. M. Barcus

Association for the Protection of Rural Scotland
3rd Floor, Gladstone's Land, 483 Lawnmarket, Edinburgh EH1 2NT
Tel: 0131-225 7012/3
Fax: 0131-225 6592
E-mail: aprs@aprs.org.uk
Web: http://www.aprs.org.uk
Director: Mrs J. Geddes

Association of Deer Management Groups
Dalhousie Estate Office, Brechin, Angus
DD9 6SG
Tel: 01356-624566
Fax: 01356-623725
E-mail: dalhousieestates@btinternet.com
Chairman: S. C. Gibbs
Secretary: R. J. J. Cooke

Association of Head Teachers in Scotland
Room B34, Northern College of Education,
Gardyne Road, Dundee DD5 1NY
Tel: 01382-458802
Fax: 01382-455622
E-mail: info@ahts.calinet.co.uk
General Secretary: J. C. Smith

Association of Registrars of Scotland
77 Bank Street, Alexandria G83 0LE
Tel: 01389-608980
Fax: 01389-608982
Hon. Secretary: A. P. P. Gallagher

Association of Scotland's Self-Caterers
Dalreoch, Dunning, Perth PH2 0QJ
Tel: 01764-684100
Fax: 01764-684633
Chairman: D. M. A. Smythe
Secretary: Mrs W. W. Marshall

Association of Scottish Community Councils
21 Grosvenor Street, Edinburgh EH12 5ED
Tel: 0131-225 4033
Fax: 0131-225 4033
E-mail: ascc@compuserve.com
Web: http://www.ascc.org.uk
Chairman: J. Mackintosh
Secretary: D. Murray

Association of Speakers Clubs
Beanlands Chase, 20 Rivermead Drive, Garstang,
Preston, Lancashire PR3 1JJ
Tel: 01995-602560
Fax: 01995-602560
E-mail: natsecasc@lineone.net
National Secretary: Ms D. M. Dickinson

The Automobile Association
Fanum House, Erskine Harbour, Erskine,
Renfrewshire PA8 6AT
Tel: 0141-848 8622
Fax: 0141-848 8623
E-mail: neil.greig@theaa.com
Web: http://www.theaa.co.uk
Head of Motoring Policy: N. Greig

Ayrshire Archaeological and Natural History Society
10 Longlands Park, Ayr KA7 4RJ
Tel: 01292-441915
Hon. Secretary: Dr T. Mathews
President: W. Layhe

Ayrshire Cattle Society of Great Britain and Ireland
1 Racecourse Road, Ayr KA7 2DE
Tel: 01292-267123
Fax: 01292-611973
E-mail: society@ayrshires.org
Web: http://www.ayrshires.org
Chief Executive: S. J. Thomson

BAFTA Scotland
249 West George Street, Glasgow G2 4QE
Tel: 0141-302 1770
Fax: 0141-302 1771
E-mail: baftascotland@btconnect.com
Director: Ms A. Forsyth

Barnardo's Scotland
235 Corstorphine Road, Edinburgh EH12 7AR
Tel: 0131-334 9893
Fax: 0131-316 4008
E-mail: martin.crewe@barnardos.org.uk
Web: http://www.barnardos.org.uk
Director of Children's Services:
  H. R. Mackintosh

Birth Centre
40 Leamington Terrace, Edinburgh EH10 4JL
Tel: 0131-229 3667
Fax: 0131-229 6259
E-mail: NadineEdw@aol.com
Co-ordinators: Ms N. Edwards;
  Ms A. McLaughlin; Ms D. Purdue;
  Ms E. Mollan

Botanical Society of Scotland
c/o Royal Botanic Garden, Inverleith Row,
Edinburgh EH3 5LR
Tel: 0131-552 7171
Fax: 0131-248 2901
Hon. General Secretary: R. Galt

Boys' and Girls' Clubs of Scotland
88 Giles Street, Edinburgh EH6 6BZ
Tel: 0131-555 1729
Fax: 0131-555 5921
E-mail: bgcf@freezone.co.uk
Web: http://www.freezone.co.uk/bqcscotland
Chief Executive: T. Leishman

The Boys' Brigade – Scottish Headquarters
Carronvale House, Carronvale Road, Larbert
FK5 3LH
Tel: 01324-562008
Fax: 01324-552323
E-mail: carronvale@boys-brigade.org.uk
Web: http://www.boys-brigade.org.uk
Director for Scotland: I. McLaughlan

British Agencies for Adoption and Fostering
40 Shandwick Place, Edinburgh EH2 4RT
Tel: 0131-225 9285
Fax: 0131-226 3778
E-mail: scotland@baaf.org.uk
Web: http://www.baaf.org.uk
Director - Scotland: Ms B. Hudson
Chief Executive: Ms F. Collier

British Association of Social Workers
28 North Bridge, Edinburgh EH1 1QG
Tel: 0131-225 4549
Fax: 0131-220 0636
E-mail: r.stark@scotland.basw.co.uk
Web: http://www.basw.co.uk
Professional Officer: Mrs R. Stark

British Deaf Association Scotland
3rd Floor, Princes House, 5 Shandwick Place,
Edinburgh EH2 4RG
Tel: 0131-221 1137
Fax: 0131-221 7960
Development Manager, Scotland
    Ms L. Mitchell

British Deer Society (Scottish Office)
Trian House, Comrie, Perthshire PH6 2HZ
Tel: 01764-670062
Fax: 01764-670062
E-mail: scottishsecretary@bds.org.uk
Web: http://www.bds.org.uk
Secretary: H. Rose

British Limbless Ex-Servicemen's Association
24 Dundas Street, Edinburgh EH3 6JN
Tel: 0131-538 6966
President: A. Delworth MBE

British Lung Foundation
Royal College of Physicians and Surgeons,
234–242 St Vincent Street, Glasgow G2 5RJ
Tel: 0141-204 4110
Fax: 0141-204 4110
E-mail: redballoon@blfscotland.org.uk
Web: http://www.lunguk.org
Manager: J. Brady

British Red Cross
Alexandra House, 204 Bath Street, Glasgow
G2 4HL
Tel: 0141-332 9591
Web: http://www.redcross.org.uk
Director: G. McLoughlin

Business for Scotland
PO Box 23087, Edinburgh EH2 4YT
Tel: 0131-225 9134
Fax: 0131-226 3009
E-mail: sbarber@busforscot.co.uk
Web: http://www.businessforscotland.org
Chairman: T. Hamilton

CancerBACUP
2/2, 30 Bell Street, Glasgow G1 1LG
Tel: 0141-553 1553
Fax: 0141-553 2686
E-mail: jennyw@cancerbacup.org
Web: http://www.cancerbacup.org.uk
Chief Executive: Mrs J. Mossman

Cancer Research Campaign
The Thain House, 223 Queensferry Road,
Edinburgh EH4 2BN
Tel: 0131-343 1344
Fax: 0131-343 6812
E-mail: bmckinlay@crc.org.uk
Web: http://www.crc.org.uk
Regional Director: B. McKinlay

Capability Scotland
22 Corstorphine Road, Edinburgh EH12 6HP
Tel: 0131-337 9876
Fax: 0131-346 7864
E-mail: capability@capability-scotland.org.uk
http://www.capability-scotland.org.uk
Chief Executive: A. Dickson

Carers National Association
3rd Floor, 91 Mitchell Street, Glasgow G1 3LN
Tel: 0141-221 9141
Fax: 0141-221 9140
E-mail: internet@carerscotland.demon.co.uk
Chief Executive: Ms D. Whitworth
Director - Scotland: J. Wilkes

Carnegie Dunfermline Trust
Abbey Park House, Dunfermline, Fife
KY12 7PB
Tel: 01383-723638
Fax: 01383-721862
Secretary and Treasurer: W. C. Runciman

Carnegie Hero Fund Trust
Abbey Park House, Dunfermline, Fife
KY12 7PB
Tel: 01383-723638
Fax: 01383-721862
Secretary: W. C. Runciman

Carnegie United Kingdom Trust
Comely Park House, Dunfermline, Fife
KY12 7EJ
Tel: 01383-721445
Fax: 01383-620 682
Secretary: C. J. Naylor OBE

Centre for Scottish Cultural Studies
University of Strathclyde, Livingstone Tower,
26 Richmond Street, Glasgow G1 1XH
Tel: 0141-548 3518
Fax: 0141-552 3493
E-mail: ken.simpson@strath.ac.uk
Director: Dr K. G. Simpson
Deputy Director: G. Carruthers

Centre for Scottish Public Policy
16 Forth Street, Edinburgh EH1 3LH
Tel: 0131-477 8219
Fax: 0131-477 8220
E-mail: mail@jwcentre.demon.co.uk
Conference Officer: P. Head

Chartered Institute of Bankers in Scotland
Drumsheugh House, 38B Drumsheugh Gardens,
Edinburgh EH3 7SW
Tel: 0131-473 7777
Fax: 0131-473 7788
E-mail: info@ciobs.org.uk
Web: http://www.ciobs.org.uk
Chief Executive: C. W. Munn

Chest, Heart and Stroke Scotland
65 North Castle Street, Edinburgh EH2 3LT
Tel: 0131-225 6963
Fax: 0131-220 6313
E-mail: admin@chss.org.uk
http://www.chss.org.uk
Chief Executive: D. H. Clark

ChildLine Scotland
18 Albion Street, Glasgow G1 1LH
Tel: 0141-552 1123. Helpline: 0800-1111
Fax: 0141-552 3089
E-mail: scotland@childline.org.uk
Web: http://www.childline.org.uk
Director: Ms A. Houston

Children 1st (Royal Scottish Society for Prevention of Cruelty to Children)
Melville House, 41 Polwarth Terrace, Edinburgh
EH11 1NU
Tel: 0131-337 8539
Fax: 0131-346 8284
E-mail: children1st@zetnet.co.uk
Chief Executive: Mrs M. McKay
Director of Children and Family Services:
  Ms C. Dewar

Children in Scotland
Princes House, 5 Shandwick Place, Edinburgh
EH2 4RG
Tel: 0131-228 8484
Fax: 0131-228 8585
E-mail: info@childreninscotland.org.uk
Web: http://www.childreninscotland.org.uk
Chief Executive: Dr B. Cohen

Christian Aid Scotland
41 George IV Bridge, Edinburgh EH1 1EL
Tel: 0131-220 1254
Fax: 0131-225 8861
E-mail: edinburgh@christian-aid.org
Web: http://www.christian-aid.org.uk
National Secretary: Revd J. Wylie

The Church of Scotland Guild
121 George Street, Edinburgh EH2 4YN
Tel: 0131-225 5722
Fax: 0131-220 3113
E-mail: atwaddle@cofscotland.org.uk
Web: http://www.cofscotland.org.uk
General Secretary: Mrs A. M. Twaddle
Information Officer: Mrs F. J. Lange

Citizens Advice Scotland
26 George Square, Edinburgh EH8 9LD
Tel: 0131-667 0156
Fax: 0131-668 4359
Chief Executive Officer: Ms K. Lyle

Clyde Area Biological Records Centre
Foremount House, Kilbarchan, Renfrewshire
PA10 2EZ
Tel: 01505-702419
Chairman: Dr J. A. Gibson

Comunn Na Gàidhlig
5 Mitchell's Lane, Inverness IV2 3HQ
Tel: 01463-234138
Fax: 01463-347470
E-mail: oifis@cnag.org.uk
Chief Executive: A. Campbell

Community Care Forum
c/o 18–19 Claremont Crescent, Edinburgh
EH7 4QD
Tel: 0131-557 2711
Fax: 0131-557 2711
E-mail: karen.jackson@scvo.org.uk
National Development Officer:
    Ms K. Jackson

Community Service Volunteers Scotland
Wellgate House, 200 Cowgate, Edinburgh
EH1 1NQ
Tel: 0131-622 7766
Fax: 0131-622 7755
E-mail: edinburgh@csvscotland.u-net.com
Web: http://www.csv.org.uk
Director, Scotland: Ms C. Stevens

Cot Death Trust
Royal Hospital for Sick Children, Yorkhill,
Glasgow G3 8SJ
Tel: 0141-357 3946
Fax: 0141-334 1376
E-mail: hb1w@clinmed.gla.ac.uk
Web: http://www.gla.ac.uk/Acad/ChildHealth
    /SCDT
Executive Director: Ms H. Brooke

Council for Arbitration
27 Melville Street, Edinburgh EH3 7GF
Tel: 0131-226 2552
Fax: 0131-226 2501
E-mail: jim.arnott@macroberts.co.uk
Chief Executive: J. Arnott

Council for Scottish Archaeology
c/o National Museums of Scotland, Chambers
Street, Edinburgh EH1 1JF
Tel: 0131-247 4119
Fax: 0131-247 4126
Director: Dr S. Fraser

Council for Single Homeless
5th Floor, Wellgate House, 200 Cowgate,
Edinburgh EH1 1NQ
Tel: 0131-226 4382
Director: R. Aldridge

Council on Alcohol
2nd Floor, 166 Buchanan Street, Glasgow
G1 2NH
Tel: 0141-572 6700
Fax: 0141-333 1606
Chief Executive: J. Law

Couple Counselling Scotland
40 North Castle Street, Edinburgh EH2 3BN
Tel: 0131-225 5006
Fax: 0131-220 0639
E-mail: enquiries@couplecounselling.org
Web: http://www.couplecounselling.org
Director: Mrs F. Love

Cruse Bereavement Care
Scottish Headquarters, 33—35 Boswall Parkway,
Edinburgh EH5 2BR
Tel: 0131-551 1511
Fax: 0131-551 5234
E-mail: crusescothq@bizline.co.uk
Chief Officer: Ms R. Hampton

Cystic Fibrosis Trust
Princes House, 5 Shandwick Place, Edinburgh
EH2 4RG
Tel: 0131-211 1110
Fax: 0131-221 1110
E-mail: hmacfarlane@cftrust.org.uk
Web: http://www.cftrust.org.uk
Chief Executive: Ms R. Barnes
Regional Support Co-ordinator:
    Ms H. Mayarlae

The David Hume Institute
21 George Square, Edinburgh EH8 9LD
Tel: 0131-650 4633
Fax: 0131-667 9111
E-mail: hume.institute@ed.ac.uk
Web: http://www.ed.ac.uk/~hume/
Director: Prof. B. Main
Administrator/Manager: Ms C. Laing

Diabetes UK
4th Floor, 34 West George Street, Glasgow
G2 1DA
Tel: 0141-332 2700
Fax: 0141-332 4880
E-mail: scotland@diabetes.org.uk
Web: http://www.diabetes.org.uk
National Manager: Mrs D. Henry

The Duke of Edinburgh's Award
69 Dublin Street, Edinburgh EH3 6NS
Tel: 0131-556 9097
Fax: 0131-557 8044
E-mail: scotland@theaward.org
Web: http://www.theaward.org
Secretaray for Scotland: Miss J. Shepherd

Dyslexia Association Scotland
Unit 3, Stirling Business Centre, Wellgreen,
Stirling FK8 2DZ
Tel: 01786-446650
Fax: 01786-471235
E-mail: dyslexia.scotland@dial.pipex.com
Chairman: Mrs E. Reilly

Dyslexia Institute
74 Victoria Crescent Road, Dowanhill, Glasgow
G12 9JN
Tel: 0141-334 4549
Fax: 0141-339 8879
E-mail: glasgow@dyslexia-inst.org.uk
Web: http://www.dyslexia-inst.org.uk
Principal: Mrs E. Mackenzie

Earl Haig Fund Scotland
New Haig House, Logie Green Road, Edinburgh
EH7 4HR
Tel: 0131-557 2782
Fax: 0131-557 5819
E-mail: earlhaigfund@hotmail.com
Chief Executive: Maj.-Gen. J. D. MacDonald,
   CB, CBE

Ecclesiastical History Society
Department of History (Medieval), University of
Glasgow, Glasgow G12 8QQ
Tel: 0141-330 4087
Fax: 0141-330 5056
Secretary: M. J. Kennedy

Edinburgh Bibliographical Society
c/o National Library of Scotland, George IV
Bridge, Edinburgh EH1 1EW
Tel: 0131-226 4531
Fax: 0131-220 6662
President: Miss B. E. Moon
Hon. Editor of the Transactions: K. Dunn

**Employment Opportunities for People with
Disabilities**
5th Floor, Portcullis House, 21 India Street,
Glasgow G2 4PZ
Tel: 0141-226 4544
Fax: 0141-248 5068
E-mail: eopps.glasgow@connectfree.co.uk
Web: http://www.opportunities.org.uk
Regional Director: G. Young

**ENABLE (Scottish Society for the Mentally
Handicapped)**
7 Buchanan Street, Glasgow G1 3HL
Tel: 0141-226 4541
Fax: 0141-204 4398
E-mail: enable@enable.org.uk
Director: N. Dunning

Engender
13 Gayfield Square, Edinburgh EH1 3NX
Tel: 0131-558 9596
E-mail: engender@engender.org.uk
Web: http://www.engender.org.uk
Convenor: Ms S. Robertson

Epilepsy Association of Scotland
48 Govan Road, Glasgow G51 1JL
Tel: 0141-427 4911
Fax: 0141-419 1709
E-mail: enquiries@epilepsyscotland.org.uk
Web: http://www.epilepsyscotland.org.uk
Chief Executive: Ms H. Mounfield

Erskine Hospital
Bishopton, Renfrewshire PA7 5PU
Tel: 0141-812 1100
Fax: 0141-812 3733
E-mail: isobel.mccartney@erskine.org.uk
Web: http://www.erskine.org/welcome.htm
Chief Executive: Col. M. F. Gibson OBE

The European Movement
6 Hill Street, Edinburgh EH2 3JZ
Tel: 0131-220 0377
Fax: 0131-220 0377
E-mail: scotland@euromove.org.uk
Web: http://www.euromove.org.uk
National Organiser Ms B. MacLeod

Ex-Services Mental Welfare Society
Hollybush House, Hollybush, by Ayr KA6 7EA
Tel: 01292-560214
Fax: 01292-560871
E-mail: rdsi@combatstress.org.uk
Web: http://www.combatstress.com
Regional Director, Scotland and Ireland:
   Wg Cdr. D. Devine

Fair Isle Bird Observatory Trust
Fair Isle Bird Observatory, Fair Isle, Shetland
ZE2 9JU
Tel: 01595-760258
Fax: 01595-760258
E-mail: fairisle.birdobs@zetnet.co.uk
Web: http://www.fairislebirdobs.co.uk
Administrator: Ms H. Craib

Family History Society
164 King Street, Aberdeen AB24 5BD
Tel: 01224-646323
Fax: 01224-639096
E-mail: enquiries@anesfhs.org.uk
Web: http://www.anesfhs.org.uk
Chairperson: Mrs G. Murton

Family Planning Association Scotland
Unit 10, Firhill Business Centre, 76 Firhill Road
Glasgow G20 7BA
Tel: 0141-576 5088
Fax: 0141-576 5006
E-mail: jackie@fpascotland.fonet.co.uk
Web: http://www.fpa.org.uk
Director: Ms A. M. McKay
Information Officer: Ms J. Nicholson

Fèisean Nan Gàidheal
Meall House, Portree, Isle of Skye
Tel: 01478-613355
Fax: 01478-618399
E-mail: feisean@dircon.co.uk
Web: http://www.feisean.org
Director: A. Cormack
Development Officer: D. Boag

Findhorn Foundation
The Park, Findhorn, Forres, Moray IV36 3TZ
Tel: 01309-690311
Fax: 01309-691301
E-mail: reception@findhorn.org
Web: http://www.findhorn.org
Co-Chairpersons: R. Alfred; Ms M. Hollander

Fishmongers' Company
Fala Acre, Fala Village, Pathhead, Midlothian
EH37 5SY
Tel: 01875-833246
Fax: 01875-833246
Salmon Fisheries Inspector: W. F. Beattie, MBE

Fraser of Allander Institute for Research on the Scottish Economy
University of Strathclyde, Curran Building,
100 Cathedral Street, Glasgow G4 0LN
Tel: 0141-548 3958
Fax: 0141-552 8340
E-mail: fraser@strath.ac.uk
Web: http://www.fraser.strath.ac.uk
Director: J. Ireland
Policy Director: B. Ashcroft

Friends of the Earth Scotland
72 Newhaven Road, Edinburgh EH6 5QG
Tel: 0131-554 9977
Fax: 0131-554 8656
E-mail: info@foe-scotland.org.uk
Web: http://www.foe-scotland.org.uk
Director: K. Dunion, OBE

The Game Conservancy Trust
Scottish Headquarters, Couston, Newtyle,
Perthshire PH12 8UT
Tel: 01828-650543
Fax: 01828-650560
E-mail: imccall@gct.org.uk
Web: http://www.gct.org.uk
Director: I. McCall

Gingerbread Scotland
1307 Argyll Street, Glasgow G3 8TL
Tel: 0141-576 5085
Fax: 0141-576 7976
Web: http://www.gingerbread.org.uk
Chairperson: J. McGuinn
Development Co-ordinator: R. Smith

The Girls' Brigade in Scotland
Boys' Brigade House, 168 Bath Street, Glasgow
G2 4TQ
Tel: 0141-332 1765
Fax: 0141-331 2681
E-mail: hq@girls-brigade-scotland.org.uk
Web: http://www.girls-brigade-scotland.org.uk
Brigade Secretary: Mrs A. Webster

Grand Lodge of Antient Free and Accepted Masons of Scotland
Freemasons' Hall, 96 George Street, Edinburgh
EH2 3DH
Tel: 0131-225 5304
Fax: 0131-225 3953
Web: http://www.grandlodgescotland.com
Grand Secretary: C. M. McGibbon
Grand Master Mason: A. D. Orr Ewing

Guide Association Scotland
16 Coates Crescent, Edinburgh EH3 7AH
Tel: 0131-226 4511
Fax: 0131-220 4828
E-mail: administrator@scottishguides.org.uk
Executive Director: Miss S. Pitches

Guide Dogs for the Blind Association
Princess Alexandra House, Dundee Road, Forfar
DD8 1JA
Tel: 01307-463531
Fax: 01307-465233
Web: http://www.gdba.org.uk
Operations Director: Ms J. Potmore

Hawick Archaeological Society
Orrock House, Stirches Road, Hawick,
Roxburghshire TD9 7HF
Tel: 01450-375546
Hon. Secretary: I. W. Landles

Hearing Dogs for Deaf People
29 Craighiehall Crescent, West Freelands,
Erskine, Renfrewshire PA8 7DD
Tel: 0141-812 6542
**Community Fund-raiser and Scottish
    Representative:** Ms M. Arthur

Hebridean Wale and Dolphin Trust
28 Main Street, Tobermory, Isle of Mull, Argyll
PA75 6NU
Tel: 01688-302620
Fax: 01688-302728
E-mail: hwdt@sol.co.uk
Web: http://www.hwdt.org
Executive Director: Ms C. Fleming
Scientific Director: Dr C. Parsons

Help the Aged
Heriot House, Heriothill Terrace, Edinburgh
EH7 4DY
Tel: 0131-556 4666
Fax: 0131-557 5115
Web: http://www.helptheaged.co.uk
Scottish Executive: Ms E. Duncan

Highland Cattle Society
59 Drumlanrig Street, Thornhill, Dunfries
DG3 5LY
Tel: 01848-331866
Fax: 01848-331183
E-mail: info@highlandcattlesociety.com
Web: http://www.highlandcattlesociety.com
Secretary: A. H. G. Wilson

Housing Association Ombudsman for Scotland
2 Belford Road, Edinburgh EH4 3BL
Tel: 0131-220 0599
Fax: 0131-220 0577
Acting Ombudsman: Ms K. Steinol

Human Rights Centre
146 Holland Street, Glasgow G2 4NG
Tel: 0141-332 5960
Fax: 0141-332 5960
E-mail: shrc@dial.pipex.com
Web: http://www.shre.pipex.com
Director: Prof. A. Miller

Immigration Advisory Service
115 Bath Street, Glasgow G2 2SZ
Tel: 0141-248 2956
Fax: 0141-221 5388
E-mail: advice@iasuk.org
Web: http://www.iasuk.org
Chief Executive: K. Best

Imperial Cancer Research Fund
Scottish Appeals Centre, Wallace House,
Maxwell Place, Stirling FK8 1JU
Tel: 01786-446689
Fax: 01786-446691
E-mail: appealsscot@icrf.icnet.uk
Web: http://www.icnet.uk
Fundraising Director: Mrs J. F. M. Cameron

Institute of Chartered Accountants of Scotland
CA House, 21 Haymarket Yards, Edinburgh
EH12 5BH
Tel: 0131-225 5673
Fax: 0131-225 3813
E-mail: icas@icas.org.uk
Web: http://www.icas.org.uk
Chief Executive: D. A. Brew

Institute of Chartered Foresters
7A St Colme Street, Edinburgh EH3 6AA
Tel: 0131-225 2705
Fax: 0131-220 6128
E-mail: icfor@charteredforesters.org
Web: http://www.charteredforesters.org
Executive Director: Mrs M. W. Dick

Inverness Field Club
Swallowhill House, Lentran, Inverness IV3 8RJ
Hon. Secretary: Mrs G. Cameron

John Muir Trust
41 Commercial Street, Edinburgh EH6 6JD
Tel: 0131-554 0114
Fax: 0131-555 2112
E-mail: admin@jmt.org
Web: http://www.jmt.org
Director: N. Hawkins

Jubilee 2000 Scottish Coalition
121 George Street, Edinburgh EH2 4YN
Tel: 0131-225 4321
Fax: 0131-226 4293
E-mail: j2000scot@networkteam.net
Web: http://www.j2000scot.org
Co-ordinator: Ms E. Hendry

Keep Scotland Beautiful
7 Melville Terrace, Stirling FK8 2ND
Tel: 01786-471333
Fax: 01786-464611
E-mail: ksb@tidybritain.org.uk
Director: J. P. Summers

King George's Fund for Sailors
HMS Caledonia, Rosyth, Dunfermline
KY11 2XH
Tel: 01383-419969
Fax: 01383-419969
E-mail: tony@kgfs.org.uk
Web: http://www.kgfs.org.uk
Area Organiser: Cdre. A.C. Herdman, RN
Assistant Area Organiser: Mrs S. Banting

Leonard Cheshire Scotland
161 Lower Granton Road, Edinburgh EH5 1EY
Tel: 0131-538 5544
Fax: 0131-538 5566
Fundraising Manager: Ms J. Pike

Leukaemia Research Fund
43 Westbourne Gardens, Glasgow G12 9XQ
Tel: 0141-339 0690
Fax: 0141-339 0690
Executive Director: D. L. Osborne
Scottish Secretary: Mrs M. Naddell

Macmillan Cancer Relief
9 Castle Terrace, Edinburgh EH1 2DP
Tel: 0131-229 3276
Fax: 0131-228 6710
Web: http://www.macmillan.org.uk
Director for Scotland and Northern Ireland:
    I. R. L. Gibson

Mental Health Foundation Scotland
5th Floor, Merchants House, 30 George Square,
Glasgow G2 1EG
Tel: 0141-572 0125
Fax: 0141-572 0246
E-mail: scotland@mhf.org.uk
Web: http://www.mentalhealth.org.uk
Director, Scotland: Ms M. Halliday

The Mission to Seafarers Scotland
Containerbase, Gartsherrie Road, Coatbridge,
Lanarkshire ML5 2DS
Tel: 01236-440132
Adminstration Manager: Mrs L. C. Boyd

Multiple Sclerosis Society Scotland
Rural Centre, Ingliston, Edinburgh EH28 8NZ
Tel: 0131-472 4106
Fax: 0131-472 4099
E-mail: admin@mssocietyscotland.org.uk
Web: http://www.mssociety.org.uk
Director: M. Hazelwood
Fundraising Manager: Ms G. Mackenzie

**The National Association for Gifted Children
in Scotland**
PO Box 2024, Glasgow G32 9YD
Tel: 0141-639 4797
Fax: 0141-778 0556
E-mail: nagcs.org@talk21.com
Chairman: D. M. Henderson
Counsellor: Mrs S. Divecha

National Asthma Campaign Scotland
29 North Charlotte Street, Edinburgh EH2 4HR
Tel: 0131-226 2544
Fax: 0131-226 2401
E-mail: scotland@asthma5.demon.co.uk
Web: http://www.asthma.org.uk
Chief Executive: Ms A. Bradley

National Childbirth Trust
Stockbridge Health Centre, 1 India Place,
Edinburgh EH3 6EH
Tel: 0131-260 9201
Administrator: Ms K. McGlew

National Foster Care Association
2nd Floor, Ingram House, 227 Ingram Street,
Glasgow, G1 1DA
Tel: 0141-204 1400
Fax: 0141-204 6588
Administrator: Ms L. Curran
Manager: B. Ritchie

National House-Building Council (NHBC)
42 Colinton Road, Edinburgh EH10 5BT
Tel: 0131-313 1001
Fax: 0131-313 1211
Web: http://www.nhbc.co.uk
Director: T. Kirk

National Schizophrenia Fellowship Scotland
Claremont House, 130 East Claremont Street,
Edinburgh EH7 4LB
Tel: 0131-557 8969
Fax: 0131-557 8968
E-mail: info@nsfscot.org.uk
Web: http://www.nsfscot.org.uk
Chief Executive: Ms M. Weir
Information Officer: I. Harper

The National Trust for Scotland
28 Charlotte Square, Edinburgh EH2 4ET
Tel: 0131-243 9300
Fax: 0131-243 9301
E-mail: information@nts.org.uk
Web: http://www.nts.org.uk
Director: T. Croft

National Union of Students Scotland
29 Forth Street, Edinburgh EH1 3LE
Tel: 0131-556 6598
Fax: 0131-557 5679
E-mail: nus.scot@dircon.co.uk
Web: http://www.nus.org.uk
President: M. Telford
Director: L. Jarnecki

National War Memorial
The Castle, Edinburgh EH1 2YT
Tel: 0131-226 7393
Fax: 0131-225 8920
Secretary to the Trustees: Lt.-Col. I. Shepherd

NCH Action for Children Scotland
17 Newton Place, Glasgow G3 7PY
Tel: 0141-332 4041
Fax: 0141-332 7002
Web: http://www.nchatc.org.uk
Director: G. O'Hara

One Parent Families Scotland
13 Gayfield Square, Edinburgh EH1 3NX
Tel: 0131-556 3899
Fax: 0131-557 9650
E-mail: opfs@gn.apc.org
Web: http://www.gn.apc.org/opfs
Director: Ms S. Robertson

Ornithologists' Club
21 Regent Terrace, Edinburgh EH7 5BT
Tel: 0131-556 6042
Fax: 0131-558 9947
E-mail: mail@the.soc.org.uk
Web: http://www.the.soc.org.uk
Secretary: Miss S. Laing

Outward Bound Scotland
Loch Eil Centre, Achdalieu, Corpach, Fort
William PH33 7NN
Tel: 01397-772866
Fax: 01397-773905
Web: http://www.outwardbound-uk.org
Director: Sir Michael Hobbs KCVO, CBE
General Manager: T. Shepherd

Oxfam in Scotland
5th Floor, Fleming House, 134 Renfrew Street
Glasgow G3 6ST
Tel: 0141-331 1455
Fax: 0141-331 2264
Web: http://www.oxfam.org.uk
Head of Oxfam Scotland: Mrs M. Hearle

PA News Ltd
124 Portman Street, Kinning Park, Glasgow
G41 1EJ
Tel: 0141-429 0037
Fax: 0141-429 1596
Web: http://www.pressassociation.press.net
Editor, PA Scotland: Ms C. Stephen

Parkinson's Disease Society - Scottish Resource
10 Claremont Terrace, Glasgow G3 7XR
Tel: 0141-332 3343
E-mail: pds.scotland@community-care.net
Regional Manager: D. R. McNiven

PDSA (People's Dispensary for Sick Animals)
Community Activities Office, Veterinary Centre,
Muiry Fauld Drive, Tollcross, Glasgow
G31 5RT
Tel: 0141-778 9229
Fax: 0141-778 9229
E-mail: crawford.lynn@pdsa.org.uk
Community Activities Manager:
   Ms L. Crawford

PHAB Scotland
5A Warriston Road, Edinburgh EH3 7SL
Tel: 0131-226 5320
E-mail: info@phab.org.uk
Web: http://www.phab.org.uk
Chief Executive: Miss F. Hird

Post Office Users' Council for Scotland
Room 306-7, 2 Greenside Lane, Edinburgh
EH1 3AH
Tel: 0131-224 5576
Fax: 0131-224 5696
E-mail: help@poucs.org
Web: http://www.poucs.org
Secretary: R. L. L. King
Complaints Manager: Mrs M. Malloch

The Poverty Alliance
162 Buchanan Street, Glasgow G1 2LL
Tel: 0141-353 0440
Fax: 0141-353 0686
E-mail: admin@povertyalliance.org
Web: http://www.povertyalliance.org
Director: D. Killeen

Prince's Scottish Youth Business Trust
6th Floor, Mercantile Chambers, 53 Bothwell
Street, Glasgow G2 6TS
Tel: 0141-248 4999
E-mail: team@psybt.org.uk
Web: http://www.psybt.org.uk
Director: D. W. Cooper
Director of Operations: Ms E. McDonald

Prince's Trust Scotland
7th Floor, Fleming House, 134 Renfrew Street,
Glasgow G3 6ST
Tel: 0141-331 0211
Fax: 0141-331 0210
E-mail: volscot@princes-trust.org.uk
Web: http://www.princes-trust.org.uk
Office Manager: Mrs Y. Murphy-Beggs

The Princess Royal Trust for Carers
Campbell House, 215 West Campbell Street,
Glasgow, G2 4TT
Tel: 0141-221 5066
Fax: 0141-221 4623
E-mail: PRTCGlasgo@ao.com
Web: http://www.carers.org
Chief Executive: Ms A. Ryan

Quarriers
Head Office, Quarriers Village, Bridge of Weir,
Renfrewshire PA11 3SX
Tel: 01505-612224
Fax: 01505-613906
E-mail: enquiries@quarriers.org.uk
Web: http://www.quarriers.org.uk
Chief Executive: P. Robinson

Queen Victoria School
Dunblane, Perthshire PK15 0JY
Tel: 01786-822288
Fax: 0131-310 2955
E-mail: enquiries@qvs.pks.sch.uk
Web: http://www.qvs.pkc.sch.uk
Headmaster: B. Raine

Queen's Nursing Institute
31 Castle Terrace, Edinburgh EH1 2EL
Tel: 0131-229 2333
Fax: 0131-229 0443
E-mail: qnis@aol.com
Web: http://www.qnis.co.uk
Director: G. D. C. Preston

Robert Burns World Federation Ltd
Dick Institute, Elmbank Avenue, Kilmarnock
KA1 3BU
Tel: 01563-572469
Fax: 01563-572469
E-mail: robertburnsfederation@kilmarnock.26
.freeserve.co.uk
Chief Executive: Mrs S. Bell

Royal Academy of Engineering
Department of Petroleum Engineering,
Heriot-Watt University, Riccarton,
Edinburgh EH14 4AS
Tel: 0131-451 3128
Fax: 0131-451 3127
E-mail: brian.smart@pet.hw.ac.uk
Scottish Convenor: Prof. B. G. D. Smart

Royal British Legion Scotland
New Haig House, Logie Green Road, Edinburgh
EH7 4HR
Tel: 0131-557 5819
General Secretary: Maj.-Gen. J. D. MacDonald,
CB, CBE, DL

Royal Caledonian Horticultural Society
6 Kirkliston Road, South Queensferry
EH30 9LT
Tel: 0131-331 1011
Secretary: T. Mabbott

Royal Celtic Society
23 Rutland Street, Edinburgh EH1 2RN
0131-228 6449
Fax: 0131-229 6987
E-mail: gcameron@stuartandstuart.co.uk
Secretary: J. G. Cameron

**Royal Highland and Agricultural Society of
Scotland**
Royal Highland Centre, Ingliston, Edinburgh
EH28 8NF
Tel: 0131-335 6200
Fax: 0131-333 5236
E-mail: rayj@rhass.org.uk
Web: http://www.rhass.org.uk
Chief Executive: R. Jones

Royal Medical Society
The Potterrow, 5/5 Bristo Square, Edinburgh
EH8 9AL
Tel: 0131-650 2672
Fax: 0131-650 267
Senior President: P. Mills
Permanent Secretary: Mrs P. Strong

Royal National Institute for Deaf People
9 Clairmont Gardens, Glasgow G3 7LW
Tel: 0141-564 1600. Textphone: 0141-564 1602
Fax: 0141-564 1601
Web: http://www.rnid.org.uk
Director: Ms L. Lawson

Royal National Lifeboat Institution Scotland
Bellevue House, Hopetoun Street, Edinburgh
EH7 4ND
Tel: 0131-557 9171
Fax: 0131-557 6943
E-mail: ro/scot@rnli.org.uk
Web: http://www.rnli.org.uk
National Organiser, Scotland: Mrs M. Caldwell

Royal National Mission to Deep Sea
Fishermen
Scottish Regional Office, Melita House, Station
Road, Polmont, Stirlingshire FK2 0UD
Tel: 01324-716857
Fax: 01324-716423
E-mail: ian.rnmdsf@talk21.com
Director - Scotland: I. Baillie

Royal Naval and Royal Marine Association
Heriot Hill House, 1 Broughton Road,
Edinburgh EH7 4EW
Tel: 0131-556 2973
Hon. Secretary: W. Tovey

Royal Scottish Academy
The Mound, Edinburgh EH2 2EL
Tel: 0131-225 6671
Fax: 0131-225 2349
Administrative Secretary: B. Laidlaw
Assistant Administrative Secretary:
   Ms M. Wilson

Royal Scottish Agricultural Benevolent
Institution
Ingliston, Edinburgh EH28 8NB
Tel: 0131-333 1023/1027
Fax: 0131-333 1027
E-mail: rsabi@argonet.co.uk
Web: http://www.argonet.co.uk/users/rsabi/
Director: I. C. Purves-Hume
Welfare Secretary: Ms E. Brath

Royal Scottish Geographical Society
Graham Hills Building, 40 George Street,
Glasgow G1 1QE
Tel: 0141-552 3330
Fax: 0141-522 3331
R.S.G.S.@strath.ac.uk
Web: http://www.geo.ed.ac.uk/~RSGS/
Director: Dr D. M. Munro

Royal Scottish Pipe Band Association
45 Washington Street, Glasgow G3 8AZ
Tel: 0141-221 5414
Fax: 0141-221 1561
Executive Officer: C. Darroch

Royal Scottish Pipers' Society
127 Rose Street Lane South, Edinburgh
EH2 4BB
Tel: 01620-842146
Secretary: Dr M. J. B. Lowe

Royal Society for the Prevention of Accidents
(ROSPA)
Slateford House, 53 Lanark Road, Edinburgh
EH14 1TL
Tel: 0131-455 7657
Fax: 0131-443 9442
Web: http://www.rospa.co.uk
Road Safety Manager - Scotland:
   M. A. McDonnell

The Royal Society for the Protection of Birds
Dunedin House, 25 Ravelston Terrace,
Edinburgh EH4 3TP
Tel: 0131-311 6500
Fax: 0131-311 6569
E-mail: rspb.scotland@rspb.org.uk
Web: http://www.rspb.org.uk
Director: S. Housden

Royal Society of Edinburgh
22–24 George Street, Edinburgh EH2 2PQ
Tel: 0131-240 5000
Fax: 0131-240 5024
E-mail: rse@rse.org.uk
Web: http://www.royalsoced.org.uk
Executive Secretary: Dr W. Duncan

Royal United Kingdom Beneficent Association
PO Box 16058, Gargunnock, nr Stirling
FK8 3YN
Tel: 01698-860446
Fax: 01698-860446
Representative: Mrs M. Graham

Royal Zoological Society of Scotland
National Zoological Park, Edinburgh Zoo,
134 Corstorphine Road, Edinburg EH12 6TS
Tel: 0131-334 9171
Fax: 0131-316 4050
E-mail: marketing@rzss.org.uk
Web: http://www.edinburghzoo.org.uk
Director: Dr D. Waugh, Ph.D.

SACRO, Safeguarding Communites - Reducing Offending
1 Broughton Market, Edinburgh EH3 6NU
Tel: 0131-624 7270
Fax: 0131-624 7269
E-mail: info@national.sacro.org.uk
Web: http://www.sacro.org.uk
Chief Executive: Ms S. Matheson
Communications Officer: Ms M. Chalmers

St Andrew Animal Fund
Queensferry Chambers, 10 Queensferry Street
Edinburgh EH2 4PG
Tel: 0131-225 2116
Fax: 0131-220 6377
E-mail: advocates.animals@virgin.net
Secretary: L. Ward

St Andrew's Children's Society Ltd
Gillis Centre, 113 Whitehouse Loan,
Edinburgh EH9 1BB
Tel: 0131-452 8248
Fax: 0131-452 8248
E-mail: info@standrews-children.org.uk
Director: S. J. Small
Chairperson: Ms M. McEvoy

St Margaret's Children and Family Care Society
274 Bath Street, Glasgow G2 4JR
Tel: 0141-332 8371
Fax: 0141-332 8393
Director: Mrs M. Campbell

Saltire Society
9 Fountain Close, 22 High Street, Edinburgh
EH1 1TF
Tel: 0131-556 1836
Fax: 0131-557 1675
E-mail: saltire@saltire.org.uk
Web: http://www.saltire-society.demon.co.uk
Adminstrator: Mrs K. Munro
Director: I. Scott

Save the Children Scotland
2nd Floor, Haymarket House, 8 Clifton Terrace,
Edinburgh EH12 5DR
Tel: 0131-527 8200
Web: http://www.savethechildren.org.uk
Programme Director: Mrs A. Davies

Scotland's Gardens Scheme
31 Castle Terrace, Edinburgh EH1 2EL
Tel: 0131-229 1870
Fax: 0131-229 0443
E-mail: sgsoffice@aol.com
Director: Mr R. S. St Clair-Ford

Scots Language Resource Centre Association
A. K. Bell Library, 2–8 York Place, Perth
PH2 8EP
Tel: 01738-440199
Fax: 01738-477010
E-mail: slrc@sol.co.uk
Web: http://www.pkc.gov.uk/slrc/index/html
Secretary: Ms L. Roe
Convener: Prof. R. Johnstone

Scots Language Society
c/o Scots Language Resource Centre,
A. K. Bell Library, York Place, Perth
PH2 8EP
Tel: 01738-440199
Fax: 01738-646505
Secretary: D. H. Brown

Scots Leid Associe
The A.K. Bell Library, York Place, Perth
PH2 8EP
Tel: 01738-440199
E-mail: d.brown1@tesco.net
Web: http://www.geocities.com/Athens/sparta/
2933/
Lallans Editor: J. Law

Scots Tung
27 Stoneyhill Avenue, Musselburgh, Midlothian
EH21 6SB
Tel: 0131-665 5440/9351
E-mail: rfairnie@talk21.com
Web: http://www.mlove.free-online.co.uk/
Convener: R. Heinsar
Secretar: F. Fairnie

Scottish Association of Law Centres
c/o Paisley Law Centre, 65 George Street,
Paisley PA1 2JY
Tel: 0141-561 7266
Fax: 0141-561 7164
E-mail: LW@PaisleyLawCentre.co.uk
Secretary: Ms L. Welsh

Scottish Accident Prevention Council
Slateford House, 53 Lanark Road, Edinburgh
EH14 1TL
Tel: 0131-455 7457
Fax: 0131-443 9442
E-mail: secretary@sapc.org.uk
Web: http://www.sapc.org.uk
Secretary: M. A. McDonnell

Scottish Tartans Society
Hall of Records, Port-na-Craig Road, Pitlochry
PH16 5ND
Tel: 01796-474079
Fax: 01796-474090
Web: http://www.tartans.scotland.net
Researchers and Archivists: Mr and Mrs K.
    Lumsden

Scottish Association for Marine Science
PO Box 3, Oban, Argyll PA34 4AD
Tel: 01631-562244
Fax: 01631-565518
E-mail: mail@dml.ac.uk
Web: http://www.ccms.ac.uk
Director: Dr G. B. Shimmield, FRSE

Scottish Association for Public Transport
5 St Vincent Place, Glasgow G1 2DH
Tel: 0141-639 3697
Fax: 0141-639 3697
E-mail: thstsg@aol.com
Chairman: Dr J. McCormick

Business in the Community
115 George Street, Edinburgh EH2 4JN
Tel: 0131-220 3001
Fax: 0131-220 3003
E-mail: sbc@sbcscot.freeserve.co.uk
Chief Executive: Ms S. Barber

Scottish Campaign for Nuclear Disarmament
15 Barrland Street, Glasgow G41 1QH
Tel: 0141-423 1222
Fax: 0141-243 1231
E-mail: cndscot@dial.pipex.com
Web: http://ds.dial.pipex.com/cndscot
Administrator: J. Ainslie

Scottish Child Law Centre
23 Buccleuch Place, Edinburgh EH8 9LN
Tel: 0131-667 6333
Fax: 0131-662 1713

Scottish Childminding Association
Suite 3, 7 Melville Terrace, Stirling FK8 2ND
Tel: 01786-445377
Fax: 01786-449062
E-mail: childminding@dial.pipex.com
Web: http://dialspace.dial.pipex.com/
    childminding
Director: Mrs A. McNellan, MBE

Scottish Church History Society
Crown Manse, 39 Southside Road, Inverness
IV2 4XA
Tel: 01463-231140
Fax: 01463-230537
Hon. Secretary: Revd Dr P. H. Donald

Scottish Civic Trust
The Tobacco Merchants House, 42 Miller
Streeet, Glasgow G1 1DT
Tel: 0141-221 1466
Fax: 0141-248 6952
E-mail: sct@scotnet.co.uk
Web: http://www.scotnet.co.uk/sct
Director: J. N. P. Ford

Scottish Council for National Parks
Erskine Court, Castle Business Park, Stirling
FK9
Tel: 01786-457700
Fax: 01786-446885
Web: http://www.sepa.org.uk
Chief Executive Officer: A. Paton

Scottish College of Complementary Medicine
c/o The Complementary Medicine Centre,
11 Park Circus, Glasgow G3 6AX
Tel: 0141-332 4924
Fax: 0141-353 3783
E-mail: ruthchappell@compuserve.com
Web: http://ourworldcompuserve.co./homepage/
    complementarymedicinecentre
Clinic Directors: B. Fleming; Ms R. Chappell

Scottish Conservation Bureau
Historic Scotland, Longmore House, Salisbury
Place, Edinburgh EH9 1SH
Tel: 0131-668 8668
Fax: 0131-668 8669
E-mail: cbrown.hs.scb@gtnet.gov.uk
Web: http://www.historic-scotland.gov.uk
Conservation Bureau Manager: C. E. Brown

Scottish Council for Voluntary Organisations (SCVO)
18–19 Claremont Crescent, Edinburgh
EH7 4QD
Tel: 0131-556 3882
Fax: 0131-556 0279
E-mail: enquiries@scvo.org.uk
Web: http://www.scvo.org.uk
Director: M. Sime
Deputy Director: H. Campbell

The Scottish Council of Deafness
Clerwood House, 96 Clermiston Road,
Edinburgh EH12 6UT
Tel: 0131-314 6075
Fax: 0131-314 6077
Administrator: Mrs L. Sutherland
Director: Ms L. Lawson

The Scottish Council of Law Reporting
26 Drumsheugh Gardens, Edinburgh EH3 7YR
Tel: 0131-226 7411
Fax: 0131-226 2934
Deputy Secretary: D. Cullen
Chairman: A. Stewart, QC

Scottish Council of Physical Education
Department of Sports Studies, Gannochy Sports
Centre, University of Stirling, Stirling
FK9 4LA
Tel: 01786-466906
Fax: 01786-466919
E-mail: r.n.gowrie@stir.ac.uk
Sports Development Co-ordinator: R. Gowrie

Scottish Crofters Union
Old Mill, Broadford, Isle of Skye IV49 9AQ
Tel: 01471-822529
Fax: 01471-822799
E-mail: crofters.union@talk21.com
Web: http://www.scc.co.uk
Director: R. Dutton
Crofting Adviser: Ms F. Mandeville

Scottish Downs Syndrome Association
158–160 Balgreen Road, Edinburgh EH11 3AU
Tel: 0131-313 4225
Fax: 0131-313 4285
E-mail: info@sdsa.org.uk
Web: http://www.sdsa.org.uk
Director: Ms K. Watchman
Office Manager: Ms P. Hernandez

Scottish Drugs Forum
Shaftesbury House, 5 Waterloo Street, Glasgow
G2 6AY
Tel: 0141-221 1175
Fax: 0141-248 6414
E-mail: enquiries@sdf.org.uk
Web: http://www.sdf.org.uk
Information Officer: Ms I. Hendry

The Scottish Genealogy Society
Library and Family History Centre, 15 Victoria
Terrace, Edinburgh EH1 2JL
Tel: 0131-220 3677
Fax: 0131-220 3677
E-mail: scotgensoc@sol.co.uk
Web: http://www.scotsgenealogy.com
Hon. Secretary: Miss J. P. S. Ferguson
Hon. Librarian: Miss M. A. Stewart

Scottish History Society
Department of Scottish History, University of
Edinburgh, 17 Buccleuch Place, Edinburgh
EH8 9LN
Tel: 0131-650 4030
Fax: 0131-650 4042
Hon. Secretary: Dr S. Boardman

Scottish Kennel Club
Suite 3, Archibald Hope House, Eskmills Park,
Station Road, Musselburgh EH21 7PQ
Tel: 0131-665 3920
Fax: 0131-653 6937
E-mail: asim@scotkennel.sol.co.uk
Secretary-General: I. A. Sim
Assistant Secretary: Mrs A. W. Fox

Scottish Landowners' Federation
Stuart House, Eskmills Business Park,
Musselburgh EH21 7PB
Tel: 0131-653 5400
Fax: 0131-653 5401
E-mail: slfinfo@slf.org.uk
Director: Dr M. S. Hankey

Scottish Law Agents' Society
11 Parliament Square, Edinburgh EH1 1RD
Tel: 0131-225 5051
Fax: 0131-225 5051
E-mail: secretary@slas.co.uk
Web: http://www.slas.co.uk/INDEX_1.html
Secretary: Mrs J. H. Webster, WS

Scottish Motor Neurone Disease Association
76 Firhill Road, Glasgow G20 7BA
Tel: 0141-945 1007
Fax: 0141-945 2578
E-mail: info@scotmnd.sol.co.uk
Web: http://www.scotmnd.org.uk
Chief Executive: C. Stockton

Scottish National Dictionary Association
27 George Square, Edinburgh EH8 9LD
Tel: 0131-650 4149
Fax: 0131-650 4149
E-mail: mail@snda.org.uk
Web: http://www.snda.org.uk
Editorial Director: Ms I. Macleod

The Scottish Naturalist
Foremount House, Kilbarchan, Renfrewshire
PA10 2EZ
Tel: 01505-702419
Editor: Dr J. A. Gibson

Scottish National Federation for the Welfare of the Blind
Thomas Herd House, 10–12 Ward Road,
Dundee DD1 1LX
Tel: 01382-227101
Fax: 01382-203553
E-mail: jduncan@dsvib.co.uk
Hon. Secretary and Treasurer: J. Duncan

The Scottish National Institution for the War Blinded
PO Box 500, Gillespie Crescent, Edinburgh
EH10 4HZ
Tel: 0131-229 1456
Fax: 0131-229 4060
E-mail: enquiries@rbas.org.uk
Secretary and Treasurer: J. B. M. Munro

Scottish Parent Teacher Council
63–65 Shandwick Place, Edinburgh EH2 4SD
Tel: 0131-228 5320/1
Fax: 0131-228 5320
E-mail: sptc@sol.co.uk
Web: http://www.sol.co.uk/s/sptc
Administrator: Ms I. Ferguson
Development Manager: Mrs J. Gillespie

Scottish Property Network
University of Paisley, Paisley PA1 2BE
Tel: 0141-561 7300
Fax: 0141-561 7319
E-mail: info@scottishproperty.co.uk
Web: http://www.scottishproperty.co.uk
General Manager: Ms A. Neilson
Technical Support Manager: P. McKay

Scottish Refugee Council
1st Floor, Wellgate House, 200 Cowgate,
Edinburgh EH1 1NQ
Tel: 0131-225 9994
Fax: 0131-225 9997
Manager/Policy Development Officer:
R. Albeson

Scottish Rights of Way and Access Society
24 Annandale Street, Edinburgh EH7 4AN
Tel: 0131-558 1222
Fax: 0131-558 1222
E-mail: srws@scotways.demon.co.uk
Web: http://www.scotways.demon.co.uk
Secretary: A. C. H. Valentine

Scottish Society for the Prevention of Cruelty to Animals
Braehead Mains, 603 Queensferry Road,
Edinburgh EH4 6EA
Tel: 0131-339 0222
Fax: 0131-339 4777
E-mail: enquiries@scottishspca.org
Web: http://www.scottishspca.org
Chief Executive: J. Morris, CBE, BSc
Support Services Director: Ms K. Bunyan

Scottish Spina Bifida Association (SSBA)
190 Queensferry Road, Edinburgh EH4 2BW
Tel: 0131-332 0743
E-mail: mail@ssba.org.uk
Chief Executive: A. H. D. Wynd
Association Administrator: K. Hasler

Scottish Wildlife Trust
Cramond House, Kirk Cramond, Cramond
Glebe Road, Edinburgh EH4 6NS
Tel: 0131-312 7765
Fax: 0131 312 8705
E-mail: enquiries@swt.org.uk
Web: http://www.swt.org.uk
Chief Executive: S. Sankey

Scottish Youth Hostels Association
7 Glebe Crescent, Stirling FK8 2JA
Tel: 01786-891400
Fax: 01786-891333
E-mail: enquiries@syha.org.uk
Web: http://www.syha.org.uk
General Secretary: W. B. S. Forsyth

Scottish Women's Aid
Norton Park, 57 Albion Road, Edinburgh
EH7 5QY
Tel: 0131-475 2372
Fax: 0131-475 2384
E-mail: swa@swa-l.demon.co.uk
National Worker: Ms K. Arnot

Scottish Youth Theatre
6th Floor, Gordon chambers, 90 Mitchell Street,
Glasgow G1 3NQ
Tel: 0141-221 5127
Fax: 0141-221 9123
E-mail: admin@scottishyouththeatre.freeserve.co.uk
Web: http://www.scottishyouththeatre.freeserve.
co.uk
Chief Executive: Ms M. McCluskey
Marketing Officer: Ms U. M.Surimatour

Scout Association Scottish Council
Fordell Firs, Hillend, Dunfermline KY11 5HQ
Tel: 01383-419073
Fax: 01383-414892
E-mail: shq@scouts-scotland.org.uk
Web: http://www.scouts-scotland.org.uk
Chief Executive: J. A. Duffy

The Sea Cadets
Northern Area HQ, HMS Caledonia, Rosyth,
Fife FK11 2XH
Tel: 01383-416300
Fax: 01383-419772
Area Office Manager: A. E. Parr

Shelter Scotland
4th Floor, Scotia Bank House, 6 South Charlotte
Street, Edinburgh EH2 4AW
Tel: 0131-473 7170
Fax: 0131-473 7199
E-mail: liz@shelter.org.uk
Web: http://www.shelter.org.uk
Director: Ms E. Nicholson

Society of Antiquaries of Scotland
Royal Museum of Scotland, Chambers Street,
Edinburgh EH1 1JF
Tel: 0131-247 4115/4133
Fax: 0131-247 4163
Director: Mrs F. Ashmore, FSA

**Society of Solicitors in the Supreme Court of
Scotland**
SSC Library, Parliament House, 11 Parliament
Square, Edinburgh EH1 1RF
Tel: 0131-225 6268
Fax: 0131-225 2270
E-mail: ssc.library@dial.pipex.com
Secretary: I. L. S. Balfour
Librarian: C. A. Wilcox

Society of Writers to HM Signet
Signet Library, Parliament Square, Edinburgh
EH1 1RF
Tel: 0131-220 3426
Fax: 0131-220 4016
E-mail: wssoc@dial.pipex.com
Web: http://www.signetlibrary.co.uk
General Manager: M. R. McVittie
Librarian: Miss A. Walker

SSAFA Forces Help
New Haig House, Logie Green Road,
Edinburgh EH7 4HR
Tel: 0131-557 1697
Fax: 0131-557 5819
Branch Secretary: Ms J. Spence

The Standing Council of Scottish Chiefs
Hope Chambers, 52 Leith Walk, Edinburgh
EH6 5HW
Tel: 0131-554 6321
Fax: 0131-553 5319
E-mail: bevkel@btinternet.com
General Secretary: George Way of Plean

Stewart Society
53 George Street, Edinburgh
Tel: 0131-220 4512
Fax: 0131-220 4512
E-mail: member@stewartsociety.org
Web: http://www.stewartsociety.org
Hon. Secretary: Mrs M. Walker

Sustrans Scotland
3 Coates Place, Edinburgh EH3 7AA
Tel: 0131-623 7600
Fax: 0131-623 7761
E-mail: sustrans@sustrans-scot.freeserve.co.uk
Web: http://www.sustrans.org.uk
Administration Manager: Ms H. Maxfield
Chief Executive: J. Grimshaw

The Thistle Foundation
Niddrie Mains Road, Edinburgh EH16 4EA
Tel: 0131-661 3366
Fax: 0131-661 4879
E-mail: jfisher@thistle.org.uk
Web: http://www.thistle.org.uk
Director: Ms J. Fisher

Turning Point Scotland
121 West Street, Glasgow G5 8BA
Tel: 0141-418 0882
Fax: 0141-420 6170
E-mail: tps_scotland@dial.pipex.com
Chief Executive: Ms N. Maciver
Fundraising Co-ordinator: K. Blackie

UNICEF in Scotland
PO Box 2006, Aberfeldy PH15 2YJ
Tel: 01887-829893
Fax: 01887-829894
E-mail: denisem@unicef.orguk
Web: http://www.unicef.org.uk/
Scotland Officer: Ms D. McNiven

Unit for the Study of Government in Scotland
University of Edinburgh, Chisholm House,
High School Yards, Edinburgh EH1 1LZ
Tel: 0131-650 2456
Fax: 0131-650 6345
E-mail: ladams@ed.ac.uk
Administrative Secretary: Mrs L. Adams
Chief Executive: Prof. D. McCrone

United Nations Association
40 Grosvenor Lane, Glasgow G12 9AA
Tel: 0141-339 5408
Fax: 0141-339 5408
National Officer: Ms F. Mildmay

Variety Club of Great Britain
437 Crow Road, Glasgow G11 7DZ
Tel: 0141-357 4411
Fax: 0141-334 4796
Executive Secretary: Mrs P. A. Jenkins

Victim Support Scotland
15–23 Hardwell Close, Edinburgh EH3 9RX
Tel: 0131-668 4486
Fax: 0131-662 5400
E-mail: info@victimsupportsco.demon.co.uk
Web: http://www.victimsupportsco.demon.co.uk
Director: Ms A. Paterson

Wildfowl and Wetlands Trust - Caerlaverock
Eastpark Farm, Caerlaverock, Dumfriesshire
DG1 4RS
Tel: 01387-770200
Fax: 01387-770539
E-mail: mail@wwtck.idps.co.uk
Web: http://www.wwtck.free-online.co.uk
Centre Manager: J. B. Doherty

Women's Royal Voluntary Service
44 Albany Street, Edinburgh EH1 3QR
Tel: 0131-558 8028
Fax: 0131-558 8014
Support Services Administrator: Miss E. Smith

Women's Rural Institutes
42 Heriot Row, Edinburgh EH3 6ES
Tel: 0131-225 1724
Fax: 0131-225 8129
E-mail: uwri@swri.demon.co.uk
Web: http://www.swri.demon.co.uk
General Secretary: Mrs A. Peacock

Woodland Trust Scotland
Glenruthven Mill, Abbey Road, Auchterarder
Perthshire PH3 1DP
Tel: 01764-662554
Fax: 01764-662553
Web: http://www.woodland-trust.org.uk
Chief Executive: M. J. Townsend
Operations Director - Scotland: Ms A. Douglas

WWF Scotland (World Wide Fund for Nature)
8 The Square, Aberfeldy, Perthshire PH15 2DD
Tel: 01887-820449
Fax: 01887-829453
Head: S. Pepper

YMCA Scotland
James Love House, 11 Rutland Street, Edinburgh
EH11 2AE
Tel: 0131-228 1464
Fax: 0131-228 5462
E-mail: ymca@zetnet.co.uk
Web: http://www.users.zetnet.co.uk/YMCA
National Secretary: J. Knox

Youth Clubs Scotland
Balfour House, 19 Bonnington Grove,
Edinburgh EH6 4BL
Tel: 0131-554 2561
Fax: 0131-555 5223
E-mail: office@ycs.org.uk
Chief Executive: Ms C. Downie

Youthlink Scotland
Central Hall, West Tollcross, Edinburgh
EH3 9BP
Tel: 0131-229 0339
Fax: 0131-229 0339
E-mail: info@youthlink.co.uk
Web: http://www.youthlink.co.uk
Chief Executive: G. Johnston
Information Officer: R. Brewster

**YWCA (Young Women's Christian Association
of Great Britain)**
7B Randolph Crescent, Edinburgh EH3 7TH
Tel: 0131-225 7592
Fax: 0131-467 7008
E-mail: ywca_scotland@compuserve.com
Director: Miss I. A. Carr
Development Manager: Ms M. Lane

ASTRONOMY
AND TIDES

ASTRONOMICAL DATA
TIDAL DATA
FORTHCOMING EVENTS
PUBLIC HOLIDAYS/CALENDAR

ASTRONOMY

LIGHTING-UP TIME

The legal importance of sunrise and sunset is that the Road Vehicles Lighting Regulations 1989 (SI 1989 No. 1796) make use of the front and rear position lamps on vehicles compulsory during the period between sunset and sunrise. Headlamps on vehicles are required to be used during the hours of darkness on unlit roads or whenever visibility is seriously reduced. The hours of darkness are defined in these regulations as the between half and hour after sunset and half an hour before sunrise.

In all laws and regulations, sunset refers to the local sunset, e.g. the time at which the Sun sets at the place in question. This common-sense interpretation has been upheld by legal tribunals. Thus the necessity for providing for different latitudes and longitudes is evident.

SUNRISE AND SUNSET

The times of sunrise and sunset are those when the Sun's upper limb, as affected by refraction, is no the true horizon of an observer at sea-level. Assuming the mean refraction to be 34′, and the Sun's semi-diameter to be 16′, the time given is that when the true zenith distance of the Sun's centre is 90°+34′+16′ or 90° 50′, or, in other words, when the depression of the Sun's centre below the true horizon is 50′. The upper limb is then 34′ below the true horizon, but is brought there by refraction. An observer on a ship might see the Sun for a minute or so longer, because of the dip of the horizon, while another viewing the sunset over hills or mountains would record an earlier time. Nevertheless, the moment when the true zenith distance of the Sun's centre is 90° 50′ is a precise time dependent only on the latitude and longitude of the place, and independent of its altitude above sea-level, the contour of its horizon, the vagaries of refraction or the small seasonal change in the Sun's semi-diameter; this moment is suitable in every way as a definition of sunset or sunrise for all statutory purposes.

TWILIGHT

Light reaches us before sunrise and continues to reach us for some time after sunset. The interval between darkness and sunrise or sunset and darkness is call twilight. Astronomically speaking, twilight is considered to begin or end when the Sun's centre is 18° below the horizon, as no light from the Sun can then reach the observer. As thus defined, twilight may last several hours; in high latitudes at the summer solstice the depression of 18° is not reached, and twilight lasts from sunset to sunrise. The need for some sub-division of twilight is met by dividing the gathering darkness into four stages.

(1) Sunrise or sunset, as defined above
(2) Civil twilight, which begins or ends when the Sun's centre is 6° below the horizon. This marks the time when operations requiring daylight may commence or must cease. In England it varies from about 30 to 60 minutes after sunset and the same interval before sunrise
(3) Nautical twilight, which beings or ends when the Sun's centre is 12° below the horizon. This marks the time when it is, to all intents and purposes, completely dark
(4) Astronomical twilight, which begins or ends when the Sun's centre is 18° below the horizon. This marks theoretical perfect darkness. It is of little practical importance, especially if nautical twilight is tabulated

To assist observers the durations of civil, nautical and astronomical twilights are given at intervals of ten days. The beginning of a particular twilight is found by subtracting the duration from the time of sunrise, while the end is found by adding the duration to the time of sunset.

JANUARY 2001

SUNRISE AND SUNSET (GMT)

	Edinburgh 3° 11' h m	55° 56' h m	Glasgow 4° 14' h m	55 °52' h m	Inverness 4° 12' h m	57° 28' h m
1	8 44	15 49	8 47	15 54	8 58	15 43
2	8 43	15 51	8 47	15 55	8 58	15 44
3	8 43	15 52	8 47	15 57	8 57	15 46
4	8 42	15 53	8 46	15 58	8 57	15 47
5	8 42	15 55	8 46	15 59	8 56	15 49
6	8 41	15 56	8 45	16 01	8 56	15 50
7	8 41	15 58	8 45	16 02	8 55	15 52
8	8 40	15 59	8 44	16 04	8 54	15 53
9	8 39	16 01	8 43	16 06	8 53	15 55
10	8 38	16 03	8 42	16 07	8 52	15 57
11	8 38	16 04	8 41	16 09	8 51	15 59
12	8 37	16 06	8 40	16 11	8 50	16 01
13	8 36	16 08	8 39	16 12	8 49	16 02
14	8 35	16 10	8 38	16 14	8 48	16 04
15	8 34	16 11	8 37	16 16	8 47	16 06
16	8 32	16 13	8 36	16 18	8 45	16 08
17	8 31	16 15	8 35	16 20	8 44	16 10
18	8 30	16 17	8 34	16 22	8 43	16 12
19	8 29	16 19	8 32	16 24	8 41	16 15
20	8 27	16 21	8 31	16 26	8 40	16 17
21	8 26	16 23	8 30	16 28	8 38	16 19
22	8 24	16 25	8 28	16 30	8 36	16 21
23	8 23	16 27	8 27	16 32	8 35	16 23
24	8 21	16 29	8 25	16 34	8 33	16 25
25	8 20	16 31	8 23	16 36	8 31	16 28
26	8 18	16 33	8 22	16 38	8 30	16 30
27	8 16	16 35	8 20	16 40	8 28	16 32
28	8 15	16 38	8 18	16 42	8 26	16 34
29	8 13	16 40	8 17	16 44	8 24	16 37
30	8 11	16 42	8 15	16 46	8 22	16 39
31	8 09	16 44	8 13	16 49	8 20	16 41

FEBRUARY 2001

SUNRISE AND SUNSET (GMT)

	Edinburgh 3° 11' h m	55° 56' h m	Glasgow 4° 14' h m	55 °52' h m	Inverness 4° 12' h m	57° 28' h m
1	8 07	16 46	8 11	16 51	8 18	16 44
2	8 05	16 48	8 09	16 53	8 16	16 46
3	8 03	16 51	8 07	16 55	8 14	16 48
4	8 01	16 53	8 05	16 57	8 12	16 51
5	7 59	16 55	8 03	16 59	8 09	16 53
6	7 57	16 57	8 01	17 02	8 07	16 55
7	7 55	16 59	7 59	17 04	8 05	16 58
8	7 53	17 01	7 57	17 06	8 03	17 00
9	7 51	17 04	7 55	17 08	8 01	17 02
10	7 49	17 06	7 53	17 10	7 58	17 05
11	7 47	17 08	7 51	17 12	7 56	17 07
12	7 45	17 10	7 48	17 15	7 54	17 09
13	7 42	17 12	7 46	17 17	7 51	17 12
14	7 40	17 15	7 44	17 19	7 49	17 14
15	7 38	17 17	7 42	17 21	7 46	17 16
16	7 35	17 19	7 39	17 23	7 44	17 19
17	7 33	17 21	7 37	17 26	7 41	17 21
18	7 31	17 23	7 35	17 28	7 39	17 23
19	7 28	17 26	7 33	17 30	7 36	17 26
20	7 26	17 28	7 30	17 32	7 34	17 28
21	7 24	17 30	7 28	17 34	7 31	17 30
22	7 21	17 32	7 25	17 36	7 29	17 33
23	7 19	17 34	7 23	17 39	7 26	17 35
24	7 16	17 36	7 21	17 41	7 24	17 37
25	7 14	17 39	7 18	17 43	7 21	17 40
26	7 12	17 41	7 16	17 45	7 19	17 42
27	7 09	17 43	7 13	17 47	7 16	17 44
28	7 07	17 45	7 11	17 49	7 13	17 46

Duration of Twilight at 56° N. (in minutes)

January	1st	11th	21st	31st
Civil	47	45	43	41
Nautical	96	93	90	87
Astronomical	141	138	134	130

Moon Phases

January	d	h	m
First Quarter	2	22	31
Full Moon	9	20	24
Last Quarter	16	12	35
New Moon	24	13	07

Duration of Twilight at 56° N. (in minutes)

February	1st	11th	21st	31st
Civil	41	39	38	38
Nautical	86	83	81	81
Astronomical	130	126	125	124

Moon Phases

February	d	h	m
First Quarter	1	14	02
Full Moon	8	07	12
Last Quarter	15	03	24
New Moon	23	09	21

MARCH 2001
SUNRISE AND SUNSET (GMT)

	Edinburgh 3° 11', 55° 56'		Glasgow 4° 14', 55°52'		Inverness 4° 12', 57° 28'	
	h m	h m	h m	h m	h m	h m
1	7 04	17 47	7 08	17 51	7 11	17 49
2	7 02	17 49	7 06	17 53	7 08	17 51
3	6 59	17 51	7 03	17 56	7 05	17 53
4	6 57	17 53	7 01	17 58	7 03	17 55
5	6 54	17 55	6 58	18 00	7 00	17 58
6	6 51	17 58	6 56	18 02	6 57	18 00
7	6 49	18 00	6 53	18 04	6 55	18 02
8	6 46	18 02	6 50	18 06	6 52	18 04
9	6 44	18 04	6 48	18 08	6 49	18 07
10	6 41	18 06	6 45	18 10	6 46	18 09
11	6 39	18 08	6 43	18 12	6 44	18 11
12	6 36	18 10	6 40	18 14	6 41	18 13
13	6 33	18 12	6 37	18 16	6 38	18 15
14	6 31	18 14	6 35	18 18	6 35	18 18
15	6 28	18 16	6 32	18 20	6 33	18 20
16	6 25	18 18	6 30	18 23	6 30	18 22
17	6 23	18 20	6 27	18 25	6 27	18 24
18	6 20	18 22	6 24	18 27	6 24	18 26
19	6 18	18 24	6 22	18 29	6 22	18 29
20	6 15	18 27	6 19	18 31	6 19	18 31
21	6 12	18 29	6 17	18 33	6 16	18 33
22	6 10	18 31	6 14	18 35	6 13	18 35
23	6 07	18 33	6 11	18 37	6 11	18 37
24	6 04	18 35	6 09	18 39	6 08	18 40
25	6 02	18 37	6 06	18 41	6 05	18 42
26	5 59	18 39	6 03	18 43	6 02	18 44
27	5 57	18 41	6 01	18 45	5 59	18 46
28	5 54	18 43	5 58	18 47	5 57	18 48
29	5 51	18 45	5 56	18 49	5 54	18 50
30	5 49	18 47	5 53	18 51	5 51	18 53
31	5 46	18 49	5 50	18 53	5 48	18 55

Duration of Twilight at 56° N. (in minutes)

March	1st	11th	21st	31st
Civil	38	37	37	38
Nautical	81	80	82	84
Astronomical	124	125	129	136

Moon Phases

March	d	h	m
First Quarter	3	02	03
Full Moon	9	17	23
Last Quarter	16	20	45
New Moon	25	01	21

APRIL 2001
SUNRISE AND SUNSET (GMT)

	Edinburgh 3° 11', 55° 56'		Glasgow 4° 14', 55°52'		Inverness 4° 12', 57° 28'	
	h m	h m	h m	h m	h m	h m
1	5 43	18 51	5 48	18 55	5 46	18 57
2	5 41	18 53	5 45	18 57	5 43	18 59
3	5 38	18 55	5 43	18 59	5 40	19 01
4	5 36	18 57	5 40	19 01	5 37	19 04
5	5 33	18 59	5 37	19 03	5 35	19 06
6	5 30	19 01	5 35	19 05	5 32	19 08
7	5 28	19 03	5 32	19 07	5 29	19 10
8	5 25	19 05	5 30	19 09	5 26	19 12
9	5 23	19 07	5 27	19 11	5 24	19 14
10	5 20	19 09	5 24	19 13	5 21	19 17
11	5 18	19 11	5 22	19 15	5 18	19 19
12	5 15	19 13	5 19	19 17	5 16	19 21
13	5 12	19 15	5 17	19 19	5 13	19 23
14	5 10	19 17	5 14	19 21	5 10	19 25
15	5 07	19 19	5 12	19 23	5 08	19 27
16	5 05	19 21	5 09	19 25	5 05	19 30
17	5 02	19 23	5 07	19 27	5 02	19 32
18	5 00	19 25	5 04	19 29	5 00	19 34
19	4 57	19 28	5 02	19 32	4 57	19 36
20	4 55	19 30	4 59	19 34	4 54	19 38
21	4 53	19 32	4 57	19 36	4 52	19 41
22	4 50	19 34	4 55	19 38	4 49	19 43
23	4 48	19 36	4 52	19 40	4 47	19 45
24	4 45	19 38	4 50	19 42	4 44	19 47
25	4 43	19 40	4 47	19 44	4 42	19 49
26	4 41	19 42	4 45	19 46	4 39	19 52
27	4 38	19 44	4 43	19 48	4 37	19 54
28	4 36	19 46	4 40	19 50	4 34	19 56
29	4 34	19 48	4 38	19 52	4 32	19 58
30	4 31	19 50	4 36	19 54	4 29	20 00

Duration of Twilight at 56° N. (in minutes)

April	1st	11th	21st	31st
Civil	38	40	42	44
Nautical	85	90	96	105
Astronomical	137	148	167	200

Moon Phases

April	d	h	m
First Quarter	1	10	49
Full Moon	8	03	22
Last Quarter	15	15	31
New Moon	23	15	26
First Quarter	30	17	087

MAY 2001

SUNRISE AND SUNSET (GMT)

	Edinburgh 3° 11'	Edinburgh 55° 56'	Glasgow 4° 14'	Glasgow 55 °52'	Inverness 4° 12'	Inverness 57° 28'
	h m	h m	h m	h m	h m	h m
1	4 29	19 52	4 34	19 56	4 27	20 02
2	4 27	19 54	4 31	19 58	4 24	20 05
3	4 25	19 56	4 29	20 00	4 22	20 07
4	4 22	19 58	4 27	20 02	4 20	20 09
5	4 20	20 00	4 25	20 04	4 17	20 11
6	4 18	20 02	4 23	20 06	4 15	20 13
7	4 16	20 04	4 21	20 08	4 13	20 15
8	4 14	20 06	4 18	20 10	4 11	20 17
9	4 12	20 08	4 16	20 12	4 08	20 20
10	4 10	20 10	4 14	20 13	4 06	20 22
11	4 08	20 12	4 12	20 15	4 04	20 24
12	4 06	20 13	4 10	20 17	4 02	20 26
13	4 04	20 15	4 09	20 19	4 00	20 28
14	4 02	20 17	4 07	20 21	3 58	20 30
15	4 00	20 19	4 05	20 23	3 56	20 32
16	3 58	20 21	4 03	20 25	3 54	20 34
17	3 57	20 23	4 01	20 27	3 52	20 36
18	3 55	20 25	3 59	20 28	3 50	20 38
19	3 53	20 26	3 58	20 30	3 48	20 40
20	3 52	20 28	3 56	20 32	3 46	20 42
21	3 50	20 30	3 54	20 34	3 44	20 44
22	3 48	20 32	3 53	20 35	3 43	20 45
23	3 47	20 33	3 51	20 37	3 41	20 47
24	3 45	20 35	3 50	20 39	3 39	20 49
25	3 44	20 36	3 48	20 40	3 38	20 51
26	3 42	20 38	3 47	20 42	3 36	20 53
27	3 41	20 40	3 46	20 43	3 35	20 54
28	3 40	20 41	3 44	20 45	3 33	20 56
29	3 39	20 43	3 43	20 46	3 32	20 58
30	3 37	20 44	3 42	20 48	3 31	20 59
31	3 36	20 45	3 41	20 49	3 29	21 01

Duration of Twilight at 56° N. (in minutes)

May	1st	11th	21st	31st
Civil	45	49	53	57
Nautical	106	121	143	TAN
Astronomical	209	TAN	TAN	TAN

Moon Phases

May	d	h	m
Full Moon	7	13	53
Last Quarter	15	10	11
New Moon	23	02	46
First Quarter	29	22	09

TAN Twilight all night

JUNE 2001

SUNRISE AND SUNSET (GMT)

	Edinburgh 3° 11'	Edinburgh 55° 56'	Glasgow 4° 14'	Glasgow 55 °52'	Inverness 4° 12'	Inverness 57° 28'
	h m	h m	h m	h m	h m	h m
1	3 35	20 47	3 40	20 51	3 28	21 02
2	3 34	20 48	3 39	20 52	3 27	21 04
3	3 33	20 49	3 38	20 53	3 26	21 05
4	3 32	20 51	3 37	20 54	3 25	21 06
5	3 31	20 52	3 36	20 55	3 24	21 08
6	3 31	20 53	3 35	20 57	3 23	21 09
7	3 30	20 54	3 35	20 58	3 22	21 10
8	3 29	20 55	3 34	20 59	3 21	21 11
9	3 29	20 56	3 33	21 00	3 21	21 12
10	3 28	20 57	3 33	21 00	3 20	21 13
11	3 28	20 58	3 32	21 01	3 19	21 14
12	3 27	20 58	3 32	21 02	3 19	21 15
13	3 27	20 59	3 31	21 03	3 19	21 16
14	3 26	21 00	3 31	21 03	3 18	21 16
15	3 26	21 00	3 31	21 04	3 18	21 17
16	3 26	21 01	3 31	21 05	3 18	21 17
17	3 26	21 01	3 31	21 05	3 18	21 18
18	3 26	21 02	3 31	21 05	3 18	21 18
19	3 26	21 02	3 31	21 06	3 18	21 19
20	3 26	21 02	3 31	21 06	3 18	21 19
21	3 26	21 03	3 31	21 06	3 18	21 19
22	3 27	21 03	3 31	21 06	3 18	21 19
23	3 27	21 03	3 32	21 07	3 18	21 19
24	3 27	21 03	3 32	21 07	3 19	21 19
25	3 28	21 03	3 32	21 07	3 19	21 19
26	3 28	21 03	3 33	21 06	3 20	21 19
27	3 29	21 03	3 33	21 06	3 20	21 19
28	3 29	21 02	3 34	21 06	3 21	21 19
29	3 30	21 02	3 35	21 06	3 22	21 18
30	3 31	21 02	3 35	21 05	3 23	21 18

Duration of Twilight at 56° N. (in minutes)

June	1st	11th	21st	31st
Civil	58	61	63	62
Nautical	TAN	TAN	TAN	TAN
Astronomical	TAN	TAN	TAN	TAN

Moon Phases

June	d	h	m
Full Moon	6	01	39
Last Quarter	14	03	28
New Moon	21	11	58
First Quarter	28	03	19

JULY 2001

SUNRISE AND SUNSET (GMT)

	Edinburgh 3° 11' 55° 56'		Glasgow 4° 14' 55 °52'		Inverness 4° 12' 57° 28'	
	h m	h m	h m	h m	h m	h m
1	3 32	21 01	3 36	21 05	3 23	21 17
2	3 32	21 01	3 37	21 04	3 24	21 17
3	3 33	21 00	3 38	21 04	3 25	21 16
4	3 34	20 59	3 39	21 03	3 26	21 15
5	3 35	20 59	3 40	21 02	3 27	21 15
6	3 36	20 58	3 41	21 02	3 29	21 14
7	3 37	20 57	3 42	21 01	3 30	21 13
8	3 39	20 56	3 43	21 00	3 31	21 12
9	3 40	20 55	3 45	20 59	3 32	21 11
10	3 41	20 54	3 46	20 58	3 34	21 10
11	3 42	20 53	3 47	20 57	3 35	21 08
12	3 44	20 52	3 48	20 56	3 37	21 07
13	3 45	20 51	3 50	20 55	3 38	21 06
14	3 47	20 50	3 51	20 53	3 40	21 04
15	3 48	20 48	3 53	20 52	3 41	21 03
16	3 49	20 47	3 54	20 51	3 43	21 02
17	3 51	20 46	3 56	20 49	3 45	21 00
18	3 53	20 44	3 57	20 48	3 46	20 58
19	3 54	20 43	3 59	20 47	3 48	20 57
20	3 56	20 41	4 00	20 45	3 50	20 55
21	3 57	20 40	4 02	20 44	3 52	20 53
22	3 59	20 38	4 04	20 42	3 53	20 52
23	4 01	20 36	4 05	20 40	3 55	20 50
24	4 03	20 35	4 07	20 39	3 57	20 48
25	4 04	20 33	4 09	20 37	3 59	20 46
26	4 06	20 31	4 11	20 35	4 01	20 44
27	4 08	20 29	4 12	20 33	4 03	20 42
28	4 10	20 28	4 14	20 31	4 05	20 40
29	4 11	20 26	4 16	20 30	4 07	20 38
30	4 13	20 24	4 18	20 28	4 09	20 36
31	4 15	20 22	4 20	20 26	4 11	20 34

AUGUST 2001

SUNRISE AND SUNSET (GMT)

	Edinburgh 3° 11' 55° 56'		Glasgow 4° 14' 55 °52'		Inverness 4° 12' 57° 28'	
	h m	h m	h m	h m	h m	h m
1	4 17	20 20	4 21	20 24	4 13	20 32
2	4 19	20 18	4 23	20 22	4 15	20 30
3	4 21	20 16	4 25	20 20	4 17	20 27
4	4 23	20 14	4 27	20 18	4 19	20 25
5	4 24	20 12	4 29	20 15	4 21	20 23
6	4 26	20 09	4 31	20 13	4 23	20 21
7	4 28	20 07	4 33	20 11	4 25	20 18
8	4 30	20 05	4 35	20 09	4 27	20 16
9	4 32	20 03	4 37	20 07	4 29	20 14
10	4 34	20 01	4 39	20 05	4 31	20 11
11	4 36	19 58	4 40	20 02	4 34	20 09
12	4 38	19 56	4 42	20 00	4 36	20 06
13	4 40	19 54	4 44	19 58	4 38	20 04
14	4 42	19 52	4 46	19 55	4 40	20 01
15	4 44	19 49	4 48	19 53	4 42	19 59
16	4 46	19 47	4 50	19 51	4 44	19 56
17	4 48	19 44	4 52	19 48	4 46	19 54
18	4 50	19 42	4 54	19 46	4 48	19 51
19	4 52	19 40	4 56	19 44	4 50	19 49
20	4 54	19 37	4 58	19 41	4 53	19 46
21	4 56	19 35	5 00	19 39	4 55	19 44
22	4 58	19 32	5 02	19 36	4 57	19 41
23	4 59	19 30	5 04	19 34	4 59	19 38
24	5 01	19 27	5 06	19 31	5 01	19 36
25	5 03	19 25	5 08	19 29	5 03	19 33
26	5 05	19 22	5 10	19 26	5 05	19 30
27	5 07	19 20	5 12	19 24	5 07	19 28
28	5 09	19 17	5 14	19 21	5 09	19 25
29	5 11	19 15	5 16	19 19	5 12	19 22
30	5 13	19 12	5 18	19 16	5 14	19 20
31	5 15	19 10	5 19	19 14	5 16	19 17

Duration of Twilight at 56° N. (in minutes)

July	1st	11th	21st	31st
Civil	61	58	53	49
Nautical	TAN	TAN	144	122
Astronomical	TAN	TAN	TAN	TAN

Duration of Twilight at 56° N. (in minutes)

August	1st	11th	21st	31st
Civil	48	45	42	40
Nautical	120	106	96	89
Astronomical	TAN	205	166	147

Moon Phases

July	d	h	m
Full Moon	5	15	04
Last Quarter	13	18	45
New Moon	20	19	44
First Quarter	27	10	08

Moon Phases

August	d	h	m
Full Moon	4	05	56
Last Quarter	12	07	53
New Moon	19	02	55
First Quarter	25	19	55

SEPTEMBER 2001

SUNRISE AND SUNSET (GMT)

	Edinburgh		Glasgow		Inverness	
	3° 11'	55° 56'	4° 14'	55 °52'	4° 12'	57° 28'
	h m	h m	h m	h m	h m	h m
1	5 17	19 07	5 21	19 11	5 18	19 14
2	5 19	19 04	5 23	19 09	5 20	19 12
3	5 21	19 02	5 25	19 06	5 22	19 09
4	5 23	18 59	5 27	19 03	5 24	19 06
5	5 25	18 57	5 29	19 01	5 26	19 03
6	5 27	18 54	5 31	18 58	5 28	19 01
7	5 29	18 51	5 33	18 56	5 30	18 58
8	5 31	18 49	5 35	18 53	5 32	18 55
9	5 33	18 46	5 37	18 50	5 35	18 52
10	5 35	18 44	5 39	18 48	5 37	18 50
11	5 36	18 41	5 41	18 45	5 39	18 47
12	5 38	18 38	5 43	18 42	5 41	18 44
13	5 40	18 36	5 45	18 40	5 43	18 41
14	5 42	18 33	5 47	18 37	5 45	18 38
15	5 44	18 30	5 49	18 34	5 47	18 36
16	5 46	18 28	5 50	18 32	5 49	18 33
17	5 48	18 25	5 52	18 29	5 51	18 30
18	5 50	18 22	5 54	18 27	5 53	18 27
19	5 52	18 20	5 56	18 24	5 55	18 24
20	5 54	18 17	5 58	18 21	5 57	18 22
21	5 56	18 14	6 00	18 19	6 00	18 19
22	5 58	18 12	6 02	18 16	6 02	18 16
23	6 00	18 09	6 04	18 13	6 04	18 13
24	6 02	18 06	6 06	18 11	6 06	18 11
25	6 04	18 04	6 08	18 08	6 08	18 08
26	6 06	18 01	6 10	18 05	6 10	18 05
27	6 08	17 59	6 12	18 03	6 12	18 02
28	6 10	17 56	6 14	18 00	6 14	17 59
29	6 12	17 53	6 16	17 57	6 16	17 57
30	6 14	17 51	6 18	17 55	6 18	17 54

OCTOBER 2001

SUNRISE AND SUNSET (GMT)

	Edinburgh		Glasgow		Inverness	
	3° 11'	55° 56'	4° 14'	55 °52'	4° 12'	57° 28'
	h m	h m	h m	h m	h m	h m
1	6 16	17 48	6 20	17 52	6 21	17 51
2	6 18	17 45	6 22	17 50	6 23	17 48
3	6 20	17 43	6 24	17 47	6 25	17 46
4	6 22	17 40	6 26	17 44	6 27	17 43
5	6 24	17 38	6 28	17 42	6 29	17 40
6	6 26	17 35	6 30	17 39	6 31	17 37
7	6 28	17 32	6 32	17 37	6 33	17 35
8	6 30	17 30	6 34	17 34	6 36	17 32
9	6 32	17 27	6 36	17 32	6 38	17 29
10	6 34	17 25	6 38	17 29	6 40	17 27
11	6 36	17 22	6 40	17 27	6 42	17 24
12	6 38	17 20	6 42	17 24	6 44	17 21
13	6 40	17 17	6 44	17 21	6 46	17 19
14	6 42	17 15	6 46	17 19	6 49	17 16
15	6 44	17 12	6 48	17 16	6 51	17 13
16	6 46	17 10	6 50	17 14	6 53	17 11
17	6 48	17 07	6 52	17 12	6 55	17 08
18	6 50	17 05	6 54	17 09	6 57	17 05
19	6 52	17 02	6 56	17 07	7 00	17 03
20	6 54	17 00	6 58	17 04	7 02	17 00
21	6 56	16 57	7 00	17 02	7 04	16 58
22	6 58	16 55	7 02	16 59	7 06	16 55
23	7 00	16 53	7 04	16 57	7 09	16 53
24	7 03	16 50	7 07	16 55	7 11	16 50
25	7 05	16 48	7 09	16 52	7 13	16 48
26	7 07	16 46	7 11	16 50	7 15	16 45
27	7 09	16 43	7 13	16 48	7 18	16 43
28	7 11	16 41	7 15	16 46	7 20	16 40
29	7 13	16 39	7 17	16 43	7 22	16 38
30	7 15	16 37	7 19	16 41	7 24	16 36
31	7 17	16 34	7 21	16 39	7 27	16 33

Duration of Twilight at 56° N. (in minutes)

September	1st	11th	21st	31st
Civil	39	38	37	37
Nautical	89	84	82	80
Astronomical	146	135	129	126

Duration of Twilight at 56° N. (in minutes)

October	1st	11th	21st	31st
Civil	37	37	38	40
Nautical	80	80	81	83
Astronomical	125	124	124	126

Moon Phases

September	d	h	m
Full Moon	2	21	43
Last Quarter	10	19	00
New Moon	17	10	27
First Quarter	24	09	31

Moon Phases

October	d	h	m
Full Moon	2	13	49
Last Quarter	10	04	20
New Moon	16	19	23
First Quarter	24	02	58

NOVEMBER 2001

SUNRISE AND SUNSET (GMT)

	Edinburgh 3° 11'	55° 56'	Glasgow 4° 14'	55 °52'	Inverness 4° 12'	57° 28'
	h m	h m	h m	h m	h m	h m
1	7 20	16 32	7 23	16 37	7 29	16 31
2	7 22	16 30	7 26	16 35	7 31	16 29
3	7 24	16 28	7 28	16 32	7 33	16 26
4	7 26	16 26	7 30	16 30	7 36	16 24
5	7 28	16 24	7 32	16 28	7 38	16 22
6	7 30	16 22	7 34	16 26	7 40	16 20
7	7 32	16 20	7 36	16 24	7 43	16 18
8	7 34	16 18	7 38	16 22	7 45	16 15
9	7 36	16 16	7 40	16 20	7 47	16 13
10	7 39	16 14	7 42	16 19	7 49	16 11
11	7 41	16 12	7 45	16 17	7 52	16 09
12	7 43	16 10	7 47	16 15	7 54	16 07
13	7 45	16 09	7 49	16 13	7 56	16 05
14	7 47	16 07	7 51	16 11	7 58	16 03
15	7 49	16 05	7 53	16 10	8 01	16 02
16	7 51	16 03	7 55	16 08	8 03	16 00
17	7 53	16 02	7 57	16 06	8 05	15 58
18	7 55	16 00	7 59	16 05	8 07	15 56
19	7 57	15 59	8 01	16 03	8 09	15 55
20	7 59	15 57	8 03	16 02	8 11	15 53
21	8 01	15 56	8 05	16 00	8 13	15 51
22	8 03	15 54	8 07	15 59	8 16	15 50
23	8 05	15 53	8 09	15 57	8 18	15 48
24	8 07	15 52	8 11	15 56	8 20	15 47
25	8 09	15 50	8 13	15 55	8 22	15 45
26	8 11	15 49	8 14	15 54	8 24	15 44
27	8 12	15 48	8 16	15 53	8 26	15 43
28	8 14	15 47	8 18	15 52	8 27	15 42
29	8 16	15 46	8 20	15 51	8 29	15 40
30	8 18	15 45	8 21	15 50	8 31	15 39

DECEMBER 2001

SUNRISE AND SUNSET (GMT)

	Edinburgh 3° 11'	55° 56'	Glasgow 4° 14'	55 °52'	Inverness 4° 12'	57° 28'
	h m	h m	h m	h m	h m	h m
1	8 19	15 44	8 23	15 49	8 33	15 38
2	8 21	15 43	8 25	15 48	8 35	15 37
3	8 22	15 42	8 26	15 47	8 36	15 37
4	8 24	15 42	8 28	15 46	8 38	15 36
5	8 25	15 41	8 29	15 46	8 40	15 35
6	8 27	15 40	8 31	15 45	8 41	15 34
7	8 28	15 40	8 32	15 45	8 43	15 34
8	8 30	15 39	8 33	15 44	8 44	15 33
9	8 31	15 39	8 35	15 44	8 46	15 33
10	8 32	15 39	8 36	15 43	8 47	15 32
11	8 33	15 38	8 37	15 43	8 48	15 32
12	8 35	15 38	8 38	15 43	8 49	15 32
13	8 36	15 38	8 39	15 43	8 50	15 31
14	8 37	15 38	8 40	15 43	8 52	15 31
15	8 38	15 38	8 41	15 43	8 53	15 31
16	8 39	15 38	8 42	15 43	8 54	15 31
17	8 39	15 38	8 43	15 43	8 54	15 31
18	8 40	15 39	8 44	15 43	8 55	15 32
19	8 41	15 39	8 45	15 44	8 56	15 32
20	8 41	15 39	8 45	15 44	8 57	15 32
21	8 42	15 40	8 46	15 44	8 57	15 33
22	8 42	15 40	8 46	15 45	8 58	15 33
23	8 43	15 41	8 47	15 46	8 58	15 34
24	8 43	15 42	8 47	15 46	8 58	15 35
25	8 44	15 42	8 47	15 47	8 59	15 35
26	8 44	15 43	8 47	15 48	8 59	15 36
27	8 44	15 44	8 48	15 49	8 59	15 37
28	8 44	15 45	8 48	15 50	8 59	15 38
29	8 44	15 46	8 48	15 51	8 59	15 39
30	8 44	15 47	8 48	15 52	8 59	15 40
31	8 44	15 48	8 47	15 53	8 59	15 41

Duration of Twilight at 56° N. (in minutes)

November	1st	11th	21st	31st
Civil	40	41	43	45
Nautical	84	87	90	93
Astronomical	127	130	134	137

Duration of Twilight at 56° N. (in minutes)

December	1st	11th	21st	31st
Civil	45	47	47	47
Nautical	93	96	97	96
Astronomical	138	141	142	141

Moon Phases

November	d	h	m
Full Moon	2	13	49
Last Quarter	10	04	20
New Moon	16	19	23
First Quarter	24	02	58

Moon Phases

December	d	h	m
Last Quarter	7	19	52
New Moon	14	20	47
First Quarter	22	20	56
Full Moon	30	10	40

──── TIDAL DATA ────

Constants

The constant tidal difference may be used in conjunction with the time of high water at a standard port shown in the predictions data to find the time of high water at the places listed below.

These tidal differences are very approximate and should be used only as a guide to the time of high water at the places below. More precise local data should be obtained for navigational and other nautical purposes.

All data allow high water time to be found in Greenwich Mean Time; this applies also to data for the months when British Summer Time is in operation and the hour's time difference should be allowed for.

Example

To find the time of high water at Stranraer at 2 January 2001:

Appropriate time of high water at Greenock	
Afternoon tide 2 January	1720 hrs
Tidal difference	-0020 hrs
High water at Stranraer	1700 hrs

The columns headed 'Springs' and 'Neaps' show the height, in metres, of the tide above datum for mean high water springs and mean high water neaps respectively.

Port	Diff.	h	m	Springs	Neaps
Aberdeen	Leith	-1	19	4.3	3.4
Ardrossan	Greenock	-0	15	3.2	2.6
Ayr	Greenock	-0	25	3.0	2.5
Glasgow	Greenock	+0	26	4.7	4.0
Lerwick	Leith	-3	48	2.2	1.6
Oban	Greenock	+5	43	4.0	2.9
Rosyth	Leith	+0	09	5.8	4.7
Scrabster	Leith	-6	06	5.0	4.0
Stranraer	Greenock	-0	20	3.0	2.4
Stromness	Leith	-5	26	3.6	2.7
Ullapool	Leith	-7	40	5.2	3.9
Wick	Leith	-3	26	3.5	2.8

Predictions

The following tidal data are daily predictions of the time and height of high water at Greenock and Leith. The time of the data is Greenwich Mean Time; this applies also to data for the months when British Summer Time is in operation and the hour's time difference should be allowed for. The datum of predictions for each port shows the difference of height, in metres, from Ordnance data (Newlyn).

JANUARY 2001 *high water* GMT

		LEITH				GREENOCK			
		Datum of predictions 1.62 below				Datum of predictions 2.90 below			
		hr	ht m	hr	ht m	hr	ht m	hr	ht m
1	M	06 42	4.7	18 46	4.8	04 25	3.1	16 34	3.3
2	TU	07 30	4.6	19 34	4.7	05 12	3.0	17 20	3.2
3	W	08 24	4.5	20 32	4.6	06 02	3.0	18 12	3.1
4	TH	09 24	4.5	21 37	4.6	06 56	2.9	19 12	3.0
5	F	10 28	4.6	22 44	4.7	07 59	2.9	20 25	3.0
6	SA	11 29	4.8	23 47	4.9	09 09	3.0	21 39	3.1
7	SU	–	–	12 26	5.1	10 14	3.2	22 41	3.2
8	M	00 45	5.2	13 18	5.3	11 08	3.3	23 36	3.3
9	TU	01 38	5.5	14 05	5.6	11 56	3.5	–	–
10	W	02 27	5.7	14 50	5.7	00 28	3.4	12 42	3.7
11	TH	03 16	5.9	15 36	5.8	01 21	3.4	13 27	3.8
12	F	04 04	5.9	16 23	5.8	02 12	3.5	14 12	3.9
13	SA	04 53	5.8	17 12	5.7	03 01	3.4	14 57	3.9
14	SU	05 45	5.5	18 05	5.6	03 49	3.4	15 41	3.9
15	M	06 38	5.2	19 01	5.3	04 37	3.3	16 28	3.8
16	TU	07 37	4.9	20 05	5.1	05 26	3.2	17 17	3.6
17	W	08 39	4.7	21 10	4.9	06 19	3.1	18 10	3.4
18	TH	09 42	4.5	22 14	4.7	07 18	3.0	19 09	3.2
19	F	10 47	4.5	23 21	4.7	08 38	3.0	20 32	3.0
20	SA	11 53	4.6	–	–	09 49	3.1	22 00	3.0
21	SU	00 24	4.8	12 51	4.8	10 44	3.2	22 59	3.1
22	M	01 19	4.9	13 38	4.9	11 29	3.3	23 47	3.1
23	TU	02 04	5.0	14 17	5.1	–	–	12 10	3.4
24	W	02 43	5.1	14 52	5.2	00 28	3.1	12 49	3.5
25	TH	03 17	5.1	15 23	5.2	01 06	3.1	13 23	3.5
26	F	03 49	5.1	15 54	5.3	01 39	3.1	13 54	3.5
27	SA	04 22	5.1	16 26	5.3	02 11	3.1	14 24	3.5
28	SU	04 55	5.1	16 59	5.2	02 44	3.1	14 56	3.5
29	M	05 31	5.0	17 34	5.1	03 19	3.1	15 30	3.4
30	TU	06 09	4.9	18 12	5.0	03 56	3.1	16 07	3.3
31	W	06 51	4.7	18 54	4.8	04 34	3.1	16 46	3.2

FEBRUARY 2001 *high water* GMT

		hr	ht m	hr	ht m	hr	ht m	hr	ht m
1	TH	07 38	4.6	19 42	4.7	05 16	3.0	17 29	3.1
2	F	08 34	4.5	20 43	4.6	06 03	2.9	18 22	3.0
3	SA	09 41	4.5	22 00	4.6	06 59	2.8	19 32	2.9
4	SU	10 52	4.6	23 18	4.7	08 16	2.8	21 06	2.9
5	M	12 00	4.8	–	–	09 43	3.0	22 25	3.0
6	TU	00 27	5.0	12 59	5.2	10 48	3.2	23 26	3.2
7	W	01 25	5.4	13 50	5.5	11 40	3.4	–	–
8	TH	02 16	5.7	14 36	5.7	00 21	3.3	12 29	3.6
9	F	03 03	5.9	15 21	5.9	01 14	3.4	13 16	3.8
10	SA	03 49	5.9	16 07	6.0	02 03	3.4	14 01	3.9
11	SU	04 36	5.8	16 53	5.9	02 48	3.4	14 44	3.9
12	M	05 22	5.6	17 42	5.7	03 29	3.4	15 25	3.9
13	TU	06 11	5.3	18 33	5.4	04 08	3.4	16 07	3.8
14	W	07 01	4.9	19 29	5.0	04 48	3.3	16 49	3.6
15	TH	07 56	4.6	20 31	4.7	05 29	3.1	17 33	3.4
16	F	08 57	4.4	21 37	4.5	06 17	3.0	18 23	3.1
17	SA	10 02	4.3	22 49	4.4	07 15	2.8	19 22	2.8
18	SU	11 17	4.3	–	–	09 06	2.8	21 37	2.7
19	M	00 04	4.4	12 28	4.5	10 20	3.0	22 47	2.8
20	TU	01 04	4.6	13 21	4.8	11 09	3.2	23 35	2.9
21	W	01 50	4.8	14 01	5.0	11 52	3.3	–	–
22	TH	02 26	5.0	14 35	5.1	00 15	3.0	12 31	3.4
23	F	02 58	5.1	15 05	5.2	00 52	3.0	13 05	3.4
24	SA	03 28	5.2	15 34	5.3	01 23	3.0	13 34	3.3
25	SU	03 58	5.2	16 04	5.3	01 51	3.0	14 02	3.3
26	M	04 30	5.2	16 35	5.3	02 19	3.1	14 32	3.4
27	TU	05 04	5.1	17 08	5.3	02 50	3.1	15 06	3.4
28	W	05 39	5.0	17 44	5.1	03 23	3.2	15 41	3.3

MARCH 2001 *high water* GMT

LEITH
Datum of predictions 1.62 below

		hr	ht m	hr	ht m
1	TH	06 18	4.9	18 25	5.0
2	F	07 02	4.7	19 13	4.8
3	SA	07 54	4.5	20 13	4.6
4	SU	09 02	4.4	21 33	4.5
5	M	10 24	4.4	23 00	4.6
6	TU	11 40	4.7	–	–
7	W	00 14	5.0	12 43	5.1
8	TH	01 13	5.3	13 34	5.4
9	F	02 02	5.6	14 19	5.7
10	SA	02 46	5.8	15 03	5.9
11	SU	03 30	5.9	15 47	6.0
12	M	04 13	5.7	16 31	5.9
13	TU	04 57	5.5	17 17	5.7
14	W	05 41	5.2	18 05	5.3
15	TH	06 26	4.9	18 57	5.0
16	F	07 15	4.6	19 54	4.6
17	SA	08 12	4.3	20 59	4.3
18	SU	09 17	4.2	22 11	4.2
19	M	10 32	4.2	23 34	4.2
20	TU	11 54	4.3	–	–
21	W	00 40	4.5	12 53	4.6
22	TH	01 25	4.8	13 35	4.9
23	F	02 00	5.0	14 09	5.1
24	SA	02 31	5.1	14 39	5.2
25	SU	03 00	5.2	15 08	5.3
26	M	03 30	5.3	15 38	5.4
27	TU	04 02	5.3	16 10	5.4
28	W	04 36	5.3	16 45	5.4
29	TH	05 12	5.2	17 23	5.2
30	F	05 51	5.0	18 06	5.1
31	SA	06 36	4.8	18 57	4.8

GREENOCK
Datum of predictions 2.90 below

hr	ht m	hr	ht m
03 58	3.1	16 17	3.2
04 35	3.1	16 57	3.1
05 17	2.9	17 46	2.9
06 11	2.8	18 53	2.7
07 25	2.7	20 46	2.7
09 18	2.8	22 19	2.9
10 31	3.1	23 20	3.1
11 25	3.4	–	–
00 12	3.2	12 13	3.6
01 01	3.3	13 00	3.7
01 45	3.4	13 44	3.8
02 25	3.4	14 25	3.9
03 01	3.4	15 04	3.8
03 35	3.4	15 43	3.7
04 10	3.3	16 21	3.5
04 49	3.2	17 02	3.3
05 32	3.0	17 49	3.0
06 25	2.8	18 44	2.7
07 39	2.7	20 04	2.6
09 49	2.8	22 26	2.7
10 43	3.0	23 12	2.8
11 26	3.2	23 51	2.9
–	–	12 04	3.2
00 26	3.0	12 38	3.2
00 56	3.0	13 06	3.2
01 22	3.1	13 35	3.2
01 50	3.1	14 07	3.3
02 20	3.2	14 42	3.3
02 53	3.3	15 18	3.3
03 28	3.2	15 55	3.2
04 04	3.2	16 36	3.0

APRIL 2001 *high water* GMT

LEITH

		hr	ht m	hr	ht m
1	SU	07 28	4.6	19 59	4.6
2	M	08 39	4.4	21 22	4.5
3	TU	10 05	4.4	22 48	4.7
4	W	11 22	4.7	–	–
5	TH	00 01	5.0	12 24	5.1
6	F	00 58	5.3	13 14	5.4
7	SA	01 44	5.6	13 59	5.7
8	SU	02 26	5.7	14 42	5.9
9	M	03 07	5.7	15 25	5.9
10	TU	03 49	5.6	16 10	5.8
11	W	04 30	5.4	16 54	5.5
12	TH	05 11	5.2	17 40	5.2
13	F	05 53	4.9	18 29	4.8
14	SA	06 38	4.7	19 22	4.5
15	SU	07 30	4.4	20 21	4.2
16	M	08 34	4.2	21 27	4.1
17	TU	09 44	4.1	22 42	4.2
18	W	11 01	4.2	23 56	4.4
19	TH	–	–	12 08	4.5
20	F	00 45	4.7	12 55	4.7
21	SA	01 23	4.9	13 32	5.0
22	SU	01 56	5.1	14 05	5.2
23	M	02 28	5.3	14 37	5.3
24	TU	03 01	5.4	15 11	5.4
25	W	03 35	5.4	15 46	5.5
26	TH	04 11	5.4	16 25	5.4
27	F	04 49	5.3	17 07	5.3
28	SA	05 30	5.1	17 54	5.2
29	SU	06 17	4.9	18 48	4.9
30	M	07 13	4.7	19 54	4.7

GREENOCK

hr	ht m	hr	ht m
04 46	3.0	17 27	2.8
05 41	2.8	18 41	2.6
06 58	2.7	20 46	2.6
08 58	2.8	22 12	2.9
10 12	3.1	23 08	3.1
11 06	3.3	23 56	3.2
11 53	3.5	–	–
00 41	3.3	12 39	3.6
01 22	3.4	13 22	3.7
01 58	3.4	14 03	3.7
02 31	3.4	14 41	3.7
03 04	3.4	15 18	3.6
03 38	3.4	15 57	3.4
04 16	3.3	16 37	3.2
04 58	3.1	17 24	2.9
05 49	2.9	18 20	2.7
06 54	2.7	19 30	2.6
08 43	2.7	21 37	2.6
10 04	2.9	22 34	2.8
10 50	3.0	23 15	2.9
11 27	3.1	23 50	3.0
12 00	3.1	–	–
00 21	3.0	12 31	3.2
00 50	3.1	13 05	3.2
01 21	3.2	13 42	3.2
01 54	3.3	14 20	3.3
02 29	3.4	15 00	3.2
03 05	3.4	15 41	3.1
03 44	3.3	16 28	3.0
04 28	3.1	17 28	2.8

MAY 2001 *high water* GMT

LEITH
Datum of predictions 1.62 below

GREENOCK
Datum of predictions 2.90 below

		hr	ht m	hr	ht m	hr	ht m	hr	ht m
1	TU	08 27	4.5	21 14	4.6	05 26	2.9	18 55	2.6
2	W	09 50	4.6	22 34	4.8	06 49	2.8	20 39	2.7
3	TH	11 02	4.8	23 42	5.0	08 37	2.9	21 53	2.9
4	F	–	–	12 02	5.1	09 48	3.1	22 47	3.1
5	SA	00 37	5.2	12 53	5.4	10 43	3.3	23 33	3.2
6	SU	01 23	5.4	13 38	5.6	11 30	3.4	–	–
7	M	02 05	5.5	14 22	5.7	00 16	3.3	12 16	3.5
8	TU	02 45	5.5	15 06	5.7	00 55	3.3	12 59	3.5
9	W	03 25	5.5	15 50	5.5	01 31	3.4	13 40	3.5
10	TH	04 05	5.4	16 34	5.3	02 04	3.4	14 18	3.4
11	F	04 45	5.2	17 18	5.1	02 38	3.4	14 56	3.3
12	SA	05 24	5.0	18 03	4.8	03 13	3.4	15 35	3.2
13	SU	06 06	4.7	18 51	4.5	03 49	3.3	16 17	3.1
14	M	06 54	4.5	19 44	4.3	04 30	3.1	17 05	2.9
15	TU	07 51	4.3	20 41	4.2	05 18	2.9	18 00	2.7
16	W	08 56	4.2	21 43	4.2	06 18	2.8	19 01	2.6
17	TH	10 02	4.3	22 47	4.3	07 28	2.7	20 10	2.6
18	F	11 05	4.4	23 46	4.6	08 51	2.8	21 27	2.7
19	SA	12 00	4.6	–	–	09 55	2.9	22 24	2.9
20	SU	00 34	4.8	12 47	4.9	10 39	3.0	23 06	3.0
21	M	01 16	5.1	13 28	5.1	11 18	3.1	23 44	3.1
22	TU	01 54	5.3	14 06	5.3	11 57	3.1	–	–
23	W	02 32	5.4	14 45	5.4	00 19	3.2	12 38	3.2
24	TH	03 09	5.5	15 26	5.5	00 56	3.3	13 21	3.2
25	F	03 49	5.5	16 09	5.5	01 34	3.4	14 05	3.2
26	SA	04 30	5.4	16 55	5.5	02 12	3.5	14 50	3.2
27	SU	05 15	5.3	17 45	5.3	02 51	3.5	15 38	3.1
28	M	06 05	5.1	18 41	5.1	03 34	3.4	16 33	3.0
29	TU	07 04	4.9	19 46	4.9	04 22	3.3	17 39	2.8
30	W	08 15	4.8	21 00	4.8	05 22	3.1	18 55	2.8
31	TH	09 30	4.8	22 11	4.8	06 39	3.0	20 14	2.8

JUNE 2001 *high water* GMT

		hr	ht m	hr	ht m	hr	ht m	hr	ht m
1	F	10 37	4.9	23 16	4.9	08 07	3.0	21 23	2.9
2	SA	11 37	5.1	–	–	09 20	3.1	22 19	3.0
3	SU	00 13	5.1	12 32	5.2	10 18	3.2	23 07	3.1
4	M	01 02	5.2	13 20	5.3	11 08	3.3	23 51	3.2
5	TU	01 45	5.3	14 06	5.4	11 54	3.3	–	–
6	W	02 26	5.3	14 51	5.4	00 30	3.3	12 38	3.3
7	TH	03 06	5.3	15 34	5.3	01 08	3.3	13 19	3.2
8	F	03 44	5.3	16 16	5.2	01 43	3.4	13 59	3.2
9	SA	04 22	5.2	16 57	5.0	02 17	3.4	14 37	3.1
10	SU	04 59	5.0	17 37	4.8	02 52	3.4	15 17	3.1
11	M	05 38	4.9	18 20	4.7	03 28	3.3	15 59	3.0
12	TU	06 22	4.7	19 06	4.5	04 06	3.2	16 45	2.9
13	W	07 11	4.5	19 56	4.4	04 49	3.0	17 34	2.8
14	TH	08 07	4.4	20 51	4.3	05 40	2.9	18 27	2.8
15	F	09 06	4.4	21 49	4.4	06 38	2.8	19 21	2.7
16	SA	10 07	4.4	22 48	4.5	07 42	2.8	20 20	2.7
17	SU	11 06	4.6	23 44	4.7	08 49	2.8	21 24	2.8
18	M	–	–	12 01	4.8	09 50	2.9	22 21	2.9
19	TU	00 36	5.0	12 52	5.0	10 42	3.0	23 10	3.1
20	W	01 23	5.2	13 39	5.2	11 29	3.1	23 54	3.2
21	TH	02 06	5.4	14 25	5.4	–	–	12 17	3.2
22	F	02 48	5.5	15 10	5.6	00 36	3.3	13 06	3.2
23	SA	03 31	5.6	15 56	5.7	01 19	3.4	13 56	3.2
24	SU	04 16	5.6	16 44	5.6	02 01	3.5	14 47	3.2
25	M	05 03	5.5	17 35	5.5	02 44	3.6	15 39	3.1
26	TU	05 54	5.4	18 30	5.3	03 29	3.6	16 34	3.1
27	W 2	0 651	5.2	19 30	5.1	04 18	3.5	17 32	3.0
28	TH	07 56	5.1	20 36	4.9	05 13	3.3	18 33	2.9
29	F 2	0 904	5.0	21 42	4.8	06 16	3.2	19 37	2.9
30	SA	10 10	4.9	22 46	4.7	07 28	3.1	20 45	2.9

JULY 2001 *high water* GMT

		LEITH hr	ht m	hr	ht m	GREENOCK hr	ht m	hr	ht m
		Datum of predictions 1.62 below				Datum of predictions 2.90 below			
1	SU	11 12	4.9	23 47	4.8	08 46	3.1	21 48	2.9
2	M	–	–	12 12	5.0	09 54	3.1	22 41	3.0
3	TU	00 41	4.9	13 07	5.1	10 50	3.1	23 28	3.1
4	W	01 30	5.0	13 56	5.1	11 39	3.1	–	–
5	TH	02 12	5.1	14 40	5.1	00 11	3.2	12 24	3.1
6	F	02 51	5.2	15 20	5.1	00 50	3.3	13 06	3.0
7	SA	03 28	5.2	15 58	5.1	01 26	3.3	13 45	3.0
8	SU	04 03	5.2	16 34	5.0	02 01	3.3	14 22	3.0
9	M	04 37	5.1	17 11	4.9	02 34	3.3	14 59	3.0
10	TU	05 13	5.0	17 49	4.8	03 07	3.3	15 38	3.0
11	W	05 52	4.9	18 29	4.7	03 42	3.2	16 18	3.0
12	TH	06 34	4.8	19 14	4.6	04 20	3.1	17 01	2.9
13	F	07 19	4.6	20 03	4.5	05 02	3.0	17 46	2.9
14	SA	08 11	4.5	20 58	4.4	05 51	2.9	18 35	2.8
15	SU	09 11	4.5	21 58	4.5	06 48	2.8	19 28	2.8
16	M	10 16	4.5	23 00	4.6	07 56	2.8	20 31	2.8
17	TU	11 21	4.7	–	–	09 09	2.8	21 41	2.9
18	W	00 01	4.8	12 23	4.9	10 15	2.9	22 42	3.0
19	TH	00 56	5.1	13 18	5.2	11 11	3.1	23 33	3.2
20	F	01 45	5.3	14 08	5.5	–	–	12 04	3.2
21	SA	02 30	5.5	14 56	5.7	00 20	3.4	12 58	3.2
22	SU	03 15	5.7	15 43	5.8	01 06	3.5	13 51	3.2
23	M	04 01	5.8	16 30	5.8	01 52	3.6	14 42	3.2
24	TU	04 48	5.8	17 19	5.7	02 36	3.7	15 31	3.2
25	W	05 37	5.7	18 11	5.4	03 20	3.7	16 19	3.2
26	TH	06 30	5.5	19 05	5.1	04 05	3.6	17 06	3.2
27	F	07 29	5.2	20 05	4.9	04 52	3.5	17 54	3.1
28	SA	08 34	5.0	21 08	4.7	05 44	3.3	18 46	3.0
29	SU	09 40	4.8	22 12	4.6	06 41	3.1	19 50	2.9
30	M	10 48	4.7	23 19	4.6	07 56	2.9	21 13	2.9
31	TU	11 56	4.7	–	–	09 34	2.9	22 18	3.0

AUGUST 2001 *high water* GMT

		hr	ht m	hr	ht m	hr	ht m	hr	ht m
1	W	00 23	4.7	12 57	4.8	10 40	2.9	23 09	3.1
2	TH	01 17	4.9	13 47	4.9	11 31	3.0	23 54	3.2
3	F	02 01	5.0	14 29	5.0	–	–	12 16	3.0
4	SA	02 38	5.2	15 05	5.1	00 34	3.3	12 56	3.0
5	SU	03 12	5.2	15 39	5.1	01 11	3.3	13 32	3.0
6	M	03 43	5.3	16 10	5.1	01 44	3.3	14 05	3.0
7	TU	04 14	5.3	16 43	5.1	02 14	3.3	14 37	3.0
8	W	04 47	5.2	17 18	5.0	02 44	3.3	15 10	3.0
9	TH	05 22	5.1	17 55	4.9	03 16	3.3	15 45	3.1
10	F	05 59	5.0	18 35	4.8	03 51	3.2	16 22	3.0
11	SA	06 39	4.8	19 19	4.6	04 28	3.1	17 02	3.0
12	SU	07 25	4.7	20 10	4.5	05 10	3.0	17 46	2.9
13	M	08 21	4.5	21 12	4.4	06 01	2.8	18 38	2.8
14	TU	09 32	4.5	22 22	4.5	07 09	2.7	19 42	2.8
15	W	10 49	4.6	23 32	4.7	08 36	2.7	21 05	2.8
16	TH	–	–	12 01	4.9	09 59	2.9	22 19	3.0
17	F	00 34	5.0	13 03	5.2	11 03	3.1	23 16	3.3
18	SA	01 27	5.4	13 54	5.6	11 57	3.2	–	–
19	SU	02 13	5.7	14 41	5.9	00 05	3.5	12 50	3.3
20	M	02 57	5.9	15 26	6.0	00 52	3.6	13 40	3.3
21	TU	03 42	6.0	16 11	5.9	01 38	3.8	14 27	3.4
22	W	04 27	6.0	16 57	5.8	02 22	3.8	15 10	3.4
23	TH	05 15	5.9	17 45	5.5	03 03	3.9	15 50	3.4
24	F	06 05	5.6	18 35	5.2	03 44	3.8	16 29	3.3
25	SA	07 00	5.3	19 30	4.8	04 26	3.6	17 10	3.2
26	SU	08 03	4.9	20 31	4.6	05 10	3.4	17 54	3.1
27	M	09 11	4.6	21 37	4.4	06 00	3.1	18 48	2.9
28	TU	10 22	4.5	22 49	4.4	07 01	2.8	20 17	2.8
29	W	11 39	4.5	–	–	09 25	2.7	21 56	3.0
30	TH	00 02	4.6	12 45	4.7	10 35	2.8	22 50	3.1
31	F	01 00	4.8	13 34	4.9	11 22	3.0	23 35	3.3

SEPTEMBER 2001 *high water* GMT

		LEITH				GREENOCK			
		hr	ht m	hr	ht m	hr	ht m	hr	ht m
1	SA	01 44	5.0	14 12	5.1	–	–	12 02	3.0
2	SU	02 20	5.2	14 45	5.2	00 15	3.4	12 40	3.1
3	M	02 51	5.3	15 15	5.2	00 52	3.4	13 13	3.1
4	TU	03 19	5.4	15 44	5.3	01 23	3.3	13 42	3.1
5	W	03 49	5.4	16 15	5.2	01 50	3.3	14 09	3.1
6	TH	04 20	5.4	16 48	5.2	02 18	3.3	14 38	3.2
7	F	04 53	5.3	17 23	5.1	02 49	3.3	15 10	3.2
8	SA	05 28	5.1	18 00	4.9	03 22	3.3	15 44	3.2
9	SU	06 08	5.0	18 42	4.8	03 58	3.2	16 20	3.1
10	M	06 54	4.8	19 32	4.6	04 36	3.1	17 01	3.0
11	TU	07 50	4.6	20 34	4.5	05 22	2.9	17 50	2.9
12	W	09 03	4.5	21 52	4.5	06 31	2.7	18 57	2.8
13	TH	10 29	4.6	23 09	4.7	08 17	2.7	20 35	2.9
14	F	11 46	4.9	–	–	09 55	2.9	22 01	3.1
15	SA	00 14	5.1	12 48	5.3	10 57	3.1	22 58	3.4
16	SU	01 07	5.5	13 37	5.7	11 48	3.3	23 47	3.6
17	M	01 53	5.8	14 22	5.9	–	–	12 35	3.4
18	TU	02 36	6.0	15 04	6.0	00 34	3.7	13 21	3.5
19	W	03 19	6.2	15 48	6.0	01 19	3.9	14 03	3.5
20	TH	04 04	6.1	16 32	5.8	02 02	3.9	14 41	3.5
21	F	04 51	5.9	17 17	5.5	02 42	3.9	15 16	3.5
22	SA	05 40	5.6	18 04	5.2	03 20	3.8	15 52	3.5
23	SU	06 33	5.2	18 55	4.8	03 59	3.6	16 30	3.4
24	M	07 34	4.8	19 54	4.6	04 41	3 4	17 13	3.2
25	TU	08 41	4.5	21 01	4.4	05 28	3.1	18 04	3.0
26	W	09 53	4.3	22 14	4.4	06 26	2.8	19 13	2.9
27	TH	11 14	4.4	23 32	4.5	09 10	2.7	21 24	3.0
28	F	–	–	12 23	4.6	10 18	2.9	22 24	3.2
29	SA	00 33	4.8	13 10	4.9	11 00	3.0	23 09	3.3
30	SU	01 18	5.0	13 47	5.1	11 38	3.1	23 48	3.4

OCTOBER 2001 *high water* GMT

		hr	ht m	hr	ht m	hr	ht m	hr	ht m
1	M	01 53	5.2	14 17	5.2	–	–	12 12	3.2
2	TU	02 23	5.3	14 46	5.3	00 24	3.4	12 44	3.2
3	W	02 51	5.4	15 14	5.4	00 55	3.4	13 11	3.2
4	TH	03 21	5.5	15 45	5.4	01 21	3.4	13 37	3.3
5	F	03 52	5.5	16 18	5.3	01 50	3.4	14 06	3.4
6	SA	04 26	5.4	16 53	5.2	02 23	3.4	14 38	3.4
7	SU	05 04	5.3	17 31	5.1	02 57	3.4	15 12	3.4
8	M	05 45	5.1	18 13	4.9	03 33	3.3	15 47	3.3
9	TU	06 34	4.9	19 03	4.7	04 12	3.1	16 26	3.2
10	W	07 32	4.7	20 07	4.5	04 59	2.9	17 16	3.1
11	TH	08 48	4.6	21 30	4.5	06 13	2.7	18 26	2.9
12	F	10 14	4.7	22 49	4.8	08 13	2.7	20 13	3.0
13	SA	11 29	5.0	23 53	5.1	09 47	3.0	21 40	3.2
14	SU	–	–	12 28	5.4	10 44	3.2	22 37	3.5
15	M	00 45	5.5	13 17	5.7	11 31	3.4	23 26	3.7
16	TU	01 31	5.9	14 00	5.9	–	–	12 15	3.5
17	W	02 14	6.1	14 41	5.9	00 12	3.8	12 57	3.6
18	TH	02 57	6.1	15 23	5.9	00 57	3.9	13 35	3.6
19	F	03 42	6.0	16 06	5.7	01 39	3.9	14 10	3.7
20	SA	04 29	5.8	16 49	5.5	02 19	3.8	14 45	3.7
21	SU	05 17	5.4	17 33	5.2	02 57	3.7	15 20	3.6
22	M	06 09	5.1	18 21	4.9	03 36	3.6	15 58	3.5
23	TU	07 05	4.7	19 17	4.6	04 17	3.3	16 40	3.4
24	W	08 08	4.4	20 22	4.4	05 04	3.1	17 31	3.2
25	TH	09 15	4.3	21 33	4.3	06 02	2.8	18 34	3.0
26	F	10 29	4.3	22 46	4.5	07 22	2.7	20 14	3.0
27	SA	11 41	4.5	23 51	4.7	09 36	2.9	21 44	3.1
28	SU	–	–	12 32	4.8	10 23	3.0	22 33	3.3
29	M	00 39	4.9	13 10	5.0	11 02	3.2	23 14	3.4
30	TU	01 16	5.1	13 42	5.2	11 38	3.3	23 49	3.4
31	W	01 49	5.3	14 13	5.4	–	–	12 10	3.3

LEITH Datum of predictions 1.62 below

GREENOCK Datum of predictions 2.90 below

NOVEMBER 2001 *high water* GMT

LEITH
Datum of predictions 1.62 below

GREENOCK
Datum of predictions 2.90 below

		hr	ht m	hr	ht m	hr	ht m	hr	ht m
1	TH	02 20	5.4	14 44	5.4	00 20	3.4	12 38	3.4
2	F	02 53	5.5	15 17	5.5	00 51	3.4	13 06	3.4
3	SA	03 28	5.5	15 51	5.4 •	01 24	3.4	13 38	3.5
4	SU	04 05	5.5	16 28	5.4	02 00	3.4	14 12	3.6
5	M	04 45	5.4	17 07	5.2	02 38	3.4	14 47	3.6
6	TU	05 30	5.2	17 51	5.0	03 17	3.3	15 25	3.5
7	W	06 21	5.0	18 43	4.8	04 01	3.1	16 06	3.4
8	TH	07 21	4.8	19 49	4.7	04 55	2.9	16 58	3.2
9	F	08 36	4.7	21 11	4.7	06 17	2.8	18 10	3.1
10	SA	09 56	4.8	22 27	4.9	08 02	2.8	19 48	3.1
11	SU	11 07	5.0	23 29	5.2	09 24	3.0	21 12	3.3
12	M	–	–	12 06	5.3	10 20	3.3	22 13	3.5
13	TU	00 22	5.5	12 55	5.5	11 07	3.4	23 03	3.6
14	W	01 09	5.7	13 38	5.7	11 50	3.5	23 50	3.7
15	TH	01 54	5.9	14 20	5.7	–	–	12 30	3.6
16	F	02 39	5.9	15 01	5.7	00 34	3.7	13 08	3.7
17	SA	03 25	5.8	15 43	5.6	01 17	3.7	13 44	3.7
18	SU	04 11	5.6	16 25	5.4	01 58	3.7	14 20	3.7
19	M	04 58	5.3	17 06	5.2	02 37	3.6	14 56	3.7
20	TU	05 45	5.0	17 50	5.0	03 16	3.5	15 34	3.6
21	W	06 35	4.7	18 40	4.7	03 58	3.3	16 15	3.5
22	TH	07 29	4.5	19 38	4.5	04 46	3.1	17 02	3.3
23	F	08 27	4.3	20 42	4.4	05 41	3.0	17 59	3.1
24	SA	09 29	4.3	21 47	4.4	06 45	2.9	19 06	3.0
25	SU	10 32	4.4	22 49	4.6	07 59	2.9	20 28	3.0
26	M	11 32	4.6	23 45	4.7	09 19	3.0	21 40	3.1
27	TU	–	–	12 20	4.8	10 14	3.1	22 29	3.2
28	W	00 31	5.0	13 02	5.1	10 57	3.3	23 09	3.3
29	TH	01 12	5.1	13 39	5.3	11 33	3.4	23 45	3.3
30	F	01 51	5.3	14 16	5.4	–	–	12 06	3.4

DECEMBER 2001 *high water* GMT

		hr	ht m	hr	ht m	hr	ht m	hr	ht m
1	SA	02 29	5.4	14 52	5.5	00 23	3.3	12 41	3.5
2	SU	03 07	5.5	15 29	5.5	01 03	3.4	13 16	3.6
3	M	03 48	5.5	16 08	5.5	01 44	3.4	13 54	3.7
4	TU	04 32	5.5	16 50	5.4	02 27	3.3	14 32	3.7
5	W	05 19	5.4	17 37	5.2	03 11	3.3	15 13	3.7
6	TH	06 11	5.2	18 30	5.1	04 00	3.2	15 58	3.6
7	F	07 09	5.0	19 33	4.9	04 59	3.0	16 51	3.4
8	SA	08 18	4.9	20 47	4.9	06 12	2.9	17 56	3.3
9	SU	09 31	4.8	21 59	5.0	07 32	3.0	19 15	3.3
10	M	10 39	4.9	23 02	5.1	08 49	3.1	20 37	3.3
11	TU	11 40	5.1	23 59	5.3	09 50	3.2	21 45	3.4
12	W	–	–	12 32	5.2	10 41	3.3	22 41	3.5
13	TH	00 51	5.4	13 19	5.4	11 26	3.5	23 31	3.5
14	F	01 40	5.5	14 03	5.5	–	–	12 08	3.5
15	SA	02 27	5.5	14 44	5.5	00 17	3.5	12 47	3.6
16	SU	03 13	5.5	15 25	5.4	01 01	3.5	13 25	3.7
17	M	03 57	5.4	16 05	5.4	01 42	3.4	14 01	3.7
18	TU	04 40	5.2	16 44	5.2	02 22	3.4	14 38	3.7
19	W	05 22	5.0	17 23	5.1	03 01	3.3	15 15	3.6
20	TH	06 04	4.8	18 06	4.9	03 42	3.2	15 54	3.5
21	F	06 49	4.6	18 53	4.7	04 26	3.1	16 35	3.4
22	SA	07 37	4.5	19 47	4.6	05 13	3.1	17 21	3.2
23	SU	08 31	4.4	20 45	4.5	06 05	3.0	18 14	3.1
24	M	09 28	4.4	21 46	4.5	06 59	2.9	19 12	3.0
25	TU	10 26	4.4	22 45	4.5	07 59	2.9	20 19	3.0
26	W	11 25	4.6	23 43	4.7	09 06	3.0	21 29	3.0
27	TH	–	–	12 19	4.8	10 08	3.1	22 27	3.1
28	F	00 36	4.9	13 08	5.1	10 56	3.2	23 16	3.2
29	SA	01 24	5.1	13 51	5.2	11 39	3.4	–	–
30	SU	02 09	5.3	14 32	5.4	00 02	3.3	12 19	3.5
31	M	02 52	5.5	15 12	5.5	00 48	3.3	13 00	3.6

⸻ FORTHCOMING EVENTS ⸻

January
10–28   Celtic Connections, Glasgow
*17–30   Re-enactment at Burns' Birthplace, Alloway
*25   Lerwick Up Helly Aa

March
*9   Real Ale Festival, Dundee
*24   Spring Flower Show, Lossiemouth

April
5–8   Bright Ideas, Glasgow
6–15   Gatehouse of Fleet Festival
*7–8   City of Dundee Flower Show
7–17   Edinburgh International Science Festival
27–29   Isle of Bute Jazz Festival
*28   Dumfries Book Fair

May
4–6   Highlands and Islands Music and Dance Festival, Oban
18–20   Ceilidh Gall Gallowa', Carsphairn
19–20   Borders Vintage Agricultural Show, Kelso
19–27   Strichen Festival
21–24   Royal Highland Show, Ingilston, Edinburgh
21–26   Dundee Jazz Festival
25–3 June   Dumfries and Galloway Arts Festival
25–9 June   Highland Festival

June
3   Borders Vintage Automobile Club Historic Extravaganza, Mellerstain
*3   Pipe Band Contest, Turriff
3–23   West End Festival, Glasgow
9–16   Guid Nychburris, Dumfries
22–27   St Magnus Festival

July
1–7   Carnoustie Gala Week
4–8   Glasgow International Jazz Festival
7–8   Game Conservancy Scottish Fair, Perth
7–8   Scottish Traditional Boat Festival, Portsoy

August
1–11   Aberdeen International Youth Festival
3–25   Military Tattoo, Edinburgh
5–27   Edinburgh Festival Fringe
6–7   Turriff Show
11   Scottish Horse Show, Kelso
11   World Pipe Band Championships, Glasgow Green
12–16   Edinburgh International Film Festival
18–19   Scottish Championship Horse Trials, Thirlestane Castle
19   Dumfries and Galloway Horse Show
19   Champion of Champions Pipe Band Contest, Mintlaw

September
1–8   Borders Walking Festival, West Linton
*7–9   Dundee Flow and Food Festival
8–17   Techfest, Aberdeen

October
*12-20   Aberdeen Alternative Festival

SPORTS EVENTS

Badminton
4–6 February   National Championships, Edinburgh

Bowls
12–14 July   Women's National Championships, Ayr
2–4 August   Men's National Championships, Ayr

Curling
20–25 February   Men's and Women's Final, Braehead

Football
14-15 April   Scottish FA Cup Semi-Finals, Hampden Park

26 May	Scottish FA Cup Final, Hampden Park

Golf

4–9 June	Amateur Championships, Prestwick
8–10 August	Seniors Open Amateur Championships, Royal Portrush

Horse Racing

20–21 April	Scottish Grand National, Ayr

Motor Sports

8–10 June	RSAC Scottish Rally, Dumfries

Rugby

Six Nations

4 February	France v. Scotland, Paris
17	Scotland v. Wales, Murrayfield
3 March	England v. Scotland, Twickenham
17	Scotland v. Italy, Murrayfield
7 April	Scotland v. Ireland, Murrayfield

Rugby Final

28 April	BT Cellnet Cup Final, Murrayfield

Shinty

2 June	Camanachd Cup, *Glasgow

Snooker

*8–15 April	Regal Scottish International Open, Aberdeen

Yachting

31 May–3 June	Bergen to Shetland Yacht Race
30 June–3 July	Halliburton North Sea Yacht Race, Macduff
20–26 June	North Sea Triangle International Yacht Race, Shetland

* provisional

GAMES AND GATHERINGS

There are about 100 Gatherings each year, mostly in towns and districts in the Highlands but also in other parts of Scotland. Details can be obtained from the Scottish Games Association (Tel: 01738-627782) and the various local tourist boards (*see* list below).

RIDINGS
Ridings of the Marches and Common Ridings are held in the Borders between June and August. Of some antiquity, the ridings symbolise the patrolling of the disputed border areas, or Marches, between Scotland and England, and the laying of claim to common lands. Details can obtained from various local tourist boards.

TOURIST BOARDS
Aberdeen and Grampian
27 Albyn Place, Aberdeen AB10 1YL
Tel: 01224-632727; Fax: 01224-581367
Email: info@agtb.org
Web: http://www.agtb.org

Angus and Dundee
21 Castle Street, Dundee DD1 3AA
Tel: 01382-527527; Fax: 01382-527551
Email: enquiries@angusanddundee.co.uk
Web: http://www.angusanddundee.co.uk

Ayrshire and Arran
Unit 2, 15 Skye Road, Prestwick, Ayrshire KA9 2TA
Tel: 01292-288688; Fax: 01292-288686
Email: ayr@ayrshire-arran.com
Web: http://www.ayrshire-arran.com

Dumfries and Galloway
64 Whitesands, Dumfries DG1 2RS
Tel: 01387-253862; Fax: 01387-245551
Email: info@dgtb.ossian.net
Web: http://www.dumfriesandgalloway.co.uk

Edinburgh and Lothians
4 Rothesay Terrace, Edinburgh EH3 7RY
Tel: 0131-473 3800; Fax: 0131-473 3881
Email: esic@eltb.org
Web: http://www.edinburgh.org

Fife
Haig House, Balgonie Road, Markinch
KY7 6AQ
Tel: 01592-750066; Fax: 01592-611180
Email: fife.tourism@kftb.ossian.net
Web: http://www.standrews.co.uk

Greater Glasgow and Clyde Valley
11 George Square, Glasgow G2 1DY
Tel: 0141-204 4480; Fax: 0141-204 4074
Email: corporate@seeglasgow.com
Web: http://www.seeglasgow.com

Orkney
6 Broad Street, Kirkwell, Orkwell KW15 1NX
Tel: 01856-872856; Fax: 01856-875056
Email: info@otb.com.net
Web: http://www.orkneyislands.com

Perthshire
Lower City Mills, West Mill Street, Perth
PH1 5QP
Tel: 01738-627958; Fax: 01738-630416
Email: info@ptb.ossian.net
Web: http://www.perthshire.co.uk

Scottish Borders
Shepherds Mill, Whinfield Road, Selkirk
TD7 5DT
Tel: 01750-20555; Fax: 01750-21886
Email: sbtb@scot-borders.co.uk
Web: http://www.scot-borders.co.uk

Shetland Islands
Market Cross, Lerwick, Shetland ZE1 0LU
Tel: 01595-693434; Fax: 01595-695807
Email: shetland.tourism@zetnet.co.uk
Web: http://www.shetland-tourism.co.uk

Stirling
Castle Esplanade, Stirling FK8 1EH
Tel: 01786-479901; Fax: 01786-451881
Email: info@scottish.heartlands.org
Web: www.scottish.heartlands.org

Western Isles
Web: http://www.witb.co.uk

—— INDEX ——

434 Index